THE BOASTFUL CHEF

The Boastful Chef

The Discourse of Food in Ancient Greek Comedy

JOHN WILKINS

OXFORD
UNIVERSITY PRESS

OXFORD

UNIVERSITY PRESS

Great Clarendon Street, Oxford OX2 6DP

Oxford University Press is a department of the University of Oxford.
It furthers the University's objective of excellence in research, scholarship,
and education by publishing worldwide in

Oxford New York

Athens Auckland Bangkok Bogotá Buenos Aires Calcutta
Cape Town Chennai Dar es Salaam Delhi Florence Hong Kong Istanbul
Karachi Kuala Lumpur Madrid Melbourne Mexico City Mumbai
Nairobi Paris São Paulo Shanghai Singapore Taipei Tokyo Toronto Warsaw

with associated companies in Berlin Ibadan

Oxford is a registered trade mark of Oxford University Press
in the UK and in certain other countries

Published in the United States
by Oxford University Press Inc., New York

© John Wilkins 2000

The moral rights of the author have been asserted
Database right Oxford University Press (maker)

First published 2000

British Library Cataloguing in Publication Data

Data available

Library of Congress Cataloging in Publication Data

Wilkins, John, 1954–
The boastful chef : the discourse of food in ancient Greek comedy / John Wilkins.
p. cm.
Includes bibliographical references and index.
1. Greek drama (Comedy)—History and criticism. 2. Dinners and
dining—Greece—History. 3. Food habits—Greece—History. 4. Dinners and dining in
literature. 5. Cookery—Greece—History. 6. Food habits in literature. 7. Cookery in
literature. 8. Cooks in literature. I. Title.
PA3166 .W55 2000
882'.0109355—dc21 00-035643
ISBN 0-19-924068-X

1 3 5 7 9 10 8 6 4 2

Typeset in Imprint by
Jayvee, Trivandrum, India
Printed in Great Britain
on acid-free paper by
Biddles Ltd., Guildford and King's Lynn

PA
3166
.W55
2000

CONTENTS

ACKNOWLEDGEMENTS

I wish to thank my Exeter colleagues for their encouragement and support, in particular David Braund, Richard Seaford, Emma Gee, and Christopher Gill for reading parts of the book. I also thank the Press Readers and Geoffrey Arnott for helpful advice. The greatest encouragement and inspiration has come from my wife, Heather Chadwick, to whom this book is dedicated.

ABBREVIATIONS

AJA	*American Journal of Archaeology*
AJP	*American Journal of Philology*
APF	J. K. Davies, *Athenian Propertied Families* (Oxford 1971)
BCH	*Bulletin de Correspondance Hellénique*
BICS	*Bulletin of the Institute of Classical Studies*
BSR	*Proceedings of the British School at Rome*
CAH	*The Cambridge Ancient History*, vol. 5^2, ed. D. M. Lewis, J. Boardman, J. K. Davies, and M. Ostwald (Cambridge 1992); vol. 6^2, ed. D. M. Lewis, J. Boardman, S. Hornblower, and M. Ostwald (Cambridge 1994).
CGFP	*Comicorum Graecorum Fragmenta in Papyris Reperta*, ed. C. Austin (Berlin 1973)
CJ	*Classical Journal*
CQ	*Classical Quarterly*
CR	*Classical Review*
FGrH	*Die Fragmente der griechischen Historiker*, ed. F. Jacoby (Berlin, 1923–)
FHG	*Fragmenta Historicorum Graecorum*, ed. C. Müller (Paris, 1841–70)
GRBS	*Greek, Roman and Byzantine Studies*
HSCP	*Harvard Studies in Classical Philology*
IG	*Inscriptiones Graecae*
JHS	*Journal of Hellenic Studies*
JRS	*Journal of Roman Studies*
LIMC	*Lexicon Iconographicum Mythologiae Classicae* (Zurich 1981–)
LSCG	*Lois sacrées des cités grecques* (Paris, 1969)
LSJ	*A Greek-English Lexicon*[9], ed. H. G. Liddell, R. Scott, and H. J. Jones (Oxford)
LSS	*Lois sacrées des cités grecques. Supplément* (Paris)
OCD	*Oxford Classical Dictionary*[3], ed. S. Hornblower and A. Spawforth (Oxford 1996)
PCPS	*Proceedings of the Cambridge Philological Society*
PMG	*Poetae Melici Graeci*, ed. D. Page (Oxford, 1962)
P.Oxy	*The Oxyrhynchus Papyri*
QUCC	*Quaderni Urbinati di Cultura Classica*

RE	*Pauly's Real-Encyclopädie der klassischen Altertumswissenschaft* (Stuttgart, 1894–)
SH	*Supplementum Hellenisticum*, ed. H. Lloyd-Jones and P. Parsons (Berlin and New York, 1983)
SIG	*Sylloge Inscriptionum Graecarum*, ed. W. Dittenberger (Leipzig, 1915–24)
SVF	*Stoicorum Veterum Fragmenta*
TGrF	*Tragicorum Graecorum Fragmenta 4*, ed. S. Radt (Göttingen, 1977)
ZPE	*Zeitschrift für Papyrologie und Epigraphik*

INTRODUCTION

Foods, the ways in which they are processed and cooked and the social context in which they are consumed, contribute to the self-definition of a culture and distinguish it from its neighbours. Greek culture was no exception. The Greeks farmed the animals and plants which grow in the Mediterranean area, they caught fish, birds, and other wild animals from the natural environment, and they supplemented this diet to a limited extent with foods imported from elsewhere.[1] They consumed these products as foods (with some regional variation) throughout the Greek-speaking world according to religious and social rules which reflected both their relations with their gods and networks between friends, kinsmen, and fellow-citizens. Religious and social practice distinguished them from Persians, Scythians, or Egyptians. There was an additional factor which particularly distinguished the Greeks from their neighbours, namely the extent to which they represented these forms of eating in poetry and literature from Homer through to late antiquity. In two different cities, Syracuse and Athens, they developed the dramatic form of comedy in whose discourse food was a major element.

From the earliest times Greek poetry incorporated food and eating into its verse. In the *Iliad* heroes sacrificed cattle, cut them up as prescribed by ritual, offered the thigh-bones to the gods in the smoke of sacrifice, and divided the remainder among the human participants in equal portions. These rituals were performed partly to sustain the human body—they ate until they had satisfied the desire for food and drink, in Homer's formulaic phrase. The sacrifice of cattle also constituted the human contribution to the reciprocal relationship between the heroes and their gods, while the accompanying commensality or its failure indicated good or bad relations at the human level. In the *Odyssey* foods consumed by those whom Odysseus and his men

---

[1] Grimm (1996), 1–13, provides the basic data from modern psychology and medical biology for the nutritional requirements of the human body.

met identified their difference from Greek eaters, who did not consume human flesh or lotus plants; in the later books, the behaviour of the suitors of Penelope at table and their treatment of men begging for food in the house of Odysseus indicated their moral failings. Later writers such as Plato, the comic poet Eubulus, and Athenaeus commented on the special codes which the Homeric poems appeared to follow for the consumption of foods: unusually for Greeks, the heroes ate plenty of cattle but no fish. What did this signify? Odysseus visited the Phaeacians who lived in a semi-paradise with self-generating plants. Did this indicate luxury? Circe demolished the boundaries between man and pig with her magical skills. What were the implications of her magic?

Hesiod, in *Works and Days* and the *Theogony*, gave a mythical aetiology for sacrifice, and in *Works and Days* set out a literary farmer's calendar which, somewhat selectively, advised when to plant and harvest certain crops. Later authors incorporated feasting and eating into their texts. Elegiac and lyric poetry had a particular interest in sympotic themes which were probably linked to the circumstances of performance, while elegiac and especially iambic poetry developed representations of the lower levels of social life and more humble forms of eating, often combined with the poetry of insult and invective. By the fifth and fourth centuries, Greek writers could thus look back to various representations of eating composed in a number of different cities. This was a culture which gave a prominent place in its literature to food and eating, even though in many parts, particularly in mainland Greece, food supplies were unpredictable and difficult to manage. Small farmers did not know from one year to the next whether the barley harvest would be adequate; fishermen did not know whether the expected shoals of fish would in fact arrive. Such practical difficulties were of no concern to the heroes and demigods of the Homeric poems, who only considered sources of supply such as fish and game when in the direst straits, but they were a concern to anyone with an eye to the daily sustenance of the people in town and country. The literary genre which most closely addressed these concerns was comic drama.[2]

---

[2] Micha-Lampaki (1984) has studied food in comedy but from the perspective of diet rather than literary discourse.

In 486 BC Athens first included comedy in the dramatic competition at the festival of the City Dionysia. From this date, if not before, comedy was played to a large audience. Comedy was probably an ancient form, with links to iambic invective and possibly to komoi or songs and dances in honour of Dionysus.[3] Comedy in Syracuse may have pre-dated its Athenian counterpart—certainly comedy was later thought to have originated in Doric-speaking states. Too little is known of the predecessors of Epicharmus—the greatest comic poet in Syracuse—and the circumstances of production in that city. Further, the plays of Epicharmus are difficult to date. Most comedies in both traditions were written in the period 500 BC to 250 BC. Any account we give for this phenomenon cannot rest on local and political considerations alone, for these cities spoke different dialects of Greek and, in the early period of comedy at least, Syracuse was ruled by tyrants and Athens was a democracy which recognized comedy as suitable drama for official production at festivals of Dionysus organized by the city state. The two comic traditions appear to have been very different. Attic comedy was based on festivals of Dionysus, with choruses, great metrical variety, political invective, and obscenity, while Syracusan comedy appears to have rested on mythological burlesque and narrative, with no clear use of either choruses or invective. This study centres on Attic comedy, since the remains of Epicharmus are meagre and less still is known of his successors, let alone of comedies that were never committed to texts. By 350 BC, however, after more than a century of development, some of it influenced from outside, Attic comedy appears to have become more like its Syracusan equivalent, with plots, characters, and the use of burlesque becoming more prominent.

---

[3] It is possible, even probable, that scenes of feasting in Attic comedy derive from parts of a sacrifice to Dionysus and the following komos, but too little is known of the origins of comedy to make such speculation worthwhile. The attempt of Cornford (1914) to construct a hypothesis for the ritual origin of Attic comedy based on the death, resurrection, and marriage of a Vegetation Spirit has not found favour, largely because the supposed vestiges of that ritual in the plays of Aristophanes cannot be shown to support the theory. In the absence of such a theory for the *origins* of comedy, I simply point out the ubiquity of feasting in the surviving plays of Aristophanes and Menander and the assimilation of feasting to themes of marriage and festival in the polis.

This book uses the conventional division of Greek comedy into four parts: Syracusan Comedy, Attic Old Comedy (486 BC to the late fifth century), Attic Middle Comedy (early fourth century to the time of Menander—his first play was put on in 322/1),[4] and New Comedy. The divisions between phases of Attic comedy are not rigidly dateable, since some elements of Middle Comedy appeared in Old even before the last two surviving plays of Aristophanes. It is not possible to chart the exact distinctions between Middle and New, since no Middle plays survive and of New only a few plays of Menander survive. It would be accurate to say that Old Comedy modulated into New over a long period, some of which we term Middle. Few comedies survive intact, only eleven of Aristophanes' from Attic Old Comedy and one of Menander's, along with substantial fragments of half-a-dozen more of his plays. Apart from these, all that remains of the hundreds of comedies composed are thousands of fragments preserved in quotations and on torn pieces of papyrus texts. These fragments are currently being edited in the splendid edition of R. Kassel and C. Austin,[5] which provides the text used in this book (with the exception of the fragments of the Sicilian poets (I use Kaibel) and the larger fragments of Menander (I use Sandbach and (where available) Arnott).[6]

In the earliest comedies to have survived, albeit in fragmentary form (namely those of Epicharmus in Syracuse and Ecphantides and Magnes in Athens), it is clear that foods and the way they were eaten were part of the genre. Too little of Sicilian comedies survives to allow us to form a full picture of the role of food there, though I offer some suggestions in Chapter 7. In Athens, on the other hand, the role of food in comedy can be studied with much more confidence. Four aspects immediately distinguished it from its literary predecessors. First, its range is enormous, over social groups, institutions, classes of foods, and all the pots and pans linked with the preparation of food. Second, the consumption of food in comedy is at least as prominent as the drinking of wine. In this respect comedy diverges from sympotic

---

[4] See Schröder (1996), 35–48.

[5] *Poetae Comici Graeci* (*PCG*) (Berlin and New York, 1983–).

[6] The book fragments of Menander have been published in Kassel–Austin (1998), vol. VI/2. Vol. VI/1 with the longer papyrus fragments is awaited.

literature. Third, its audience was enormous and gathered together on one occasion. Comedy was also a self-conscious genre which readily commented on its reception by the audience. Few other genres were so closely in contact with a mass audience. While nearly all of Old Comedy was played to the democratic polis, New Comedy was played to an Athenian audience under a variety of administrations, running from democracy to military governors imposed by Macedon. For this study I have assumed that, whatever the political affiliations of the playwright (about which in most cases we know nothing), the comedy was played to a large audience, a considerable proportion of the population of either Athens or Syracuse when compared with genres that were not performed at public festivals. Comedy, then, was forced, at least in Athens under the democracy, to take account of a large number of citizens. In this sense it was probably more representative of the wider polis than, say, sympotic poetry. Comedy constructs a 'comic polis' parallel to the historical polis; in this construction food and feasting play a key role, and the powerful, identified by comedy as leading politicians, poets, and philosophers, are often excluded from the feast and replaced by comically acceptable diners, notably the chorus and the audience. As Davidson (1997) has noted, in comedy there is a very loose definition of 'us', the Athenian people included in the comic feast; broadly, 'we' are everyone but the very prominent, who are set apart in humiliating exclusion.[7]

One other genre, tragedy, produced alongside comedy to large audiences at civic festivals in Athens, occupies an extraordinary place in the literature of food. In tragedy, in comparison with most other Greek poetry, almost no food is eaten or wine drunk. Comparison with Homer, which in other respects influenced tragedy strongly, makes this clear. There is little feasting and little drinking; this is partly explained by the disruption of sacrifice in tragedy and its perversion either by ritual act or metaphor into murder and kin-killing. Many tragedies present the collapse of relations between humans and gods and between humans themselves in sacrificial terms. Since sacrificial killing in tragedy is

---

[7] Powerful people may have been delighted to have been considered of sufficient note to be ridiculed in comedy. Nevertheless, the comedies take the part of the majority.

often ambiguous and problematic, there is little place for the consumption of food that should follow. A great feast in Euripides' *Ion* (at which murder is planned) shows what tragedy could have done with feasts, had the poets so wished.[8] The hospitable offering of cheese and wine by Electra to her disguised brother in Euripides' *Electra* is a notable exception to this rule—in a play characterized in other respects as deviant from the canons of tragic composition. Tragic poets appear to have deflected themes on eating and drinking into their fourth, burlesque or satyr play, of which Euripides' *Cyclops* is a good example.

Sacrifice in comedy proceeds without difficulty, with much of the ritual either enacted on stage or reported. Comic sacrifice is, however, rarely of Homeric proportions. Animals are often small or skinny,[9] they are usually killed singly, and in comic references to civic festivals there are no descriptions of the hundreds of animals that were frequently sacrificed. Rather, plays refer only to parts of single animals or to single sacrifice within the period of the festival. This is curious, since comedies reflect other aspects of the festivals of Athens, in two of which they were themselves staged. The explanation appears to lie in the genre's commitment to the domestic and small-scale level of the individual citizen. Both tragedy and comedy explored major ethical and political issues at the level of the *oikos* or household. Tragedy presents the royal household that rules the city, normally the household of a mythical king. The household is either destroyed or threatened with destruction, often from within. Comedy also often focuses on the household, sometimes reducing the major institutions of the city to a domestic level, as in Aristophanes' *Knights* and *Wasps*.[10] Comic eating is very often presented on the

---

[8] See Schmitt-Pantel (1992).

[9] See Dunbar (1995), on *Birds* 901–2 and Gomme and Sandbach (1973) on Menander, *Samia* 399–402. These small sacrifices resemble those often made by individuals and by the demes: see Gomme and Sandbach on Menander, *The Sicyonian* 184.

[10] Although many comedies on mythological themes were written (in Attic comedy mainly from the fifth century until about 350 BC), none survive to a sufficient extent to demonstrate how comic eating in myth was presented. Some burlesque comedies parodied tragedy, others presented very unusual feasts, such as the banquet of fish enjoyed by the gods in the *Muses or Marriage of Hebe* of Epicharmus. On burlesque and its decline in the fourth century see Webster (1953), 82–97, Nesselrath (1990), 188–241, and Arnott (forthcoming).

domestic level. Even when major festivals are celebrated, eating by the individual within his community is what is shown.

Athenian drama of the fifth and fourth centuries thus developed distinctive codes of eating in comparison with other literature: sacrifice was disrupted and eating suppressed in tragedy, while in comedy and satyr plays both were pursued on a large scale. Comedy and satyr plays probably treated the disrupted sacrificial eating of tragedy,[11] but in comedy the sacrifice as an expression of proper relations with the gods appears to be so strong that even when the theme of a play is the overthrow of the gods, as in Aristophanes' *Birds*, the sacrifice of a goat proceeds without difficulty. At the heart of sacrifice is the containment of violence—the taking of life—by ritual. Tragedy concerns itself with the failure to contain that violence, comedy with the extension of the violence of sacrifice into the cutting and chopping of every kind of food for human consumption. This demarcation in codes of eating between tragedy and comedy appears to be firm and is explicitly exploited in some comedies.[12]

Comedy had a further mighty counterpoint in Athens as the fifth century progressed, namely philosophy. The development of abstract thought in Greece was influential in Athens. Even if the major early thinkers were from elsewhere in Greece, philosophers came to Athens and expanded many areas of thought. For the most part such developments were confined to the intellectual elite. Comedy attacked both elite and abstraction in a resolute pursuit of the material and gritty realities of Athenian life. Philosophy, like tragedy, was exploited by the comic poets to sharpen comedy's own identity. We shall see both philosophers and tragic poets fitting uncomfortably into the city as comedy presented it, with jarring juxtapositions of comic materialism against abstraction and comic foods forced into tragic verse. This militant approach was tempered in the fourth century, by which time abstract thought had to some extent been accommodated in

[11] Euripides' *Cyclops* and Aristophanes' *Proagon* (frr. 477 and 478) are two examples.

[12] My approach differs from that of Scodel (1993a), who interprets the comic sacrifice in Menander's *Dyscolus* as a decline and 'trivialisation' of tragic sacrifice. Scodel is supported, from a different perspective by von Reden (1998): see Chap. 1 below.

the city. Now it could be incorporated into a discourse of food in the speeches and theorizing of the comic cook.

Although comedy purports to show 'gritty reality', there is much in the comic representation of food and eating which is far from 'real'. The comic world reflects the 'real' world of the polis, but at a remove. Hence the adoption as my subject in this book of the *comic discourse* of food. Comic discourse represented a selection of ways of talking about food, of things that can be said about food. I have already said that comedy did not represent the hecatombs sacrificed at festivals. Comedy also expanded the divisions between town and country and frequently opposed war, which the historical city was unable or unwilling to do. We shall see in Chapter 3 a construction of the city which denies festivals and sympotic pleasures to wartime, even though we know that such events did take place, for example, during the Peloponnesian War. In its promotion of the interests of the ordinary citizen comedy also exploited the discourse of luxury which set forth the dangers of excessive desire among the wealthy. James Davidson has recently published a study of the discourse of desire, to which I return in Chapters 5 and 6. Davidson (1997) made four particularly germane points about eating which I develop further in this book:

1. Even though the consumption of food and drink is inherently pleasurable to the palates of all humans, the Greeks imagined certain foods to be extraordinarily desirable, fish above all.
2. The discourse of desire imagined a development from earlier restraint—the fish which in Homer's poems were represented as a resource of no value had become the object of fevered scenes of desire at the fish-stalls in Athens.
3. Fish was a category of food known as an *opson*, a supplement to the staple diet of cereals, and one which in some texts was construed as a luxurious danger to society.
4. Since appetite is felt by all humans, the discourse of desire speaks to all. The wealthy might spend the most and consume the most, but everyone in a comic or any other audience knew what desire was.

Davidson shows that the discourse of desire is to be found in many texts of the fifth and fourth century BC, comedy prominent among them. I shall demonstrate in this book that comedy exploited this discourse, which in many texts is negative and used for invective and political attack. But comedy also expanded it. In comedy the discourse of desire turns the audience against greedy politicians and certain rich and powerful men, but the desires of others whom comedy approves are encouraged and fulfilled. Protagonists and audiences, choruses and young lovers about to marry, eat to their heart's content.

Eating empowers. The eater triumphs over the eaten, the full belly over the starving, the people whose food supplies are abundant over those whose next meal is in peril. Furthermore, many of the foods that are consumed in comedy are *opsa*, those supplements characterized as dangerous (Davidson 1997: 20–35). We shall meet many comic meals based on wheat, and in particular on barley cakes, the dietary staple of the Greeks; but many too are the comic characters who consume vegetables and fruits, meat and fish, and all the made dishes which are defined as *opsa*. Eating in comedy is not confined to endless bowls of reconstituted barley-meal porridge, the virtuous consumption of which might have allowed the comic representatives of the Athenian masses to denounce the meals of large fish enjoyed by the rich.[13] Rather, comic food reflects the wide range of the Athenian diet, from anchovies to figs, from thrushes to honey cakes and sweet wines. These comic meals which include many different foods are also feasts of words. A number of the birds listed in D'Arcy Thompson's *A Glossary of Greek Birds* and a much larger number of fish in his *Glossary of Greek Fishes* appear in comic texts as foods for consumption.[14] The Greeks ate much of the wildlife around them and hundreds of species of birds and fish were consumed. Comedy lists many. Why all these names for fish, in Attic and Syracusan comedy? If comedy wished to show a rich young man unable to control his desire, why does that desire extend to so many varieties? Why do the gods in the *Muses or Marriage of Hebe* of Epicharmus eat dozens of species of fish, including cheap

---

[13] Davidson probably exaggerates the status of fish by concentrating on notorious examples. It is likely that the average Athenian ate fish more often than meat, which was reserved for special occasions.

[14] D'Arcy Thompson is not always reliable in identifying ancient species. See also, on fish, A. C. Campbell (1982); Palombi and Santorelli (1960); A. Davidson (1981); and on birds, Capponi (1979).

and unfavoured categories? Would a dozen courses of the most favoured fish not suffice? Comedy clearly reflects the abundance of species fished from the sea. Both quantity and the range of species are important. Some or all comic poets wished to incorporate into their dramatic texts long lists of names. They could not do this with farmed animals since the domestic species are few. But they could list the many fruits and vegetables, types of cereal and pulses, types of wine, and the types of vessels in which all these foods and drinks were prepared, cooked, and served. All of these were the *things* of the ordinary world which were incorporated into comic texts in profusion. And if varieties of any thing consumed were important, then nothing had more categories or species than fish.

D'Arcy Thompson was anticipated by a number of ancient authors who listed the species of Greek fish and birds. Dorion *On Fish* and Aristotle *On the History of Animals* had done so in different ways in the fourth century BC.[15] Athenaeus of Naucratis, writing his *Deipnosophistae* at the end of the second century AD or at the beginning of the third, also compiled lists of Greek fish and shellfish, drawing on Dorion, Aristotle, and comedy, among others. Many of his species are illustrated by quotation from comedies. Athenaeus, indeed, is the major source for the comic fragments which mention fish and for many of the other categories of food and social practice discussed in this book. Writing under the Roman Empire, with access to libraries, glossaries, and compendia of earlier literature, Athenaeus was able to compose a literary symposium at which semi-fictional diners ate a series of large meals and listed every literary precedent they could bring to mind for the food they were currently eating or the social aspect of eating they were enacting. Much of their evidence depends on citation from the hundreds of comedies known either directly to Athenaeus or indirectly through his sources. Athenaeus tells us there were 800 comedies classified as 'Middle' Comedy alone. He thus gives access to hundreds of plays otherwise lost.

---

[15] Davidson (1997), 3–20, connects the interest in the taxonomy of fish with these and other authors of the fourth century. But Epicharmus had listed many species a century earlier. Taxonomy simply built on an older comic approach.

Athenaeus lists dozens of fish, as well as wines, vegetables, fruits, birds and animals, cakes and drinking cups, drawing on the many lists he found in the texts of comedies. Listing of material objects—including many foods and drinks—was one way in which the material world had been represented in comedy. The genre was intensely materialist, opposing the myriad objects and variety of the world of the Greek polis to the abstractions and unifying definitions of the philosophers.[16] Athenaeus adopted this discourse based on material *things*. He also adopted from comedy (among other sources) the discourse of luxury and desire to which I referred above. Further, he surveyed many of the cities of the Greek world and beyond in his fourth and twelfth books, presenting many different forms of eating according to the social composition of the community. His comic material is mainly Athenian, reflecting the branch of the comic tradition which produced most of the texts. Chapters which follow on the material world (1), the social world (2), and on the symposium (5) and luxury (6) interpret comedy through the discourse of the *Deipnosophistae*, which is a close relative. Though Athenaeus' audience was very different—a small audience of the learned elite—he attempts a similar type of discourse, one that also tries to represent the material world of food and drink in literature. Athenaeus went so far as to survey the stock comic characters of the parasite (see Chapter 2 below), the cook (see Chapter 8 below), and the courtesan, the first two of which gave expression respectively to the needy eater and to the skills of the kitchen. Where Athenaeus differed from comedy was in his use of the sympotic, rather than the 'popular-festive', medium to which comedy belonged.[17]

The exploitation of other genres such as epic, tragedy, and philosophy contributed to comedy's development of its own discourse, which commented on all around it and concerned itself with language and terminology, with ways of turning material reality into verse. The texts of comedy in turn became an early subject for Hellenistic scholarship, which tried to elucidate for a

---

[16] This book has benefited from Emily Gowers (1993), whose study of Roman comedy (pp. 50–108) approaches the material world from a perspective which is different from, but complements, those adopted in Chap. 1 below.

[17] A number of studies of Athenaeus are forthcoming in Braund and Wilkins (forthcoming).

later generation all the detail that the poets had managed to incorporate into their texts. This scholarship developed into the scholarly tradition used by Athenaeus, who was able to give an analysis of antiquity built in no small measure on the testimony of comedy. Thus, despite the comparatively late date of the *Deipnosophistae* (late second century AD), Athenaeus builds his text in part on many fragments of comedies written in the fifth and fourth centuries BC. Some of them he merely quotes, while others he locates in their cultural context.

It is a commonplace to observe that our knowledge of Greek comedy is severely distorted by Athenaeus, since he is the source of so many quotations from lost plays and yet his preoccupation is with eating and drinking and social practice. The purpose of this book is to interpret all of Greek comedy, both fragmentary and surviving plays, from this perspective and to claim that, while Athenaeus' portrait of comedy is indeed one-sided, it is a perspective that is fundamental (among others) to comedy of all periods. Food and eating were always important to the comic poet; no matter what his period, his own approach to his material, or the particular demands of the play he was writing, he was likely to draw on the comic discourse of food. In the surviving plays of Aristophanes, as we shall see in Chapter 8, the protagonist is normally in charge of the provision and cooking of food. In the few plays lacking such provision, other reference to food is not lacking. As Attic comedy changed from Old to New, so the representation of eating changed and the early protagonist who had presided over the provision and cooking of food was replaced by a professional cook who was a subsidiary character within a plot. The cook is present in Menander's *Dyscolus*, *Samia*, and *The Arbitration*. Plays of the New Comedy were written in which no cook appeared. But few were the plays which gave only a passing mention to food. Some readers may consider that extravagant claims are being made for Old, Middle, and New Comedy on the basis of very fragmentary material which is probably unduly influenced by our much better knowledge of Aristophanes and Menander. The claims are necessarily made on the basis of the fragments that have survived, in full recognition that if complete plays of Cratinus, Alexis, and Diphilus, for example, were to be found, a very different picture might emerge. I have counteracted the difficulty as well as I have been able by bearing in mind what is known of the rivals of Aristophanes,[18] and by drawing on the commentaries of Hunter and Arnott for the later dramatists.[19] Furthermore, my comments on the complete or nearly complete plays of Aristophanes and Menander are intended to balance the picture provided by hundreds of plays known only from a handful of fragments.

Many books on Greek comedy readily recognize the presence of food and feasting in the plays and move on to other matters. Feasting in comic utopias and at weddings, sympotic and Dionysiac scenes, the interminable speeches of parasites and cooks, are noted and abandoned. Feasting, however, is no small matter. It may have been a daily occurrence for kings, tyrants, and some of the wealthy elite in the Greek world, but for the vast majority of inhabitants of city-states (poleis), feasting represented the communal consumption of surplus agricultural production—which was never guaranteed. Harvests regularly failed. Anxieties faced by small farmers are the major theme of such works as Garnsey (1988), Sallares (1991), and Gallant (1991), while Gallant (1985) has argued that supplies of fish too were subject to similar problems of shortage and abundance. A rich polis such as Athens could provide for additional feasting at civic expense, but the underlying anxieties over the harvest still remained. If feasting appears in comedy as a period of merry-making and fun for one and all, this is aspirational rather than normal. Comedies were echoing other voices in the polis who were praying that the gods would provide. Guaranteed supplies of food belong to certain countries in the modern world but not to their ancient counterparts. Comic appeals to the gods to provide sufficient nourishment and to save the city are deadly serious. That the feast is provided at the end of a comedy is an indication, not that comedy reflected well-being but that it was part of comic discourse to promote that aspiration and the communal benefits that came with surplus.

Six strands can be detected in the comic discourse of feasting. First, to judge from the comedies to have survived—all Attic—comedy is a civic genre dependant on the city but with a strong

---

[18] For the recent research see Harvey and Wilkins (forthcoming), and Belardinelli *et al.* (1998).

[19] Hunter (1983) and Arnott (1996).

interest in the countryside and frequently with a desire to draw attention to distinctions between town and country. The principal distinction between town and country rests on money. Second, the city is the centre for commerce, on which the comic discourse has much to say—the much-desired fish belong to the market-places of the city rather than the small fishing communities in which they were often caught. While commerce is not always viewed in a negative light in comedy—we shall see in Chapter 4 much reflection of trade and the market-place in comedy—this reflects the anxiety that the world of money and commodities might have overtaken traditional and ritualized areas of life such as sacrifice and even politics. Commerce might allow feasting to get quite out of hand, supplying tasty dishes to consumers who cannot control their appetites. The third and fourth strands tend to raise anxieties about the role of money. Commensality, eating with friends, neighbours, and fellow citizens, is the desired form of social interaction, guaranteed as it is by tradition and ritual forms. Those who do not conform to the approved patterns of eating are ridiculed.[20] Commensality is accompanied by the symposium, the ritualized communal drinking of a group of men. Murray (1990) has argued that the symposium was the preserve of the elite in Athens, but I try to show in Chapters 2 and 5 that, in comedy at least, the symposium was part of the shared world of comic characters and their audience. Both commensality and sympotic drinking might threaten the good health of the comic city if pursued by exclusive groups with unlimited wealth who did not respect traditional restraints against excess, and who exploited their appetites at the market against the common interest. Comic discourse thus ranges over acceptable and unacceptable forms of commensality and symposia. Ambiguities in these areas are increased by, fifthly, comedy's focus on the domestic scale of eating. Families and friends are normally the area of operation of eating, even if the occasion is a civic feast. Lastly, as Attic comedy developed from Old to New, the public and civic sphere came to be replaced by the domestic, enabling further concentration on acceptable and unacceptable behaviour in that context.

---

[20] On commensality in ancient Greece see Schmitt-Pantel (1992) and Belardinelli *et al.* (1998).

Comic discourse negotiates its way between tradition and innovation, between ritual and the commercial world. In these negotiations, food plays a key role. The suggestion is often made by comic characters that ritual forms of consumption are no longer respected. We shall meet this claim with civic dining (in Aristophanes' *Knights*) and with the decline of the parasite from ritual eater to scrounger, for example. The cooking of food may have followed a similar trajectory. Dalby (1995) suggests that there were significant developments in cooking and gastronomy in the period 500–250 BC, and that cooking was advanced by new methods and new skills. His social-historical approach to food produces a very different picture from the one offered here,[21] which is sceptical of such development. The developments, in my view, were largely in the literary discourse of food, not in the way that it was eaten. The new foods brought from the East after Alexander seem to have made little impact on comedy. Admittedly, the late fourth century falls towards the end of the period covered in this book, but before Alexander foods introduced from the East (such as the domestic fowl and pepper) were known but little exploited as foods in comic or sub-comic texts and recipes. For the most part the Greeks ate what they always had and used the same methods of cooking. Foreign influences were few—we shall find little evidence of luxury sauces (Chapter 6). Their interest in cooking, however, changed dramatically. It became a topic for literary elaboration, particularly in comedy and sub-comic genres. Suddenly comic poets put on stage cooks who explained how a fish should be cooked and even identified the book in which they had found the best recipe. I have written elsewhere of related literature, namely Greek recipe books[22] and the parodic guide to fish-eating by Archestratus of Gela,[23] to both of which I refer in Chapter 7. My study of the recipes of Mithaecus was informed by Goody (1982: 97–9). He defined the cultural desiderata for the production of a cookery book as: a wide range of ingredients, some imported; a broad elite which includes discerning and critical eaters; attitudes which promote the pleasure of eating; practical skills, including the skill of committing alternative modes of cooking (recipes) to books. I have

---

[21] See J. Wilkins, *CR* 48 (1998), 387–8, reviewing this book.
[22] Wilkins and Hill (1996).   [23] Wilkins and Hill (1994).

discussed elsewhere the question why the work of Mithaecus appeard in about 400 BC and not 500 BC. The answer, I believe, is a literary one, that such treatises were not written at that date; and not a culinary one, that is, that in 500 BC Greek 'cuisine' had not developed sufficiently to produce a cookery book. It is difficult to believe that the Ionian cities of the sixth century or such Italian and Sicilian towns as Sybaris and Syracuse lacked the agricultural base, the ingredients, and the attitude that promoted pleasure among the elite—but they did lack the literary form of the treatise. Cooking methods became of interest to literature and drama—that is the major change. This may have had a significant impact on social practice, though I have not been able to detect it. We hear of specialist cooks outside comedy, but their impact outside comedy is difficult to demonstrate.[24] Xenophon, for example, does not mention *mageiroi*, and refers to the older *opsopoioi* in a neutral fashion.[25] Plato and Aristotle mention *mageiroi*, but by this term they mean agents of sacrifice or butchers as often as cooks. Only at *Gorgias* 518 does Plato make a significant reference to a cook, and that is to the book of Mithaecus. Recipe books appear to have become quite common in the fourth and third centuries but their social impact was limited. I suspect that much of Dalby's 'gastronomy' was literary and its practical effect, even on the elite, small in the fourth century. The impact on comedy with its huge audience of perhaps 17,000 people[26] was, however, immense, not just because the emerging character of the comic cook was waiting for a repertoire but because comedy had long concerned itself with matters related to Goody's desiderata, that is, with agricultural production, the import

---

[24] Comedy provides much of the evidence, but had been subject to great changes itself. Comedy now had its stock cook, along with the stock courtesan and stock parasite. Were there, therefore, more numerous and more sophisticated courtesans and parasites in fourth-century than in fifth-century Athens? It would be rash to assume so. Comedy's massive provision of evidence in these areas is demonstrated by Davidson (1997), who considers the discourse of desire in the orators, philosophers, and historians. These texts—unlike comedy—are not concerned with the many different species of fish or different sauces or different kinds of courtesan.

[25] Berthiaume (1982) lists inscriptions recording *mageiroi* hired for cult purposes. These again are scarcely heralds of new fashions in cookery.

[26] This figure is disputed. See Pickard-Cambridge (1988), 263, and Green (1994), 10, with n. 24.

of ingredients, and the problematizing of pleasure. Further, commentary on other literary genres had long been a major preoccupation of comedy. All of these could be harnessed in Attic comedy at the end of the fifth century, at the very time that comedy was turning from its early civic form (with protagonist and chorus) into a comedy based on the household and the characters within it. The shift from the protagonist who cooks to the stock character of the cook is enormous. For comedy, cooking (as distinct from eating) was no longer an activity of central importance to the plot. The amount of space given to it may not have changed, but the occasion has become important, the wedding or funeral, while the cooking itself has become both more complicated and more satirized—because given to the comic cook.

I do not aim to present definitive interpretations of passages of complete plays, let alone of fragments torn from their context. My aim is to convey the general character and main types of comic discourse on food. The discourse reflects intense interest in certain areas of eating and certain pressures. Thus, if we consider, for example Hermippus fr. 63 on foods and sympotic goods imported into Athens,[27] we might stress the presence of Dionysus and urge that this is a celebration of Athenian strength in trade approved by the god, or we might concentrate on the varied provenances of the goods, from Carthage, the Hellespont, and Phoenicia, and conclude that the main focus is the import of 'luxuries' into Athens. Both explanations, indeed, may be possible. Such passages often balance various aspects of the discourse, as do the scenes of Dicaeopolis' celebrations at the end of *Acharnians* which have been interpreted in many different ways. It may be, also, that in my consideration of the ritual control in Athens represented by public dining at the prytaneion (in Chapter 4) I have underestimated the levels of 'luxury' allowed in such public buildings. I consider there some evidence for elaborate dining in a public building in the agora found recently by archaeologists. Further, an ancient scholar on Lucian[28] suggests that women at the Haloa festival in Athens dined on all the foods of earth and sea (with a few exceptions), some of which might come within the discourse of luxury.

---

[27] Quoted at the beginning of Chap. 4.   [28] 279.24 Rabe.

One of my Exeter colleagues once remarked how boring he found the series of passages from Old Comedy on comic utopias blessed with automatic provision of food and drink.[29] These are seven variations on an alimentary theme written by six poets in serious competition with each other. In the Athenian comic theatre there appears to have been a constant demand for long speeches, sometimes serious and sometimes parodic, listing the elements of feasts and modes of preparation. Such speeches are often interrupted with complaints of their length or inappropriate content—we shall see this in the long speeches of the boastful cook in Chapter 8. But the poets did not cease to write such speeches. The speaker was designed to be engagingly boring, but the content was not. Comedy was the cultural form which dwelt on culinary detail since food was a subject for discourse, a subject for both anxiety and for celebration, but above all a subject of quite extraordinary importance for the Athenian theatre.[30]

[29] Athenaeus 7.267e–270a, quoted in Chap. 3.

[30] Peter Garnsey's excellent *Food and Society in Classical Antiquity* (1999) arrived too late for consideration in this book. Garnsey surveys the production and distribution of food in antiquity and problems of approaching ancient sources.

I
Comedy and the Material World

1.1. THE SCOPE OF THIS CHAPTER

Comedy is a particularly materialist form of drama; if the subject is lawcourts, voting funnels and the bar of the court will come into play, if peace, hoes and mattocks will be wielded by farmers; in the context of eating, the verses of comedy are filled with foods, with the pots and pans in which food was prepared and served and with the cups and bowls in which liquids were contained. In this chapter I consider first the *things*, the inanimate physical objects of the polis.[1] And secondly, the nature and structure of bodies, with which comedy is greatly concerned: both the fish and animals that were consumed by humans and the human body itself, the mouth which took the food into the body, the belly which benefited from the nourishment, and the rectum from which waste matter was extruded. For this chapter, the human (and even the divine) body is considered as a physical entity.

Comedy manipulates these 'things': it puts their nature under the spotlight—the material fabric of a clay pot, the texture of a fish-head—and explores their places in the social and religious world: a barley cake may be part of a poor man's meal, or of a rich man's meal in another social context, or of an offering to a god in another. Ties between objects and their social or religious places are a particular concern, since comedy challenges these ties and often confuses or transgresses them. As for bodies, in comedy the body of the animal or fish is dissected, while the human body is presented with an emphasis on its apertures rather than the surface whole of the 'person', and even the divine body (in human form) is rendered susceptible to beating and the need to be fed. In this sense the comic body challenges through assimilation the

---

[1] On *things*, see esp. Appadurai (1986), discussed below.

accepted hierarchy of animal, human, and divine—fish are compared with women and gods with pigs. Furthermore, animate and inanimate are assimilated: the cooked body of a fish (outside comedy no longer a creature but a 'food') promotes its own cooking[2] and is able to dance,[3] the statue of a goddess bends down and whispers,[4] and even utensils form a religious procession[5] and give evidence in court.[6]

In the following pages comic foregrounding of the material world will be evident in many areas of cultural life. Two in particular may be highlighted here. In religious ritual such objects as a robe, a knife hidden in a basket of cereal grains, and a pot of boiled pulses carried enormous significance: the object may have a practical purpose, it may be a gift to the god, it may be supported by a myth which 'explains' its presence at the ritual. However used, the object is indispensable. At *Peace* 922–38 Aristophanes' characters argue over the range of possible offerings to Peace and, once a sheep is selected, rehearse the dismemberment of the animal into its parts. In all sacrifice the parts of the animal carry particular meanings and are destined for particular participants, human and divine, but comedy will emphasize those parts because of its special interest in the material body. At the same time, materialist comedy addresses itself to abstract thought. The abstract was increasingly important in Athens of the late fifth century as theory and philosophy developed. Comedy confronts this in its relentless promotion of the material. In *Clouds*, for example, the cosmos of the school of Socrates is illustrated with the analogy of the domed bread-oven or *pnigeus*. The heavens are represented by the clay dome, while we humans are the charcoal with which it is heated (94–7).[7] Physicists had borrowed images from the known material world as analogies for the cosmos;[8] comedy takes this further and forces the philosophical speaker to move from the language of physics to comedy's own world of the kitchen. Philosophy was familiar only to a few, the kitchen to all. Promotion of the material thus sometimes allowed comedy to oppose abstraction to the world of the common people

---

[2] Crates fr. 16.   [3] In e.g. Diphilus fr. 64.4 (cited below).
[4] *Peace* 661–7.   [5] *Ecclesiazusae* 730–45.
[6] *Wasps* 936–66.   [7] See O'Regan (1992), 28–30.
[8] Dover (1968), on l. 96, discusses the possibility that Hippon and Meton compared the sky with a *pnigeus*.

and so to give an ideological component to material concerns. A similar phenomenon is evident in comic citation of tragedy. Material objects play an important role in tragedy, but comedy presents foods as its own and allows foods incongruously to invade the tragic discourse: in his list of requests to Euripides, Dicaeopolis in *Acharnians* asks for one last thing, 'give me some chervil that you've got from your mother' (478). The joke rests on the supposed trade in vegetables (*lachana*) which his mother plied: market trading in a humble product is, it is implied, a humiliating occupation for the mother of a tragic poet whose genre (unlike comedy) excluded the items of such a trade.

Just as comedy inhabits the material world to a strong degree, so foods themselves have a robust materiality. *Wealth* 189–93 makes the point:

CHREMYLUS: You can have a surfeit of all other things, sex . . .
CARIO: Loaves,
CHREMYLUS: Culture,
CARIO: Nibbles,
CHREMYLUS: Honour,
CARIO: Flat-cakes,
CHREMYLUS: Courage,
CARIO: Dried figs,
CHREMYLUS: Competitiveness,
CARIO: Barley cake,
CHREMYLUS: Campaigning,
CARIO: Lentil soup.[9]

Chremylus the master lists abstract terms, while his slave Carion confines himself to foods. To a large extent the focus on foods reflects the lower cultural level inhabited by the low-status slave. This example shows that comic poets always had the option of presenting the material world in clear distinction from the abstract within its own discourse—without any need to refer to philosophy or tragedy. Often, however, such distinctions within

9

XP.: τῶν μὲν γὰρ ἄλλων ἐστὶ πάντων πλησμονή,
ἔρωτος ΚΑ.: ἄρτων XP.: μουσικῆς ΚΑ.: τραγημάτων
XP.: τιμῆς ΚΑ.: πλακούντων XP.: ἀνδραγαθίας ΚΑ.: ἰσχάδων
XP.: φιλοτιμίας ΚΑ.: μάζης XP.: στρατηγίας ΚΑ.: φακῆς.
Cf. the exchange between Dionysus and Heracles over Euripides and pea soup at *Frogs* 55–67.

the comic text are blurred. On many occasions comedy uses material objects to represent its own nature and objectives. Plays often identify themselves with traditional values, for example. In *Ecclesiazusae* conservatism in the polis is exemplified in a list of practical activities performed by women,[10] while in the parabasis of *Frogs* unwelcome political developments are compared with the debasement of the city's coins.[11]

1.2. APPROACHES TO THE MATERIAL WORLD

The following analysis of the material world in comedy rests on three principal observations. First, objects of the material world fill the text; comedy claims the material as its own and represents it largely in verbal form, within comic discourse. It is often for this reason that comedy is so frequently quoted by authors such as Athenaeus and Pollux, for whom the texts of comedy attest the terms for everyday objects of earlier periods. Verbal representations were further supported by gesture and props which are prominent in comedy.

Second, objects are presented in their social and cultural context which have a place in a hierarchy. Power mystifies itself by abstraction and the endowment of symbolic significance to the trappings of office. 'Popular-festive' forms of literature oppose such abstraction with elements of the material world such as foods; with the activities of the common people such as market traders and craftsmen; with an emphasis on the body, in particular with the apertures of the body rather than its generalized surface, and with the 'lower stratum', that is the anus and generative

---

[10] 214–32: 'PRAXAGORA: I will demonstrate how women are better than us in their conduct. To start with, they dye their wool with hot water, according to ancient custom. All of them. And you won't see them introducing any changes either. By contrast, if the city of Athens has any institution that is doing fine, it does not look after it, unless some new light on it can be devised. The women sit down to roast their barley, just as they used to. They carry things on their head, just as they used to. They bake flat-cakes just as they used to. They worry their husbands to death, just as they used to. They have lovers in the house, just as they used to. They like their wine neat, just as they used to. They enjoy sexual intercourse, just as they used to. Therefore, gentlemen, let's not drone on about handing the city over to them and let's not bother to enquire what it is they propose but simply let them run things.'

[11] 718–37.

organs; and with an emphasis on death and the underworld. Bakhtin (1968) has used this approach particularly well in his study of the grotesque in Rabelais. While the grotesque in Greece in the fifth century BC had not developed many of the characteristics seen in the Middle Ages,[12] comedy employs a number of related features and shares the perspective of festivity and the voice of the people. Nowhere is this better illustrated than in *Knights*, a play in which two politicians of Athens are declared to be uneducated, to be craftsmen in the two malodorous trades of tanning and black-pudding-making. They process the hides and guts of animals into commodities which they sell as market traders with dishonest sales techniques. The traders dismember animals and process both the hides and the inner parts; but they also make reference to the apertures of their own bodies, the shouting mouth and the defecating and farting anus which might also be an avenue for buggery. The politician-traders have suffered loss of status and are slaves, while the most humiliated, Cleon/Paphlagon, is subjected to the ritual violence of expulsion as the scapegoat, possibly at the Thargelia festival. These elements are studied further in Chapter 4. *Knights* is not unique: similar treatments of the body of the politician and other prominent citizens are to be found, for example, in *Acharnians* and in fr. 99 of the *Demes* of Eupolis. Two passages will suffice here. Early in *Acharnians* ambassadors, notorious purveyors of the trappings of power in pompous language, report to the Athenian assembly their sufferings during an embassy to the king of Persia (65–87):

AMBASSADOR: You sent us to the great king on expenses of two drachmas a day while Euthymenes was archon.
DICAEOPOLIS: Alas for the drachmas!
AMBASSADOR: Then we were exhausted with our travels under awnings

---

[12] See Carrière (1979), 29–32. The grotesque in Greece is exemplified in the Furies of Aeschylus' *Eumenides*, who are repulsive creatures of the nether regions. Nothing comparable is known in comedy apart possibly from Aristophanes' description of Cleon at *Wasps* 1032–5 = *Peace* 755–8: 'the most dread gleams shone from the eyes of Cynna; a hundred heads of groaning flatterers encircled his head with licking tongues; he had the voice of a torrent giving birth to destruction, the smell of a seal, the unwashed testicles of Lamia, and the anus of a camel.' Plays with the title *Lamia* were written by Euripides and Crates. The farting of Lamia is the subject of Philocleon's attempt at an after-dinner story at *Wasps* 1177.

over the plains of the Cayster, reclining softly on special wagons. It almost ruined us.

DICAEOPOLIS: I was trying to keep myself going lying among the debris by the parapet [of the long walls].

AMBASSADOR: We were entertained and under duress drank sweet unmixed wine from cups of crystal and gold.

DICAEOPOLIS: O city of Cranaus, don't you realize how you are mocked by the ambassadors?

AMBASSADOR: The barbarians believe real men to be only those able to eat and drink the most.

DICAEOPOLIS: With us it's the buggers and the bum boys.

AMBASSADOR: In the fourth year we arrived at the king's court. But he was away with an army in the bog and was shitting for eight months on the golden hills.

DICAEOPOLIS: For how long did he keep his arse shut?

AMBASSADOR: For the full moon. Then he went home. Then he entertained us and served us with whole oven-roast oxen.

DICAEOPOLIS: And who ever saw oven-roast oxen? What imposture!

Later in the same play Dicaeopolis, who seems to be identified with Aristophanes himself,[13] describes how he was attacked by the politician Cleon. The images of insult are those of a torrent rather than bodily fluids of vomit, urine, and excrement, but the orifices of the politician are implied (377–82): 'I myself know what I suffered at Cleon's hands over last year's comedy. Dragging me into the council chamber, he slandered and tongued lies against me. He rushed like the stream of Cycloborus and washed me so thoroughly that I almost died from his filthy dealings.'

The ambassador to Persia reported in 'popular-festive' mode both the bowel movements of the Great King and the material objects of the banquet, expensive cups, whole animals roasted, and mobile couches.[14] These indicated the exclusiveness as well as the excess and foreignness of the hospitality. A popular-festive approach is particularly suited to the study of Old Comedy; in New Comedy obscene and bodily elements are much reduced, but even here material objects are linked with characters of low

---

[13] Dicaeopolis has a complex identity: see Foley (1988) and A. M. Bowie (1993) 28–9, with n. 42.

[14] That is not to say that obscenity and material objects are theoretically equivalent, but that the latter may be incorporated into the rude ways of the 'popular-festive' mode.

status such as cooks, parasites, and *hetaerae* who often prevail against the authority of the dominant male.[15]

It is rare for material objects to be culturally neutral. The third observation arises from the collection of essays edited by Appadurai (1986) and by Douglas and Isherwood (1979), in their analyses of the modern consumer economy in comparison with other cultures. These anthropologists and historians insist on the needs of the people for material goods in broad cultural terms: goods carry social and cultural meaning—for the pleasure they bring, for their relation to society, and their facility for placing the individual within social networks and groups. Thus, while the academic economist may disapprove of luxury, for example, for the individual luxury brings identity and meaning. Luxury is important for the present study since, although *tryphe* is presented in negative terms in comedy as in much of Greek literature, the desires of the individual whom comedy approves are normally met. The discourse of luxury is ideological, and comedy—certainly Old Comedy—often endorses the amassing of goods, luxurious or otherwise, by approved persons, normally the protagonist, chorus, and demos of Athens.[16]

Material goods may be identified with commodities;[17] alternatively they may be endowed with a special cultural or religious significance and set apart. Goods may also move from the category of commodity to a special category, according to circumstances. Commodities, in Kopytoff's words, have 'use value and

[15] In Menander's *Dyscolus*, for example, the cook and slave twice torment Cnemon, the senior male, with scenes in which they attempt to borrow cooking equipment (456–521, 889–958); in his *Samia* the senior male misunderstands a kitchen scene in which his partner (a former *hetaera*) is suckling a child (206–82).

[16] On luxury (which in ancient thought has strong hints of decadence) and pleasure see further Chap. 6 and Murray (1995).

[17] I adopt the broad definition of Appadurai (1986), 3: a commodity is an object of economic value. Kopytoff writes (in ibid. 68), 'I assume commodities to be a universal phenomenon. Their existence is a concomitant of the existence of transactions that involve the exchange of things (objects and services), exchange being a universal feature of human social life and, according to some theorists, at the very core of it . . . Where societies differ is in the ways commoditization as a special expression of exchange is structured and related to the social system, in the factors that encourage or contain it, in the long-term tendencies for it to expand or stabilize, and in the cultural and ideological premises that suffuse its workings.'

can be exchanged in a discrete transaction for a counterpart'. Money is a sign that something is a commodity and a commodity differs from a gift in being 'discrete' and part of a finite transaction.[18] Saleability implies goods in common, that can be exchanged.[19] Cultures make order by carving out differences in value and classifying areas of homogeneity and hierarchy. 'The counterdrive to this potential onrush of commoditization is culture. In the sense that commoditization homogenizes value, while the essence of culture is discrimination' (Kopytoff 1986: 73). Appadurai (1986), building on Kopytoff, points out (p. 13) that 'things can move in and out of the commodity state'. Buyer and seller may relate in various ways to each other and to the prevailing cultural boundaries and expectations.[20] Similarly, Douglas and Isherwood (1979: 59) suggest that goods are needed (in addition to subsistence and competitive display) for 'making visible and stable the categories of culture'.[21]

----

[18] 'Gifts are given in order to evoke an obligation to give back a gift, which in turn will evoke a similar obligation—a never-ending chain of gifts and obligations. The gifts themselves may be things that are normally used as commodities (food, feasts, luxury goods, services) but each transaction is not discrete and none, in principle, is terminal.'

[19] 'The perfect commodity would be one that is exchangeable with anything and everything else, as the perfectly commoditized world would be one in which everything is exchangeable or for sale. By the same token, the perfectly decommoditized world would be one in which everything is singular, unique and unexchangeable.'

[20] Social arenas will affect matters; weddings bring women particularly into exchange; dealing with strangers may 'bring to commodity status things that are otherwise protected from commoditization'; 'auctions accentuate the commodity dimension of objects (e.g. paintings) in a manner that might well be regarded as deeply inappropriate in other contexts. Bazaar settings are likely to encourage commodity flows as domestic settings are not' (p. 15). Commodities help to shape human values; if you have x, you are an x type of person (p. 20).

[21] 'More effective rituals use material things, and the more costly the ritual trappings, the stronger we can assume the intention to fix the meanings to be. Goods, in this perspective, are ritual adjuncts; consumption is a ritual process whose primary function is to make sense of the inchoate flux of events. . . . The most general objective of the consumer can only be to construct an intelligible universe with the goods he chooses.' 'The choice of goods continuously creates certain patterns of discrimination, overlaying or reinforcing others. Goods then are the visible part of culture. They are arranged in vistas and hierarchies that can give play to the full range of discrimination of which the human mind is capable' (1979: 65–6).

These anthropological approaches can be usefully applied to the study of Greek comedy, since the exchange of goods between individuals differently placed in the hierarchy is a major comic preoccupation and that hierarchy is often challenged and reconfigured. In *Ecclesiazusae* the hierarchy is inverted and goods and property are held in common; in *Birds* exchanges between humans and gods are modified; in other utopian plays goods and exchange take on new values. The protagonist of *Acharnians*, for example, rejects and establishes markets at will and sets up new values of exchange which are to his benefit since others are suffering a wartime economy: a Megarian exchanges his daughters for garlic and salt (812–14), a Boeotian eels for market tax and a sycophant in a pot (895–7, 904–5); as for gifts, a ruined farmer's request for peaceful eye-ointment is rejected (1018–39), while a bride's request for her husband's penis to stay at home is accepted and stay-at-home ointment given (1058–68).[22] In *Peace* there is much delight that the market-place is full again (974–1015) and that the agricultural market has improved at the expense of the arms trade (1197–267). Comedy sometimes sides ideologically with those opposed to commerce, at other times with individual citizens who spend their allowance earned from jury service and other civic duties (see Chapter 4). The elite expressed its power both by spending large sums (see Chapter 6.5) and in lavish displays of hospitality and gift-giving (see Anaxandrides, fr. 42, quoted 278–80).

Comedy is the genre in which money played a significant part. Prices are attached to goods to a greater extent than in other literary texts of the period. The spectrum of commodity and 'culture' is an issue in these plays. Comedy tends on the one hand to reduce everything to a monetary equivalent, to commodity status, while on the other to pick out special cultural features, whether for the purposes of a joke or to make an ideological point. *Knights* provides the best example. In this play everything is for sale, leather, black-puddings, and politics. But in the grand

[22] The husband himself offers meat in exchange for peace-libations and is rejected (1048–55). These various exchanges are subject only to the whim of the protagonist, who is following a Dionysiac/festive agenda, though he does not consistently support peace and farming as might be expected (see Chap. 3), nor does he wish to share the sweet benefits of peace with all, as the chorus observe (1037–9).

coup at the end of the play black-puddings receive extra validation as the meat of sacrifice, and politics returns to an idealized
state in which price is subordinated to traditional values.[23] Von
Reden (1998) has argued that Menander, on Kopytoff's spectrum of commodity and culture, presents characters or individuals who degrade sacrifice and marriage by reducing them to the
level of commodities for sale.[24] The clearest example is *Drunkenness (Methe)* fr. 224:[25]

then do we not do business and sacrifice in similar ways? Where for the
gods I bring in a nice little sheep that I've bought for ten drachmas, for
a little less than a talent I can get pipe-girls and perfume and harp-girls
[. . .] Thasian wine, eels, cheese, and honey. It follows that we get a
blessing worth ten drachmae, if, that is, good omens have accompanied
the sacrifice to the gods and we offset these benefits against the expense
on these luxury items. But how can this not be a doubling of the evils of
sacrifice? Now if I were the god, I would never allow a loin of meat to be
put on the altar unless the dedicator did not also consecrate an eel: in
that way, Callimedon would be dead, one of the kinsmen of the eel.[26]

The speaker cleverly or ironically combines two areas of consumption that are elsewhere put in separate categories—animal
sacrifice and the luxury meal. As the speaker acknowledges,
money and sacrifice were connected in ancient Greece—money
was used to acquire sacrificial victims and raised from the sale of
hides. Novelty arises from the suggestion that the metaphorical
currency of sacrifice has the same system of value as the commercial market-place for luxury goods. The valuation of sacrificial meat had been presented as ambiguous at least since the time
of Hesiod.[27] Finally, whatever the ideological position adopted in
a comic passage to the ambiguous or symbolic value of money,

[23] I am grateful to Richard Seaford for the observation that in the Greek
polis of this period money is not separated from the sacred. Cults regularly
bought animals for sacrifice and earned income both from the lease of land for
grazing and from the sale of hides of sacrificial animals (Schmitt-Pantel 1992).

[24] See Chap. 2 for a different interpretation of her evidence.

[25] She also cites (1998: 266–9) *Dyscolus* 448–52, *The Arbitration* 206–11, and
Samia 189–95.

[26] On this fragment see Gomme and Sandbach (1973). They suggest that
Callimedon would be so upset to see his favourite food as a burnt offering for the
gods instead of a tempting dish for human consumption that he would sacrifice
his life in an attempt to save it. On Callimedon see Chap. 6.

[27] Hesiod, *Theogony* 535–616.

the comic text retains an interest in the material reality of coins. Epicharmus has numerous references in his meagre fragments to the *litra* (a Sicilian silver coin); Attic comedy often cites prices, which, though baffling to ancient economists,[28] constitute the commodification of objects. Money itself has various roles in a culture: Pherecrates took this further, apparently writing a whole play, *Crapataloi*, based on an imaginary currency in the underworld. One *crapatalos* was, according to Pollux 9.83, worth two breadcrumbs.

Exchanges of commodities, in whatever form, take place in certain parts of the polis. Comedy is conscious of civic space, the city or *astu* and the countryside and villages (*chora*); of the agora, whether the imagined market-place of Dicaeopolis in *Acharnians* or the Athenian agora with its complex of commercial, civic, and sacred spaces; of sacred space such as the acropolis, of political space such as the pnyx (which was converted into a sacred space during the festival of the Thesmophoria), and, in particular, of domestic space. Crane (1997), who recognizes the material essence of the comic polis,[29] examines comedy's negotiation between civic and domestic space. We might expect a number of lost plays to have exploited this rich area, such as the *Kitchen or All-Night Festival*[30] of Pherecrates, whose title may imply location in both domestic and sacred space. While comedy to some extent reflects cultural norms in not representing the interior of the home and in particular female space, it also presents the oikos on stage as much as does tragedy. Women (their status cannot always be determined in fragments)[31] are seen with their make-up and their drinking cups, and male activity normally conducted in civic space is transferred to the home. Notable examples are the household of Demos in *Knights*, in which politicians are reduced to the status of house slaves preparing food for

[28] Many attempts have been made to compare prices in comic texts and on inscriptions. There has been much discussion of the inscription setting fish-prices in the Boeotian town of Acraephia: see Feyel (1936), 27–36; Schaps (1987), 293–6; Davidson (1993), 55–6 and (1997), 186–90; Schaps (1985–8); Dalby (1995), 67; Gallant (1985), 39–42.

[29] A 'somatic, sensible entity shaped by intellectual forces yet present in its parts and its grainy particularity'.

[30] *Ipnos or Pannychis*.

[31] Aristophanes, *Thesmophoriazusae B* fr. 332 presumably concerns a woman of citizen status.

their old master (here the polis is imagined to be an oikos, with the civic hearth now a domestic hearth). When Trygaeus drives the arms dealers from his wedding in *Peace* they are sent packing from an ill-defined house (1221). The domestic trial of the dog for the theft of cheese in *Wasps* is a well-known case in which the home is used instead of the courtroom, and many details of the kitchen are incorporated, just as earlier in the play the old protagonist is pursued through the tiny interstices of the house, the oven/kitchen, the chimney, and the roof-tiles. The use of the kitchen is remarkable since the average Athenian kitchen was not fitted out in the manner of modern kitchens with fixed equipment such as cookers (see below). Often the domestic kitchen was linked with the 'kitchen of state' and the 'kitchen of sacrifice', and with the individual's links with community and cult. It was usually the utensils and cooking techniques that were important rather than the kitchen space, and these could be deployed in secular and sacred spaces at will, as seen in the hired cooks of Middle and New Comedy and, probably, in the *Fryers* (*Tagenistae*) of Aristophanes, the remit of whose chorus is sadly lost to us.[32]

1.3. THE RAW MATERIALS

The text of comedy is crammed[33] with all the materials of daily life, and that text too exerts itself upon material objects. Thus in *Clouds*, when gender in language is under discussion it is the gender of a feeding-trough that is considered (670–93). When metaphors or images are sought to characterize the verse of Euripides in *Frogs*, it is the medicines of the doctor and the raw ingredients of the kitchen which are presented as doing so best (see below). Aristophanes polarizes Aeschylus and Euripides, presenting them respectively as the poet of war and myth and the poet of the contemporary and domestic; in this way Euripides' plays are imagined to resemble comedy in content.[34]

---

[32] See further Kassel–Austin (1984), p. 264.

[33] Gowers (1993), 70–6 discusses the stuffing of comic and satirical verse and the analogy with stuffed foods.

[34] In the fourth century a speaker (a *mageiros*?) in Anaxilas *Mageiroi* fr. 19 declares 'A: It seems to me much better than the verses of Aeschylus to roast little fish. B: What are you saying? Little fish? You'll make the guests sea-sick.

1.3.1. The Lentil

A food that is not likely to appear in a tragic text is the lentil, a legume of particularly low status and therefore exploitable by comedy if its poets wished to flaunt their claims to the everyday and the ordinary. At *Wealth* 1004–5 Chremylus declares, 'now he is wealthy he no longer enjoys lentil soup. In the past, because of his poverty, he ate everything.' The material structure of the lentil, as with most plants, does not lend itself to comic elaboration in the ways that are possible for meat and fish. Rather, lentils constitute an earthy basis for the diet, probably for all, but in particular for the impoverished and those opposed to 'luxurious' and high-status dishes. Lentils are often consumed in the form of soup, such as that enjoyed by Procleon at *Wasps* 811–15. Athenaeus[35] introduces his survey of the lentil with the *Parekdidomene* (= *Woman Secretly Married*(?)) of Antiphanes, whose character pronounces (fr. 185): 'I swear to you, gentlemen, by the god through whom we are all enabled to get drunk, that this is the life I choose rather than the excess of King Seleucus: it is sweet to guzzle lentil soup without fear; to sleep luxuriously and softly but in fear is wretched.' The humble lentil, the food of the common people, excels all the unstable luxury of the tyrant. Antiphanes exploits the notion that lentils and wine are the foods of the Athenians; no one takes the lentil to excess, and any excess at the symposium is sanctioned by Dionysus himself; the foreign tyrant, by contrast, knows no restraint. In Athenaeus' survey, a typical tour de force that ties lentil consumption to his own place or origin, Roman Egypt, and revels in its 'erudition concerning the lentil' (4.158d), the two principal consumers of lentils are the poor and philosophers who identify the lentil as virtuous food. The 'Symposium of the Cynics' by Parmeniscus,[36] a sub-comic text which is a mini-version of the *Deipnosophistae*, presents a

More [. . .] to boil extremities, snouts, trotters . . .' The reference to Aeschylus may be modelled on the rhetorical phrase 'X is a greater matter than the capture of Troy': cf. Eubulus fr. 6.2, quoted on p. 95.

[35] 4.156c–160d. As with the majority of his discussions of foods, Athenaeus' survey of the lentil is based on comic quotation. I have chosen his treatments of the lentil and meats boiled in water to illustrate two features, one the extent of material reference to a particular food in comedy, the other the exploitation of those foods to form poetic material within comic discourse.

[36] An author known only from the quotation by Athenaeus at 4.156c–157d.

group of non-Athenian philosophers who meet during the Athenian Dionysia and, apparently ignoring the festival, exchange witticisms on lentils which take the form of phrases from tragedy into which are inserted the incongruous terms 'lentil' and 'lentil soup'.[37] Lentils belong to comedy and readily deflate the pretension of philosophy and tragedy, not to mention the serious presentation of myth. Athenaeus makes the point by inserting a comic text from a play on a mythical topic, Diphilus' *Daughters of Pelias* (fr. 64): 'A: The dinnerette was splendid and very well done—a large bowl full of lentil soup was placed by each man. B: For a start that is not splendid! A: After that a huge *saperdes* waltzed in, carrying itself into our midst, though rather foul-smelling. B: That is the sacred *anthias*, which makes the wrasses keep it at a distance.'[38] An example drawn from tragic myth in art follows (Sophilos fr. 10): 'lentil soup is a tragic item, for they say that Agatharchus once painted a picture of Orestes guzzling lentil soup when he had got over his illness.'[39] There are straight comic examples also: Aristophanes, *Amphiaraus* fr. 23, 'you who abuse lentil soup, that most tasty of opsa'; Antiphanes, *Similars* fr. 171, 'it turned out well, for one of the inhabitants of the place taught me to boil lentil soup'.[40] Sopater, *Bacchis* fr. 1, gives a new twist to the humble lentil: 'I could not, if I could see the huge bronze Colossus, eat lentil bread.' Humble it remains in Pherecrates, *Corianno* fr. 73:

A: Come on, I'll recline on the couch. Bring out a table and a drinking cup and something to eat, so that I'll enjoy the drink better.

B: Look, here's your cup and table and lentils.

A: No lentils for me, by Zeus. I dislike them. If you eat them, your mouth smells bad.

[37] For other examples of this sympotic game see Athenaeus 1.4a–d, discussed in Wilkins (forthcoming, a).

[38] This is typical comic blending of the categories of good taste and the sacred which were discussed above by Kopytoff (1986). The *saperdes* and *anthias* are not securely identified: see Thompson (1947), 14–16, 226. The *saperdes* is sometimes identified with the meagre and other poorly regarded fish, while the *anthias* is 'a celebrated fish' (Thompson).

[39] Further sub-comic citations include Timon of Phlius on Stoics spicing lentil soup and verses by Chrysippus in mixed metres on tassel hyacinth-and-lentil soup.

[40] And Ar. *Gerytades* fr. 165, Epicharmus, *Dionysuses* fr. 33.

Comedy may have exploited the bad breath induced by lentils elsewhere: in Strattis, *Phoenician Women* fr. 47, Jocasta says: 'I want to give you some good advice—if you boil lentil soup, don't add perfume'; Sopater, *Nekuia* fr. 14, 'Odysseus of Ithaca at your service. As the saying goes, the perfume is in the lentil soup. Be brave, my heart.' Perfume may, however, have served some other purpose in these passages which manage to combine the great aristocrats of myth with what is clearly the poor man's food.[41] Outside Attic comedy the lentil expanded its role in texts. Hegemon has himself addressed as 'Foul Lentil Soup' in epic parody: 'as I thought on these things, Pallas Athene stood beside me holding her golden wand. She drove me on and said, "Foul Lentil Soup who have suffered such torments, go forth to the contest". Then I took heart and sang all the more.'[42] Sopater wrote a comedy entitled *Lentil Soup*.[43]

The lentil remains doggedly at the bottom of the hierarchy of foods. Along with other legumes/pulses it is readily available to all at low cost and is not subject to elaborate cooking or processing. Thus the lentil is not to be found in fourth-century poetic texts which overtly celebrate luxurious foods, *The Life of Luxury* of Archestratus of Gela, *The Attic Dinner* of Matro, or the *Dinner* of Philoxenus.[44] These texts help us to distinguish the lentil from other legumes, such as the chickpea which appears as an item of dessert in Philoxenus (*PMG* 836 (e) 20) and in Archestratus

---

[41] A survey of the incidence of φακῆ in Aristophanes, to set as a control against the selection of Athenaeus used here, reveals nothing out of line with the notion that lentil soup is the poor man's standby: *Wasps* 811, 814, 918, 984; *Wealth* 192, 1004; frr. 23, 164, 165. Fr. 164 is the most neutral example, simply listing 'trotters, breads, langoustes, tassel hyacinths, lentil soup'.

[42] Φακῆ βδέλυρε (Hegemon fr. 1.18–21 Brandt), introduced by Athenaeus (8.406b–407a) among the legumes and pulses. Brandt (1888: 40) does not accept as genuine the further couplet cited by Athenaeus from Chamaeleon of Pontus and addressed by Foul Lentil Soup to the audience, 'here are the stones. Let anyone who wishes throw one at me. Lentil soup is a fine thing both in winter and in summer.' On Hegemon's parodies and their relation to comedy see Chap. 7.

[43] Athenaeus playfully follows comedy's lead at 4.158d in calling Sopater ὁ Φάκιος, for ὁ Πάφιος. Comedies with titles named after foods are rare. Cf. the *Sausage* of Epicharmus. The closest Attic title is probably the *Cooking-Pot* of Alexis, though the title may refer to a pot that contained treasure: see Arnott (1996). The fragments indicate the presence of a *mageiros*. The *Oinos* (*Wine*) of Alexis is a further possibility: see ibid.

[44] On these texts see Chap. 7.

fr. 62.10–16: 'Have nothing to do with those Syracusans who drink only in the manner of frogs and eat nothing. No, do not be taken in by them, but eat the foods I set forth. All those other *tragemata* are a sign of wretched poverty, boiled chickpeas, broad beans, apples and dried figs. I do though applaud the flat-cake born in Athens.' The discourse of Archestratus in mock-epic hexameters overtly promotes luxury in a form that is alert to comic mockery, but makes a useful distinction in the hierarchy of foods. He has no time for foods that are available to the poor, such as apples and chickpeas,[45] but at least they gain access to his text, as lentils do not.[46] He also praises the Attic flat-cake.

1.3.2. Cereals and Flour

Cereal products, which, like lentils, are the staple diet of Greeks of all classes, are admitted to the texts of Archestratus, Matro, and Philoxenus, and not merely confections based on wheat and yeast, which, because of their comparative rarity, achieved a higher status in Greece. Flat-cakes (that is, breads without yeast) were available to all, as, more significantly, was barely cake, *maza*. *Maza*, above all else, was the cereal staple of ancient Greece, but it gained access to texts lauding luxury because it could be processed into refined forms that marked distinction.[47] The grain could be selected for quality and milled to high

[45] On *tragemata* see n.158 below. On other despised foods in Archestratus cf. fr. 4: 'Tassel hyacinths. I bid farewell to vinegar-dishes (*oxubapha*) of tassel hyacinths and plant stalks, and to all other side-dishes (*paropsides*).' On tassel hyacinth bulbs and stalks see Wilkins and Hill (1994), 42–3 and Olson and Sens (forthcoming); on *oxybapha* and *paropsides* see below and Chap. 5.

[46] As far as surviving fragments reveal. On chickpeas see Pherecrates fr. 89 and Athenaeus 2.54e–55b.

[47] For unrefined barley cakes see Poliochus fr. 2, 'twice a day each of us had a little blackened barley cake kneaded with chaff and a few figs; sometimes we roasted a mushroom and when the dew was on the ground we hunted for a snail. There were greens grown from the very soil, a crushed olive, and a negligible wine of doubtful quality.' Also Antiphanes fr. 225.1–6, 'dinner is a barley cake bristling with chaff, presented economically, a single tassel hyacinth, and side-dishes of thistle or mushroom or such wretched fare as this wretched place affords us. Such is our way of life, with no fire and no heat.' Contrast Amphis, *The Madness of Women* fr. 9, 'A: Have you ever heard of the "milled" way of life? B: Yes. A: Clearly that is what we have here. Milk cakes, sweet wine, eggs, sesame, perfume, a garland, a pipe-girl. B: O Dioscuri, you have listed the names of the twelve gods!' On Amphis fr. 9 see Chap. 6.

specification. Thus, Archestratus praised barely breads above wheat (fr. 4.1–15), Philoxenus the whitest barley cake (*PMG* 836 (b) 6), and Matro admitted *maza*, albeit grudgingly.[48] Higher-grade still was finely sifted *amulon* from which came the luxurious cakes (*amuloi*) praised by Philoxenus in dithyrambic elaboration (*PMG* 836 (e) 5–10, 18). Such confections might be served at the end of the meal, during the symposium, or earlier: comic texts of utopia present *amuloi* as a bed on which to serve fish and meat.[49] Many forms of breads and cakes appear in comic texts.[50]

1.3.3. The Vine

The plant which above all is elevated beyond its material form into a complex and rich symbol is the vine, the premier gift of Dionysus. It is essential to the sacrifice, it identifies the Greek symposium and civilized drinking, and it seals many cultural exchanges. Comedy, in its elevation of the material, picks out such vinous transactions. *Acharnians*, a text particularly rich in Dionysiac imagery, presents a peace-treaty in the material form of wine in wineskins (187–200) and the rejection of war in the refusal to drink with War personified because he pours away wine and burns vine-props (983–6). In its sour form, as vinegar, wine has many comic uses.[51]

1.3.4. Parts of Animals

Comedy pays much attention to the animals consumed by humans, animals of land, sea, and air—sacrificial animals, hunted animals, birds, and fish. Very often a part of an animal is consumed either because it is a particularly tasty or sought-after part or because comedy wishes to emphasize that the meat or fish being consumed is a former creature. Analysis of fish and meat provides a different picture from the cereals and pulses investigated above. Where in British culture texture is no longer enjoyed and the lesser cuts of meat are ground into sausages, pies, and burgers, in Greece these textures were sought out. Thus, lesser

---

[48] For comic texts praising white barley cakes see Arnott (1996), on Alexis fr. 145.7 and add Teleclides, *Amphictyons* fr. 1.5–6. On the lesser cereals in comedy see Dalby (1995), 89.

[49] Pherecrates, *Miners* fr. 113.17 and Metagenes, *Thuriopersians* fr. 6.11.

[50] See Chap. 6; Athenaeus 3.109b–115b, 14.643e–648c; Dalby (1995), 91.

[51] Dalby (1995), 89.

cuts such as heads, ears, wombs, and trotters appear in contexts of luxury as well as in the diet of the poor. This cultural valuing of material texture in meat and fish offered the comic poets much more scope than did cereals and pulses. Intense interest in the parts of animals also allowed the comic poets to engage with other poetic forms, in particular tragedy. It will be evident in the fragments that follow that comic adaptations of tragic and other forms of myth introduced either elements unknown in the genre that is being parodied (such as fish-heads in the myth of the Seven against Thebes) or more grotesque elements. Where Aeschylus pictured the eating of children in the feast of Thyestes in an analogy with the sacrificial division of an animal into vital organs, flesh, and entrails,[52] Aristophanes has Thyestes speak of the tripe-sausages and snouts of his children (see below).

Fragment 16 of Amphis, 'whole *glaukos*[53] and portions of nice fleshy head-meat', illustrates the contrasting textures of the fish's body—in a play derived from tragic myth, *Seven Against Thebes*: the objectives of the gourmet meet the comic version of the tragic myth of Polynices and Eteocles. Similarly, Anaxandrides, *Nereus*, fr. 31,[54] presents a mythological discoverer (*protos euretes*) for the textures of fish: 'the first to discover the lavish great head of the *glaukos* sliced up and the frame of the blameless tuna and the other comestibles from the watery brine [was] Nereus who inhabits the entirety of this place.' Texture may be promoted both by the cut of fish and the cooking process: Antiphanes writes in *Cyclops* fr. 130, 'let there be grey mullet sliced, electric ray stewed, perch split, squid stuffed, dentex baked, the front cut of a *glaukos*, the head of a conger, the belly of an angler-fish, the flanks of a tuna, the back of a ray, the lion of a barracuda, [. . .] of a sole, a sprat, a prawn, a red mullet, a wrasse. Let none of these be missing.' Notable elements in this text are the mythological subject of the play, the extraordinary range of the list over species and modes of preparation, and the animated anapaestic rhythm.[55] All three passages, among others, are listed by

---

[52] *Agamemnon* 1221–2.

[53] No certain species can be identified: see Thompson (1947), 48.

[54] See also p. 390.

[55] Nesselrath (1990), 267–80 discusses the anapaestic diameter in Middle Comedy. I discuss the use of such rhythms in the early speeches of the boastful cook in Chap. 8.

Athenaeus in his gazetteer entry on the *glaukos* (7.295b–297c); of the last he writes (295f), 'Antiphanes outshoots the epicure Archestratus'. Athenaeus probably refers to the gourmandise, but Antiphanes has produced a comic tour de force that contributes as much to poetic as to edible texture; it is likely, in addition, that these are the words of a satirized character, whether host, chef, or gourmet. There are many comparable examples[56] where the wider cultural implications of texture and taste are examined. These include advice from medical texts which indicate that more than the pleasure of eating is at issue.

Animal extremities are reviewed in Athenaeus' category of 'meats boiled in water' (3.94c–101f): 'feet, heads, ears, jaws, together with intestines, tripe and tongues.' Athenaeus ties his review apparently to his own experience, the boiled-meat shops[57] of Alexandria, downriver from his native Naucratis, but the contents are almost exclusively comic. Comedy's combining of Attic diction with material content made it a source beyond compare for Athenaeus. Thus, says Athenaeus,[58] the boiled-meat shops were given (comparatively) ancient validation in Posidippus, *Paidion* fr. 22. The choice of Aristophanes' *Knights* as the first comedy to attest such foods may be significant since, of surviving plays, it appears to have been the boiled-meat play of all time (see Chapter 4). Athenaeus selects 300–2 in paraphrase ('I will denounce you for selling untaxed guts') and in quotation 160–1 ('Sir, why don't you leave me to wash my guts and sell my black-puddings? Why do you mock me?'), 356–8 ('I will gulp down the gut of a cow and the tripe of a pig, and then, drinking up their soup, without washing my hands I'll out-bawl the politicians and confuse Nicias'), and 1178–9 ('the goddess with the mighty father gave me meat boiled in soup and a slice of gut, cow-stomach, and belly').[59] Also from the fifth century BC, Athenaeus adds

---

[56] Some are listed in Wilkins and Hill (1994a).

[57] ἐφθοπώλιαι.

[58] The text is epitomized at this point and speakers assigned in the original text of Athenaeus have been excised.

[59] Athenaeus selects process (cleaning tripe, boiling in stock), metaphor, and aggressive boasting—not a bad representation of *Knights*, as I argue in Chap. 4. His selection may, however, rest solely on a word-search of the terms κοιλία and ἤνυστρον. Athena at *Knights* 1178–9 is attributed material functions not normally considered part of her role in the polis. Cf. her advice above to Hegemon, 'Foul Lentil Soup', a protégé somewhat different from the hero of the *Odyssey*.

Cratinus, *Wealths* fr. 174, Sophocles, *Amycus* fr. 112 Radt (a satyr play),[60] and Epicharmus, *Orya* (*Sausage*).[61] Moving to Middle and New Comedy, Athenaeus cites Alexis, *Leucadia* fr. 137, Antiphanes, *Weddings* fr. 73, and many others.[62] Now, although Athenaeus appears mainly to have concerned himself with listing passages—and he achieves this to telling effect—other features intervene. Considering snouts, he cites Anaxilas, *Circe* fr. 13, 'it's a terrible thing, Cinesias, having a pig's snout'. Given the play's title, Circe's transformation of the companions of Odysseus is a probable plot and, whatever the role of Cinesias[63] in the play, similarities and differences between humans and pigs are suggested by fr. 13. This raises the matter of the relationship of the human and animal body, which Athenaeus takes further. He cites fr. 478 of the *Proagon* of Aristophanes: 'What a wretch

[60]   Also *Clouds* 455–6; Cratinus, *Wine Flask* fr. 205; Eupolis, *Goats* fr. 34.

[61]   For the title cf. n. 43 above. On the *Orya*, Kaibel (1899), 110 notes Hesychius' entry, ὀρούα· χορδή, καὶ σύντριμμα πολιτικόν, εἰς ὃ Ἐπιχάρμου δρᾶμα. The term 'political cuts' is obscure, but might mean that the metaphorical application of meat-processing terms to the political process was to be found in Syracusan as well as Attic comedy.

[62]   On feet, ears, and snout (= *akrokolia*), Alexis, *Crateia or The Drugseller* fr. 115.15–6; Theophilus, *Pancratiast* 8 (quoted p. 94 n. 173); Anaxilas, *Mageiroi* 19 (cited above, n. 34); *Calypso* fr. 11; Anaxandrides, *Satyrias* fr. 44; Axionicus, *The Chalcidian* fr. 8; Pherecrates, *Leroi* fr. 107. Trotters have good texture: Aristophanes, *Aeolosicon* fr. 4, 'and indeed the whatshisname, I boiled four trotters for you till they were soft'; *Gerytades* fr. 164, 'trotters, breads, flat lobsters'; Pherecrates, *Miners* fr. 113.14 (see p. 112); *Slave-Teacher* fr. 50,'A: Tell us how they are coming along with the dinner. B: Well, there is eel steak for you, squid, lamb meat, a slice of sausage, a boiled foot, liver, a rib, a multitude of birds, cheese in honey, a portion of meat'; Ecphantides, *Satyrs* fr. 1, 'whenever he had to buy and eat boiled pig's feet'. The tongue: Aristophanes, *Fryers* (*Tagenistae*) fr. 520, 'That's enough whitebait for me. I'm bloated from scoffing fatty food. Bring me [. . .] a piece of liver or the neck of a young boar. If not that, then bring a rib or a tongue or some spleen or the womb of a young autumn pig with some hot rolls.' The womb: Alexis, *The Man From Pontus* fr. 198 'everyone wishes to die for his country but Callimedon the Crayfish would perhaps offer to die for a boiled womb' (but on the text see Arnott 1996); Euphron, *Paradidomene* fr. 8, 'my teacher prepared a womb and served it to Callimedon and made him jump as he was eating it—whence the name Crayfish'; Dioxippus, *Anti-Pimp* fr. 1, 'What foods he desires! How cultured! Stomachs, wombs, guts'; *Historian* fr. 3, 'Amphicles burst into the stoa and pointing to two wombs hanging up said "send him if you see him"'; Eubulus, *Deucalion* fr. 23, 'little livers, an intestine jejunum, lungs, a womb'.

[63]   See 1.5 below.

am I! I have tasted the sausage of my children. How can I gaze upon their charred snout?'[64] In this comic version of the feast of Thyestes[65] the horror of cannibalism is comically expressed in terms suitable to the animal rather than human physiognomy. Noting that 'snout'[66] properly applies to pigs, Athenaeus illustrates the term applied to other animals and humans in Archippus, *Amphitryo* fr. 1, 'and that even though he [some animal other than a pig] has such a long snout', and Araros, *Adonis* fr. 1, 'for the god is turning his snout towards us'. The latter play may have presented a porcine Adonis or perhaps, given his death at the tusk of a boar, the reference is to another god. At all events the term properly applicable to an animal is applied to the human and divine.[67]

1.4. THE BODY, ANIMAL, HUMAN, AND DIVINE

Comedy regularly blurs the boundaries between animal, human, and god in its relentless pursuit of mocking bathos and its aggressive attack on established boundaries, especially those marking status. That is not to say that comedy fails to represent the established boundaries. The sacrificial procession of the Rural Dionysia in *Acharnians* (237–61) or the sacrifice of the sheep in *Peace*, for example, are two of the best surviving descriptions of sacrifice outside Homer, to set beside such passages as Euripides, *Electra* 774–858. The sacrifice in *Peace* combines both preliminary consecration and details of the distribution of the body parts. To these straight sacrifices are added a number of comic elements, above all the redefinition of who will participate in the sacrifice and who will not: in *Acharnians* the participating body is declared by the protagonist to be his household and not the warlike chorus (200, 249); in *Peace* the chorus are included along with the audience and the priest is excluded along with other officials and all warriors (956–1121).

In *Peace* and *Birds* the gods Hermes and Heracles are marked

[64] Not all snouts, evidently, were boiled in water.
[65] The play appears to concern the process of selecting plays preliminary to the dramatic festivals.
[66] ῥύγχος.
[67] Compare the pig-daughters of the Megarian at *Acharnians* 729–817.

by their gluttony and desire for meat in the form normally consumed by humans rather than the smoke of the sacrificial fire. In *Peace* the loathsome dung-beetle is the vehicle for Trygaeus to approach the gods in the heavens—comedy as it were approaches divinity—and the comic discovery is made that some at least among the gods enjoy bodily pleasures and excrete much as humans do.[68] In *Birds* and *Frogs* Heracles is presented as the gluttonous god whose desire for pea soup is as strong as his appetite for meat (on which see Chapter 2). In *Frogs* Dionysus' mind is on higher things than satisfying physical appetite (Heracles thinks rather of women and food, 52–67), though Charon calls him *gastron*, 'big-belly' (200). But later Dionysus is subjected to physical pressures and both fouls himself in fear and is subjected to bodily torture: the play dwells on the god's physicality, on his bodily form and the sudden evacuation of the divine gut:

XANTHIAS: You there, what have you done?
DIONYSUS: I've shit myself. Call the god.[69]
XANTHIAS: You figure of fun! Won't you stand up before someone else sees you?
DIONYSUS: But I'am all yellow.[70] Bring that sponge against my heart.
XANTHIAS: Here, take it and apply it.
DIONYSUS: Where is it?
XANTHIAS: O golden gods, do you have your heart down there?
DIONYSUS: Yes I do. My heart was terrified and slipped to the bottom of my belly.

(479–85)

DIONYSUS: I declare that I am immortal, Dionysus son of Zeus, and that this man is a slave.
DOORKEEPER: You hear that?
XANTHIAS: Affirmative. He is to be whipped all the more. If he's a god he won't feel it.

[68] 'TRYGAEUS: Where will the wretched beetle get its food from? HERMES: It will eat the "ambrosia" of Ganymede' (723–4). 'SLAVE: I wouldn't give three obols for the gods if they are prostitutes' pimps like we mortals' (848–9). Divinity and excreta do not readily mix: cf. Antiphanes, *Woman of Corinth* fr. 124, 'A: And then too a pig's trotter to Aphrodite? Ridiculous! B: You do not realize. In Cyprus, master, she takes such pleasure in pigs that she prevents the animal from eating excrement and forces that task on the cattle.'

[69] κάλει θεόν 'was uttered after the pouring of a libation on certain ritual occasions' (Dover).

[70] Colour of excrement.

DIONYSUS: Well then, since you declare that you too are a god, why won't you too receive the same blows as I do?
XANTHIAS: Fair enough. And whichever one of us you see weeping first or claiming greater rights when struck, consider him not to be the god.

(631–9)

In *Birds* the natures of gods, humans, and birds are brought under scrutiny in the most absurd and searching ways by changing human and divine forms and institutions into avian versions. The body of Tereus illustrates the point. Aristophanes takes the Sophoclean version of the myth of Tereus' transformation into a hoopoe: the tragic poet is said to have shown humans how to metamorphose into birds but to have deformed the body of the avian Tereus by giving him a beak and feathers which were defective.

EUELPIDES: We are not laughing at you.
HOOPOE: At what then?
EUELPIDES: Your beak seems ridiculous to us.
HOOPOE: Well that is how Sophocles did me, Tereus, harm in his tragedies.
EUELPIDES: Why, are you Tereus? Are you a bird or a peacock?
HOOPOE: I'm a bird, me.
EUELPIDES: Where are your feathers then?
HOOPOE: They've fallen off.
EUELPIDES: Because of some illness perhaps?
HOOPOE: No. In winter all birds shed their feathers and then we grow new ones.

(98–106)

The tragedy *Tereus* appears to have included the metamorphosis of King *Tereus* into a bird (see Radt *TGrF* IV (1977), 435), but *Birds* probably explores the matter further because of the particular interest of comedy in bodily detail. Later in *Birds* problems of cooking birds—who are now the new gods—for human consumption come into play. Aristophanes sidesteps the issue by concentrating on particular modes of presentation: it is more humiliating for birds to be prepared in a sauce (531–8);[71] birds

---

[71] 'Nor then, if they've decided to do this, do they simply roast and serve you up but they grate over you cheese, oil, silphium, vinegar, and mix up a further sauce that is sweet and rich and then pour all this hot stuff over you as if you were carrion.'

may be roasted if they are politically unsound (1579–86).[72] Preparation in a sauce is insulting to birds because, says Peisetaerus, it implies they are dead meat or carrion. Eating of the dead body is to be distinguished from the body freshly killed: the former is a corpse, the latter 'meat'. The point is made at Aristophanes fr. 714,[73] and is linked to anxiety over those birds of prey whose natural food is carrion contaminating meat at sacrifice.[74] Dead bodies at an intermediary stage between carrion and the meat of sacrifice are those of non-sacrificial animals such as dogs and donkeys. Black-puddings from this category are to be sold by the humiliated Cleon/Paphlagon, the scapegoat at the end of *Knights* 1398–9). *Knights* provides the most inventive text on the interchange between the human and animal body. I analyse in Chapter 4 the ways in which the Black-Pudding-Seller and his adversary Cleon/Paphlagon the tanner, one a processor of animal intestines, the other of animal hides, apply the violence suitable to their trades on each other and in a number of ways themselves become animals. They screech and scream like animals, they claw and bite each other; Cleon/Paphlagon's head becomes the pig's head in the butcher's stall (357–81).[75]

1.5. THE HUMAN BODY: EATING AND BODY-SIZE

The comic text is interested in the human body as much as in the bodies of fish, animals, and plants. In a number of plays in Old Comedy the chorus became animals themselves. The drama had developed, in ways that are not entirely clear to us, from fertility rituals in which men disguised themselves as animals, sometimes insects, sometimes edible animals such as wild beasts, goats, and fish. In fragmentary plays known to us, the *Beasts* of Crates, the

---

[72] On the cooking and sacrifice of birds in the play see further Wilkins (forthcoming, b).

[73] 'I don't eat carrion. When you have a sacrifice, call me.'

[74] See *Peace* 1099–100; Dunbar (1995) on *Birds* 865 and 892; and Berthiaume (1982), 81–93.

[75] For the identity of human and pig, cf. *Peace* 928—a pig is an unsuitable victim with which to inaugurate the statue of Peace since it suggests the swinishness of Theogenes—and Menander, *Fishermen* fr. 25 on Dionysius of Heracleia, who was 'a fat pig who lay upon his snout'.

Goats of Eupolis, and the *Fishes* of Archippus, choruses raise the problem of predation between humans and other animals and often make clear that they do not wish to be consumed by humans.[76] Other comedies allude to human fears of consumption by fish.[77]

Eating is a physical and aggressive process, ingesting one body, whether plant or animal, into another. The eater is likely to benefit more than the eaten, and eating is generally a good in comedy, a benefit to the eater—though the eater may not be approved, particularly the excessive or gluttonous eater and the exclusive eater, such as Cleon/Paphlagon in *Knights*. Eating may take a variety of forms: *Peace* 1305–10, 'For the rest, it's the job of the rest of you here to crush and pound all of these foods in your teeth, and not to leave your stomachs empty. But strike in manly fashion and grind down with both jaws. For, my poor friends, there's no use in having white teeth if they don't chew the food.' There is something here of the physiology, and of the pleasure of eating. Other terms in the comic vocabulary for eating include χορτάζειν ('to eat fodder'),[78] ῥοφεῖν ('to guzzle'),[79] μασᾶσθαι ('to chew'),[80] λαφύσσειν ('to gulp down like an animal'),[81] καταβροχθίζειν ('to swallow down')[82] and τρώγειν ('to nibble').[83]

Eating is a further part of the physical and material comic world that can be used to counter the pretention of other systems of thought. At *Clouds* 385–93 Socrates uses Strepsiades' guts as an illustrative model of meteorological phenomena:

---

[76] See further Wilkins (forthcoming, b).

[77] See Plato fr. 57; Antiphanes, *Butalion* fr. 69; *Kouris* fr. 127; Alexis, *Hellenis* fr. 76; Olson and Sens (forthcoming) on Archestratus 23.16–7; Purcell (1995), 133–4.

[78] Athenaeus (3.99f–100b) cites Cratinus, *Odysseuses* fr. 149, 'you sat eating white milk as fodder all day'; Aristophanes, *Gerytades* fr. 162,'nurture him/her and feed on a fodder of monodies'; Amphis, *Ouranos* fr. 28; Eubulus, *Dolon* fr. 29, 'I'm foddered up pretty well, gentlemen, in fact I'm full—to such an extent that whatever I try and do I can barely do up my shoes'; Sophilos, *Phylarchus* fr. 7, 'It'll be lavish gourmandise. I can see the start of it [. . .] I shall feed myself on fodder. By Dionysus, gentlemen, I'm already up for it (στρηνιῶ)'; Menander, *Trophonius* fr. 353.

[79] A verb used particularly of the ingestion of soup, e.g. at *Wasps* 814. Human pigs 'guttle' at *Acharnians* 807, ῥοθιάζουσι.

[80] *Wealth* 321.   [81] Eupolis fr. 166.   [82] *Knights* 357 and 826.

[83] Especially of fruit and dessert (*tragemata*).

SOCRATES: I will use you as an example to instruct you. Were you nicely filled up with meat soup at the Panathenaia and then felt upset in your stomach, and did a sudden noise rumble through it?

STREPSIADES: Yes by Apollo. It gave me grief straightaway and was upset and like thunder that little bit of soup rumbled and made a terrible crack, gently at first, pop, pop, and then it came on more, pop, pop, pop, and when I crapped, all at once it thundered pop, pop, pop, just like those clouds do.

SOCRATES: Consider then how you farted from this little stomach of yours. How is it not reasonable that this great Ether in all its measureless extent should not thunder loudly?

A little later (403–11):

STREPSIADES: What then is lightning?

SOCRATES: Whenever dry wind is raised up and enclosed in the clouds, it inflates them like a bladder, and then breaking out from them with great force it is carried fiercely though the thick air, catching fire under the pressure of the whirling motion and its own strength.

STREPSIADES: By Zeus, that's the very thing I experienced once at the Diasia when I was roasting an animal stomach for my relatives and took my eye off it. It inflated and then suddenly burst open and spattered my eyes, and burnt my forehead.

These passages illustrate comedy's debunking approach to science through the deployment of its own fields of interest, namely physical details of the human body, particularly internal organs, the similarity between human and animal stomachs and bladders, and the social setting of the festival (Panathenaia and Diasia) as the locus at which the animal body is likely to be consumed, in the form of meat soup or a stuffed stomach. The material, as often, is integrated into the social and religious structures of the polis, and it is at festivals that the majority of citizens expected both to eat meat and watch comedies.[84]

Comedy concentrates on the human body: *Acharnians* 30–2, 'I groan, I yawn, I stretch, I fart, I lose my purpose, I sketch, I pull out a few hairs, I do a calculation, . . .'. The comic character displays fewer inhibitions than others in the culture, behaving sometimes as one from a more refined part of the community might expect a dog to behave—in ignorance of the niceties of polite society. At *Ecclesiazusae* 311–73 Blepyrus defecates on stage.

---

[84] See Chaps. 2 and 3 below.

The stomach plays a large part. Some insatiable men have a hollow stomach (Eupolis fr. 187), others are *gastrimargoi* (with a gluttonous stomach) and *encheirogastores* (filling their stomach with the work of their hands). The last is the title of a play by Nicophon. So too the neck, considered in many texts to be the seat of the pleasure of taste, with the greater pleasure going to the person with the longer, more crane-like neck. Some men were lickers of plates, others chasers after the steam of the frying-pan (Eupolis fr. 190). This comic phenomenon has a long history, extending back at least to an elegy of Asius.[85]

A body of excessive weight is a frequent object of satire,[86] exemplified by Antiphanes, *Aeolus* fr. 20, 'because of his glugging of wine and the fat of his body all the locals call him Wineskin'.[87] The ambassador at *Acharnians* 88–9, describing the size of animals roasted whole by the Persians, declares, 'yes by Zeus, and a bird three-times the size of Cleonymus, and it was called imposter'. Fat is frequently a political issue in comedy, large body-size being invoked within the rhetoric of political invective against greed. Cleonymus is by implication a bad politician as well as an excessive consumer. Aristophanes returns to the theme at *Clouds* 674–7; Peisander is a similar target at *Birds* 1556–64, Eupolis, *Demes* fr. 99.1, and elsewhere.[88] Comedy similarly had views on bodies of insufficient weight. Emaciation was attached to certain categories of person, in particular some philosophers[89] and the dithyrambic poet Cinesias, who, according to Athenaeus (12.551d), belonged in this category.[90] Those who received inadequate nourishment, in particular the poor and the dead, belong here: Athenaeus says that Hermippus listed emaciated persons

---

[85] Fr. 14 West. See further Chap. 2.

[86] On obesity in antiquity see Gourevitch and Grmek (1987), 355–67.

[87] Wineskins (ἀσκοί) are also found in this sense at *Acharnians* 1002, *Clouds* 1237–8, and Alexis, *Hesione* fr. 88. Pickard-Cambridge (1968), 222 compares *Frogs* 663 and Anaxandrides fr. 70, together with costumes for fat men and the 'fat men' depicted on Corinthian vases who may be linked to early comedy (discussed in Pickard-Cambridge (1962), 169–71).

[88] Athenaeus 10.415d cites these two as targets for comic abuse.

[89] Antiphanes fr. 120.4=Athenae 3.98f: philosophers are *leptoi, asitoi, figmen*.

[90] See further Dunbar (1995) on *Birds* 1387; Aristophanes fr. 885; Plato fr. 200, 'withered, with no bum and carrying reed-thin legs'; and Cameron (1991), 534–8. In contrast, the dithyrambic poet Philoxenus of Cythera was a notable eater (see Chap. 7).

in his *Cercopes*, for example in fr. 36, which was addressed to Dionysus: 'For the poor are already sacrificing to you maimed little cattle that are thinner than Leotrophides and Thoumantis.' There were emaciated poets in Aristophanes, *Gerytades* fr. 156 (Athen. 12.551a–b), though the fragment itself does not mention emaciation:[91] comedy[92] is represented by the emaciated Sannyrion, tragedy by Meletus, and dithyramb by Cinesias. Sannyrion himself in *Laughter* fr. 2 writes 'Meletus the corpse from the Lenaion'. Thinness and the dead are further linked in jokes against Philippides in the fourth century: Alexis in *Thesprotians* fr. 93 appeals to Hermes as conductor of the gods[93] and owner of Philippides; Aristophon writes (*Plato* fr. 8), 'A: in three days I will reveal him thinner than Philippides. B: You make them corpses like that in so few days?'[94]

1.6. EXCRETA

Comedy's concentration on the body reaches its most extreme form in the treatment of excrement and vomit. These malodorous products from the body, in Athenian as in many other cultures, are contained within what might be termed *cordons sanitaires*. In some literary genres they are not mentioned at all, through decorum or for other reasons.[95] Constipation, however, is not advisable and comedy implicitly recommends regular bowel movement (see *Frogs* 1–21, discussed below).[96] Comedy

---

[91] The poets listed are said to ride on thin hopes, and thin bodies are implied by the ease with which they will be swept away by the river of diarrhoea.

[92] Bentley emended τραγωιδῶν to τρυγωιδῶν.

[93] But see Arnott's comments (1996).

[94] Add Menander, *Anger* (*Orge*), fr. 266, 'if the famine you're suffering bites him it will reveal him a corpse thinner than Philippides'. Also Alexis, *Woman Under the Influence of Mandrake* fr. 148, 'A: you're in a terrible state. By Zeus, you're almost a sparrow. You've been Philippidized. B: Don't chatter on at me with your new phrases. I'm all but dead. A: Poor you. You've suffered wretchedly.' (On the text, see Arnott 1996.)

[95] On excrement and toilets see Henderson (1991), 187–203; Ussher (1973) on *Ecclesiazusae* 320–2; and Hunter (1983) on Eubulus fr. 53.

[96] Cf. Brillat-Savarin (1970), 181: 'comic poets will be found among the regular, tragic poets among the constipated, and pastoral and elegiac poets among the lax: whence it follows that the most lachrymose of poets is only removed from the most comic of poets by a degree of digestionary coction.'

confronts bodily evacuation squarely, placing excrement in the heavens, in the underworld, and in the streets of Athens. The dung-beetle of *Peace*, Aristophanes' finest creation in this area, brings dung-consumption to Olympus in a play in which excrement is part of an aggressive discourse against poets, politicians, and arms dealers.[97] Gods and excrement do not happily coexist: comic allegations of excrement-eating among the gods (*Peace* 42: Zeus the Excrement-eater; *Wealth* 706: farting causes Asclepius no distress since he is an 'excrement-eater')[98] are buffoonish asides by slave characters. But, since in comedy gods can be imagined to eat the same foods as humans, comic gods will even be tempted to eat the excrement of the parrot-wrasse (Epicharmus, *Marriage of Hebe* fr. 54). In *Peace* the recently dead Cleon is imagined to eat excrement in the Underworld, where, according to *Frogs* 146 and *Gerytades* fr. 156, rivers of dung and diarrhoea are to be found. Dung has its uses, as Xenophon points out,[99] and may be spread on the fields to promote the fertility so eagerly sought in a number of comedies: thus the distraught farmer in *Acharnians*, who appeals to Dicaeopolis for help after the theft of his oxen, declares (1025–6), 'they nourished me in the manure to which I was accustomed'.

Fear in comedy induces failure of bowel control, both in gods (Dionysus cited above) and humans. A further likely occasion for bodily evacuation arose at the symposium, where excessive indulgence in food and wine might take its toll.[100] While the excreta of gods and men, Greek or foreigner,[101] are suitable subject-matter for comedy, much greater attention is afforded the buttocks and anus, the latter serving a double purpose as the channel for excreta and for buggery.[102] Farting often receives ingenious attention, for example in political debate (*Knights* 638–42) and in a riddle at Eubulus, *Sphinx-Carion* fr. 106.

[97] See Henderson (1991), 64.

[98] The scholiast suggests a reference to doctors who were accustomed to tasting faeces and urine.

[99] See Pomeroy on *Oeconomicus* 16.12, 17.10, 18.2–3.

[100] Aristophanes, *Wasps* 1127–8; *Gerytades* fr. 157 on vomit and excrement after playing the *kottabos* game. On the sympotic chamber-pot, see Chap. 5.

[101] The Persian golden hills of *Acharnians* 80–2 were cited above. The excreta of women appears not to be a topic for comedy.

[102] See Davidson (1997), 167–82, within his excellent chapter on bodies (pp. 139–82); Dover (1978), 145, 152; and Henderson (1991), 52–4, 187–219.

1.7. THE PROCESSES OF GROWING AND COOKING FOOD

All of these areas of comic interest, the foods, the ingesting body, and the body's waste products, both test and transgress the boundaries of the polite and acceptable and contribute to capturing the essence of Athenian identity. Comedy is not simply presenting what might be termed an anti-form of what is acceptable elsewhere, a transgression of epic, tragedy, or philosophy; in addition to such transgression it also offers a representation of the material world of the polis of Athens. That identity is further expressed in the processes by which food was prepared, cooked, and served. The preparation of food in many cultures is gendered and stratified in a hierarchy. In Greece much food preparation was the preserve of women and slaves, and even the sacrifice of animals, although the honorific preserve of priests and private citizens of both sexes, was conducted—that is the throat was cut—by the *mageiros*, whose status was low.[103] The kitchen is, as we have seen, a particular preserve for comedy: on the one hand all the material foods and pots and pans are present in profusion, along with the low-status servants and humble preparers of dishes, and on the other comedy extends its kitchen into areas of the polis hitherto unconnected with it, such as the lawcourt of *Wasps* and the government of *Knights* and *Ecclesiazusae*. The kitchen of comedy may also extend naturally into the kitchen of sacrifice,[104] since sacrifice to the Olympians was normally based on cooking as much as on blood-letting. Nowhere is this better illustrated than in the *Dyscolus* of Menander, whose cook enters the stage with his sheep for sacrifice and occupies two matching scenes in which he attempts to borrow cooking utensils from Cnemon the misanthrope. Cnemon does not manage to synthesize sacrifice and cooking with communal eating, unlike the protagonists of Old Comedy who are masters of these skills in great comic detail.[105] Dicaeopolis organizes the cooking of his meal for the Anthesteria as follows: 'boil away, get roasting, turn to, draw off the hare meat quickly, wreathe the garlands. Bring the small

---

[103] Detienne (1989); Berthiaume (1982); Athenaeus 14.658e–662d.
[104] 'The Cuisine of Sacrifice' is the phrase of Detienne and Vernant (1989).
[105] See further Chap. 8.

spits so that I can spear the thrushes. . . . Rake out the fire'
(*Acharnians* 1005–14).

Menander's misanthropic farmer is a comic exaggeration who
will be considered again in Chapter 2. Comedy is generally well-
disposed towards farmers and producers of foods and has much
interest in vine-dressing and hoeing and ploughing: Old Comedy in particular sets up an opposition between the honest and
peaceful toil of the countryside and the bellicose and luxurious
city.[106] In *Peace*, the tools and utensils of agricultural production
triumph over the arms dealers:

TRYGAEUS: Look at the faces of the people in the audience, so that you
can identify their trades.
HERMES: Yuk, poor wretch!
TRYGAEUS: Yes, don't you see that crest-maker tearing his hair?
HERMES: Yes, and the hoe-manufacturer just farted in the face of that
sword-maker.
TRYGAEUS: And don't you see how happy the sickle-maker is, and how
he jeered at the spearman?
HERMES: Come on, tell the farmers to go away.
TRYGAEUS: Listen out, you people! Farmers, go off to the fields taking
with you all your farm equipment as fast as you can, without spear
and sword and javelin.

(543–53)

Later in the play (1198–269), agricultural implements such as the
sickle command high prices, while the weapons of war are converted into sympotic equipment. The crest can be sold for dried
figs as a table-wipe. The breastplate can be reused as a chamber-
pot, the trumpet as a *kottabos* stand, the spears for vine props.

Once the plants had been grown they were processed into food
through various forms of winnowing, grinding, sifting, and
kneading, listed, for example, by Aristophanes, *Dramas or Centaur*
fr. 282 and Pherecrates fr. 197.[107] Many utensils were needed for
the boiling and roasting of vegetables and meats. Athenaeus
gathers together fragments citing cooking utensils,[108] among
them Anaxippus, *Citharodist* fr. 6, 'would you bring a soup ladle,
a dozen little spits, a meat hook, a mortar, a baby cheese-grater, an
axe-haft, three bowls, a knife, four choppers. And before that,

---

[106] See Chap. 3.   [107] The latter is quoted in Chap. 8.
[108] *Mageirike skeue* (4.169b–170c). Cf. Pollux 10.95–104.

you abomination to the gods, bring the little cooking-pot and the things from the soda shop. Late again? And the impressive axe?'[109] Various shapes of the stewing-pot or *caccabe* follow,[110] demonstrating copiously comedy's incorporation of the 'earth-born' pot[111] of clay into its own light and inventive text and its delight in playing with variations on a material theme, whether in linguistic exuberance or for the purpose of satirizing the speaker, who is in many cases a boastful cook of some kind. Athenaeus is less interested in the basic cooking-pot or *chutra* which is widely found in comedy,[112] and the *lopas* or general stewing-pot.

Foods that were not to be boiled might be fried, in the *teganon* or *tagenon*.[113] Athenaeus (6.228e–229b) cites Eubulus, *Titans* fr. 108, 'and, smiling, the stewing-pot splutters with barbarian chattering,[114] while fish jump in the middle of the frying-pans'.[115]

---

[109] The text is uncertain at the end of the fragment. The speaker appears to be a hired cook.

[110] *Caccabe*: Aristophanes, *Women Setting Up Festival Tents* fr. 495; *Banqueters* fr. 224; Antiphanes, *Pro-Theban* fr. 216, 'everything is now ours. The Boeotian eel whose name coincides with our mistress indoors is mingling in the hollow depths of the *caccabe* and is heating, rising up, boiling, and spluttering' (on eels resembling women see below). *Batanion*: Antiphanes, *Euthydicus* fr. 95; Alexis, *Asclepiocleides* fr. 24. *Patanion*: Antiphanes, *Wedding* fr. 71, 'stewing-pots (*patania*), beet, silphium, pots (*chutrai*), lamps, coriander, onions, salt, oil, a bowl (*trublion*)'; Philetaerus, *Oenopion* fr. 14; Antiphanes, *Parasite* fr. 180, 'A: after this another will come, huge, the size of a table, of noble birth. B: Who do you mean? A: Nurseling of Carystus, earth-born, seething. B: Aren't you going to tell me? Go on. A: I mean the *caccabos*. Perhaps you would call it stewing-pot (*lopas*). Do you think I care about the name? Whether some folk take pleasure in calling it *caccabos* or *sittybos*? All I need to know is that it's a cooking-vessel' (see Chap. 8). Of Eubulus, *Ion* fr. 37, 'bowls (*trublia*) and *batania* and *caccabia* and stewing-pots and *patania* all with varied notes when struck, and— I couldn't recite them if I recited them'; Hunter notes the unreliable testimony of comedy to these dialect terms: see further the discussion of Arnott (1996) on Alexis fr. 24. The important point for the present study is their exploitation as material for the comic text.

[111] In the phrase of Antiphanes.

[112] Sparkes (1962), 130; *Knights* 1174; *Birds* 78; *Frogs* 983; *Ecclesiazusae* 1092; *Wealth* 673, 683, 686; fr. 606.

[113] On the dialect forms see Arnott (1996) on Alexis fr. 115.12. Sparkes (1962), 129 notes that the *tagenon* appears to have acted also as a pan for holding hot charcoal over which food was cooked.

[114] Cf. Antiphanes fr. 216.4 and Cleon/Paphlagon in *Knights*, the barbarian slave, who splutters (919–22).

[115] Athenaeus lists Pherecrates, *Leroi* fr. 109 's/he said s/he'd eaten whitebait

Athenaeus adds inventive applications of the utensil in Eubulus, *Orthannes* fr. 75 (7–8), (1–2) 'every beautiful woman in love is in attendance and luxuriates with the frying-pan',[116] and 'the fan arouses the dogs of Hephaestus, sharpening them up with the hot breath of the frying-pan'.

1.8. POTS AND PANS AND WINE-CUPS

The archaeologists who excavated the remains of clay pots and pans in the Athenian agora could look to comedy above all to identify the myriad forms and shapes of these vessels, since comedy enthusiastically incorporated cups and pots into its text for such occasions as festivals or private symposia and parties, and sometimes commented on shape and materials used by potters, as we have seen.[117]

The skills of the kitchen might be deployed by members of the household or by a hired cook. The kitchen as a part of the house does not in itself play a large part in comedy, though the activities linked to it are widely exploited. Pherecrates, *Ipnos or Pannychis* appears to have presented the *ipnos* or kitchen in some form.[118] One fragment, 66, describes a man blowing on the fire and getting ash in his face. Archaeology seems to support the comic picture in suggesting that the room was one of the less important in many houses, though a room (*optanion*) is clearly indicated at *Knights* 1033 and the cooks of Middle and New Comedy needed extensive

from the frying-pan'; *Persians* fr. 133; *Ant-Men* fr. 128; Phrynichus, *Tragedians* fr. 60, 'it is sweet to benefit from the frying-pan without making a contribution'; Philonides, *Buskins* fr. 2, 'to welcome with kneading-troughs and frying-pans', and 'smelling the aroma of the frying-pans'. The smell of caramelizing food is particularly appealing, hence Eupolis' description of parasites in fr. 374, 'the friends of the frying-pan and the after-lunch variety'.

[116] The play appears to concern a fertility god. The *teganon* is elsewhere linked with pleasure at Eupolis fr. 385.

[117] See Sparkes (1962) and Amyx (1958), 163–307. Sparkes and Talcott (1970) note the rarity of plates. *Pinakes* are found at *Wealth* 813 and Sopater, *Orestes* fr. 15.

[118] Hesychius identifies the ἰπνός as part of the house, as the kitchen, in this play. The term may also signify an oven, a lamp (*Peace* 839), or a toilet. See the discussion of Sparkes (1962), 127–9 and of Dunbar (1995) on *Birds* 436. At Antiphanes, *Omphale* fr. 174 a speaker, possibly Heracles, praises the 'white-bodied' bread cooked in the ἰπνός of the house—of Omphale?

space in which to prepare the meals they describe.[119] Cooking might also be performed outside, as the cook at Menander, *Samia* 291 indicates. For the most part, ovens and braziers were as portable as the cooking vessels they supported and the professional comic cook expected to supply his own utensils as often as they were available from his employer. The brazier or *eschara* is frequently mentioned, along with the fan to encourage the flames[120] and the spits on which the meat or other food cooked.[121] Space was needed for storage vessels, the large container or *sipue* and *amphorae* for liquids,[122] such as those filled by the god at *Wealth* 807: 'the *sipue* is full of white flour and the *amphorae* of fragrant dark wine.' There were pots and basins, the *stamnos* for wine,[123] and *lekanis/lekanion* for food.[124] The pestle and mortar often appear in comedy, sometimes as metaphors.[125] The tray on which to knead bread was the *kardopos* or *maktra*.[126] The utensil for parching barley and beans was the *phrugetron* or *seison*.[127] Water was carried in the *hydria, kalpis*, or *kados*.[128] Other comic

[119] See esp. Sparkes (1962), 125–32. At Menander, *Samia* 291 the hired cook asks if the oven is indoors. On the *optanion* see Arnott on Alexis, *All-Night Festival (Pannychis)* fr. 177.13–5.

[120] e.g. *Acharnians* 669, 888, 'slaves, bring me out the brazier and the fan'; Eubulus fr. 75.7.

[121] e.g. *Acharnians* 1007; *Birds* 357.

[122] On the *sipue* see *Knights* 1298; fr. 555; Pherecrates fr. 151; Eupolis fr. 324. Sparkes (1962), 124 considers also the *kypsele* holding six *medimni* at *Peace* 631. See schol.

[123] At *Frogs* 22, Dionysus' statement 'I am Dionysus son of *Stamnos*' humorously claims for the god the wine-jar as a parent made of material fabric, presumably clay.

[124] *Acharnians* 1110: 'give me the *lekanion* for the hare meat.'

[125] *Doidux* may signify either a rubbing-stone for a quern (Sparkes 1962: 125) or a pestle, *torune* and *hyperon* pestles, *thueia* a mortar of varied shape, shallow or less shallow. Comic examples may be found at *Knights* 984, *Clouds* 676, *Wasps* 924, and *Wealth* 710–11, the last specified as a stone mortar, in a temple. In *Peace*, War proposes to grind up the Greek cities as if they were foods in a giant mortar (236–88), with Cleon and Brasidas as pestles (282).

[126] *Clouds* 669–76, *Wealth* 545. Kneading equipment is listed in Aristophanes, *Merchant Ships* fr. 431, 'bowls (*skaphides*), kneading-trays and barley cake trays (*mazonomias*) from the Mossynoici'.

[127] Polyzelus fr. 6; Alexis fr. 139; Axionicus fr. 7, 'ᴀ: bowls (*trublia*), a pot (*chutra*), a little stewpot, a vinegar-pot, a chamber pot, a flat bowl, a mortar, a cup, a parcher, a lamp. ʙ: You've got a ship's complement of pots there, old woman.'

[128] Details in Sparkes (1962), 129–30. The *kados* was the pot for the

kitchen utensils include the butcher's knife or cleaver,[129] meat-hook, and cheese-grater.[130] Comedy also interested itself in the personnel of the kitchen, whether women of the household, slaves, or hired servants (see Chapter 2). In Old Comedy cooking is done apparently on stage (*Acharnians* 1005–17, *Peace* 1039–62, *Birds* 1579–89) and off; in Middle and New it is largely transferred to verbal reports of cooking processes such as those presented in the speeches of *mageiroi* (see Chapter 8).

The small-scale provision of the Greek kitchen might be supplemented by the utensils brought or hired 'at the place where pots are available for hire by *mageiroi*' (Alexis, *The Fugitive* fr. 259.3–4), who were themselves usually hired.[131] Food was brought by servants or slaves to table and served to the reclining diners. Many comedies describe the physical details of the *deipnon* and symposium, which may be compared with the extended descriptions in the comic utopias, and in Philoxenus, Archestratus, and Matro.[132] Couches were prepared[133] and water brought for washing hands; tables were then carried in with food in dishes. During the meal, hand-wipes made of bread (*apomagdalia*) might be used and discarded on the floor as dog food.[134] More water was supplied for washing hands and then came all the sympotic equipment, including the mixing-bowls, ladles,[135]

---

well: *Ecclesiazusae* 1002–4; Menander, *Dyscolus* 190, 576, 582, 626. Both plays have much comic exploitation of a simple implement.

[129] The *machaira* and *kopis* of the *mageiros*: see Berthiaume (1982), and Arnott (1996) on Alexis fr. 179.11.

[130] Sparkes (1962), 132. The meat-hook (*kreagra*) is cited at *Knights* 772, *Ecclesiazusae* 1002 (same term, different use), the cheese-grater (*turoknestis*) at *Wasps* 938, 963, *Birds* 1579, *Lysistrata* 231–2 (the last a sexual metaphor).

[131] See Arnott (1996) on Alexis 259. Utensils were brought by cooks to private houses in comedy as well as to alfresco sacrifices such as that in Menander, *Dyscolus*. At *Dyscolus* 262 the cook appears to be hired at Phyle, though at 490 he boasts of his clientele in Athens: see Gomme and Sandbach (1973) on 262.

[132] Utopias are cited in Chap. 3, the three poets in Chap. 7.

[133] Athenaeus 2.47f–48a cites Antiphanes fr. 292, 'gathering the three of you into a three-couch room'; Phrynichus fr. 69, 'there was a fine room with seven couches and then another with nine'; Eubulus fr. 119, 'A: Set the seven-couch room. B: Here it is. A: And five Sicilian couches. B: Say anything else you have to say. A: Five Sicilian cushions'; Amphis fr. 45; Anaxandrides fr. 72. Hunter (1983) on Eubulus fr. 119 discusses the possibility of the couches being set up on stage.

[134] *Knights* 413–6; Pollux 6.93; Sparkes (1962), 127.

[135] Sparkes (1962), 131–2. Wine-ladles are to be found at the beginning of

strainers, cups, and *kottabos* stands described in Chapter 5. Cups are listed,[136] often with comment on material fabric and size,[137] and on the silver and gold cups of the wealthy.[138] Even the *kylikeion* or *kylix* cupboard is mentioned.[139] Comic incorporation of the physical material of the symposium is, in short, extensive.

1.9. FOOD AND SEX

In sympotic or quasi-sympotic contexts, women, normally women of low status, may be consumed by men as part of their diet of pleasure, as they may consume a bowl of soup or an eel:

HERMES: Quickly, take away Festival here and give her to the Council, to whom she once belonged.

TRYGAEUS: O lucky Council to get Festival! How much of her soup will you guzzle up in three days, how many boiled black-puddings and meats will you eat up!

(*Peace* 713–17)[140]

Athenaeus, Book 10.424a–d: Plato, *Phaon* fr. 192; *Presbeis* fr. 128; Archippus, *Fishes* fr. 21; 'Cratinus and Aristophanes in many passages'; *Wasps* 855; Phrynichus, *Poastriae* fr. 42.

[136] e.g. Dionysius of Sinope, *The Woman Who Saved* fr. 5, 'A: How many shapes of fine Thericlean cups there are, my lady, *gualai*, two-*kotule* cups, three-*koyule* cups, a huge *dinos* holding a full measure, a boat-cup, bowls, drinking-horns. B: The old woman eyes up the cups but nothing else at all!' See Chap. 5, and n. 131 there on Thericlean cups.

[137] Athenaeus lists many comic passages in his gazetteer of drinking-cups at 11.782d–503f (781–4 are misplaced in the MSS and should follow 466d), and cites comment on fabric at 464a–d. Cf. Richter and Milne (1953).

[138] Athenaeus discusses silverware at 6.229b–231b, starting with the transformation of a family's clay pots into precious materials by the god Wealth (*Wealth* 812–15): 'all the vinegar vessels and the stewing-pots and boiling-pots became bronze. And the shoddy fish-plates you could see were of gold. Our oven had suddenly been changed into ivory.' Athenaeus insists, influenced probably by comic and moralizing historical sources such as Theopompus, that gold and silver tableware indicates vulgarity (*phortikon*) and new money, citing Philippides, *The Loss of Money* fr. 9; Alexis, *Agonis or Hippiscus* fr. 2; Nicostratus, *Kings* fr. 8; Antiphanes, *Lemnian Women* fr. 143; Sopater, *Orestes* fr. 15; *Lentil Soup* fr. 19; Diphilus, *Painter* fr. 43; Philemon, *Doctor* fr. 35; Menander, *Self-Tormentor* fr. 78; *Hymnis* fr. 366. Add Xenarchus fr. 10.

[139] Athenaeus (11.460d–f) cites Aristophanes, *Farmers* fr. 106; Anaxandrides, *Melilot* fr. 30; Eubulus, *Leda* fr. 62; Hunter (1983) on *Semele or Dionysus* fr. 95 (his 96); *Harp-Girl* fr. 116; Cratinus the Younger, *Cheiron* fr. 9.

[140] See Chap. 3 and Henry (1992). Festival is a personification of all city

O dearest one, and long-desired!
How desired you are by the comic chorus—and by Morychus!
Slaves, bring out the brazier and the bellows,
look, slaves, at this best of eels,
arriving with difficulty in this the sixth year without her.
Address her, children! I'll bring you charcoal
for the sake of this female guest.
Bring her in! Not even when I am dead may I be
without her wrapped up in beet!

(*Acharnians* 885–94)[141]

Eels are prominent in the discourse of luxury,[142] whether because they were expensive in Attica or because their fatty flesh was particularly prized, or both.[143] They came from Lake Copais in Boeotia, a neighbouring region whose agricultural fertility was the envy of the Athenians and source of much comic comment.[144] Eels came too from the sea, as is attested by Archestratus of Gela and other authors, but it is the Copaic eel that fascinated comedy.[145] In many passages the Copaic eel is a

festivals where meat was eaten over a period of three or so days (cf. 900). The three days of festival contrast with the three-day rations of the soldier which comedy frequently disowns. The terms for meat and soup belong to the obscene vocabulary: see Henderson (1991), 145, 186. Henderson has many other examples of terms drawn from the natural and culinary world and applied to the sexual organs and sexual activity. Eubulus has a character say in *Cercopes* fr. 53, 'I went to Corinth. There in a pleasant kind of way I nibbled on some greens and corrupted Herb-Basil [a *hetaera*].'

[141] This is an elaborate parody of the *Alcestis* of Euripides, with the eel longed for by protagonist, chorus, slaves, and glutton Morychus superimposed on the dead wife and grand language of the tragic original.

[142] See Chap. 6.

[143] Eels, like the heads and feet of animals discussed above, have a distinctive texture and flavour.

[144] On the gluttony of Thebans see Chap. 2 and Gilula (1995), 386–91.

[145] Eels other than Copaic eels are found in comedy in Antiphanes, *Thamyras* fr. 104 (from the River Strymon). Certain foods that became comic standbys, such as the Boeotian eel and the Milesian sea bass may be suspected of little material reality, but the suspicion is ill-founded. Other texts attest the excellence of the Copaic eel (Dorion and Agatharchides ap. Athenaeus 7.297c, Pausanias 9.24). Ancient authors appear not to have considered how the eel reached Lake Copais, presumably because they believed them to be generated in the mud of the lake (Aristotle fr. 311 Rose, *HA* 570a2–25, summarized by the Athenaeus at 7.298b–d). By a curious historical coincidence, the discovery of the life-cycle of the eel—its journey to the Sargasso Sea to mate and die and the return to

woman, 'the *hetaera* next door' at *Lysistrata* 701, the bride at
Eubulus fr. 34, the goddess at Eubulus frr. 36 and 64.[146] Eels
resemble women in being intensely desirable to male consumers.
There are other aspects of women and eels[147] which were important to men, but in this respect they had a similar ability to satisfy
appetite. *Hetaerae* might be compared with and named after
other fish, in particular in Archippus, *Fishes* fr. 27 and Antiphanes, *Fisherwoman* fr. 27. In these instructive passages both
men and women might be given the names of fish, but the significance is almost certainly not gender-neutral. The women are
hetaerae for consumption,[148] the men something different. A
number of men are compared with fish in comedy, most notably
Callimedon the Crayfish in the fourth century. They acquire
these names in part because they consume fish excessively, not
because they are eaten (on this see further Chapter 6).[149] Here
again, the discourse of comedy is relentlessly a male discourse.[150]

1.10. THE MATERIAL OF ATHENAEUS

The ways in which women and men resemble fish fascinated
Athenaeus. Comic discourse and the inventive adaptation of the
material world into literary texts are central to his work, which
rests on the elevation of the material to cultural and sympotic
discourse.[151] The *Deipnosophistae* is a massive work, which is

Europe of the elver—came almost at the same time as the draining of Lake
Copais at the end of the last century. The eels presumably reached the inland
lake by swimming through the River Kephissos which ran underground to the
sea. The nineteenth-century traveller W. M. Leake tasted the eels and inspected
the underground river (1835: ii. 281); see also *RE* I (1894), 1–4 s.v. 'aal'; Wallace
(1979), 67–73.

[146] See further Gilula (1995), 390–1; Degani (1995), 423–5 (on the sub-comic
Attic Dinner of Matro).

[147] Eels are mentioned as goddesses in Egypt at Antiphanes, *Lycon* fr. 145 and
Anaxandrides, *Cities* fr. 40.

[148] Women may also be compared with animals for sacrifice, in particular
pigs: see further Chap. 3 for an analysis of women as recipients of sexual favours
who are imagined as sacrificial victims.

[149] Arnott (1996) on Alexis fr. 57 gives further reasons for Callimedon's
nickname.

[150] Food may also be used as a medium for seducing boys: see esp. Gilula
(1995), 143–56.

[151] His discussion of eels (7.297c–300d) is a good example. Listed

difficult to read because of the mass of quotation that is not digested into a fluent text; in places lists are formed which survey vegetables, breads, fish, meats, drinking cups, or cakes without full regard to the discourse into which they are inserted. Significant advances have recently been made in understanding the organization and considerable sophistication of the work, particularly as an example of a library, a repository of the finest works of an earlier age.[152] This is important for the present study since it was the libraries and associated scholars of the Hellenistic world who first lighted upon the text of the comic poets as material particularly in need of scholarly exegesis and who are the ancestors of Athenaeus' own work.

The contribution of Athenaeus to the present work is enormous and may be assessed under two headings, the sheer mass of quotation from hundreds of lost plays—a quantity that exceeds all other sources—and his reading of comic discourse which, though at times perverse, reveals more than any other the place of comedy in Greek culture, in particular in relation to sub-comic and other genres such as epic parody, sympotic literature, letters, poetic biography, moralizing histories, and anecdote embedded in various genres. This reading partakes in such discourses as luxury, the containment of pleasure within social ritual, and the privileging of the cerebral over the physical.

Much of the organization of this book is by topic or by food rather than by play. Some of the topics are prompted by Athenaeus—luxury and parodic literature in particular—as are many of the surveys of foods—lentils and head meat in this

---

alphabetically between the *gnapheus* or fuller-fish and the *elops*, both unidentified, the entry on the eel begins with a citation from Epicharmus (see Chap. 7), cites Copaic eels, and diverts into the sacrifice of eels and other fish. The general exclusion of fish from sacrifice, while recognized as a diversion (298b), is a large issue for the present book and its interest in the discourse of luxury in Chap. 6. Athenaeus proceeds to Aristotle on the generation of eels, to eels as attractive to gluttons and the luxurious, to the dialectical variants of the term *enchelus* (here are included jokes on eels and plagiarism from Old Comedy), to comedy on eels in Egyptian culture, and to eels wrapped in beet leaves (these are the passages from Middle Comedy identifying women with eels). This entry contains many of the elements necessary to place the eel in Greek culture, though they are not systematically presented or placed in a well-ordered argument.

[152] The papers of a conference held in Exeter in 1997 are to be found in Braund and Wilkins (forthcoming).

chapter, wines in Chapter 5, and fish in Chapter 6. Foods are thus approached through the vehicle which preserves the fragments as well as through the plays in which they originally appeared.

1.11. THE MATERIAL OF THE COMIC TEXT

Since comedy is an intensely self-reflective form of drama, it has much to say about how the material world of food and the body is incorporated into its text. Surviving comedy (with the notable exception of *Acharnians*) is less forthcoming on the physical details of eating and drinking at the festivals in which it was produced, though it seems likely that a play such as Ephippus, *Obeliaphoroi (Spit-Loaf-Bearers)*[153] made some reference at least to events at the Dionysia.[154] At both the Lenaea and the City Dionysia, there were offerings of animal victims and bloodless sacrifice, while at the latter there was a komos and other foods were offered, including the loaves called spit-loaves.[155] The citizens consumed food and drink at these festivals (wine at the Dionysia at least) before they came to the theatre. Philochorus goes so far as to say that the audience had eaten and drunk before the Dionysia, that they arrived wearing garlands and drank during the performances, ate nuts and fruit (*tragemata*), and gave wine to the chorus.[156] Aristotle also attests[157] the eating of *tragemata*—when the plays were poor.[158] We may well view these claims with considerable scepticism; my purpose is to examine not what the audience and indeed chorus *did* consume but the claims made for festive consumption in the comic texts. A number of comedies claimed that they were feasting the audience,

---

[153] On the spit-loaf bearers see p. 335.

[154] Cf. *Thesmophoriazusae* which, for all its interest in gender and tragedy, refers in passing to sacrifice (284–5), the goddesses (295–311), the day of fasting (947–52), and tent-mates (624). On festivals see Chap. 2.

[155] Pickard-Cambridge (1988), 25–36, 57–63.

[156] *FGrH* 328 F 171 = Athenaeus 11.464f.

[157] *Nicomachean Ethics* 1175b12.

[158] See further Pickard-Cambridge (1988), 272–3, 'the audience naturally provided itself with refreshments'. *Tragemata* were foods that could be munched or chewed, similar to the *trogalia* (nibbles) noted below at *Wealth* 798. These foods often comprise fruit and nuts but can also include cakes and such savoury dishes as sow's womb and birds. *Tragemata* were eaten either as snacks or at the dessert stage of a meal, at the so-called 'second tables' that were eaten during the symposium. See further Arnott (1996) on Alexis 168.2.

offering light meals and dining at the festival as a metaphor for their relationship with their audience. While the audience might feel hungry during a tragedy,[159] comedy sent away the citizen body politically and poetically nourished. There is also an ideological element to these claims in so far as the meal comedy provides is to be consumed in a community purged of undesirable elements in the polis. I discuss these claims in Chapter 2.2 and 2.11.

There are some comic passages in which *real* food and drink appear to be offered rather than the food of comic discourse. In Pherecrates, *Crapataloi* fr. 101, which is preserved in paraphrase, someone declares, 'whoever in the audience is thirsty can swirl down a large cup full of wine'. Philochorus[160] appears to refer to a related passage when he cites Pherecrates as saying that no one went home hungry after a performance. It is unlikely that Pherecrates' play was making any more than a poetic claim about the relationship between comedy and its audience. On several occasions Aristophanes refers to foods—similar to these same *tragemata*—that were thrown to the audience by the actors. At *Wealth* 796–801 such practices are deprecated:

WEALTH: Then we should avoid grossness,[161] for it is not seemly for the producer of a play to throw dried figs and nibbles to the audience and force them to laugh in return.
WIFE: You speak well. Because Dexinicus here is standing up in order to snatch the dried figs.

This passage occurs in the middle of scenes with important material content—the restoration of the sight of Wealth in the Asclepieion is attended by much farting, a greedy priest who snatches food from the altar, and an 'excrement-eating' god (665–711), while after the reception of Wealth all the utensils of the house are turned to gold and silver (802–18). The passage itself is spoken in the context of traditional gifts offered by households to the god Wealth. There is a correct way for exchanges based on food to be made, says the god, both in the home and in the theatre, whether the food offered is substantial or symbolic. Food should not be thrown to the audience, since the exchange between actors and audience ought to be based on

---

[159] *Birds* 787.   [160] In the fragment cited above.   [161] τὸ φόρτον.

comic discourse only. A different picture is presented in the sacrifice of the sheep at *Peace* 955–73, where Trygaeus instructs his slave to throw barley over the audience. These are grains thrown not as food but in a ritual of inclusion. Despite farcical additions (the pun on *krithe*[162] and the dousing of the chorus in lustral water), the throwing of barley incorporates the audience symbolically into the sacrifice; later, at 1115, they are invited to share in tasting the vital organs of the animal. The character of the exchange between actors and audience is of the greatest importance in comedy[163]—and foods have their part to play. In *Wasps* Aristophanes went further in rejecting such exchanges as figs for laughter and transferred such 'grossness' to Megara. Xanthias says:

Come on then, let me tell the audience the theme of the play, and first by way of preface in several small matters let me tell them not to expect anything too big from us, nor indeed any humor pinched from Megara. For we do not have a couple of slaves chucking nuts to the audience from a basket nor Heracles cheated of his dinner nor again Euripides presented in disgusting mode; nor if Cleon is prominent at the moment through some chance event will we again grind the same man into a sauce again. Rather, we have a sensible little themelet.

(54–64)

Megarian grossness appears again in Ecphantides fr. 2 and Eupolis fr. 261: 'Heracles! Your joke is disgusting and Megarian and distinctly cold.'[164] Negative presentations of Megarian comedy, about which we are sadly ill-informed,[165] have much more to do with the self-identity of Attic poets than with any rival tradition.[166] While filling their verses with material derived from eating and the body and with all kinds of 'grossness', the poets denied such material to themselves and ascribed it to their rivals. *Frogs* 1–24 is a classic example:

XANTHIAS: Shall I say one of the usual gags, master, that the audience always laugh at?

---

[162] Barley grain/penis: see Henderson (1991), 119–20.
[163] Goldhill (1991).
[164] Neither poetry nor food should be 'cold' in Greek culture.
[165] Pickard-Cambridge (1962), 178–87; MacDowell (1971), on *Wasps* 57, Henderson (1991), 223–8.
[166] All the items listed in *Wasps* appear in a number of Attic comedies.

DIONYSUS: Yes, by Zeus, whatever you like, as long as it isn't 'I'm hard pressed'. Avoid that. That really gets the bile going.

XANTHIAS: Nor some other witticism?

DIONYSUS: As long as it isn't 'I'm under pressure'.

XANTHIAS: What? Shall I say the really funny one?

DIONYSUS: Yes, by Zeus, say it boldly. But be careful not to say . . .

XANTHIAS: What?

DIONYSUS: Shifting the burden round, that 'you're desperate for a crap'.

XANTHIAS: Nor that I am carrying around such a burden that if someone doesn't relieve me I shall fart?

DIONYSUS: No indeed, I beseech you. Unless when I need to throw up.

XANTHIAS: Why then did I have to carry all this gear if I'm not going to make one of the jokes Phrynichus usually makes and Lycis and Ameipsias?

DIONYSUS: Now, don't do it! Because when I go to the theatre and see one of these clever jokes I always go away more than a year older.

XANTHIAS: O my wretched neck, how it's burdened and won't speak the gag.

DIONYSUS: Now is it not hubris and outrageous living that I, Dionysus, son of wine jar, am on foot and labouring, and carry this man so that he shouldn't suffer or carry any burden?

Aristophanes combines the routine of the comic slave who is carrying a burden and takes the opportunity to introduce jokes about constipation and farting with rejection of the routine and ascription of that option to rivals who are by implication lesser poets. To this he adds comment on drama from the god of the theatre, giving him also physical characteristics as the statue brought into the theatre every year ('when I go to the theatre . . . a year older') and as the wine god, born as it were from the wine jar.[167] These are well-known passages,[168] adduced here because in

---

[167] The parabasis of *Clouds* plays a similar game, claiming a modest form of comedy with no need for gross physical action: 'see how she is by nature modest. She doesn't come on with a stitched leather [phallus] hanging down all red and thick at the end in order to give the children a laugh; nor does she mock the bald or drag out a *kordax* dance nor is there an old man leaning on a stick with which he belabours a character in order to obscure bad jokes. Nor does she rush in with torches and shout help help!, but she comes in confident in herself and in her words. And I am the sort of poet who doesn't have long hair nor do I seek to deceive you by bringing on the same stuff two or three times, but I am full of cleverness, bring on new forms, none of them like any other, and all full of wit' (537–48).

[168] See Dover on both *Clouds* (1968) and *Frogs* (1993), and Goldhill (1991), 220–1.

denying slapstick and the use of the physical, corporeal, and material they are in fact embedding such material into the text of comedy. A number of Aristophanes' plays revel in jokes about farting and many kinds of bodily reference: their rejection reminds the audience of them, and to contrast them with wit and invention is merely a rhetorical device to celebrate them. Both grossness and poetic invention are essential to Old Comedy. In similar mode Aristophanes denies *bomolocheumata* to his plays. The term is often translated as 'buffoonery', but refers literally to the low-life character who lurks at altars in the hope of stealing meat. The *bomolochus* is one who does not belong to those participating in the feast, but such a religious and social outcast has too much to offer for him to be ignored by the comic poet.[169] Like the *alazon* or boaster,[170] he may be insulted but he may also be incorporated into the plot—as is the Black-Pudding-Seller in *Knights*[171]—or give rise to related low-life characters such as the parasite, who generate much comic material. Comedy is well aware of all these possibilities, and in passages such as the opening of *Frogs* revels in its own ambiguities and playfulness.

Comedy, after all, uses stage props and physical impedimenta far more than any other dramatic genre. In tragedy, as Richard Seaford has pointed out, props are almost always lethal, gifts given by one character that have deadly consequences for the recipient—such as the sword of Ajax or the robes given by Medea to Glauce and by Deianeira to Heracles. Comic props, by contrast, celebrate the physicality of the material world. Notable examples are the dung-beetle of *Peace*, and in *Acharnians* the Megarian girls in a sack wearing snouts (744–5), the sycophant wrapped up for export (927–8), and the contrasting military and sympotic equipment of Lamachus and Dicaeopolis in the final scene.

Comic discourse manipulates all the aspects of the material world reviewed above into its own poetic material, setting the verbal or the metrical against the textures of pots or fish, inserting vegetables and meats into verses where they do not belong or where they are not found in other poetic genres.[172] Examples

---

[169] The *bomolochus* is discussed in Chap. 2.
[170] Ribbeck (1882); Cornford (1914), 115–33; Pickard-Cambridge (1962).
[171] For his triumphant *bomolochia* see Chap. 4.
[172] At *Lysistrata* 457–8 the protagonist calls women to her aid from the

include the anapaestic list of fish prepared in Antiphanes, *Cyclops* fr. 130 (quoted above) or the grilling of small fish in the parabatic lyric of *Acharnians* 665–75. Comedy has its own special forms. The list, for example, allows the compression of the material into a short space and, while stylistically unpromising, offers an expression of abundance and plenty. Furthermore, a degree of variation is attainable, in syndetic and asyndetic lists, hints of tragedy and myth, and satirical colouring.[173] Homer had used a form of the list in his catalogue of ships in *Iliad, 2*;[174] the comic poets imitated him in hexameters (Hermippus fr. 63, quoted in Chapter 4) and in trimeters and anapaests (Mnesimachus, *Horse-Breeder* fr. 4, the latter probably influenced by the parodic verse discussed in Chapter 7).[175] Sometimes foods and drinks listed are brought by a human agent, sometimes they come of their own accord,[176] and there is much variation in single-word lists and more elaborate phrasing. All these effects modulate what might have been a dry inventory. Lists reviewed in later chapters include the many good things in the utopian feasts (see Chapter 3), lists of imports into the markets of Athens (see Chapter 4), lists in luxurious banquets, such as Anaxandrides, *Protesilaus* fr. 42 (see Chapter 6), the lists of fish in Epicharmus and elsewhere (see Chapter 7), and the lists of foods prepared by comic cooks (Chapter 8). Long lists, such as those of the utopias and comic cooks, are sometimes interrupted by bored or frustrated interlocutors—a further means of dramatizing the list *in situ*.

market-place but they are comically inflated stallholders: 'O seed-of-the-agora-soup-sellers-of-vegetables, O garlic-landlady-breadsellers.' These Rabelaisian concoctions resemble the longest word in the Greek language, coined for the finale of *Ecclesiazusae*.

[173] For a survey of lists in Alexis see Arnott (1996), 33 and 876. In Antiphanes fr. 131 repeated reference to castration and cheese strike an obsessive note in the pastoral Polyphemus who is presumably the speaker of what appears to be a wedding list: 'of land animals the following will come to you from me, an ox from the herd, a billy-goat that wanders the forest, a nanny-goat from heaven, a castrated ram, a well-castrated boar, a ram not castrated, a grown pig, a shaggy-foot [hare], kids, [. . .] fresh cheese, dry cheese, chopped cheese, grated cheese, sliced cheese, thickened cheese.'

[174] On which see Minchin (1996) and Spyropoulos (1974).

[175] Sometimes the list is presented as a breathless *pnigos*, on which see Hunter (1983) on Eubulus fr. 63, and Gilula (forthcoming).

[176] See Hunter (1983) on Eubulus fr. 36.1 (his 37.1).

The list is taken over by Athenaeus, who uses many comic citations to fill the material world on which the *Deipnosophistae* is built. At 4.170a–c, for example, Athenaeus cites two passages of Alexis which, in their magnificent lists, demonstrate the irascible or distracted cook but at the same time enumerate many of the flavourings of the ancient Mediterranean: *Cooking-Pot* fr. 132.

A: Don't give me any excuses, any 'I haven't got that'. B: Well say what you need. I will get hold of everything. A: OK. First of all go and get some sesame. B: There's some in the house. A: Chopped raisins, fennel, dill, mustard, silphium stalk, silphium,[177] dried coriander, sumach, cummin, capers, marjoram, onion, anise, thyme, sage, new wine, pepper, rue, leek.[178]

The second fragment of Alexis is from *All-Night Festival or Hired Workers* fr. 179,

I'll have to run around in a circle and shout if I need anything. You'll ask me for your dinner as soon as you arrive. I've got no vinegar, no dill, no marjoram, no fig-leaf, no oil, no almonds, no garlic, no sweet wine, no onion, no tassel hyacinth, no heat, no cummin, no salt, no egg, no wood, no bowl, no pan, no well-rope—I've seen no cistern, no well. There's no wine jar. Here I stand in complete lack of everything with knife in hand and my tunic fastened round my waist.

Athenaeus cited these passages simply as catalogues of seasonings in Alexis. On other occasions, such as Eubulus, *Olbia* fr. 74 which includes fruits, vegetables, and equipment for the legal system, a list incorporates items that confuse categories normally kept separate in Athenian society. In this respect the list may be used as a destabilizing anti-structural device that confuses categories.

Comedy portrays animals with speech, utensils on the march, gods eating meat and fish,[179] and humans defecating according to a well-defined agenda. A number of well-established boundaries are transgressed for clear objectives. Like myth and some festivals, particularly those linked with Dionysus, comedy confuses categories in order to destabilize the existing power structure and integrate the community into a new whole. In this respect

---

[177] On silphium see Arnott's note (1996).
[178] Herbs and spices are a frequent material component in comic lists.
[179] The latter in particular in *The Muses or The Marriage of Hebe* of Epicharmus.

the 'comic polis' differs markedly from the real polis while evoking all the detail of everyday life. The material world is thus not merely the low-level reality down to which comedy drags more illustrious areas of thought such as tragedy and philosophy. It is the bedrock of comedy, the essential reality of the polis. Comedy, according to Aristotle,[180] derived from performances of phallic songs, from celebrations of Dionysus or other fertility gods who would honour the city with harvests of fruits and (in related festivals of Demeter such as that celebrated in *Thesmophoriazusae*) the conception of babies. The physical presence of foods in festivals is a constant concern of comedy, in particular the objective to be secured at the end of some Old Comedies. So too the securing of marriage or equivalent sexual unions at the end of plays of all periods. These are the good things, the *agatha* for which Greeks, particularly Greeks in comedies, prayed. They are also upbeat, representative of surplus or near-surplus rather than grinding poverty at subsistence level. Many other aspects of life are portrayed in comedy in similar terms. The *agatha* are material; other benefits for the polis are much larger, but tied to these material *agatha*. At all times *agatha* for the polis are stressed, sometimes specifically as feasting for the demos. The material world is ideologically charged, for Greek politicians since Hesiod and Homer had been devourers of bribes: comedy puts on stage politicians who do just that. Cleon/Paphlagon eats all that comes his way in *Knights*, and in *Wasps* the revenues of the Athenian empire are imagined to be foods and wines given as gifts to Cleon and other politicians.[181] Cities in the Athenian empire did indeed send material goods to Athens, money, oxen, and phalli made of wood; Aristophanes has transformed these from gifts to the city to bribes in the form of foods and sympotic equipment which can be put to private use.

Comic treatment of the all-important relations with the Olympian gods is similar. The gods of comedy are often venal and bent on material gain. Hermes in *Peace* can be bribed with meat and gold cups in as direct a way as any human.[182] The ideology of sacrifice in which humans eat the mortal parts of an animal and the gods the less mortal parts, in particular the marrow and

---

[180] *Poetics* 1449a11–13. [181] 675–7.
[182] 192–3, 378–9, 423–32.

vital organs,[183] is cast in more material terms: gods desire meat as well as smoke. They experience hunger. Thus it becomes possible in *Birds* and *Wealth* to starve the gods into submission by denying them sacrificial smoke.[184] In these plays the Olympians do indeed benefit from the fragrant smoke of sacrifice, but that smoke can be cut off—in *Birds* by the building of a wall in the sky—and the gods denied nourishment. The gods are imagined to feed off the fragrant and fatty smoke. Again, comedy builds on ambiguities inherent in sacrifice and exaggerates them by emphasizing the material elements. The same is seen in the comic utopias where the dead or primitive Greeks are imagined to eat to their hearts' content without the necessity of labour: work is made redundant, but the desire to eat remains as important as ever.

The exploitation of the material world in *Peace* is instructive, and may be borne in mind in the myriad fragments cited in later chapters for the kind of text in which the fragment was originally written. Human society organizes the material world in its desired patterns of meaning, order, hierarchy, and so on. The play opens in malodorous disorder: the household slaves are making cakes, not of barley but of excrement. Humans do not eat excrement, but the play presents the dung-beetle, which does. The beetle is a comic device to fill in what tragedy has omitted. Euripides in his *Bellerophon* supplied the winged horse Pegasus and Bellerophon, the hero who flew to heaven: Aristophanes' version also has the flight to heaven, but only after devoting much attention to the provision of fodder for the beetle. The hard work of grinding excrement cakes, the quality of the food, and the provision of food are all set out. The beetle is as much a fastidious consumer who takes pleasure in his food as any comic eater. Dung as food, however, is an affront to human society and serves in the comedy to mark the disorder expected at the beginning of a play which will contrast with the good order and good smells of the wedding feast at the end. As we have seen, the beetle also enables us to imagine the excrement of the gods, at least

---

[183]   Detienne and Vernant (1989).

[184]   In this respect and others, such as the bribing of gods who always have their hands out for gifts (*Ecclesiazusae* 777–83), the comic gods contrast with those of Plato's *Symposium* who, Socrates declares, need nothing. In comedy their needs are material.

the ambrosial excrement of Ganymede. The beetle, whose normal role in the food chain of the fauna of Greece[185] does not bring it close to human society, now invades human society and links it with the divine—an inventive exploitation of normally discrete elements of the material world—and the greatest affront to eating at the beginning of any play.[186] Inventive use of the material continues. Trygaeus arrives in heaven on his flying beetle to be greeted by a hostile Hermes as 'foul, totally foul, most foul' (183)—without reference to the nature of the beetle. Hermes proves to be both gluttonous for meat (192–3)—material meat rather than the etherial smoke of the sacrificial fire—and guardian of the pots and pans of the gods (201–2).

Material content breaks down further boundaries. The terrible ogre War (*Polemos*, chosen by Aristophanes in place of Ares the god of war) grinds up the cities of Greece as if they were the ingredients for a tasty dish—leeks represent Prasiae, garlic Megara, cheese Sicily, honey Attica. Trygaeus, in a literal reading of his name, the Vintage Man, is to marry Opora, Harvest, and the two will reproduce and create not children but plants, little grapes. Much of the comic concern with farming and the countryside rests on fertility ritual and similarities between plant and human reproduction: here the two become one.[187] Women too in *Peace* are linked both with plants and animals for sacrifice, comparable to the piglet daughters of *Acharnians*. All these comically creative ideas bring together material aspects and implications with surprising directness and juxtaposition, working partly through metaphor and partly through energetic pursuit of the material.

The comic celebration of the material world derives both from the search for good things (*agatha*) linked with festivity and from the perspective adopted by the comic voice, the voice from the streets of the ordinary citizen, male or female, who has little interest in the pretension and puffed-up flummery with which the powerful protected themselves. Hence the return to first principles, materialist principles, and the search for objectives,

[185] See Beavis (1988), 157–64.

[186] Further linguistic jokes on the beetle are allowed: the *kantharos* is also a drinking-cup and a boat.

[187] Cf. the Thesmophoria and the Rural Dionysia in *Acharnians* 247–79, which take on an unusually strong interest in human reproduction.

fantastic or utopian but available to all, or at least to the protagonist and chorus. The comic presentation of tragedy and philosophy is instructive. In *Frogs* the issues are large and abstract, the saving of the city and the relative merits of the verses of Aeschylus and Euripides. But the protagonist is the buffoonish comic god Dionysus, whose material qualities we have already noted. His devotees in the underworld, furthermore, concern themselves with salvation and purity, but also with comedy and meat; and the inhabitants of the underworld resemble more the innkeepers and working women of contemporary Athens than the glorious dead.[188] Once Dionysus addresses himself to Aeschylus and Euripides, the poets turn to some extent to materialist considerations. Aeschylus' treatment of tragedy, claims Euripides, was fantastical and overblown (939–44): 'when I took over the art from you first of all its body was swollen with pompous words and heavy phrases. First I slimmed her down and reduced her weight with light verses and walks and white beet, administering a juice from gibbering chatter taken from unusual books. Then I fed her up on monodies [. . .]' A little later Aristophanes has Euripides, with help from Dionysus, change the metaphor from medicine to the domestic economy (973–91):

EURIPIDES: . . . I introduced calculation to the art and consideration, thorough knowledge of various matters and in particular how to run their homes better than before and to examine, 'how is this so?', 'how is this so for me?', 'who took this?'
DIONYSUS: Yes, by the gods. Now every Athenian goes home and bawls to his slaves and enquires, 'Where is the cooking-pot? Who has eaten the head off the sprat? The old bowl has died on me. Where's yesterday's garlic? Who's nibbled the olive?' In the past they were simple-minded and sat gawping.[189]

These passages satirize tragedy but they also assimilate it to comedy and celebrate it. We can add the weighing of tragic verse like cheese (1364–9), the little pot (*lecythion*) added by Aeschylus to

[188] Dionysus asks Heracles to tell him about the route to the underworld when he came in search of Cerberus, the 'harbours, breadshops, brothels, inns, the right turnings to take, fountains, paths, cities, ways of life, landladies, where there are fewest bugs' (110–15).
[189] For the domestic instruction in Euripides cf. *Thes.* 383–432 on husbands learning about their wives' drinking and their lovers.

all the prologues Euripides can cite from his own plays,[190] and his wife's supposed lover Cephisophon who also appears at fr. 596. At Teleclides fr. 41 Mnesilochus is parching a new drama as if it were barley and Socrates is adding the kindling underneath.

We have seen how comedy adds the material to philosophy, in *Clouds* linking the theoretical work of the comic Socrates with bread-making and farting. It should be noted that this technique in part resembles the starting-point—though not the objective —of Plato in a number of dialogues. Plato's Socrates drew his initial positions from the artisans of Athens;[191] although he consorted with such members of the elite as Callias and Alcibiades, he remained down-to-earth and unpretentious. There is an excellent example in the discussion of pots, soup, and ladles in *Hippias Major* 288c–291a, and of whether a golden ladle is better for the purpose than one made of fig-wood. Plato follows a similar approach in his dialogue on love and the body-beautiful, the *Symposium*. In a most sympathetic portrait Plato's Aristophanes accounts for sexual attraction in the overtly material terms of a myth of bodies divided by an angry Zeus as if he were cutting up apples or eggs. The portrait appears as sympathetic to Aristophanes' art as to the poet himself. So too Plato's Alcibiades describes the qualities of Socrates by comparison with a statue of Silenus used at shrines.[192] Plato admits the material world into his dialogues, and moves from the material to the ethical and metaphysical. This is where his latter-day disciple Athenaeus falls short of the master's lead. For Athenaeus, the material world is all, and ethics and aesthetics are contained within it. Thus, while he models his *Deipnosophistae* on Plato's *Symposium* and to some extent follows Plato's ethical approach, his book is so stuffed with the foods and paraphernalia of the visible world of the Greek polis, particularly as presented in the texts of comedies, that he remains always materialist.

---

[190] See 1200, with Dover's note.

[191] See e.g. *Apology* 23c9–e5, with Burnet's note (1924).

[192] Cf. also Plato *Meno* 80a, in which Meno compares Socrates with a νάρκη or torpedo-fish.

2

Food in the Comic Social Order

2.1. THE SCOPE OF THIS CHAPTER

The material things of the previous chapter, which are so important to comedy, were rarely presented in a cultural and social vac-
cum. Next I consider the social context of eating: first, 'normal'
eating in comedy and then infringements of that 'normality'—
the solitary eater, the glutton, the parasite or unequal eater at the
feast, the comic cook who prepares food as well as discourse, the
foreign eater, and finally Heracles, the paradigmatic eater of
myth who accordingly appeared in many comedies. The
relationship between comedy and certain forms of eating and
drinking will be of particular concern.

2.2. EATING IN THE COMIC POLIS

2.2.1. Comedy on Festivals

Many of the forms of eating to be considered in this chapter took
place at civic festivals. It was on these occasions of public commensality that the Athenians most clearly affirmed their own
identity in relation both to their gods and to other Greeks. Private commensality also took place on these days. Festivals and
other forms of festivity are made possible, in a community whose
economy is largely built on agriculture (as at Athens), when production is in surplus. Feasting, as Mary Douglas has shown,[1] is
often a product of abundance.[2] An individual uses festivity to
display to the community his well-being and the major stages in
the life-cycle of his family, such as birth and marriage.[3] The

---

[1] Douglas (1978).

[2] Festivity may also take place in times of shortage, either as part of an
appeal to the gods to favour the community with better supplies or as an assertion of well-being which will be followed by abstemious living.

[3] Individuals also use such display for networking and extending their

community, acting as a super individual, spends surplus wealth generated in the agricultural and wider economy[4] to stage festivals which go far beyond the traditional rites of the religious calendar. The citizens share their common good fortune in eating together, and, like the wealthy individual, develop their networks by, for example, inviting allies and foreigners to join the audience in performances of comedy and tragedy at the City Dionysia. Comedy as a genre—certainly Old Comedy—tended to favour the group over the individual and to adopt the perspective identified by the Old Oligarch as that of the demos.[5]

Festivals formed a major part of the religious year, marking out the calendar and emphasizing the relationships of the community both internally and towards the gods and other communities. Comedy, itself produced at three of the civic festivals of Dionysus,[6] constituted a part of the display of wealth by the community, produced as it was on the same occasion as other income was put on show, such as tribute, oxen, and fig-wood phalli sent by the allies.[7] Comedy appears to concern itself with some festivals and not others, and selects certain aspects—sometimes apparently minor aspects—of what were complex rituals, to the exclusion of others. Sometimes a festival is mentioned only in passing;[8] at other times a festival is alluded to and not directly named.[9] Again, a pattern of events might be presented which appears to reflect less the ritual aspects of a festival than the myth

influence, as do, to take comic examples, Callias in the *Flatterers* of Eupolis and Cimon in the *Archilochoi* of Cratinus, fr. 1. The latter appears to refer to the practice of Cimon and others of opening up orchards (units of agricultural production) to provide free feasts for the people.

[4] In an imperial city such as Athens the wider economy embraced revenue from subject cities which was partly ploughed into such festivals as the Panathenaia and City Dionysia.

[5] [Xenophon], *Constitution of the Athenians* 2.9–10 (quoted in Chap. 3, n. 182) and 18.

[6] City Dionysia, Lenaea, Rural Dionysia, and perhaps informally at the Anthesteria: see Pickard-Cambridge (1968), 15–16.

[7] Ibid. 58–63.

[8] The Apaturia at *Acharnians* 146, the Diasia and Panathenaia at *Clouds* 386 and 408, but in all three cases the sense of belonging to the community or to a group of kinsmen is strong.

[9] I discuss in Chap. 4 Aristophanes' possible use of either the Pyanopsia or the Thargelia in *Knights*.

linked with that festival (if the two can be separated).[10] Reference to festivals is not confined to those of the polis; Panhellenic gatherings such as those at the Isthmus and Olympia were also exploited. Athenian festivals of particular importance to Old Comedy were those which stressed the identity of the polis (the Panathenaia and City Dionysia), belonging to the community (the Apaturia), the reproduction of plants and humans (festivals of Dionysus and Demeter—in particular the Rural Dionysia, Anthesteria, Eleusinian Mysteries, Scira, and Thesmophoria), gendered festivals (especially the women's festivals of the Thesmophoria and Adonia), and festivals for new gods such as the Bendideia.[11] In Middle and New Comedy festivals continued to be of importance. Dorpia, one of the days of the Apaturia, was personified and spoke the prologue in the *Heracles* of Philyllius,[12] while the *Dodecate* of the same poet is named after one of the days of the Anthesteria festival. Feasting at civic festivals had a role to play, and a new element was developed, the sexual encounter of a citizen woman at a festival, whether extramarital sex or rape.[13]

At many festivals foods and drinks were consumed. This element was a major concern for comedies of all periods,[14] often closely allied to comedy's generic interest in feasting as a representation of itself (on which see 2.11). Comedies gave particular attention to the consumption of wine and the meat of sacrificial

[10] A. Bowie (1993). This survey makes no attempt to list exhaustively all the festivals alluded to in comedy. I explore in the next chapter general reference to civic festival in Old Comedy and the comic use of festivals which allude to otherwise unknown elements. When some parts of festivals are not mentioned (as is often the case), it is open to interpretation whether or not they are alluded to: see e.g. ibid. on the role of Orestes at the Anthesteria which may be hinted at in *Acharnians*.

[11] Parker (1996), 170–5. The festival of Bendis was at least mentioned in Cratinus, *Thracian Women* and Aristophanes, *Lemnian Women*. On the festivals of Bendis and other foreign gods in comedy see A. Bowie (forthcoming). In the fourth century Timocles wrote a *Dionysiazusae* and Philippides an *Adoniazusae*.

[12] Fr. 7. A. Bowie (1997), 4 suggests that the *protenthai* of the Apaturia, referred to at *Clouds* 1198–200, contribute to the theme of the reintegration of Strepsiades and Pheidippides into the community.

[13] See e.g. Menander, *The Arbitration, Plokion, The Ghost*, and *Samia*.

[14] There are, to be sure, many occasions on which comedy dwells on aspects of festival other than eating.

victims which constituted for the citizens both nourishment and a celebration of commensality. Comedy extended 'festival' to more general festivity,[15] licence, and such combinations of communal and private interests as the 'marriage' of the protagonist of Old Comedy. We might add the *pannychis*, or all-night festival, which was on some occasions part of a festival of the polis such as the Panathenaea and on others an impromptu celebration for women.[16] Some *pannychides* appear to have resembled sympotic festivity.[17] For Old Comedy, at least, festivity was the goal to which the movement of the play was directed: in *Acharnians* the peace brokered by Dicaeopolis is rapidly celebrated with a procession at the Rural Dionysia, and the play concludes with the Anthesteria; in *Peace* Attendence at the Festival (Theoria) is a personified (though silent) character. In Middle and New Comedy negative aspects of the festival emerge in plays which feature rape; in these plays resolution is found in citizen marriage rather than festival.

We must be quite clear, however, that what comedy does not represent is carnival in the late-medieval sense of the term so influentially presented in Bakhtin (1968). There are aspects of carnival which Old Comedy in particular shares, the prioritizing of the body and all-consuming belly, the frequent interest in the market-place of the city, and the ubiquitous concentration on foods and eating. Comedy also presents a topsy-turvy world in which the powerful are brought low, whether the politicians of Old Comedy or the heads of household in Middle and New. There is reference to, but no apparent exploitation of the Cronia, the festival in which the roles of master and slave were reversed.[18] But what is crucially lacking in Old Comedy, as Carrière (1979), Goldhill (1991), and Edwards (1993) have pointed out, is the political attack on authority. The polis sponsors the dramatic festivals and comedy respects strongly that civic context of the festival and the controlling authority of the demos. Comedy is

---

[15] The content of the *Heortae* or *Feasts* of Plato is not known.

[16] Menander, *Dyscolus* 857, *Samia* 38–46.

[17] See Rosen (1989), 356–7 on Eubulus fr. 3; Athenaeus 15.668c–d; *Clouds* 1069; Aristophanes fr. 715; Posidippus, *Dancing-Women* fr. 28.22; and Gomme and Sandbach (1973) on Menander, *Dyscolus* 858.

[18] See Chap. 3.

thus not carnival, though it must be stressed that comedy does attack authority as vested in individuals, as the Old Oligarch recognized.[19] In Old Comedy in particular, political and military leaders are reviled, as are such leaders of the cultural elite as philosophers and tragic poets. Furthermore, Old Comedy also criticizes such democratic institutions as the assembly and the lawcourts, contrasting them unfavourably with idealized forms of government from the past. There is a limited but not fundamental reversal of power. I discuss below (2.11) the comic reconfiguration of society in which citizens, audience, chorus, and other friends of comedy are invited to the feast and such enemies as politicians, generals, officials, and tragic poets are expelled. In this way comedy offers a special festive fare of its own, combining its special discourse of feasting and consumption with the festivals that took place in the wider polis and offering itself as modest nourishment to the audience of citizens. Comic texts show respect to the demos but present a special agenda that stresses agriculture and peace in a form the polis could not follow. The comic polis was, furthermore, resolutely masculine—women of low status were consumed in sympotic excess along with tasty food and wine (see Chapter 1.9 and Chapter 3).

In much comic festivity there is a tension between two contrasting features; on the one hand, comic festivity offered commensality with other citizens and the city's gods and promoted civic identity; on the other, it brought licence and release from everyday restraints. The slave in *Peace* exemplifies the second feature, reducing a festival at Brauron to a riot of drinking and sexual pleasure on the road to, and at Brauron.[20] The *Mercator* of Plautus includes both elements (64–72): the young lover describes his father's early life as a hard, dirty, but rewarding life on the farm, with the city as a centre of temptation from which he was kept by the grandfather. The father went to town only once every four years for the Panathenaea, and as soon as he had seen the new robe for Athena he was sent back to the countryside—before he could join in the wider festivities or the immoral life of the city.

---

[19] [Xenophon], *Constitution of the Athenians* 2.18.
[20] See below, Chap. 3.

2.2.2. Mealtimes

Too little is known in detail of 'normal' eating in Athens, but the general pattern appears to be two meals a day, a light meal or *ariston* and a more substantial meal or *deipnon*. Writers sporadically remark on the oddity of eating once a day;[21] medical writers allow for patients eating once or twice daily.[22] In his seventh *Epistle* (326b) Plato wrote disapprovingly of Italian and Sicilian citizens who were dedicated to eating, to filling themselves with food twice a day and never sleeping alone at night. In many societies elaboration is attached to the more substantial meal, and it is to this that guests who are not kinsmen or well-known to the family are likely to be invited. The smaller meal, whether 'breakfast' or 'lunch', is likely to be less elaborate and probably more conservative. Here will be foods that are not innovative but those with which the eaters feel at ease. It is no coincidence that it is with this meal that comedy frequently identifies itself rather than the more ostentatious *deipnon*, where display and foreign influences were more likely to be felt.[23] Much eating in ancient Athens was 'public', at festivals organized by the polis or deme or within religious clubs or *orgeones*. Comedy often identifies itself also with this form of eating. It is not always easy to separate public and private, since it was often the case that citizens might eat at home with friends 'privately' while participating in one of the festivals of the city. Very often it is context alone that determines whether a particular form of eating is in good order or not. Eating in Greek culture was gendered, women of status being likely to eat at *ariston* and at home, or at a festival or wedding, while *deipna* and symposia normally appear to have been reserved for men and their *hetaerae* or female companions.

---

[21] e.g. Phylarchus, *FGrH* 81 F13 = Athenaeus 2.44b, '[Phylarchus] says that all the Iberians drink water despite being the richest of men and always eat once a day through meanness while wearing the most expensive clothes'.

[22] Passages collected by Arnott (1996) on Alexis fr. 271: Hippocrates, *Ancient Medicine* 11, *Regimen in Acute Diseases* 11, 28, 32; Galen 10.544 Kühn; Philumenus in Oribasius *Medical Compilations* 45.29.55.

[23] I am grateful to Geoffrey Arnott, however, for pointing out that New Comedy at least is more commonly occupied with a *deipnon*, largely because the span of the stage time was from dawn to dusk, and the meal comes at the end of the play.

2.2.3. Comedy on Two Meals a Day

On mealtimes in comedy Athenaeus notes[24] 'the one-meal man' at Alexis fr. 271 and Plato fr. 296:[25] 'whenever you see a private individual eating one meal a day[26] or a poet showing no desire for song and lyric, consider the one to have lost half of his life and the other half of his art. They are both barely alive'; 'he did not eat once a day but sometimes dined twice daily'.[27] For the most part, however, comedy does not raise the issue; further, it is not always clear how a *deipnon* is distinct from an *ariston*: the *ariston* at Diphilus, *The Painter* fr. 43 is 'select', comes 'dancing in' and includes novel and desirable varieties of fish and meat together with silver vessels—all features normally expected of the *deipnon*. At Alexis fr. 296,[28] indeed, the two are combined. Similarly, in the *Dyscolus* of Menander the post-sacrificial meal prepared by the cook is described as an *ariston* (555), despite massive emphasis on the elaboration of the meal. The *deipnon* was normally eaten in the evening,[29] but there are exceptions: at Aristophanes, *Cocalus* fr. 360 a character says, 'but it is well into midday, father, the time when the young men must have their *deipnon*'.[30]

2.2.4. Comedy on Domestic Eating

At *Wasps* 605–16 Philocleon describes the pleasures of life at home:

[24] 2.47 a–e. Noting the oddity of 'eating one meal', Athenaeus adds phrases which describe other deviations: the parasite who is ἄνηστις, 'very hungry' (Cratinus fr. 45) and ὀξύπεινος, 'sharply hungry' (Diphilus fr. 95, Antiphanes fr. 249, Eubulus fr. 10), the man who is *apositos* or 'off his food' (Philonides fr. 1), the man who is *anaristetos*, 'unbreakfasted' (Eupolis fr. 77), the man who is *anankositos* 'forced to eat' (Crates fr. 50). The note both demonstrates the lexical voraciousness of Athenaeus and draws on the culture's plethora of terms distinguishing deviations from the assumed norms of eating.

[25] On the term μονοσιτεῖν see Arnott (1996) on Alexis fr. 271.1.

[26] Arnott argues for this sense of μονοσιτεῖν, though 'eating alone' is an (otherwise unattested) possibility.

[27] οὐ μονοσιτῶν ἑκάστοτε ἀλλὰ κἀνίοτε δειπνῶν δὶς τῆς ἡμέρας.

[28] 'From which we can have a brief *aristodeipnon*.'

[29] *Clouds* 175; *Wasps* 1401; Kassel–Austin (1986) on Ar. fr. 360.

[30] The unorthodox hour may indicate that a very long symposium is to follow. Arnott (1996) suggests a practical solution: the *ariston*, whether taken in the morning or afternoon, came before the *deipnon* (taken in the afternoon or evening). Precise times varied according to the time of year, with the *deipnon* being taken earlier in winter than midsummer. See Heath (1998), 215–18.

when I go home with my jury pay, then everyone is pleased to see me on account of the silver. First, my daughter gives me a wash and oils my feet and leans forward to kiss me and, speaking fondly to her father, fishes the three obols out of my mouth with her tongue. And my little wife flatters me and gives me a barley cake and then sits beside me and urges me on, 'eat this, nibble this'. I love it, and have no need to look to you or your steward whenever he serves an *ariston* with curses and grumbles. But if he does not knead me a barley cake I have the money as a shield against misfortune, as a protective instrument against missiles. And if you do not pour out wine for me to drink, I bring home for myself this donkey here full of wine and then tip it up and pour myself a drink.

The speech first concerns the freedom brought to poorer citizens by jury pay: they are able to exert influence at home and go to market and buy extra essentials. Here the freedom is from the old man's allegedly overbearing son, but the increase in money for a number of citizens probably increased small-scale commercial activity in the agora and contributed to comedy's ambivalent attitude to commerce and commodities. Shopping plays an ambivalent role in comedy, as I set out in Chapter 4.[31] The scene at home shows that those who normally ministered to Philocleon were his female kin or a slave, while his son controlled the wine. There is no sexual segregation when strangers are not present; snacks or light meals are served.[32]

2.2.5. Comedy on Gendered Eating

Comedy represents the categories of women in Athenian society, the citizen class and the non-citizen, whether *hetaera*, foreigner, or slave. For citizen women, eating was segregated from male eating on the formal occasion of the *deipnon* and symposium and on other occasions. Segregation is particularly evident in the new social order in *Ecclesiazusae*, where such radical changes as the communal ownership of property and communal organization of sexual intercourse do not extend to dining. Women wait outside

---

[31] This is one of those comic passages (MacDowell (1971), on 609 and 791, adds *Birds* 503, *Ecclesiazusae* 818, frr. 3 and 48) in which men carried tiny Attic coins in their mouths. Whether or not this really was an Athenian practice, all these passages occur in contexts which include food, the money in the mouth representing nourishment for which it will be exchanged.

[32] Dalby (1995), 15 takes this passage as evidence that women served their husbands before themselves. Ancient detail to support this idea is lacking.

male eating and drinking parties and pick up partners afterwards (626–9). It is evident too in the *Dyscolus* of Menander, in which the sacrifice to Pan and the communal eating (prior to marriage) is wholly organized by a woman of status for her family, yet the festivities are divided into a symposium for the men and an all-night festival for the women—presumably because men and women who are not an exclusive group of kinsmen or close friends are present together.[33] Family *deipna*/symposia were perhaps not segregated; they were rarely described in comedy, as far as I know, though Menander, *Bridegroom* fr. 186 provides a good example: 'it's quite a business to fall headlong into a family symposium,[34] where first of all the father takes the cup and leads the discussion and then, his advice delivered, drinks up. Second comes the mother, then an aunt makes a rambling aside, then a deep-voiced old man, the aunt's father, then an old woman who calls the young man "darling". He nods to all these advisers.' This is a sympotic scene where advice to a bridegroom appears to replace the usual entertainment. At the formal wedding-feast segregation returned, to judge from Menander, *Samia* 287–9[35] and Euangelus, *The Bride Unveiled* fr. 1, where there are six tables for the men and four for the women.[36] Comedy reflects other Athenian literature in concentrating on male eating, but female eating is not neglected. Menander's *Women Lunching Together* was probably a notable example. Fr. 340 implies *deipna*: 'it was a clever idea not to gather the women together and give dinner to a crowd, but to have the wedding based on food at

[33] Segregation was not complete since either Getas or Sicon must have been present at the women's festival in order to describe female behaviour at 943–53. On female commensality outside comedy see Burton (1998).

[34] Literally *triklinon*, 'three-couch [symposium]'.

[35] 'If I can find out how many tables you're going to have, how many women there are, what time dinner will be . . .' This passage (which is not conclusive on this point) is a typical list of questions by a hired cook: for further examples see Chap. 8.

[36] 'A: I told you, four [. . .] tables of women and six of men, a full dinner and lacking in nothing. We want this to be a dazzling wedding. I mustn't find out details from an intermediary but will instruct on the basis of personal inspection. [corrupt text], as many kinds as you wish. For meat, you've got a calf, pigs, piglets, and hares. B: What a boaster the wretch is! A: Fig leaves, cheese, moulded cakes. COOK(?) Slave! Dromon! A: Lydian sauce, eggs, fine-meal [. . .]. And finally, the height of the table will be four feet so that the diner will raise himself up if he wants to get anything.'

home.'[37] *Lysistrata* opens with a list of festivals attended by women, a private festival of Dionysus[38] and celebrations for Pan and Aphrodite Colias and Genetyllis, while at 700–1 a woman invites her neighbour to share in an 'entertainment' in honour of Hecate.

Festivals and meetings with neighbours provide by far the greatest opportunities for commensality among comic women.[39] On both these occasions comedy appears to concentrate on drinking over eating, on strong wine in particular. Athenaeus, prior to his survey of barbarian drinkers, endorses the cliché of women as heavy drinkers, 'that the race of women love their wine is commonplace'.[40] *Thesmophoriazusae* provides a well-known example, allocating much more space to wine than to the day of fasting or the final feast of the festival; *Lysistrata* offers another, for the women's objective of peace is threatened by concerns about wine, not food. Drinking in the neighbourhood often relates to the local general store and bar, *kapeleion*,[41] whose wine for consumption on or off the premises is a frequent topic of comment among female speakers. An example is provided by Antiphanes, *Akontizomene* fr. 25: 'One of my neighbours is a *kapelos*. This guy, whenever I go there with a thirst, is the only one who knows how to mix my wine. I don't know that I've ever had too watery or too strong a drink.'

Many comic fragments present women in sympotic environments whose social context is unclear. In fragments describing symposia with men and women together it is usually certain that the women are *hetaerae* and social inferiors who entertain with music and in many other forms, including sexual favours.[42]

---

[37] Further evidence for this play is provided by a mosaic in Naples which shows three women at table and by Plautus *Cistellaria*, which is based on Menander's play. See Trendall and Webster (1971), 145 and Csapo and Slater (1995), 73–5.

[38] See the scholiast and Henderson on these lines.

[39] A similar picture could be given of 'real' women: see Burton (1998) and bibliography. Since gender-stereotyping is a strong element in comic discourse—as I discuss in Chaps. 1 and 6—it would be particularly unwise to elide comedy with 'reality' in this area.

[40] 10.440d–442a.   [41] On which see Chaps. 4 and 5.

[42] See e.g. Chap. 5 on the *kottabos* game with kisses as one of the prizes. In Menander, *The Arbitration* fr. 1, the young master has the harp-girl, Habrotonon, in his house even though he has just been married. See further 589–695.

These *hetaerae* might need to be regulated by the city authorities,[43] but the comic fragments appear to be more interested in
the supervisors of citizen women, the *gunaikonomoi*, who
checked their numbers at symposia, weddings, and sacrifices.[44]
When a comic fragment presents a discussion between two
female drinkers it is often impossible to identify their status, for
example in Antiphanes, *Female Initiate* fr. 163: 'A: Do you want a
drink, dear? B: I'm fine thanks. A: Give it to me then. They say we
should honour the gods as far as three cups' worth.' More examples are given in Chapter 5.

Eating at mealtimes follows preparation of the food, often in
laborious and time-consuming processing of raw materials, particularly cereals. Much of this labour is likely to have been undertaken by slaves in wealthy households, but, as Aristotle noted,[45]
in families without those resources such tasks were performed by
women.[46] A number of comedies refer to the labour of grinding
cereals. 'The woman singing while grinding the *kakrus* [parched
barley]' at *Clouds* 1358 is probably a slave;[47] other comedies
describe wives undertaking such tasks. At *Ecclesiazusae* 214–32
(quoted in Chapter 1) women are said to roast their own barley
and bake their own cakes; at Pherecrates, *Agrioi* (*Savages*) fr. 10
it is implied that this is no longer the case: 'in those days nobody
had a slave, a Manes or a Sekis, but the women had to do all the
household labour themselves. In addition, they used to grind the
grain early in the morning so that the village echoed to the touch
of the mills.'[48] Once the food was prepared, it was served by
slaves or women. Women normally serve their husbands their
morning *ariston* (*Ecclesiazusae* 469), and may join a neighbour
for *ariston* at her house (*Ecclesiazusae* 348–9).

---

[43]   See Fisher (forthcoming) and Davidson (1997), 82–3.
[44]   Athenaeus 6.245b–c, citing Timocles, *Court-Lover* fr. 34; Menander,
Kekruphalos fr. 208; Philochorus, *FGrH* 328 F 65. On this sumptuary legislation see further Bayer (1942); Habicht (1997), 55–6; Fisher (forthcoming); and
Ogden (1996).
[45]   Dalby (1995): *Politics* 1323a4.   [46]   See further Wilkins (forthcoming, c).
[47]   On Women's work songs see ibid.
[48]   *Savages* is a play about early Greek society. One explanation for comic
inconsistencies over women's work may be ambiguity over the class of woman
described. Comedy sometimes describes all citizen women, sometimes only the
elite.

2.3. EATING IN THE COMMUNITY

Everyday eating is much less evident in comedy than eating on special occasions with kinsmen or guests. Domestic eating was not an area of life which was a major concern, though comedy has a greater interest in it than other forms of literature. We have seen examples above. All the same, a major investment in the domestic sphere had to wait for many centuries and very different forms of literature. Communal eating took many forms, some of them overlapping with eating in private. So, at the Panathenaia festival animals that had been sacrificed on the acropolis were taken for distribution to the Cerameicus—and consumed there or at home.[49] At *Clouds* 409[50] Strepsiades—presumably at home—is roasting a paunch for his kinsmen at the Diasia; Lysistrata honoured Hecate with her neighbour. At Eubulus fr. 148 the speaker claims it is customary to have a slap-up meal during the Amphidromia, the ceremony at which a newly born child was accepted into the family.[51] Parker[52] suggests that food preparation at a number of festivals of the polis, including perhaps the boiling of beans for the Pyanopsia and the solitary drinking of the Anthesteria, took place certainly at deme level and possibly at household level. In many of the speeches of boastful cooks that I survey in Chapter 8, the cook is first concerned with the occasion that he is cooking for. Almost by definition he will not have been hired for a standard domestic meal, but many of the possibilities extend beyond a grand private dinner. The cook might ask[53] how

---

[49] There are many inscriptions recording the regulations for sacrifice—for example the Attic calendars—which stipulate whether or not the meat can be taken home and whether or not shared among men *and* women. Comedy exploits the phrases ἐκφορά/οὐκ ἐκφορά at *Wealth* 1138, Theopompus fr. 71, Euphron *Brothers* fr. 1.20. On the meat at the Ceramicus see Fisher (forthcoming).

[50] Quoted in Chap. 1.

[51] 'It was the Amphidromia, at which it is customary to roast a slice of cheese from the Chersonese, to boil a cabbage glistening with oil, to roast some fat breast of lamb, to pluck doves, thrushes, and finches, to nibble cuttlefish and sprats, to beat many octopus with great vigour, and to drink many cups of strong wine.' Hunter (1983) on this passage notes the remark of the *Suda* (α 1722) that relatives sent gifts on the occasion of the Amphidromia, in particular, octopus and cuttlefish.

[52] (1987) 42.

[53] Diphilus, *The Woman Who Left Her Husband* fr. 17. On cooking for weddings see Chap. 8.

many are invited to a wedding and whether they include merchants as well as Athenians; different foods may be served for
those returning from a funeral;[54] the person in charge of the sacrifice or *deipnon* must be discovered—whether merchant or
wastrel or a *hetaera* celebrating the Adonia.[55] A notable occasion
on which women ate at festival was at a *pannychis* or all-night festival. These might be private occasions (the wedding in *Dyscolus*)
or public festivals. Four plays were written with the title *Pannychis*, by Pherecrates, Eubulus, Alexis, and Hipparchus. While
some or all of these titles may refer to the name of a *hetaera*,[56] it is
possible that nightly celebrations were the subject, with the possibility of seduction (as Arnott suggests). Alexis' play has a significant role for a cook.

There were many *orgeones* and *thiasoi*, or religious groups established to honour a local hero or other divinity, at which citizens
sacrificed and ate together;[57] there were meals organized by *demes*
(local administrative units), *phratries* (kinship groups), and *gene*
(the Athenian tribes). More informal meals for dining in groups
appear to have been *deipna sumbolaia* to which people contributed.
One person appears to have collected contributions from all in
order to buy the food and wine and possibly hire a cook. At Alexis,
The Man Who Has Got Glaucoma fr. 15 (one example of many),
there is a dispute over how much the contribution is to be.[58] There
were also *deipna asumbolaia* where everything was provided:
Amphis fr. 39, 'whoever is late at a dinner where no contribution is
expected you can immediately expect to desert the battle-line'.[59]
As we shall see below, parasites were in particular need of meals
without a contribution of their own. Kassel and Austin list examples (see Timocles fr. 10). Fragments refer to various groups

[54] Hegesippus, *Brothers* fr. 1.
[55] Diphilus, *Painter* fr. 42. Cf. Anaxippus, *Behind the Veil* fr. 1, which distinguishes lovers, philosophers, and tax-collectors.
[56] See Hunter (1983) and Arnott (1996), *ad loc.*
[57] Athenaeus 5.185f–186a; Ferguson (1944), 61–140; Parker (1996), 109–11,
333–42; Fisher (forthcoming). A deme festival is celebrated at Menander, *The
Sicyonian* 183–6.
[58] Arnott (1996) on this fragment gives details of the *deipnon sumbolaion* or
apo sumbolon. See also Hunter (1983) on Eubulus fr. 72, and Gow (1965) on
Machon 44.
[59] At Plautus, *Aulularia* 106–12 Euclio fears it would arouse suspicion if he
avoided a free handout (this time, of money).

eating together. At Aristophanes fr. 419 the speaker boiled up the soup for the *eranistai* (a loan syndicate: compare Cratinus fr. 494); at Alexis fr. 260 there are complaints of the food served for the *tetradistai* (people celebrating on the fourth day of the month), who, says Athenaeus, were feasted by a cook also for a festival of Aphrodite Pandemos at Menander, *Flatterer* fr. 1.[60] Festivity, as I have said, is a goal of comedy, Old Comedy in particular, the point at which the play often reaches its successful conclusion. Festive eating generally overshadows the domestic. At the end of *Acharnians* Dicaeopolis and his slaves cook a meal for the Anthesteria, as they would cook for a private meal; he is then invited to the house of the priest of Dionysus. He takes his food as a contribution to a feast which is already well supplied (1085–234), and participates in a symposium (1135, 1142) with the priest of Dionysus at a polis festival. Public and private, sacred and secular are all combined at the end of *Acharnians* in a form that is most instructive for this study.

I wish to draw attention to the sympotic element in comic festivals, for which *Acharnians* provides ample evidence. I argue in Chapter 5 that I do not believe that comic texts support the contention of Oswyn Murray and Pauline Schmitt-Pantel that the symposium at the end of the fifth century BC in Athens was an institution of the elite. The parts of the symposium are often referred to without rancour in comedy, and I am not aware of any comic text which identifies the symposium as the preserve of the elite. Certainly there are such plays as the *Flatterers* of Eupolis, the *Wasps*, and many plays of Middle and New Comedy which set forth elegant symposia, but the features of mixing wine with water, drinking together, wearing garlands, and reciting poetry and singing songs appear to be widely known and practised. Decisive for comedy are those passages which reject war in favour of sympotic activity: the symposium is presented as the home ground of comedy, to be enjoyed with that other unalloyed comic good, peace.[61] Fisher (forthcoming) has recently argued a similar case against Murray, drawing attention also to evidence for symposia in public buildings in the agora and to provision for

---

[60] Fisher (forthcoming), 13. See Arnott (1996) on Alexis fr. 260 for further detail on the *tetradistai*.

[61] See in particular the closing scenes of *Acharnians*, *Peace* 1140–58, 1240–49, and Hermippus, *Moirai* fr. 48. On comedy and the symposium and the very difficult interpretation of Ian Ruffell, see further below.

andrones, or sympotic rooms, in comparatively modest homes in the Peiraeus which do not appear to belong to the elite. (However, if Murray is right to restrict the symposium to the elite in the polis, then this is another part of society in which the comic polis constructs an alternative social configuration.)

Eating among the elite, whether the wealthy or political leaders, was of major interest to comedy. As we shall see in Chapters 4 and 6, comedy portrays politicians abusing privileges of public dining at the prytaneion and often presents corruption in the form of excessive appetite and consumption. The wealthy have access to foods out of the reach of the people of Athens, luxuries among which fish are pre-eminent. In this context, excessive private dining is contrasted with forms of communal eating that are contained by ritual. Thus, the *mageiroi* who cut the throats of animals at sacrifice and sell surplus meat in the market become for the rich in comedy hired experts in the art of fine cooking. The comic poet can select where to place them on a range between masters of the sacrifice and purveyors of luxury—Menander in *Dyscolus* explores the ambivalence in this range. The *protenthai*, the 'pre-tasters' at the Apaturia festival, may in comedy become identified with gluttony and the more private *tenthai*.[62] Comedy[63] converts the honoured officials who 'ate with' the gods, the parasites, into hangers-on at the feast of the rich. Comic texts on occasion refer to regulation of the markets by such officials of the democracy as *agoranomoi* or *oinoptai*[64] in order to contain excessive consumption at the point of sale. As Arnott observes, *mageiroi* often speak their boastful piece en route from the market to the private house for which they are to cook. In all these examples comedy explores the area of concern around unregulated private dining and revels in details of excess, real or imagined. Eating in ancient Athens was almost always a communal, a social activity. In some plays comedy raised the spectre of the exception, the man who ate alone.[65]

---

[62] Though *Clouds* 1198 is the only clear example cited by Athenaeus at 4.171c–f. Dover (1968) urges caution. On *tenthai* see *Peace* 1009, 1120.

[63] Alexis, to be precise: see 2.6.

[64] Athenaeus (10.425a–b) cites Eupolis, *Cities* fr. 219, '[men] whom you wouldn't have chosen even as wine-inspectors in the past are now generals. O polis, polis, how your good fortune exceeds your good sense!'

[65] I am not aware of any comic examples of solitary dining by women.

2.4. THE SOLITARY EATER

It is part of the agenda of comic poets to highlight those who do not eat and drink with the community: the lone eater who refuses to participate, the glutton who satisfies appetite before sharing in commensality, and the parasite who is too poor to contribute his share either at a *deipnon sumbolaion* or in a reciprocal invitation to his home for a host who has fed him. All these are deformations of what is considered correct eating in the polis as far as comedy is concerned. A number of comedies featured the solitary eater or *monophagos*, who is denounced as criminal at Ameipsias fr. 23, 'go to hell, solitary eater and criminal', and Antiphanes fr. 291, 'you are eating alone. Already you are doing me harm.'[66] In both Greek and Roman society the man who ate alone transgressed the essential solidarity of commensality.[67] Among surviving plays with protagonists who defy commensality are the *Dyscolus* of Menander and (in Latin) *The Pot of Gold* of Plautus. Cnemon and Euclio[68] respectively want as few dealings as possible with shopping for food, preparation of meals, and feasting. These two share characteristics with other misanthropes[69] in such lost plays as the *Monotropos* of Phrynichus[70] and Anaxilas and the *Timon* of Antiphanes. The *Agrioi* of Pherecrates went a stage further, since the whole chorus was misanthropic, at least for part of the play.[71] Menander's *Dyscolus* best brings out the failure of commensality in the misanthrope. Cnemon objects to the proximity of the shrine of Pan next door to his house and to the people who come to sacrifice to Pan. He is an antitype of the good citizen, ignoring human contact as far as he can, critical of the way in which the neighbouring gods were worshipped, and negligent of both farm

[66] Cited by Athenaeus near the beginning of the *Deipnosophistae* (1.7f–8e) in the context of deviation from socially acceptable eating.

[67] Morton Braund (1996). The same can be said of the solitary drinker, on whom see Villard (1992), 77–81.

[68] *Aulularia* 371–89.

[69] At *Dyscolus* 6 Cnemon is described by Pan as ἀπάνθρωπός τις ἄνθρωπος: on the range of the term *apanthropos* over 'remote', 'unsocial', even 'inhuman' see Gomme and Sandbach (1973), *ad loc.*

[70] The misanthrope of fr. 19 leads 'the life of Timon and is unmarried . . . quick to anger, unapproachable, *unlaughing*, difficult to exchange dialogue with and idiosyncratic'.

[71] As attested by Plato, *Protagoras* 327d.

and oikos in failing to invest in farming potential and a marriage for his daughter. As an extreme example of self-sufficiency or autarky, he also serves the important function, emphasized by von Reden (1998), of isolating the self-interest and less-than-ideal conduct of other characters. She notes the invasion of money and commodities into the sacred and social world, the hired cook, and the shared meal used for self interest, together with Cnemon's denunciation of the sacrifice as an excuse for gluttony under the pretence of religion. Von Reden presents Menander as a conservative poet who attempts to resist further commodification, but in my view she puts the case far too strongly. As we saw in Chapter 1, there is in all Greek comedy a potential fight to be won in the conflicting concerns of commodification and 'culture': in the fifth century Aristophanes exposed Cleon as an honorand who did not use the prytaneion with gratitude but in order to satisfy his gluttony; Cimon's conversion of his home into a public space or prytaneion might be seen either as a benefaction to the people or as an attempt to buy support and subvert the political order.

In his self-sufficiency Cnemon is deviant, though he does not go so far as to reject the gods or take up criminal monophagy. But he is extreme enough. As he says, if everyone lived like him there would be no courts, no prisons, and no war (743–5)—nor would there be any polis. His farming is partly characterized by wild fruits—the wild pear—rather than the fruits of agriculture; he avoids human contact wherever possible, and therefore complains about his divine neighbours (444–7) because humans come to offer sacrifice to Pan and the nymphs. To be sure the people he censures are faintly ridiculous and perhaps self-interested— the woman who organizes the sacrifices is excessively given to such devotion; her rich son is out of place in a rustic environment—but it would be an unusual comedy that supported the man who refused to attend the wedding feast, and this comedy highlights his failure to feast by repeating the scene in which he is asked to lend pots and pans for the sacrifice and feast. Sicon the cook is indeed hired,[72] but his ritual function is stressed by his

---

[72] How else could a woman perform a sacrifice in a lonely place? She was not likely to kill the animal herself: see Detienne (1989), with the reservations of Osborne (1993), 392–405.

arriving with a sacrificial sheep on his shoulders; he attempts to borrow rather than hire equipment; there is no indication of shopping for food;[73] and the very sacrifice is initiated not by the zealous mother of Sostratos but by Pan.[74] Cnemon's denunciation of the self-serving humans at the sacrifice[75] is a comic version of the ambiguity of the Greek sacrifice that was highlighted as early as Hesiod: in a sacrifice offered by the polis or by an individual[76] the gods always receive the parts of the animal considered inedible by humans. There is certainly a case to be made for the commodification of sacrificial eating and feasting in comedy, but von Reden (1998) has not chosen a suitable play in *Dyscolus*. The deviance of Cnemon is manifested in the crucial area of communal life and social eating, and those he criticizes show few signs of gluttony or deviant eating themselves.[77]

2.5. GLUTTONS

The comic glutton resembled the solitary eater. The most striking example is the trial of the dog in *Wasps*, where the defendant has eaten without sharing and is declared to be the 'most-solitary-eating man of all dogs' since 'he shared nothing, not with the community, with me, that is' (917–23).[78] The dog represents

[73] As there is, for example, in the wedding preparations in *Samia*. In *Dyscolus* the food is perhaps provided from household supplies: see Gomme and Sandbach (1973) on *Samia* 228.

[74] Compare *Aulularia*, in which the Lar ensures the daughter is properly married, against opposition to feasting and shopping from Euclio.

[75] On which see Chaps. 2 and 6.

[76] Except for a holocaust to the gods of the underworld.

[77] Cnemon accuses his tormentors when they sacrifice of being social undesirables rather than gluttons (447) since they trouble him in asking for utensils, his portable property. At Ameipsias fr. 23 (cited above) the solitary eater was classed with the criminal as an antisocial element.

[78] Similarly, at *Acharnians* 1038–9 the chorus reflects on the good fortune of the protagonist and his unwillingness to share with anyone else, thus lending support to those who see Dicaeopolis as a selfish citizen (Foley 1988 and Fisher 1993). The immediate person with whom Dicaeopolis refuses to share his peace is Dercylus the farmer, a surprising exclusion given Old Comedy's orientation towards the country-people. He also appears to exclude the chorus (1044–6), but they are invited to join his procession at the end of the play (1231). This refusal to share his feast should be contrasted with his restoration of traded foods and participation in festivals of Dionysus (on which see Chap. 3), though

the general Laches, who like Cleon is alleged to have profited from campaigns overseas. The clear implication is that, whether a general or simply a consumer of food, everyone must put communal benefit and consumption first. Those identified as gluttons in Old Comedy, such as Morychus, Glaucetes, and Teleas in *Peace*,[79] have no other objective but to satisfy their appetite. They must be elbowed out of the way by the people and forced to make the good things available to all. Later comedy developed the fish-lover as the principal glutton whose appetite drove him to consume, whatever the cost to himself or others.

The most important parts of the glutton's body were the belly and the throat, as we saw in Chapter 1. The glutton represents the body out of control, hopelessly at the mercy of appetite. In his discussion of the *opsophagos*,[80] Davidson highlights the gourmet's sacrifice of all to appetite. He must have his food instantly, piping hot and straight from the pan. There can be no waiting for the niceties and rituals of dinner; in fact the meal sometimes fades from the picture. The appetite of women for strong drink is a similar theme.[81] There is also a social aspect to the belly, first seen in the early elegist Asius:[82] 'lame, a branded slave, exceeding old, like a beggar he came, the fat-flatterer, when Meles got married, uninvited, in urgent need of soup. In the midst of all the hero stood, rising up from the mud.' While those of excessive appetite may be the rich and famous, the politician and the tragic poet, the poor and despised may also have an appetite to satisfy, those whose need overrules protocols of status and drives to shameless parasitism through flattery. Such citizens are driven by the smell of food, particularly the aroma of fat, to satisfy their craving. So Amphis, *Gunaikomania* fr. 10: 'Eurybatus, you fat-licker. [. . .] There is no way you are not a person who finds happiness in his belly.' Such is the parasite, who is characterized by need and little self-respect and who barges in uninvited.

A. M. Bowie (1993) and Fisher (1993) would link his attendance at the Anthesteria with the solitary drinking of Orestes, who is perhaps to be linked with 'Orestes the bandit', referred to at 1166. See also A. M. Bowie (1997), 18.

[79] 1006–15.   [80] Davidson (1995), 209.
[81] See Chap. 6 for the comic discourse of appetite.
[82] Fr. 14 West=Athenaeus 3.125d.

2.6. PARASITES

The parasite, who occasionally appeared in other guises in Old
Comedy, becomes one of the great stock characters of Middle and
New Comedy. First seen, as far as we know, in Epicharmus, the
parasite and his close relative the flatterer or *kolax* highlight in
their exclusion the importance of commensality in the polis.
'Uninvited', or in need of a special invitation, the parasite must
gain access to the feast through other means, normally witty
remarks, games, and self-abasement. Comedy often emphasizes
the physical needs of the parasite, his appetite for the sustenance
that he desperately craves: Athenaeus cites Cratinus fr. 47, 'for
you are not the first uninvited guest who comes to the *deipnon* in
great hunger', Diphilus fr. 95, 'I enjoy seeing the sharply hungry
with cloaks off and eager to know everything before the proper
time', and Antiphanes fr. 249, 'A: he has this one illness: he is
always sharply hungry. B: He means that the man is an utter
Thessalian.'[83] The uninvited guest is introduced early in the
Deipnosophistae (1.7f–8d)[84] and given a historical perspective:
Archilochus (fr. 124(b) West) attacked one, Pericles, 'drinking
much unmixed wine, you neither brought your share [. . .] nor
invited [. . .][85] you came, as if a friend (*philos*). It was your belly
that led your mind and heart astray into shameless conduct.'
From Middle Comedy Athenaeus cites Eubulus fr. 117

Out of our guests who have been invited to the dinner are two who are
invincible, Philocrates and Philocrates—for though he is one I count
him as two great [. . .], three even. They say that he was once invited to
dinner by a friend?[86] who said 'come when you measure the marker at
twenty feet'. At dawn as soon as the sun rose he began to measure, and
when the shadow was longer than two feet he appeared! Then he said
that he had come a little late because of a business commitment—at
daybreak!

The deviant confirms the correct behaviour of the other diners
who are not driven by their bellies to ignore the proper time and
other proprieties, such as an invitation or the obligation to recip-
rocate. At the same time, much comic ingenuity could be applied
to the position of the parasite. Athenaeus continues with two

---

[83] Athenaeus 2.47 = n. 24 above. On Thessalians see 2.10.
[84] Just prior to the *monophagoi* cited above, p. 67.
[85] There are lacunae in the text.   [86] The text is corrupt.

fragments of Antiphanes which are probably ironic—frr. 252 and 253, 'that is the life of the gods, when you have the means of dining at the expense of others with no need to attend to adding up', and 'this is a blessed life! I must always seek out some new way to provide a bite for my jaws' (the text is corrupt), concluding with the significant, 'for we poets always sacrifice without smoke'.[87] The parasite, for all his humble position, relies heavily on what he can in fact offer in exchange, words, jests, songs, and poetry. The jests may often be at his own expense, but the poet, even the comic poet, may share something of the parasite's role.

Sympotic entertainment, after all, is not only provided by the underdog, the parasite, but by all participants, and in a symposium in a comedy the audience is not just the fellow-drinkers but the theatre audience also. The parasite, as we shall see, is a man of many names and many turns of phrase who can invent new strategies to defend his position and new ways to delight his audience. He can transform the material foods that he desperately needs into discourse: he can embody food, amuse by his consumption of it, amuse by his requests, his *bons-mots*, his neat turns of literary phrases and enthusiasm for sympotic games. Comedy's use of food in the discourse of the parasite enables the poet to draw on wider aspects of flattery and clientship in the polis—the undesirability of a powerful man gathering together a crowd of dependants in the manner of a tyrant, for example, or the similarity of the parasite and the blackmailer[88]—and to present such issues at a tangent, as a discourse about food and drink and the good order of the dinner.

The parasites were originally officials of status who in comedy became scroungers of food. This supposed decline in the status of the parasite mirrors our remarks above on comedy's concern that eating should be contained by ritual. If parasites are now directed solely by status and appetite, that decline is to be deplored. Diodorus of Sinope plays on this explicitly in *The Heiress* fr. 2:

I want to show you clearly that this is a revered and recognized invention of the gods. It was wise men and no god who revealed the other arts, but the art of the parasite was discovered by Zeus the god of friendship

---

[87] 'Live at the expense of others', Gulick.
[88] See further Davidson (1997), 269–74.

himself who everyone agrees is the greatest of the gods. For this god enters houses, making no discrimination between poor or rich, and wherever he sees a nicely covered couch and a table set beside it with all that is necessary, straightaway he reclines with the diners in good order, feasts[89] himself, eats and drinks and goes home without paying his corner.[90] And this is what I too do now. When I see couches covered, tables ready, and an open door, I go in there quietly and make myself the good guest so as not to disturb my fellow-drinker, and, after taking my pleasure in everything that is laid out and having a drink, I go home like Zeus the god of friendship. That this procedure was always honoured and held in high regard can be understood more clearly from this: when the polis honoured Heracles with a glittering feast she made sacrifice in all the demes and did not ever take lots to select the parasites for these sacrifices or take those who happened to be available for the purpose; rather she chose twelve men carefully from the citizen body, selecting those who were born citizens by male and female descent, who owned property, and who led an upstanding life. Then, later, in imitation of Heracles some of the better-off selected parasites and invited them to be fed, choosing not the most elegant but those able to flatter and to praise everything. When a man belches in front of them after eating radishes or a rank *silouros*[91] they say he has just eaten violets and roses. And when he is reclining with one of them and farts, the parasite brings forward his nose and begs him to say 'where do you get this incense from?' Because of such patrons and such foul usage what was honoured and fine is now shameful.

The speaker of this fragment warms to the theme of ritual order that has been abused. The appeal based on *theoxenia* for Zeus Philios and the honoured officials of Heracles resembles other evidence adduced by Athenaeus who is, once again, our major source for this office. What is particularly important in parasitism as a religious ritual is its location in the polis and the demes, and its links in particular with Heracles, whose place in comic eating is considered below.[92] Diodorus also picks out two other aspects, the analogy between eating in private homes and

---

[89] ἀριστίσας.

[90] Cf. Antiphanes fr. 252 above.

[91] A large fish, not certainly identified, but possibly a catfish. It is linked with the *glanis* in some authors. See Thompson (1947), 233–5 and Willis (1991).

[92] Heracles had many sacred precincts in Attica: see Woodford (1971), Parker (1996), 333–4, who mentions in passing the evidence for the chorus of the *Banqueters* of Aristophanes dining in a precinct of Heracles.

eating with a god and the relationship 'now' between 'secular' parasites and powerful patrons, a relationship into which exchanges based on words have entered (*kolakeuein*) in addition to eating and drinking. Further, the power relation has changed, the god who had formerly been the guest is replaced by the patron who provides food and expects a return from his flatterer. Athenaeus tracks this perceived decline with extensive comic quotation and evidence, including inscriptions, from Atthidographers and others (6.234c–235f). Cults of Heracles were not alone in using parasites: Apollo and the Dioscuri are also mentioned, and cults outside Athens are cited. Diodorus differs from Athenaeus' quotation of Polemon in stressing that parasites of Heracles should be drawn from Athenians of two Athenian parents: Polemon cites an inscription from Cynosarges stipulating 'bastard' officials of mixed birth. This discrepancy aside,[93] Diodorus and the other sources used by Athenaeus attest the importance, antiquity, and strict regulation of the 'parasites' who 'ate beside' their god.[94] Although Diodorus compares ancient honours with present dishonour, one inscription cited by Athenaeus dates to 432–1 (6.234f) and Clearchus claims (6.235a) that parasites in his day were still honoured officials in most poleis.[95]

The comic parasite normally reflects, with more or less frankness, on the unacceptability of his way of life, whether or not by reference to the past. The assimilation of the parasite with the flatterer appears to have been made by Alexis in his *Parasite*. Even though in earlier comedies flatterers had long offered discourse in exchange for food, they had not been called parasites. This is the conclusion of Arnott (1968) on the basis of Athenaeus' report of Carystius of Pergamum's work *On Didascalia* (6.235e–f).[96] Athenaeus himself disputes this claim, but we have no firm evidence that the term 'parasite' was applied to the comic character before Alexis. Athenaeus adduces the earliest manifestation in frr. 34 and 35 of the *Hope or Wealth* of Epicharmus: 'but another man walked in here(?) on the heels of the first, a man

---

[93] Diodorus wrote of 'all the demes': his speaker may be mistaken, or he may have excluded the special case of Cynosarges and the bastard officials.

[94] See further Bruit (1995); Schmitt-Pantel (1992), 100–4; Avezzù (1989).

[95] The inscription lists parasites at Pallene.

[96] On Arnott see further below.

whom you will easily find(?) easy to buy and ever-eating. Come what may he drinks up his life like a cup, in one swift gulp.' Epicharmus makes his 'parasite' say the following to any enquiry:

I dine with anyone who asks—he just has to invite me—and indeed anyone who does not—and there's no need for an invitation. There(?) I am witty and provide much mirth and praise my host. And if someone wishes to say something against him, I am ready with insults and matter to make myself hated. Then, after much eating and much drinking, I depart. I have no slave to hold up a light for me, but drag myself along, lonely and slipping in the darkness. If I meet any patrols, this is the one blessing that I account to the gods, that they want no more than to beat me. When I at last get home, dead beat, I sleep without any covers and take no note(?) of the preliminaries [of the day?] as long as the unmixed wine has me in its grip and takes over my mind.

This Sicilian prototype of the poor man without honour, indifferent to his reception at the feast[97] provided he scrounged and consumed successfully, and as dishonoured away from the meal as when he was performing, had many Attic successors. Avezzù (1989) picks up the essential twin features of the man driven by his belly and the man of low status, the latter, she claims, particularly appropriate to the Athens of the fourth century.[98] The patronage of the poor by the rich is always problematic, a concern picked up by comedy at all periods.[99] Fr. 172 of the *Flatterers* of Eupolis (probably from the parabasis) makes the point at the height of the democracy in the fifth century:

[97] Epicharmus twice used the lines 'someone unwillingly asked you to dinner, and you came willingly, on the run', at *Hope or Wealth* fr. 37 and *Periallos* fr. 110.

[98] After Epicharmus, Athenaeus cites Diphilus fr. 61: 'When a rich man invites me to a dinner he is putting on, I pay no attention to the triglyphs or the ceiling, nor do I rate the Corinthian jars, but I watch closely the smoke produced by the cook. If it rises up straight and in great strength, I am delighted and pleased and am all aflutter. But if it drifts about and is thin I instantly realize that this is a dinner for me but one that has no blood in it.' For the obligation on the polite guest to admire the house of the host, Gulick compares Aristophanes, *Wasps* 1214–15 and Homer, *Odyssey* 4, cited by Athenaeus at 5.179b and 181e.

[99] Nor is unequal status the only difficulty. A friend (*philos*) might have an invitation to a feast and still be unwelcome at the *deipnon* and symposium: a speaker in Pherecrates, *Cheiron* fr. 162 counsels against such treatment of a guest.

but we will recite for you the life that flatterers enjoy. Listen to how we
are smart men in every situation. First, we have a slave who normally
belongs to someone else [. . .].[100] Then I have these two elegant cloaks [. . .]
always change into the other one and issue forth into the market-place.
There, when I notice some rich innocent, I'm instantly all over him.
And if this rich guy makes some comment I praise it strongly and am
beside myself in appearing to take pleasure in his words. Then we go to
dinner, each of us in a different direction, to a barley cake that belongs
to another.[101] There the flatterer must instantly make many witty
remarks or be thrown out of doors.[102] I know that Acestor the branded
slave suffered this fate, for he made some distasteful joke and the slave
dragged him out to the door with a wooden collar applied and handed
him over to Oeneus.[103]

Many of the elements common to the comic parasite are here:
flattery of the rich, the access to food bought with witty remarks,
the perils of expulsion and humiliation. A fourth element is the
inclusion of Acestor among the parasites. Callias, the rich man
who is portrayed in the play of Eupolis as squandering his estate
on flatterers,[104] surrounds himself with such intellectuals as Protagoras and Acestor.[105] Both philosopher and poet may be construed in comedy as parasites for their receipt of patronage from
one of the Athenian elite. While their position may be similar to
that of poets and philosophers at the courts of tyrants, such as
Pindar at the court of Hiero, Plato at the court of Dion, or
Euripides at the court of Archelaus, Athens was not Syracuse or
Pella. Both the flatterer who is the recipient of patronage and the
host who provides it are areas of concern for the democracy. Poets
are a small concern for the democratic polis when compared with
powerful politicians such as Cimon, Pericles, or Cleon, but tragic
and comic poets have a high profile in comedy. Thus Acestor falls

---

[100] Corrupt text.
[101] On the possible parodic allusion to the suitors of Penelope seeking ἀλλότριον
βίοτον see Ribbeck ap. Kassel–Austin (1986).
[102] Cf. the similar claims in Epicharmus fr. 35.
[103] That is, to be thrown into the *barathron* or pit of punishment, which was
in the district of the tribe Oeneis: see Kassel–Austin (1986) and Arnott (1996) on
Alexis fr. 159.1.
[104] On his luxurious provision of fish and women see Chap. 6.
[105] Acestor was a tragic poet, who was satirized also by Cratinus (fr. 92),
Aristophanes (*Wasps* 1227), and others. As for Protagoras, see Eupolis testimonium ii KA = Athenaeus 5.218b–d, on Plato's *Protagoras*.

into the category of gluttonous parasite that was noted above for Morychus, Glaucetes, and Teleas in *Peace*. Comedy frequently reviews these concerns either by satirizing patron and client or by adducing ritualized forms of exchange which provide contrasting restraint against such private excess. The exchange of food is frequently the area of concern, and rituals against which parasitism is tested include *sitesis* (eating) in the prytaneion (see Chapter 4 on *Knights*) and the honoured eating by official parasites that pre-dated Alexis' transfer of the term to scroungers.

According to Alexis, *Helmsman* fr. 121, parasites fall into two categories:

PARASITE: There are two kinds of parasite, Nausinicus. One is the common kind satirized in comedy, we black ones. Now the other kind, [. . .] the well-named high-class parasites, act out in their lives, eyebrows at the ready, parasite satraps and distingusihed generals, running through estates of a thousand talents. Do you know the kind and the general picture?
NAUSINICUS: I certainly do.
PARASITE: The type of operation of each of these kinds is one and the same, a contest in flattery. As generally in men's lives, fortune assigns some of us to great patrons, others to the less prominent. Thus some of us are well off, others in a frenzy of despair. Am I setting it out clearly, Nausinicus?
NAUSINICUS: Right on target. But if I praise you any further, you'll ask me for something!

The text of this fragment is corrupt in lines 3–6. I have followed Arnott (1996) and others against Kassel–Austin (1986) in interpreting the high-class parasites as satraps and generals rather than the parasites of satraps and generals listed from non-comic sources by Athenaeus at 6.248c–252f. Arnott proposes Chabrias and Nicostratus of Argos as possible targets for this satire. There are few comic passages which describe foreign courts, though Arnott cites Antiphanes fr. 200 on the luxuries of Paphos.[106] Arnott notes reference to satraps in Menander, *Flatterer*. Alexis appears to have extended to new heights satire

---

[106] Athenaeus (6.260c) cites a fragment of the *Dionysius* of Eubulus on the flatterers at the court of Dionysius II of Syracuse (fr. 25): 'he is rougher towards the dignified and all the flatterers, but good-tempered towards those who mock him. Thus he believes that these alone are free men, even if they are slaves.' Other courts: *Acharnians* 65–87; Euphron fr. 10.

against the circles of influential Athenian generals such as Cleon in *Wasps*, whose associates are portrayed as flatterers who drink with him.[107] The contests in *Knights* between Cleon/Paphlagon and the Black-Pudding-Seller at the 'court' of Demos are based on flattery and the consumption of food.[108] Later, there are the attentions paid to Demetrius of Phaleron in New Comedy and the supposed flattery of their new overlords by the Athenian demos.[109] Alexis, *Crateia or the Drug-Seller* fr. 116 contains a toast to 'King Antigonus for his victory . . . to the young Demetrius Poliorcetes and . . . to Aphrodite Phila'.[110]

Alexis fr. 121 makes the important claim that, while 'parasitism' may include political influence at court, parasites truly belong to the comic stage. Politician-parasites 'act out' in their lives what truly belongs to comic discourse. On the stage, parasites compete for attention (in the 'contest of flattery'), while the poets compete with each other in ingenious variations on the theme. Notable examples of such invention are Diphilus, *Parasite* fr. 62 'don't you realize what is contained in the curses, if one does not point out the road properly or kindles a fire or pollutes the water *or hinders someone intending to give a dinner?*', fr. 63, 'one mustn't be a parasite if one is hard to please', and Eubulus, *Oedipus* fr. 72, 'the first inventor of dining at the expense of others[111] was a democrat in his ways, it seems, and whoever invites someone to dinner, whether friend or stranger, and demands a contribution, let him become an exile and take nothing with him from his home'.[112]

---

[107] 42–51, 1219–21 (the list of *sumpotai* includes the son of Acestor and such politicians as Theorus, Alcibiades, Aeschines, and one Phanos): see further the perceptive comments of Fisher (forthcoming).

[108] See Chap. 4.

[109] Athenaeus 6.252f–254c.

[110] On the date and the occasion (in 306) see Arnott (1996), 309–11, 324–9.

[111] On the *protos heuretes* as a form of expression favoured by the comic parasite see Hunter (1983) on this fragment and Arnott (1996) on Alexis fr. 27. It is found also in the context of fish-eating in Anaxandrides, *Nereus* fr. 31 (cited in Chaps. 1.3.4 and 7) and in Critias fr. B2 West, which combines such discoveries with the provenance of sympotic and other practices (see Chap. 4.1).

[112] Further comic variations on the role and status of the parasite include Axionicus, *The Chalcidian* fr. 6, 'when still young I first fell in love with the life of the parasite, in the company of Philoxenus the Ham-chopper, I withstood blows from fists, bowls, and bones that were so great that I sometimes had at

Two fragments pick up the themes of Diodorus fr. 2 and Eupolis fr. 172. Timocles, *Dracontium* fr. 8 returns to Diodorus' themes of gods as parasites and ritualized dining, this time in the prytaneion:

so shall I allow anyone to speak ill of the parasite? Far from it. For in such matters there is no class of person more serviceable. Now if friendship and comradeship count among the good things in life, a man who is a parasite offers these to perfection. You are in love? He becomes a fellow-lover who is never repelled. You have some business? He will be at your side to transact all the necessaries, defining justice just as does the man who feeds him. He is full of wonderful praise as if one of your friends. So they enjoy the pleasures of dining without paying their corner? But what mortal does not? Or what hero or what god distances himself from such a style of life? Not to speak at length all day long on many examples, I think I will adduce one mighty proof to show how the life of parasites is held in high regard. The same prize is given to them for their excellence as is given to winners at the Olympic Games[113]— free food in the prytaneion. Wherever contributions are not demanded, all of these places are known as prytaneia.

Antiphanes, *Twins* fr. 80 echoes Eupolis fr. 172:

for if you consider the matter properly, the parasite shares in both a man's fortune and his life. No parasite prays that his friends will suffer

least eight wounds [. . .]. For I am at the mercy of pleasure and in time, in a certain way, I came to think that the situation was worthwhile. For example, if someone loved quarrels and wanted a fight with me, I turned to him and immediately agreed with his abuse and received no injury. Then, if a bad man claims to be good, I sing his praises and go off with his gratitude. If today I eat a boiled slice of *glaukos*, I am not upset if tomorrow I have it warmed up. Such is my way and my nature.'Add Timocles, *Boxer* fr. 31, 'you will find one of these foodseekers who dine on the food of others to the point of bursting, offering themselves as punch-bags for the athletes to thrash'; Pherecrates, *Old Women* fr. 37, 'A: Smicythion, won't you go quickly to seek food? B: What is this man to you? A: I take him everywhere as a gluttonous foreigner on a fee'; Diphilus, *Synoris* fr. 75, 'A: He is angry? He's a parasite and angry? B: No, but he's anointed the table with his bile and will wean himself off it like babies'; and fr. 76, 'A: Then you can eat, parasite. B: See how he abuses my profession. Don't you know that the parasite gets the next place to the harp-singer?'

[113] For the athletes and others awarded *sitesis* at the prytaneion in Athens see the inscription cited in Chap. 4. Athletes are a good choice on the part of Timocles since they too were the subject of satire as less 'useful' recipients of civic favour: Athenaeus 10.413c–414c cites Xenophanes fr. 2 West and Euripides fr. 282 N². See Arnott (1996) on Alexis, *Apobates* (pp. 105–6), and below on Heracles.

misfortune; quite the reverse, that all will always prosper. If someone is lavish in his lifestyle, he does not begrudge that but rather stays with him and prays to have a share in it all. He is also a noble and trusty friend, not belligerent, not sharp in anger, not malicious, good at bearing another's anger. If you mock him, he laughs. He is amorous, a joker, cheerful in his character. Then again, he is the good soldier, to a hyperbolical degree provided there is a dinner ready as his food ration.

Parasites often claim or are given a nickname.[114] It is the contention of Arnott (1968) that the *kolax* or flatterer was first called 'parasite' in Alexis' play of that name: (fr. 183) 'all the young blades[115] call him by the nickname Parasite. He doesn't care. He dines as silently as Telephus,[116] merely nodding to those who question him, so that often the host who has invited him prays to the mysteries of Samothrace that he will stop blowing a gale and restore calm waters. That young fellow is a winter's storm to his friends.'[117] The parasite may be so named for his insatiable hunger, which swoops down like a storm.[118] He may also acquire his name in recognition of his favourite food, often fish or meat stock. Alexis has a long list at *Pancratiast* fr. 173: 'A: first, I can tell you, there was Callimedon the Crayfish, then the Lark, Goby,

---

[114] Nicknames cover a range that extends far beyond foods and eating. Anaxandrides, *Odysseus* fr. 35 gives examples: 'you are forever jesting at one another's expense, I know. If a man is handsome, you call him Sacred Marriage. If he is a little man of pronounced shortness you call him Droplet. A dazzling fellow has come forward: instantly he is Nancy Boy. Well-oiled Democles walks round the town: he is named Black Soup. Another takes pleasure in being rough and dirty: he is revealed to be Dust-cloud. A flatterer follows behind someone: he receives the name Dinghy. A man who walks round the town dinnerless: he is Fasting-mullet. If a man gazes at the beautiful young men, he is the New Theatre-maker. For a joke someone robs a shepherd of a lamb: he is called Atreus. If it's a ram, he's Phrixus. If it's a fleece, Jason.'

[115] Arnott (1996), 543–4 notes that it is the *neoteroi* who are frequently responsible for the coining of telling names for parasites.

[116] Cf. the fishmonger who adopts the silence of Telephus at Amphis, *Planos* (*Vagabond/Entertainer*) fr. 30.

[117] Why is he a storm? The likeliest explanation is his overwhelming voracity. Another may be that the parasite comes with the expectation of words and flattery and in this case enrages fellow diners by eating relentlessly and offering no reciprocal jests.

[118] The image of the storm is applied to parasites also at Antiphanes, *Ancestors* fr. 193.11 and Anaxippus, *Lightning* fr. 3. A man may also descend on the fish-market like a sudden storm: see Chap. 6.

Bran,[119] Mackerel and Finest Flour. B: Dear Heracles, woman! You speak of foods at market, not a symposium.' Similarly, Alexis, *Isostasion* fr. 102: 'A: They were drinking on a contributory basis, looking only to dance, nothing else, and took the names of tasty foods. B: Of tasty foods? A: Yes, Crayfish, Goby. B: Of cereals? A: Yes, Finest Flour.'[120] Some of the Athenians with nicknames derived from foods were politicians who could be regarded as parasites—such as Callimedon the Crayfish and Eucrates the Lark—others are only known by their nickname. The nickname may be acquired for various reasons, whether gluttony, addiction to luxurious eating, insatiable hunger, or a supposed incident in a life.[121] Parts of his body may be indentified, in particular the belly.[122] Many of these cases indentify the human consumer closely with his distinctive food: he has become what he eats. He embodies aspects of the material world identified in Chapter 1, whether in an overdeveloped part such as the belly or in assimilation with what is consumed. These aspects are extensively exploited in Middle and New Comedy but were already present in Old, possibly in such plays as the *Encheirogastores* of Nicophon and the *Fishes* of Archippus (fr. 27).[123]

Other variations were possible. Athenaeus collects many terms either synonymous with 'parasite' or related to it. These reflected both comic invention and the culture's engagement in deviant eating over a broad lexical range. We have already seen the term 'sharply hungry' (*oxupeinos*); to these Athenaeus adds (6.247e) 'food-seeker' (*episitos*),[124] 'eating at home' (*oikositos*),[125]

---

[119] Or Bean-Pod.   [120] I have followed the text of Arnott (1996).

[121] On possible explanations for the nicknames Tithymallos and Lark see ibid.

[122] *Frogs* 200, and see Chap. 1.   [123] Arnott (1996), 510–11 lists more.

[124] Crates, *Dares* fr. 37.1, 'he cultivates the food-seeker, but though he freezes in the house of Megabyzus, he will receive food for his pay'; Aristophanes, *Storks* fr. 452, 'for if you prosecute one criminal, twelve food-seekers will bring counter-evidence for other criminals'; and Eubulus, *Daedalus* fr. 20, 'he wishes, without pay, to remain with them as a food-seeker'. All three fragments link the food-seeker with pay, the *Storks* passage at least working in the area of food and sycophancy explored by Aristophanes in *Wasps* (where the topic is jury pay and civic revenues).

[125] Anaxandrides, *Huntsmen* fr. 25, 'a son who eats his own food is a pleasant thing'; Antiphanes, *Scythian* fr. 198, 'soon the assemblyman eats his own food';

'bread-cutter' (*sitokouros*),[126] 'self-feeder' (*autositos*),[127] 'bad-
eater' (*kakositos*),[128] 'little-feeder' (*oligositos*),[129] 'crumb-flatterer'
(*psomokolax*),[130] These terms, along with 'parasite', attest a
deep interest in proper and improper social engagement with
eating. The parasite may be uninvited, thereby acknowledging
his inferiority, but is sometimes invited and behaves wrongly.
The parasite may promote undesirable behaviour in the patron,
who may squander his wealth on too many flatterers and other
distractions. The self-abasement of the parasite may be more or
less tasteful. But all variations reflect a culture in which eating
with others is paramount and therefore worthy of endless explor-
ation. Hence the unease that surrounds the comic parasite and
the exuberant elaboration of the type.

The belly of the parasite, who is always male, is the counterpart of the belly of the *hetaera*.[131] Both are a potential drain on the
resources of the rich. The belly may be a liability to the parasite
himself, while the poet may exploit the literary tradition of the
demanding belly.[132] Parasites are fed, just as prostitutes are by

Menander, *The Ring* fr. 98, 'we have found a bridegroom who eats his own food
and has no need of a dowry'; *Harpist* fr. 6, 'you get an audience (ἀκροατὰς) that
does not eat its own food'. All these citations are based on the merits of self-
sufficiency and constitute a counter-example to the parasite.

[126] See Arnott (1996) on Alexis, *All-Night Festival* (*Pannychis*), fr. 182, 'you
will be a peripatetic bread-cutter'. Menander brings out the wretchedness of the
'bread-cutter': *As Brave as a Lion* fr. 185, 'hesitant, dithering over everything,
a bread-cutter who acknowledges that he is fed by someone else'; *Sold* fr. 352,
'you wretch! You're still standing at the door with your bag on the ground!
We've taken into the house a bread-cutter, a miserable, useless specimen.'

[127] Crobylus, *Hanged Man* fr. 1, 'a self-feeding parasite. At least you feed
yourself for the most part when you are a *suneranistes* with the master.'

[128] Eubulus, *Ganymede* fr. 16, 'sleep feeds him when he eats badly'.

[129] Phrynichus, *The Recluse* (*Monotropos*) fr. 24, 'Heracles the little-feeder—
what's he doing there?'; Pherecrates (or Strattis), *The Aristocrats* fr. 1.3–4,
'what a little-feeder you turned out to be! You eat food fit for a trireme the long
day through!'

[130] See Aristophanes, *Gerytades* fr. 172; Sannyrion, *Io* fr. 11; Philemon, *The
Woman Who Renewed Youth* fr. 7; Philippides fr. 8.

[131] Avezzù (1989) compares Hesiod on the *gaster* of the parasitic woman: see
further Vernant (1989).

[132] Arnott (1996), 613, on Alexis, *Dying Together* fr. 215, 'you may learn what
an evil for mankind is the belly, what it teaches us and what it forces us to. If
someone were to remove from us that part of the body, no one would ever wrong
another in any way nor willingly commit an outrage on him. As it is, because of

pimps: Araros, *The Wedding Hymn* fr. 16, 'there is no way you are not a parasite, darling. And this Ischomachus is the man who is feeding you.'[133]

All these aspects of the parasite are as prominent as his poverty, which was present from the beginning, in Epicharmus fr. 35. The comic parasite may often be a poor man but has a place in the comic discourse of eating for three overriding reasons, need, the irresistible demands of his belly (which indicates his bad character), and his attendance at the meals of others who are his betters. The poor man eating with his peers is not a comic parasite nor is the man who feasts at a public festival. Old Comedy is instructive in this respect. The flatterer or parasite appears at private dinners and does not always enjoy the support of the protagonist. (He enjoys such support in Menander, *Flatterer* and Terence, *Phormio.*) He normally lacks a commanding presence both in the movement of the play and in his social position, which is always dependent on another. The protagonist may be among the needy, as in *Peace* and *Wealth*, but is never a parasite because the demands of his appetite do not lead him to plead a place at the meals of others. Rather, he finds his own method for providing for himself and his fellow-citizens. We shall see[134] that the protagonist of Old Comedy on occasion shares some characteristics with the cook. The two stock characters of parasite and cook, therefore, come to Middle and New Comedy from different origins in Old Comedy, but once there have similar characteristics. First, in a number of plays the claims of the parasite are contained in a long speech. We shall see in Chapter 8 that speeches of similar length by boastful cooks in Middle and New Comedy

---

the belly, everything is very difficult.'A character in Diphilus likewise ascribes all world events to the belly: *Parasite* fr. 60, 'Golden Euripides has spoken well of many things: "Need and my wretched belly overcome me" [fr. 915 N]. There is nothing more wretched than the belly, into which you will throw [the text is corrupt] another vessel. In a bag you might carry bread, but not meat soup or you will spoil it. You will throw barley cakes into a basket, but not lentil soup, a little wine into a vessel, but not a langouste. But into this belly hated by the gods goes everything even though they do not agree with each other. I don't add the rest since universally everything happens on account of that wretched belly.' (All four fragments of this play refer to parasitism.)

[133] On feeding parasites (*trephein*) see Davidson (1997), 270–2.
[134] In Chap. 8.

invite ridicule. In his negative social role the parasite draws attention to what all free citizens are imagined to be doing, that is, eating together as equals. Some speeches make this explicit by contrasting the parasite with such rituals of commensality as meals of the parasites of Heracles, eating in the prytaneion, and well-ordered eating in the past. The parasite's inferiority, further, is reinforced by forms of humiliation, physical or otherwise, meted out by his betters.

At the same time, the parasite has many positive aspects on which the comic poet can draw. Unlike the cook, whose proper domain is the kitchen, the parasite's place is at the *deipnon* and symposium and it is for him to supply wit and sympotic entertainment. While the cook is often concerned with the guest list and requisite preparations, the parasite attends the meal and entertainment itself. Both translate bodily needs for material fuel into social and sympotic discourse. The variety and inventiveness of the parasite can add lustre to the play in which he appears.

Diphilus offers two examples of the ability of the parasite to turn a clever phrase for sympotic entertainment. Diphilus, *Parasite* fr. 60 (quoted in note 132 above) recasts traditional wisdom in the form of general reflections on the power of the belly to include Euripides, the specialist in general reflections, and much physical detail. Reflections on Euripides can be taken further. Athenaeus (6.247a–b) introduces Diphilus, *Synoris* fr. 74 as follows:

Diphilus in *Synoris* (Synoris was the name of a *hetaera*) mentions Euripides (a throw of the dice was called Euripides), playing on the name of the poet and on the subject of parasites, like this:

A: You've done nicely with that throw.
B: You're a clever one. Put down your drachma.
A: I put it down ages ago.
B: How can I throw a Euripides?
A: Euripides would never save a woman. Don't you see how he hates them in his tragedies? But he loved parasites. He says at one point, 'the man who is well-off and does not support at least three others without expecting a contribution—may he perish and never achieve his journey home to his native land!'
B: Where in the god's name is that from?
A: What do you care? It's not his play but his thought that we are looking at.

It is worth assessing the contribution of Athenaeus in this area. Much of the history and the social implications of the parasite are brought out in great detail. He demonstrates, further, how jokes and anecdotes attached to parasites by the comic poets transferred to other forms of literature. Thus, Diphilus the comic poet and Philoxenus nicknamed the Ham-chopper feature in Machon's *Chreiae* (anecdotes in iambics), Eucrates nicknamed 'Lark' and Chaerephon in Lynceus (another anecdotist); the *Ludicrous Chronicles* of Aristodemus and historians such as Theopompus extend the phenomenon into the courts of the Macedonian and Hellenistic kings.[135] Philip II of Macedon is said to have collected the sayings of 'parasites' in an Athenian eating club,[136] and surrounded himself with parasites. The occasional comic fragment on the subject of parasites at the courts of foreign tyrants is susceptible to endless elaboration in these other forms. Arnott's study of Chaerephon[137] illustrates the connections well. Almost all we know derives from Athenaeus; Chaerephon was satirized by Alexis and Menander, and outside comedy by Matro in his *Attic Dinner* 9,[138] Machon 10–24, and in prose by Lynceus of Samos.[139] Chaerephon himself wrote a short prose *Deipnon*, dedicated to Epicrates, nicknamed Curebion ('Bran'), another parasite, mentioned in Alexis fr. 173 above. Lynceus links him with 'Lark',[140] also mentioned in Alexis fr. 173, and Machon with the *hetaera* Gnathaena. He travels to Corinth at Alexis, *Dying Together* fr. 213, displaying the same desire as Archestratus to

---

[135] Cf. Chap. 7 on Philoxenus of Cythera at the court of Dionysius I.

[136] According to Hegesander of Delphi ap. Athenaeus 6.260a–b.

[137] (1996), 610. This is a later Chaerephon than the parasitic companion of Socrates. There was a third, cited in Apollodorus of Carystus fr. 29.

[138] On which see Chap. 7.

[139] The same writers also pick up the 'Lark' and Philoxenus the Ham-chopper: see Athenaeus 6.241d–242c.

[140] Who was also the subject of anecdotes in Lynceus, along with Philoxenus the Ham-chopper. Lynceus links them with the court of one of the Ptolemies, but there are no comic examples. For comic anecdotes of Lark see Cratinus the Younger, *Titans* fr. 8; Timocles, *Spiteful man* fr. 11; Alexis, *Demetrius or Philetaerus* fr. 48; *Nurse* fr. 229; *Poets* fr. 188, 'I very much want to be the one who is laughed at and always says comical things—the best of the Athenians after Lark'. As Arnott (1996) observes *ad loc.*, the speaker presents himself as the *gelotopoios*, the versatile entertainer at the symposium, on whom see Davidson (forthcoming).

travel for the pleasure of his belly.[141] Most of the comic anecdotes on Chaerephon are specific to hunger and scrounging meals and do not extend to other topics.[142] Chaerephon is a good example of a comic parasite who may or may not be a literary construct,[143] but whose comic and sub-comic curriculum vitae connects him with comic writers, comic anecdote, and the area of invention built upon food and witticism. There is an element of the normative in this comic censure—his constant scrounging of food is simply 'not done'—but also of invention: comedy itself lives off endless variation and elaboration of the theme. Chaerephon is comparable with Archestratus of Gela and Philoxenus of Cythera, themselves composers of works on eating who were subject to comic and sub-comic anecdote on this area of life which was the life-blood of comedy itself.[144] And similarly with the *Deipnosophistae*, which in turn censures practitioners of the very art of eating that comprises its own literary material (see Wilkins and Hill 1994: 25–8). Chaerephon in these varied but mutually nourishing genres is the ideal subject of the anecdote which was developed by Machon and greatly exploited by Athenaeus.[145] The nicknames given to parasites aided the progress of such anecdotes, since the audience came to know what to expect.

---

[141] 'Chaerephon went to dinner in Corinth uninvited. Already he is flying over the sea. So sweet is it to eat the food of others.' On the travels of Archestratus see Chap. 7. In the same passage (4.164f–165a) Athenaeus cites Alexis, *The Fugitive* fr. 259 on the ingenuity of Chaerephon: 'Chaerephon is always devising some trick. Even now he is making provision for non-contributory dinners. For to the place where pottery may be hired by cooks he goes to stand from the break of day. If he sees a rental for a feast, he finds out the name of the host from the cook and if he comes upon the door gaping wide, is the first to go inside.' This misplaced ingenuity again recalls that of Archestratus which finds censure in Athenaeus.

[142] Athenaeus 6.243a–244a cites Menander, *Kekruphalos* fr. 215; *Anger* fr. 265; *Drunkenness* fr. 225; *Androgenous or the Cretan* fr. 55; Timocles, *The Letters* fr. 9; Antiphanes, *Scythian* fr. 197; Timotheus, *Puppy* fr. 1; Apollodorus of Carystus, *Priestess* fr. 29; and *The Girl Who Was Sacrificed* fr. 31.

[143] Callimachus tells us that he wrote the prose *Deipnon* (fr. 434 Pfeiffer = Athenaeus 6.244a). This should probably be accepted.

[144] Cf. Anaxandrides, *Drug-prophet* fr. 50, 'you censure me for being a boaster? But why? This art beats all the others by far, with the exception of flattery. This is superior.'

[145] On the comic anecdote see Hunter (1983) on Eubulus fr. 117.

2.7. THE COOK

The parasite is a more important creation than the comic cook: the latter did not take on a life elsewhere, except in such texts as Archestratus and Roman satire, while the parasite was transferable to the royal courts of the Hellenistic world and to the anecdotes of Machon, Lucian, and Athenaeus. The cook deserves preliminary consideration here.[146] He is a character of low status who is of no account in Old Comedy (but for the crucial provision that part of his role is performed by the protagonist), yet he came to dominate scenes in Middle and New Comedy. Like the parasite, he was given to long and witty discourse, though he was not part of the smart circle of the dinner and symposium. He deserves mention here since he brings vividly to the stage reports of the guest list, the necessary shopping, and what is happening in his kitchen. He brings practical skills to the stage, albeit liberally larded with boastful claims. He brings into the comic text long lists of ingredients and makes much of the labour he must put in: he is often responsible for introducing the materials of meals and the methods of preparation into the texts. We saw in Chapter 1 two examples from Alexis: *Cooking-Pot* fr. 132 and *Pannychis or Erithoi* fr. 179. At the end of the latter he declares himself to have his knife in his hand and his tunic ready tied.[147] The cook sometimes had retainers, and there was a hierarchy of the kitchen, including the table-maker and table-server:[148] Antiphanes, *Metic* fr. 150, 'I also went and got this table-maker, who will wash the dishes, prepare the lamps, make up the libations, and do everything else he should', Alexander, *The Drinking Session* fr. 3, 'tomorrow I must get a pipe-girl. I will get a table maker and a *demiourgos* (confectioner). This was what my master sent me here for from the country.' There were also slaves for shopping: Menander, *Phanium* fr. 390, 'he was a sparing and modest purchaser at market', Aristophanes, *Tagenistae* (*Fryers*) fr. 517, 'how that man who went shopping delayed our lunch!'

---

[146] The main discussion is reserved for Chap. 8.
[147] On knife (*machaira*) and tunic see Arnott (1996), 536–8.
[148] So Athenaeus 4.170d–171a.

2.8. THE *BOMOLOCHUS*

The role of the parasite and cook in comedy is illuminated by comparison with the *bomolochus*, one who lurks by the altar in the desperate hope of snatching offerings for his own consumption. This is the definition of Harpocration (76.9), who quotes Pherecrates *Tyrannis* fr. 150, 'then so that we would not be called *bomolochi*—because we were lurking round altars all over the place—Zeus made an absolutely enormous chimney'. *Bomolochia*, for which 'altar-lurking' appears not to be a false etymology, is the lowest form of social life, which everyone, including the gods, strives hard to avoid. Pherecrates humorously presents the gods as feeling particularly vulnerable to the charge, since they are the recipients of sacrificial offering. Harpocration says that seers and pipers might also be charged with inappropriate feasting on offerings (Aristophanes describes such theft at *Peace* 1118 and *Wealth* 676–8, without using the term *bomolochus*; a piper at *Peace* 950–5 is 'uninvited'), and then considers the metaphorical sense of *bomolochus*, a low-life person who waits for gain and makes jokes and playful remarks. Here the sacrificial context of unacceptable conduct is extended to something analogous to the parasite. The *bomolochus*, the one who does not belong to the circle of sacrificers but tries unofficially to partake in the food which is strictly the by-product of the ritual, metaphorically becomes a needy jester with time on his hands. Harpocration illustrates this sense with Aristophanes, *Gerytades* fr. 171, 'you make witty and playful jokes against us and play the *bomolochus*'. Old Comedy seems to have used the term for various forms of inappropriate and coarse behaviour, as Dover (1993) notes on *Frogs* 358 (compare Aristotle, *Nicomachean Ethics* 1108a24–5, 1128a4–7). Euripides' immoral advice is rejected in these terms by Aeschylus at *Frogs* 1085 (cf. 1521), as is bad music at *Clouds* 969 and a bad public speaker at *Knights* 1358. We shall meet several examples from the Black-Pudding-Seller in *Knights* in Chapter 4, for he combines the theft of meat (417–20, 1192–206) with cheap tricks (902, 1194). A striking extension of all this inappropriate *bomolochia* was its application to comic poetry. Aristophanes dismisses the work of his rivals as *bomolocheumata* (crude and inferior work) at *Peace* 748 and apparently at *Frogs* 358 (see Dover). The context of *Gerytades* fr. 171 is unknown, but the play was at least in part devoted to dramatic poetry (compare Chapter 1.5). The *bomolochus* appears to be a construction of comic and iambic discourse—there are few literary attestations of the *bomolochus* at work. Rather, in his deviation from the sacrificial code, his purpose is to reinforce the sense of order and what is right.[149] He is, as it were, an invented deviant who confirms the structure of the ritual and in comparison with whom comic identities can be drawn.

The *bomolochus* resembles the parasite as a comic construction of the social deviant. If these two were to be placed in Athenian society they would normally be drawn from among the poor. But comedy has little to say about the poor, beyond concerns for general impoverishment found in *Peace* and *Wealth*. As Davidson has observed, comedy tends to blur social distinctions: Old Comedy speaks broadly from the point of view of the small farmer and the ordinary male and female citizens, while Middle and New Comedy tends to be based on somewhat richer property-owning families. References to the individual poor are few, three striking examples being Poliochus fr. 2, Antiphanes fr. 225 (cited in Chapter 1), and Eriphus, *Meliboea* fr. 3, 'there are things the poor cannot buy, the belly of a tuna or the head of a sea bass or a conger or a cuttle, that not even the blessed gods would look down on, I believe'. In terms of resources, the poor and the gods find themselves at opposite extremes since the poor have little, while for the gods everything is available. Comedy brings the gods closer to human society than many other literary genres; in *Birds*, for example, human powers exceed those of the Olympians. As far as eating is concerned, comic gods dine on fish (Epicharmus, *The Marriage of Hebe*) and are often imagined, as in Eriphus fr. 3, to desire to eat fish,[150] to drink wine (Hermippus fr. 77) or to lead the life of a parasite (Timocles fr. 8.11–12). The gods in the polis were imagined to eat the same foods as humans at *theoxeniai*; this is taken up by comedy[151] and extended, so that on some comic occasions the gods eat the same foods as humans, while on others they subsist on the smoke of sacrificial offerings.

---

[149] See further Berthiaume (1982), 90–1, on meat in various respects sacrificed improperly (81–93).

[150] Cf. Philemon fr. 82.22–4.

[151] e.g. Chionides fr. 7, in which the gods are feasted on cheese, barley cake, olives and leeks.

Within the broad spectrum running from impoverished humans to the Olympian gods, poor citizens in comedy can be helped to feast like gods in the utopias of Old Comedy, while the gods might be portrayed either as feasting like the rich elite (of Syracuse in *The Muses or The Marriage of Hebe*) or as desperately in need of food, like the poor. Certain minor gods play a large role in comedy in this respect, notably Hermes and Heracles who are constructed as intermediaries between gods and mortals.

2.9. HERACLES

In the discussion of parasites, Heracles was shown to be an important deity in Athens at whose precinct sacred eating of an important kind took place. Heracles as a comic character has a less honoured but related role to play. In the surviving plays of Aristophanes Heracles plays the burlesque role of the glutton who is as subject to the demands of his belly as any parasite of fourth-century comedy. He experiences the parasite's hunger, but invariably lacks his wit and verbal dexterity. In *Birds* he appears with Prometheus, Poseidon, and the Triballian god at the moment in which Peisetaerus is roasting some birds (1579–90):

PEISETAERUS: Someone give me the cheese-grater. Bring the silphium. Someone bring the cheese. Stoke up the charcoal.
POSEIDON: We three gods greet the man.
PEISETAERUS: Grate some silphium over them.
HERACLES: This is the meat of which animal?
PEISETAERUS: Some birds have tried to revolt from the democratic birds and decided to break the law.[152]
HERACLES: So you grate silphium on them first then?
PEISETAERUS: O welcome Heracles! What's the problem?
POSEIDON: We have come as ambassadors of the gods to seek a truce from the war.
PEISETAERUS: There is no olive oil in the flask.
HERACLES: Yes indeed. It's right that bird-flesh should be gleaming with oil.

In this exchange Peisetaerus deflects the solemn business of the gods by concentrating on his roasting and seasoning of birds,[153]

---

[152] On the roasting of birds in the new order where birds are gods see Wilkins (forthcoming, b).

[153] Cf. the roasting of birds by Dicaeopolis at *Acharnians* 1005–7, 1104, 1106,

and easily diverts Heracles from his prescribed negotiations, for the hero can see preferable uses for olive oil. As Poseidon puts it (1604), 'what, you wretch? You are a simpleton and glutton.'[154] Similarly in *Frogs*, the encounter in the underworld between Heracles and Dionysus (himself a buffoon in the play) is marked by Heracles' great expertise in pea soup (63–5) and in the brothels and food outlets of the underworld (112–15).

Later in *Frogs* Heracles is revealed on a more epic scale. Dionysus, now disguised as Heracles, discovers details of the hero's journey in the underworld, both his strangling of Cerberus (467–8) and his consumption of food. For the return of Heracles[155] Persephone has made preparations (505–18): 'she has baked loaves, has boiled two or three pots of pea soup, has roasted a whole ox, and has baked rolls and flat-cakes . . . She has roasted birds, toasted sweet cakes and mixed very sweet wine.' Pipe-girls and dancing girls are waiting for him to make the *deipnon*/symposium complete, and the *mageiros* has slices of meat and tables ready.[156] Shortly afterwards (549–76) Dionysus-Heracles is pursued by a landlady for debts incurred, for seventeen loaves, roast meat at twenty half-obols a portion, garlic, fresh cheese consumed, baskets and all, none of it paid for since Heracles became violent, appeared to be mad, and made off with drinking-cups. Now the aggrieved party declares (571–3), 'o foul gullet! How sweet it would be to knock out with a stone the molars which guzzled my goods' and (575–6) 'I'd like to cut out your throat with the sickle that you used to snatch the entrail-sausages'. Significant elements in the last scene are the massive appetite of Heracles and the commercial nature of the transaction: just as at a private dinner the jaws and throat of the parasite may be emphasized, so in this inn are those of Heracles. Where the parasite makes no contribution but pays in kind with jests at his own expense or physical humiliation, here Heracles avoids reciprocity by threats of physical violence and the deformations of madness. These excerpts portray the two complementary aspects of

---

1108, 1116, also in preparation for the final feast of the play and in the context of tormenting his opponent Lamachus.

[154] γάστρις εἶ. Cf. *Frogs* 200 (of Dionysus), γάστρων.

[155] In fact the slave Xanthias, who has taken over the disguise from Dionysus.

[156] Why is Heracles the welcome guest? Because he is a (distant) kinsman? Dover (1993), on 503–48, suggests that Persephone 'fancied Heracles'.

Heracles which concern us here, the pea soup glutton and the epic eater on the grand scale, the consumer of whole oxen and rolls by the dozen. The gluttonous Heracles is rejected by Aristophanes as suitable material for his comedy at *Wasps* 60 and *Peace* 741.[157] The scholiast on *Peace* 741 cites another instance of Heracles in Aristophanes;[158] we know too little of the dramatist's work to be able to assess whether he is rejecting *buffoonish* treatment of Heracles either as glutton or as performer of menial tasks (but not other treatments of Heracles the great eater) or whether his denial is merely strategic and not to be taken literally.[159] *Birds* 1579–90 and *Frogs* 63–115 appear to indicate that the denials are not to be taken at face value. Surviving examples of the gluttonous buffoonery of Heracles in the plays of the rivals of Aristophanes are not many: titles reveal little and fragments are few.[160] Plato, *Zeus Wronged* fr. 46[161] is one example, Phrynichus, *Monotropos* fr. 24 another. There are more in Middle and New Comedy,[162] but given the fragmentary state of the evidence it is not possible to distinguish the 'purely buffoonish' from the 'mythological'. The distinction is probably false, since in plays which portrayed the burlesque of myth, such as the *Omphale, Cercopes, Auge,* and *Amaltheia* of Eubulus, the poet was likely to take the hero who travelled through the world and the underworld both to epic encounters and to drinking sessions at symposia and commercial bars. In the *Amaltheia* of Eubulus, for example, Amaltheia may have been the goat with the horn of plenty or an innkeeper.[163]

The rejection of the buffoonish Heracles at *Wasps* 60 may refer not to Attic but to Megarian comedy (57).[164] We do know that Heracles played a role in the Dorian drama of Epicharmus, but all instances, as far as we can tell, refer to mythological burlesque. All

---

[157] Respectively 'Heracles cheated of his dinner' will not be part of the first; 'he [Aristophanes] was the first to drive out Heracleis making barley cakes and those starving characters'.

[158] *Aeolosicon.*

[159] See pp. 40–51 on comparable statements, and Goldhill (1991).

[160] Pherecrates, *Anthropheracles*; *False Heracles*; Nicochares, *Heracles Gets Married* and *Heracles Choregos*; Archippus, *Heracles Gets Married*.

[161] Quoted in Chap. 5.

[162] Anaxandrides, *Heracles*; Alexis, *Linus* fr. 143 (quoted in Chap. 7); Arnott (1996) on Alexis *Hesione, Kyknos,* and fr. 263; Diphilus, *Heracles*; Philyllius, *Heracles.*

[163] See Hunter (1983).   [164] On which see Chap. 1.

that survive are the titles of five plays (out of thirty seven in Kaibel) in which Heracles is likely to have appeared: *Alcyoneus, Busiris, The Muses or Marriage of Hebe*,[165] *Heracles and the Belt*, and *Heracles Guest of Pholus*. Heracles the mighty eater with the terrible jaws is first seen in surviving comedy in Epicharmus, *Busiris* fr. 21: 'first of all, if you were to see him eating, you'd die. His throat thunders within, his jaw rattles, his molar rings out, his canine grinds, he sizzles in his nose, he waggles his ears.' This is a heightened description of the eater, from a play in which the bearer of Greek civilization presumably conquered the cannibal king of Egypt. There is more here than 'simple' burlesque. Comic treatment of Heracles differs from that of Odysseus or other epic heroes who may be shown eating instead of performing more 'heroic' feats.[166] Heracles, as part of his repertoire of labours and clearing of monsters from the mythical world, was also the culture-hero who brought cattle—and the sacrifice of cattle—to Greece.[167] He contributed to aspects of eating in Greek culture and was so recognized in cult, hence his role as the particular patron of the 'parasites' at Cynosarges and elsewhere in Attica.

Attic comic poets differed from Epicharmus in, among other respects, writing within a dramatic context which included tragedy and satyr plays, in both of which Heracles played a significant role. Heracles the burlesque eater was not likely to appear in tragedy,[168] but did appear in satyr plays and comedy. We are not in a position to evaluate how, say, the *Busiris* of Cratinus resembled the *Busiris* of Euripides in its treatment of Heracles, not least because a chorus of satyrs might be found in both satyr play and comedy.[169] Heracles proved attractive to comic poets because of ambiguities in his nature. Just as comedy appears largely to have avoided the destructive aspects of Dionysus[170] in favour of his great gifts of wine, plants, and festival, so

---

[165] On this play see Chap. 7. Two plays with similar titles in Attic were *Heracles Gets Married* by both Archippus and Nicochares.

[166] On Odysseus eating see Athenaeus 10.412b–d.

[167] On the master of animals see Burkert (1979), 78–98.

[168] He appears in the quasi-satyric *Alcestis*.

[169] Satyr choruses were to be found in, for example, the *Dionysalexandros* and *Satyrs* of Cratinus.

[170] There were exceptions, such as the *Bacchae* of Epicharmus and the *Semele or Dionysus* of Eubulus.

with Heracles his homicidal madness is left to tragedy and his
eating celebrated in comedy. This can be treated with some
ambiguity, normally as excessive but with no damaging results.
Thus, for all his excess his eating cult can be compared
favourably with parasites in Athens (Diodorus fr. 2, quoted
above) since this is regulated eating which is strongly promoted
by the polis, in contrast with the social damage brought by parasitism within the human social sphere. Athenaeus explores these
and further aspects of Heracles in his study of gluttony at the
beginning of Book 10. Satyr and comedy appear to be closely
related in his citation of Astydamas, *Heracles* 60 F 4,[171] Epicharmus, *Busiris* fr. 21, and Ion, *Omphale* 19 F 29, 'driven on by fierce
hunger he swallowed down the haunches and the charcoal'.
Athenaeus explores the competition between Heracles and
Lepreus in a contest of excessive eating, the meat-eating athletes
Theagenes of Thasos and Milo of Croton,[172] and the verses
against athletes by Xenophanes and Euripides noted above.
Theagenes and Milo were consumers of whole oxen, Milo 'alone
consuming a bull in one day'. Heracles the athlete, the super-
consumer and demigod, shares something with the meat-eating
athlete who might also be a solitary eater, both figures criticized
in the polis.[173] These links make him more significant a meat-
eater than Hermes, who in comedy, as we have seen, much
prefers a good steak to the fragrant smoke of sacrifice usually
offered to the gods. The comic poets sought to give Heracles
speeches in which he would enthuse over foods and wines from

---

[171] Quoted below. This is a text of a satyr play in comic eupolideans commenting on sending the audience home well fed, as might comedy.

[172] 10.412d–413d. On Milo see Detienne (1977), 42–5.

[173] On athletes and appetite Athenaeus quotes, among other fragments,
Philetaerus, *Atalanta* fr. 3, 'and if necessary I can speed over more stades than
Sotades, exceed Taureas in my regime and outrun Ctesias in eating'; Anaxip-
pus, *Thunderbolt* fr. 3, 'A: I can see one of my friends coming towards me from the
wrestling school. It is Damippus. B: Are you talking about *that* Damippus . . .
A: Yes, the one his friends now call the Thunderbolt because of his bravery.
B: Quite right. I reckon he makes tables holy ground by crashing down on them
with his jaw.' Also Theophilus, *Pancratiast* fr. 8 (of an athlete), 'A: Of boiled
dishes nearly three minas. B: Tell us more. A: A snout, a ham, four pigs' feet.
B: Heracles! A: Three ox-feet and a bird. B: Apollo! Tell us more. A: Two minas
of figs. B: And you drank how much with that? A: Twelve *kotulai* of neat wine.
B: Apollo, Horus, and Sabazius!'

the perspective of his heroic background. Strattis, *Callipides* fr. 12
presents Heracles the meat-eater, 'instantly he snatched[174] the
slices and the hot flamed cuts of boar and wolfed them down all
together', while Archippus, *Heracles Gets Married* fr. 10 has,
'there were together trotters of little pigs, flamed cuts of a large-
horn ox, and the long flamed cuts of a boar'. At Eubulus,
Amaltheia fr. 6 he gives meat an endorsement with an epic
flavour:

whether fairly hot or fairly crispy or medium, this is a greater matter for
each man than capturing Troy. I haven't come here to graze on silphium stalks and silphium juice, on godforsaken and bitter side dishes
or tassel hyacinths. No, but on what comes first in the diet and promotes
strength and good health—all this is my customary dining fare, a great
piece of boiled beef not mucked about, a decent piece of foot and snout,
three roast bits of pork[175] sprinkled with salt . . .

The great meat-eater rejects hors d'oeuvres familiar in many
comic dinners with quotation from Euripides[176] and Homeric
phrases for meat consumption put to uses unseen in the texts of
Homer—he has arrived at the symposium and can play the
games of citation and allusion well enough.[177]
    In Plato, *Zeus Wronged* fr. 46 a pimp offers Heracles a game of
kottabos in which there are amorous prizes.[178] He accepts with
pleasure: 'Ye gods! This contest is approaching, greater than the
Isthmian Games.' When presenting the mighty athlete and master
of animals, the comic poet was at liberty to stress his strength,
his appetite, his simplicity, or his ability to manipulate sympotic

---

[174] On the verb ἁρπάζειν in the context of eating see Chap. 6.
[175] The text is uncertain here.
[176] 'This is a greater matter for each man than capturing Troy' is taken from
Andromache 369.
[177] Eubulus wrote a comparable sympotic speech referring to the absence of
fish in Homer's text (fr. 118): 'where has Homer spoken of one of the Achaeans
eating a fish? All they did was roast meat, for he has none of them boiling it, not
even a bit. Nor did any of them see a *hetaera*. No, they masturbated for ten years.
A bitter campaign they saw, for they captured one city and came back with arses
much wider than the gates of the city they'd captured.' This fragment is introduced by Athenaeus at 1.25b–c as the playful comic wit of Eubulus—the poet
was reading Homer in terms belonging to the fourth century and in the light of
the sympotic themes of homo- and heterosexual love. Athenaeus' reading of
Homer is explored in Chap. 6.
[178] The fragment is quoted in Chap. 5.

themes. A further sympotic scene unfolds in Alexis, *Hesione* fr. 88, 'eventually he was restored to his right mind and demanded a cup and, grabbing it, drank off draughts thick and fast, draining the cup, in the words of the proverb, the man was always the well-termed wine skin, the well-termed meal-sack'. The drunken Heracles epitomizes better than most the similarity between the pot-belly and the wine-skin, the wine's container now being the consumer's belly.[179] *Hesione* fr. 89 may also describe Heracles distracted from a pretty girl by food: 'when he saw two men carrying in the table bursting with an array of varied dishes, he no longer looked at me.' Alexis also has Heracles in the library of Linus (fr. 140),[180] in which his choice of book proves to be a cookery book by Simus. Linus comments on the obsession with eating,[181] to which Heracles replies, 'but I'm starving'.

This synthesis of epic gourmandise Athenaeus attaches loosely to further fragments on gluttony and parasites, including Alexis, *Parasite* fr. 183 (quoted above) and Diphilus, *Heracles* fr. 45: 'can't you see I've been drinking and am now half-cut and angry and have lunched on this cheese-cake, my twelfth, and it's bigger than Asterion?' Heracles presides over and contextualizes much excessive eating in comedy, in Athens and elsewhere.[182] On Thebes, the native city of Heracles, Athenaeus quotes Eubulus, *Mysians* fr. 66 '[Heracles], you, as you say, have left the plain of Thebes, the best men at eating necks all day long,[183] and near to the toilets . . .'.[184] In tragedy Thebes was constructed by the Attic

---

[179] Cf. Epicharmus fr. 246, 'this is the nature of men, inflated wine-skins', and Chap. 1. See further Arnott (1996) on *Hesione* fr. 88.

[180] Quoted in Chap. 7.

[181] Whether of Simus or Heracles is unclear: see Arnott (1996), *ad loc.*

[182] This also is picked up by Athenaeus, who quotes the fragments of Eubulus cited below at 10.417b–f. They are cited in alphabetical order of play and presumably indicate Athenaeus' use of a particular papyrus rather than any special interest Eubulus may have had in Thebes.

[183] Necks of mussels? Or of larger animals? See Kassal–Austin (1986).

[184] Theban eating also created a strong demand for toilets at Eubulus, *Cercopes* fr. 52, 'after that I came to Thebes where the whole night and whole day long they dine and each has a toilet by the door where for the mortal who is full there is no greater boon. Since when a man wishes to crap and has a long walk, a man who has eaten a lot and is biting his lip is ludicrous to behold'. Athenaeus' list also includes *Antiope* fr. 11 (in dialect but corrupt), on the Thebans eating and

dramatists as the setting of the most horrible crimes against kinsmen, including Heracles' frenzied murder of his family;[185] the
comic analogue may recall tragic myth but is also a city of unrestrained eating, endless loosening of the bowels, and an excessive
preoccupation with the physical demands of the body.

2.10. THE COMIC CONSTRUCTION OF BOEOTIAN AND OTHER GREEK DIETS

The Athenians distinguished their regimes of eating from those
of their neighbours and other foreigners, as part of the construction of the civic identity of abstemious eating and restraint.
Eubulus makes the point in *Antiope* fr. 9, 's/he orders Zethus to
go and live in holy Thebes—and it seems they sell cheaper bread
there. And you are very hungry. The more artistic Amphion is to
go to famous Athens where the sons of Cecrops are always hungry, snapping at the air and feeding on hopes.' Athenaeus in Book
4 establishes the contrast between the Athenian self-image of
light eating and the heartier eating of others. The diets of neighbours might be characterized by 'luxury',[186] by the sheer ingestion of food in quantity, or in Sparta's case as quite unique. On
Sparta, Attic comedy seems content to have noted their communal dining and black soup; there appears to be nothing to compare with the bon mot of a citizen of Sybaris cited by Athenaeus:
'the Spartans are rightly the bravest men of all, for anyone of
sound mind would prefer to die ten-thousand times rather than
partake of that cheap fare.'[187] A number of passages commented

drinking much and the Athenians talking much and eating little; *Europa* fr. 33,
'found the city of the Boeotians, the best men at eating throughout the day'; *Ion*
fr. 38, 'so much is he Boeotian in his ways that, so they say, not even at dinner
does he feel full up'.

[185] Zeitlin (1990).

[186] Luxury is defined and discussed in Chap. 6.

[187] Athenaeus 4.138d. He cites Antiphanes, *Archon* fr. 46, 'you were in
Sparta? Then you must follow their laws. Go to their messes for dinner. Enjoy
their black soup. [. . .] moustaches. Do not be proud. Do not seek after any other
delights. In their customs, be old-fashioned.' Also Philyllius fr. 15; Eupolis,
Helots fr. 147; Epilycus, *Coraliscus* fr. 4, 'I think I'll go to the *kopis* [festival]. At
Apollo's temple at Amyclae there is much barley cake and wheat-loaves and a
very fine black soup.' Cratinus also referred to the *kopis* (*Wealths* fr. 175), 'is it

on the luxurious and innovative cooking of the Sicilian Greeks.[188] The 'gluttony' of the Boeotians was a product of their rich agricultural land which furnished crops in plenty (augmented by the eels of Lake Copais),[189] and allowed varied exports to Athens that are celebrated in Old and Middle Comedy.[190] On the negative side, Boeotians could be seen as 'too agricultural'—it was convenient for Attic poets to attribute rusticity to their neighbours rather than themselves. Thus Cratinus fr. 77 introduces some 'Boeotian swine'.[191] The rich land of Thessaly produced a similar crop of comments in Attic drama, on their lavish tables (Eriphus, *Peltast* fr. 6) and on the size of portions:[192] for example, Philetaerus, *Torch-Bearers* fr. 10, 'and meat of swine flesh of Thessalian cut, as heavy as your hand'. Other non-Athenian eating is examined in Chapter 6. The background to much comedy written in the fourth century may be seen in the historiography and anecdotal literature collected by Athenaeus in Book 6 on parasites and on the appetites of Dionysius I, Demetrius Poliorcetes, Philip II, and Alexander. All around for the Athenians to behold were alternative forms of totalitarian government in which the powerful leader indulged his appetites to his heart's content and to the adoring praise of his parasites. Some echoes of this found their way into comedy, in the *Dionysius* of Eubulus; Mnesimachus wrote a *Philip*, in which appeared a militaristic symposium (fr. 7): 'don't you know that you will have to fight against men who dine on sharpened swords? As a relish we gulp down blazing torches. Straight after that a slave brings us after-dinner *tragemata* of Cretan arrows like chickpeas and broken shafts of spears, and we have for cushions shields and breastplates, and at our feet slings and bows, while we are garlanded with catapults'.

true as they say that all visitors who go there can feast well at the *kopis*? That in the public buildings there are blood puddings hanging up on nails for the old men to bite at?'.

[188]   These are cited in Chaps. 6 and 7.   [189]   On which see Chap. 1.
[190]   See e.g. *Acharnians* 870–80.   [191]   *Suoboiotoi*.
[192]   Athenaeus 10.418c–e offers the following variations: Crates, *Lamia* fr. 21, 'three-cubit words cut in Thessalian style'; Hermippus, *Fates* fr. 42, 'Zeus took no notice of any of these, shut his eyes, and rustled up a little Thessalian morsel'; Aristophanes, *Tagenistae* fr. 507, 'A: How do Lydian and Thessalian dinners compare? B: The Thessalian are much more like their chariots' (alluding both to the size of meals and the horses that could be reared on the rich Thessalian plain).

2.11. COMIC EATING

In this chapter I have reviewed comedy's presentation of eating in the polis and beyond. Athenian comedy reflects eating in the city according to its own codes and priorities which often do not coincide with those of the 'real' polis. Comedy, for example, often mentions festivals of the city, but rarely the mass sacrifice of victims that took place on such days; if comedy is to present a festival, attention is more likely to be given to a minor part of the feast or to a broad aspect of commensality. Nor does comedy merely comment on eating in the city according to its own satirical discourse; the provision of food is often at the centre of the plot or a scene of a play, and the beneficiaries of such comic meals are often very different from those who enjoyed commensality in the polis. In this way comedy reconfigures the Athenian community as the comic community.

Eating is so much part of comic discourse that the play itself may be represented by metaphors of eating. Comedy offers nourishing food to its audience in various forms. Of the two meals a day normally eaten by the Greeks, the lighter meal or *ariston* sometimes represents comedy. The work of Crates is described thus in the parabasis[193] of *Knights* (537–9): 'what anger Crates bore from you, what harsh blows! With modest expense, he sent you away with a good *ariston*; from a mouth full of cabbage he kneaded the most urbane ideas.' In the parabasis of *Birds* one of the claimed benefits of wings, now that humans can become birds, is to avoid tragedy in the civic drama festival (785–9): 'there is nothing better or more pleasant than to grow wings. If a member of the audience had wings and was hungry and suffering during the tragic choruses, he could instantly fly off and go home for his *ariston* and then, nicely filled up, he could fly back down to our comic competition.' The audience feel hungry during a tragedy; a full stomach is suitable for a comedy. (In *Peace* the tragic poets themselves do not go hungry but are presented as gluttons who set themselves apart from the eating of the demos.)[194] The comic *ariston* links the genre with that other area

---

[193] The part of an Old Comedy in which above all the poet reflects on the form of the drama.

[194] See Chap. 3 on the gluttonous tragic poets at *Peace* 801–16.

of restrained eating, public dining at the prytaneion.[195] Peisetaerus at the end of *Birds* offers to make peace with the gods if Zeus agrees to hand over his sceptre, saying (1601–2), 'if we can have a deal on this basis, I will invite the ambassadors to an *ariston*'. The triumph of the comic protagonist over the king of the gods is to be sealed with a light meal as if they were ambassadors invited to the prytaneion.[196] The light meal is not the only food offered by comedy, for in Old Comedy festive eating is also much in evidence. Quantities of food are available for protagonist, chorus, and audience, provided they are all of one mind and concur with the wish of the demos as proclaimed by the protagonist.[197]

Many good things are on offer at the end of *Acharnians* and *Ecclesiazusae*. Elsewhere, two plays present drama as a rich confection offering novelty and variety, a *deipnon* rather than a simple *ariston*. In Metagenes, *Lover of Sacrifices* fr. 15, a fragment probably from the parabasis, the poet declares, 'I change my discourse episode by episode so that I can feast the theatre with many new side-dishes'. A character in the satyr play *Heracles* of Astydamas (II, 60 F 4) declares, 'but the wise poet must provide for the spectators something like the varied feast of a rich *deipnon*, so that each may leave with it, having eaten and drunk what he delights in—and the preparation should not have been unitary in its art'. Two other fragments apply metaphors of eating to comedy; Cratinus, *Pylaia* fr. 182 adapts the proverb 'the best people go effortlessly to the feasts of the best people' to 'the best people go effortlessly to the feasts of the smart spectators', and Aristophanes in the second *Thesmophoriazusae* (fr. 347) calls comic composition, as exemplified by the riddling food imagery of Crates, a 'major food'.

Food, as we saw in Chapter 1, is so much part of comic discourse that when comedy attacks another genre, as when Aristophanes comments on Euripides in *Acharnians* or *Frogs,* food may be employed in that attack. At *Old Age* fr. 128, Aristophanes says

---

[195] See Chap. 4, and esp. Chionides, *Beggars* fr. 7, 'the Athenians served the Dioscuri in the prytaneion with an *ariston,* placing on the tables cheese, barley cake, ripe olives, and leeks'.

[196] Dunbar (1995) on these lines links the offer of Peisetaerus with the formulae of inscriptions which record invitations to the prytaneion, ἐπὶ ξένια.

[197] *Acharnians, Peace, Birds,* and *Eccelsiazusae* provide the best examples. The audience is explicitly invited in the second and last.

of Euripides' verse, 'with vinegar sauce, silphium sauce, a tassel hyacinth, beet leaves, a pounded sauce, a fig-leaf confection, brains, marjoram—these are buggery for big meat'. A character in Anaxilas, *Mageiroi* fr. 19 (cited in Chapter 1, note 34) prefers little fish to the verses of Aeschylus.

In comic texts, the way that the consumption of food is approached often depends on rhetorical considerations, on its place in the discourse of the play. In many plays food, sometimes including a sacrificial victim, is prepared and consumed in the final scenes of festivity, whether a wedding, festival of the polis, or other feast.[198] By that late stage those who are to attend the feast have been determined. The *deipnon* which follows the sacrifice remains as the goal of many comic plots, rarely displaced, as in other literature, by the rituals of the symposium. In comedy sympotic elements are strong but remain the adjuncts to eating. In Old Comedy the sacrifice is performed by the protagonist, in Middle and New by the *mageiros*.[199] The sense of community is often special, and in Old Comedy has been orchestrated by the protagonist who is the master of the discourse and declares who will eat and who will not, who is the unwelcome *alazon* and who the acceptable member of the group. Sometimes the community of the Athenians is stressed against an unwelcome outsider, most notably the renegade Cleon/Paphlagon who in *Knights* is expelled from the prytaneion (into which he had been placed by the demos in 425 in recognition of his achievements at Pylos). He is the extreme case which illustrates how comic commensality differs considerably from commensality in the polis. Comedy redefines the community of citizens to exclude certain prominent members, particularly leaders identified by comedy at least as bellicose (such as Cleon, Lamachus, or Hyperbolus), prominent men who are considered to have benefited at popular expense, and a number of priests, officials, and poets who are stripped of their authority. We shall see in Chapters 3, 4, and 6 how the powerful are vilified or expelled from the meal—Cleon from the prytaneion in *Knights*, Lamachus from the Anthesteria in *Acharnians*, the tragic poets Morsimus and Melanthius in *Peace*, and in Middle and New Comedy politicians and certain

---

[198] For the details in surviving plays see Chap. 8.2.
[199] See Chap. 8.

rich citizens who were able to afford lavish meals in private houses. In the later comedy the cook is no longer in control of affairs as was the protagonist-cook of Old Comedy. He himself has been demoted to the role of *alazon*. Sometimes those he cooks for are the beneficiaries of the final feast (as in Menander, *Dyscolus*), sometimes politicians and young bloods who are satirized. As an *alazon,* he speaks interminable speeches. In Old Comedy, certainly in Aristophanes, the protagonist-cook is rhetorically more nimble, setting the feast in place in short speeches and rapid exchanges. Long descriptions of foods, such as the utopian passages cited in the next chapter, are therefore prima facie unlikely to have passed without adverse comment.

In the following four chapters I examine the comic polis from the perspectives of agriculture (which is often idealized in Old Comedy), the market-place (on which comedy has ambiguous views), the symposium, and the discourse of luxury. These extend the analysis of eating in comic society discussed here to take account of aspects of eating in the countryside and rural demes, of tensions between city and rural demes, and of the *agoraioi* or people of the market-place who form part of the personnel of comedy but also inhabit a part of the city which housed both commercial interests and the ancient institutions of the democracy. Chapter 5 explores how ritualized drinking, again an ambivalent institution in the democratic city, was incorporated into the comic polis, and Chapter 6 deals with luxurious eating, with the comic discourse hostile to the displays of the rich at table. All of these chapters set out the tensions intrinsic to eating between pleasure and restraint, relaxation and excess—on which comedy has much comment. Each chapter demonstrates comedy's construction of its own society, parallel to but essentially different from Athenian society itself.

3
Comedy on Agriculture and the Blessings of Peace

This chapter explores the idealizing of the Attic countryside in Old Comedy and the blending of agriculture, comic gods, festivals, and peace into a comic version of Athens that had markedly different objectives, particularly during the Peloponnesian War, from the real polis in which comedy was produced. In this version of the comic polis, war is rejected and the protagonist and his entourage enjoy sympotic pleasures and the festivals of Dionysus. These festive symposia anticipate the full treatment of the comic symposium in Chapter 5.

3.1. COMEDY ON THE COUNTRYSIDE AND AGRICULTURE

The Greek polis normally obtained food supplies from three sources, its own countryside (in agriculture and hunting), imports, and the sea.[1] The identity of Attic Old Comedy, which from 486 BC at least was an essentially urban cultural form,[2] was to a large extent based on the Attic countryside which it praised lavishly, even going so far as to contrast it favourably with other areas of agricultural fertility such as Boeotia and the prolific Nile Delta. With the support of the gods of agricultural fertility, farmers could compensate for what the rocky hillsides of Attica naturally lacked.[3] Dionysus, Demeter, and a rustic pantheon of lesser gods were invoked in Old Comedy both to foster the growth of plants and to receive honour in feasts and festivals for crops successfully harvested. Some plays, such as the *Dyscolus* of Menander,

---

[1] On the last two see Chaps. 4 and 6 respectively.

[2] On the role of the Rural Dionysia after 486 see Pickard-Cambridge (1968), 42–56; Csapo and Slater (1995), 121–32.

[3] On the danger of crop-failure and the uncertainties of agriculture in ancient Attica and Greece see Garnsey (1988), Gallant (1991), and Foxhall and Forbes (1982).

reflected the hard work of agricultural life, but far more idealized the countryside. The objectives were normally two: to contrast the country with the supposed luxury and innovation of the city, and to win the blessing of the gods for agriculture.

Towards the end of the *Peace* of Aristophanes (1320–28), as the wedding rites are about to commence, the chorus ask the gods to 'give wealth to the Greeks and to help us all grow a large crop of barley together with a good supply of wine and figs to nibble; grant that our wives will bear us children and that we get back to the beginning and gather together all the good things that we've lost and put aside the shining sword'. The comedy concludes with a number of standard elements, some or all of which are found at the end of nearly all Old Comedies: a feast or festivity, the renewed support of the gods, the plea for fertility in humans and plants, a return in some sense to happier times, and an end to war.

A major priority for Old Comedy was to secure *agatha* or blessings, the wealth and resources of Attica, the chief revenues of which were identified by Xenophon at least[4] as deriving from agriculture, fishing, and the mining of marble and silver; what the polis lacks, says Xenophon, is easily imported by sea. Comedy's approach to wealth is often very different from that of Xenophon, or indeed of Thucydides or Aristotle;[5] the import of grain, a contentious political issue and a top priority for the democratic assembly, is of less interest to the comic poets, while fishing in comedy is a matter less of catches than of merchandizing (fishing is discussed in Chapters 6 and 7). Nevertheless, Xenophon's categories are broadly followed, especially in Old Comedy: the success of agriculture is the central issue in *Peace* and other plays; mining was of much less importance in comedy, though mining, possibly for silver at Laurion, is likely to have been the subject of the *Miners* of Pherecrates;[6] and trade was an important element

---

[4] *Ways and Means* 1.3–7.

[5] On Thucydides 1.2.2.–5, Aristotle, *Politics* 1319a4–38, see Osborne (1987), 113–14.

[6] A variation on mining and agriculture is found in a character's praise of Paros in Alexis. The island has marble quarries and flat-cakes (*Archilochus* fr. 22): ὦ τὴν ἠϋτυχῆ [Arnott: Kassel–Austin read εὐτειχῆ with Dindorf] ναίων Πάρον, ὄλβιε πρέσβυ, | ἣ κάλλιστα φέρει χώρα δύο τῶν συναπασῶν, | κόσμον μὲν μακάρεσσι λίθον, θνητοῖς δὲ πλακοῦντας. Note that the gods receive the long-lasting marble, mortals the perishable flat-cakes.

in various plays.[7] Some of these forms of wealth-production might be problematized in comedy and contrasted with each other—agriculture and trade, for example[8]—but in general comedy sought to preserve the city by ensuring the wealth and well-being represented by those *agatha*, which, whether imported or locally produced, constituted the abundance which is so much desired and celebrated with festival, feasting, and song at the end of many plays. Agriculture is the premier form of wealth for Old Comedy; the drama centres on the surplus that the agricultural economy can produce with the gods' help and shows that surplus being used for communal festivity and formal festivals to reinforce the internal solidarity of the community and to attempt to gain the god's favour for the next harvest.

Old Comedy broadly favoured agriculture. There is, to be sure, much incidental humour at the expense of rustics, but comedy's heart was in the Attic countryside, perhaps because, as Thucydides says (2.14), much of the population lived outside the city itself.[9] In the well-known opening scene of *Acharnians* Dicaeopolis longs for his rural deme with its system of barter and wishes to escape from the city with its markets and its system of exchange based on money (33–6). In *Peace*, once peace is restored, the farmers are urged (551–5) 'to pick up your farming tools and go back to your farm with all speed, leaving behind spear and sword and javelin because now everthing here is filled with ripe peace. Let everyone go back to work in the fields singing a paean': physical labour on the farm is seen as delightful in comparison with the works of war. Farming personified is a character in Aristophanes' second *Peace* (fr. 305):

FARMING:[10] Of Peace dear to all men I am the faithful nurse, her manager, her fellow worker, her steward, her daughter, her sister: she made use of me in all these ways.

---

[7] Which are discussed in Chap. 4.

[8] As Aristophanes brings out in *Islands* fr. 402, 'you fool, you fool! Everything is provided there. This man can live in his farm on a little plot of land, freed from the hurly-burly in the agora and owner of the family yoke of oxen. He can listen to the bleating of the sheep and the sound of the vintage as it's pressed into the pot and for his special dishes (ὄψωι) eat baby finches and thrushes and not hang around for wretched three-day-old little fish in the agora, overpriced and weighed out by the lawless hand of the fishmonger.' The ancient *Life* of Aristophanes (1.59–60 Kassel–Austin) noted doubts over the authenticity of this play.

[9] On the rustic and the polis see Borgeaud (1995).   [10] Γεωργία.

B: What's your name then?
FARMING: What is it? Farming.

In surviving plays there are several farming protagonists. Dicaeopolis in *Acharnians*, Trygaeus in *Peace*, Strepsiades in *Clouds*, Demos in *Knights*, and Chremylus in *Wealth* all look to the countryside, for 'barley-grains and salvation' (*chidra kai soteria*), in the words of *Peace* (595) and *Knights* (806), for sustenance and divine protection. *Chidra* or barley grains are precisely what suffers in wartime. Comedy is on the side of the cereals, against warfare. In all these examples the comic countryside is idealized and divinely blessed: at *Acharnians* 36 we are told the deme 'used to produce everything itself'. The phrase may reflect a reality,[11] but it is strongly redolent of the language of autarky and utopia discussed below.

The division between city and country is familiar in the mental landscape of Attica[12] but at odds with the reality of political and family allegiances. Many citizens had interests in both town and country, and many 'countrymen'—even comic countrymen—were influential in prolonging war and litigation, which comedy sometimes presents as urban concerns.[13] Furthermore, there is more to the rural economy than agriculture: the chorus of Acharnians in the play of Aristophanes are charcoal-burners based in uncultivated woodland while they also tend vines.[14] In many ways Athens and Attica formed an integrated polis of urban and rural demes,[15] within which tensions inevitably arose, tensions which were reflected in politics, drama, and literature. In order to mark distinctions, the country could be seen to represent all that the city, with its 'luxury' and 'political corruption', was not. Conversely, country and town could come together in a joint

[11] Osborne (1987), 130, notes the apparent low number of market-places in rural demes.

[12] e.g. Thucydides 2.14–6, Aristotle, *Politics* 1318b.

[13] The belligerent chorus of the Acharnians of Aristophanes is a good example. Acharnae was not some rural backwater but the largest deme of the polis: see Whitehead (1986) and Hornblower (1991), on Thucydides 2.20.4. Eupolis wrote a *Prospaltians*, apparently with a chorus drawn from a proverbially litigious rural deme.

[14] Their charcoal comes from M. Parnes (348). On cultivated and uncultivated land see Borgeaud (1995).

[15] Osborne (1985; 1987) and Whitehead (1986).

representation of the polis such as is to be found in the second half of *Acharnians*, where rural deme and city appear to be blurred. Dicaeopolis vigorously champions his deme at the expense of the city, but farming plays a smaller role in the play than trading in imported foods, both farmed and wild, the 'pigs' (who are young women in disguise) from Megara (729–817), and from Boeotia (873–80) 'marjoram . . . ducks, jackdaws, black francolins, coots, wrens, little grebes . . . geese, hares, foxes, moles, hedgehogs, cats, badgers(?), martens, otters, Copaic eels'. The one Attic farmer who comes on stage as a victim of a border raid rather than as a provider of foods is treated unsympathetically. In this play farming, which Dionysus supports (see below), is subsidiary to the festivals of the god for the whole polis, whether the Rural Dionysia in the fields or the Anthesteria at which the new wine was drunk. It is also quite unclear whether the private market is set up in an urban or a rural deme, or where the Anthesteria is taking place—is the house of the priest of Dionysus, to which Dicaeopolis is invited, in the city or not? Comedy itself was a hybrid, deriving, according to Aristotle, from rustic celebrations,[16] but taking its full form only when officially produced at urban festivals. Plays put on at those festivals and celebrating country life share something with the festivals themselves, many of which bring to the centre of the polis ancient rural rites. The Anthesteria, Thesmophoria, Thargelia, and possibly Lenaea are prominent examples, all of them represented in comedy. Celebration of these festivals helps to secure the city's well-being—by appealing for divine favour and promoting agricultural productivity.

3.2. THE AGRICULTURAL GODS OF OLD COMEDY

The divine support that comedy was seeking came from the gods of the polis, Athena,[17] Poseidon, Apollo,[18] and other gods of the Athenian festivals, in particular those gods who promoted Attic agriculture, Dionysus and Demeter, with whose favour the city

[16] From those leading the phallic songs, *Poetics* 1449a11–12.

[17] 'Sacred to Athena are both the city and likewise the whole land of Attica, and no matter which other gods are ordained for worship in the demes, they offer Athena no less honour', Pausanias 1.26.6.

[18] 'Thargelia: an Athenian festival named from thargelia, all the fruits of the

sought to maintain its food supply and even to have a surplus. The ideological importance the city put on the support of Demeter and Persephone is illustrated by a decree regulating first-fruit offerings at Eleusis:[19] all Attic farmers were required to contribute a quantity of barley and wheat, as were farmers in the allied cities. All Greeks were to be encouraged (but not forced) by the hierophant and torchbearer (senior priests of the mysteries) to contribute 'in obedience with tradition'. The text concludes: 'those who do this shall have many blessings and rich and fruitful harvests, those that is who do not harm the Athenians, the city of Athens or the two goddesses.'

In a strongly ideological passage Xenophon identified Attica as a land of great fertility,[20] and at least one comedy, the *Seasons* of Aristophanes, appears to have explored this claim.[21] Others, though, emphasized the thin soil and the need for imports in peace as well as wartime.[22] Osborne (1987) argues that statistically Attica in the fifth century could have been self-sufficient, but in practice was not. There was thus a need to secure improved fertility and production with the help of the gods who favoured agriculture, an aim to which Old Comedy gave its support. Divine aid was a much higher priority for comedy than the hard work the small farmer must put in merely to subsist. Trygaeus in *Peace* (quoted above) urged farmers to pick up their tools, but also to sing a paean as they returned to work; it is the goddess Peace who converts the chorus from warriors into farmers (560–70). Later, the scythe-maker thanks Trygaeus for improved sales of tools, but little work is in evidence (1198–206). Hard work fades into the background as the gods provide abundantly for agricultural feasting and that abundance is spent on sympotic and nuptial celebrations (1140–58, 1316–57). In Aristophanes, *Farmers* fr. 111, a speaker thinks of relaxation after work: 'deep-wealthed Peace and my little yoke of oxen, if only I could, after giving up any involvement in the war, get digging and pruning the vines and, after taking a bath, drink deep of the

earth. Celebrated in the month Thargelion. To Artemis and Apollo.' (*Etymologicum Magnum* 443.18–25)

[19] *IG* I² 76 = Meiggs and Lewis no.73, variously dated between 445 and 415.
[20] Gauthier (1976: 45–6) is strong in support of this claim.
[21] On Aristophanes, *Horae* see below.
[22] Thucydides 1.2.5–6 (with Gomme and Hornblower), Plato, *Critias*.

vintage and eat bread rich in oil and a radish!' The surviving
fragments of *Farmers* seem to be broadly similar to *Acharnians*
and *Peace* fr. 112 in synthesizing town and country,[23] fr. 109 suggesting that 'we go' to take our leisure in the countryside,[24] and
fr. 102 asserting that 'you' are impending agriculture.[25] Nothing
remains of the *Farmers* of Timocles, though some have thought
that fr. 38 comes from it: 'FARMER: . . . figs, oil, dried figs, honey.
B: You're talking about the *eiresione*, not farming.' The *eiresione*
was a festive bough hung on doorways at the Thargelia or
Pyanopsia festival. The fragment appears to contrast the riches
of the harvest festival with the reality of farming itself.

There are exceptions to this semi-utopian picture of agriculture supported by the gods of the countryside. The plays of
Aristophanes, after all, were produced during the damaging
years of the Peloponnesian War (see below);[26] the troubles of the
Attic countryside in the early fourth century find some comic
reflection,[27] and Menander's *Dyscolus* reflects a bleak life for
farmers on the rocky hillsides of the northerly deme of Phyle,
even though the eponymous bad-tempered old farmer works to
excess because he wishes to be isolated on his farm from polis and
social, indeed civilized, life. Hard work in that play is contrasted
strongly with the life of the city boy who has soft hands.

The following sections pursue those aspects of the treatment
of agriculture in comedy which centre on the good things promoted by the comic gods. A number of plays portray an ideal—
the effortless provision of food in abundance—most notably in
passages treating the 'Age of Cronos' before the introduction of
agriculture, an age to which comic agriculture aspires, often with
success. We have seen that agricultural labour is often of less

---

[23] 'O beloved polis of Cecrops, Attica who sustains herself, hail, rich plain,
udder of this fine land.'

[24] 'Let us now go from the city into the countryside since we should long
since have gone to take our leisure in the bronze (?; the text is corrupt).' The chorus appear to be the speaker.

[25] 'A: I want to farm. B: Well who's stopping you? A: You lot. Since I'll give a
thousand drachmas if you release me from civic office. B: We accept. That makes
two thousand with the thousand from Nicias.' 'You lot' are the Athenian people
or some section of them.

[26] See Garnsey (1988), 132; Hanson (1983).

[27] *Wealth* 218–26. These troubles have been challenged. See e.g. Hanson
(1983), 137–43; Strauss (1986), 59–63, 163.

interest to comedy than the production of food, and opportunities to consume some of those products and relax in festive celebration are eagerly sought. Such celebrations bring together both worship of the gods and networking in the comic polis; the main celebrants are the protagonist, chorus, and audience. Alongside divine support runs a strong element of nostalgia. At *Peace* 571–2, for example, it is his memory of the 'ancient way of life'[28] which inspires Trygaeus to go back to work with his mattock. That way of life, provided by Peace, comprised 'pressed dried fruit, figs, myrtle, sweet wine lees, violets by the well, and the olives we long for'. Trygaeus may refer simply to the period before the beginning of the Peloponnesian War ten years before, but a longer perspective is possible, particularly in view of a series of comic passages which look back much further into history.

3.3. FOOD IN ABUNDANCE IN THE AGE BEFORE AGRICULTURE

Athenaeus, in his sixth book (267e–270a), introduces an apparently different comic version of the 'ancient way of life',[29] by which he means the period of human development before the advent of agriculture when food was provided 'automatically', a period in which no slaves were needed. This is a time that corresponds to Hesiod's Age of Cronos, to which comic characters could be magically returned. Eight plays are cited, according to Athenaeus in chronological order:[30] Cratinus, *Wealths*; Crates, *Beasts*; Teleclides, *Amphictyons*; Pherecrates, *Miners* and *Persians*; Aristophanes, *Fryers* (*Tagenistae*); Nicophon, *Sirens*; and Metagenes, *Thuriopersians*. Cratinus places his, apparently the first, version in the time of Cronos (inspired probably by Hesiod). Those who followed also described food provided automatically, but without the aid of Cronos—in a future utopia in Crates, by an unidentified god in Teleclides, in the underworld in Pherecrates' *Miners*, by Zeus and Plutus in his *Persians*, by the

---

[28] ἡ δίαιτα ἡ παλαιά.

[29] ὁ ἀρχαῖος βίος.

[30] 6.268e. The last two are not necessarily the last chronologically: Athenaeus (270a) put them last because they were not produced in the theatre.

elements in Nicophon, by rivers in Metagenes. Food is provided, in short, by the divine and natural world (where we are told the provider). Athenaeus writes: 'when the poets of Old Comedy discourse on the ancient way of life they set forth the following to show that there was at that time no need for slaves. Cratinus [says] in *Wealths* (fr. 176), "for them Cronos was their king in the old days, when they played dice with wheat-loves and barley cakes were put down as payment in the gymnasia. Aeginetan they were, tree-ripened and topped with nobbly bits".'[31]

Better than these is Teleclides in *Amphictyons* (fr. 1):

I will speak now of the life that I originally provided for mortals. First of all there was peace like water over the hands.[32] The earth bore neither fear nor disease but all that was needed was there automatically. Every torrent flowed with wine and barley cakes fought with bread outside the mouths of men, begging them to swallow them up if they had any liking for the whitest loaf. Fish came to the house, baked themselves, and presented themselves on the tables. A river of soup flowed by the couches, swirling with hot meats; there were pipes of rich meat trimmings for those who wanted them so that there was unlimited opportunity to gulp

---

[31] Crates, *Beasts* fr. 16 follows:

A: Then will no one own a male slave or female slave, but will have to do the work for himself even if he is old?
B: Not at all, because I will make everything walk.
A: Well, how will this help them?
B: Then each of the household items will come forward whenever the call is made. 'Put yourself beside me, table. You there, set yourself. Little kneading -trough, knead. Ladle, pour in the wine. Where is the cup? Go and wash yourself up. Get up, barley cake. The pot should have poured out the beet. Fish, walk.' 'But I'm not yet baked on the other side.' 'Well why don't you turn over and sprinkle yourself with oil and salt?'

Straight after this the speaker taking the opposite position to him says (fr. 17): 'Now put this beside your suggestion. I on the other hand for my supporters will first draw these hot waters in reverse, on columns, like the ones at the doctor's clinic, from the sea. For each man they will flow into a small bath. The water will say "Stop!" Then the perfume flask will straightaway come automatically, along with the sponge and the sandals.' In fr. 18 of *Beasts* the chorus of beasts declare that men must stop eating meat. The utopia of frr. 16 and 17 thus seems to be combined with a restoration of friendship between humans and animals. Cf. Empedocles, *Katharmoi* fr. 130 DK on amity between men, birds, and beasts, and Plato, *Politicus* 272b–e on men and animals conversing in the Age of Cronos (which they do not do in Hesiod).

[32] See Arnott (1996) on Alexis fr. 263.2 for hand-washing at the beginning of the meal.

down a mouthful after making it soft and moist. On dishes there were cakes(?)[33] sprinkled with tasty flavours; roast thrushes with milk cakes flew into the throat. There was uproar as flat-cakes jostled for position at the jaw; slaves could play dice with slices of sow's womb and crackling. Men were fat in those days and mighty giants.

Pherecrates says in his *Miners* (fr. 113):

A: everything there had been mixed together with wealth and worked in all blessings in every way. Rivers full of porridge and black soup flowed babbling through the narrow places, bread-spoons and all, and bits[34] of cheese-cakes so that mouthfuls could go easily, automatically, and well-oiled down the throats of the dead. Blood puddings and boiling slices of sausage sizzled and had been scattered beside the rivers like shells. Also present were well-roasted cutlets, well turned out with sauces of every kind, and bits of eel wrapped up in beet. Near to them on delicate plates the tenderest whole hams[35] on the bone and boiled trotters steaming fragrantly and ox tripe and pork ribs nicely browned lay daintily sitting on fine cakes. Present too was cracked wheat with a snow of milk in shallow pots and slices of beestings.
B: Oh god, you'll be the death of me if you stay here any longer when you can easily dive down to Tartarus as you are.
A: What then will you say if you hear the rest? Roast thrushes prepared for a further roasting flew near our mouths begging us to swallow them down, as they were strewn on a bed of myrtle and anemones. And apples were hanging above our heads, the finest of the fine to see, but growing on no tree. Girls just come to puberty, with public hair shaved and wearing fine shawls of woven hair, filled cups through funnels with dark fragrant[36] wine for those who wished to drink. And whenever one of them took something to eat or drink, twice as much came back again as at the start.

And in the *Persians* (fr. 137) he says:

What need do we now have for your ploughmen and yoke-makers, your sickle-makers or bronze-smiths or seed or vine-propping? For automatically over the crossroads rivers of black soup with sprinkled cakes and Achillean barley cakes[37] will flow, gushing forth abundantly from the springs of Plutus, waiting to be drawn up. And Zeus, raining with smoky wine,[38] will run you a bath over your roof-tiles, and from the

---

[33] The text is uncertain.
[34] There may be a pun on τρύφη, 'broken pieces', and τρυφή, 'luxury'.
[35] So Gulick (1929).   [36] On ἀνθοσμίας see Athenaeus 1.31f–32a.
[37] On Achillean barley cakes see Athenaeus 3.114f.
[38] On οἶνος καπνίας see Plato fr. 274; Anaxandrides, *Protesilaus* fr. 42.71.

roofs pipes of grapes with cheesecakes will be channelled down along with pea soup and a thick soup of lilies and anemones.[39] Then the trees on the mountains will bear leaves of entrails of roast kid and tender little squid and roast thrushes.[40]

The theme of *utopian* abundance produced without slave or other labour runs through these passages;[41] labour is redundant since nature or the gods provide abundantly (*Persians* explicitly declares agriculture redundant). At the same time, what is provided are the *fruits of agriculture, ready-cooked*—the foods of culture.[42] Furthermore, in these magnificent feasts the appetite for consumption comes as much from the foods themselves as from the consumers. Fish, birds, and cakes wish to be consumed and with their utensils are endowed with various forms of locomotion, walking, flying, and swimming. In a novel development on the material world of the kitchen examined in Chapter 1, fish and birds can move even when cooked and kitchen utensils in *Wild Beasts* are able magically to wash themselves up and make cakes in a striking anticipation of modern electrical gadgets. Rivers provide the favoured form of movement, existing rivers in *Thuriopersians*, rivers flowing through dining-rooms in *Miners* and

[39] Perhaps a form of barley cake and not anemones: see Kassel–Austin (1989) and cf. *Miners* fr. 113.25.

[40] Athenaeus continues, 'why need I add to these the lines of the *Fryers* (*Tagenistae*) of the delightful Aristophanes? You are all sated with his strong humour. I will bring my words to a close with mention of the *Thuriopersians* of Metagenes after sending packing the *Sirens* of Nicophon in which he writes: "Let it snow barley-meal, let it hail wheat-loaves, let it rain pea soup; let soup roll meat through the streets and the flat-cake urge itself to be eaten." And Metagenes says (fr. 6): "the River Crathis brings down for us the biggest barley cakes automatically kneaded, while the other river pushes a wave of cheese-cakes and meats and boiled rays slithering to the very place. And these little streams flow on one side with baked squid and sea bream and crayfish and on the other with sausages and minced meat, whitebait this side, pancakes on that. And cutlets automatically stewed at heat dart into the mouth from above, while others come up from foot level. Fine cakes swim round us in a circle." '

[41] For studies of the utopian passages see Graf (1845); Zielinski (1931); Baldry (1953); Fauth (1973); Hunter (1983) on Eubulus fr. 74; Ceccarelli (1996); and Ruffell (forthcoming). On individual passages see the bibliographies in Kassel–Austin (1983–9).

[42] Contrast the foods cooked 'naturally' by those who live near to the gods in other texts: see J.-P. Vernant, 'Food in the Countries of the Sun', in Detienne and Vernant (1989).

through streets in *Persians* and *Sirens*.[43] I discuss rivers and agricultural production below. The only place in extant Old Comedy which comes close to these gargantuan feasts is the festive conclusion of *Acharnians*, set at the Anthesteria, where too automation is on hand. In both festive (*Acharnians*) and utopian versions, food is consumed in the context of the *deipnon*/symposium, whether the diners be dead or alive, Greek or non-Greek. In whole or in part these passages share a number of features with comic treatments of Attic or more generally Greek agriculture—even though (the most striking point) each is set 'somewhere else', outside Greece itself.

These descriptions of utopian eating are as ample as the foods themselves. The texts constitute a discourse of excess across Old Comedy that is analogous to the speeches of boastful cooks in Middle and New Comedy.[44] The foods are anxious to be eaten and the speakers do not know when to stop. Particularly striking is the comment by a bored interlocutor in *Miners*, a feature often found in characters subjected to the speeches of comic cooks. The texts are metrically varied, indicating for some of them a probable comic situation in agones (formal comic debates) and possibly parabases (formal statements by the chorus). Some of these texts appear to constitute one side of an argument that was contested. There is every reason to believe these speeches were popular, for all their excess, since the poets of Old Comedy picked up the theme from each other and developed it in a competitive spirit across a number of plays. Behind the strong parodic element in this sequence of citations lies a rich vein of comic material,[45] for these descriptions contain characteristics that may be developed positively or negatively. Negative features include their length and their setting outside Attica, which may imply luxury in contrast to the Athenian discourse of simple and restrained eating. The length of the speeches indicates excessive material and invites a dismissive or incredulous response (contrast the lively exchanges in Dicaeopolis' utopia at the end of

---

[43] On rivers see below. The foods are piped in channels in *Amphictyons* and *Persians*: cf. the similarly fantastic pipes by which the Sybarites were said to transport their wines from estate to shore for export (Athenaeus 12.519d).

[44] Discussed in Chap. 8.

[45] The best analysis of these texts is to be found in Ceccarelli (1996), discussed below.

Acharnians). On the positive side, nature and the gods provide for plenty, which is desired by all.

Some of these positive features derive from the age of Cronos, from the mythical period before Zeus ordained a life of toil based on sacrifice, agriculture, and that form of 'civilization' which led to the development of the classical polis. The following sections demonstrate the similarities between comic agriculture and the effortless production of foods at the time of Cronos. While the Cronia, the festival of Cronos in Athens, is notably absent from the list of festivals prominent in Old Comedy and texts of the fifth century, aspects of the myth of Cronos appear to be significant. Too little is known of the *Cronos* of Phrynichus to determine whether the play dealt in any way with the Cronia.

3.4. COMIC UTOPIAS AND COMIC AGRICULTURE

3.4.1. The Age of Cronos

Consider the temporal and spatial locations of this profusion. Cratinus sets his *Wealths* in the time of Cronos (fr. 176); Crates has a speaker in his *Beasts* set proposals in a future where men and beasts live together; the speaker in Teleclides fr. 1 describes the way of life he ordained 'from the beginning'; Pherecrates fr. 113 describes the underworld, and fr. 137 the future (in Persia?); the *Fryers* (*Tagenistae*) of Aristophanes is cited but not quoted (Athenaeus may have in mind fr. 504, quoted below, which describes the underworld); fr. 21 of the *Sirens* of Nicophon gives no location; fr. 6 of the *Thuriopersians* of Metagenes is set at the rivers Crathis and Sybaris in southern Italy. From the perspective of comedy in the Athenian polis, each passage is located somewhere else, in the distant past, in the animal kingdom, in the rich areas of Persia to the east or Magna Graecia to the west, or in the underworld.[46] This distancing is characteristic of the myth or Age of Cronos.[47] In the words of Versnel (1993: 97), 'as the geographical

---

[46] Cf. Herodotus 2.13.4 on the 'automatic' flooding of the Nile which rendered labour unnecessary, in contrast with the Greeks who rely only on rainfall and must labour. Lloyd (1975–88) on this passage suggests that Herodotus is thinking only of ploughing, which is not necessary in the Nile valley, but that he ignores the heavy work needed to maintain the irrigation system.

[47] Vidal-Naquet (1981), 15–16. He and Vernant (1989: 164–9) compare the

horizon expanded, Kronos moved further to the West . . . on the other hand he was placed in the East in Phrygia. His realm was thought to have existed either before historical times . . . [or] it was sometimes situated in the earth.' The age of Cronos preceded agriculture in human culture and, since food was available automatically, no labour and hence no slaves were required.[48]

These evocations of utopia which draw on the myth of Cronos are put by Athenaeus in the mouth of his character Democritus. Cynulcus comments (6.270b), 'gentlemen and messmates, although I am extremely hungry, Democritus has feasted me rather pleasantly in taking us through rivers of ambrosia and nectar. But "even though I have been moistened in my soul I am very hungry" because I have been gulping down only words. As a result, let us now put a stop to such interminable discourse.'[49]

Democritus, though, as we have seen, has not cited ambrosia and nectar but the foods of culture available to the ordinary Athenian. What then is the relation between these comic passages and the Athenian polis? The Age of Cronos is situated elsewhere,[50] but it manifested itself in Attica in ritual form at the Cronia, a festival attested for Attica in later authors. Philochorus reports, in the paraphrase of Macrobius,[51] 'that Cecrops first set up an altar to Saturn and Ops in Attica and worshipped those gods in place of Jove and earth; he ordained that fathers of families should eat with slaves when all the crops and fruits had been gathered in. For the slaves had shared with the masters the long toil of agriculture, and the gods were pleased by the honouring of slaves.' According to Plutarch,[52] 'when the slaves feast at the Cronia or go round celebrating the rural Dionysia, you wouldn't be able to bear their wails and rumpus brought about by joy and

---

Ethiopians reported by Herodotus to have their meat cooked by the sun (3.18) and whose water provides a smell like violets, a sheen to the skin like oil, and a long life (3.20).

[48] For other comic accounts of the past see Chap. 4.4 on the ritual simplicity of Chionides fr. 7 and Chap. 8.7 on the progress from savagery in Athenion fr. 1.

[49] There is the threat of interminable discourse at 6.262b. Contrast the *Satyricon* of Petronius, whose narrator Encolpius is excessively full both of food and words at the dinner of Trimalchio.

[50] On the Age of Cronos in Athenian political discourse see below.

[51] *FGrH* 328 F 97 = Macrobius, *Saturnalia* 1.10.22.

[52] *Moralia* 1098b–c.

unlimited fineness as they did these things and said' (fr. 745 of an unknown comic author follows). Accius says that[53] 'a large part of Greece and especially Athens offer sacrifices to Saturn which they always call the Cronia. They keep the day a holiday. In fields and towns alike nearly everyone is delighted with feasts, and each citizen attends to his slaves.'[54] Impressive though this evidence is, it cannot be formally confirmed for the fifth century.[55] Nor does the Cronia appear to be a major concern for comedy; quite the reverse in fact, if *Clouds* 398, declaring the festival obsolete, is taken literally.[56] For comedy the myth of Cronos is potent, while the festival is passed by despite its superficial suitability to the genre.

Versnel is the most recent of many scholars to bring out the ambiguities attached to Cronos in myth and ritual. The myth is constructed around polarities between merrymaking and plentiful food (such as those found in the comic passages under discussion) and the violent castration of his father Ouranos, the chaining of Cronos himself, and myths of human sacrifice;[57] the ritual celebrates plenty and at the same time reverses the social order of master and slave and is set at the disruptive period of the year end. One feature of that disruption of order is gambling, where chance replaces the established hierarchy. At the Roman Saturnalia, which is related to the Cronia, gambling was allowed uniquely in the Roman year,[58] and in Teleclides fr. 1 slaves play games of chance with pieces of food.[59] So profuse is the supply of

---

[53] *Annals* fr. 2–7 Warmington = Macrobius, *Saturnalia* 1.7.36.

[54] This and similar festivals in Rome and other cities are collected by Athenaeus at 14.639b–640a. See also Versnel (1993), 103–4.

[55] Though it would be strange if the festival were obsolete by the fifth century but attested by Philochorus in the fourth.

[56] 398. Dover (1968) suggests, not implausibly, that the Cronia is considered antique not in itself but because Cronos belonged to the older generation of gods and was considered superannuated: see Arnott (1996) on Alexis fr. 63.2. Parker (1996: 270), lists the Cronia among festivals obsolescent in the fourth century.

[57] Versnel (1993), 99–102.

[58] Martial 4.14.7–9, 'dum blanda vagus alea December | incertis sonat hinc et hinc fritillis | et ludit tropa nequiore talo'. The game of tropa is played with 'Dionysiac acorns' at Cratinus, *Pylaia* fr. 180: see further Pollux 9.103, who says different kinds of acorns were often used instead of dice. Sow's womb (in Teleclides fr. 1) is another matter.

[59] The cakes which appear to function as currency in Cratinus fr. 176.2–3 resemble the *popana* offered at the Attic Cronia.

food that it can be toyed with.[60] The presence of the slaves at play, although suitable for the Saturnalian context, appears problematic after Athenaeus' introduction of meals without the need for slaves.[61] Perhaps he means to say that slaves were not needed to toil in food production and preparation. They were still thought to exist, either as gamblers or as servers at table.[62] On these comic passages Versnel[63] observes that gambling gives 'an answer . . . to the obvious question: "we are often left wondering what people actually *did* in the Golden Age".'

While the eight passages cited by Athenaeus draw on motifs of the Age of Cronos, it is not possible to say how they were exploited in each of their respective plays. In a sense, comedy is filling in a missing part of Hesiod's myth of the Golden Race 'who existed at the time of Cronos, when he ruled in heaven; they lived like gods, with hearts free from care, separated from work and grief. Shameful grief was not present, and, always similar in hands and feet, they took pleasure in feasts, far from all evils. They died as if overcome by sleep, and many good things were theirs. The life-giving earth bore fruit automatically, much of it and without stint.'[64] Hesiod is not concerned with how the golden race feasted, or on what food. In the comic versions it comes as no surprise that foods are the centre of attention, the cooked foods of culture, marked out as special only in their profusion and automation. These passages do not link automation with agricultural production—quite the reverse in *Persians*—but the sources of supply resemble those which promote agriculture, namely rivers and friendly gods.[65]

---

[60] Such dicing with food is seen also in Cratinus fr. 176.2 (bread loaves, cited above) and Epicharmus, *CGFP* fr. 84.132 (figs)—there is no indication that the players are slaves. Athenaeus (3.114a) attests a tetragonal bread known as 'dice'.

[61] Ruffell (forthcoming) suggests that Athenaeus has conflated the passages quoted with passages that do exclude slaves, producing a confusing picture.

[62] Comedy sometimes presents alternative solutions in the use or non-use of slaves in utopias. In Pherecrates, *Agrioi* fr. 10 the absence of male and female slaves results in women doing all domestic chores themselves. In *Ecclesiazusae* plentiful food and social and sexual equality for citizens is based on agricultural production by a labour force of slaves.

[63] (1993), 122–6.   [64] *Works and Days* 110–18.

[65] The *Golden Race* of Eupolis may draw on the myth of the Golden Race: the fragments do not allow a decision.

3.4.2. *Fertile Rivers*

In the comic utopia the automatic movement of food often takes liquid form, in rivers of wine (Teleclides, *Amphictyons* fr. 1), rivers of soup, channels of sauce-trimmings, and swimming fish. In Pherecrates' *Miners* rivers of broth push along pieces of cakes, while there are sausages on the riverbanks; in his *Persians* rivers of black broth flow from the springs of Wealth (Plutus), as if all were orchestrated by the god of the underworld (see below). Liquids pour in profusion not just in the form of rivers, but also as rain, snow, and hail (*Persians* fr. 137.6, *Sirens* fr. 6).[66]

Ample provision goes hand in hand with this automation, for the most part in rivers flowing by the couches (and birds flying into the mouth). Often the foods are hot and shiny with oil as they demand to be eaten. Aspects of the river are combined with sympotic and dining motifs, the irrigation of plants provided by water merging into irrigation of the throat in the form of sauces and dressing with oil, all the more necessary with food served as hot as possible in order to stimulate the appetite. The comic poets are drawing on the ancient association of rivers with wealth, primarily in supporting agriculture, but in some remote places also in supplying gold.[67] Rivers springing from the mysterious underworld presided over by Plutus, Wealth himself, brought agricultural wealth to farmers and poleis.[68] In the comic utopia the stages of plant and animal husbandry, harvesting, slaughter, processing, preparation, and cooking are all rendered superfluous by the rivers of automated cooked food. Rivers of cooked food belong to the absurd, but they share elements with rivers as the Greeks imagined them.[69] Some of the utopian rivers are divinely prompted—by an unknown god, by Plutus, and by Zeus; rivers of Greece, too, were part of the mythical and divine world.[70] Many shrines of Demeter were sited by rivers.[71]

---

[66] For Zeus raining cf. Cratinus, *Nomoi* fr. 131 (raining dried grapes).

[67] Richardson (1974) cites Aeschylus, *Prometheus Vinctus* 806.

[68] The exceptional river in the Mediterranean was the Nile, which brought such fertility that it was imagined as an automated form of agriculture (Herodotus 2.14.4).

[69] Epicharmus in *The Muses or the Marriage of Hebe* fr. 41 lists rivers who are daughters of Pieros and Pimpleis, 'Fat' (or 'Richness') and 'Fullness' respectively: see Chap. 7.

[70] See further 'fluvii' in *LIMC* IV I 139–48.   [71] Cole (1993), 204–7.

Acheloos,[72] in many ways the most important and archetypal of Greek rivers,[73] was linked in myth with Dionysus,[74] through King Oeneus and his sons who lived in the region watered by the river. Some texts went further and blended the waters of Acheloos with the wine of Dionysus to form the wine-and-water mixture of civilized drinking.[75] Acheloos in poetry became a mentonym for water,[76] even the water to be mixed with wine at the symposium.[77] Indeed, in what is probably a Dionysiac miracle, Acheloos is imagined to be flowing with wine in Sophocles, *Athamas* fr. 5 R. The comic utopias with their rivers of solid foodstuffs have gone a stage beyond the sympotic liquids of water and wine, both of which might be divinely supplied. The notion is supported by the symbolic link of rivers, and Acheloos in particular, with the horn of plenty, as in comedy is Amaltheia,[78] with whom Acheloos is associated.[79] The horn of plenty brings forth fruit and good things in abundance that may be represented by ambrosia, such fruits as apples, or by Opora (Harvest personified). In addition to river-water, other life-giving liquids may be caused to flow from the earth by gods such as Dionysus, who produces milk, honey, and wine: Euripides, *Bacchae* 706–10, 'one bacchante brought down her narthex to the ground, and the god sent forth a spring of wine for her. Those who desired a white drink scratched the earth with their finger-

[72] *LIMC* I 1.12–36, s.v. Acheloos.

[73] Macrobius, *Saturnalia* 5.8, Mynors (1994), on Virgil, *Georgics* 1.9.

[74] Mynors (1994) on *Georgics* 1.9.

[75] Ibid. on *Georgics* 1.7–9 cites Nicander fr. 86, 'Staphylus Oenei pastor', in Servius on this passage of the *Georgics*, and Cerasus at Hyginus 274, who uses Acheloos. Add Apollodorus 1.8.1 and Hyginus 129 on Oeneus who was given the gift of the vine and how to grow it as a reward for turning a blind eye to Dionysus' seduction of his wife Althaia. Virgil takes it this way at *Georgics* 1.7–9, where Liber (Dionysus) and Ceres (Demeter) bring cereals to replace the primitive acorn and new vines to mix in cups of the water of Acheloos.

[76] e.g. Aristophanes, *Lysistrata* 381; Euripides, *Bacchae* 625–6.

[77] Aristophanes, *Cocalus* fr. 365; Achaeus 20 F 9.1 Sn., μῶν Ἀχελῶιος ἦν κεκραμένος πολύς;

[78] Kassel–Austin (1984) list comic references to Amaltheia and wealth on Aristophanes fr. 707, 'the city is the Horn of Amaltheia'. Eubulus' play *Amaltheia* is said to have featured a female tavern-keeper who attracted Heracles.

[79] The two are linked at Apollodorus 2.7.5. At Ovid, *Metamorphoses* 9.85–8 Amaltheia is the daughter of Haemonias, another river-god.

nails and had streams of milk.' The god *sends forth*[80] both liquids, while earlier in the play, under his influence, the earth 'flows with milk, flows with wine, flows with the nectar of the bees' (141–3). These are the raw liquids on the margins between nature and culture[81] which precisely do not flow from the earth in the comic utopia. Rather, rivers flow with slices of beestings, honey cakes, and cheese cakes and wine is drunk sympotically—in most cases at the instigation of a god. In the miraculous production of Attic agriculture to be considered shortly, a god will again be imagined to produce the cooked foods of festival.[82] Gods are not always needed to promote the automatic production of food: sometimes the earth can do so herself.[83] Nor need the products be confined to agricultural plants. In Cratinus fr. 363 [the earth] 'automatically[84] bears spurge and sage-apple in addition, asparagus and tree medick—she revels in her youth in flower-strewn valleys—and unlimited supplies of mullein at hand for all the fields'.[85]

---

[80] ἀνιέναι.   [81] See Daraki (1985), 45–58.
[82] Cf. Xenophon, *Anabasis* 5.3, an idealized passage in which Xenophon founds a cult to Demeter, offers her a tenth of the first-fruits, and in return all worshippers are offered by the goddess barley groats, bread, wine, *tragemata*, and sacrificial meat. While the goddess is not said to produce these good things automatically, she feeds her worshippers on these foods of civilization.
[83] Cf. Solon fr. 38 West:

> πίνουσι καὶ τρώγουσιν οἱ μὲν ἴτρια
> οἱ δ' ἄρτον αὐτῶν, οἱ δὲ συμμεμιγμένους
> γούρους φακοῖσι. κεῖθι δ' οὔτε πεμμάτων
> ἄπεστιν οὐδ' ἕν, ἄσσ' ἐν ἀνθρώποισι γῆ
> φέρει μέλαινα, πάντα δ' ἀφθόνως πάρα.

('They drink and eat, some of them honey-cakes, others bread, others cakes mixed with lentils. There not one cake is missing of all those that the black earth provides among men. All are present in abundance.')

[84] Cratinus, *Malthakoi* fr. 105.8, κύτισος αὐτόματος, is not a compelling example of divine blessing since the *kutisos* (Medicago arborea or tree medick) is probably the product of human agency (see KA). Cf. the automatic arrival of a parasite's food at Diphilus, *Aplestos* fr. 14.

[85] αὐτομάτη δὲ φέρει τιθύμαλλον καὶ σφάκον πρὸς αὐτῶι ἀσπάραγον κύτισόν τε, νάπαισιν δ' ἀνθέρικος ἐνηβᾶι, καὶ φλόμον ἄφθονον ὥστε παρεῖναι πᾶσι τοῖς ἀγροῖσιν. Comedy presents a further category of river, the streams of dung and diarrhoea in the underworld (in Aristophanes, *Gerytades* and *Frogs*) which reflect both the social practice of depositing human waste in the earth and (possibly) the agricultural potential of such human manure. See Chap. 1.

3.4.3. The Comic Golden Age and Athenian Politics
My discussion of the comic utopia has concentrated on the myth of Cronos and the production of abundance by natural and divine forces. Of other approaches, the best is the essay by Ceccarelli (1996), who synthesizes poetic form, cultural context, and contemporary debate. She divides the utopian fragments into those which are set in a form of the Golden Age (*Wealths, Beasts, Amphictyons*), and the remainder which (as she sees it) develop the theme as part of an established comic routine. Since a number of the passages appear to belong to an agon,[86] there is good reason to suppose that they are not narratives but part of a contesting discourse which appears to have an ideological component at this period (430s–420s). The Age of Cronos was linked with various, usually oligarchic, politicians (Peisistratus, Aristeides, Cimon) who claimed to have brought well-being to the polis.[87] This well-being was traditional and tied to agricultural production. Agriculture was seen to have suffered under the strategy of Pericles, the opponent of the oligarchs, at the beginning of the Peloponnesian War (see below). Pericles abandoned the fields to the Spartans while putting the defence of the city into the hands of the navy (which was manned by the demos) and supplies for the city into the hands of the merchant ships. Democrats could thus show that the sea could provide virtually unlimited supplies of goods to Athens, while oligarchs cried up the sufferings of domestic agriculture. These utopian passages may, then, reflect claim and counter-claim of the benefits or perceived dangers of democratic ideology. Automatic food, according to Ceccarelli, is put to satirical use, contrasting with food

[86] Whether by metre or content or context: *Wealths* fr. 176; *Beasts* frr. 16 and 17; *Amphictyons* fr. 1; *Persians* fr. 137; and possibly *Sirens* fr. 21 (Ceccarelli 1996). See further Gelzer (1960) and Perusino (1968).

[87] Ceccarelli (1996) cites (p. 141) on Peisistratus, [Aristotle], *Athenaion Politeia* 16.7; on Hippias, Plato, *Hipparchus* 229b; on Aristeides, Plutarch, *Aristides* 24.3; on Cimon, Plutarch, *Cimon* 10.7, acknowledging that all these sources post-date the fifth century. Comedy to some extent supports this case, Cratinus, *Archilochoi* fr. 1 being part of Plutarch's evidence on Cimon and *Wealths* fr. 175 possibly linking the Golden Age of Cronos with the oligarch's ideological ally Sparta. But there are counter-examples, such as the Golden Age of Themistocles: see Teleclides, *Prytaneis* fr. 25.

traditionally produced by farmers.[88] Utopian elements in *Birds* can be shown to question Athenian policy, but, as Ceccarelli concedes (p. 157), that play demonstrates ideological complexity rather than clear cases for democrats or oligarchs.[89] In principle, Ceccarelli's case is strong. I accept that the metrical form of the utopian speeches and their non-Athenian location indicates some satirical intent. However, I differ from her in interpreting the abundance in utopia and the celebration of abundance at the conclusions of the plays of Old Comedy as similar expressions of the human desire for generous supplies of foods. For Ceccarelli, the final scenes of the plays are merely formulaic.[90] In my view she underestimates the unifying role of Dionysus, who, as god of agriculture and komos and recipient of polis cult in numerous festivals, including those in which comedy was produced, promoted something akin to agricultural utopias in several plays and made utopia attainable at the end of the play (see below). The automation in utopia in the fragmentary plays, parodic or not, is prompted by gods and is found also at the end of *Acharnians* and *Peace* in a context of agriculture, trade in agricultural products, and festive symposia.[91] Gods, just as they promoted utopias, supported agriculture and through their powers promoted the festivals of the comic polis. The most prominent god in agriculture is Dionysus, and it is he who promotes trade by sea in Hermippus fr. 63, which is seen by Ceccarelli as the maritime side of the opposition between 'democratic' fleet and 'oligarchic' farmers.[92] I turn now to the comic gods.

[88] I discuss in Chap. 4 Thucydides 2 and [Xenophon], *Constitution of the Athenians* 2.7, on which Ceccarelli bases her case.

[89] See Dunbar (1995) on *Birds* (Introduction, pp. 4–6); Konstan (1997); and Dobrov (1997a).

[90] Baldry (1953), 59 is much more reductive: 'talk of such things was confined to comedy because they were now regarded as comic. . . . Each playwright took one version or other of the traditional picture . . . in order to make fun of it by fantastic exaggeration.'

[91] And not exclusively at the end of these plays: the celebration of the Rural Dionysia towards the beginning of *Acharnians* has utopian and komastic elements.

[92] I give a different interpretation of Hermippus fr. 63 in Chap. 4. Ceccarelli is mistaken in viewing Dionysus *naukleros* (owner of a merchant ship) as analogous to Dionysus the poor rower of *Frogs* (1996: 150, n. 112)—the functions are quite distinct. Ceccarelli recognizes the ambiguities of Aristophanes, *Seasons* fr. 581, on which see below.

3.5. AGRICULTURE AND AGRICULTURAL GODS

In Attica, *agatha*, 'good things', were the products of agriculture, whether grown locally or imported. These products were guaranteed not by mighty rivers[93] but by the benevolence of the agricultural gods who shared the foods of humans in sacrifices and festivals. A number of the festivals of Dionysus and Demeter were linked to the products of agriculture and harvest.

The element of automation is to be found in some of the extant plays of Aristophanes, *Acharnians, Peace,* and *Wealth,* which are not set 'elsewhere' but in Attica (in *Peace,* in Attica and the rest of Greece), and they share a vital feature with some of the utopian passages reviewed above. Consider the *Wealths* of Cratinus. The Wealths, as they announce in anapaests that seem to indicate that they are the chorus (fr. 171, 11–12), are Titans who gained the name 'Wealths' (Pluti) in the reign of Cronos. In fr. 172 'a god sends up good things automatically for them',[94] and in fr. 176 (one of the utopian passages above) Cronos (or another god) gives them food enough to play dice with.[95] The equivalent of these Titanic Wealths in the reign of Zeus (in which most comedies are set) is Plutus (singular), the god Wealth, one of a class of lesser gods who are appropriate to the genre, and have a more limited function than the Olympians. These gods are often to be found in association with Dionysus and Demeter, whom they assist in promoting the growth of plants and humans and the general prosperity of the city. They are Peace and Wealth and the associated nymphs, the Horae (or Seasons) and the Charites.[96] Peace and the Horae are, according to Hesiod,[97] daughters of

---

[93] The Eridanus and Ilissos are not celebrated in this context in the way we saw above of the Acheloos, though the supplies of water in Athens were venerated, and springs were often linked to cults of Demeter and Persephone. See Richardson (1974) on the *Homeric Hymn to Demeter* 99, and Daraki (1985) on Enneacrounos and Callirhoe.

[94] αὐτόματα τοῖσι θεὸς ἀνίει τἀγαθά. Cronos? Or perhaps Wealth (Plutus): see Kassel–Austin (1983) *ad loc.*

[95] Contrast the utility of the good things available to Dicaiopolis at *Acharnians* 975. It is not clear how the Spartan feast or *kopis*, in which old men could nibble at sausages in public places (fr. 175), was linked with the Cronian elements of the play.

[96] On the Charites and their links with Aphrodite and Dionysus see *LIMC* III 1.191–203.

[97] *Theogony* 901–2.

Zeus and 'rich Themis who bore the Horae, Eunomia ['Good Order'], Justice and flourishing Peace'.[98] The Charites too are daughters of Zeus,[99] while 'Demeter . . . gave birth to Wealth [Plutus], mingling in delightful love with the hero Iasion in fallow land turned over three times'.[100] These minor gods and goddesses are prominent in literary contexts of prosperity, agricultural and otherwise, in poetry later than Hesiod,[101] and particularly in Old Comedy.[102] Both Aristophanes and Cratinus wrote a *Horae*, the former much concerned with the gods who preside over the fertility of Athens,[103] while in *Peace*, when that goddess is implored to return, libations are offered as the beginning of '*many good things* for all Greeks' (456), to Hermes,[104] the Charites, the Horae, Aphrodite, and Desire.[105] In that play Peace, who had been buried in the earth, is dug up.[106] The earth is a suitable place for the retreat of a goddess who promotes agriculture, the earth which comprises both the soil and the underworld where the dead reside, and plays a crucial role in Old Comedy as the place from which good things are *sent up* to mortals.

Wealth, embodied as Plutus, comes from the earth and is

---

[98] Themis is λιπαρὴν, suggesting prosperity, while Peace is 'flourishing' like a plant because (West) 'cities flourish under her rule'.

[99] Hesiod, *Theogony* 907–9.   [100] Ibid. 969–71.

[101] Peace is daughter of Zeus and Themis at Pindar fr. 30.

[102] See e.g. Aristophanes, *Farmers* fr. 111, Εἰρήνη βαθύπλουτε ('deep-wealthed Peace', cited above in 3.2). The fragment draws out in an overtly *agricultural* context what was already clear in Euripides, *Cresphontes* fr. 71 Austin: Εἰρήνα βαθύπλουτε καὶ καλλίστα μακάρων θεῶν ('deep-wealthed Peace, the most beautiful of the blessed gods'). Peace has καλλιχόρους ἀοιδὰς φιλοστέφανους τε κώμους ('songs with beautiful dances and komoi that delight in garlands') and is the suppressant of *stasis* (civil war) and *eris* (strife). Peace, in other words, fosters the city, nurturing and protecting its safety. Such ideas are as important in comedy as in tragedy, but when transferred from the one to the other, the idea is complemented with an emphasis on agricultural plenty.

[103] See below and Parker (1996), 159–63 on Sabazius and, in the context of fertility, Orthannes, Priapus, and other 'comic' minor gods in the city.

[104] Hermes is the speaker of this list.

[105] On the connection of Aphrodite with the Charites see n. 96.

[106] It appears that Aristophanes displayed much originality in the staging of the statue of Peace, since it was parodied by both Plato and Eupolis (frr. 86 and 62 respectively). Peace may not have been personified in bodily form before this. I am grateful for the advice of Emma Stafford on this point.

closely linked with Demeter[107] and Persephone, whether as
Pluto, the old husband of Persephone, or as Plutus the divine
child.[108] Comedy draws on both. Hades is 'the wealthy one', as
etymologized by Plato at *Cratylus* 403a:[109] 'Pluto is so named for
his gift of wealth because wealth comes out of the earth from
below. And Hades—most people seem to me to assume that the
name refers to the unseen—is feared, and they call him Pluto.'
The names Pluto and Plutus are often linked.[110] Aristophanes,
Fryers (Tagenistae) fr. 504[111] develops the theme:

How come he was called Pluto unless he received the best? I'll tell you
one thing, how much better the underworld is than the part Zeus has.
Now whenever you weigh something, the scale of the balance moves
downwards, while the empty pan moves towards Zeus[. . .][112] if they
weren't bound to start drinking as soon as they got to the underworld.
For this reason they are called the blessed. The words on everyone's lips
are, 'the blessed man has departed. He sleeps. He is happy because he
will feel no pain.' And we sacrifice to them as to the heroic dead, as if
they were gods, and when we pour libations to them we beseech them to
send us up good things.[113]

---

[107] Demeter, one of whose cult titles is Anesidora, 'Sender up of Gifts', is
described sending up fruits from the fields when she restores agriculture in the
Homeric Hymn to Demeter 471–3.

[108] See Farnell (1896–1909), iii. 132–153.

[109] τὸ δὲ Πλούτωνος, τοῦτο μὲν κατὰ τὴν τοῦ Πλούτου δόσιν, ὅτι ἐκ τῆς γῆς κάτωθεν ἀνίεται
ὁ Πλοῦτος, ἐπωνομάσθη . . . καὶ φοβούμενοι τὸ ὄνομα [sc. τοῦ Ἅιδου] Πλούτωνα καλοῦσιν αὐτόν.

[110] See scholiast on *Wealth* 727 and Pearson on Sophocles fr. 273, who notes
'the wealthy one' as a euphemism for Hades and comments on Plutus as an
attendant of Zeus Ktesios (as he is in Aristophanes, *Wealth* 123–46). Farnell
shows that at a later period Pluto and Plutus are more likely to be distinguished:
cf. e.g. Lucian, *Timon* 21, in which Pluto sends Plutus to earth, being πλουτοδότης
('the giver of wealth') and μεγαλόδωρος ('the great giver').

[111] One of Athenaeus' seven utopian plays, though he does not quote the precise text he has in mind.

[112] The text is corrupt, but appears to connect the garlanding of the dead with
the garlands worn at symposia.

[113] Kassel–Austin (1984) on this fragment cite Photius a 1993 ἀνίει τὰ ἀγαθά·τοῖς
τεθνεῶσιν ἔθος εἶχον λέγειν. Φρύνιχος Κωμασταῖς· ἡμῖν δ' ἀνίει δεῦρο σὺ τἀγαθὰ τοῖς τήνδ' ἔχουσι
τὴν πόλιν ἵλεως ('Send up good things: it was customary for them to say this to the
dead. Phrynichus says in his *Comastae* (Revellers), "graciously send up here
good things to us who live in this city".' On Phrynichus, *Comastae* fr. 16 see
Chap. 5). Cf Aeschylus, *Persians* 222 and *Choephori* 147. On the dead as blessed,
especially in mystery cult, see Richardson (1974), 313–14. Cicero reformulates the
idea of the wealth of Hades in *De natura deorum* (2.66): 'terrena autem vis omnis

Wealth (Plutus) dwells underground as the promoter of both agricultural and mineral wealth. Strabo[114] quotes Posidonius on the Spanish mines, whose deposits are so rich that 'among those people in truth the underworld is inhabited not by Hades but by Wealth'.[115] Of Attic miners at Laurion, Posidonius cites Demetrius of Phaleron's dictum that they work hard 'as if they were about to excavate Pluto himself'.[116] It is not known whether this idea was exploited by Pherecrates in *Miners* (the miners of Laurion?) fr. 113, cited above, though the fragment begins with the phrase 'everything there was mixed together with wealth and worked with blessings'. Plutus, then, embodies wealth; he is the god who presides over the wealth in the soil, both botanical and mineral; as Pluto, he rules the dead who are imagined in some circumstances to enjoy the wealth under the soil; and he sends up some of that wealth to mortals.[117] He may also be a vehicle for the gifts of other gods, who are then termed 'givers of wealth',[118] namely the *daemones*,[119] Demeter,[120] Zeus,[121] Peace,[122] and Iacchus,[123] who is linked with both Plutus and Dionysus.[124]

It was at Eleusis, in the mysteries of Demeter and Persephone, that Wealth (Plutus) was particularly to be found, as the divine

atque natura Diti patri dedicata est (qui Dives, ut apud Graecos πλούτων), quia et recidunt omnia in terras et oriuntur e terris.'

[114] 3.2.9, cited by Athenaeus 6.233e.

[115] παρ' ἐκείνοις ὡς ἀληθῶς τὸν ὑποχθόνιον τόπον οὐχ ὁ Ἅιδης ἀλλ' ὁ Πλούτων κατοικεῖ.

[116] ὡς ἂν προσδοκούντων αὐτὸν ἀνάξειν τὸν Πλούτωνα.

[117] Cf. Aeschylus, *Eumenides* 945–6. It is not clear whether the phrase '*gonos* . . . *ploutochthon*' refers to the human or plant population of Attica. Sommerstein (1989), *ad loc.*, is probably right to understand the human population and its wealth derived from Laurion. The scholiast notes ὁ κάρπος ὁ ἐκ γῆς πλουτίζων.

[118] πλουτοδόται.

[119] Hesiod, *Works and Days* 122–26.

[120] Diodorus Siculus 1.12.4 (an Orphic text = 302 Kern).

[121] Lucian, *Sat.* 14.15, Orphica 73.4.

[122] *PMG* 1021, 'and the poets say "O sweet Peace, giver of wealth to mortals"'.

[123] *PMG* 879 (1), in the Lenaean contests of Dionysus the *daidouchos* holding a torch says 'call the god' and the celebrants respond with the shout 'Iacchus, son of Semele, giver of wealth' (= scholiast (RV) on *Frogs* 479). See further Pickard-Cambridge (1968), 34. Herodotus (8.65) attests the shout 'Iacchos' as early as 480 BC.

[124] See Richardson (1974), 27 and 316–21.

child linked with the life and fertility of the grain.[125] It is no surprise, then, to find Plutus in the list of gods at *Thesmophoriazusae* 296–300: 'pray to the two goddesses of the Thesmophoria, Demeter and Kore, and to Plutus and to Calligeneia [the goddess of good birth], and to Earth the nourisher of children and to Hermes and the Charites.' The gods are asked to protect the women and the polis of Athens, and to give blessings (300) to the women. The citizens, the female population in particular, will benefit, in the fertility of the soil and of themselves. The women of the city nurse their children just as Demeter and Persephone are *kourotrophoi* (nurses) of the divine child, who at the same time bring agricultural wealth. This role of Wealth (Plutus) appeared in various popular cults and religious verse in addition to comedy.[126] In art, Plutus carried the cornucopia.[127] In the Athenian agora, near the statues of the eponymous heroes, there was in the fourth century a statue of Peace carrying the infant Wealth (Pausanias 1.9.2.).[128]

The comic utopias quoted by Athenaeus constructed a world similar to that ascribed by Hesiod to the time of Cronos.[129] A related utopia is achieved in a number of the surviving plays of Aristophanes and made available to the population of Athens, or at least that part of it approved by the protagonist. In *Acharnians, Peace,* and *Wealth,* peace, blessings, and food in abundance are provided by Amphitheos, Peace, and Wealth respectively; in *Frogs* Dionysus goes down to the underworld and meets Pluto. The lord of the underworld does not send up food or riches, but allows Dionysus to send the tragic poet Aeschylus with the message (1462) 'send up the blessings' in order to 'save our city' (1501). The chorus sing finally, '*daemones* who live under the earth, give a good journey to the poet returning to the light and give the city "good plans for great good things"'. The form of provisioning in these plays is far from the daily round of the agricultural year. In a sense they return to the life of the golden

---

[125] See ibid., n. 122.

[126] On the Eiresione song, the 'Crows', and the Boeotian expulsion of Boulimos (Hunger) see Richardson (1974), 317; Athenaeus 8.359d–360e.

[127] Richardson (1974), 318–19. On the cornucopia see above on Acheloos and Amaltheia.

[128] A Roman copy survives in the Glypothek Museum, Munich.

[129] *Works and Days* 42–119.

race of men described by Hesiod, who had all good things, no ageing,[130] automatic food, and delight in feasting, and when they died out they were replaced by *daemones* who warded off evil (*alexikakoi*) and gave wealth (*ploutodotai*) (121–6).

Automation is achieved in *Wealth, Peace,* and *Acharnians.* In the first, Wealth is not hidden in the earth but wanders helplessly and blindly, Although the play follows a version of the myth alternative to sending up wealth from the earth, when the sight of Wealth is restored, 'a heap of good things'[131] bursts into the house, not from the earth, but good all the same, and in profusion.[132] Towards the end of *Peace*, before the wedding takes place, the chorus declares that for those who were hungry before there is food in profusion, 'for it is not every day that it is possible to come across flat-cakes wandering about unclaimed' (1313–14). In *Acharnians* Dicaeopolis, the countryman who restored peace, embraced the products of Dionysus, and set up his private market, is praised by the chorus for his intelligence and the 'goods for trade, that he has to deal in after making his libations' (972): peace has brought him goods for trade, some of them useful for the house and some 'hot to eat' (974–6), and 'all these good things are provided automatically for this man'. The form in which these good things are enjoyed in the polis resembles that found in the utopian passages above. The polis, though, is greatly concerned with the source of these good things, as the inhabitants of utopia were not. Supplies arrive in the form appropriate to an agricultural community, with the earth as the source of wealth and good things, and the fertility gods of Attica the facilitators.

It should now be clear that the utopia achieved for Attica in some plays of Old Comedy resembles the comic utopias located elsewhere, with important differences. In Attica, the comic utopia is a special form of the overall representation of agriculture. The facilitating fertility gods include Dionysus, who presided over comedy and who was honoured in a number of Attic festivals. I now turn to other aspects of agriculture and festivity in Old Comedy which demonstrate further that comic

---

[130] Some of Aristophanes' comic heroes are rejuvenated: see n. 190.

[131] ἀγαθῶν σωρός: cf. the cult title Polusoros ('Provider of many heaps [of grain]') of Demeter.

[132] Cf. the ever-replenished supplies of food and drink in Telecleides, *Amphictyons* fr. 1.32–3, cited above.

discourse represents Athens and Attica in a special form that does not always coincide with the life of the city that experienced the Peloponnesian war.

3.6. OLD COMEDY ON FESTIVITY

In Attica, as we have seen, the wealth of agricultural produce came through the benevolence of the gods, since there were no rivers to provide fertility on the scale achieved by the Acheloos or the Nile. We shall see in *Acharnians* and *Peace* that this abundance is celebrated in a number of ways, which include festivity, whether a formal festival of the polis or feasting at a private event such as a wedding. Such feasting is desired by communities whose food supply is based on agriculture and is not guaranteed. We saw in Chapter 2.2 that feasting is not only a celebration of an agricultural surplus and a point of reference on the religious calendar but also an affirmation of commensality. We saw, further, in 2.11 that feasting in comedy is a goal to which the plays of Old Comedy were directed and that comic commensality was extended to a group of diners who did not coincide with the elite in the polis. This reconfiguration is a strong theme in *Acharnians* and *Peace*—indeed *Peace* even modifies the circumstances in which festivals take place.

Comedy is sometimes crude or reductive in its approach to festivity, with much emphasis on male enjoyment of food and women without status.[133] The Anthesteria is respresented at the end of *Acharnians* as an occasion for the protagonist to eat and have sex with *hetaerae*,[134] while the slave in *Peace* recalls the Brauronia (or the Dionysia at Brauron) as a time of drinking and 'banging' a *hetaera*. This endorsement of pleasure is notable since in other circumstances, most notably in the discourse of desire,[135] pleasure is problematic. Furthermore, what the comic individual experiences as personal pleasure the wider culture might see as of more general benefit; themes of fertility are often present in the comic festival when the rites of Dionysus and

---

[133] Whether *pornae* ('prostitutes') or *hetaerae* ('companions'): the terms are not mutually exclusive. On sex see Chap. 1.9.

[134] This is not the form of the festival normally highlighted in other texts.

[135] Discussed by Davidson (1997) and in Chap. 6.

Demeter are at issue—in the fertility festival of the Thesmophoria of *Thesmophoriazusae* the women pray for their love-life (331–51), while in *Peace* the marriage of the protagonist with the *hetaera* Harvest will produce a harvest of grapes, implying increase of both children and crops.

3.6.1. Dionysiac Festivals in Acharnians[136]

In *Acharnians* peace is secured by Amphitheos, an immortal descendant of Triptolemos and Demeter, the married pair of the Eleusinian mysteries: resembling one of the fertility gods discussed above, Amphitheos brings back the libations for peace (*spondai*), in the material form of wine in wineskins. He is doing the gods' bidding (51–2), for they, as in *Peace*, do not support war. Once these libations for peace have been poured, utopia beckons: 'O Dionysia! This libation smells of ambrosia and nectar' (195–6). The restoration of peace enables Dicaeopolis to celebrate the festival of the Rural Dionysia in honour of the wine god. Dicaeopolis' festival comprises a phallic procession and sacrifice and a comic hymn to the god Phales, who is construed as a drunken reveller, a komast. Since the peace is 'private', only his family takes part.[137] His unnamed wife is told to look from the roof of the house, his daughter is basket-bearer, Xanthias the slave phallus-bearer. Dicaeopolis sings the phallic hymn (263–79):

Phales, companion of Bacchus, fellow komast, night-wanderer, adulterer and pederast, in this the sixth year I address you with pleasure on my return to my deme. I have made myself a peace treaty and freed myself from troubles and battles and Lamachuses. It is far pleasanter, O Phales, Phales, to find a young female slave wood-gatherer stealing, the Thracian slave of Strymodorus from Phelleus and, grabbing her and lifting her up and throwing her down to take out her kernel, O Phales Phales. If you become our fellow drinker, after a hangover, first thing, you will guzzle up a bowl of peace, and the sheild will hang up in the chimney.

This hymn, perhaps traditional in form,[138] describes a Dionysiac komos that accompanies or follows the procession and

---

[136] The Dionysiac festivity discussed here contains many elements which belong to the symposium. The symposium is dealt with in Chap. 5.

[137] The play places much emphasis on this private peace; I discuss below problematic aspects of this exclusive deal, bearing in mind that comedy often presents civic space as private space (Chap. 1.3).

[138] Parker (1997), 126–8.

sacrifice.[139] Sexual pleasure and drinking are prominent features, and to be enjoyed by the group of revellers with their god, who at the end is formally invited to drink with them.[140] These are the hedonistic benefits of festival that I noted above; at the same time, these pleasures coincide with the restoration of the domain of the wine god and of wider fertility. The phallus here appears to be both the reproductive phallus and the instrument of aggression to be used against a powerless slave-woman—aggression is clear in the hymn, but in the preparations for the procession Dicaeopolis speaks of a husband and the possibility of reproduction for his daughter (254–6).[141] With Peace restored and wine tasted, Dionysus and his acolyte are once more honoured in the countryside. The vine suffers particularly in war (see below), and towards the end of the play war and wine are set in opposition to each other,[142] represented respectively by Lamachus the warrior and Dicaeopolis the festival-goer. War damages vines, vine-poles, and the wine, while festival promotes the vine god, the drinking of his wine, and communal eating. The vines take their revenge on Lamachus,[143] who goes off to face a wintry campaign, while Dicaeopolis celebrates hot sympotic pleasures (1141–2).

This division between war and sympotic enjoyment is explicit in the second parabasis (978–87). The chorus chant,

---

[139] There is no good evidence for a komos at the Rural Dionysia. As Pickard-Cambridge (1968), 44–5 points out, December is too late for the vintage and too early for the opening of the new wine, which was ritually celebrated two months later at the Anthesteria. In adding these elements to the Rural Dionysia, Aristophanes has modified the festival actually celebrated in Attica. Similarly, in presenting the celebration of the Anthesteria at the end of the play he has telescoped the period of more than two months which separated these festivals.

[140] 277 Phales is 'our fellow-drinker'.

[141] On the Rural Dionysia see Deubner (1932), 134–8; Simon (1983), 101–4. On the phallus as a symbol of aggression and the marking of boundaries see Burkert (1983), 69–72.

[142] Cf. *Peace* 267, where Trygaeus appeals to Dionysus to restrain the terrible gods of war.

[143] He is wounded by a vine prop (1178). Parody of Euripides' play *Telephus* is prominent in this play. In the Telephus myth (though not attested in the fragments of the *Telephus* of Euripides), Telephus was caught by a vine prior to being wounded by Achilles because he failed to honour Dionysus: see Apollodorus, *Epitome* 3.17; Eustathius 1.40–1 (on Homer *Iliad* 1.59). This tragic reminiscence distances Lamachus further from Dionysus and Dicaeopolis.

I will never receive Polemos [War] into my house, nor will he, reclining by my side, sing the Harmodius *skolion* [144] because by nature he is disagreeable in his wine (*paroinikos*) and came as an extra reveller (*epikomasas*) among people who had all good things. He did many bad deeds and turned over and poured out the wine jars and fought. And furthermore when I kept inviting him 'drink, lie back, take the cup of friendship', he kept setting fire to the vine-poles all the more and forcibly poured the wine out of our vines.

War is the enemy of the wine-grower and symposiast, as unwelcome at the symposium as at the komos. The separation of war from the symposium is of special concern to comedy. Military themes are to be found, for example in surviving examples of the drinking songs known as *skolia*:[145] in particular, two of the Harmodius *skolia* begin 'in a branch of myrtle I will carry my sword . . .'[146] The current passage appears to wish to separate the sympotic myrtle of Aphrodite handed out to symposiasts from the sword. In the place of War, the chorus welcome Diallage, Reconciliation, as 'fellow nurseling with Aphrodite and the Charites'. She, as a woman, cannot be a fellow-symposiast but takes the role of *hetaera* or object of sexual interest. Once again, agricultural elements are introduced. Thinking of sex,[147] the chorus describe planting out the vine and the fig: 'first to push in a long row of young vines, then next to it young shoots of fig, and thirdly a row of cultivated vine' (995-7). Dicaeopolis, propelled as if by wings (970, 988), proceeds to the celebration of the Anthesteria, the new wine festival. He takes his own contribution to the *deipnon* in the house of the priest of Dionysus (1087), a huge range of foods and variety of cooking methods, while Lamachus experiences snow and discomfort.[148] Already provided

---

[144] Harmodius, one of the tyrannicides in 510 (Thucydides 6.53-9), was a symbolic figure claimed by both aristocrats and democrats. For the political aspects of Harmodius in the period see Gomme, Andrews, and Dover.

[145] *Skolia* are collected by Athenaeus at 15.693f-696a and Page, *PMG* 884-917.

[146] *PMG* 893 and 895.

[147] According to the scholiast. See Sommerstein (1980). The passage recalls the intercourse of Demeter and Iasion in a thrice-ploughed field of human and plant fertility at Hesiod, *Theogony* 969-71 (quoted above), on which see West (1966) and Richardson (1974) on the *Homeric Hymn to Demeter* 489. The 'child' of the union was Plutus (Wealth).

[148] There is much emphasis on the heat of the food (976) and on cooking (in

at the priest's house are the essential items for the *deipnon* and symposium: 'couches, tables, pillows, garlands, perfume, dessert, prostitutes, starchcakes, flat-cakes, sesame cakes, honey cakes, and beautiful dancing-girls' (1090–3).[149] Symposium and festival, sexual intercourse and vine-growing come together in a comic construction of the Anthesteria.

3.6.2. Festival in Peace

Similar events unfold in *Peace*. The goddess is restored by the farmers who drag her statue out from under the ground. Trygaeus spells out the activities brought by peace, which prove to be a mixture of festive, sympotic and bodily pleasures: 'you will be able to sail away, stay at home,[150] have sex, go to sleep,[151] attend big festivals, feast, play *kottabos*, live like a Sybarite,[152] and cry out "hurrah! Hurrah!"'[153].'[154] None of these activities was impossible in the polis in wartime, but they may well have been disrupted; in this and other comedies, however, they are rigorously separated from war. Here again, comedy is reconfiguring aspects of life in the polis. When the statue of Peace comes into sight, Trygaeus addresses her as 'queen, giver of the grapeclusters' (520), and declares (530–2) that she smells of 'autumn fruit, entertainment, the Dionysia, pipes, tragedies, songs of

---

the sense of applying heat): 1005, 1014, 1041, 1043, 1047, 1102. A choregus who failed to feast his chorus at an earlier Lenaea is also to be taunted, with hot squid (1156–61).

    [149] On the *deipnon* at the Anthesteria see Henrichs (1990) and Parker (1987).
    [150] An end to travelling on military campaigns?
    [151] That is, in your own home? At 867–8 Trygaeus claims to have saved the Greeks by restoring safe sex and sleep 'in the fields'—on their own farms.
    [152] Live luxuriously? This is the first gloss of the scholion, but the second is attractive, 'tell sybaritic tales or refrains (*epiphthegmata*)'. Sybaritic tales, we are told by the scholia to *Birds* 471 and *Wasps* 1259, were about humans, as opposed to the animal fables of Aesop. The two are mentioned as sympotic entertainment at *Wasps* 1259 and they appeared also in Epicharmus fr. 215 and Mnesimachus fr. 6. The *Sybarismos* of pipers (whatever that means), appears in Phrynichus fr. 67. A sympotic tale makes good sense in the list after playing *kottabos*.
    [153] 'Iou, iou': the cry was uttered in a festive context at the Oschophoria (Plutarch, *Theseus* 22.3).
    [154] (338–45): ἀλλ' ὅταν λάβωμεν αὐτήν, τηνικαῦτα χαίρετε καὶ βοᾶτε καὶ γελᾶτ'· ἤδη γὰρ ἐξέσται τόθ' ὑμῖν πλεῖν, μένειν, κινεῖν, καθεύδειν, εἰς πανηγύρεις θεωρεῖν, ἑστιᾶσθαι, κοτταβίζειν, συβαριάζειν, ἰοὺ ἰού' κεκραγέναι. (NB θεωρεῖν.)

Sophocles, thrushes, little lines of Euripides', again a mixture of sympotic and festive elements, with tragedy now added.

In what sense can Peace be said to 'smell of' tragedy and the Dionysia?[155] Tragedies of Sophocles and Euripides were produced during the Archidamian War, and the Dionysia were performed irrespective of the war. Later, Peace is hailed as 'queen of the choruses, queen of weddings' (976): again, choruses were danced and weddings performed in the polis at war, but comedy puts a special construction on them.[156] One of the personified women who returns with Peace is Theoria ('Showtime'),[157] implying that attending the festival was a peace time activity. This appears to be no more the case in Attica than in Athens itself: to the best of our knowledge Attica was only invaded during the Archidamian War in early summer, for a maximum of forty days.[158] There was, then, no apparent impediment to the celebration of the Rural Dionysia in Poseideon, the Eleusinian Mysteries in Boedromion, or any other Attic festival outside May and June.[159] Yet *Peace* implies that there were no festivals and *Acharnians* 267 that there had been no Rural Dionysia since the beginning of the Peloponnesian War. If the war did not in practice prevent the citizens of Attica from celebrating rural rites, were they restricted in travelling outside Attica to the 'big festivals' cited above, to such Panhellenic festivals as the Isthmian Games, which was the only Panhellenic festival celebrated during the fighting season?[160] *Peace* 879–80 implies that there was no access to the Isthmian Games. Some evidence suggests that this is unlikely during the Archidamian War, for, later in the war, when

---

[155] In addition to the evocation of the material smells of these items picked up by the nose, for which cf. *Acharnians* 186–98.

[156] Cf. *Acharnians* 1048–66, where Dicaeopolis distinguishes a wartime bridegroom (a combatant) from the bride (a non-combatant).

[157] Sommerstein's translation. *Theoria* means literally 'Attending the Festival'.

[158] Forty days maximum (in 430), Thucydides 2.57. Thucydides mentions invasions of Attica also in 431 (2.18–24), 428 (3.1), and (the shortest at fifteen days) 425 (4.2–6). See further Hanson (1983), 112–43.

[159] The Brauronia, another festival possibly mentioned in *Peace*, may have been affected *if* it was held in Mounichion. It is placed in the same month as the festival of Artemis Mounichia by Parke (1977), but not by Mikalson (1975). Deubner (1932), 207 gives no date.

[160] Osborne (1987).

the Athenians faced worse restriction through the Spartan occupation of Deceleia, they continued to enjoy access to the Isthmian Games. Thucydides (8.9–10) writes, 'the Athenians were called to the festival and attended'. I conclude that, as far as the comic polis was concerned, festivals were only celebrated in peacetime, when sympotic culture too was restored, as we have seen in *Peace* 338–45. In removing festivity and the rituals of the symposium totally from the realm of war, comedy is constructing a special world different from the world of the real polis, a comic world with rigid boundaries drawn around wartime and peacetime.[161] In the real polis there was no such division, and festivals and sympotic drinking continued to function in wartime.

That is not to say that festivity and other forms of worship were not disrupted by war in the polis. The Spartans were prevented from attending the Olympic Games during disputes with Elis in 420.[162] The first provision of the Peace of Nicias of 421 allowed free access to Panhellenic temples for 'anyone who wanted' to travel, to consult the oracles and attend the games (Thucydides 5.18), while Panhellenic festival sites guaranteed the peace: *stelai* were to be set up at Olympia, Delphi, and Isthmia as well as in Athens and Sparta (Thuc. 5.18.10), and Spartans and Athenians were to attend each-others' most politicized festivals (5.23.4). The free access for individuals specified by the peace treaty is probably different from the immunity granted to official delegations, and recalls the sailing away and staying at home of *Peace* 338 and the 'taste of peace' which, according to Dicaeopolis, says 'to my mouth "Go wherever you please"' (*Acharnians* 198). If access to festivals was not officially impaired by the ten years of war, it is likely to have been disrupted, at least in some respects, for ordinary citizens; but the comic construction has it that festivals were totally dislocated, and that this dislocation was related to the destabilization of agriculture in war.

---

[161] Comedy, as we have seen, had a large investment in festivals. A number of comedies appear to have titles implying festivity or festival. Likely titles are the *Thearoi* of Epicharmus (fr. 79 apparently contains dedications at Delphi listed by the chorus), the *Feast or Islands* of Epicharmus (suspected by Kaibel), the *Women Setting Up Festival Tents* of Aristophanes, the *Feasts* of Plato, and in mime the *Women Attending the Isthmia* of Sophron.

[162] Thucydides, 5.49–50.

If Old Comedy places a special construction on festivals, identifying them as a phenomenon of peacetime, and on the symposium likewise, what of agricultural production in wartime? Were the farmers of Attica as badly hit as comedy would have us believe? *Peace* implies that no farming was possible until the restoration of Peace. Some have thought otherwise:[163] cereals and mature trees were probably damaged little in Spartan raids; the vine and young trees possibly suffered badly.[164] It is the plants of Dionysus that may have suffered, just as his symposia and festivals suffered. And as with supposed disruption to festivals, the damage to agriculture, especially the vine, may have been greater in the mind than in reality. Overall damage may not have been disastrous, though for individual farmers the picture may have been very different.[165] Thucydides certainly suggests that the farmers suffered when they were forced to abandon their fields, homes, and shrines, implying disruption to their economic, domestic, and religious life.[166] It should be added, though, that Thucydides makes it quite clear that agriculture, at least the growing of cereals, continued in Attica during the Archidamian War, since crops were standing in the fields when the Spartans invaded in 428 and 425.[167]

The solutions to this assault on agriculture are again very different in comedy and in the polis. For comedy, the answer was the total elimination of war and the establishment of the closest links between peace, the gods of peace, and agriculture. The polis had other ways of dealing with disruption to agriculture and festivals. In the ephebic oath sworn by young recruits to the hoplite army, they pledge to honour their holy weapons and to stand by their comrades in defence of the city's shrines, calling as witnesses,

---

[163] Details in Hanson (1983) and Foxhall (1993).

[164] Foxhall (1993), though Hanson (1983), 58, claims that it is not easy to destroy vines at their stage of development in May and June.

[165] Much depends on the settlement patterns of Attica and the distribution of farmland: see Hornblower (1991), on Thucydides 2.16.1, Osborne (1987), Foxhall (1993).

[166] Naturally, for the historian there is a political case to argue, focusing on the policy of Pericles: see Ceccarelli (1996) discussed above.

[167] See n. 158. Add 7.27.4 where he says (a propos the fortifying of Decelea) that previous invasions had not prevented the Athenians from benefiting from their farm land. Furthermore, the Athenian cavalry deterred Spartan troops from wandering too far from their main forces (e.g. 2.22).

among others, Thallo, Auxo, Hegemone,[168] the boundaries of the fatherland, the wheat, the barley, the vines, the olives, and the figs.[169] This version of the oath was found in the deme Acharnae, and broadly reflects the position of Aristophanes' chorus of Acharnians who resist peace with the Spartans because 'with them we share no altar, no trust, and no oath'(308) and they have trampled down the vines of the deme (223–33). Just as hoplites fought to defend crops, so, later in the Peloponnesian War, troops were used to protect the overland route to Eleusis, enabling initiates to approach their festival by the sacred road and not by water.[170] Alcibiades deployed his troops thus to display his piety towards the Eleusinian goddesses, after risking their displeasure a decade earlier when charged with parodying the mysteries in a private symposium.

Old Comedy, then, in plays which concentrate on the countryside and on peace, takes up a special position on agriculture, highlighting the damage caused to plants and the benefits to be gained by recalling peace-loving fertility gods. In other plays and other contexts, divinities—not least Athena—appear as supportive of both comedy and war.[171] In these latter contexts, comedy comes closer to the traditional reflections of Greek poetry—such as those seen on the shield of Achilles in *Iliad* 18—in which the benefits of peace and the troubles of war are contrasted and ruefully accepted.

In both *Acharnians* and *Peace* the protagonist is a winegrower[172] who restores the growth of plants with the help of a fertility god or goddess. When peace is celebrated, though, it is not in an exclusively rustic setting; rather, city and country events are merged into a whole. Henrichs[173] has shown how comedy brings together rural and civic, especially in festive contexts. This is a comic extension of the festivals which bring the rural into the city (the new wine of the Anthesteria, or the statue of

---

[168] All three are Horae.   [169] Tod (1948), ii. 204.

[170] Plutarch, *Alcibiades* 34; Xenophon, *Hellenica* 1.4.20.

[171] At *Knights* 581–5 Athena rules over the most holy land that is pre-eminent in war, poets, and power and is offered comic victory to assist in campaigns and battles.

[172] Dicaeopolis (*Acharnians* 512) and Trygaeus from Athmonon, an accomplished vine-grower (*Peace* 190).

[173] (1990), 269–71.

Dionysus brought from Eleutherae to the theatre in the precinct of Dionysus in Athens). The Dionysia of *Peace* 530, as we have seen, are unlikely to include only the city festivals of City Dionysia, Lenaia, and Anthesteria: also included are the rural festivals, of which several are known in deme calendars and another may be added at Brauron, if the scholiast to *Peace* 890 is to be believed.[174] The festivals at deme level almost certainly complemented the city celebrations of the Anthesteria and City Dionysia. There appears to have been a domestic element to ancient festivals, with private celebrations complementing civic sacrifice,[175] and these small-scale and private celebrations in cult appear to coincide with comedy's interest in the domestic.

The restoration of agricultural fertility in *Acharnians* and *Peace* is celebrated in the consumption of cooked foods, the foods produced by agriculture supplemented by hunting, and cooked in ways similar to those found in the comic utopias. In *Peace* there are cakes, birds, hare, and rolls (1195–6) to accompany the flat-cakes which wander round in automatic form waiting to be eaten (1313–14), and in *Acharnians* there are many foods and cooking processes, including some which might be classed as 'luxurious'—such as the hare stew[176] of line 1112—were the eating not contained within the ritual of the Anthesteria. There are soup and a flat-cake also at the Rural Dionysia in *Acharnians* 245–6. This festive food approaches the utopian delights and is achieved by the favour of the gods that has made Athens comparable to much more favoured places.[177] This is food to be shared, often in a sympotic context, to the exclusion of opponents. In the celebration of the Rural Dionysia in *Acharnians* Dicaeopolis and others 'drink with' Phales and reject the shield (276–9). In the Anthesteria at the end of the play Dicaeopolis enjoys food and sympotic pleasures to the exclusion of Lamachus, the representative of war. Lamachus is forced to endure the very limited foods of the soldier's ration while on campaign, and is excluded both from the rituals of the festival and the foods consumed in profusion. At the end of *Peace* there is drinking with like-minded people to the

---

[174] On the Dionysia at Brauron see below.   [175] See Chap. 2.2.

[176] *Mimarkys* was a dish of hare, especially its entrails, stewed in its own blood. See Hesychius μ 1371, Pollux 6.56, and the scholion to *Acharnians* 1112.

[177] The major difference, as noted above, lies in the rhetorical presentation which in some of the utopias takes the form of a tedious excursus.

exclusion of war. In all this festivity and communal drinking, comedy is reconfiguring social relations from the wartime pattern that excludes agriculture and other features to a festive pattern in which warriors are excluded as anti-festive and anti-sympotic. There are other exclusions also. Festival makes possible the enjoyment of food, wine, and sexual partners; in this context of fertility achieved, luxury and pleasure are not carefully screened out in the way described in Chapter 6. An abundance of fine food is on offer in addition to the ritual elements of the drinking con-test of the Anthesteria or the hymns of the Rural Dionysia. The festival is enjoyed by the protagonist, his friends, and often the chorus and the audience. *Peace* closes with the chorus inviting the audience to follow and eat flat-cakes (1364), the very confec-tion which was said to be wandering round as if automated food from the comic utopia. The comic festival has brought the audi-ence close to the automatic dining of the comic utopia. If the audience is included, excluded (along with Hyperbolus and any-one else associated with war) is Antimachus, the choregos who allegedly failed to feed a chorus at the Lenaea (*Acharnians* 1150–73), thereby identifying himself as an enemy of comedy. The world of the play takes itself out to the larger world of one of the festivals of Dionysus. Festivals, of course, are complex, and not every play treats festival in quite so straightforward a way. In the closing scenes of *Acharnians* the chorus appear not to be included in Dicaeopolis' preparations for the festival, though I suspect their words in fact underline how desirable Dicaeopolis' achievement is.[178] It is the warlike Lamachus who is explicitly excluded and suffers the reverse of each of Dicaeopolis' pleas-ures, while at the end of the play the chorus follow Dicaeopolis, the victorious drinker, and his wine-skin (1231–4). Dicaeopolis is taking part in the festival, is joined in procession by the chorus, and is invited to the home of the priest of Dionysus. This has led many to see him as a problematic hero lacking civic and commu-nal virtues.[179] The selfishness of Dicaeopolis is, to be sure, an

---

[178] 'I envy you your present feast' (1009–10), 'the man has found something tasty in the treaty, but seems not to share it with anyone' (1037–9), 'you will kill me and my neighbours with hunger, shouting like that and with that savoury smell' (1044–6).

[179] Foley (1988); Bowie (1993); Fisher (1993); MacDowell (1995), 77–9; Slater (1995).

issue in the play, but it is difficult to take the argument far, given his celebration of two festivals of Dionysus, his partial identification with the poet,[180] and his appearing on the side of plants and peace against the enemy, war.[181]

3.6.3. The Demos and the Festival

There is a political aspect to this festivity. The Old Oligarch says[182] that the Athenian demos supported the poor who could not individually afford sacrifices, shrines, and feasts by making it possible to have state-funded sacrifice and the allocation of the meat to the people. Old Comedy is democratic in precisely this respect, including in its feasts the demos and audience, and excluding the rich, the gluttonous, and those who would set themselves apart:[183] so Morsimus and Melanthius are wished no chorus for their tragedies because they are gluttons (*Peace* 801–11), while Trygaeus hopes that the gluttons Morychus, Teleas, and Glaucetes will be elbowed away from the food market by 'all of us' now that food is not restricted (*Peace* 1006–9). Similarly in *Acharnians*, the chorus sing (836–59) of Dicaeopolis who will enjoy all the fruits of the agora at the expense of all the usual tiresome and wealthy people in power. Where before the few ate at the expense of the many, comedy ensures that the appetite of the many is fed.

In the parabasis of *Peace*, the Muse of Aristophanes is asked to spit on Morsimus and Melanthius, and 'joins in play' at the 'feast'.[184] The victory of Aristophanes will be celebrated at 'the table and at the symposia'(770), and the poet will be given food to

---

[180] See p. 6.

[181] A. Bowie (1983) would draw on the myth of Orestes at the Anthesteria to support a difficult and ambiguous role for Dicaeopolis.

[182] [Xenophon] 2.9: θυσίας δὲ καὶ ἱερὰ καὶ ἑορτὰς καὶ τεμένη γνοὺς ὁ δῆμος ὅτι οὐχ οἷόν τέ ἐστιν ἑκάστωι τῶν πενήτων θύειν καὶ εὐωχεῖσθαι καὶ κτᾶσθαι ἱερὰ καὶ πόλιν οἰκεῖν καλὴν καὶ μεγάλην, ἐξεῦρεν ὅτωι τρόπωι ἔσται ταῦτα. Θύουσιν οὖν δημοσίαι μὲν ἡ πόλις ἱερεῖα πολλά· ἔστι δὲ ὁ δῆμος ὁ εὐωχούμενος καὶ διαλαγχάνων τὰ ἱερεῖα. ('As for sacrifices and shrines and feasts and holy precincts, the demos is aware that not each one of the poor is able to sacrifice and have a feast and set up shrines and live in a city which is beautiful and great, and has worked out how to make these things available. The city sacrifices many victims at public expense and it is the demos that enjoys the feast and gets the victims.') See also Chap. 8.2.

[183] See Chap. 2.2.

[184] Lines 815–17 ὧν καταχρεμψαμένη μέγα καὶ πλατὺ Μοῦσα θεὰ μετ' ἐμοῦ ξύμπαιζε τὴν

nibble (772). In other words, the spectators (*hoi theomenoi*) are encouraged to support a victory for Aristophanes at symposia outside the theatre: his drama will transcend the theatrical space into the sympotic.[185] The Muse will reject war, dance with her friend, and celeberate 'the weddings of gods, the feasts of men, and the festivities of the blessed'[186] (779–80). Comedy demonstrates that rituals of eating are related to the experience of watching, creating shared bonds of solidarity. The audience of *Peace* participates in the ritualized forms by which the women (as female personifications) are incorporated into the community: Peace through sacrifice (see 3.6.5 below), Autumn Fruit through marrige (see 3.6.4), and Showtime through the control of the members of the Council sitting in the audience (see 3.6.6).

3.6.4. Marriage

The female companions of Peace are Opora (Autumn Fruit) and Theoria (Showtime). The play concludes with a wedding between Trygaeus, 'Vintage Man', and Autumn Fruit, 'Harvest Woman'.[187] At 706–8 Hermes says, 'take Autumn Fruit here to be your wife, and then when you are living together in the country make for yourselves bunches of grapes'. Trygaeus makes sexual advances on her (709–11). The vines and fruits and other plants will flourish along with the human population of Attica and the whole of Greece. Peace is said to be 'rotting' (like a vintage wine)[188] at 554, as if she were not only the 'giver of grape clusters' (520) but an ageing wine, comparable perhaps to the treaties in *Acharnians*. Water and nuptial couch are prepared (843–4), and the wedding cakes of sesame and flat-cakes made ready.[189] The old bridegroom now feels dazzling and rejuvenated

---

ἑορτήν. ('Spit on them in a really big way, goddess Muse, and join with me in play at the feast.')

[185] Cf. the songs of Cratinus sung at symposia (*Knights* 529–30 and Chap. 5).

[186] θεῶν τε γάμους ἀνδρῶν τε δαῖτας καὶ θαλίας μακάρων—quoted from Stesichorus.

[187] *Opora*, according to Hesychius, signified the fruit of the vine in particular. Alexis wrote an *Opora* which, according to Athenaeus (10.443e, 13.567c), was named after a *hetaera*. Arnott (1996), 497–8 brings out the strong links of Opora in myth and art with the followers of Dionysus, who include Peace, Oenopion, Silenus, and Desire.

[188] σαπρᾶς.

[189] τὰ τῆς πυγῆς are declared καλά, and ὁ πλακοῦς πέπεπται, σησαμῆ ξυμπλάττεται, καὶ

(859–62).[190] When harvest comes, he will show how good a citizen he has been for all (912).

The wedding ceremonies again entail the exclusion and inclusion of certain groups. Those not invited to the feast are arms dealers, whose wares are converted into sympotic equipment and whose children must sing songs on the subject of feasting rather than fighting. Invited are all the people of Greece (except the politician Hyperbolos)—the chorus[191] and the audience, who, at the end of the play, are urged to eat flat-cakes such as those wandering around unclaimed in the rich, virtually 'automatic', agricultural production. In singing the wedding song, the chorus participate in the honouring of bride and groom whose sexual organs and sexual pleasure are expressed in agricultural imagery of figs and harvest. Trygaeus' treatment of his bride lacks the restraint expected at a wedding of Athenian citizens (709–11), but Autumn Fruit has no specified status and both bride and groom represent the fertility of plants as much as of humans. We might compare the third day of the Thesmophoria festival, Calligeneia, 'the day of fine birth', on which fertility in humans as well as in plants appears to have been at issue.[192] The role of Trygaeus is essentially active, restoring the wine harvest, while Opora is 'harvested' at her wedding (1337–8).

3.6.5. Sacrifice

The statue of Peace is to be incorporated into the comic community not with the ritual of *hidrusis* ('setting up a statue'), by which statues were normally dedicated, but by sacrifice.[193] The scholiast notes, 'when they wanted to dedicate alters or statues of the

---

τἄλλ' ἀπαξάπαντα· τοῦ πέους δὲ δεῖ (869–70). ('All of her bum is beautiful. The flat-cake is cooked, the sesame-cake kneaded, and everything else is there. All that's missing is a penis.')

[190] The chorus in *Acharnians*, who had earlier complained of the harsh treatment of the old (676–18), declare during their song on the achievements of Dicaeopolis (993) that they are not as old and decrepit as they appear.

[191] Peace is hailed as Queen of Choruses, Queen of Weddings (974): Peace presumably supports many forms of choral dancing, including the present chorus.

[192] On the Thesmophoria see below and Cole (1994), 202.

[193] The sacrifice in *Peace* is notable for the rejection of pots and the use of blood sacrifice for peace. Peace certainly received animal sacrifice in 334/3, 71 oxen in fact (Rosivach, 1994: 69), as she did from Cimon in the fifth century (Plutarch, *Cimon* 16). Stafford (1998) casts doubt on the evidence of Plutarch.

gods they performed a preliminary rite by boiling pulses; they gave thanks to the dedicates for the first diet'.[194] This notional memory of the 'first diet', the boiling of pulses before the development of cereals in agriculture, such as was enacted at the Anthesteria and Pyanopsia,[195] is rejected in favour of the Promethean sacrifice. Peace is declared too important to be dedicated with boiled pulses: only blood sacrifice will be adequate for the goddess who has brought back agriculture and the full functioning of the poleis of Greece, perhaps because blood-sacrifice above all other sacrifice expresses Greek culture in relation to agriculture and includes all members of the polis.[196] Trygaeus and his slave ritually incorporate the chorus by dousing them in lustral water (970–2), and the audience by sprinkling them with barley grains (962–5). The audience is later invited to share in the vital organs (1115). Once again, those included in the comic polis differ from those in the polis of Athens: Trygaeus, the bringer of wine, the 'good man for all citizens'[197] and 'saviour for all men',[198] the man 'who has endured much and saved the holy city',[199] is warned to avoid the dreadful musician Chaeris who scrounges food though not invited.[200] Stilbides the diviner is made redundant, and the professional priest Hierocles is driven away. These last two are unwelcome professionals, *alazones*, opponents of peace, opponents, that is, of the good things provided for the ordinary folk by the comic protagonist. Hierocles will be driven from his place at the civic hearth and fed by the city no more.[201] On stage he is drawn by the smell of the sacrificial fat,

---

[194] ὁπότε μέλλοιεν βωμοὺς καθιδρύειν ἢ ἀγάλματα θεῶν, ἕψοντες ὄσπρια ἀπήρχοντο τούτων, τοῖς ἀφιδρυμένοις χαριστήρια ἀπονέμοντες τῆς πρώτης διαίτης, ὡς οὗτος εἶπεν ἐν Δαναΐσι·
μαρτύρομαι δὲ Ζηνὸς ἑρκείου χύτρας,
μεθ' ὧν ὁ βωμὸς οὗτος ἱδρύθη ποτέ.
(Aristophanes fr. 256, 'I call as witness the pots of Zeus of the Courtyard with which this altar was dedicated.') Our passage resembles *Wealth* 1197, where Plutus is to be installed with an offering of pots. In both passages Aristophanes makes jokes at the expense of *hidrusis* ('setting up a statue') and animal sacrifice, none though to challenge the ritual itself.

[195] Burkert (1985), 240.   [196] Detienne and Vernant (1989), 1–86.

[197] χρηστὸς ἀνὴρ πολίταις . . . ἅπασιν (909–10)—a feature that will only be known in full, he says, 'when you harvest the grapes'(ὅταν τρυγᾶτ' 912).

[198] σωτήρ . . . ἅπασιν ἀνθρώποις—a claim that will be all the stronger, he says, 'when you drink off a great cup of new wine' (916 ἐπειδὰν ἐκπίῃς οἴνου νέου λεπαστήν).

[199] πόλλ' ἀνατλὰς ἔσωσε τὴν ἱερὰν πόλιν (1035–6).   [200] 950–5 ἄκλητος.

[201] On the prytaneion see Chap. 4.

a scavenger resembling the kite that he himself refers to (1099–100),[202] and tries (1118–20) to seize the vital organs of the sheep,[203] only to be beaten for being 'a glutton and an imposter'.[204] In this scene Aristophanes runs the quintessential comic undesirables of uninvited parasite, glutton, and imposter out of the most important ritual of the polis.

The comic protagonist performs part of the task of the *mageiros*,[205] and for the comic configuration of the polis reorganizes those who are to be included in or excluded from the ritual: out go the officials of the polis, in are brought chorus, audience, and other favoured groups. The protagonist as quasi-*mageiros* and organizer of participants at the feast is a feature of other plays. Sacrifice in *Knights* is jointly controlled by Demos (who controls the sacrifice) and the Black-Pudding-Seller (the purveyor of sacrificial meat); together they drive out Cleon/Paphlagon and replace him with the Black-Pudding-Seller. In *Birds* sacrifice is reorganized so that birds as well as gods receive the smoke of sacrifice and the priest is no longer a participant. An unspeaking *mageiros* assists Peistetaerus, who, now a god, celebrates his own sacred wedding. Dicaeopolis in *Acharnians*, as soon as he makes his peace, welcomes the Dionysia and celebrates the Rural Dionysia with a sacrifice. Later, at the Anthesteria, he prepares food for the festival, and while the preparation is not a sacrifice, Dicaeopolis, who is in charge of cooking for a meal at the festival (1085), prepares 'like a *mageiros*, with cleverness, in a dining fashion' (1016–17) and appears to exclude the chorus (1037–46). The problem for the chorus, however, is one of words: the cook's lists are too exciting to bear. The words anticipate the interminable speeches of the *mageiroi* of Middle and New Comedy, men who have the skills for sacrifice and catering for banquets, but no longer control the sacrificial space, nor indeed the comedy.[206]

The female part of the population are not included in the sacrifice of *Peace*, perhaps because they may not have been part of

---

[202] On the kite at sacrifice see Dunbar on *Birds* 892 and 1624.

[203] σπλάγχνα ἁρπάζεσθαι.   [204] ὅτι τένθης εἶ σὺ κἀλαζὼν ἀνὴρ.

[205] At 1017–18 he is told to sacrifice the sheep 'like a *mageiros*'.

[206] See Scodel (1993), and Chap. 8 on Giannini (1960), Dohm (1964), and Nesselrath (1990).

the comic audience.[207] Through a pun on the word *krithe*, 'barley', the women of the city will not be sprinkled with sacrificial barley grains but will enjoy intercourse with the penis, *krithe*, of their men (962–7). The omission of women from the sacrifice of the sheep for Peace is notable, given the close association between women and peace elsewhere in Old Comedy. Women occupy a special place in *Peace*; they have no speaking-parts and play a passive role, representing the three personifications Autumn Fruit, Festival, and Peace. At the same time, those personifications represent all that is most precious to the comic world, the very features of culture that must be incorporated into it.

3.6.6. Male Control of the Hetaera

If Opora as a personification was treated as the passive recipient of the desires of the protagonist, her sister personification Theoria (Showtime) is the object of the desires of characters and audience.[208] Theoria represents not only the running of the festival but also having a good time, particularly in the relaxing of male inhibitions.[209] The comic characters illustrate what this means on the body of Theoria. Restoration of the Isthmian Festival is represented by a slave as an opportunity for finding a 'tent for my penis' (879–80),[210] while he remembers the Brauronia as an occasion for drunkenness and sex with Theoria (874–6).[211] The scholiast on line 876 writes, 'in Brauron, one of the Attic demes, there were many prostitutes. The Dionysia was celebrated there, and in each deme, at which festival they got drunk. When drunk, they picked up many prostitutes . . . Every four years they attended the festival of the Dionysia.' Some have thought that the

---

[207] See Pickard-Cambridge (1988), 263–5. The best survey of this vexed question is Goldhill (1994). Csapo and Slater (1995), 286–7 believe that the audience did include women. Alexis, *Gunaikokratia* fr. 42 refers to women watching from the block of seats at the back, but it is not known whether this reflects actual practice or comic invention: see Arnott (1996).

[208] Many people have erections at the prospect of both women (728).

[209] On the sexual and excremental themes of *Peace* see Henderson (1991), 62–6.

[210] We might compare the tents put up by women at the Thesmophoria and Aristophanes' play *Women Setting Up Festival Tents*.

[211] ἢν ἡμεῖς ποτε ἐπαίομεν Βραυρωνάδε ὑποπεπωκότες. ('Whom we once banged when we were drunk on the way to Brauron'.)

scholiast has invented a Dionysia at Brauron,[212] in order to
account for the slave's remark. The Brauronia was a four-yearly
festival, with a procession from Brauron to Athens;[213] if the slave
refers to this festival, then he has incongruously attached to a festival for the incorporation of young women into adulthood the
general characteristics of 'festivity', particularly Dionysiac festival, sexual licence, and drinking. If the scholiast is right about a
four-yearly Dionysia or at least the Rural Dionysia at Brauron
with many prostitutes, then we might perhaps compare the Tau-
ropolia at Halae Araphenides, a festival, like Brauron, of Artemis,
at which sexual encounters might take place. Such an encounter
is the occasion of the problematic pregnancy in Menander, *The
Arbitration*.[214] Sexual encounters at Halae may have taken place
as an annex to the main festival. Whatever the festival at Brauron
referred to by the slave, the aggressive sexual treatment offered to
Theoria as representing the prostitutes there is similar to the fate
of the Thracian slave girls in the hymn to Phales at *Acharnians*
271–6 and the second parabasis of *Peace* (1138–9).

Trygaeus and the slave also attend to eating rituals with Theoria. She is placed among the *theomenoi*, the watching audience
(882): actors and spectators, characters and watchers are brought
together into a group, as they will be when they share the vital
organs of the sheep in the sacrificial ritual (1115). The sacrifice is
a vital element in establishing this community of characters and
audience, for when Peace first appeared she refused to speak to
the audience because she was angry with them for their unpeace-
ful politics.[215] Theoria is given to the boule (Council) and prytaneis (872, 878, 887, 905–6). There is some evidence, in addition
to this passage, that the members of the boule sat together in the

---

[212] See Deubner (1932), 138; Rhodes on [Aristotle] *Athenaion Politeia* 54.7. I
am grateful to Emma Stafford for drawing my attention to a frieze on a round
altar that was found at Brauron and dates to 410–400 BC. On the altar are
depicted Dionysus and Peace, among others. See further Stafford (1998),
201–2; E. Simon, *LIMC* III 1 704. The frieze supports some presence of
Dionysus in cult at Brauron.

[213] For the presentation of the festival at Brauron in comedy see Henderson
(1987) on *Lysistrata* 645.

[214] Another such encounter is implied at Menander, *Ghost* 97–8.

[215] 658–9 She also did not speak because she was a statue! Censure of the audience is found outside the parabasis (where it is normally to be found) probably
because the play is engaging with forms of watching and festive participation.

theatre.[216] Why is the boule singled out to receive Theoria? Hardly to attack them as powerful politicians, as if they were generals like Cleon or orators like Ariphrades (883). Rather, they are responsible for the affairs of the polis represented by Theoria, that is, the sending of religious missions to festivals such as the Isthmian Games, the supervising of festivals such as the Brauronia in Attica, and the staging of the dramatic festivals in Athens. While [Aristotle], *Constitution of Athens* makes it clear that the archon was responsible, with *epimeletai*, for the City Dionysia (56.4),[217] and ten *hieropoioi* selected by lot were responsible for such festivals as those held at Delos, Brauron, and Eleusis (54.7), the boule still had responsibilities in these areas. Rhodes observes (on 54.6), from inscriptional evidence, that there were many boards of *hieropoioi* in Athens, often appointed from the boule. In the *Constitution of Athens* religious delegations and provision for theatrical production are cited in proximity (56.3). In the theatre, the boule may have had some responsibilities for the selection of judges.[218]

Just as Autumn Fruit, given in marriage to Vintage Man, represents the restoration of human and plant fertility after war, so Theoria, given to the boule, represents the restoration of the city to full religious contact with its own festivals, both within the gates and in the hinterland—such as the Brauronia—and with festivals of other poleis, whether at pan-Greek gatherings such as the Isthmia or within formerly hostile states such as Sparta.[219] Theoria may also restore Athenian drama to its full glory, though this is less clear. I have noted above that tragedy had been performed in war anyway, but that the comic polis presents the matter differently. The union between Trygaeus and Autumn Fruit was celebrated with much consumption of food, and anticipated consumption of the bride by bridegroom and chorus. Theoria too is to be consumed. The boule, who (if Winkler is right) were sitting in the central wedge of the theatre and therefore the most prominent *theomenoi* (those watching), are asked to observe how

---

[216] Dunbar (1995) on *Birds* 794, 'the *bouleutikon*', discusses whether this part of the theatre was the most easily visible to all. See also Pickard-Cambridge (1988), 269–70; Winkler (1990), 38.

[217] The *archon basileus* was responsible for the Lenaea (57.1).

[218] Pickard-Cambridge (1968), 96–7.

[219] Compare the provisions of the Peace of Nicias cited above.

many blessings[220] Trygaeus is giving them (888) when he presents to them Theoria, 'the act of watching'. He says (889–91) the result will be that if 'you lift her legs in the air you can then celebrate an *anarrhusis*. Look at her oven here.'[221] Here are combined ideas of agricultural plenty (*agatha*), of sexual fulfilment for the *bouleutae* in the context of a day of sacrifice at the Apaturia,[222] and of the woman's sexual organs as an oven. The Apaturia was a festival that cemented communal identity, for its main purpose was to incorporate new members—specifically, young boys or brides— into the phratry or clan. Community and well-being were expressed in sacrifice; in *Peace* that idea is transferred to male enjoyment of sexual intercourse.[223] The point had been made ear- lier (439–42), when the chorus had said that part of 'living life at peace' was 'having a *hetaera* and poking her coals', and Dionysus was asked to make sure warriors had none of this but were kept at the front. 'Poking her coals' belongs to the same sacrificial metaphor of men cooking sexually with women of low status under the patronage of Dionysus. The association of intercourse with sacrifice and cooking in a context of festival is to be found also at *Acharnians* 729–835. The starving Megarian pretends his daughters are pigs, punning on the term *choiros*, 'young pig' or 'vulva', and offers them both as pigs for sacrifice and women for sex. They are described as pigs for sacrifice at the Mysteries at 747 and 764. At 795–6 their flesh is succulent when speared—on a spit or by a penis. These passages from *Acharnians* and *Peace* clearly present the woman's body for male consumption.

In *Peace* sacrifice (890), the cooking of meat in an oven (891), the accommodating of trivets[224] under the oven (893), the making of a meat-based soup, and the eating of boiled black-pudding and meat[225] all express order in various respects (man's domination

---

[220] ἀγαθά.

[221] ὥστ᾿ εὐθέως ἄραντας ὑμᾶς τὼ σκέλει ταύτης μετεώρω κᾆτ᾿ ἀγαγεῖν ἀνάρρυσιν. τουτὶ δ᾿ ὁρᾶτε τοὐπτάνιον. *Anarrhusis* was the name for the second day of the Apaturia fes- tival. The term *optanion* may signify either her 'oven' or her 'kitchen'.

[222] Henderson (1991), 173, against Sommerstein (1985).

[223] For sacrifice and cooking as a metaphor for intercourse see Henderson (1991), 177–8.

[224] λάσανα. The term also means 'chamber-pots'.

[225] ζωμός (soup) 716, 885; black-pudding and meat 717. Arnott (1996) on Alexis fr. 145.8 claims that *zomos* (soup) was thick and meatless. His discussion includes the famous black soup of Sparta and soup produced by gypsies in

over the animal world, his joining in as one of the community) within the reassurance and well-being of festivity represented by the woman. If transferred to heterosexual intercourse, then the order, the domination, and the sense of male community is over a woman. As meat is desirable and an object of pleasure, so is a non-citizen woman. At the symbolic level, Theoria represents the sacrificial meats of festivals Athenian, Attic, and beyond, and the sense of well-being in the populace. Festivity expresses that well-being. Drama festivals were part of this—many cattle, for example, were slaughtered at the City Dionysia of 334/3,[226] and a number at the Lenaea of that year.[227] The audience then expected to eat at the festival, possibly to drink, as well as to watch drama. In addition, the chorus might be fed—or not fed[228]—by the choregos.[229]

Theoria expresses order in a different form at *Peace* 894–908: she is to enter into a series of sporting activities with alternative sexual connotations. The images from sport probably allude once more to the large Panhellenic gatherings such as the Isthmia (where the slave hoped to house his penis, 879–80)[230] or Olympic Games, reflecting their importance just as above we saw the Peace of Nicias guaranteeing peace for Athens and Sparta at the major athletic games.

The well-being of males enjoying the prospect of consuming Theoria in *Peace* is aggressively expressed. Theoria herself has no voice,[231] though this is partly accounted for in her personifying an abstract team.[232] The interests of women in festivals are

Lancashire in the 1940s. While some *zomos* may have been meatless, I believe he goes too far in excluding meat altogether. Aristotle refers to thick *zomoi* made from animals ('fatty animals such as horse and pig' at *History of Animals* 520a8–10 and *zomoi* that are like blood at *Parts of Animals* 651a28–9), and Pollux (6.57) says that the term *haimatia* was applied to Spartan *zomos*, which suggests it was thickened with blood (*haima*).

[226] 81, e.g. at the City Dionysia in 334/3 (figure from Rosivach (1994), 70). See also Schmitt-Pantel (1992), 121–43, and esp. 130–1, and Pickard-Cambridge (1968), 61–3.

[227] 34 in Rosivach (1994).   [228] *Acharnians* 1150–61: cited above, p. 140.

[229] Scholiast on *Clouds* 339; Pickard-Cambridge (1968), 89.

[230] Aeschylus wrote a satyr play entitled *Theoroi or Isthmiastae* (*The Watching Audience or Isthmian Spectators*). At Plato fr. 46.10 Heracles refers to the Isthmian Games in a sexual context.

[231] Zweig (1990).   [232] On the implications see Warner (1985).

not neglected in other plays. *Thesmophoriazusae* takes place on the second day of the Thesmophoria, the day of fasting (947–52), negativity, and suspicion of men.[233] Despite the inauspicious day, the women include prayers to many gods for the well-being of themselves and Athens (295–371, 953–1000, 1136–59), addressing in particular Demeter and Persephone and the lesser fertility gods linked with them, and also Athena who is asked to come with 'peace which is the friend of festivity' (1147). The day of sacrifice at the Thesmophoria, the third day, Calligeneia, is not part of the play, though the goddess Calligeneia is mentioned among other fertility gods at 298; she also spoke the prologue of *Thesmophoriazusae b* of Aristophanes.[234] The comic poets might in addition adapt or invent festivals where consumption and sexuality are brought together. Such appears to be the case in Plato, *Phaon* fr. 188, unless Courotrophos (the Nurse who is speaking) was a god or goddess in the festival of Adonis. The fragment develops the theme of female consumption of the male in a religious context, though animal sacrifice is largely replaced with other foods. Courotrophos[235] says:

Well now, ladies, [. . .] I've been praying for some time that your madness be changed into—wine. As the proverb goes, when you're in the wine shop[236] you have no sense at all. If you want to see Phaon, you must make many preliminary sacrifices first, as follows. The first sacrifice to me, Courotrophos, should be an uncastrated flat-cake, a pregnant meal-cake, sixteen whole thrushes covered in honey, and twelve moon-shaped hare pies. [. . .][237] Listen, now. Three half-measures of tassel hyacinths to Orthannes, to Conisalus and the two attendants[238] a plate of myrtles plucked by hand—for the gods dislike the smell of the lamp.[239] [. . .] to the Dogs and the Hunters. A drachma for Lordon, three obols for Cubdasus, for the hero Celes a hide and an offering of flour, oil, and wine. There are the expenses. If you pay then you can go in. If not, then you can have a vain attempt at a fuck.[240]

---

[233] Burkert (1985); Bowie (1993).

[234] According to the scholiast of *Thesmophoniazusae* 298.

[235] An aspect of Aphrodite?   [236] Reading ἐν τῶι καπήλου (Casaubon).

[237] The text is corrupt.   [238] Testicles.

[239] The myrtle is slang for the vulva. Plucking and singeing refer to pubic hair.

[240] For the obscene language see the commentary in Kassel–Austin (1989) and *Ecclesiazusae* 1–18, which lists intimate preparation of the body prior to discussion of the Scria festival.

3.6.7. A Blessing Too Far?

Comedy sought the blessings of the gods to support Attic agriculture. With the gods' support, near-utopian results could be achieved. We saw above that the Horae or Seasons were numbered among the minor gods in the entourage of Dionysus. Three comedies were written with the title *Horae*, by Aristophanes, Cratinus, and Anaxilas. Little survives except fr. 581 of Aristophanes, which might have portrayed how agricultural fertility could be too successful. The pattern of life set by the Seasons for the agricultural year and major festivals seems to have been modified by the arrival of a new god or gods, probably Sabazius (fr. 578). Fr. 581 offers a striking exchange:

A:[241] You will see in the middle of winter cucumbers,[242] bunches of grapes, the fruits of summer, garlands of violets.

B: Yes and blinding dust as well, I reckon.

A: And the same man sells thrushes, pears, honeycombs, olives, beestings, gut-puddings, swallows [or dried figs], cicadas, embryos. There is a chance to see baskets of figs and myrtle berries in snowy profusion.[243]

B: Then they sow gourds alongside turnips, so that no one knows where in the yearly cycle they are.

A: Well is it not the greatest good fortune to get whatever you like throughout the year?

B: It is the greatest misfortune. If there was not the opportunity, there would not be the demand nor the expenditure. My way would be to offer them for a short time and then remove them.

A: In fact I do that for other cities, but not for Athens. These facilities are provided for them because they honour the gods.

B: A fine benefit then for paying you honour!

A: How do you mean?

B: You have made their city Egypt, not Athens.

---

[241] The speakers are difficult to identify (see Kassel–Austin). Speaker A may be Athena. Speaker B may be Sabazius. Some have thought that the chorus intervenes in these exchanges also. I have followed Kassel–Austin in marking only two speakers.

[242] Theophrastus, *Characters* 14 describes a man who chides his slave for not buying cucumbers in winter.

[243] νειφομένους appears to be a pun indicating both the snow of winter and profusion. The verb is cleverly used since winter snow implies the reverse of agricultural growth: cf. *Acharnians* 1075 and 1141, where Lamachus is dispatched to wintry campaigning while Dicaeopolis enjoys the Anthesteria and the accompanying symposium.

Is excessive agricultural production unnatural and foreign, akin to the seasons of the Nile? This is quite different from the tone of *Peace* and *Acharnians*, where the provision of good things, though not necessarily their distribution, is unproblematic. The extraordinary fertility and unseasonable produce here set out, possibly by Athena, or by Sabazius or one of the foreign gods mentioned by Cicero,[244] appears, at least in one speaker's view, to be inappropriate to Attica. The food products in this fragment are both on sale (πωλεῖ) and are locally grown (ἀροῦσιν): the conflation of praises of agriculture and the breadth of foods for sale at market resemble *Acharnians* 719–976 and *Peace* 999–1015. Objections appear to be based on the inflationary influence of 'demand' and 'expenditure' (which might imply the encouragement of luxury) and on the transformation of Attica with its self-image of hard work and spare living into Egypt. Normally Athens imported Egyptian goods: here she appears to have taken on Egyptian soil and climate also. There is always the potential, in declarations on plenty, that a speaker may prefer a leaner and more austere option, hence claims for the simplicity of Athenian cooking in the fourth century. The passage most resembles one of the utopian passages in style. Written in iambic tetrameters, it is part of a debate, not a joyful celebration at the end of a play. Among the issues in the debate are probably the nature of the anonymous god,[245] the desirability of observing seasonal changes, and the quality or otherwise of Athenian agriculture. The new god may have threatened the moderating influence of the Seasons, to whom, according to Philochorus, victims were boiled rather than roasted in order to keep excessive heat away from the crops.[246] Kassel and Austin on fr. 581 collect passages both celebrating the unusual fertility of Athens—among them the sober Xenophon in idealizing mode[247]—and praising famous areas of fertility abroad.[248]

---

[244] *Laws* 2.37. He refers to this passage but does not quote it.

[245] See Parker (1996), 159–62 on Sabazius. He mentions similar gods, Courotrophos and the Priapic figure of Orthannes, in Plato, *Phaon*. These are new gods in Athens, with whom *Horae* shares something.

[246] *FGrH* 328 F 173 = Athenaeus 14.656a.

[247] Xenophon, *Poroi* 1.3, οὐκοῦν τὸ μὲν τὰς ὥρας ἐνθάδε πραοτάτας εἶναι καὶ αὐτὰ τὰ γιγνόμενα μαρτυρεῖ· ἃ γοῦν πολλαχοῦ οὐδὲ βλαστάνειν δύναιτ' ἄν, ἐνθάδε καρποφορεῖ. ὥσπερ δὲ ἡ γῆ, οὕτω καὶ ἡ περὶ τὴν χώραν θάλαττα παμφορωτάτη ἐστί. καὶ μὴν ὅσαπερ οἱ θεοὶ ἐν ταῖς ὥραις

To conclude, the rituals of festival have a particular importance for comedy. In the first place, comedy often presents festival in terms of foods or wine consumed, whether Dionysia, Thesmophoria, Panathenaia, or Diasia. Thus the comic Anthesteria of *Acharnians* has the shared *deipnon* uniquely among ancient sources. This reflects comedy's interest in the material and consumable items discussed in Chapter 1. Then the comic polis does not directly represent the 'real' polis: in the comic version, festival is associated with agriculture and the fertility of humans and plants more closely than in the real polis. War and festival are separated in Old Comedy in a way they were not in the Archidamian War: the warrior in the city was not excluded from festivity as is Lamachus in *Acharnians*. In this respect comedy may be thought in a limited way to share something with carnival: it topples, or rather starves, the powerful and mounts a limited ideological attack on the political order of the democracy. The demos in comedy is able to retrieve its power from the political leaders it had elected. Festivity is a part of comedy: this is the dramatic form which reflects the communal life of the polis. Commensality binds the city together and expresses the civic sense of celebration based on adequate, if not bountiful, resources, based above all on sacrifice. The civic dimension has such an important part to play in comedy that the gods Dionysus, Demeter, and their associates are brought up in support. Comedy plays with other forms of provision supplied by the gods, utopia and a land flowing with the riches of the Nile, but it is agricultural provision that is at the centre, agriculture backed up by the Promethean system of sacrifice based on the cooking of meat. Vegetable offerings retreat before the cooking of meat; and sexual intercourse, even between partners who personify the world of plants, is presented as a further form of festive sacrifice. Dionysus the provider of streams of milk and honey, the god of

ἀγαθὰ παρέχουσι, καὶ ταῦτα πάντα ἐνταῦθα πρωιαίτατα μὲν ἄρχεται, ὀψιαίτατα δὲ λήγει. ('The very products testify to the fact that the seasons are gentle here. At least things that could not grow in many places here bear fruit. Like the land, the sea which surrounds it is also very productive. Indeed, all the good things that the gods provide in their season here come on very early and die back very late.')

[248] Josephus, *Jewish War* 3.518: Genezareth (a fertile plateau near Galilee) is said to produce wine and figs over ten months and other fruits over twelve. Kassel–Austin (1984) also compare Virgil *Georgics* 2.149.

nature in a wilder form, belongs not to comedy but to the sister genre of tragedy, in which other wild aspects such as maenadism and the destruction of the household are portrayed. While Henrichs (1990) rightly contends that in comparison with the tragic Dionysus his comic manifestation is closer to the jolly Bacchus of Hellenistic and Roman literature, comedy nevertheless stands some way from that untroubled world in placing the god in the rituals of festival and symposium which cemented the social coherence of the polis. The symposium does in fact share much with comedy.[249] There is common ground in the shared komos which might follow both symposium and festival. Plays entitled *Comastae* were written by Epicharmus, Phrynichus, Ameipsias, and Eubulides (though these may reflect the myth of Hephaistos, as, apparently, did the version of Epicharmus). The chorus in New Comedy is normally a komos. Comedy goes further beyond that shared ground and incorporates so many sympotic details with approval that they cannot for the most part be seen as an element of upper-class life alien to the protagonist, as portrayed in *Wasps*.

Drinking rituals are the subject of Chapter 5. First I turn to the agora or market-place of Athens, the urban territory of comedy which, although problematic in comic discourse, is not dismissed as rapidly as might be supposed from the enthusiastic endorsement of agriculture just discussed. Comedy creates a special agora of its own, just as it creates its own version of agricultural production—by establishing a tension between the commercial sector of the market-place and the ancient institutions also housed there.

---

[249] Here I contest the views of Ian Ruffell, who believes that the democratic comic festival is structurally opposed to the oligarchic symposium: see further Chap. 5.

4
The Comic Agora

4.1. DIONYSUS *NAUKLEROS*

The previous chapter set out how the comic countryside, with the support of Demeter and Dionysus and minor gods associated with them such as the Horae, provided agricultural wealth and other good things for the city-state. In both *Acharnians* and *Peace* it was envisaged that these agricultural goods would be traded in markets. One comic passage imagines Dionysus himself bringing similar good things from outside Athens, by sea: Hermippus describes, in fr. 63 of his *Basket-Bearers*,[1] Dionysus as a merchant who brings cargoes of foreign products to Athens:[2]

[1] The basket-bearers of the chorus appear to be porters who carry goods to market, specifically goods from ships or from the Peiraeus. David Braund (private communication) suggests to me that this must have been a major source of employment at Athens: cf. Brunt (1980), 92 on Rome and Ostia. Baskets large and small, for trading and shopping at market, are material objects often mentioned in comedy: see e.g. Aristophanes *Horae* fr. 581.5 (baskets of figs—cf. Alexis fr. 133.3); *Merchant Ships* fr. 427; *Triphales* fr. 557 (three kinds, for *opsa*); Epicharmus fr. 113 (three kinds); Pherecrates, *Corianno* fr. 83. The last two mention *koikes*, which, according to Hesychius, were vessels woven from leaves of trees, or *phormoi*, the containers used here.

[2]

ἔσπετε νῦν μοι, Μοῦσαι 'Ολύμπια δώματ' ἔχουσαι,
ἐξ οὗ ναυκληρεῖ Διόνυσος ἐπ' οἴνοπα πόντον,
ὅσσ' ἀγάθ' ἀνθρώποις δεῦρ' ἤγαγε νηὶ μελαίνηι.
ἐκ μὲν Κυρήνης καυλὸν καὶ δέρμα βόειον,
ἐκ δ' 'Ελλησπόντου σκόμβρους καὶ πάντα ταρίχη,
ἐκ δ' αὖ Θετταλίας χόνδρον καὶ πλευρὰ βόεια·
καὶ παρὰ Σιτάλκου ψώραν Λακεδαιμονίοισι,
καὶ παρὰ Περδίκκου ψεύδη ναυσὶν πάνυ πολλαῖς.
αἱ δὲ Συράκουσαι σῦς καὶ τυρὸν παρέχουσαι
.   .   .   .
καὶ Κερκυραίους ὁ Ποσειδῶν ἐξολέσειε
ναυσὶν ἐπὶ γλαφυραῖς, ὁτιὴ δίχα θυμὸν ἔχουσι.
ταῦτα μὲν ἐντεῦθεν· ἐκ δ' Αἰγύπτου τὰ κρεμαστὰ
ἱστία καὶ βίβλους, ἀπὸ δ' αὖ Συρίας λιβανωτόν.

Tell me now, Muses who live in houses on Olympus, of the good things that Dionysus brought here for men in his black ship from the time when he ran his merchant ship over the wine-faced sea. From Cyrene he brought silphium stalks and ox-hides, from the Hellespont mackerel and all sorts of salt fish, again, from Thessaly crushed wheat and barley[3] and ox ribs. From Sitalces an itchy rash for the Spartans and from Perdiccas falsehoods in a great number of ships. Syracuse supplies pigs and cheese [. . .] and may Poseidon destroy the Corcyreans in their hollow ships because they are divided in their hearts. These are the goods from these places. From Egypt he brought rigged sails and papyrus, from Syria incense. Fair Crete provides cypress-wood for the gods, Libya much ivory for sale, and Rhodes dried grapes and dried figs which bring sweet dreams. From Euboea he brought pears and fat apples, slaves from Phrygia and mercenaries from Arcadia. Pagasae furnishes slaves and branded slaves, the Paphlagonians the acorns of Zeus and shining almonds. These are the adornments of the feast. Phoenicia[4] sends the fruit of the date-palm and finest flour (*semidalis*),[5] Carthage rugs and multicoloured cushions.[6]

Hermippus appears to draw on the myth of Dionysus the travelling god,[7] a myth which may have been enacted in cult with the

> ἡ δὲ καλὴ Κρήτη κυπάριττον τοῖσι θεοῖσιν,
> ἡ Λιβύη δ' ἐλέφαντα πολὺν παρέχει κατὰ πρᾶσιν,
> ἡ Ῥόδος ἀσταφίδας τε καὶ ἰσχάδας ἡδυονείρους.
> αὐτὰρ ἀπ' Εὐβοίας ἀπίους καὶ ἴφια μῆλα,
> ἀνδράποδ' ἐκ Φρυγίας, ἀπὸ δ' Ἀρκαδίας ἐπικούρους.
> αἱ Παγασαὶ δούλους καὶ στιγματίας παρέχουσι.
> τὰς δὲ Διὸς βαλάνους καὶ ἀμύγδαλα σιγαλόεντα
> Παφλαγόνες παρέχουσι· τὰ γὰρ τ' ἀναθήματα δαιτός.
> †Φοινίκη δ' αὖ† καρπὸν φοίνικος καὶ σεμίδαλιν,
> Καρχηδὼν δάπιδας καὶ ποικίλα προσκεφάλαια.

[3] Χόνδρος was coarsely ground cereal (or 'groats': see Arnott (1996) on Alexis, *Ponera* fr. 196). Thessalian *chondros* was highly regarded, as Arnott notes. Wheat and beef were imported from the rich plain of Thessaly, on which see Chap. 2. Cf. Antiphanes, *Anteia* fr. 36, in which three kinds of *chondros* are on sale in baskets: 'A: Whatever is in the baskets, my friend? B: In three of them, best Megarian *chondros*. A: But don't they say that Thessalian is good? B: [. . .] from Phoenicia [. . .] best-grade flour (*semidalis*), sifted down very finely?'

[4] The text is uncertain.

[5] On *semidalis* in comedy see Arnott (1996) on Alexis fr. 102.4.

[6] For a bibliography of this fragment see Kassel–Austin (1986) and Gilula (forthcoming).

[7] See Euripides, *Bacchae* 1–22; Daraki (1985), 19–44, and esp. 31–4; and the cup painted by Exekias (Munich 2044) portraying Dionysus on a ship whose mast has become a vine and whose crew of pirates have been changed into dolphins.

ship-cart as his Anthesteria festival.[8] That festival falls at the opening of the sailing season when trade resumes after the winter. The role of Dionysus as a trading sea-captain seems to be a novel comic proposal, combining his noted travels by sea with an interest in trade, of which other gods such as Hermes Agoraios or Zeus Agoraios are more common patrons. Dionysus brings goods from all corners of the Mediterranean, thereby representing Athens' influence in trade with all these areas, some of whose inhabitants—such as the Corcyreans—allegedly do not deserve the god's or his city's attention. Hermippus' representation of the god of comedy as a sea-captain can be compared with Aristophanes' lost play *Dionysus Shipwrecked* and many other comic presentations of Dionysus.[9] The form of this fragment is as unusual as its content. While lists are common in comedy, this example is written in hexameters—reminiscent of the catalogue of ships in *Iliad* 2. Hexameters, though rare in the surviving plays of Aristophanes, are found in the fragments of Old Comedy and in New Comedy;[10] Hermippus may have had a particular interest in hexameter composition since he was also a composer of hexameters in the genre of parody.[11] Hexameter parodies of the late fifth and fourth centuries often chose food and eating as their subject-matter and adapted Homeric phrases as Hermippus has done here.[12] In his presentation of Dionysus as a merchant and in his choice of metre, Hermippus has brought trade into comic discourse in a strikingly new form.

Certain goods are said by Hermippus to derive from specific areas; the distribution of these products of various cities, many of

---

[8] Pickard-Cambridge (1968), 8 and 12 reviews the evidence on the *katagogia* of Dionysus (with bibliography). Burkert (1983) would put the ship-cart at the later festival of the Dionysia.

[9] Which are reviewed in Chap. 5.

[10] See Menander, *Theophoroumene* 36–41, ?50, 52, 56 (Arnott).

[11] See Chap. 7. It is unclear whether Polemon (cited by Athenaeus at 15.699a) means to say that Hermippus and Cratinus composed 'parodies' as well as comedies, and quite what he meant by the term. When he speaks of Hermippus, Cratinus, and Epicharmus, has he in mind such passages as fr. 63? *Phormophoroi* was certainly a comedy, for Athenaeus explicitly contrasts the play with the *Iamboi* of Hermippus at 15.700d. The non-dramatic iambic and tetrameter fragments of Hermippus are edited in West (1972), 67–9.

[12] 'Fat apples' (for the Homeric 'fat sheep'), 'these are the adornments of the feast'. Many more adaptations are noted by Kassel–Austin.

them foods, is celebrated also in long lists in Middle Comedy. A number of these are quoted with Hermippus fr. 63 by Athenaeus at 1.27d–28d: Antiphanes fr. 233,[13] 'from Elis a cook,[14] from Argos a stewing-pot, wine from Phlius, covers from Corinth, fish from Sicyon, pipe-girls from Aegion, cheese from Sicily [. . .], myrrh from Athens, eels from Boeotia'; Eubulus, *Glaucus* fr. 18, 'and mustard and scammony juice from Cyprus, and pepperwort from Miletus and onion from Samothrace and silphium and silphium stalk from Carthage and thyme from Hymettus and marjoram from Tenedos', and fr. 130, 'pots from Cnidus, pans from Sicily, vats from Megara'. The addition of the provenance of items is a further refinement of the comic list.[15] Concern with such provenances is not confined to comedy, for Athenaeus adds Pindar fr. 126 Sn–M and Critias fr. B2 West. Provenance is what concerns Athenaeus in Hermippus fr. 63 and the other fragments, which are quoted in the middle of a description of wines (1.25f–2.47a). A later quotation, indeed, from Amphis (fr. 40), is quoted for its wine: 'oil in Thurii, in Gela lentils, Icarian wine and Cimolian dried figs.' It is worth noting here that many of the comic fragments that Athenaeus cites in his survey of wines (including Hermippus fr. 77, which is also written in hexameters) also list provenances. It appears that when the comic poets were working lists into their texts, two frequent contexts were considered to be particularly suitable, namely the foods to be used by the boastful cook (Eubulus fr. 18 is probably an example) and the wines and paraphernalia of the symposium.[16] But in Hermippus fr. 63 there is a notable absence of wine, given that the cargo is brought by the god of wine himself.[17] The goods comprise many items to be found at the *deipnon*/symposium, which are enumerated in the order followed in a Greek meal, that is, fish

---

13

ἐξ Ἤλιδος μάγειρος, ἐξ Ἄργους λέβης,
Φλιάσιος οἶνος, ἐκ Κορίνθου στρώματα,
ἰχθῦς Σικυῶνος, Αἰγίου δ᾽ αὐλητρίδες,
τύρος Σικελικός, . . .
μύρον ἐξ Ἀθηνῶν, ἐγχέλεις Βοιώτιαι.

[14] For the cooks of Elis cf. Epicrates, *Merchant* fr. 6 and Chap. 8.
[15] Discussed in Chap. 1.11.
[16] I examine sympotic lists further in Chap. 5.
[17] Note by E. L. Bowie (1995).

and meat followed by the incense, fruit and nuts (the 'second tables'—see Chapter 5), and cushions used at the symposium. The speaker in fact acknowledges that the sympotic items are 'the adornment of the feast'. This sympotic element constitutes a further striking aspect of fr. 63.[18]

To be sure, foods are not the only goods to be linked with places of origin or manufacture: just as Hermippus fr. 63 lists hides, slaves, fabrics, and papyrus, so earlier texts list provenances for fabrics and other 'luxury' goods. The links between foods and particular places are frequently invoked in comedy, the cheese of Sicily, the sea bass of Miletus, the eels of Copais, the fish of Sicyon, the silphium of Cyrene, the salt fish of Byzantium, the incense of Syria. Such associations derive from various influences—silphium was a unique local product; Milesian sea bass and Copaic eels were apparently particularly fine; products from the Black Sea were said, as a kind of shorthand, to come from Byzantium or the Hellespont.[19] There is little reason to think that these specialities have been dreamt up by the comic poets.[20] Dalby (1996:124–9) examines the extensive evidence for provenances of foods in Greek literature of the fifth and fourth centuries, and demonstrates conclusively that these are not comic fabrications.[21] At the same time, these associations become comic clichés—so eels, for example, usually seem to come from Lake Copais—and places associated with particular foods are mentioned with the foods as a matter of course. There is always additional scope for humour, as in the assertion in *Acharnians* that Athens specializes in blackmailers.

4.2. ATHENS/PEIRAEUS AS A MAJOR PORT

Of the products listed by Hermippus, the central theme is that all these goods are brought here, to Athens, as a divine favour to mortals and to the Athenians in particular. Athens/Piraeus is the

---

[18] The political figures of Sitalces and Perdiccas, along with the Corcyreans, are included in this list of imports: for the confusion of categories in comic lists see Chap. 1.11.

[19] Braund (1995).

[20] Archestratus of Gela takes the links between foods and places much further in the fourth century: see Chap. 7.

[21] Occasionally these items appeared on the coins of Greek cities, e.g. silphium at Cyrene.

great port of the Mediterranean[22] whose myriad imports ('good things' in Hermippus fr. 63.3) are made available to her by a protecting god. Athens is presented not only as an entrepôt between trading cities but as the point of exchange between gods and humans. The chorus of basket-bearers presumably reinforced this sense of plentiful variety which celebrates the good fortune of the city. Some of the products complemented goods that Athens could produce herself; others supplemented home production, and may have been luxurious alternatives to the native product. Gallo (1989: 217–18) notes that Hermippus fr. 63 lists imported products in which Athens specialized, notably dried grapes and figs. Athenians presumably made cheese; they certainly produced pigs: imported pigs and cheese from Sicily may have simply augmented inadequate local supplies or may have provided variety, a high-quality imported product, as was Phoenician flour.

The Old Oligarch has a gloss to put on this: 'if one is to refer to lesser matters, first of all through their command of the sea the Athenians have had dealings in various ways with various peoples and have discovered forms of feasting. Whatever is a delicacy in Sicily or in Italy or in Cyprus or in Egypt or in Lydia or in the Pontus or the Peloponnese or anywhere else, all these things are brought to one place because of their command of the sea.'[23] After a comment on influences on the Attic dialect from other Greek cities, the Old Oligarch notes the generous provision made by the Athenian demos for the establishment of shrines, feasting, and sacrifices for all citizens, rich and poor alike.[24] This is a significant combination of ideas. The provision of special food for feasting, he says, while not a matter of central importance, is linked with developments in the democracy which allow non-aristocrats to feast in a way traditionally closed to all but

---

[22] Xenophon, *Ways and Means* 6–8.

[23] [Xenophon], *Constitution of the Athenians* 2.7, εἰ δὲ δεῖ καὶ σμικροτέρων μνησθῆναι, διὰ τὴν ἀρχὴν τῆς θαλάττης πρῶτον μὲν τρόπους εὐωχιῶν ἐξεῦρον ἐμισγόμενοι ἄλληι ἄλλοις· ὅ τι ἐν Σικελίαι ἡδὺ ἢ ἐν Ἰταλίαι ἢ ἐν Κύπρωι ἢ ἐν Αἰγύπτωι ἢ ἐν Λυδίαι ἢ ἐν τῶι Πόντωι ἢ ἐν Πελοποννήσωι ἢ ἄλλοθί που, ταῦτα πάντα εἰς ἐν ἠθροίσθη διὰ τὴν ἀρχὴν τῆς θαλάττης. The Old Oligarch's list comprises many of the regions identified by Athenians as luxurious (see Chap. 6). By the Peloponnese I imagine he has Corinth and Sicyon in mind ahead of Sparta.

[24] Discussed in Chap. 3.

the rich. Desirable imported luxuries, which he describes as 'sweet' or 'pleasant', are combined with civic cult at the expense of the rich and powerful. Athens, thanks to her influence in so many poleis and her maritime importance, is a collecting-point for products from many areas, the majority of which are identified with 'luxury' in other texts. Luxury, which in some contexts is a problematic issue,[25] loses its threat if properly contained by religious and social ritual. Luxury, provided it is democratic, is ideologically desirable for the Athenian demos.[26] I would interpret Hermippus fr. 63 similarly: 'luxuries' are brought to Athens by one of the city's gods—a particularly important god for comedy—and therefore constitute 'blessings' rather than a threat.

A notable omission from the list of the Old Oligarch and from Hermippus fr. 63 are Athenian grain imports from Egypt and the Black Sea: grain is not 'sweet' or 'pleasant', but an essential staple.[27] This omission leads me to doubt the contention of Ceccarelli that Hermippus fr. 63, which is probably to be dated to the Archidamian War, should be read as a critique of the policy of Pericles and the promotion of the Athenian navy at the expense of her land forces.[28] She notes in particular the comments of Thucydides on Athens' *autarkeia*, self-reliance, based on imports (2.36.3, 2.38.2). Others have certainly interpreted the agricultural plays of Aristophanes and other comic poets as conservative, as a plea for a return to an older way of life in which distinctions of class were more evident.[29] Luxuries were indeed identified as goods which come from outside, in particular from places either associated with the riches of the orient or with fertile land that could sustain an extraordinary sense of well-being, such as that found near Syracuse or Tarentum. If more goods were being imported because of the war in which Pericles favoured imports over protection of agricultural land, then *tryphe* (luxury) may have been encouraged by the Peloponnesian War. But, as the Old Oligarch says, luxuries are lesser matters—in contrast with

[25] As I demonstrate for the Athenians and for comedy in particular in Chap. 6.

[26] See Braund (1994).

[27] Note in Hermippus fr. 63 that the *chondros* from Thessaly and the *semidalis* from Phoenicia are processed grains, not wheat and barley. On *chondros* see Arnott (1996) on Alexis fr. 196.

[28] Ceccarelli (1996), 141–58. See also pp. 122–3 above.

[29] Ste. Croix (1972); Cartledge (1990); and in particular Henderson (1990).

the volume of grain imports on which Pericles' policy depended; and, I repeat, Old Comedy generally does not satirize 'luxury' provided it goes to the right people, that is, the demos.

It is not possible to pursue this theme through the plays which commented on the Athenian empire and control of the sea (*Babylonians* and *Islands* of Aristophanes and *Cities* of Eupolis) because too little survives. In *Babylonians*, which, according to the scholiast on *Acharnians* 378, was an attack on Cleon and the administration of the empire, Dionysus was apparently prosecuted by the demagogues (fr. 75 = Athenaeus 11.494d). In *Islands* fr. 402 (quoted in Chapter 3) a speaker praises farming in the country over buying fish in the city, but other fragments on food reveal little: fr. 405, 'a meal cake, salt fish, beestings, dried figs, lentil soup' and fr. 406, 'one harvesting the grapes, the other picking the olives'.[30] So too in Eupolis, *Cities* the cities are picked out, but in the fragments which remain no foods are associated with them—only a list of equipment for the symposium (fr. 218) and the raising of quails (226), possibly by Demos son of Pyrilampes (227). The allies of the Athenian empire brought tribute each year to Athens at the Dionysia, together with an ox and a phallus.[31] At *Wasps* 675–9 Aristophanes converts this tribute first into the offering of food and the good things of the symposium to the Athenian people, and then twists it so that all the good things become bribes taken by the politicians at the expense of the ordinary citizen [the allies] 'give bribes to them of jars of salted fish, wine, rugs, cheese, honey, sesame oil, pillows, cups, blankets, garlands, necklaces, cups, health-wealth, but to you who rule them by rowing over land and sea they give not even a head of garlic for your boiled fish.' In this image of the empire, luxuries are seen to accrue to some Athenians, but not to the demos at large. They are, further, divinely approved luxuries, as the inclusion of 'health-wealth' implies.[32]

Trade was clearly a theme of Aristophanes, *Merchant Ships*, which was, according to the Argument of *Peace*, a play about

---

[30] Varieties of olive also appear in fr. 408.

[31] See Chap. 2.2.

[32] On πλουθυγίεια—a compound of two desiderata provided by the gods and often found in prayers and unique to Artistophanes—see *Knights* 1091 and Dunbar (1995) on *Birds* 731.

peace.[33] Fr. 428[34] lists grains, 'wild chickling, wheat, barley gruel, crushed wheat and barley, spelt, darnel, fine flour'.[35] There is a similar list of fish (fr. 430) and bread-making vessels in anapaests (fr. 431). Trade of this kind, whatever the political context, depends upon the naval power of Athens. If the grain imports of Pericles were to be attacked by a comic poet this might be the play in which it was done, but too little is known of the content of *Merchant Ships*.

4.3. THE COMIC MARKET-PLACE

Once landed, these imported goods, these *agatha*, went to market along with those grown on Attic and neighbouring farms. Goods, whether brought by land or by sea, were distributed within the polis itself (and re-exported), in the various *agorai*, or markets for the exchange of foods, on which the polis depended.

The markets were part of Athenian life. On the agora, Thompson and Wycherley write,[36] 'the Athenian going to buy goods (*agorazein*) here might say he was going to the Agora, no less than when he was attending a political meeting'. The market-place is where the *agoraioi* were to be found, the frequenters of the market-place, the common citizens, whose voices are frequently those of comedy, and whose opinions were often dismissed by the elite.[37] The agora was a place of sale and a place of discourse, as is illustrated by the cripple who speaks in Lysias 24.[38] He claims that certain citizens are accustomed to frequent his place of trade (unspecified) and spend time there, as they might equally at the perfume-seller, barber, or leather-cutter (cobbler); the closer the shop to the agora, the more popular it was likely to be. It is clear from many texts that the market traders set up their stalls both in the agora proper and in adjacent areas such as the

---

[33] Testimonium iii KA.   [34] In anapaests (from parabasis or agon?).

[35] Cf. Pherecrates fr. 201, 'beans, wild chickling, spelt, darnel, *akeanos* [apparently another legume]'.

[36] (1972), 170.

[37] See Aristotle, *Politics* 1319a24–30 and n. 139 below.

[38] The following list of sellers and talkers is expanded from Wycherley (1957), 185–206.

Cerameicus.[39] Pollux,[40] drawing on comedy, lists the sectors (the *topoi* or *mere*) of the market, the book sector, the sectors for *opsa*,[41] wine,[42] olive oil[43] and pots. He cites Eupolis fr. 327, 'where books are sold. . . . I went round to the garlic sector, to the onion, to the incense, straight to the perfumer, and round to the fancy goods'. Pollux also identifies the place where cooks were hired, 'walking from the cooks' area and pushing into the *opsa* sector',[44] and to the *kukloi* or circles where slaves were sold[45] and the women's agora. Within these sectors traders operated from a variety of stalls. There were *skenai* ('booths'), *gerra* (structures of wicker),[46] *trapezai* ('tables'),[47] and there were almost certainly traders operating from baskets and portable stands.[48]

Comic characters often refer to specific traders, many of whom include purveyors of food.[49] There is the *alphitopolis* (barely meal market) of *Ecclesiazusae* 686[50] and the traders in barley meal,

---

[39] Thompson and Wycherley (1972: 170, n. 3) note the distinction in Demosthenes 18.169 between *kata ten agoran* ('in the region of the agora') and '*en thi agorai*' ('in the agora'). See below on *Knights*.

[40] 9.47–8 and 10.18–19.

[41] *Opsa* may be fish or any kind of protein to supplement cereal: see Davidson (1995), (1997); Arnott (1996) on Alexis frr. 47.6 and 129.2.

[42] Aristophanes, *Heroes* fr. 310.   [43] See Menander fr. 700.

[44] Antiphanes, *Soldier* fr. 201. Traders were combined with other pursuits: the scholion to Euripides, *Medea* 68 cites 'the draughts'—the gamblers—with other extravagant attractions, the sale of *opsa* and perfume. Pollux lists the *asoteia*, *petteia*, and *kubeia* at the 'more shameful' end of his survey of sectors.

[45] Illustrated by Alexis, *Calasiris* fr. 104; Diphilus, *Mainomenos* fr. 55. On Menander, *Ephesian* fr. 171, Pollux (7.11) writes, 'the *kukloi* are the places in New Comedy in which slaves are sold'. Arnott (1996) on Alexis fr. 104 challenges the claim of Pollux that other goods were sold in the 'circles'.

[46] Wycherley prefers the interpretation 'hurdles', or 'partitions'. The nature of these *gerra* is not clear: they may be identical with the *skenai*, part of their structure, or another structure. See Wycherley (1957), 190–2 on Demosthenes 18.169 (together with Wankel's commentary), and Harpocration s.v. *gerra*.

[47] These appear to be the tables of money-changers and of other traders who displayed their wares.

[48] Such as the Black-Pudding-Seller (*Knights* 152 and 169), the Megarian selling his 'pigs' in a sack in *Acharnians*, the trays of birds in *Birds*, and traders in the early modern city: see e.g. Berrouet and Laurendon (1994). They cite Fournel (1887). I discuss the noise of the market-place below.

[49] Wycherley (1957) draws heavily on comic references.

[50] There was another at Peiraeus with which this one might be confused: Wycherley (1957), 193; Ussher (1973), *ad loc.*

possibly on a smaller scale, at *Clouds* 640, *Birds* 491,[51] and *Ecclesiazusae* 424 and 817–19; there were bread-sellers (see below),[52] fish-merchants,[53] and butchers selling meat (*Knights* 418 and 1245–6),[54] and possibly donkey meat (*Knights* 1399)[55] and carrion.[56] There were sellers of birds (*Birds* 13–14), cheese (*Knights* 854),[57] vegetables (*Lysistrata* 557, Arnott on Alexis fr. 47.8), honey (*Knights* 854, Antiphanes fr. 123), figs (*Lysistrata* 564, Alexis fr. 133), and (for the symposium and sacrifice) garlands (*Thesmophoriazusae* 448, *Ecclesiazusae* 302, and the eponymous *Garland-Sellers* of Eubulus' play), and perfume (*Knights* 1375, Eupolis *Cities* fr. 222, Philemon *Sculptor* fr. 41).[58] This list mentions a few of the many market traders who appear in the verses of comedy. They reflect the hustle and bustle of the market-place and are an essential element in the popular culture that comedy often represents.[59] In some fragments it is not possible to discern whether or not a list of foods is being bought or sold. In Nicophon, *Encheirogastores*[60] fr. 6, for example, a character says, 'I [?] wheat bread, barley cake, pancake, barley flour, rolls, spit-bread, honey cake, moulded cakes, barley gruel, flat-cakes, *dendalis* cakes, fried cake'. He or she may (or may not) be selling this wide range of confections, though I am not aware of any cook who lists such a range of breads and cakes. In fr. 10 of the same play the following sellers are listed: 'anchovy-sellers, charcoal-sellers, dried-fig-sellers, hide-sellers, barley-meal-sellers, bread-spoon-sellers, booksellers, sieve-sellers, honey-cake-sellers, seed-sellers.' The poet appears to be revelling in the rhythm of the list at least as much as he reflects the trades in the market.

[51] See Dunbar (1995).
[52] It is not clear whether 'market-bread' indicates bread that was sold in the market in Lynceus of Samos ap. Athenaeus 3.109d, Archestratus fr. 4.
[53] *Knights* 1247 (salt fish); *Wasps* 491–9 (quoted below), 788–91; *Frogs* 1068; Antiphanes, *Cnoiditheus* fr. 123; and many fragments reviewed by Arnott (1996) on Alexis fr. 16; Davidson (1997); and in Chap. 6 below.
[54] See Berthiaume (1982), 44–61; Machon 300–8; Theophrastus, *Characters* 9.4, 22.7.
[55] See below and Pollux 9.48.
[56] See Berthiaume (1982), 89 and Erotian, *Glossarium Hippocraticum* 82.8.
[57] Cf. Lysias 23.6.
[58] Thompson and Wycherley (1972), 170–3 warn that trading-sites may not have been as fixed as these sources imply until the Roman period.
[59] See Bakhtin (1968).
[60] The chorus appears to comprise men who feed their bellies with the work of their hands.

To the specialist dealers reviewed above must be added three categories of trader who are particularly satirized. These correspond to the three basic elements of the diet, wine, bread or barley cakes, and *opson*, in particular fish.[61] *Kapeloi* sold a range of goods, but in particular wine; they sometimes also provided a bar.[62] In comedy the provision of drink appears to have been the main function of the *kapelos*. The *kapeleion* is of particular interest because of its apparent ubiquity (several passages refer to the neighbourhood bar—it was not necessary to go to the agora for this service)[63] and its association with women drinkers and poorer citizens (on which see Chapter 5). A number of comic references treat the *kapelos/is* as dishonest or disliked, particularly by women,[64] and the *kapeleion* as the site of excessive drinking, again by women.[65] The inn landlady, *pandokeutria*, is a fearsome character in *Frogs* 549–76 and *Wealth* 426. Pollux includes the *kapelos* in his list of livelihoods that bring reproach;[66] it is hard to separate this list from the discourse of comedy, particularly in view of the choice of the ubiquitous pimp and the tanner and black-pudding-seller, who come together in *Knights*.[67]

Bread-sellers (*artopolides*) are not included in Pollux's list of reproachful livelihoods,[68] despite the low esteem they often share with *kapeloi* in comedy and invective. Comedy's treatment of bread-selling is complex. The sale of *artos*, wheat-bread, is the subject of satire, but there is no abuse against sellers of *maza* (barley cake). It appears that *maza* was for the most part made at home from barley flour that had been bought.[69] It may be that

[61] On *opson* in comedy see Arnott (1996) on Alexis fr. 47.6. For the tripartite division see in particular Davidson (1997), 3–35 and Marr (1994).

[62] Davidson (1997), 53–9.

[63] *Wealth* 435–6; Nicostratus fr. 22 (this *kapelos* sells torches and vinegar as well as wine); Antiphanes fr. 25; Davidson (1993).

[64] *Thesmophoriazusae* 347–50; *Wealth* 435–6.

[65] *Lysistrata* 466; *Thesmophoriazusae* 735–7; Plato, *Phaon* fr. 188.4; Antiphanes fr. 25.

[66] 6.128: βίοι ἐφ' οἷς ἄν τις ὀνειδισθείη, πορνοβοσκός, κάπηλος, ὀπωρώνης, ὀπωροπώλης . . . βυρσοδέψης . . . ἀλλαντοπώλης—the keeper of prostitutes, the general merchant, the fruit-seller, the tanner, the black-pudding-seller.

[67] Cf. Dalby (1995), 93, n. 1 on Pollux on cookery-book writers.

[68] Bread is listed elsewhere, in Pollux 6.32–3.

[69] See Arnott (1996) on Alexis fr. 145.7. High-grade barley cakes were sold at market (according to Archestratus fr. 4). There were specialist sellers of barley cakes, such as the *enchrides* (honey-cakes) mentioned by Nicophon above.

artopolai/ides, bread-sellers, reflected the higher status of their product and put on airs. This may account for their being insulted by the rejuvenated old men in Aristophanes' plays *Wasps* and *Old Age*.[70] In Anacreon 388 *PMG* female bread-sellers,[71] together with *ethelopornoi*, willing male prostitutes, are part of the undesirable society kept by one Artemon, who is 'discovering a counterfeit life'. Hermippus wrote a *Bread-Sellers* (*Artopolides*), which had something to do with Hyperbolus' mother, a supposed bread-maker, though whether in an extended metaphor similar to the black-pudding-selling of *Knights*, or in passing like the vegetable-selling of the mother of Euripides is unknown.[72] Eupolis in *Marikas* fr. 209 likened the mother of Hyperbolus to a kneading tray. Comic treatment of Thearion, the Athenian master-baker named in Plato's *Gorgias*, takes a different course, placing him in tragic parody in *Aeolosicon* fr. 1 and Antiphanes, *Omphale* fr. 174;[73] Thearion appears to have been the doyen of commercial bakers in Athens.[74]

Fishmongers are the third category of vendor that is most satirized, particularly in Middle and New Comedy. Most of the surviving examples are quoted by Athenaeus at 6.224c–227b, after which follows a list of fish-eating gourmets.[75] The fishmongers are conventionally abused in comedy, so that variations on themes are offered, principally on their outrageous prices and strategies: at Xenarchus, *Purple-Shell* fr. 7, for example, the fishmongers fake fights, feign death, and throw water, apparently at each other but in fact at their fish to give it a fresh appearance. Stale or dead fish are the subject of Antiphanes, *Adulterers* fr. 159 and *Pro-Theban* fr. 217. Fishmongers are named, Hermeus of Egypt by Archippus at *Fishes* fr. 23,[76] and Micion by Alexis at *Heiress* fr. 78.

[70] See MacDowell (1971) on *Wasps* 1388 and Kassel–Austin (1984) on fr. 129.
[71] On female bread-sellers see Brock (1994), 338–9.
[72] Fr. 9, 'O rotten woman, total whore and sow', recalls the link with prostitution in Anacreon. Euripides' mother is unlikely to have been a vegetable-seller in real life: see Ruck (1975).
[73] It is not known how he was referred to in Aristophanes, *Gerytades* fr. 177.
[74] See Dalby (1995).
[75] On comic fishmongers in general see Chap. 6 and Arnott (1996) on Alexis fr. 16.
[76] He is accused of cruelty towards fish.

The presentation of these three trades, the general merchant/ wine-seller, the bread-seller, and the fishmonger, exemplify the negative approach that comedy might take to trading in the agora, the home of the shady deal. Just as fishmongers are shown to overprice their goods and pass off bad fish as good, so the *kapelides* (it is claimed) were prone to selling short measures and to excessive mixing with water when they sold wine by the *kotule*.[77] Fig-sellers are presented as dishonest in Alexis, *Cooking-Pot* (*Lebes*) fr. 133, 'why should we go on to speak of those who always sell fish in baskets? They always put the hard and bad figs at the bottom while the fine ripe ones are on top. The buyer pays the price, buying them as good figs, while the seller bites the coin in his teeth and hands over wild figs, swearing that he sells the cultivated variety.' The market vendor in comedy is seen from the purchaser's point of view and usually receives criticism.[78] The stallholders are often said to have a strong physical presence[79] and big voices, with which they can insult and cheat customers as they promote their wares.[80] At *Frogs* 858–9 Dionysus observes that poets should not trade insults like female bread-sellers.

At the other side of the counter, the buyer who approaches the stallholder in the market-place may be satirized as well, particularly the young, who enjoy the bad company and expense of the agora (*Knights* 1373–4, *Clouds* 991), and 'gluttons' whose resources enable them to pay any price, while the ordinary people suffer shortages (*Peace* 1005–15).[81] Eubulus, *Nurses* fr. 109 offers an example of a buyer who attempts restraint but has a long list of tasty items: '. . . not lavishly, but with simpliciy in mind, for the sake of piety. Small squid will suffice, and small cuttlefish, little tentacles of octopus, a fasting-mullet, a womb,

[77] *Wealth* 435–6; Arnott (1996) on Alexis fr. 9; Davidson (1997), 53–61.

[78] Dover (1993), on *Frogs* 857–8.

[79] We shall meet in Chap. 6 fishmongers who put on airs like generals and glare like gorgons. I noted above that Poverty in *Wealth* has an appalling appearance similar to a female innkeeper or pease-pudding-seller (426–7, 435–6).

[80] See n. 48 on the cries in the markets of Paris.

[81] The clients of the fishmonger, whose visits to the agora are all-too frequent and who suffer an excessive desire to consume are discussed in Chap. 6, while the cooks discussed in Chap. 8 either send out slaves to shop or take orders from the client on what should be bought.

savoury puddings, beestings, a huge sea bass head.'[82] The treatise on shopping by Lynceus of Samos[83] in the early third century probably reflects the temptations of the market stalls. The *hetaerae* of New Comedy are big spenders, often of other people's money.[84] The market traders have much to offer the comic poet. They are the main source in the polis of those material goods which are, as we saw in Chapter 1, so much a part of comic discourse; they provide the goods which the ordinary Athenian both needed and desired; they are themselves often ordinary Athenians.[85] On many occasions they are referred to in a neutral sense. A character goes to the agora and simply buys the necessary provisions. As we also saw in Chapter 1, comedy refers to coins and money more often than many other texts. Usually, however, they are viewed with hostility. Comedy shares with much other Athenian literature an ambivalence, if not a dislike, towards those dealing in commerce. Plato brings this out most clearly at *Gorgias* 518b, where Socrates lists three men who offer tempting food, Sarambus the *kapelos*, Thearion the baker, and Mithaecus the fish-cook or maker of *opsa*.[86] They are deficient in two respects, both as commercial dealers and as purveyors of food to please rather than to improve health. Plato's Socrates opposes pleasure which 'flatters' the body rather than sustains physical need. When comedy deals with vendors in the market-place, it often does so from a more ambiguous ideological perspective, as we saw in Chapter 3. When peace is established in *Peace* foods become available once more in the agora (974–1015); Dicaeopolis in *Acharnians* exchanges goods, albeit in his special private agora, with farmers from Boeotia and Megara. Trade is as natural for a comic protagonist as any other aspect of his well-being: so Dicaeopolis sets up his private market, and Trygaeus in *Peace* celebrates all the goods that will now come to the agora for the benefit of all and

---

[82]   The speaker appears to be carried away at the end.

[83]   Dalby (1995), 158 and Dalby (forthcoming).

[84]   In the sub-comic Machon, Gnathaena goes to market in search of the food-stalls (302).

[85]   When Lysistrata appeals for support (*Lys.* 456–8) she calls on the women of the market, 'O sellers-of-seeds-in-the-market,-pease-porridge-and-greens, O sellers-of-garlic,-landladies-and-bread'. These composite terms share something in comic invention with Nicophon fr. 6 above.

[86]   Dalby (1995), 109; Davidson (1997), 54.

not merely politicians and gluttons. Everyone, it is implied, desires good things, *agatha*, the demos, humanity in the myth of the Golden Age, farmers—and greedy politicians and anti-democratic elements. In the democratic polis, as we shall see further below, these *agatha* should be put to communal rather than private use, and they should preferably be provided by gods— Peace in *Peace*, Dionysus or his acolytes in Hermippus fr. 63 and *Acharnians*—or the earth itself.[87]

In the market-place goods are exchanged for money: this form of exchange is often unfavourably compared with other forms of exchange and reciprocity, most notably at the beginning of *Acharnians*, where Dicaeopolis imagines a rural economy based on barter as opposed to the hated markets of the town. Money and trading may displace the traditional exchanges of society that ensure peace and continuity, marriage between families, legitimate heirs to estates, constitutional controls against tyranny, and the notion of equal shares between participants at the symposium and the sacrifice. Money may give access to status and power that would not be attainable in the traditional system. A 'lesser' man may be able to buy his daughter a 'better' husband; a man may buy influence by putting on lavish meals beyond the means of his class. Furthermore, the market encourages consumption, appetite, and the spending of a man's estate.[88] Land and property may be frittered away on 'ephemeral' pleasures.

I mentioned in Chapter 1 anthropological approaches to commodification and the argument of von Reden (1998) for the 'commodification of symbols' in Menander, for money making available *hetaerae*, lavish meals, and luxuries in comedy. She charts a world where the 'high' discourse of politics and religion is reduced to the 'low' discourse of everyday concerns. This problematizing of money is important in comedy at a much earlier date than she allows.[89] The intervention of money to buy

---

[87] Contrast Eubulus fr. 74 (cited below) with Antiphanes fr. 177, 'A: the land bears produce, Hipponicus, better than anywhere else in the civilized world, honey, bread, figs, B: Figs certainly, by Zeus, A: flocks, wool, myrtle-berries, thyme, wheat, water, such that you'd instantly recognize Attic water when you drink it'.

[88] Davidson (1993; 1997).

[89] Von Reden looks at the link between Menander and the changes in Athens after the Macedonians took control. See also Chap. 2.

political influence that cannot be gained though democratic debate in the assembly is prominent in 'Old Comedy'—I discuss *Knights* below; in 'Middle Comedy', political institutions and the sale of food are placed side by side in the *Olbia* of Eubulus. A character claims that everything is for sale (fr. 74):

A: in the one place everything is for sale in Athens, figs,[90]
B: summons-witnesses,
A: bunches of grapes, turnips, pears, apples,
B: witnesses,
A: roses, medlars, savoury puddings, honeycombs, chickpeas,
B: lawsuits,
A: beestings, heated beestings, myrtle,
B: lot-machines,
A: hyacinth, sheep,
B: water clocks, laws, prosecutions.[91]

This fragment both satirizes and expresses a literal truth. Foods are available for sale in the agora on a scale imagined in the comic utopias[92] or Aristophanes, *Seasons* fr. 581 (cited in Chapter 3). Included are the most desirable of country products, the beestings (first milk) and heated beestings.[93] The second speaker sardonically adds the machinery of the courts among these items for sale, for the agora was more than a place of sale—it was also the administrative and legal centre of the city, exhibiting a blend of the official and the commercial. Aristotle and Xenophon indeed argued for a market in which civic and commercial elements were separated (*Politics* 1331a32–b4, *Cyropaedia* 1.2.3). Comedy frequently exploits the tension between these elements.

The food supply was a political issue, as often were food prices—certainly in the fourth century in respect of grain[94] and

[90] Hunter (1983) notes that here, in Antiphanes fr. 177 (n. 87), and elsewhere figs trigger jokes on courts and sycophants. See also Arnott (1996) on Alexis fr. 4. Figs were also a quintessentially Attic product: see Athenaeus 3.74 c–75a and Arnott on Alexis fr. 167.

[91] Wycherley (1957), 185 compares the ψηφισματοπώλης of *Birds* 1035–57, a trade supposed by Dunbar (1995)—with good reason—to have been invented by Aristophanes.

[92] See Hunter (1983).

[93] Ancient references are collected by Kassel and Austin (1983), on Cratinus fr. 149.

[94] The provision of σῖτος was (in the fourth century at least) one of the items of agenda for the *kuria ecclesia* ('principal meeting of the assembly', Aristotle,

in comedy in respect of fish prices. Elected officials, *agoranomoi*, regulated trade and prices in the market-place. Dicaeopolis attends to a comic version of such officials in his agora (*Acharnians* 723–4); the assaulted bread-seller in *Wasps* appeals to them (1407)[95] and in Alexis, *Phaedo* fr. 249 a character is told, 'A: you, if the gods so desire, shall be *agoranomos* so that you, if you are my friend, can put a stop to Callimedon blowing a gale through the fish-market twice a day. B: You're describing a task for tyrants, not *agoranomoi*. The man is warlike, though he has his uses for the city.'[96] Callimedon is one of those gourmet-politicians with a strong appetite for fish and luxury.

Wasps 488–99 gives a further perspective to the politics of the market stall. Bdelycleon responds to a charge of trying to set up a tyranny:

everything with you is tyranny and conspirators, whether it's a large or small matter of complaint. I haven't heard the word conspiracy for the past fifty years. Now it's much cheaper than salt fish! With the result that the word is being bounced around in the agora. If a man buys perch and doesn't want anchovies, instantly the man selling the anchovies in the next stall says 'that guy looks as if he's buying special fish with a view to tyranny'. And if he asks for an onion to be thrown in as a garnish for some whitebait,[97] the woman vegetable-seller, looking askance with one eye, says 'tell me. You're asking for an onion. Is that for setting up a tyranny, or do you believe that Athens produces a tribute[98] of garnishes for you?'

The stallholders hawk their foods through the buzzwords of political debate, expressing aggressive challenges in political

---

Athenaion, Politeia 43.4): Rhodes (1981) *ad loc.* compares Xenophon, *Memorabilia* 3.6.1–13 and Aristotle, *Rhetoric* 1360a12–17, περὶ τροφῆς. He also discusses (51.3–4) the function of *sitonomoi*, *agoranomoi*, and other regulatory officials.

[95] For an analysis of their functions see MacDowell (1971).

[96] Arnott (1996) explores the probable irony of the last clause. Alexis also treated the honouring of Callimedon in fr. 57, 'the fishmongers have voted, so they say, to set up a bronze statue to Callimedon in the fish-market during the Panathenaea with a roasted crayfish in its hand, in recognition of the fact that he is the one true saviour of their craft while all others do them harm'. Alexis mocks the politician in the language of decrees to public benefactors and at the major festival of the polis. The poet memorably combines the commercial traders and their customers with the institutions of state.

[97] On garnish for fish see *Wasps* 679, *Knights* 676–9.

[98] MacDowell (1971), on 499, notes the pun in Athens producing food as if it were tribute paid to a ruler.

terms when they do not get a sale. There is both a strong sense of bathos in the placing together of fish and politics and the assumption that the stallholders, as *agoraioi*, hold democratic sympathies and adapt their hostility to their customers to political discourse, implying that a purchaser who prefers a more expensive item is expressing elitist sympathies. Some texts imply a temporal division in the agora between the time for sales and an earlier hour for other business. Such is Photius' comment[99] on Pherecrates fr. 178, 'he arrived early before the agora filled up'. Aristophanes exploits this gap between the political and intellectual elite—the more usual exponents of political argument in the assembly and in literature—and market stallholders elsewhere, for example in the comic representation of the mother of Euripides as a vegetable-seller[100] and in Dionysus' observation (*Frogs* 1068) that the rich disguise themselves as poor men in order to avoid liturgies but then sneak off to the fish stall.

All these features are exploited in Aristophanes' great play about the agora and its market, *Knights*, in which the big voice of the market huckster is linked with the rhetoric of the politician. *Knights* is based on an underlying tension between the essential nature of the agora both as market and centre of government and the low-class people, male and female,[101] who populate it, and who, though citizens of the democracy, are not the elite whose views dominate in literary accounts of Athenian politics. These are the *agoraioi*, the people regularly dismissed by the great and the good.[102] Aristophanes created two extraordinary *agoraioi*, the

---

[99] a 238 = *Suda* a 306: ἀγορᾶς ὥραν· οὐ τῶν πωλουμένων, ἀλλὰ τῶν ἄλλων πράξεων τῶν κατ' ἀγοράν. ('The agora hour. This is the hour not of the market-sellers but of the other transactions in the area of the agora.')

[100] See Ruck (1975); Harding (1987).

[101] Women in the surviving plays of Old Comedy appear more in town plays than country plays (apart from the *hetaerae* of *Peace* who have neither status nor a dramatic voice). They are the plotters and market traders. Old Comedy appears to have had some interest in women working in the country, however, to judge from the lost *Poastriai* (*Haymakers?*) of Magnes and Phrynichus. On women workers in both town and country in Attica see Brock (1994) and Aristophanes frr. 829, 916; Demosthenes 57.45; Garlan (1980), 9; Herfst (1979), 13–17; Keuls (1985), 231–2. Herfst (1979), 48–9 charts some forty-one male food-traders and ten female (add *lekithopolis*)—all overlapping.

[102] 'Aeschylus' boasts at *Frogs* 1014–15 that he peopled his plays with noble characters and not men of the agora.

Black-Pudding-Seller and Cleon/Paphlagon, politician-slaves to the people, Demos, whose 'home' is the civic hearth in the prytaneion. The Black-Pudding-Seller is 'bad, from the agora and bold' (181), uncultured (188), with a foul voice, of low birth, an *agoraios* (218)—clearly not of the elite!

4.4. DINING IN THE AGORA AND THE PRYTANEION

At the end of *Knights* the Paphlagonian slave who represents the politician Cleon suffers expulsion from both the agora and the prytaneion. The agora housed the executive offices of government as well as commercial interests, and the prytaneion the sacred hearth of the polis: the two were at the heart of the Athenian polis, as they were of many Greek poleis.[103] The Athenian prytaneion had three principal functions: it housed the cult of Hestia and the city's fire (religious groups set out from here and colonists took fire to found new cities abroad),[104] it was a special court, and it contained one or more rooms for dining. It functioned as the civic hearth at which honoured guests—gods, foreign visitors, and benefactors and certain categories of honoured Athenians—were given food, *sitesis*.[105] The exact relationship between prytaneion and prytaneis in the archaic period is not clear; in the fifth century the prytaneis, the executive committee of the boule, did not, despite their name, dine here but in the tholos near to the boule. (They are unlikely to have dined here even before the building of the tholos in about 470 BC.)[106] Schmitt-Pantel draws an important contrast between the traditional nature of meals in the prytaneion, which were based on the model of earlier aristocratic commensality, and the feeding in the tholos, which was democratic and restrained civic maintenance of the executive, based on subsistence pay for the purchase of

---

[103] Thucydides (2.15.2) and Plutarch (*Theseus* 24.3) record that Theseus set up one bouleuterion and one prytaneion for the whole of Attica.

[104] Cult of Bendis: Chap. 2, n. 11. Colonies: Herodotus 1.146.2.

[105] On the prytaneion see Miller (1978); Wycherley (1957), 166–74; Thompson and Wycherley (1972), 46–7; Schmitt-Pantel (1992), 145–77; and Rhodes (1981) on *Athenaion Politeia* 3.5.

[106] Schmitt-Pantel (1992), 146.

food that was cooked on the premises.[107] The prytaneis dined at work, as did the *thesmothetai* and perhaps other officials at the *thesmotheteion*.[108]

Schmitt-Pantel's distinction between honorific dining in the prytaneion and the dining of officials in the tholos sheds crucial clarity in an area often confused in ancient sources.[109] Thus Plutarch writes[110] that 'the institutions called Andreia by the Cretans and Phiditia by the Spartans had the form of exclusive bouleuteria and aristocratic assemblies, as do, I believe the prytaneion and *thesmotheteion* here [in Athens]'.[111] Unclear too is the site of the prytaneion. Unlike the tholos and probably the *thesmotheteion*, it was not in the agora but, according to Thompson and Wycherley 'it may be regarded as an adjunct'.[112] Pausanias[113] locates it near the shrines of Aglauros and the Dioscuri, that is, somewhere on the northern slopes of the acropolis; but those shrines may have been sited towards the eastern end of the northern slopes and thus, in the words of Schmitt-Pantel, 'complètement distinct(s) et même éloigné(s) de l'agora et de la Tholos'.[114] (The precinct of the agora itself is not clearly known: only two or three boundary markers have been found.)[115]

Aristocratic or not in origin, meals at the prytaneion were, we are told, 'simple' and 'traditional'. This type of meal at the prytaneion is part of Athenaeus' argument for restrained eating in Athens,[116] contrasting with the gluttony of Thessalians and

---

[107] They resembled jurors in receiving *misthos*, subsistence pay, but differed from them in spending it on food for consumption at work rather than at home.

[108] Scholiast to Plato, *Phaedrus* 235d.

[109] Wycherley (1957), 166–74. Fisher (forthcoming) counsels against pressing the contrast too far.

[110] *Quaestiones conviviales* 7.9 = 714b.

[111] Hesychius implies a similar analogy with Crete and Sparta in listing three *sussitia* in Athens, the prytaneion, the archons in the *thesmotheteion*, and the prytaneis in the tholos. Athenaeus implies a similar approach in describing meals at the prytaneion in Athens in Book 4 just prior to his account of Spartan and Cretan messes.

[112] Thompson and Wycherley (1972), 46.   [113] 1.18.1–3.

[114] (1992), 146, n. 5. On possible earlier sites see Thompson and Wycherley (1972) and Rhodes (1981), loc. cit.

[115] See Wycherley (1957), 218; Ste. Croix (1972), 273–6; and Thompson and Wycherley (1972), 117–19. The Athenians clearly knew where the boundaries were since *atimoi* were excluded from the agora, but it is by no means clear to us.

[116] 4.137e–f. Athenaeus Book 4 is discussed in Chap. 6.

others. One model for eating in the prytaneion was the feasting of the Dioscuri, who were neighbours, as we have seen. Athenaeus says this *theoxenia* was referred to in the *Beggars* attributed to (among others) Chionides (fr. 7): 'whenever they set a light meal before the Dioscuri in the prytaneion, they put on the tables "cheese, a barley cake, tree-ripe olives, and leeks" in memory of the ancient diet.'[117] A second model was provided by Solon, who, says Athenaeus, prescribed barley cake to all those feeding in the prytaneion, but wheat-bread at festivals. Notable features in *Beggars* fr. 7 are the divine guests, a light meal of vegetarian food,[118] and antiquity; with these Athenaeus contrasts anecdotes on the irregularities of cooks at the Academy and Lyceum, who made foods appear to be what they were not. In the problematic area of eating, civic dining forms a model of restraint in contrast with luxurious consumption elsewhere, in particular in shopping for food in the agora and in private dining. Certain foods and drinks were, according to Athenaeus, specified in prytaneia in other cities: in Thasos, wine sweetened with dough (1.32d); in Naucratis, two forms of bread, pork, barley or vegetable soup, eggs, fresh cheese, dried figs, a flat-cake, and a wreath—and nothing else allowed.[119] Restraint is evident in this regulated commensality, and is seen too in civic eating beyond the prytaneion: Athenaeus says (4.185f–186a), '[in Athens] the law-givers, thought ahead to the dinners we now have and ordained dinners both at tribe and deme level and in addition the thiasoi and phratry and so-called orgeonic dinners'. He adds, 'the prytaneis dined together on a daily basis, eating dinners that were restrained and that promoted the safety of the city'.[120] This emphasis on restraint in civic dining is an ideological construction which should not be pressed too far for Athens itself (though in *Knights* restraint is a key element in the attack on Cleon/

---

[117] ὁ δὲ τοὺς εἰς Χιωνίδην ἀναφερομένους Πτωχοὺς ποιήσας τοὺς Ἀθηναίους φησίν, ὅταν τοῖς Διοσκούροις ἐν πρυτανείωι ἄριστον προτιθῶνται, ἐπὶ τῶν τραπεζῶν τιθέναι τυρὸν καὶ φυστὴν δρυπεπεῖς τ' ἐλάας καὶ πράσα, ὑπόμνησιν ποιουμένους τῆς ἀρχαίας ἀγωγῆς.

[118] Athenaeus compares it with Plato's vegetarian diet in the *Republic* (372c).

[119] Any *hieropoios* who exceeds this prescription is to be fined: 4.149d–150b. Athenaeus considers other cities where a contribution from individuals was allowed, as it was in Sparta.

[120] συνεδείπνουν δ' ὁσημέραι οἱ περὶ πρύτανιν σώφρονα καὶ σωτήρια τῶν πόλεων σύνδειπνα.

Paphlagon).[121] Some form of symposium was put on at the prytaneion[122] and excavations in the remains of a public building in the agora have revealed five types of drinking cups, some stamped as public property, mixing-bowls, some perhaps donated, and evidence for the mixing of wines, including imported wines.[123] Elaborate drinking rituals were therefore not confined to private occasions.

Mortals who ate at the prytaneion in Athens were foreign visitors (such as the 'King's Eye', the Persian ambassador Pseudartabas, in *Acharnians* 124–7), and certain honoured Athenians,[124] the Hierophant (and possibly other priests of Demeter and Kore at Eleusis), the senior living male descendant of Harmodius and Aristogeiton, and victorious athletes in gymnastics, horse-racing, and chariot racing at the Olympic, Pythian, Isthmian, and Nemean games. Others were *athlothetae* during the Panathenaia and Athenians returning from foreign missions.[125] These are the personnel in the aristocratic mode identified by Schmitt-Pantel. By far the most frequent category in honorary decrees of the fifth and fourth centuries are foreign visitors and delegations.[126] In what may have been a new departure, Cleon appears to have been granted *sitesis* in 425/4 for his victory over the Spartans at Pylos.[127] Thereafter other Athenians were granted *sitesis* temporarily or for life.

Solon is Athenaeus' second model for restrained commensality in the city. Plutarch (*Solon* 24) attests his provision for 'eating

[121] This control of eating by the polis is comparable to control of politicians who might exploit their public position for private gain. The demos thereby controls its leaders and ensures its own survival.

[122] The scholion in the B MS of Plato, *Gorgias* on 451e records that *skolia* (formal drinking songs—see Chap. 5) were sung in the Athenian prytaneion for Harmodius, Admetus, and Telamon.

[123] Rotroff and Oakley (1992); Fisher (forthcoming), who argues for symposia in other civic buildings, including perhaps the tholos since a pipe-player was employed there.

[124] See *IG* I² 77 (= A26 in Miller (1978)). Details are disputed: Osborne (1981); Schmitt-Pantel (1992), 147–168; Rhodes (1981), on *Athenaion Politeia* 24.3.

[125] *Chresmologoi* or oracle-givers may also have enjoyed this privilege, at least during the Peloponnesian War, according to the scholiast on *Peace* 1084, 'no longer will you dine henceforth in the prytaneion', but this claim appears improbable.

[126] Miller (1978), App. A.

[127] Noel Worswick has suggested to me that Cleon received this honour through his marriage to a woman descended from the tyrannicides.

at public expense',[128] which was obligatory but not to be abused by too much or too little eating. Plutarch also says that the laws of Solon were preserved in the prytaneion, as attested by Cratinus (= fr. 300):[129] 'By Solon and by Draco, on whose *kurbeis* they now parch the barley.'[130] Cratinus pictures the incongruous scene of barley-parching on the wooden blocks on which the laws of the great lawgivers were inscribed. He implies that insufficient respect is accorded the laws but from another perspective, both laws and food-preparation belong in the prytaneion and the disrespect shown is in a sense appropriate. What is clear is that the right people must eat in the prytaneion in the right way: dining there is 'traditional' and 'honorific' commensality, ideologically contrasted to the excesses of private individuals in the city. Cleon/ Paphlagon in *Knights* offends this commensality.[131]

4.5. ARISTOPHANES, *KNIGHTS*

Eating in the prytaneion had long ago been brought into domestic politics; as we saw in Chapter 2, Cimon converted his private estates into a 'prytaneion'. A politician from the elite could influence his demesmen and kinsmen by opening up his estate and its orchards to public use.[132] In his *Knights* Aristophanes reverses this, presenting the prytaneion as a house in which a general/demagogue is fed by the people. He receives *sitesis*, sometimes, as Schmitt-Pantel points out, described as receiving *ta sitia*, a soldier's ration. Cleon the demagogue general has found a vastly superior form of rations. In the play, prytaneion and agora are jointly presented as being at the centre of the city, from which the ill-favoured are expelled to the margins at the

---

[128] τῆς ἐν δημοσίωι σιτήσεως (which Solon called παρασιτεῖν, 'being a parasite'/'eating with the god'). This was honourable parasitism of the ancient kind, to be distinguished from the comic parasite: see Chap. 2.

[129] Pausanias (1.18.1–3) concurs and adds statues of Peace and Hestia (the date at which this happened is disputed). The date at which the laws were first stored in the prytaneion is also disputed, but the comic construction is my concern here.

[130] There is also alleged to be a joke here on κυρήβια, husks; cf. *Knights* 254 and schol.

[131] Cf. the historical reality of the developing concern with the 'ancestral constitution': see Finley (1975), 34–59.

[132] Schmitt-Pantel (1992), chap. 3.

Dipylon Gate and Cerameicus. Buying and selling was in fact conducted in both 'agora' proper and Cerameicus, as we have seen:[133] Aristophanes has accentuated the point made by the cripple of Lysias 24, that the more popular stalls were in the agora proper. We should add that the area at the gates was in some respects disreputable, associated in particular with prostitution.[134] On the other hand, surplus meat from the sacrifices at the Panathenaea was sold in the Cerameicus.[135] It is thus a construction of Aristophanes that Cleon/Paphlagon is expelled to the gates in great humiliation at the end of the play, to sell a lower class of sausage made from the meat of dogs and donkeys,[136] while the Black-Pudding-Seller is invited to honoured eating in the prytaneion. Earlier in life the Black-Pudding-Seller had been brought up at the gates on black-pudding-selling and prostitution (1242),[137] and then became peripatetic between the gates and the agora: he etymologizes his name 'Agoracritus' as 'the man disputing in the agora'; he stole meat from the butchers (*mageiroi*) in the agora, and has a special portable table—*eleon*—which implies mobility.[138]

Knights is a particularly striking example of a prejudicial view of the *agoraioi* and their market.[139] The play draws on a

---

[133] Authors differ on where is meant by the Cerameicus: see Wycherley (1957), 221–4. There is the further complication of an area known as Cerameicus both within and outside the Dipylon Gate.

[134] Wycherley (1957), 222–3; Davidson (1997), 72–91; Neil (1909), on *Knights* 1245–7.

[135] *SIG* I no. 271; Fisher (forthcoming).

[136] We do not know the location of *memnoneia* and *kenebreia* (stalls for donkey meat and carrion): Wycherley (1957), 186, 197. The consumption of dog-meat is occasionally attested in medical and other texts in ancient Greece (see Arnott (1996) on Alexis 223.4). The eating of dogs is often culturally distinctive: J.-L. Durand and J. Scheid have told me of their studies of dogs eaten by one African people and absolutely not by their neighbours.

[137] He sold two forms of meat, his sausages and his penis.

[138] The question to Agoracritus, 'did you sell black-puddings in the agora or at the gates?', at 1245–6 confirms that black-puddings could be sold at either place.

[139] Cf. Aelian, *Varia Historia* 2.1, 'to encourage and incite him Socrates said, "do you not despite the cobbler over there?" (Here he gave the man's name.) When Alcibiades said he did, Socrates continued, "And the man over there crying his wares in the 'rings', and the tent-maker?" When the young man agreed, "Very well", said Socrates, "the Athenian Demos is a collection of such men."' (Trans. Wycherley (1957), 188.)

dialectical opposition between the city and the countryside. In contrast with the Black-Pudding-Seller and Cleon/Paphlagon, their master Demos is a countryman in his temper (41), he longs for the groats and dried grapes of the countryside (805–7), and returns to his rustic roots at the end of the play (1394–5). Dicaeopolis, the rustic protagonist of *Acharnians*, expresses a similar orientation, longing for the countryside where the voices of the city are not heard: 'the men in the agora chatter up and down' (21), 'my deme never said "buy charcoal" nor "vinegar" nor "oil": "buy" is never sung out. My deme produces everything itself and Mr Buy is not to be found.'[140] Whether or not this passage attests a rural economy based on barter, Dicaeopolis contrasts the town, market talk, and imported foods with the rural economy. The idealizing form of this is evident in 'produces everything for itself', a phrase closely related to the automatic foods of Chapter 3 and *Acharnians* 976, as we have seen. The automated foods made available by Dicaeopolis are distributed through his apparently rural agora in which exchange is conducted by barter. *Knights* takes this refinement of the agora further, for while the man of the agora is initially dismissed as disgusting (181–93), the criteria are based on financial exchange and lack of education. By the end of the play a purified and fully acceptable agora is established.

The *agoraioi* of *Knights* work in the animal business. Butchers are attested elsewhere in comedy (see above), as are 'leather-sellers' and cobblers.[141] There are few other traders mentioned in the play other than the butchers of 418, honey- and cheese-sellers of 852–4, and the 'seller-politicians' who preceded Cleon/Paphlagon, the hemp-seller, the lamp-seller, and the sheep-seller. There is a notable absence of female traders in this play of homosexual violence. Agoracritus, the man of the agora and black-pudding-seller *extraordinaire*,[142] for all his loathsome qualities, is an insider, an Athenian, whose work, though scorned

---

[140] See above and *Islands* fr. 402.

[141] Cobblers: Wycherley (1957), 188, 200; rein-makers and leather-cutters (ibid. 200).

[142] The *allas* which Agoracritus sells appears to have been a blood pudding with garlic: see Wilkins (1994). At *Knights* 207–8, Demos says that the *allas* is long and 'a blood-drinker' like a snake. I have therefore called Agoracritus the Black-Pudding-Seller in place of the conventional Sausage-Seller. *Chorde*, also

(144), is firmly embedded in the sacrificial system.[143] Indeed, he rejuvenates Demos by means of techniques drawn from meat processing. By contrast, Cleon/Paphlagon is not of Athenian descent[144] and he eats fish and other luxury foods which elsewhere in comedy imply either tyranny or anti-democratic sentiments. Paphlagonia may have been associated with luxurious eating: in the fourth century at least Theopompus attacks Thys, the mythical king of Paphlagonia.[145] Despite these failings, the Paphlagonian also works within the sacrificial system as a tanner, deriving most if not all of his hides for tanning from temple sales.[146] As a tanner Cleon/Paphlagon is a different type of meat-processor, but closely related to the black-pudding trade. Significant though tanning is in *Knights*, Cleon/Paphlagon's appetite for food is much more prominent. We return to the prytaneion.

Cleon was the first Athenian general to be given honorific dining in the prytaneion, as far as we know.[147] The generals may have dined at state expense, in the *strategeion* or elsewhere.[148] If so, then Cleon was singled out for particular honour in the prytaneion after the victory at Sphacteria. The parabasis of *Knights* asserts that the honour was won by lobbying from Cleaenetus, Cleon's own father. Once established in the prytaneion, Cleon/Paphlagon does not eat as he ought, with the restraint and gravity of an Aristeides,[149] but displays a powerful appetite. This allows Aristophanes to develop themes of greed where there ought to be respect for the honour bestowed,[150] and from greed

sometimes translated as 'sausage', was at least sometimes in fact a blood-pudding: see Sophilus, *Fellow Runners* fr. 6.2.

[143] Wilkins (1994).

[144] A frequent accusation in comedy and political invective: see MacDowell (1993).

[145] Athenaeus 4.144f, 10.415d.

[146] Inscriptions detailing the sale of hides have been studied by Schmitt-Pantel (1992), 129–39, and Georgoudi (1990).

[147] Aristophanes appears to say at *Knights* 283 that Pericles was not thought worthy of the honour. At 573–6 he says that generals before Cleon would not even have asked.

[148] Thompson and Wycherley (1972), 89. At *Knights* 1325 Aristeides and Miltiades are said to have eaten with the demos.

[149] Aristeides is notable as a politician who was not diverted by pleasure (Athenaeus 12.511c; Plutarch, *Aristeides* 25).

[150] The generals 'say they will not fight unless they are given a seat of honour and food' (575–6).

political rapacity and corruption. Since the prytaneion in the play is the 'home' of Demos, domestic metaphors are brought to bear. The generals are slaves of Demos and prepare food for him: thus barley cakes made for Demos represent the military victory at Pylos. These barley cakes may be greedily consumed or stolen from the cook and passed off as the thief's own production.

Eating in the prytaneion has much hanging upon it. It is a sign of honour, of being included in the state in a much more prestigious way than participation in a sacrifice might be. The honour is often bestowed with the privilege of *prohedria*, the right to sit in the front ranks of the theatre.[151] If Cleon was feasting in the prytaneion, he was also entitled to sit in the front row at the theatre in which *Knights* was presented. At 702 Cleon/Paphlagon swears by the *prohedria* which he was awarded for Pylos, to which the Black-Pudding-Seller retorts (703–4), 'look at this *prohedria*! I'll see you removed from this *prohedria* to the last row of seats!' This link between theatre and honours in the prytaneion and *prohedria* is seen elsewhere in comedy: at *Knights* 535 Cratinus is said to deserve free drink rather than free food, and the right of *prohedria* beside the statue of Dionysus.[152] At *Frogs* 764 poets in the underworld are imagined to be honoured in a similar format with a throne and free food. For a comic poet actually to be feasted in the prytaneion a more political career was probably required, as seen in the recognition of the *eunoia* of Philippides at the end of the fourth century—under the successors of Alexander rather than the democracy.[153]

4.5.1. The Politics of Consumption

Knights presents the hearth of the polis in the prytaneion as if it were in the private home of Demos, the Athenian people personified.[154] The generals are the house slaves of Demos who prepare

---

[151] And, according to the scholiast on *Knights* 575, in the front row at the boule, ecclesia, and other gatherings. Gauthier notes that there seems to be no sign of a public statue for Cleon, the third of the 'greatest honours' voted to civic benefactors.

[152] On Cratinus and drinking see Chap. 5. Cole (1993) notes thrones in Delos in which Dionysus sits between two satyrs. Perhaps Aristophanes implies that Cratinus resembles a drunken old satyr.

[153] *IG* II² 657 = testimonium 3 Kassel–Austin (1989), Plutarch, *Demetrius* 12.8.

[154] For the reduction of a state institution to a private house in Old Comedy see Chap. 1.

food for their master.[155] Cleon/Paphlagon, a slave of recent acquisition, is master's favourite slave. Especially honoured by the Demos and given food in the prytaneion, he is portrayed in the play as a greedy and overbearing slave. He lords it over the other slaves and claims barley cakes made by them to be his own.[156] At the end of the play the honours are reversed. Religious ritual takes over, and Cleon/Paphlagon is driven from both prytaneion and agora as a scapegoat: his eating in the prytaneion, it emerges, has proved to be for the less distinguished but equally distinctive purpose of being fattened after selection as the *pharmakos* or scapegoat.[157] He is replaced by the Black-Pudding-Seller, who has restored the powers of Demos by boiling him in a cooking-pot.

This study of *Knights* examines three strands which prepare for the final scenes in which Demos is boiled and Cleon/Paphlagon expelled: market-trading, the consumption of food, and violence against animals.

4.5.2. Market-trading

For much of *Knights* the agora is a negative space, sneered at by the chorus of aristocratic knights and recalling the encounter in Herodotus (1.153) between Cyrus and the Spartan envoys.[158] The King is not impressed with the agora, which is a feature of the Greek but not the Persian city and is set apart in the middle of the city. There 'they all go to meet and swear oaths and cheat' and 'they go about buying and selling'. *Knights* picks up these ideas of false words and of trade: the city will be controlled by a succession of salesmen (128–45), the last of whom will have the particularly unimpressive trade of black-pudding-selling. All of this is discovered in an oracle stolen from Cleon/Paphlagon:

[155] As in most texts, the arrangements for the meals of slaves is of no interest. Evidence for food preparation in the prytaneion is slim. Better attested is food preparation in the tholos, and indeed animal bones were found in a pit under the present structure.

[156] 54–7. This barley cake prepared for the people represents the campaign against the Spartans at Sphacteria in which Cleon succeeded Demosthenes as commander.

[157] On the scapegoat see Bremer (1983) and Burkert (1983). For the scapegoat driven from the prytaneion see Herodotus 7.197, on the Achaean rituals deriving from Phrixus.

[158] See Braund (1998), 174–5.

SLAVE A: The oracle says straight off that first there is to be a hemp-seller who will be the first to control the affairs of the city.

SLAVE B: That's one seller. What next? Go on.

SLAVE A: After this one then the second is a sheep-seller.

SLAVE B: That's two sellers. What'll happen to this one?

SLAVE A: He'll rule until there's another man more foul. For Paphlagon the leather-seller comes next, a rapacious roarer with the voice of a torrent.

SLAVE B: So the sheep-seller was fated to die at the hands of the leather-seller?

SLAVE A: That's right.

SLAVE B: Alas poor me! Where could one remaining seller still be found?

SLAVE A: There's still one with an extraordinary job.

SLAVE B: Tell me, please, who it is.

SLAVE A: Shall I tell you?

SLAVE B: Yes!

SLAVE A: A black-pudding-seller is the one to destroy him.

The Black-Pudding-Seller arrives as a saviour at the end of this parody of a succession myth (147–9):[159] 'O blessed Black-Pudding-Seller, come here, come here, my dear fellow! Step up, the revealed saviour of the city and of us!' Aristophanes combines, in a political context, the language of sale and of divinity. The successive salesmen possess elemental and divine qualities as well as stalls in the market-place and low birth which, it is suggested, is the qualification for office—the Black-Pudding-Seller will become great because he is bad and from the agora and brazen (180–1), ignorant and hateful (192), with a foul voice, bad birth, and the general characteristics of the agora (218). Cleon/Paphlagon, identified above as 'a rapacious roarer with the voice of a torrent', blows a gale, against which both Black-Pudding-Seller and Aristophanes contend (429–37 and 511). The Black-Pudding-Seller takes on this elemental force[160] as an *agoraios* whose agora comprises more than a place of sale. He is told (164–5) that he will rule over 'the agora, the harbours, and the pnyx', that is, the sites of popular politics, trade, empire, and government; he will also enjoy violent pleasures against the persons of

---

[159] Bowie (1993).

[160] In one of Aristophanes' more absurd touches in this play the Black-Pudding-Seller declares that he will furl the sausages of his ship in the face of the gale (432–3).

councillors and generals (166—those currently in power). Standing on his portable black-pudding stall (168) he will be able to see the islands, the large trading areas (*emporia*), and the merchant ships, all of which made Athens a successful commercial empire (see above). At the end of the play the Black-Pudding-Seller takes over, as predicted in the oracle setting out the succession. He is the popular hero, welcome to all because, as we shall see, he has restored the rule of the Demos, the people, against those in power.[161]

Market-traders, like their customers, were sometimes imagined to exercise little restraint over their desires.[162] In his enthusiasm for fish Archestratus encourages the prospective buyer to pay any price or snatch or steal what he cannot otherwise acquire:[163] this desperate buying is matched by the greedy eating of the fish once prepared.[164] One of Theophrastus' *Characters*, the shameless man (9), shows a similar lack of restraint at the butcher's stall. In *Knights* the two specialist traders, the black-pudding-seller and leather-seller, are characterized by greed, enormous appetite, and lack of restraint. They are politically rapacious and substitute the worst aspects of the market-place for the proper control of ritual. They represent a consumer society rather than a ritually ordered respect, and flout the latter in

---

[161] On Bakhtin and my disagreement with the objections of Edwards see Chap. 1. There is, further, a theatrical dimension to this political reconfiguration. The audience, the 'rows of the people' (163) are to be the subjects of this popular hero. Cleon, the enemy of all, will not even be represented with a mask, so fearful is his visage. The audience will have to use its ingenuity to recognize him (230–4). Cleon/Paphlagon (as we have seen) will be relegated to the very back of the theatre (703–4). The Black-Pudding-Seller will have as allies the poet (511), the rich and the poor (220–4), and the chorus (247–54). When the Black-Pudding-Seller succeeds in rejuvenating Demos, he calls on the theatre to rejoice by singing a *paean* (1318).

[162] Cf. Plato, *Laws* 11.918d. See further Chap. 6, where this passage is quoted.

[163] Frr. 15, 21; cf. Athenaeus 8.342d–e.

[164] Fr. 22. This greed is matched by anecdotes in Athenaeus on Philoxenus (1.5d–6b). If that gourmet was unable to buy goods in the market, the preferred location of his appetite, he went unbidden to a wedding (that is, as a parasite) where he could earn food in return for his dithyrambs: these tales contrast the market economy with the ritualized form of the wedding. On Philoxenus and Archestratus see Chap. 7.

pursuit of appetite.[165] The Black-Pudding-Seller is accused of selling tripe without paying a proper fee to the prytaneis who administer the temple from whence it came (300–2); he is alert to whitebait prices (662, 672), and buys up monopoly supplies of coriander and onion (676–7).

It is important to stress how specialized is the market-trading in *Knights*. Perfume-sellers (1375), honey-sellers, and cheese-sellers (853–4) are mentioned, but in this play the market-place is dominated (uniquely in Greek texts, as far as I know) by meat-selling and leather-selling. The Black-Pudding-Seller claims (850–7) that the leather-sellers co-ordinate the *agoraioi* against attempts of Demos to control them. There are no female vendors except for the prostitutes at the gates.

4.5.3. *Consumption of Food*

The politicians feed Demos as if he were a man in his dotage,[166] since he gives every appearance of being too old to control events. The foods he receives are a blend of two kinds: actual food such as barley cakes (which are often metaphors for political action), and political rhetoric—both to be found in the Athenian agora. The politicians set up mealtimes to suit their own needs. Demos is encouraged to think of himself as an autocratic ruler, a king or tyrant with lackeys to keep off the flies,[167] while the politicians are

[165] Schmitt-Pantel (1992) sees in this play a comic confusion of ritualized and hedonistic eating, exemplified perhaps by oral sex in the prytaneion offered to the Black-Pudding-Seller (167) and wine in the prytaneion to Cratinus (535). I would argue, rather, that mechanisms of control are never far from the surface and are finally reimposed at the end of the play.

[166] μεμακκοακότα (62; cf. 396). Demos appears to be childlike. On the complex mechanisms of control between the provider and consumer of food we might compare the relationship between a mother and child. The mother, if not fully vigilant or too indulgent, may allow the child to swallow too much food for his or her own good health; equally, the mother may allow the child a certain kind of food and more of it than is desirable for good health. Both mother and child bring psychological and other pressure to bear on each other as they negotiate over the power relationship between them. By refusing food the child is able to exert his or her will over the mother, while the mother can strengthen the child's bond with her by offering more food. The relationship may also be reversed over time so that, at the end of her life, the mother may become the consumer of food that is provided by the adult child.

[167] For Cleon/Paphlagon keeping away other politicians as if they were flies compare the comic description of the king of Paphos cited on p. 77.

his parasites who flatter him and sponge from him. In this respect Cleon/Paphlagon's activities resemble those attributed to him in the *Wasps*:[168] (47–8) 'abasing himself, he fawned on the master, wheedled, flattered and deceived him';[169] he suggests a bath after the lawcourt and then that Demos should 'pop in a morsel, suck in some soup, nibble away, have your three obols'.[170] Four terms for false speech are followed by three special forms of eating.[171] Cleon/Paphlagon then offers an extra meal, a 'supper' or *dorpos* (52). Further, he attempts to become the sole 'carer' of Demos (59–60).[172] Cleon/Paphlagon is alleged to provide exclusive and excessive nursing and nourishment. Later (715), Cleon/Paphlagon declares he knows the right kinds of baby-food for Demos, which the Black-Pudding-Seller (716–18) interprets as masticating Demos' food as children's nurses do and putting just a little in the 'infant's' mouth (*entitheis*) while gulping down three times as much himself.[173] Cleon/Paphlagon knows how to make Demos 'wider and narrower' (720), which the Black-Pudding-Seller interprets not as making him fatter or thinner but as buggering him. The phrase reinforces the passive role of Demos.[174]

The contests later in the play are based on various offers of food to Demos. At 788–9 Demos is said to receive more little dainties. At 1101, in a metaphor for the corn supply for the people of Athens, Cleon/Paphlagon offers to provide barley and daily sustenance, which[175] the Black-Pudding-Seller counters with ready-made barley cakes and roasted *opson*: no effort was

---

[168] *Wasps* 666–79.

[169] (47–8), ὑποπεσὼν τὸν δεσπότην ἤικαλλ', ἐθώπευ', ἐκολάκευ', ἐξηπάτα.

[170] ἐνθοῦ, ῥόφησον, ἔντραγ', ἔχε τριώβολον.

[171] On the details see Neil (1909) *ad loc*. ἐντιθέναι is particularly used of nurses feeding infants, ῥοφεῖν of soups and porridges, ἐντραγεῖν of the fruits and nuts of dessert. On baby foods see Pollux 6.33.

[172] On the apparently anachronistic *dorpos* and on *therapeuein* as caring in a political context see Neil (1909).

[173] Cf. (404) the wish of the chorus that Cleon/Paphlagon will cough up the *enthesis* that he has filched.

[174] At 1162–3 Demos claims to manipulate his lovers if he does not get what he wants.

[175] 1101 κριθὰς ποριῶ σοι καὶ βίον καθ' ἡμέραν ('I will provide barley grains and daily sustenance for you'); 1104 ἀλλ' ἄλφιτ' . . . ποριῶ ('but I will provide barley meal').

needed but the eating of them.[176] The last contest between Cleon/Paphlagon and the Black-Pudding-Seller for the affections of Demos is built on gifts of food (1164–1225), with Athena purportedly providing the foods (1169–70, 1203). The Black-Pudding-Seller tells Demos to consider who offers the best for himself and his stomach (1208); he wins the contest because he has, or appears to have given, all the food he has to Demos, while Cleon/Paphlagon has kept a good deal for himself (1215–25). Throughout the play Demos has been the consumer, manipulated by the self-serving rhetoric of those offering him food. All this is a parody of what ought to happen in the prytaneion, namely recognition of the honour that the people has bestowed.

A number of speakers in *Knights* make it plain that the city is experiencing its present crisis because of the abuse of honorific dining in the prytaneion. In the past generals were strictly regulated—Pericles, for example (283). Those who did dine honourably, such as Aristeides and Miltiades (1325), ate together with Demos on an equal rather than exploitative basis. Cleon/Paphlagon has subverted the civic ritual because he does not accept *sitesis* simply as an honour:

BLACK-PUDDING-SELLER: I denounce this man, by Zeus, for running into the prytaneion with an empty gut and running back out again full.

SLAVE A: Yes, by Zeus, and he took out what is forbidden, bread and meat and salt fish, which even Pericles was not allowed to do.

(280–3)

This decline is reviewed further in the parabasis (573–6): 'not one of the generals in the past would have *asked* for *sitesis*—from Cleaenetus;[177] now on the other hand they refuse to fight unless they get food and seats of honour (*prohedria*)'. Later in the play (763–6), Cleon/Paphlagon confirms this picture when he prays to Athena to be allowed to continue to dine in the prytaneion—in return for nothing since he is one of the best of the prostitutes. What ought to be honorific and symbolic has been exploited to satisfy base appetite.

[176] The offer resembles the automated food of the utopian plays and plays based on provision by agricultural gods. The Black-Pudding-Seller claims at 1095 that Athena will pour ambrosia over the head of Demos.

[177] The father of Cleon.

Much food in the play is taken by force, from the prytaneion and elsewhere, to meet the insatiable appetite of the politicians. As we have seen, Cleon/Paphlagon snatches barley cakes prepared by others (these represent the victory at Pylos);[178] at 1030–4 he is compared to the ravenous mythical dog Cerberus who sneaks into the kitchen and licks out the stewing-pots—and the islands.[179] The Black-Pudding-Seller, in the competition for gross appetite,[180] counters with the declaration that he will emulate Cleon/Paphlagon in stealing loaves (778), and claims that he earned his spurs as a politician with the theft of meat by deception from the butchers in the agora (410–20, 428). The Black-Pudding-Seller finally vanquishes Cleon/Paphlagon by stealing his hare in the contest of offers to Demos (1192–200), in effect by repeating his trick against the butchers. This success in the contest of theft and appetite that runs through the play[181] is nothing less than a triumph of *bomolochia*. To be sure, the meat stolen is not sacrificial, but it is taken disreputably in circumstances which ought to be regulated by the city (the relationship of Demos and the honoured guests in the prytaneion). The snatching of food has an ambivalent place in comedy. On the one hand it represents an appetite out of control, like that seen in Archestratus above;[182] on the other, the comic protagonist may get away with actions normally discouraged by the moral code, and may in comic terms be praised for it—provided, as here, that the protagonist is acting for the people and the chorus against agreed opponents.[183] When the Black-Pudding-Seller steals Cleon/Paphlagon's hare, therefore, he is in part turning the tables on all of the latter's rapacity earlier in the play, and in part triumphing in his rascality—which is permissible if the means meet the comic end of benefiting the people.

[178] At 391–6 he is said to be parching the corn (that is, the prisoners of war) captured from Pylos in anticipation of sale.

[179] That is, he consumes the imperial revenues. Cf. the dog at *Wasps* 894–917.

[180] The chorus say to the Black-Pudding-Seller: 'what you say is fine, but we are alarmed by your guzzling the soup of political affairs on your own' (360).

[181] The snatching or stealing of food is reinforced by other rapacity which does not specify food. For the verb ἁρπάζειν and related terms see lines 137, 205, 248, 296, 802, 1127, 1147, 1224, 1239, 1252.

[182] See Athenaeus 8.342d–e and Chap. 6.

[183] See Chap. 2.11 and such actions as the trouncing of interfering officials by Dicaeopolis in *Acharnians* and Trygaeus in *Peace*.

Snatching and stealing in the play are supplemented with greedy eating, gulping, and other forms of swallowing. Cleon/Paphlagon is accused of consuming the property of all;[184] he also picks off magistrates under examination like ripe figs (259–60). This diet augments the food that he pretended to give to Demos but in fact kept for himself. Sometimes the mouth of Demos is open[185]—as is often the case with the 'gawping' poor of Athens—but nothing goes in: Cleon/Paphlagon gulps down the 'stalks' of the *euthunai* (accounts submitted by officials) that he has chopped off and 'spoons up'[186] public money with both hands (824–6)—bread-spoons help down the vegetables. All this contrasts with Themistocles, another of the idealized generals of the past, who gave food to the city and took none away:[187] Themistocles supplied healthy food while Cleon/Paphlagon abuses fine food (819).[188] Eating in the city has, however, not in fact been orchestrated quite as Cleon/Paphlagon planned.

At 1125–30 Demos makes an unexpected declaration: 'there is no brain under that hair of yours if you think I am not thinking straight. I put on these foolish ways on purpose. I enjoy myself childishly guzzling my daily allowance, and it is my wish to feed up one of these thieving political leaders. When he's full, I lift him up for sacrifice and strike.' The chorus reply, 'well, you do very well in that, and there's much shrewdness in your method, as you say, if you deliberately feed them up on the Pnyx as

---

[184] τὰ κοινά . . . κατεσθίεις (258).   [185] 824 χασμᾶι.

[186] Crusts served as spoons in Greece: see n. 200.

[187] Themistocles added Peiraeus as a barley cake (*maza*) for ariston (on which see Chap. 2): see Marr (1996) on the meal of *maza*, *opson*, and wine that Themistocles provided for Athens. While Themistocles is not listed with Aristeides and Miltiades among the generals of old who respected the honorific eating of the prytaneion, he is presented as a provider of good 'foods' for the city which contrast with the insubstantial infant foods provided by Cleon/Paphlagon.

[188] This theme recurs in *Wasps* 666–79: Bdelycleon asserts that Philocleon has chosen to be ruled by the politicians because he has been 'thoroughly cooked' by their little speeches (668). The politicians threaten the allies, while the people are happy 'nibbling around their sheep's feet' (672). The allies realize the people are content to be 'eking out a poor living from the voting urn and nibbling nothing' (674), and so give bribes to the leaders (679, quoted above). Bribes in the form of food have a dual function: they appear trivial beside the great affairs of state but at the same time reflect imported luxuries—extras which the privileged enjoy and the majority do not—particularly in the sense of conferring social distinction.

sacrificial animals at state expense and then whenever you run out of meat you sacrifice whichever of them is fattened and dine on him'.[189] Demos, we now discover, was in control all along: he knew the politicians were stealing his food, and makes them vomit up what they have stolen (1145–50). In his restored state at the end of the play Demos answers the question, 'if one of the offering-stealers—a public speaker[190]—should say "there is no ground barley for you unless you find guilty in this case" what will you do to this public speaker?'; 'I shall lift him up and throw him in the pit, having strung up Hyperbolus by the throat' (1358–63). Demos makes a public example of the men who previously appeared to control his decisions through diet. The ritual order of proper *sitesis* and sacrifice were, it now appears, always underpinning the city. The politicians are suitable animals for sacrifice.

4.5.4. Animal Sacrifice

Knights is a play of the Old Comedy without a chorus of animals,[191] but Cleon/Paphlagon reacts to the chorus's entrance on stage as if they were animals, 'by what animals am I gutted!'.[192] Animals in this play represent aggression and appetite, and as the contest unfolds, it is the animality of Cleon/Paphlagon and the

---

[189] ΔΗ.: νοῦς οὐκ ἔνι ταῖς κόμαις ὑμῶν, ὅτε μ᾽ οὐ φρονεῖν νομίζετ᾽· ἐγὼ δ᾽ ἑκὼν ταῦτ᾽ ἠλιθιάζω. αὐτός τε γὰρ ἥδομαι βρύλλων τὸ καθ᾽ ἡμέραν, κλέπτοντά τε βούλομαι τρέφειν ἕνα προστάτην· τοῦτον δ᾽, ὅταν ᾖ πλέως, ἄρας ἐπάταξα. ΧΟ.: χοὔτω μὲν ἂν εὖ ποιοῖς, εἴ σοι πυκνότης ἔνεστ᾽ ἐν τῶι τρόπωι, ὡς λέγεις, τούτωι πάνυ πολλή, εἰ τούσδ᾽ ἐπίτηδες ὥσπερ δημοσίους τρέφεις ἐν τῆι πυκνί, κἀιθ᾽ ὅταν μή σοι τύχηι ὄψον ὄν, τούτων ὃς ἂν ᾖ παχύς, θύσας ἐπιδειπνεῖς. The terms for meat (*opson*) and dine (*epideipneis*) could be taken to support Schmitt-Pantel's case for the confusion of luxury and ritual in the play. I propose a different interpretation. Food consumed in the prytaneion and other public buildings in Athens was, as we saw above, more than basic. It is not clear whether the terms used here refer only to food consumed in the prytaneion or also to the fattening of animals for sacrifice followed by communal dining at a civic festival such as the Panathenaia.

[190] βωμολόχος ξυνήγορος.

[191] Except in the limited reference to the knights' horses feeding on lucerne and crabs (595–610). It is perhaps possible that the chorus was composed of twelve horses and twelve riders, like the knights on a much earlier Attic black-figure amphora (Berlin 1697), for which see Sifakis (1971), 73 and pl. 1.

[192] ὑφ᾽ οἵων θηρίων γαστρίζομαι 273. Again, in suffering disembowelment he is subject to the skills appropriate to the trade of the Black-Pudding-Seller.

Black-Pudding-Seller rather than that of the chorus which is developed. The antagonists shout and bawl at each other (284–96):[193]

CLEON/PAPHLAGON: Instant death for you!
BLACK-PUDDING-SELLER: I'll shriek three times louder than you!
CLEON/PAPHLAGON: I'll shout you down with shouting!
BLACK-PUDDING-SELLER: I'll shriek you down with shrieking!
CLEON/PAPHLAGON: I'll slander you if you're elected general!
BLACK-PUDDING-SELLER: I'll dog-chop your back!
CLEON/PAPHLAGON: I'll strip you bare with my equivocations!
BLACK-PUDDING-SELLER: I'll cut off your escape routes!
CLEON/PAPHLAGON: Look at me without flinching!
BLACK-PUDDING-SELLER: I was raised in the agora too!
CLEON/PAPHLAGON: I'll take you apart if you grunt!
BLACK-PUDDING-SELLER: I'll carry you out on a shit shovel if you chatter on!
CLEON/PAPHLAGON: I acknowledge my thieving. But you're not.

They shout like animals, with animal aggression. They claim in addition enormous appetite (353–81): Cleon/Paphlagon consumes hot[194] tuna slices and neat wine before aggressive sex against the generals at Pylos, while the Black-Pudding-Seller gulps down some of his meats as a prelude to political violence.[195] Cleon/Paphlagon links his appetite with a bid for an imported luxury, a Milesian bass (361),[196] while the Black-Pudding-Seller has an appetite for (Attic) meat and mines. This competition in appetite leads into a series of butchering metaphors and threats that each will apply against the other his skills in processing animals. Working from their experience in tanning and pudding-making (314–18), they threaten summary violence (364–81):

BLACK-PUDDING-SELLER: I'll stuff your bum instead of a pudding!
CLEON/PAPHLAGON: I'll drag you outside by the buttocks, head down!

[193] Of κράζειν, βοᾶν, γρύζειν, only the second literally describes the human voice.
[194] On the stimulating effect of hot food on the appetite see Chap. 1.
[195] Much of the sexuality in the play is aggressive and is built on male homosexuality. There is the offer of sex and battery against the council at 166–7; there is the proud boast of being the prostitute who is best for Athens and who is able 'to do nothing and dine in the prytaneion' (764–6). The Black-Pudding-Seller was brought up as a prostitute (1242, 'I sold my puddings and I had sex').
[196] Cf. 930–40, where the Black-Pudding-Seller links Cleon/Paphlagon's appetite for sizzling squid with plans for extortion in Miletus. The scholiast may be right to say that Cleon was active in Miletus.

SLAVE A: By Poseidon, if you drag him off you'll have to take me too!

CLEON/PAPHLAGON: See how I'll tie you into the stocks!

BLACK-PUDDING-SELLER: I'll prosecute you for cowardice!

CLEON/PAPHLAGON: Your hide is going to be stretched!

BLACK-PUDDING-SELLER: I'll skin you to make a thief's pouch!

CLEON/PAPHLAGON: I'll peg you out on the ground!

BLACK-PUDDING-SELLER: I'll make mincemeat out of you!

CLEON/PAPHLAGON: I'll pluck out your eyelashes!

BLACK-PUDDING-SELLER: I'll cut out your crop![197]

SLAVE A: Yes, by Zeus, we'll shove a peg in his mouth like butchers do, then we'll pull out his tongue to see good and proper whether his gaping hole[198] is diseased.

Political aggression is expressed in the terms suitable to the violence of their own trades. Those trades, however, derive from the processing of animals in sacrificial ritual, as we have seen, and there are early hints that Cleon/Paphlagon is to be the 'animal' 'sacrificed' by Demos at the end of the play and the Black-Pudding-Seller the processor who will prevail. At 375–81 it is Cleon/Paphlagon's head which is the pig's head displayed in the butcher's shop.

As part of the rhetorical competition in bribery and grossness, in which insufficient shamelessness[199] incurs Cleon/Paphlagon's oath, 'may I never be present to share the vital organs sacrificed to Zeus of the agora' (410), the Black-Pudding-Seller claims (411–28) to have been brought up in the agora on a diet of bread thrown to the dogs,[200] theft of meat, and prostitution.[201] He is urged (454–6) to be brave and to 'hit him in the stomach with

---

[197] i.e. the crop of a cock, in which the bird prepares food for digestion. Athenaeus refers to a sacrifice of a cock to Athena at the Panathenaea, albeit on the evidence of Juba at a much later date (3.98b).

[198] Aristophanes writes 'arsehole' as a surprise for 'mouth'.

[199] On shamelessness and politicians compare the choral strophe at 324–32 and esp. 324–5, 'well then, Cleon/Paphlagon, didn't you from the start display your shamelessness (*anaideia*)? Shamelessness is the one single defender of politicians.'

[200] In the absence of forks and (normally) spoons the Greeks used bread to mop up food. They also used bread to wipe the fingers clean. Waste bread was thrown to the dogs. Edite Vieira (1988), 8, reports a similar practice among the rich in Portugal. Waste bread, she says, went to dogs and beggars.

[201] For the connection between meat and sex see Henderson (1991), 129.

your entrails and guts. See you gut him!'[202] The processors of animals slog it out in bestial fashion, and the guts in question are at one moment at a sacrifice (300–2), at another part of the Black-Pudding-Seller's trade (160–1), and now the antagonists' own guts (454–6). On their way to the assembly they are primed with garlic like fighting-cocks (490–7). After the parabasis and messenger speech, in which the Black-Pudding-Seller reports an outrageous bid and counter-bid to the assembly with his bribe of one hundred sacrificial cattle beaten by Cleon/Paphlagon's offer of two hundred cattle, the contest continues with aggressive eating, swallowing, and consumption (698–709):

CLEON/PAPHLAGON: I swear by Demeter that if I don't consume you utterly out of this land I won't be able to live!

BLACK-PUDDING-SELLER: If you don't consume me? Well, me too, if I don't drink you up and if, when I guzzle you up, I don't go on to burst!

. . . .

CLEON/PAPHLAGON: I'll claw your guts out with my nails!

BLACK-PUDDING-SELLER: I'll claw out the food you ate in the prytaneion!

Once Demos appears on stage (728) a new element is introduced into the contest, the offering of food as if they were his affectionate lovers (732–40, 1163) and the proving of their love by wishing their meat-processing on their own heads if they are not true lovers (767–72):

CLEON/PAPHLAGON: If I hate you and if I alone don't fight for you and support you, may I perish and be sawn up and cut into leather straps!

BLACK-PUDDING-SELLER: Me too, Demos. If I don't love you and cherish you may I be cut up and boiled as mincemeat! And if you don't believe that, may I be grated up on this table and be cooked in a savoury pie with the cheese, and may I be dragged by the bollocks to the Cerameicus on my own meat-hook![203]

Towards the end of the play (1015–34) oracles recall an earlier theme of Cleon/Paphlagon, the dog with a big voice and appetite who bites and steals food. After the oracles the antagonists outbid each other in offering titbits to Demos who reveals (as we

---

[202] γάστριζε καὶ τοῖς ἐντέροις καὶ τοῖς κόλοις, χὤπως κολᾷ τὸν ἄνδρα.

[203] This last is an imaginative adaptation of the Athenian practice of selling or distributing surplus meat from sacrifice at the Cerameicus.

have seen at 1130–40) that it is in fact he who is in ritual control of the animal-politicians. The animality brought out in the battles, though, is combined slowly with new elements, of festivity (possibly the Thargelia) and hints of ostracism and expulsion. All these features prepare the way for the boiling of Demos and the expulsion of Cleon/Paphlagon as the scapegoat.

In *Knights* food is processed, cooked, and consumed in a number of 'real' and metaphorical forms. The Black-Pudding-Seller for much of the play is a *mageiros* only in one of the three senses demonstrated in Berthiaume (1982). He is a purveyor of meat in the market, apparently cooked and uncooked. He shows few of the characteristics either of the *mageiros* who cuts the animal's throat at sacrifice or of the *mageiros* who is the hired chef of comedy in the fourth century.[204] He enters the stage with his gear (*skeue*), as do his successors in Middle and New Comedy. He sells meats that have been boiled (a lower category than meats that have been roasted).[205] The tools of his trade include his knives (412) and his portable block or table (152, 159);[206] the skills of his trade include the washing of entrails (*koiliai*, 160), the stuffing of guts, and the stirring, mixing, and spicing of ingredients (213–16). The latter process has a striking political analogue:

BLACK-PUDDING-SELLER: I'm amazed that I have the ability to oversee the people.
SLAVE A: That's easy. Do what you do! Stir and blend the pudding mixture all together,[207] always adding some fat[208] and adjusting the seasoning with some cook's phraselets.[209]

The Black-Pudding-Seller appears to be not merely a manufacturer of puddings; he also cooks them for the table. That at least is implied by his boasts about swallowing meat soup (357),

---

[204]　On whom see Chap. 8.

[205]　See Detienne and Vernant (1989) and Wilkins (1994) for his place in the sacrificial system. Athenaeus collects comic citations of meats boiled in water (3.94c–96f), as I noted in Chap. 1.

[206]　The *epikopanon* of New Comedy (Pollux 6.90). Cf. the *epixenon* of Dicaeopolis, *Acharnians* 355, 359.

[207]　Cf. Thucydides' praise of the political *sunkrasis* (8.97.2).

[208]　There is a pun on Demos, which signifies both the people and cooking-fat.

[209]　At 343 the Black-Pudding-Seller declares, 'I know how to speak in public and to make rich sauces (καρυκοποιεῖν)'. This is the only reference in the play to the Black-Pudding-Seller's preparation of a luxury dish. For *karuke* see Chap. 6.

his self-imprecation about being chopped up and boiled (769–70), and his offering of meat boiled in soup (1178), together with 216 ('cook's phraselets') and 343 (making rich sauces). Cooking terms, such as boiling and roasting, have a wide resonance in comedy, both literally and in images of violence.[210] While the contests in the play employ a range of terms of violence deployed by the bestial politicians,[211] the Black-Pudding-Seller remains close to the culinary process. We gain the increasingly clear impression from 375–81 onwards that he is the cook and Cleon/Paphlagon the pig. The latter is also imagined to be the cooking-pot, or perhaps the cooking liquid: at 919–22 he is spluttering and boiling over; the fire must be reduced and the scum skimmed.[212] (Aristophanes liked this image, and employed it later in a rhetorical sense at *Peace* 314: 'the guy splutters and shouts.')[213] Cleon/Paphlagon is imagined to be part of the *batterie de cuisine* manipulated by the cook. These images prepare for the final scenes in which the Black-Pudding-Seller, while earlier displaying some of the characteristics of an animal, controls the techniques of cooking which are at the heart of the Greek sacrifice. There is not a sacrifice at the end of the play, for Demos does not put his 'sacrifice' of politicians into practice, visiting instead the violence of scapegoating on the victim Cleon/Paphlagon.[214] Instead of cutting the throat of the fattened 'animal' victim, Demos expels the fattened *pharmakos* from the prytaneion.

---

[210] Cf. 769–72 (cited above) with *Peace* 236–70.

[211] I cited above culinary imagery at 372, 374, and 454–6.

[212] A cooking-pot is doing just that at Eubulus, *Titans* fr. 109 Hunter: 'with laughter the stewing-pot splutters in a barbarian chatter and the fish jump up in the middle of the frying-pans'. Eubulus' phrase 'barbarian chatter' may recall *Knights*, since Cleon/Paphlagon is the quintessential comic barbarian of a politician. The scholiast points out the metaphor.

[213] Cf. Timocles 17.3 on an orator *paphlazon*. Cleon/Paphlagon is also a *doidux* and *torune* (forms of pestle) at 984, another image of culinary, though not sacrificial, violence—used of him again, and of Brasidas as generals in *Peace*.

[214] For the expulsion of the scapegoat as in some sense a 'sacrifice' see Burkert (1983), Burkert (1979), 59–77. Caution is needed in identifying too closely in *Knights* the ritual violence of sacrifice with the expulsion of the scapegoat. Similarly, it is not certain that the festival implied by the *eiresione* of Demos (729) is the Thargelia rather than the Pyanopsia. I am grateful for advice from Jean-Louis Durand and Alan Sommerstein on these points.

There is also a quasi-sacrifice of Demos himself. The Black-Pudding-Seller puts Demos in his pot and rejuvenates him by boiling (1321). This action, according to the scholiast, is built on the mythological paradigm of Medea's cooking of Pelias which had been treated in the *Nurses of Dionysus* of Aeschylus. This mythological echo has not come into the play from nowhere. The Black-Pudding-Seller, as we saw above, is hailed as a saviour early in the play; throughout the play he concerns himself with the processing of animals; now he uses those same techniques to save Demos by restoring him to his youthful powers. How does he boil Demos?[215] As one who prepares and sells cooked food, the Black-Pudding-Seller dismembers animals. In his section on 'meats cooked in water' (2.94c), Athenaeus lists four of his sixteen quotations from *Knights*.[216] The Black-Pudding-Seller does not cook animals whole, he boils parts of them, the intestines in particular but also the extremities.[217] Demos is boiled discreetly: we are not told how it was done, but are left, like the scholiast, to imagine something like Pelias in the Medea myth.[218]

[215] Aristophanes may be helped by the pun on the word demos (see n. 208). He uses this pun at 954, where Demos declares that his seal is a 'roasted fig-leaf savoury (*thrion*) of cow fat'. We should perhaps imagine that the boiling of Demos resembles the refining of fat. Pollux (6.57) says that the making of a *thrion* starts with 'boiled pig fat' (στέαρ ὕειον ἑφθόν).

[216] For which see Chap. 1 on cooking utensils and bodily dismemberment.

[217] Feet are referred to at 291, the animal head at 375–81.

[218] Medea persuaded the daughters of Pelias that she could rejuvenate their father as she had restored Jason's father Aeson to his youth. This was a trick to punish Pelias for his injustice towards Jason. Aeson had been rejuvenated by a boiled mixture of magic herbs (see Homeric cycle *Nostoi* fr. 6; Ovid, *Metamorphoses* 7.251–96). The daughters of Pelias were shown how Medea could rejuvenate a ram by cutting it up and boiling it in a pot. They imitated the process, cut up their father, and boiled him. He died horribly (see Frazer (1921) on Apollodorus 1.9.27; Ovid, *Metamorphoses* 7.297–349; Hunter, 'Medea', *OCD³*, 944). Aeschylus' play *The Nurses of Dionysus* apparently portrayed Medea's rejuvenation of the nurses and their husbands. This is noted by ancient scholars in the hypothesis of Euripides' *Medea* and on *Knights* 1321, and may have been the most familiar scene of rejuvenation by boiling to Athenian audiences. The hypothesis to *Medea* also mentions Medea's rejuvenation of Jason in versions by Simonides and Pherecydes. Since the phrase Aristophanes uses is 'to boil off' or 'refine' Demos, we are presumably to imagine that he is boiled in a pot like the ram Medea boiled (and presumably the nurses of Dionysus) rather than given the kind of blood-transfusion imagined by Ovid for Aeson. Unfortunately, the

The Black-Pudding-Seller is an early example of the vendor of boiled or cooked meats which Athenaeus attests in Alexandria in the second century AD.[219] This is a trade that is low in the social hierarchy; early in the play, as we have seen, the Black-Pudding-Seller is invited to leave his guts and become ruler of the citizens, of the agora, harbours, and pnyx. I have demonstrated in this chapter that the agora was at the heart of the polis; *Knights* reflects this and, in problematizing the agora with the trades of Cleon/Paphlagon and the Black-Pudding-Seller, demonstrates that the agora must be a regulated space and not subject to the limitless ambition and appetite of politicians and salesmen. Athens as a polis regulated her agora and harbours with officials responsible to the council; in *Knights* that regulation is imposed by the ritual constraints of sacrifice and a sense of order that appeals to tradition. Demos is restored to his antique beauty (1321) and is now able to reject Cleon/Paphlagon's seat of power, the lawcourts (1317, 1358–61), in favour of those who row in the fleet and fight in the army (1366–71). The young, those who are particularly prone to irresponsible expense at fish-stalls and elsewhere, as we shall see in Chapter 6, are no longer to be allowed into the agora (1373), and no longer will young leather-sellers be able to flout the desire of the Demos to ostracize whom it chooses (852–7).

I have demonstrated elsewhere[220] that the organization of food within the play is carefully regulated: sacrificial meats are under the control of Demos and the Black-Pudding-Seller, while fish, game, and other foods are enjoyed by Cleon/Paphlagon, the rival meat-processor whose production includes nothing edible.[221] Demos' control of sacrifice is undeclared until the end of the play; once he recognizes and accepts the Black-Pudding-Seller's powers he submits to a quasi-magical transformation and is boiled in the cauldron of rejuvenation (1321), receiving great

hypothesis to *Medea* does not give details of how Medea effected all these rejuvenations (with the exception of the *Nostoi* fragment, which it quotes).

[219] See p. 19 above.   [220] Wilkins (1994).

[221] There are minor exceptions to what I wrote in 1994—the Black-Pudding-Seller refers rhetorically to *karuke* sauce, he offers sardines to the assembly, and oracles relating to him include mackerel—but these do not seriously undermine my case, for cheap fish are not included in the discourse of luxury in comedy: see Chap. 6.

agatha from the Black-Pudding-Seller (1335–6). The 'sacrifice' of Cleon/Paphlagon takes a different form, the violent expulsion of the *pharmakos*, perhaps in the context of the Thargelia. A hint of the festival is to be found in Demos' drawing attention to his *eiresione* or harvest-bough (728–9), while the expulsion of the *pharmakos* was linked with the Thargelia in Athens and other cities. The Black-Pudding-Seller proves to be a miracle-worker; despite his apparently unfavourable origins (he is not one of the elite), he is an Athenian and has, it turns out, always been on the right side, like all protagonists of Old Comedy. He belongs, with the audience, to the community of citizens, for all his baseness, shamelessness, and buffoonery.[222]

The expulsion of the *pharmakos* Cleon/Paphlagon in this play is a literal enactment of what is found widely in comedy, the violent exclusion, the comic ostracism, of those in power in the polis. In *Knights* Cleon/Paphlagon was fed in the prytaneion, is driven outside the city gates, and is called a *pharmakos* (1405). Cleon/Paphlagon suffers literally what is wished on, for example, Lamachus in *Acharnians* (exclusion from feast and festival) and Hyperbolus in *Knights* (1363) and *Peace* (Hyperbolus is excluded from the feast).[223] Cleon is made to suffer in the theatre (1318). Aristophanes has converted political honour in the city—*sitesis* for Cleon in the prytaneion—into ritual humiliation on the stage.

Knights demonstrates the richness of the agora in its civic and commercial dealings and the need for regulation in all the activities taking place in the heart of the city. This play feeds into the notion of restraint that was part of the self-definition of Athens. Hermippus fr. 63 demonstrates the importance of Athenian markets (whether in the Athenian agora or in the Peiraeus) in the import, export, and possible re-export of foods from elsewhere. Imported foods might be contrasted with indigenous products, and their desirability or strangeness registered. So, in *Acharnians*, the well-being of the community is linked with the ability to

---

[222] Bowie (1993), 74–7 explores the mythological background to the scapegoating of Cleon/Paphlagon and the transformation of the Black-Pudding-Seller.

[223] After these humiliations on stage Hyperbolus suffered political ostracism in 417.

import foods from Megara and Thebes. It is immediately obvious how those cities differ from Athens. Thebans have more food,[224] Megarians less. Athenians claimed a comparatively lower intake of food, and simpler foods at that[225]—though not as low as a city under siege such as Megara. Others could be identified by their sauces, their greater luxury, and their gluttony. This self-definition is unlikely to correspond entirely, if at all, with 'reality' or indeed with other literature. Matro's *Attic Dinner* demonstrates that lavish dinners could be imagined in Attica. It is likely that some new influences from other cities were felt but that much of what we read are reactionary Athenian views which claim lower consumption, praise simplicity, and develop the discourse of luxury explored in Chapter 6.

This and the previous chapter have demonstrated that, although there is a polarity in comedy between the countryside and the city, the two are usually integrated into a whole polis. The comic agora is an integral part of the polis, though it may be perverted by the self-seeking politician and the unscrupulous trader. Both rural and urban demes benefit from the assertion of communal values and commensality as guaranteed by the comic gods and religious and civic ritual. If the supply of food from fields and trade is running smoothly and the distribution of food is not diverted for the benefit of the elite, then the comic polis flourishes.

The next chapter extends the theme of the present chapter, excess contained by the rituals and regulations of the polis and its gods, to drinking. Just as meat was a natural product laden with cultural significance, so too was wine.

---

[224] See Gilula (1995) and Chap. 2.
[225] See Athenaeus 4.131f–138b and Chap. 6.

5
Dionysus and His Wine in Comedy

We have seen in Chapters 2 and 3 some aspects of the comic representation of the cult of Dionysus in festivals of Dionysus—the Rural Dionysia and Anthesteria in *Acharnians*—and the major interest in the gods of the underworld, particularly those fertility gods associated with Demeter and Dionysus, who include Wealth, the Seasons, and the *Charites* or Graces. These gods linked with the underworld are related to the Mysteries of Dionysus in *Frogs*.[1] The god plays two major roles in comedy, first as the Dionysus of Chapter 3 who is invoked in some Old Comedies to protect the crops and the people against war, perhaps like the god of the ancient cult statue, the *xoanon*, of figwood or vinewood, who offered protection to the fig and the vine in Sparta and Naxos.[2] In his second role, which I explore in this chapter, the god takes on a different aspect, and shows an interest in the refined life of the polis, the cultivation of the arts, as opposed to the cultivation of plants. In this context Dionysus and other gods drink Mendean and other 'luxury' imported wines (Hermippus fr. 77), they enjoy the pleasures of conviviality and drinking just as humans do,[3] and Dionysus sets the limits on what is right and wrong in the symposium. The comic Dionysus also draws on the representation of the god in other forms of poetry and in the visual arts, in particular vase painting.

A number of recent studies of the symposium set some of the terms for the discussion that follows. Oswyn Murray, in a number of works, has contended that the symposium was an aristocratic institution of the archaic polis which even in the late fifth century remained the preserve of the elite.[4] Ian Ruffell, in an

---

[1] The initiates into the Eleusinian Mysteries in *Frogs* share much with initiates into the Mysteries of Dionysus: see Lada (1999).

[2] Athenaeus 3.78c.   [3] Oswyn Murray in Murray (1995), ch. 1.

[4] Murray (1982), (1983), (1990).

unpublished essay, has applied Murray's symposium to the comic fragments, contending that the comic poets constructed an ideological opposition between the private symposium of the elite and the comic festival which belonged to the wider, democratic community. By contrast, N. R. E. Fisher (forthcoming) argues that the symposium was not as narrowly based in the polis as Murray supposes, and to some extent collapses the opposition of Ruffell between the private symposium and public festival. Meanwhile James Davidson (1997) broadly accepts Murray's symposium as a preserve of the elite and promotes the *kapeleion*, or commercial bar, as the alternative drinking venue of the poorer citizen. In this chapter I broadly accept the arguments of Fisher and Davidson, though this study centres resolutely on comic representation rather than the social structures and history of the polis itself.

There have been valuable studies, too, in sympotic poetry, prominent among which are West (1974), Gentili (1988), and on elegy E. L. Bowie (1986). Comparison between elegaic, iambic, and lyric poetry and comedy is instructive, since for the first three genres the rituals of drinking frequently provide both the occasion for the poem and a point of reference for the content. The rituals of eating and banqueting are less prominent, at least in elegy and lyric. In comedy, conversely, the *deipnon* and the symposium are taken together and the food is at least as prominent as the wine. At 2.39d–e Athenaeus adapts an (unnamed) ancient source to assert, 'from dry food no jokes arise nor any impromptu poetry . . . Boasting and jesting and merriment do not come from well-being and fullness but from what alters the mind and turns it to falseness, which arises only through drunkenness'. While this observation is true of sympotic poetry and indeed of comedy as far as drunkenness is concerned, comedy resolutely rises to the challenge of food-based boasting and jesting, as we saw in Chapter 4 and will see again in Chapter 8. It is the very materiality of food that challenges the comic poet to take it on and convert that apparently unyielding substance into comic discourse (compare Chapter 1).

In many cultures wine and other intoxicating beverages have a special place because of their mind-enhancing properties, for good or ill. Their consumption is incorporated into social and religious ritual across the world, and it is partly owing to this

cultural embedding of wine in Greece that comedy has so much
to say about its consumption. The comic poet may draw on,
comment on, or satirize any one of these ritual acts. A degree of
secularization may invade the sacred in a culture where the two
are rarely distinct. Ritualized drinking has become a subject for
anthropological study in Douglas (1987).[5]

5.1. APPROACHES TO THE COMIC SYMPOSIUM

Let us begin with two scenes of drinking from Old Comedy. The
first is from the second parabasis of *Peace* (1140–58):

there is nothing more pleasant than to get the seed in, to see the god
raining nicely on it, and for your neighbour to say, 'tell me,
Comarchides, what shall we do now? I'd like us to drink together since
the god has been good to us. Wife, parch three measures of beans, mix
in wheat with them, and get out some of the figs. Let Syra chase in
Manes from the fields because it is not possible to tend the vines today
or break up the soil because the land is wet. Let someone bring out from
my place the thrush and the two chaffinches. And there were also some
beestings in the house and four portions of hare, unless the ferret(?) got
one last night. There was a noise last night, I don't know what. It was
certainly making a racket. Slave, bring out three for us and one for
father. Ask Aeschinides for some fruiting myrtle boughs and while
you're there get Charinades to come so that he can drink with us—
because the god has done good to us and favoured our ploughing.'[6]

The second is fr. 16 from the *Comastae* of Phrynichus, 'send up
here good things (*agatha*) for us who live joyfully in this city'.
Together these passages recall the themes of Chapter 3, the
comic delight in agriculture, crops, and the plea to the gods to
send up *agatha* for the benefit of mortals. In *Peace* 1140–58 the
comic farmer has a drink with his friends when he is at leisure in
early winter. Many of the details of the symposium are included,

---

[5] Davidson (1997: 36–9) has instructive comment on the desire of some
anthropologists to concentrate on socialized drinking over alcoholic excess.

[6] An antistrophe follows: 'when the cicada sings its sweet song, I enjoy
watching my Lemnian vines, to see if they are ripening now (the plant is an early
variety) and looking to see if the figs are swelling and then when they're ripe I go
for it and eat some and recite "dear Seasons" and grind and mix up some thyme.
And I get fat at that time in the summer.' A denunciation of war follows in more
trochees.

the men drinking together, the myrtle for garlands, the tasty foods that might form a *deipnon* or might comprise 'the second tables', or the dessert foods eaten in the drinking session. The chorus leader is called, significantly, Comarchides, the leader of the komos or revel. This is clearly not a gathering of the elite, but it seems to me perverse to deny that a symposium is envisaged, if a less formal and prestigious version than those enjoyed by the elite. This symposium should be compared with the strophe of the chorus at *Acharnians* 971–87 (quoted in Chapter 3), in which War personified is declared an unwelcome fellow-symposiast on the drinking-couch, and with Dicaeopolis' preparations for the symposium at the house of the priest of Dionysus in that play. The comic chorus and protagonist in these plays enjoys the prospect of a symposium at the end of the play as part of the festivity organized for the triumphant protagonist and denied his enemies. Earlier in *Acharnians* Dicaeopolis sings a sympotic hymn to Phales (also quoted in Chapter 3). There is no sign there either that an institution of the elite is envisaged.

We know nothing of the context of Phrynichus fr. 16, but the Alcaic metre in which it is expressed might indicate a sympotic song, possibly a *skolion*. Comedy, as we shall see, incorporated into its text many other poetic forms, a number deriving from the symposium. These two passages establish two major themes of this chapter, the social context of comic symposia and comic exploitation of sympotic features. Comic presentation of the paraphernalia of the symposium constitutes a third element.

Murray has argued[7] that the symposium was an institution of the elite in Athens, at least at the end of the fifth century. The elegant furniture, sympotic equipment, and wines that went with it, together with aristocratic songs, marked it out and at times of political tension made the symposium the object of suspicion among the people and the democrats. In addition to distinctions conferred by wealth, the symposium was often a private gathering at which conspiracies might be hatched or at least suspected. Some studies have suggested that the symposium may not have been restricted to the elite. In two studies of the upwardly mobile in Athenian society, Fisher (1998, forthcoming) has argued that the symposium may have been less exclusive

---

[7] See n. 4.

than Murray supposes. Houses excavated in the Piraeus and in other Greek cities suggest that the *andron*, or room for the male symposium, was to be found in comparatively modest homes;[8] as we saw in Chapter 2, some festivals of the polis appear to have included symposia, while more citizens than the elite participated in quasi-religious local cults and clubs, and we saw in Chapter 4 that, for all the emphasis on restraint and tradition at the prytaneion, and more so on simplicity at the tholos in Athens, some sympotic elements are to be found there and in other civic buildings. It appears to have been possible to recline and drink together in Athens in a civic context. Fisher's case is that symposia were more varied and available to a wider section of the community than Murray and others allow.

Davidson,[9] who does not challenge Murray,[10] has suggested that the poorer citizens of Athens bought their drinks from commercial *kapeleia*. Traces of such an establishment may have been found in the Athenian agora,[11] if remains of drinking-cups and amphorae containing Attic and other Greek wines do indeed indicate a commercial building. Davidson argues for the popularity of 'taverns' in such cities as Athens and Corinth, and reviews adverse comment on them by authors of the fourth century, such as Aristotle, Hyperides, and Theopompus who criticized the democrats of Byzantium for leading a frivolous life in the bars of the agora and harbour.[12] These *kapeleia* are often mentioned in comic texts, as we have seen in Chapter 4, and are said to be a resort of women, as I noted in Chapter 2. Davidson well brings out their role as neighbourhood bars in such passages

---

[8] W. Hoepfner and E.-L. Schwandner, *Haus und Stadt im Klassischen Griechenland* (Munich 1994), 24–43. Fisher considers also the debates between Michael Vickers and others on the use of metalware as opposed to pottery at symposia and the case for pottery production dedicated largely to votive uses. Whether or not the elite did use pottery, Fisher argues that the extensive remains of pottery probably indicate wide-scale use—by the living as well as the dead.

[9] (1997), 53–61.

[10] He notes (p. 53) 'the lingering connotations of elitism' in the symposium in *Wasps* and quotes Murray's phrase, 'to the fifth-century audience, the *symposium* is an alien world of licence and misbehaviour'.

[11] Shear (1975).

[12] Aristotle, *Rhetoric* 1411a24; Theopompus, *Philippica*, *FGrH* 115 F62 = Athenaeus 12.526d–e; Hyperides fr. 138 Jensen = Athenaeus 13.566f.

as *Wealth* 435, 'the female *kapelis* of the neighbourhood', Eubulus, *Pamphilus* fr. 80, 'and I watched out for the nurse of the girl
in the big new *kapeleion* right opposite the house', and Nicostratus, *Patriotai* fr. 22, 'the *kapelos* in this neighbourhood'. Davidson makes a good case for the popularity of taverns, for the
suspicions held by writers of the elite that they were meeting-
places of the lower orders (the *agoraioi* of comedy), and for their
retailing wine ready-mixed with water for instant consumption,
which led to complaints of short measures and excessive watering down of the wine. All of this we can accept, with the proviso
that the *kapeleion* was only one of the locations of popular drinking, to be added to symposia of various kinds at festivals, weddings, and other occasions. To accept the contrast of ritualized
symposia for the rich with drinking in a commercial context for
the majority seems to me a serious distortion, at least for drinking in the comic polis, which is my concern. In my view it should
not be imagined that the vast majority of the population that did
not belong to the elite (over 90 per cent) only drank in company
in a commercial bar.

Some plays, to be sure, appear to present the symposium as an
institution of the elite. The most-cited is *Wasps*, in which old
Philocleon is instructed in sympotic ritual by his *arriviste* son.
The old man knows what a symposium is—there is no need to
explain to him that drinkers recline or mix their wine with water
or wear garlands—but he is wanting in elegance and in the correct use of etiquette, the right kind of song, the right kind of
remark. So too in the *Flatterers* of Eupolis, the elegant drinking
and dining of Callias and his supporters such as Protagoras the
philosopher appear to have been satirized. Elsewhere comic
characters seem not to distance themselves from a symposium—
as in the second parabasis of *Peace*.

Some clarification is needed. The following assumptions
inform my argument. First, all or nearly all Greeks drank wine
mixed with water, either with their food or after it.[13] If this eating

---

[13] Eating and drinking were not as rigidly divided in ancient Greece as is
sometimes asserted. The 'second tables' at symposia provided a range of foods
during the drinking session and it is not credible that diners at the *deipnon*
worked their way through their food without any liquid: cf. the elaborate
deipnon and symposium of the *Deipnon* of Philoxenus (*PMG* 836, discussed in
Chap. 7) at which (39) the diners move on to the symposium when they have

and drinking extended to friends and kinsmen on special occasions, formal drinking (for men only) might be separated from the *deipnon* in the form of a symposium. Since eating by the average Athenian beyond the family circle is prominent in comedy, it would be surprising if such symposia were excluded—that is, defining symposia very broadly as 'drinking with' male friends with greater or lesser formality, as for example in *Peace* 1140–58.[14] A symposium of this kind, affordable by most citizens and not necessarily requiring an *andron*, should, I believe, be added to the commercial drinking described by Davidson (1997)—at least as far as comedy is concerned. Second, versions of the symposium which used a formal *andron* appear to have taken place in the polis in an unknown number of private homes beyond the elite—if Fisher is right, against Murray—and on special occasions such as festivals and weddings. For the comic audience, the symposium appears to have been familiar. Third, the symposium plays an ideological role in comedy. The elegant symposia of the rich are presented, perhaps sometimes to astound,[15] but on other occasions to be satirized. Symposia are as much part of the reconfiguration of Athenian society that we saw in Chapters 2 and 3 as is dining—the two cannot be separated. Both are enjoyed, in Old Comedy at least, by the protagonist and his approved entourage.

E. L. Bowie (1995) argues for the absence of drinking at formal festivals in Old Comedy, particularly at the Lenaea and City Dionysia where we might expect it, either on stage or off stage. He acknowledges the possibility of ritual drinking in such lost plays as Aristophanes, *Banqueters* (*Daitales*) and the *Satyrs* of Ecphantides, Cratinus, Phrynichus, and perhaps Callias. At

'reached their fill of food and drink'. That said, there was a formal division between *deipnon* and symposium, marked by the washing of hands and the drinking of toasts of unmixed wine to the gods. On the unity of eating and drinking see also A. Lukinovitch, 'The Play of Reflections between Literary Form and the Sympotic Theme in the *Deipnosophistae* of Athenaeus', in Murray (1990), 263–71.

[14] Fisher (forthcoming) comments on the wide range of dinners that might inform notions of a 'dinner-party' in Britain.

[15] The Press Reader observes that audiences might enjoy seeing plays about people better off than themselves, as they did in 'Greek tragedy and indeed [in] most European drama until Ibsen; it was true too of lighter British drama until the 1930s'.

women's festivals, conversely, such as in Aristophanes, *Thesmophoriazusae* and *Women Setting Up Festival Tents* fr. 487, drinking is attested in a comic representation of festival. Ritual symposia also appear to be rare on stage; there are no choruses of symposiasts, though Bowie allows that the *Comastae* of Ameipsias and Phrynichus may have represented ritual drinking by the chorus.[16] There is also little drunkenness on stage in Old Comedy, beyond Philocleon in *Wasps* and Dicaeopolis in *Acharnians*.[17] Drinking in Old Comedy, Bowie argues, is presented as part of the good life and is generally approved when the drinker is of the zeugite category, and often disapproved when the drinker is female, slave, or a male of a higher or lower category than zeugite, especially when drinking alone. I believe that some of these categories are too exclusive. I agree with the social divisions, which accord with comic approval of the society configured by the protagonist and his supporters. The division between private and festive drinking is, however, too strong: at the end of *Acharnians* Dicaeopolis ritually empties his jug at the Anthesteria *and* attends a symposium with the priest of Dionysus.[18] It is indeed notable that little festive drinking by males (let alone drinking at a festival of Dionysus) is represented by surviving fragments of Old Comedy; but festive eating *is* represented, as we saw in Chapter 2. It is thus festive drinking that is absent, rather than festive commensality altogether, and the latter may, anyway, imply the former. I dissent strongly from Bowie's initial claim (p. 113) that 'features of the presentation of wine . . . cohere with many other elements of Old Comedy which show that, like tragedy, it had detached itself almost wholly from its religious context'.[19]

Ruffell argues for a different ideological approach, that comedy, as a 'metafestive' genre, appropriates certain forms of drinking for itself, that is, those that belong to the Dionysiac komos of the public festival, while it distances itself from the private symposium of *Wasps*, Eupolis, *Flatterers*, and such plays as the *Apokottabizontes* of Ameipsias and the *Moirai* of Hermippus.

---

[16] Ameipsias, *Apokottabizontes* is another.
[17] See below on the scholarly tradition which claimed the poets (Epicharmus and Crates in comedy) represented drunks on stage.
[18] See Chaps. 2 and 3.   [19] See Chaps. 2 and 3, and below on Dionysus.

Attractive though this approach is, it relies on the elitist symposium of Murray, which cannot be sustained for comedy. There are too many occasions in which aspects of both public and private symposia are presented in comedy with approval. Ruffell cites Hermippus, *Moirai* fr. 48: 'woolly cloaks have been thrown aside and everyone is buckling on their breastplate, the greave is fitted round the shin and there's no desire left for the white slipper. You will see the *kottabos* rod rolling in heaps of chaff and Manes doesn't hear the winedrops. As for the wretched disk,[20] you could see that by the hinge of the garden door in a pile of rubbish.' According to Ruffell, fr. 48 depicts the rejection of the sympotic luxuries of the elite in favour of the hoplite warfare undertaken by the whole polis. This interpretation seems to me unlikely in view of the hostility to war that I demonstrated in Old Comedy in Chapter 3. Towards the end of *Peace* the arms dealers come on stage with their obsolete weapons and are advised to adapt them into various sympotic and farming items. Trygaeus suggests a trumpet be converted into a *kottabos* stand. Peace is a sufficiently emotive subject in the comic polis to persuade me that the *kottabos* is an item welcome to protagonist and chorus, just as is the crest converted into a table-wipe, the breastplate into a chamber-pot, and the spear into a vine-prop. The merging of public and private worlds in many comic passages, as we have seen in earlier chapters, does not help Ruffell's case, nor does the sheer weight of references to symposia in Old, Middle, and New Comedy in terms that often seem to imply no censure. We might add the presence of Dionysus in a number of sympotic contexts in Old and later comedy. It is difficult to believe that this god of the democratic polis, who mixes up all citizens alike, becomes an ideologically different god in the comic symposium.

Finally, A. M. Bowie (1997), drawing in part on sympotic themes on painted pottery,[21] brings out the ubiquity and ingenious applications of these themes, in particular with reference to the domestic 'symposia' of *Wasps* and *Clouds* and the ambivalent endings of *Acharnians* and *Ecclesiazusae*, which appear to problematize the role of symposia both in the polis and in the final scenes of comedies. By using a broad definition of sympotic themes, he traces them through much of *Knights* and *Wasps*,

---

[20] On the game of *kottabos* see 5.5.2 below.   [21] In Lissarrague (1990).

from the initial discussions of the slaves to (in *Wasps*) the 'komos' of the parodos and the following domestic symposia. For *Knights* he brings out the sympotic elements in the contests for the favour of Demos and in the restored spendour of Demos at the end of the play.

5.2. SYMPOTIC DISCOURSE IN COMEDY

The symposium plays a large role in comedy for a number of reasons. First, as a companion to food, wine offered the comic poets opportunities to elaborate on varieties, mixtures with water, and accompanying events and entertainments—a further reflection of the material and social world. The symposium also gave comedy access to public and private rituals in honour of Dionysus and other gods and, more importantly, provided varied forms of discourse drawn from earlier and contemporary genres of sympotic poetry, from sympotic games, and from those rituals of Dionysus. Many of these sympotic elements in Aristophanes have been discussed by A. M. Bowie (1997) and in Old Comedy more widely by E. L. Bowie (1995). In this chapter I review sympotic fragments from comedies of all periods, many of which have been preserved by Athenaeus. It is worth considering the contribution of Athenaeus to our understanding of the comic symposium, for three reasons. First, he gathers together fragments on similar topics and illustrates similar themes in different poets over a long period, independently of the plot and particular circumstances of the play (though he occasionally contributes to our knowledge of plot also). Thus, wines and their mixtures with water are offered in abundance in Books 1 and 2, hearty drinkers and riddles in Book 10, wine cups in Book 11, the *kottabos* game, garlands, and *skolia* (drinking songs) in Book 15. Second, he synthesizes sympotic detail on an unparalleled scale from a wide range of sources in addition to comedy. What appear in the works of, for example, Pickard-Cambridge (1968), Lada (1999), W. J. Slater (1976), and Lissarrague (1990) to be references to drinking and the worship of Dionysus drawn from a very wide range of Greek authors are in fact in many cases drawn from quotations in Athenaeus. This network of interlocking pieces of information from Philochorus and the Attidographers, elegy, comedy, and little-known scholarly sources provides valuable pointers and terms of reference for the present study. At 11.464e–f, for example, Athenaeus cites Philochorus on the Athenians attending the theatre after drinking and offering wine to the chorus, as attested by Pherecrates fr. 101, and builds Philochorus' claim into a broader picture and the current discourse of the Deipnosophistae. We may not believe Philochorus either literally or at all; we may suspect his use of Pherecrates and we may suspect Athenaeus' use of Philochorus.[22] Nevertheless, links between theatre, drinking, and sympotic ritual are proposed and developed. The third strength of Athenaeus lies in this development of sympotic themes into what one of his characters calls 'Dionysiac chat' (11.463c).[23] The *Deipnosophistae* revels in its ability to convert material objects and foods into discourse; thus, for example, we find the Deipnosophistae feeding each other with discourses on the comic utopia (6.270b) and adding a small *opson* of fish-discourse to their long discourse on fish (8.331c).[24] This conversion of the material to discourse often refers explicitly to comic antecedents (Archippus, *Fishes* fr. 30 at 8.331c; the comic utopias cited in Chapter 3 at 6.270b; Alexis, *Tarentines* fr. 222 at 11.463c) and to other genres on which comic discourse also drew, on dithyramb and iambic poetry, for example (11.461e):

'Plutarch will teach us about this. It is the hour to recline on our couches'. When we had reclined, Plutarch said, 'according to Pratinas the poet of Phlius, "not ploughing land already ploughed but seeking out unturned soil", I am going to cup-talk,[25] though I am not one of the Cylicranians[26] whom Hermippus the comic poet satirized in his *Iamboi*[27] when he says "I walked on and arrived at the spongy plain of the Cup-people. So I saw Heracleia and a very fine city it was."'

Athenaeus' adaptation of dithyramb, iambics, and comedy demonstrates his familiarity with the sympotic invention of comedy and its sister genres. The conversion of sympotic themes into discourse was almost certainly more developed than such themes on food. As I have noted above from Athenaeus 2.39e, it was

---

[22] See Chap. 1.11.   [23] Διονυσιακαὶ λαλιαί.
[24] Cf. 7.277b, 8.354d.   [25] κυλικηγορήσων.
[26] The inhabitants of a city in Trachis whose name sounds like *kylix* (drinking cup).
[27] On Hermippus as a writer of comedy and other genres see Chap. 7.

claimed that wine excelled dry food in promoting jests.
Athenaeus concludes his section on wine mixtures and Dionysus
with his own flourish (2.40f), 'he wine-discoursed in this way (or
talked about wines), gulping down the names of the wines'.[28] I
give now a selection of his quotation of comic fragments in order
to provide the context for the later discussion of comic symposia.

5.3. ATHENAEUS ON COMIC SYMPOSIA AND SYMPOTIC DISCOURSE

5.3.1. Origins

In a number of books Athenaeus draws on a scholarly tradition
which read sympotic themes into the authoritative texts of
Homer: the rituals of drinking (1.13.d–14d, 16b–c), seated symposia (as opposed to reclining, 1.17f, 10.428b), personal conduct
(5.186d–180e),[29] heavy drinking by some heroes, such as Nestor
(10.433b–d), and to a small extent allegory. Dionysus' flight from
Lycurgus into the sea in *Iliad* 6.135 signifies that wine-making
had long been known, 'because wine is sweet when sea water is
poured in' (1.26b). Homer is said to commend dark wine, which,
according to Theopompus, originated in Chios,[30] a polis founded
by Oenopion son of Dionysus (1.26b–c).[31] Other mythical figures and origins of wine are listed: Maron (1.33d–e), Phytius
('Grower') and Oeneus ('Wine-man') in Aetolia (2.35b), the discovery of the vine at Olympia (1.34a), the development of
tragedy and 'trugedy' (comedy)[32] at Icaria/Icarium in Attica
(2.40a–b), and the place of Orestes at the Anthesteria festival.[33]
Dionysus taught the Athenian king Amphictyon how to mix

---

[28] The sentence is abbreviated in the Epitome and the speaker is unclear.

[29] The pages of Book 5 have been reordered.

[30] 1.26b. The locating of a feature of wine-making or associated ritual in his
own polis (Theopompus was Chiot) is comparable to Eparchides locating
Pramnian wine on Icaros (1.30b–d) and Philochorus on Dionysus instructing
Amphictyon how to mix wine with water in Athens.

[31] Alexis fr. 113, (*Kouris*) exploits Oenopion: 'Well my son has become the
sort of person you have just seen him to be, an Oenopion or a Maron or a
kapelos or indeed Timocles. He's just as drunk as they. Now my other son—how
can I light on a name for him? Clod, plough, earthborn man.' On the use of
Oenopion and the Homeric name Maron see Arnott (1996) on this fragment.

[32] See Taplin (1983).

[33] 10.437b–d (from Phanodemus).

wine, how to stand upright after drinking,[34] and how to honour the Good Daimon and Zeus Soter (from Philochorus at 2.38c–d).[35] Priapus is linked with Dionysus in Lampsacus and shares the god's cult titles Thriambos and Dithyrambos.[36]

5.3.2. Wines

Athenaeus lists a number of wines, Italian and Greek.[37] The Greek wines are normally supported by quotations from comedy, of which some refer in a neutral way to a particular wine but many are ornamented with mythological and other allusions and invention.[38] On Thasian,[39] Athenaeus quotes Antidotus fr. 4, 'pour in Thasian. For [. . .][40] my heart, but when I drink some of that, it is immediately healthy again. Asclepios has given me a soaking.'[41] On Lesbian he offers Clearchus fr. 5, 'Lesbian wine, which Maron himself made, it seems';[42] Alexis fr. 278, 'sweet indeed is Bromios,[43] who puts no tax on Lesbian for those importing the wine here.[44] Whoever is caught sending even a

[34] Amphictyon also founded the cult of Dionysus Orthos in the shrine of the Seasons who ripened his fruit on the vine: on this cult see Niafas (forthcoming).

[35] The passage is repeated at 179e. At 11.464f–465a Philochorus links Dionysiac festival, drinking, and sharing drink with the audience, as we have seen.

[36] On Priapus and related gods in comedy and the comic tradition see Hunter (1983) on Eubulus, *Orthannes*; on the dithyramb in comedy see below on Cratinus, *Wine-Flask (Pytine)*.

[37] At 1.28d there is a brief note on non-Greek consumption: the supply of Chalybonian wine to the king of Persia.

[38] On these wines see Dalby (1995); Davidson (1997), 38–53; Lambert-Gócs (1990); Arnott (1996), 658–9 (on Thasian), 769 (on Lesbian).

[39] Also Epilycus fr. 7, 'Chian and Thasian strained'. See Aristophanes fr. 334; Hermippus fr. 77; Alexis fr. 232 (all cited below); and Antiphanes fr. 138.1.

[40] The text is corrupt.

[41] For 'soaking' applied to drink see Athenaeus 1.23a. On the medical image cf. *Com. Adesp.* fr. 101 (Kassel–Austin 1995).

[42] The text is defective. The attribution to Maron imparts a Homeric pedigree (cf. *Odyssey* 9.197); Maron is also found (in Homeric parody) in the *Odysseuses* of Cratinus, where someone says (fr. 146), 'I have never yet drunk such a Maron, nor will I ever again', and in Alexis fr. 113 (cited in n. 31).

[43] 'The Boomer', Dionysus, alluding to the thunder and his Bacchic powers. For the metonymy see Arnott (1996) on Alexis fr. 225. On lightning see below on Cratinus, *Wine-Flask (Pytine)*.

[44] I have translated the text of the epitome of Athenaeus (MSS CE). On the text see Arnott (1996).

ladleful to another city is to be put down for confiscation of his property'; Eubulus fr. 121, 'taking Thasian or Chian or old Lesbian that drips nectar'.[45] Peparethan[46] is attested by Aristophanes, *Thesmophoriazusae b* fr. 334, 'I will not permit the drinking of Pramnian or Chian or Thasian or Peparethan or any other that raises the ram'.[47] Mendean is represented by Cratinus, *Wine-Flask* (*Pytine*) fr. 195 and Hermippus fr. 77. On Icarian[48] Athenaeus cites Amphis fr. 40, 'in Thurii olive oil, in Gela lentils, Icarian wine, Cimolian figs';[49] from Icaros also comes Pramnian, according to the local historian Eparchides and Semos of Delos (30c–e).[50] On Acanthian Amphis writes (fr. 36), 'A: Where are you from? Tell me. B: Acanthus. A: Then why in the gods' name are you, a member of the city with the best wine, so sour, and you have the name of your homeland [thorn] in your manner, but you lack the manners of your fellow citizens?'[51] Also listed are Corinthian,[52] Euboean,[53] Naxian, Ismarian,[54] Sciathian,[55] and Bibline.[56] Many wines, including the much-favoured Chian, are praised in Hermippus fr. 77 (quoted below)

---

[45] Athenaeus also lists Alexis frr. 276–7; Ephippus fr. 28; Antiphanes fr. 238; Eubulus fr. 136; and Anaxandrides fr. 73. On wines and nectar see n. 72.

[46] From modern Scopelos, adjacent to Sciathos, whose wine is cited below.

[47] The ram at the prow of a fighting trireme, for the penis.

[48] The island, not the Attic deme.

[49] A list of imports similar to Hermippus 63.

[50] For the enormous importance of Pramnian see on Homer, 1.10b, 11.492f; there is Pramnian also from Lesbos (28f), and near Ephesus (31d). Semos writes of the Pramnian *pharmakites* on Icaros. Athenaeus reports the testimony of Eparchides on the terms for the Pramnian of Icaros, 'sacred' among *xenoi* but 'Dionysias' among the citizens of Oenoe ('Wine city') on Icaros. No credence is given to Icarian Pramnian by Jacoby.

[51] On similarities between wines and humans see below.

[52] Alexis fr. 292, 'there was imported wine available. Corinthian is sheer torture' (see Arnott, 1996).

[53] Alexis fr. 303 (see Arnott).

[54] Eupolis, *Taxiarchs* fr. 271, 'give me Naxian almonds to chew and wine to drink from Naxian vines'. Dionysus was a character in this play and Athenaeus has more to say on Dionysus' special links with Naxos (3.78c). Archilochus compared Naxian wine to nectar (fr. 290 West) and mentioned Ismarian wine (fr. 2 West).

[55] Strattis fr. 64.

[56] Epicharmus fr. 174 and Achaeus fr. 41 (a satyr play). There is a note on the location of Bibline at 1.31a–b.

and Philyllius fr. 23: 'I will provide Lesbian, rotting Chian,[57] Thasian, [. . .], Bibline, Mendean—and no one will have a hangover.'[58] Non-grape wines are listed, including date wine at Ephippus fr. 24, 'walnuts, pomegranates, dates, other things to nibble, and little jars of date wine', and barley wine and beer at 10.447a–e.

5.3.3. *Mixing Wine with Water*[59]

The strength of the wine/water mix is often at issue in the citations given by Athenaeus: Diphilus, *Pederasts* fr. 57, 'A: Pour us a drink. B: By Zeus, boy, give us something a bit stronger. For everything that is watery is an evil to the soul'; Ephippus, *Ephebes* fr. 10, 'he gave each girl a cup after mixing the wine really strong in the Homeric way'.[60] Equal measures of wine and water are specified in Archippus, *Amphitryo* fr. 2, Cratinus, *Wine-Flask* (*Pytine*) fr. 196; there follow mixtures of three parts water to one wine, four to one, four to two, five to two, two to three:[61] Alexis, *Nurse* fr. 228, 'A: Look. Here's the wine. Shall I pour in [. . .] B: Much better would be one and four. A: You're talking of a watery mix! All the same, drink off [. . .] and let's make conversation to go with our drink';[62] Hermippus, *Gods* fr. 24, 'Then, whenever we drink or have a thirst let us pray to meet the occasion, "drinking-horn, change into wine!" Then I take it to the *kapelos* and make my jokes, and immediately it has become five and two.'[63]

---

[57] On rotting wines see n. 101.

[58] On hangovers, Athenaeus (1.34c–e) has a note on cabbage as a remedy. This is a comic theme, cited in Alexis fr. 287, Eubulus fr. 124, Anaxandrides fr. 59, Nicochares fr. 18, Amphis fr. 37, and Apollodorus of Carystus fr. 32.

[59] Sometimes the proportion of wine is given first, sometimes of water: see Arnott (1996) on Alexis fr. 278.2.

[60] Add Antiphanes, *Twins* fr. 81; *Melanion* fr. 147; *Lampon* fr. 137; Clearchus fr. 1; Amphis, *Erithoi* fr. 18; Xenarchus, *Twins* fr. 3.

[61] Menander, *Hero* fr. 212; Hesiod, *Works and Days* 596; Anaxilas, *Nereus* fr. 23; Diocles, *Bees* fr. 7; Ion of Chios, *Foundation of Chios* fr. 14 *FGH*; Nichochares, *Amymone* fr. 2; Ameipsias, *Apokottabizontes* fr. 1; Eupolis, *Goats* fr. 6; Philetaerus, *Tereus* fr. 15; Pherecrates, *Corianno* fr. 76; Alexis, *Dorcis or Smacker* fr. 59; Xenarchus fr. 9, μὰ τὸν Διόνυσον, <ὃν> σὺ λάπτεις (κάπτεις Hunter) ἴσον ἴσωι; Alexis, *Suppositious Child* fr. 246.3–4.

[62] The text is uncertain: see Arnott (1996).

[63] The text of this fragment is corrupt and the version given here depends on emendation: see Kassel–Austin (1986).

Anacreon fr. 11 has the mixture two to one, fr. 64 five to three.
Further mixtures are offered in Ephippus, *Circe* fr. 11, 'it would
be much safer if you drank watery wine. B: Certainly not, by the
earth. I want three and four. A: Tell me are you going to drink it
neat?[64] A: What are you saying?'; Timocles, *Conisalus* fr. 22, 'I'll
beat you into speaking the whole truth with half and half in big
cups'; Alexis, *Moneylender or Liar* fr. 232, 'A: Don't give it to him
completely watery, OK? Mix half and half. TRYPHE.[65] Fine.
A: That drink is nice and sweet. Where does that Bromios come
from, Tryphe? TRYPHE: It's Thasian. A: Equitable and just it is
that foreigners should drink foreign wine and natives their local
product.'[66] Athenaeus turns to the water part of the mixture at
2.40f–47a, specifically to the waters and the water-drinkers[67] of
Greece. Water is one of the great products of Attica, according to
Antiphanes fr. 177 (cited above). Attacks on water-drinkers
include Phrynichus fr. 74, '. . . the dirge at the death of Lamprias,
a water-drinking fellow, a mincing sophisticate, skeleton of the
Muses, plague of nightingales, hymn of Hades'.[68]

The passages on wines and wine/water mixtures listed above,
which are a small selection of the many listed by Athenaeus (to
which may be added those quoted by others and those appearing
in the surviving plays of Aristophanes and Menander), indicate
great familiarity with wines imported into Athens in comic texts
and an informality at least in some cases in mixing wine with
water. Many of these texts appear not to depend on the formal
occasion of the symposium and the formal guidance of a symposiarch. These informal symposia (if such they are) enable the
comic poets to introduce into comic discourse much invention as
well as themes of excess and lack of control.[69] At the same time,

---

[64] This text illustrates that the term 'neat' need not be meant literally.
Cf. Davidson (1997), 46–7, on Sophilos, *Dagger* fr. 4.

[65] 'Delicate, luxurious woman'. See Arnott (1996) on this fragment.

[66] Athenaeus adds other mixtures at 1.31f–32b, including wine 'scented'
with sea-water or perfume. On perfumed wines see Aristotle, *On Drink* frr. 96
and 97 (cited by Athenaeus at 11.464c–d).

[67] Of a water-drinker Plutarch says (*Table Talk* 620c) that he is unsavoury
(*aedes*) and fit only for looking after children.

[68] See below on Cratinus, *Wine-Flask*.

[69] On the dangers of alcoholic excess in comic and other texts see Davidson
(1997).

the naming of wines, the details of mixtures, and the great variety of mixing-bowls (*craters*), wine-coolers, and in particular drinking-cups (listed exhaustively by Athenaeus in Book 11) allowed the comic poets every opportunity to draw on the material resources of the symposium.

5.3.4. *Wine, Wisdom, and Poetry*

A few fragments challenge the orthodoxy that wine brings wisdom, such as Eubulus fr. 133 = Ophelion fr. 4 ('water makes us inventive, while wine darkens our thought'—in paraphrase), and perhaps Amphis fr. 41, 'so there was then some reason (*logos*) even in wine, so it seems; and some water drinkers are pretty foolish'. Many more, however, explore the contribution of wine to invention, for example Diphilus fr. 86 on the transforming power of Dionysus: 'O Dionysus, cleverest and most benign to all those of sense, what a sweet one you are! You alone make the little guy think big, the scowling man to laugh, the weak to do something daring, and the coward to be bold'. Antiphanes fr. 268 recommends moderation: 'if he fills himself continually a man gets careless, but if he drinks below the limit he has plenty of ideas.'[70] We shall see below numerous examples of *poetic* invention inspired by drinking. In Book 10 (428e–429a), Athenaeus draws on the tradition linking drama and Dionysus himself with drunkenness: it is wrong to show statues of Dionysus drunk in festival, sculpture, and painting since this suggests that even the god cannot hold his wine. In drama Aeschylus was the first to portray drunks on stage in tragedy (in the *Cabeiri*), and was himself drunk while composing;[71] he was anticipated by Epicharmus in comedy, and imitated by the Athenian comic poet Crates in *Neighbours*. This theme was developed in the *Wine-Flask* of Cratinus, as we shall see below.

5.3.5. *The Nature of Wine and the Nature of Man*

Dramatic poets were thought to be inspired by Dionysus; they worked in one of his genres and were imagined to be made drunk by his wine, indeed in some cases to resemble his wine. Some comic poets developed elaborate analogies between humans and

---

[70] See below on Cratinus, *Wine-Flask*.
[71] Athenaeus cites Chamaeleon on Aeschylus writing by inspiration.

wine as part of their sympotic inventiveness alluded to above.
Athenaeus, writing on Pramnian wine (1.30b–c), paraphrases
Aristophanes (fr. 688) as follows: 'Pramnian is a variety of wine
and it is neither sweet nor thick but dry and harsh and possessed
of unusual strength. Aristophanes says that the Athenians did
not like it, with the remark that the Athenian demos did not like
poets who were harsh and stiff, nor Pramnian wines that force
the eyebrows and guts to contract. What they liked was fragrant
and ripe [wine] dripping with nectar.'[72] The similarities between
wine and men in general[73] are set out at Alexis, *Demetrius or
Philetaerus* fr. 46, 'in a way, man is very similar in nature to wine.
For young wine must needs boil over and do violence first of all,
as must man: but when fermentation dies down and it becomes
harder and passes the crisis of all the things I mention and this
mad froth on the top is skimmed off, then it is drinkable and settles to a sweetness and continues like that henceforth for all
drinkers.' Arnott on fr. 46 suggests that this analogy was developed by one speaker in the play, to which the speaker of Alexis
fr. 280 responded: 'A: Man bears no relation to wine in his nature:
as a man grows old he loses his sweetness, while we enthuse over
the oldest wine. B: Well, the old man bites, but the wine makes us
merry.' The theme of age in a wine is extended to female drinkers

---

[72] 'Fragrant' wine, ἀνθοσμίας, is mentioned as a term of praise at *Frogs* 1150,
Wealth 807, and fr. 351. Lesbian wine is called 'old, dripping with nectar' at
Eubulus fr. 121, on the 'dithyrambic' form of which see Hunter (1983). We
might compare Aristophanes' likening of poets to Pramnian and sweeter wines
with Phrynichus fr. 68, in which the poetry of Sophocles is called οὐ γλύξις, οὐδ᾽
ὑπόχυτος, ἀλλὰ Πράμνιος. The fragment is quoted by Diogenes Laertius 4.20, but is
best glossed by Athenaeus 1.31d–e: 'Pramnian wine was produced at Latoreia.
Timachidas of Rhodes calls one of the wines of Rhodes "hypochutos" [with
something added], similar to "gleukos" [must, sweet new wine]. "Gluxis"
[sweet, insipid wine] is the name for wine that has been boiled.' On such sweet
wines see Schmitt-Pantel (1995), n. 10. Polyzelus fr. 13 appears to be related,
'not sharp and lees-like in their words, nor indeed sweet'. Athenaeus also quotes
Polyzelus fr. 1, which is too corrupt to reveal whether 'home-made' wine was a
term applied to people. The term is cited also in Teleclides fr. 10. See further
Bowie (1995), who adds Cratinus' comparison of Eupolis with smoky wine
(καπνίας) at fr. 38. On καπνίας cf. Pherecrates fr. 137.6.

[73] Cf. *Peace* 996–8, where a medical metaphor (see Platnauer 1964) seems to
imply a drinking metaphor also: 'mix us Greeks again from the beginning with
the juice of friendship and mix our minds with gentler understanding.'

at Eubulus fr. 122, 'it is strange that always among *hetaerae* old wine has a good reputation, but not an old man. A man must be younger', and Alexis, *Dancer* fr. 172, 'A: For women everything will do if there is sufficient wine to drink. B: Well then, by the two goddesses, there will be as much as we want, and it will be very sweet, lacking teeth, already rotting,[74] [. . .] and miraculously aged.'[75] These comic conceits on the nature of man and the nature of wine draw on more than sympotic themes—a body of medical theory on the heating qualities of wine also lies behind some of them—nor are such links exclusive to comedy. Athenaeus (10.440b–d) cites Plato, *Laws* 666a on the correct age for attending festivals of Dionysus: a boy's nature is too fiery to allow him to drink wine; only at 40 may a man go to the festivals and *telete* of Dionysus.

5.3.6. The Later Stages of the Symposium

Athenaeus contributes many comic passages on the positive and negative effects of drinking, on disorderly and creative aspects of the symposium.[76] Excessive drinking may lead to violence, as the god describes in Eubulus, *Semele or Dionysus* fr. 93, a version of Epicharmus fr. 148 (both are cited below). Examples of heavy drinking are provided by Menander, *Brothers a* fr. 2, 'someone kept shouting out to pour eight and twelve cups [*kyathoi*] until he shook everyone down in his competitive zeal', and Alexis, *Apokoptomenos* fr. 21, 'Chaereas was not so much the symposiarch as the executioner, proposing twenty cups of toasts.'[77] A character asks in Crobylus fr. 3 (from *The Woman Leaving Her Husband*), 'what pleasure does continual drunkenness bring, for it deprives the drinker while still alive of reason, the greatest good our nature possesses?' Wine taken in lesser quantities, on the other hand, stimulates discourse, whether clever or

---

[74] On rotting wine see n. 101.

[75] On the development of the thought of this fragment see further Arnott (1996) and his article in *GRBS* 11 (1970), 43–7.

[76] Lada (1999) examines the comic presentation of the ambiguity of Dionysus in myth and cult.

[77] Add Diodorus of Sinope, *Aulos-Girl* fr. 1; Alexis, *Aesop* fr. 9.11–12, in which Solon contrasts 'Hellenic drinking' which is based on talk and jesting with the other sort—drinking out of wine-coolers and water-jugs—which is death.

garrulous: Ephippus fr. 25: 'A: A large amount of wine forces you to chatter a great deal. B: Don't they say that drunks tell the truth?'[78] Similar inventive defences of drinking are offered, such as Alexis fr. 285, 'no man who loves his drink is bad, for two-mother Bromios takes no pleasure in bad men or a life without education', and Amphis fr. 33 on the lack of restraint induced by wine. In addition to poetry, Dionysus and his wine promoted forms of words, playfulness, and patterns of thought at the symposium. Athenaeus lists riddles, toasts,[79] libations, and the history of the game of *kottabos*, together with many songs, *skolia*, and the sub-comic sympotic literature discussed in Chapter 7.[80]

5.3.7. *Great Drinkers*

Athenaeus introduces a list of the great drinkers of the past. These include tyrants such as Dionysius II of Syracuse, who forced men to drink. Nestor is identified as the heaviest drinker in Homer; of the Macedonian kings, Alexander exemplifies the strength of the desire to drink,[81] and Philip his father was both drinker and glutton. Athenaeus surveys Persian drinking, and reports from Theopompus, Herodotus, Polybius, and others on various kings and peoples who were drinkers: the Byzantine democrats,[82] Argives, the people of Tiryns,[83] Thracians, and Rhodians. Comic treatments of these non-Athenian drinkers

---

[78] On wine revealing all see Philochorus at 2.37e.

[79] According to Theophrastus, *On Drunkenness* (*Peri Methes*).

[80] The main discussion of *skolia* in Athenaeus comes at the end of his feast of words, at 15.693f–696d.

[81] Despite his drinking, he was killed by Dionysus for besieging the god's home city of Thebes. Menander, *Flatterer* fr. 2:

BIAS: In Cappadocia I drank up a full golden *kondy* [an Asian cup] three times, Strouthias. It held ten *kotulai*.
STROUTHIAS: You've drunk more than King Alexander.
BIAS: Well, it certainly isn't less, by Athena.
STROUTHIAS: It's an enormous amount.

[82] Menander, *Arrephoros or Flute-Girl* fr. 66, 'Byzantium makes all the merchants drunk. We were drinking the whole night long because of you, and it was a strong mixture I think. At least, I'm standing up with four heads.'

[83] Athenaeus cites Ephippus, *Busiris* fr. 2: 'HERACLES: Don't you know me for an Argive from Tiryns, in the name of the gods? They fight all their battles drunk. B: That's why they always run away.'

appear to be rare, though they are part of the construction of others in line with the gluttony of non-Athenians discussed in Chapter 2. Two fragments of Antiphanes reflect on excessive drinking in a tragic context. In *Arcadian* fr. 42 a character moralizes on the man who fails to recognize human limitations: 'for a sober man ought never, father, to lose control to drink, nor when drinking is called for ought he to be too rational. And whoever has more than mortal thoughts [. . .] trusting in his own small change, will see when he gets to the toilet that he is like everyone else. If he studies the marks of life like a doctor, which ways the veins go, some spreading up, some down, by which all human life is guided [. . .]' In *Aeolus* fr. 19 a tragic exemplum is taken from the myth of Aeolus: 'Macareus, struck with love for one of his sisters, managed to control his misfortune and contain himself, for a while. Then he took on wine as his general, who, alone of mortals, leads a man's boldness beyond his good counsel. At night he went up and got what he wanted.'

This summary overview of Athenaeus on sympotic themes in comedy is intended to supply a context for the rest of this chapter, which studies particular sympotic elements and particular plays. This overview has, I hope, provided a synthesis of elements on which comedy readily draws. In the first place, Athenaeus uses passages of comedy more often than many other literary genres. Second, although his approach is often convoluted and lacks the wit of many comic poets, he imitates, as we have seen, comic approaches towards the material and social world and their conversion into literary discourse. Third, he draws on many other literary forms, as does comedy. In placing elegiac and iambic poetry beside fragments of comedy, for example, he constructs a text which resembles comedy's incorporation of such poetry into its own discourse. Finally, his synthesis contributes towards an overview of sympotic themes expressed in many small fragments. I have tried as much as possible to be guided by this overview and not to consider particular circumstances in particular plays, as have, for example, Hunter on Eubulus and Arnott on Alexis—to very good effect. Thus, for example, while it would be possible to speculate from the three surviving fragments of Anaxandrides, *Farmers* that the play presented at least in part countrymen who were unfamiliar with passing round cups to the right at Attic symposia (fr. 1), with enjoying large feasts (fr. 2), and with drinking from large cups (fr. 3), I do not normally do so.

5.4. DIONYSUS ON THE COMIC STAGE

Although a title reveals little about the characters or direction of a play, a number of plays name Dionysus in their title and probably related to the god and/or his spheres of influence in some way. Among these were the *Birth of Dionysus* by Polyzelus,[84] Anaxandrides, and Demetrius, the *Semele or Dionysus* of Eubulus, the *Dionysus*[85] of Magnes, the *Dionysus in Training*[86] of Aristomenes and the *Dionysus* of Timocles, the *Dionysus Shipwrecked* of Aristophanes, and the *Dionysuses* and the *Dionysalexandros* of Cratinus. There were other plays in which he was a character, though not named in the title: the *Frogs* of Aristophanes,[87] the *Taxiarchs* of Eupolis; and a further group in which his influence was strong: the *Acharnians* of Aristophanes, the *Wine-Flask* of Cratinus, and possibly the *Dionysiazusae* of Timocles. Plays with a chorus of satyrs—the followers of Dionysus—were written by Cratinus (*Satyrs*, *Dionysalexandros*), Ecphantides, Phrynichus, Ophelio, and Timocles. Antiphanes and Diocles wrote a *Bacchae*. Other possible plays with a Dionysiac content may include Cratinus, *Boucoli*, in which there was a dithyramb, the *Comastae* of Ameipsias, Phrynichus, and Epicharmus, and the *Female Initiate* of Antiphanes. In the Sicilian tradition Epicharmus wrote a *Dionysuses* and a *Bacchae*. In these plays we can expect much variation over a range, from a mythological play on events in the life of Dionysus to a play in which Dionysus does not appear in person at all, but is represented in some form by his followers, such as satyrs or drinkers, or by wine and dramatic poetry. He appeared both in mythic or ritual guise and as a character from the polis, a soldier, an athlete, or a symposiast. Versatile as he was, the god appeared in many forms within this

---

[84] On plays about the birth of gods see especially Nesselrath (1991), 203, 229–30 and Arnott (forthcoming).

[85] Two versions of this play are attested by Athenaeus.

[86] Dionysus was an athlete in this play(?) On athletics in satyr plays see Seaford (1984), 36–40.

[87] Which I do not deal with here in view of the excellent study of Lada (1999).

range—in the *Dionysalexandros* of Cratinus, for example, Dionysus appeared with divine regalia (fr. 40, 'A: What attributes did he have at least? Tell me that. B: A thyrsus, his yellow and his variegated garments, and the carchesion cup'), but also apparently as Paris and as an allegorical figure for Pericles (test. i). In the *Babylonians* of Aristophanes (fr. 75) Dionysus speaks of his prosecution by demagogues and their demand for drinking-cups (*oxybapha*). Note, furthermore, that in both of these fragments the god appeared in association with drinking-cups. Fragments which made mythological references to the god, such as 'two-mother Bromios' at Alexis fr. 285, may refer only playfully to the god's birth, with no mythological development of the story in the play at all. Plays with satyr choruses may or may not have been mythological—they may have been simply a chorus of eaters or drinkers. It is possible that, whatever the role of Dionysus in the *Dionysus Shipwrecked* of Aristophanes, some link was made with the nautical metaphor for drinking which was, as we shall see, a theme at the symposium and in sympotic poetry.[88] Limited treatment of the myths of Dionysus (if it was limited) does not, however, preclude frequent reference to the god in the context of drinking and of dramatic and other poetry.

Myths of the arrival of Dionysus in Greece appear to have been treated in comedy, to judge from the plays on the Birth of Dionysus and perhaps the *Bacchae* plays. Whether the story of Icarius introducing wine to Attica was treated is uncertain—the *Icarian Satyrs or Satyrs* of Timocles appears a good candidate. Some have thought that the *Amphictyons* of Teleclides may have portrayed Dionysus demonstrating the mixing of wine and water to King Amphictyon, and that the utopian speech from Athenaeus 6.268a may have been spoken by the king or the god.[89] Comedy could represent or allude to the early history or origins of wine in more ways than straightforward versions of myths. Dionysus might be at the symposium in person or in imagination; the drinkers might perform rituals ordained by him, offer libations of neat wine, and honour his cups, songs, and plants.

---

[88] Hunter considers to good effect the sympotic and mythological possibilities for the *Semele or Dionysus* of Eubulus.

[89] Teleclides fr. 1 is quoted in Chap. 3. See further the comments of Kassel–Austin (1989). Hunter (1983) discusses the possibility of Cecrops appearing with Dionysus in the *Semele or Dionysus* of Eubulus.

Athenaeus[90] quotes two important speeches made by Dionysus on drinking among men and gods, the first from Eubulus, *Semele or Dionysus* fr. 93:

Eubulus makes Dionysus say, 'three bowls [craters] only do I mix for those of sound mind. One is for Hygieia,[91] which they drink up first; the second is for love and pleasure, the third for sleep. When they have drunk this one, those called wise walk home. The fourth is no longer ours, but belongs to hybris. The fifth belongs to shouting, the sixth to revels,[92] the seventh to black eyes, and the eighth to the summons. The ninth belongs to bilious anger, and the tenth to madness leading to the throwing of stones.[93] This is because a large amount of wine poured into one small vessel effortlessly trips up the drinkers.'

Dionysus speaks as symposiarch, apparently to men rather than gods. He does not prescribe the proportions of the mixture in the crater, but rather concentrates on the effects of the number of craters drunk. At the same time he is the god who describes in sympotic terms what happens to his devotees (here the symposiasts). The phrases 'those of sound mind', 'hubris', 'revels', and 'madness', which are appropriate to the ritual followers of the mystery cult of the god—as presented in the *Bacchae* of Euripides, for example—are transposed to the social ritual of drinking and to the city.[94] Dionysus also speaks in

[90] 2.36b–c and 1.29d–e.

[91] See below on toasts to the Good Daimon, Hygieia, and Zeus Soter.

[92] Revels, κῶμοι: some version of the Dionysiac komos, formal or informal, was presumably the subject of *Comastae* by Ameipsias, Phrynichus, and Epicharmus.

[93] I follow Hunter (1983) in interpreting the (unspecified) throwing as being of stones. Another possibility is the throwing of furniture attested by Timaeus at the 'trireme' symposium at Acragas, Athenaeus 2.37c.

[94] There are other reminiscences of Euripides' play transferred to the realm of the symposium: see Arnott (1996) on Alexis fr. 285 (Athenaeus 2.39b), 'no man who loves his drink is evil. For Bromios the god with the two mothers takes no delight in the company of bad men or the life of the unenlightened.' At 10.447d–448a Athenaeus cites Ion of Chios (fr. 26 West) on the revelations by 'king wine' of the nature of *agatha* and on Dionysus, father and prytanis of the symposium. In Amphis, *Philadelphi* fr. 33 a speaker argues for the beneficial effect of drinking on the mind: 'on many counts I praise the life of us drink lovers above the lives of you who are accustomed to have sense only in your heads. For the cast of mind that is directed to strict and definitive order by examining everything subtly and cunningly fears to advance on events decisively, while the mind that does not analyse closely what will result from each event takes action that is hot and youthful.'

fr. 94[95] of the same play, 'defining precisely' or 'giving clear orders'[96] on sacrifice. He is commenting in some way on the foods the gods receive in sacrifice.[97] At all events, in *Semele or Dionysus* the god gives some kind of commentary on the rituals of the symposium and the sacrifice. Furthermore, in fr. 93 Eubulus appears to have adapted to his Dionysiac theme a much older idea exemplified in a passage from an unnamed play of Epicharmus which Athenaeus quotes immediately afterwards (fr. 148 Kaibel).[98]

Dionysus is also the speaker of Hermippus fr. 77, cited by the epitome of Athenaeus (1.29e) from an unnamed play:

Hermippus somewhere makes Dionysus mention several wines, '... the gods themselves pee[99] Mendaean wine on their soft covers. Magnesian which is sweet with its gifts and Thasian, over which runs the scent of apples, I judge much the best of all the other wines after blameless Chian which causes no pain.[100] Now there is a wine which they call "mellow",[101] the bouquet of which rises from the mouth of jars as they are opened, a scent of violets, a scent of roses, a scent of hyacinth. The divine scent takes over the whole of the high-roofed house, ambrosia and nectar combined. This is nectar, and this is what I must provide for my friends in the rich feast, but for my enemies, wine from Peparethos.'

---

[95] From Clement of Alexandria, *Stromateis* 7.6.30. The text of the fragment is corrupt.

[96] διαστελλόμενος.

[97] Dionysus may be complaining that the gods receive the parts of the beast that are least desirable to mortals, who reserve for themselves the good things of the feast. On this comic topos see Chap. 6.

[98] The speakers are not specified. 'A: After the sacrifice comes the feast, after the feast the drinking. B: Very nice, in my opinion. A: Yes but after the drinking comes the revel (κῶμος MSS, μῶκος Meineke), and after the revel (κῶμου MSS, μῶκου Meineke) swinishness, and after swinishness a lawsuit [. . .] and after a lawsuit a judgement, and after the judgement shackles and the stocks and a fine.' Hunter (1983) notes that the theme was common enough for Eubulus to derive it from a number of sources. Athenaeus adds similar sentiments from Panyassis (fr. 13 Kinkel) and Euripides (*Cyclops* 534).

[99] The first line is corrupt and the syntax unclear.

[100] Cf. Sophocles, *Dionysiskos* fr. 172 in which the flower of the vine is 'without pain'.

[101] σαπρός, literally 'rotten'. Philyllius fr. 23 speaks of 'rotten Chian' (Athen. 1.31a). σαπρός has a negative sense at *Wealth* 1086, τρὺξ παλαιὰ καὶ σαπρά.

The gods drink named wines just as humans do: comedy conflates the human and divine worlds,[102] symbolizing the overlap in the play by means of ambrosia, a term both for strictly divine food and sweet wines.[103] It is not possible to establish whether or not these wines are mixed with water since the lines quoted concern varieties and their fragrance, perhaps the part of the wine most suitable for a god. This speech, in hexameters and with epic phrasing recalling Hermippus, *Basket-Bearers* fr. 63, is assigned by some scholars to that play. Whether or not they are right, frr. 63 and 77 share the comic features of adapting earlier poetry (in this case epic) to comic verse, listing foods and wines, and apparently approving respectively luxury products and foreign wines through the endorsement of Dionysus.

In Eubulus fr. 93 and Hermippus fr. 77 Dionysus speaks of one of his own particular concerns, the drinking of wine among friends. In some plays he is associated even more closely with wine. In three fragments quoted together[104] Dionysus is the wine, particularly wine mixed in the proportion of five water to two wine. These are Ameipsias, *Men Playing at Kottabos* (*Apokottabizontes*)[105] fr. 4, 'DIONYSUS: For you all I am Dionysus, five and two';[106] Eupolis, *Goats* fr. 6, 'Dionysus, hail! Five and

---

[102] As does vase painting. An Attic red-figure calyx crater (*ARV*² 1057,96) portrays Dionysus staggering towards a house in which a woman waits. He follows a boy silen carrying a torch and *oinochoe* and walks 'shakily, precariously balancing a full kantharos on the palm of his hand. He wears a broad fillet and leather boots and carries a knobbly stick and a cloak, articles of clothing that are worn by men to symposia or in a komos, not by a god of nature': Hedreen (1992), 46. Note that this vase, which Hedreen thinks may portray a satyr play, probably does not portray a comedy: painters, like poets, appear to maintain the division between comedy and satyr play, despite the common ground in subject-matter.

[103] Athenaeus 2.38f–39b on ambrosia and nectar as food and drink says that Homer knows nectar as a drink, while it appears to be a food at Alcman and Anaxandrides fr. 58, τὸ νέκταρ ἐσθίω | πάνυ μάττων διαπίνω τ' ἀμβροσίαν, καὶ τῶι Διὶ | διακονῶ, καὶ σεμνός εἰμ' ἑκάστοτε | Ἥραι λαλῶν καὶ Κύπριδι παρακαθήμενος. ('I eat nectar after kneading it well and I drink ambrosia on and off. I minister to Zeus and I pride myself from time to time on chatting to Hera and sitting beside Aphrodite.') On nectar and ambrosia in liquid and solid states see West (1966), on Hesiod, *Theogony* 640, and Richardson (1974) on the *Homeric Hymn to Demeter* 237.

[104] Athenaeus 10.426e–f.   [105] On this play see p. 235.

[106] ἐγὼ δὲ Διόνυσος πᾶσιν ὑμῖν εἰμι πέντε καὶ δύο.

two or not?'; and possibly Nicochares fr. 2, in which Dionysus may be hailed by Oenomaus as 'five and two'.[107] We may add a fourth passage cited earlier in Book 10, Xenarchus fr. 9, 'by Dionysus whom you gulp down equal measure with equal measure'.[108] In some of these cases (*Men Playing at Kottabos*) Dionysus may have been a character on stage, in others Dionysus may be present only by metonymy for wine.[109] The presence of Dionysus, whether on stage or not, enabled the comic poets to blend aspects of the divine world (both Olympian and in the underworld) with the human world. This was possible with a number of comic gods, but Dionysus brought with him the additional ambiguities of sympotic ritual and their representation, the richness of which in vase painting has been analysed extensively in recent years. Lissarrague (1990) demonstrates the complex games played between cup, drinker, and the image on the drinker's cup and on the crater. Dionysus was particularly associated, in poetry and in vase painting, with certain drinking cups, the *kantharos*,[110] the *karchesion*, and the *kotule*.[111] The *kantharos*, of which the *karchesion* of *Dionysalexandros* fr. 40 was a special refinement, was a large vessel.[112] Both large drinking-cup and boat, it is discussed below in the section on sailing at the symposium since it often appears in such comic contexts as Xenarchus, *Priapus* fr. 10, 'you, boy, don't carry on pouring into the silver cup, but let's put out into the deep sea. Pour into the *kantharos*, boy, into the *kantharos*, by Zeus.' The *lepaste* too was a very large cup: after drinking from it a character in Hermippus, *Fates* fr. 45 says, 'if anything happens to me when I drink off this *lepaste*, I bequeath all my possessions to Dionysus'.

---

[107] The proposal of Kock.

[108] μὰ τὸν Διόνυσον, <ὃν> σὺ λάπτεις ἴσον ἴσωι (Kock: κάπτεις MSS). The wine speaks (but not as Dionysus) at Eubulus, *Mulothris* fr. 65.

[109] Arnott discusses the metonymy on Alexis fr. 225.

[110] A draught from the *kantharos* gave the drinker a large amount of the wine of Dionysus, hence, perhaps, its suitability also for Heracles: see Carpenter (1986), 98–123.

[111] On the names of wine-cups see Richter and Milne (1953). For comic citations of the *kotule* see Hermippus, *Gods* fr. 29; Plato in *Zeus Wronged* fr. 48; Aristophanes in *Babylonians* fr. 68; Eubulus in *Odysseus* fr. 71.

[112] See esp. Davidson (1997), 64–5.

5.5. SYMPOTIC ELEMENTS IN COMEDY

Plato, *Spartans* fr. 71 sets the scene for a symposium:[113]

A: Have the men already finished their *deipnon*?

B: Pretty well all.

A: Good. Why don't you run off and bring out the tables? I'm off to pour the water.

B: And I to sweep up.

A: Then I'll pour out the libations and set up the *kottabos*-stand near them. The pipes should have been available for the girl-player by now and she should be warming up. I'm going to pour the perfume from Egypt and the orris-root. Then I'll carry in the garlands and give one to each of the symposiasts. Get someone to make a new mixture of wine.

B: It's already mixed.

A: Place the incense . . .

The poet continues:

'The libation's over and they're well advanced in drinking. The *skolion* has been sung, and the *kottabos*-stand is coming out. A young girl with pipes is playing some Carian tune to the symposiasts. I saw another girl with a triangular harp to which she sang an Ionian song.'

Plato has two slaves who have come from the *deipnon* describe the symposium which could not be portrayed in full on the stage.[114]

---

[113] Lines 1–14:

> A: ἄνδρες δεδειπνήκασιν ἤδη; B: σχεδὸν ἅπαντες. A: εὖ γε·
> τί οὐ τρέχων σὺ τὰς τραπέζας ἐκφέρεις; ἐγὼ δὲ
> λίτρον παραχέων ἔρχομαι. B: κἀγὼ δὲ παρακορήσων.
> σπονδὰς δ' ἔπειτα παραχέας τὸν κότταβον παροίσω·
> τῆι παιδὶ τοὺς αὐλοὺς ἐχρῆν ἤδη πρὸ χειρὸς εἶναι
> καὶ προαναφυσᾶν. τὸ μύρον ἤδη παραχέω βαδίζων
> Αἰγύπτιον κἀιτ' ἴρινον· στέφανον δ' ἔπειθ' ἑκάστωι
> δώσω φέρων τῶν ξυμποτῶν. νεοκρᾶτά τις ποιείτω.
> A: καὶ δὴ κέκραται. B: τὸν λιβανωτὸν ἐπιτιθεὶς †εἶπε
>   .   .   .   .
> σπονδὴ μὲν ἤδη γέγονε καὶ πίνοντές εἰσι πόρρω·
> καὶ σκόλιον ἦισται, κότταβος δ' ἐξοίχεται θύραζε.
> αὐλοὺς δ' ἔχουσά τις κορίσκη Καρικὸν μέλος τι
> μελίζεται τοῖς συμπόταις· κἄλλην τρίγωνον εἶδον
> ἔχουσαν, εἶτ' ἦιδεν πρὸς αὐτὸ μέλος Ἰωνικόν τι.

[114] E. L. Bowie (1995). The sympotic description is thus from the outside, from those not participating, as is often the case with descriptions of feasting.

The meal has reached the transitional stage between *deipnon* and symposium,[115] and this exchange is a companion-piece to the exchanges a comic cook might make with a slave in preparation for the *deipnon*. Exchanges such as this enable the poet both to list activities and (when he wishes) to satirize the symposium inside. All of these activities were familiar to comic audiences, if only from earlier comedies. They did not need to hear these details for information, and so were given them for another purpose, which may have been identical with Athenaeus' purposes for his own work (15.665a–b): 'I could not recall, Timocrates my friend, what was said so often in our enthusiastic symposia—on account of the variety (*poikilia*) and similarity (*homoiotes*) of the devices that were always being revealed in new ways. Indeed, we often discussed the order of the courses as well as the events brought on after the dinner—so much so that I have trouble counting them. One of our number recounted the iambic verses of Plato's *Spartans*.' Listing of items singly or of tasks more elaborately, as here, appears to be a feature of the comic symposium. I remarked in Chapter 1 that the list was a distinctive element in comic discourse, one of whose purposes was to emphasize an impression of plenty and well-being. A fragment of Antiphanes (fr. 238)[116] explicitly links a short list with plenty, which leads the speaker to a further sympotic pleasure, sex: 'there is a good fish, which is very enticing, and Thasian wine and perfume and garlands. For the Cyprian goddess is to be found when there is plenty all around. For those mortals who are badly off, Aphrodite is nowhere to be seen.' I noted at the beginning of Chapter 4 that Hermippus fr. 63 and other fragments, not all of them comic, appeared to constitute *sympotic* lists.

Such lists sometimes, as here, elaborate a series of tasks and at

---

Such a description may be neutral or critical (as Ruffell suggests for this passage and many others), or may develop the obsessions of the speaker, as in the speeches of the boastful cooks.

[115] The question 'have the men dined?' appears to be a common feature: Aristophanes, *Proagon* fr. 480, 'it's time for me to wander off for my master. I think they'll have dined by now'; *Danaids* fr. 260, 'you've come to my house already drunk before dinner'; Epicrates, *Amazons* fr. 1, 'The men seem to me to have dined in very good time'—all cited at Athenaeus 10.422e–f. Cf. Menander, *Dyscolus* 779.

[116] Athenaeus 1.28f.

others itemize, often asyndetically,[117] tasks[118] and foods to be consumed from the tables mentioned by the slave above. These are the 'second tables' on which a wide selection of foods were brought in to nibble or munch[119] during the drinking-session. Athenaeus cites examples of such lists in his discussion of the second tables at 14.641c–643f, the most magnificent example of which is provided by the *Deipnon* of Philoxenus quoted in Chapter 6. Many of these lists provide a lead-in for a witticism by one of the speakers: in Amphis, *Madness of Women* fr. 9 the list is compared with the twelve gods;[120] in Alexis fr. 168 the speaker declares his preference for *tragemata* and then contradicts himself;[121] in Ephippus, *Ephebes* fr. 8 there is food enough to feed some parasites. The speaker of such a list might comment on its inordinate length—this seems to be the point of Philippides, *The Miser* fr. 20, 'flat-cakes, *epidorpismata*, eggs, sesame—the day would end before I finished listing them!' Alexis provides a clever variation in *Polykleia* fr. 190,[122] 'the first inventor[123] of *tragemata* was a clever guy. He found a way of passing the time at the symposium and of ensuring our jaws were never idle.' Where this speaker sees *tragemata* as material for endless mastication by the jaws, the comic poets saw opportunities for the ever-more ingenious elaboration of lists by the organs of speech.

5.5.1. *Comedy on Drinking-Cups*

Promising material was also to be found in the drinking-cups of the symposium. Cups of many shapes, mixing-bowls (craters), ladles, strainers, coolers, and all the paraphernalia of the symposium are mentioned in many comic fragments, as I noted in Chapter 1. Athenaeus surveys the shapes of drinking-cups in

---

[117] See Arnott (1996), 33.

[118] Arnott surveys comic and other lists of these tasks on Alexis, *Philiscus* fr. 252, 'the table must be removed, water provided for hand-washing, a garland provided, together with perfume, a libation, incense and an incense-burner. *Tragema* must be provided, and we must still get hold of a flat-cake.'

[119] Aristotle (fr. 104 Rose, quoted by Athenaeus 14.641d–e) distinguishes the nibbling (τρώγειν) of these foods (τραγήματα) from the eating of the *deipnon* proper. On *tragemata* see Arnott (1996) on Alexis fr. 168.2.

[120] Quoted in Chap. 6.   [121] See Arnott (1996).

[122] On the text see ibid.

[123] On the 'first inventor' in comedy see p. 78 n. 111.

Book 11, with much comic evidence.[124] Characters with various motives describe the cups from which they drink and allow the poet to elaborate in verse some of the visual elements of the symposium and to produce in speech and on the stage some of the clever products of potters and craftsmen of sympotic ware. Lissarrague (1990) has shown how images were manipulated on vases to play with both the material and shape of the vessel and also with ambiguous aspects of Dionysus which were explored at symposia, in particular the tension between loss of control through drunkenness and the need for skill and balance to perform sympotic games. At Antiphanes, *Female Initiate* fr. 161 an old woman rejects a small cup (*oxybaphon*)[125] for a larger cup:

A: But do have a drink.
B: I'll agree to that. The shape of the larger cup is enticing somehow, and worthy of the glory of the festival. Where we were just now we drank out of earthenware *oxybapha*. Now may the gods give many blessings on the craftsman who made you, my child. Ah, your fine proportions, your simplicity!

Athenaeus says (11.494c) that the woman was a wine-lover, only interested in the size of the cup. Inebriation may be her aim, but the poet manages to bring in the shape and material fabric also. Alexis in fr. 272[126] describes a cup in much more detail:

A: Shall I tell you first of all what the cup looked like? It was round, very small, old, with crushed handles, and had letters in a circle.
B: Were they the eleven letters in gold spelling 'of Zeus Soter'?
A: Yes, no other.

The detailed description of this cup may indicate that it was a recognition token[127] but, as Arnott notes, silver cups, such as this appears to be, with gilt lettering are attested, as are ceramic versions with similar dedications to Dionysus, Hygieia, and Zeus Soter, the gods of the libation at the beginning of the symposium. Other comedies and satyr plays, according to Athenaeus, mentioned such inscriptions: Eubulus, *Neottis* fr. 69 describes an

---

[124] For the names of cups see Richter and Milne (1953).

[125] A saucer-cup also used for the game of *kottabos*, described below.

[126] Introduced by Athenaeus (11.784f–467c) under the heading of the lettered cup (*grammatikon ekpoma*). He mentions a comparable silver cup.

[127] As used in tragedy and in comic versions of recognition scenes. See Arnott (1996), who notes the paratragic language, and Nesselrath (1990), 282, n. 1.

inscribed cup used for recognition;[128] in the satyric *Omphale* of
Achaeus the satyrs described a cup with the inscription 'property of Dionysus'. An elaborate cup is also described at Alexis,
Hippeus fr. 100, 'A: and these *kymbia* cups, did they have the faces
of girls in gold? B. Yes they did. A. A wretched woman am I!'[129]
These are unusually elaborate comic cups. Size and depth were
more common themes attached to special cups, such as the
therikleos in Theopompus, *Nemea* fr. 33:

SPINTHER: Come over here, faithful child of Thericles, noble form,
   what name shall I give you? Are you not the mirror of a man's
   nature?[130] If you are offered when full then that is just what you are.
   Come on then, I'll fill you up. Old woman! Theolute! Old woman!
THEOLUTE: Why are you calling darling?
SPINTHER: So I can kiss you. Come here, Theolute, to your new fellow-
   slave. There, that's nice.
THEOLUTE: Spinther, you wretch, you're fondling me?
SPINTHER: Yes, something like that. But I'm going to drink a toast to
   you in this loving-cup. Take it, and when you've drunk as much as
   you want, hand back what's left.

The cup gives an image of the man's nature, whether as a reflection in the wine or as a mind-changing drug. Athenaeus offers
many comic examples of visual images and verbal elaboration,
with Thericleans (11.470e–472e),[131] Eubulus, *Dolon* fr. 30, *Dicers*
fr. 56, *Campylion* fr. 42, 'o potter's earth, what Thericles was it
who fashioned you and broadened the depth of your hollow
sides? A man it was who knew well the nature of women, how it
rejoices not in small drinking-cups.'[132] Many of these fragments
dwell on the amount of wine to be consumed, by men and
women. Many fragments link large cups with the appetites of
women for drink.

---

[128] In Aristophanes fr. 634 the letters of a cup are said to be recognizable.
[129] Arnott (1996) discusses what these golden faces might have been in his note.
[130] Cf. Aeschylus fr. 393: bronze is the mirror of one's form, wine of the mind.
[131] Arnott (1996) on Alexis fr. 5 surveys the evidence both for Thericles and
Thericlean pots, which appear to be not a particular shape of cup but a form of
black high-lustre ware, and decorated designs which included mixing-bowls.
[132] Add Alexis, *Hippeus* fr. 101; *Agonis* or *Little Horse* fr. 5; *Swan* fr. 124;
Apollodorus of Gela, *Philadelphi* fr. 4; Aristophon, *Philonides* fr. 13; Theophilus,
Boeotian Woman fr. 2; *Daughters of Proetus* fr. 10. The visual element is found
also in Alexis, *Dropides* fr. 60. Cratinus *Drapetides* fr. 54, Theopompus, *Althaea*
fr. 4, and Pherecrates, *Persians* fr. 134 list *phialai* with bosses.

Two fragments (frr. 75 and 76) from the *Corianno* of Pherecrates, an early example of the *hetaera* play,[133] portray women,
presumably *hetaerae*, mixing and drinking wine in quantity:

A: I've come from the baths boiled through. My throat is really dry.
B: I'll give you a drink.
A: Well, my saliva is sticky, by the two goddesses.
B: [. . .] the little cup.
A: Certainly not the small one. It gets my bile[134] rising straightaway,
ever since I drank my medicine from that kind of cup. Now pour it
into this nice big cup of mine.

A: It's undrinkable, Glyke.
GLYKE: Has she poured it in too watery for you?
A: Yes, it's 100 per cent water.
GLYKE: What have you done? How did you pour it you wretch?
B: Two parts water, mummy.
GLYKE: How about the wine?
B: Four parts.
GLYKE: Go to hell! You should have been pouring wine for frogs.

The *lepaste* was a large cup suited to women's needs.[135] At
Antiphanes, *Asclepius* fr. 47 a sick old woman is enticed back to
life with a large *lepaste*; at Theopompus, *Pamphila* frr. 41 and 42
one or more women drink strong wine from a *lepaste* in honour of
the Good Daemon (see below); at Philyllius, *Auge* fr. 5 old
women appear to drink with men: 'everywhere was full of men
and youths drinking, together with [. . .] old ladies . . . taking
pleasure in great *lepastai* of wine.'[136]

5.5.2. Later in the Symposium

Once the drinking was well established the symposiasts turned
their attention to various word games and amusements, the most
striking of which was the *kottabos* game. Athenaeus[137] gives many

---

[133] Cited in Athenaeus' list of such plays at 13.567c.

[134] For the medical terminology see n. 41.

[135] A name which Athenaeus (11.485a) derives from 'men who spend a great
deal on drinking and extravagance, whom we call gourmands (λαφύκται)'.

[136] Text uncertain.

[137] 10.427d–e, 11.479c–e s.v. *kottabis*, 11.782e, 15.665a–668f. The elegy of
Critias noted in Chap. 4.1 (B2 West) is cited again by Athenaeus in his main
description of the game, because Critias attests a Sicilian (Athenaeus claims
Sicel) origin. This is confirmed for Athenaeus by citation from Anacreon fr. 70

attestations from Old and Middle Comedy, together with satyr plays of Aeschylus, Sophocles, and Euripides and other forms of poetry, including lyric (Anacreon fr. 70, Pindar fr. 128 Sn–M) and elegy.[138] Comedy thus shares a rich literary tradition representing this game; there are in addition a number of *kottabos* scenes in vase painting.[139]

A number of passages refer, like Plato fr. 71, to setting up the *kottabos* game for the symposiasts: one of these comes from *Men Playing at Kottabos*[140] by Ameipsias, in which, to judge from the title, the game appears to have been of more than passing interest.[141] In fr. 2 a character says, 'Mania, bring the *kottabos* saucers and the *kantharoi* and the footbath and pour in the water', and in fr. 4 Dionysus announces himself as the wine-and-water mixture of the symposium (see above). Fr. 2 refers to the version of *kottabos* in which saucers (*oxybapha*) were floated on water in a vessel and wine was flicked at them until the winner managed to sink one (or perhaps more).[142] The other version, using the 'Manes' statuette, is described in Antiphanes, *The Birth of Aphrodite* fr. 57:[143]

PMG (at 10.427d–e), Callimachus fr. 69, and the treatise *On Alcaeus* of Dicaearchus, who says that the term *latage* is Sicilian and that special rooms were built for the game. Miller (1972), 78–9, believes he has found a circular *kottabos* room at Vergina, perhaps of the kind attested by Dicaearchus. Others denied the Sicilian provenance of *latage*, arguing for Thessaly and Rhodes: thus Cleitarchus at 15.666c.

[138] Dionysius Chalcus in frr. 3 and 4 West combines *kottabos*, its associations with love and the nautical metaphor. These lyric and elegiac examples are all preserved by Athenaeus. On the game in Dionysius Chalcus and Athenaeus see Borthwick (1964), 47–53. On *kottabos* in general see K. Schneider, in *RE* 11.2, 1532–3.

[139] Sparkes (1960), 202–7; Vickers (1974), 158.   [140] *Apokottabizontes.*

[141] See Rosen (1989). Ruffell may be right to suppose that the chorus comprised young men at play in the symposia of the rich. The role of Dionysus is unclear.

[142] This version is found also at Cratinus, *Nemesis* fr. 124, whose text is badly damaged. There are hints in the manuscript tradition and in an emendation of Bothe that the *oxybapha* were seen as boats on the sea.

[143]

A: τονδὶ λέγω, σὺ δ' οὐ συνιεῖς; κότταβος
τὸ λυχνεῖον ἐστι. πρόσεχε τὸν νοῦν· ὠὰ μὲν
<   > πέντε νικητήριον.
B: περὶ τοῦ; γελοῖον. κοτταβεῖτε τίνα τρόπον;

A: This one here I mean. Don't you understand? The lampstand is a *kottabos*. Pay attention. Eggs [. . .] five [. . .] the prize.[144]
B: What's it all about? It's ridiculous. How do you play *kottabos*?
A: I'll teach you. It depends on the player throwing at the disk and making the *kottabos* fall—
B: The disk? What disk?
A: This little thing placed up on the top.
B: You mean the little plate?
A: Yes. That is the disk.—This player is the winner.
B: How will anyone know?
A: If he just touches it it will fall on the *manes* and there'll be a mighty clatter.
B: In the gods name! There'll be a Manes with the *kottabos*, like a slave?'

Shortly afterwards he continues

B: Show me the rules for taking up the cup.
A: Like a piper you must bend your fingers and then pour in a little wine and not too much. Then you throw.
B: How?
A: Watch this. Like this.
B: By Poseidon! That's really high!
A: That's how you do it.
B: I couldn't reach that even with a sling.
A: Well, learn!

A: ἐγὼ διδάξω· καθ' ὅσον ἂν τὸν κότταβον
    ἀφεὶς ἐπὶ τὴν πλάστιγγα ποιήσηι πεσεῖν
B: πλάστιγγα; ποίαν; A: τοῦτο τοὐπικείμενον
    ἄνω τὸ μικρόν B: τὸ πινακίσκιον λέγεις;
A: τοῦτ' ἔστι πλάστιγξ—οὗτος ὁ κρατῶν γίγνεται.
B: πῶς δ' εἴσεταί τις τοῦτ'; A: ἐὰν θίγηι μόνον
    αὐτῆς, ἐπὶ τὸν μάνην πεσεῖται καὶ ψόφος
    ἔσται πάνυ πολύς. B: πρὸς θεῶν, τῶι κοττάβωι
    πρόσεστι καὶ Μάνης τις ὥσπερ οἰκέτης;

    ὧι δεῖ λαβὼν τὸ ποτήριον δεῖξον νόμωι.
A: αὐλητικῶς δεῖ καρκινοῦν τοὺς δακτύλους
    οἶνόν τε μικρὸν ἐγχέαι καὶ μὴ πολύν·
    ἔπειτ' ἀφήσεις. B: τίνα τρόπον; A: δεῦρο βλέπε·
    τοιοῦτον. B: ὦ Πόσειδον, ὡς ὑψοῦ σφόδρα.
A: οὕτω ποιήσεις. B: ἀλλ' ἐγὼ μὲν σφενδόνηι
    οὐκ ἂν ἐφικοίμην αὐτός. A: ἀλλὰ μάνθανε.

[144] Athenaeus cites this fragment at 15.666e–f. At 667d he refers back to the prizes of this line, listing them as eggs, little cakes, and *tragemata*. The exact wording is lost.

Instructor and pupil are unknown. Since the *kottabos* game had been referred to in drama since the time of Aeschylus,[145] it is unlikely that some strange practice of the elite was being revealed to the audience.[146] It is possible, in view of the mythological title of the play, that the pupil was a god. The Manes[147] version is found in mythological settings in satyr plays by Euripides (*Pleisthenes* fr. 631), 'great clattering of *kottaboi* echoed its melodious song in the palace', and Sophocles, *Salmoneus* (fr. 537 Radt), 'here is tickling and the sound of kisses. I am setting up prizes for the best *kottabos* player and hitter of the bronze head.' The amorous theme is picked up also by Sophocles, *Inachus* (fr. 277 Radt), 'the golden wine-drop of Aphrodite is resounding round the whole house'.

Other comedies linked the *kottabos* with sex in a burlesque setting. In Plato, *Zeus Wronged* fr. 46 Heracles and someone else are told to play *kottabos* while a *deipnon* is being prepared. Heracles, ever the man for a party and undaunted at the prospect of *kottabos* before the meal, calls for mortar, water, and cups and proposes to play for kisses. His host deplores unseemly games and proposes as prizes a girl's boots and Heracles' own cup. Heracles anticipates a contest greater than the Isthmian Games. In another fragment (fr. 47) Heracles is told to bend his arm for a good rhythm in the throw.[148] Cratinus in fr. 299 strikingly introduced the *kottabos* into a parody of the *Stheneboea* of Euripides in which, according to Athenaeus (10.427e), the queen, supposing Bellerophon to be dead, dedicated scraps of food to him. Cratinus converted Stheneboea into a symposiastic *kottabos* player and her dedications 'to the Corinthian stranger' into 'to the Corinthian penis': 'it is death to drink wine with the water added, but two jars of strong wine mixed half and half she particularly

---

[145] In his satyric *Bone-Collectors* (*Ostologoi*) fr. 179.

[146] Though the game itself *may* have been restricted to the elite—we simply do not know.

[147] The Manes statuette represents a figure of no status awaiting the humiliation of a blow from the falling disc. The Athenians also had a Manes cup, cited in Nicon, *Kitharodos* fr. 1, 'And indeed one said with brilliant timing, "Fellow countryman, I drink a toast to you". He took a stout ceramic *manes* holding perhaps five *kotylai*. I took it up.'

[148] Heracles plays *kottabos* again in the satyr play *Linus* of Achaeus (fr. 26) '. . . hurling, throwing about, smashing, telling me god knows what. O finest little Heracles, the wine-drop . . .'

drinks, and tosses the winedrops with bended arm[149] to the Corinthian—penis.'

Athenaeus (15.667d) lists further comedies in which details of the game were given.[150] Aristophanes, *Banqueters* fr. 231 may refer[151] to the dissolute brother in the play who was perhaps conversant with *kottabos*, just as in fr. 225 he appears to be at home with Syracusan and Sybaritic food. Eupolis, *Dippers* fr. 95 might also imply a dissolute or elitist setting for the game. Cephisodorus, *Trophonius* fr. 5 and Callias, *Cyclopes* fr. 12 appear prima facie to indicate a mythological setting.[152] When comic players are identified they appear to be gods, a tragic queen, and possibly of the elite. The involvement of women and the theme of love are echoed in vase paintings of the game.[153]

5.5.3. All at Sea at the Comic Symposium

Dionysus was represented in Hermippus fr. 63 as the shipowner bringing goods to Athens. He and his ship and other nautical images appeared in vase paintings, exemplified most memorably on the cup of Exekias.[154] The god and his boat or the broader metaphor of sailing for drinking were common too in sympotic poetry.[155] Many of the literary citations come from Athenaeus: Pindar fr. 124a.6–7 Sn.,[156] 'on the sea of wealth rich in gold we all sail equally towards the false shore'; Dionysius Chalcus fr. 5 West, 'and some taking wine in the rowing of Dionysus, sailors of the symposium and oarsmen of their cups'; Choerilus Samius fr. 9 Kinkel, 'in my hands I hold the chipped fragment of a cup shattered all around, the shipwreck of men at the feast, such as a blast from Dionysus often throws up on the shores of hybris'; and the story from Timaeus of Tauromenium of the young men who got so drunk that they thought their house in Acragas a

---

[149] Athenaeus claims *ankyle* was a type of cup, but Borthwick (1964) insists on the bended arm here.

[150] If we can take at face-value the statement that these authors διεξέρχονται, 'go thoroughly through', the game.

[151] The text is too corrupt to make out more than a reference to a bronze *kottabos* stand and garlands.

[152] Nicochares, *Spartans* fr. 13 mentioned the *manes* figure.

[153] Sparkes (1960); Lissarrague (1990), 80–6.

[154] Munich 2044. See Lissarrague (1990), 107–22.

[155] See Slater (1976); Davies (1978); and Lissarrague (1990).

[156] Quoted in full below.

trireme that was about to sink and lightened the load by throwing the furniture out of the house.[157] The nautical metaphor is a familiar and versatile device to represent the disorientation or madness induced by alcohol. This is well expressed by Eratosthenes fr. 34 Hiller,[158] 'wine, which has a strength like fire when it enters men, makes great waves like the north or south wind over the Libyan sea, revealing what was hidden in the depths. It utterly shakes out a man's mind.'[159] Here I extend the survey to comedy.[160]

'You see how I too am beginning to drop off a bit myself. For that unmixed cup to the Good Daemon that I drank off shook me[161] up completely. And the cup to Saviour Zeus rapidly wrecked me and tossed me, a sailor, into the sea' (Xenarchus, *Twins* fr. 2): the speaker has drunk too much of the neat wines offered to certain gods at the beginning of the symposium. Xenarchus, *Priapus* fr. 10[162] links 'going out into the deep' with drinking from the large *kantharos*, the cup of Dionysus. The *kantharos* was also the name for a boat, and the related *karchesion* is reported in Athenaeus (11.474f) to be derived from the masthead of a ship. Because of its size[163] it was readily associated with drunkenness. Other cups with the names and shape of boats were *akatos*[164] (Antiphanes, *Farmer* fr. 3, 'the Harmodius was called in, the paean sung, and someone raised a great *akatos* to Zeus the Saviour'), the *kymbion*,[165] another deep and tall cup, the trireme, and the merchant ship. A number of ship-cups appear in

---

[157] Pindar fr. 124 Sn.–M is quoted at 11.480e and 15.782d; Dionysius Chalcus fr. 5 at 10.443c; Choerilus fr. 9 at 11.464a; Timaeus at 2.37b–e.

[158] Quoted by Athenaeus at 2.36f.

[159] Athenaeus has numerous citations of Aristotle and his followers on alcohol: Aristotle, *On Drink*; Theophrastus, *On Drink*; Chamaeleon, *On Drink*. On the latter see the discussion of Wehrli (1969), 73–5. There is further evidence in Plutarch, *Table Talk* 623d–625c, 656c–657a and Stobaeus περὶ ἀκρασίας.

[160] Slater (1976) has few comic passages, Lissarrague (1990) many more.

[161] ὑποσείειν: Cf. Athenaeus on κατασείειν, 10.431b–c, and Philemon, *The Ghost* fr. 87, 'Rhoda has drunk a cup (*kumbion*) of strong wine: all of a sudden she has shaken you down.'

[162] Quoted above.

[163] Eubulus, *Pamphilus*, fr. 80; Davidson (1997); Epigenes, *Heroine* fr. 4.

[164] Also Theopompus, *Althaea* fr. 4.

[165] Athenaeus (11.481f–482d) cites Anaxandrides, *Farmers* fr. 3; *Nereids* fr. 33; Alexis, *Hippeus* fr. 100; Ephippus, *Ephebes* fr. 9; *Omoioi* or *Obeliaphoroi* fr. 16.

Antiphanes, *Chrysis* fr. 223: 'A: The bridegroom, so they say, as rich as a satrap, has cash by the talent, slaves, servants, teams of beasts, camels, bedding, silverware, saucers, triremes, goat-stags, *karchesia*, merchant-tubs all of gold. B: You mean boats? A: No, all the diners with their big paunches call wine jars merchant-tubs.'

The nautical metaphor was readily to hand at the comic symposium, and is used too by Athenaeus' symposiasts.[166] Ulpian says (5.221a), 'you seem to be completely flooded with strong words and soaked through'. I give some comic applications: Pherecrates, *Tyrannis* fr. 152,

then they had the potters make for the men cups that were flat and with no walls—only the base itself, holding not even as much as a cockle-shell full, like a tasting cup, while for themselves the women ordered deep cups like wine-carrying merchant ships, nicely rounded, delicate, bellying out in the middle. They did this not on the spur of the moment but set it up way back so that vast amounts of wine could be drunk without it being noted down. Then when we charge them with drinking up all the wine they become abusive and say they've only had one to drink. But that one is more than a thousand ordinary cups.

The cups themselves are not actually named 'merchant ships' as in Antiphanes fr. 223, but they are so large that they are compared with the ships themselves—of the wine-carrying variety.[167] This exploits the nautical metaphor in a variation on the great thirst of women. Epicrates fr. 9 maintains a three-way pun on ship-names, cup-names, and sexual intercourse with a nautical flavour: '[. . .][168] drag the old woman straight to the *karchesion*; as for the young woman, fill her up on a fair breeze. Make the pole ready, let out the ropes, and loosen the sheets.' Epinicus, *Wives With Suppositious Children* fr. 2 is unfortunately corrupt, but has three giant cups for a man to drink, one of elephant horn, the second a trireme holding a *chous*, and the third Bellerophon on

---

[166] The terms common to cups and ships are introduced as such in Book 11 (*akatos, kantharos, kymbia*) and the first three passages below are taken from that Book.

[167] In another variation Euripides' drunken Cyclops is 'loaded in my hull like a freighter, right up to the deck at the top of my belly': see Seaford (1984) on *Cyclops* 505–6.

[168] The first line is damaged; the names of two cups which are also names for boats are lost here.

Pegasus stabbing the fire-breathing chimaera. It is not clear whether the latter is one of the 'plastic' cups or a straight painting. I conclude this section with two nautical images for drinking in Aristophanes. He exploits a pun on *kantharos* at *Peace* 143: flying to heaven on his *kantharos*-beetle, Trygaeus sees no difficulty if he falls into the sea since he can steer with his phallus-rudder his *kantharos*-boat made in Naxos. A Naxian *kantharos* can also signify a drinking-cup for use later in the play.[169] At *Wasps* 675–9 Bdelycleon asserts: 'to these men, the allies give bribes of jars of salted fish, wine, rugs, cheese, honey, sesame oil, pillows, cups, blankets, garlands, necklaces, cups, health-wealth, but to you, who rule them by rowing over land and sea, they give not even a head of garlic for your boiled fish.'[170] W. J. Slater (1976) has suggested[171] that the verb translated as 'rowing'[172] might refer both to rowing and drinking, 'heaving away both in exercise and in drinking'. The rowers ought to be able to enjoy the sympotic goods whose journey to Athens they have protected, but naval rowing is all they get—no raising the arm at the symposium.

5.5.4. *Songs and Word-games*

The comic symposiast was called upon to manipulate songs and word-games as well as metaphors at the symposium. *Skolia* or traditional Attic drinking-songs were sung, a line or more at a time by each symposiast: Philocleon is instructed in the art at length in *Wasps* 1219–49.[173] The *skolia* on the tyrannicide Harmodius are cited, for example at *Acharnians* 980,[174] *Storks* fr. 444, Antiphanes, *Farmer* fr. 3, *Diplasioi* fr. 85, on Admetus at Cratinus fr. 254.[175] Comic symposiasts also sang paeans[176] and songs

---

[169] See Platnauer (1964).   [170] For this passage see also Chap. 4.2.

[171] After Van Nes (1963), 20. The suggestion is supported by Barrett's interpretation (1964), on Euripides, *Hippolytus* 1464, of the shipping and drinking language combined at Euripides, *Alcestis* 798.

[172] πιτυλεύσας.   [173] See Vetta (1983).   [174] Quoted in Chap. 3.

[175] Athenaeus lists *skolia* at 15.693f–696a (see *PMG* 884–917). See Reitzenstein (1893), 3–44, who notes (p. 7) that according to the B *scholia* on Plato, *Gorgias* 451e the singing of *skolia* to Harmodius, Admetus, and Telamon took place at the prytaneion in Athens. (The descendants of the tyrannicides were among the permanent diners at the prytaneion.) Since *skolia* were sung in this public place we should not confine them to symposia of the elite, as might be inferred from the events in *Wasps*.

[176] e.g. at Antiphanes fr. 3.

by known poets, for example Alcaeus and Anacreon at Aristophanes, *Banqueters* fr. 235, Simonides at *Clouds* 1356,[177] even comic lyrics of Cratinus (*Knights* 529–30). Songs and recitations of Aeschylus and Euripides are called for at *Clouds* 1364–72. These songs sometimes appear at comic symposia, at other times at moments of triumph (such as *Knights* 405–8) or well-being (a quotation of Stesichorus at *Peace* 779–80). The Chorus of *Peace* suggest a song in praise of Aristophanes that might be sung at dinners and symposia (769–73). The comic poets thus borrowed sympotic song for their fictional symposia, both quoting and adapting other songs, and sometimes tried playfully to insert themselves into symposia in the polis. Other forms of sympotic entertainment found their way into comedy, including dance and such informal genres as the *paegnia*, or 'playful verses' of Gnesippus.[178] Verbal games in spoken language included the riddle, 'the playful problem' that came in an interlude in the drinking (Athenaeus 10.448b–c).[179] A speaker in Antiphanes, *Cnoethideus or Big-belly* fr. 122 appears to link riddles and parasitism at the symposium; in *Aphrodisios* fr. 55 riddling language, reminiscent of the dithyramb, describes simple foods in elaborate terms—so wine is 'the sweat of the Bromiad spring' (12).[180] Arnott (on Alexis fr. 242) and Hunter (on Eubulus fr. 75) examine the exploitation of riddles and dithyrambic language in the text of comedies of the fourth century. Athenaeus has many more riddles. A number of the plays cited in note 180 illustrate the allusiveness of the comic riddle which is designed to amuse and mystify, in most cases on a sympotic subject of eating, drinking, or sexual play.

I have reviewed some of the ways in which comic poets represented and exploited for their own use the metaphors, activities and verbal games of the symposium. I cited above Athenaeus'

---

[177]   See Dover (1968) on 1353–90.

[178]   Athenaeus 14.638d–f who cites references to Gnesippus' indecent performances in Chionides, *Beggars* fr. 4, Eupolis, *Helots* fr. 148, Cratinus, *Boucoli* fr. 17, and *Malthakoi* fr. 104. On Gnesippus see Davidson (forthcoming).

[179]   See A. M. Bowie (1997), 8–9 on the riddle at *Wasps* 20–3.

[180]   Athenaeus (10.448b–459c) adds Alexis, *Sleep* fr. 242 (the riddle is on the title, sleep); Eubulus, *Sphinxcarion* fr. 106; Antiphanes, *Problem* fr. 192; *Sappho* fr. 194; and a paraphrase of Diphilus, *Theseus* fr. 49 (an obscene riddle told by women drinking at the Adonia festival).

statement at 2.39d on the power of drink over solid food to promote boasting, jesting, and ridicule, which derive 'not from con-
tentment and fullness but from the force that changes the mind
and turns all towards what is false—which happens when drunk'.
Athenaeus and his source stress the power of illusion, of not
being fully in control when under the influence of the god's wine.
Such illusion is seen in comedy in the nautical metaphor, in
scenes of drunkenness, in the blending of myth and sex with
kottabos. But by far the greatest illusion and ambiguity is to be
found in the composition of poetry under the influence of wine,
and in particular comic poetry.

5.6. THE POETS COMPOSE WHEN DRUNK: WINE AND WISDOM

Some aspects of the symposium which we have considered above
with the help of Athenaeus are exemplified in Aristophanes,
Knights 85–99:[181]

SLAVE A: Yes, but the neat wine drunk to the Good Daemon [is prefer-
able]. That way perhaps we could think up a good plan.
SLAVE B: Look at that! Neat wine! It's always drink with you. How could
a drunk think up a good plan?
SLAVE A: Really, man! You're a fountain-pot-babbler, you. You dare to
abuse wine for its inventive powers? Could you find anything that is
more suited to action than wine? See? When men drink, then they
grow rich, do business, win lawsuits, prosper, and help their
friends.[182] Bring me out a jug of wine, quick, so that I can irrigate my
mind and say something smart.
SLAVE B: Oh no! What will you do to us with your drinking?
SLAVE A: Good things. Just bring some out. I'll recline. If I get drunk,
I'll spatter all these with little plans and little ideas and little
thoughts.[183]

---

[181] A. M. Bowie (1997), 6–8 surveys sympotic themes throughout the play.
[182] Lines 92–4 are quoted by Athenaeus at 11.782c with Pindar fr. 124
Sn.–M, on which see above.
[183] Lines 85–100:

> ΟΙΚ. Α: μὰ Δί' ἀλλ' ἄκρατον οἶνον ἀγαθοῦ δαίμονος.
> ἴσως γὰρ ἄν χρηστόν τι βουλευσαίμεθα.
> ΟΙΚ. Β: ἰδού γ' ἄκρατον. περὶ πότου γοῦν ἔστι σοι.
> πῶς δ' ἂν μεθύων χρηστόν τι βουλεύσαιτ' ἀνήρ;

The slaves of Demos are in a fix: how can they deal with the tyrannical Cleon/Paphlagon? Slave A suggests that neat wine is better than the previous suggestion, suicide in the style of Themistocles, that is, to drink bull's blood. Slave A settles down for some sympotic drinking (98), but this is a travesty of a symposium, an excuse for drinking neat wine. In its proper context, immediately after the *deipnon* and just before the symposium, toasts of neat wine were drunk to the three divinities, the Good Daemon,[184] Hygieia, and Zeus Soter.[185] The plan of Slave A takes the unmixed wine out of its proper place between *deipnon* and symposium, nor does he move on to wine mixed with water as he should.[186] As the stereotypical comic slave, he is accused of twisting the rituals of drinking to meet his objective, drunkenness

OIK. A: ἀληθες, οὗτος; κρουνοχυτρολήραιον εἶ.

οἶνον σὺ τολμᾶις εἰς ἐπίνοιαν λοιδορεῖν;
οἴνου γὰρ εὕροις ἄν τι πρακτικώτερον;
ὁρᾶις; ὅταν πίνωσιν ἄνθρωποι, τότε
πλουτοῦσι, διαπράττουσι, νικῶσιν δίκας,
εὐδαιμονοῦσιν, ὠφελοῦσι τοὺς φίλους.
ἀλλ᾽ ἐξένεγκέ μοι ταχέως οἴνου χοᾶ,
τὸν νοῦν ἵν᾽ ἄρδω καὶ λέγω τι δεξιόν.

OIK. B: οἴμοι, τί ποθ᾽ ἡμᾶς ἐργάσει τῶι σωι πότωι;

OIK. A: ἀγάθ᾽· ἀλλ᾽ ἔνεγκ᾽· ἐγὼ δὲ κατακλινήσομαι.

ἢν γὰρ μεθυσθῶ, πάντα ταυτὶ καταπάσω
βουλευματίων καὶ γνωμιδίων καὶ νοιδίων.

[184] The god is not named—for reasons of prudence? Divine benevolence is sought on a broad basis. See Athenaeus 15.692f–693f. The divinities were not always the same: see Athenaeus 2.36d on a variant in Panyassis.

[185] On the three divinities and comic versions of the 'tastings' drunk in their honour, see Athenaeus 15.692f–693f and Arnott (1996) on Alexis, *Tokistes* fr. 234. Athenaeus also cites Antiphanes fr. 3; Nicostratus, *Pandrosos* frr. 18 and 19; Xenarchus fr. 2; Eriphus fr. 4; and Philochorus *FGrH* 328 F 5 on Dionysus allowing just a taste of his wine after the *deipnon* before water was mixed with the wine for mortals. Athenaeus adds that almost all the poets of Old Comedy mention the mixture to the Good Daemon—a further indication that sympotic ritual was well known to comic audiences. On the *metaniptron*, the vessel used, see 11.486f–487b. Athenaeus cites Antiphanes, *Lampas* fr. 135; Diphilus, *Sappho* fr. 70; Callias, *Cyclopes* fr. 9; Philetaerus, *Asclepius* fr. 1; Nicostratus, *Anterosa* fr. 3—toasts here are to Zeus, Hygieia, and the Good Daemon. Zeus Soter is toasted in a Thericlean vessel at Antiphanes, *Similars* fr. 172 and was inscribed on the vase in Alexis fr. 272, discussed above.

[186] Neil (1909) on this passage contrasts the ἀγαθοδαιμονισταί of Aristotle, *Eudemean Ethics* 1233b3, the men who do not proceed to the symposium.

(87, 97), as was done by the stereotypical comic women reviewed above.[187] But his own declared objective is to 'plan something good'. To be sure this is a symposium whose rituals have been travestied—neat wine, which has been stolen, is to be consumed by a slave in isolation—yet Slave A declares that drinkers are fully functioning social beings who achieve wealth and prosperity and seek reciprocal relations, in trade, law, and bonds of *philia*. And his aim is to 'water' his mind and say something clever. This successful irrigation[188] will be achieved by Slave A reclining, getting drunk, and splattering everywhere with notions and plans and ideas (99–100). This appears to be a comic version of the sympotic balance discussed above, in which grossness contrasts with admirable aims.

This splattering is a striking image, an image of spitting, spluttering, or perhaps of urination or vomiting. Whichever is meant here, the drinking of wine generates a release of bodily fluids of some kind, and that release comprises thoughts and products of the mind. *Knights* 400 appears to be related: the chorus scream an unsavoury self-imprecation against Cleon/Paphlagon, 'if I don't hate you, may I become a blanket in the house of Cratinus'.[189] Aristophanes attacked his rival Cratinus several times in *Knights*. The scholiast comments,[190]

this it seems to me spurred Cratinus back to dramatic competition, even though he had retired from competition and composition. He wrote his play *Wine-Flask* (*Pytine*) against himself and his drunkenness. This is the scheme he presents: Cratinus imagined Comedy was his wife and she wished to separate herself from living with him and charged him with ill treatment (*kakosis*). Attendant friends of Cratinus begged her to do nothing rash, and asked her the cause of her enmity. She censured him for not writing comedy any longer, but rather with wasting time with Drunkenness (*Methe*).[191]

---

[187] A woman at Theopompus fr. 42 and a man at Xenarchus fr. 2 drink more than a sip of the neat wine for the Good Daemon.

[188] Drinking irrigates the mind: Neil (1909) compares Xenophon, *Sympos.* 2.24 and Plutarch 156d, 'there is no need for a cup, but the Muses arouse and water . . .' (add Plato, *Phaedrus* 276d), and contrasts Heraclitus fr. 72–4, αὔη ψυχὴ σοφωτάτη ('a dry soul is the wisest').

[189] εἴ σε μὴ μισῶ, γενοίμην ἐν Κρατίνου κῴδιον.

[190] *Putine* Testimonium ii Kassel–Austin (1983) = *Suda* κ 2216.

[191] Then follows the corrupt fr. 193 of the *Pytine* of Cratinus.

Cratinus is said to be an old drunk who cannot control his bodily fluids. Eighteen years later, in 405 when *Frogs* was composed, the image of Cratinus in the plays of Aristophanes had improved somewhat: the chorus would exclude anyone from their rites who, among other things (357), 'had not been initiated in the Bacchic rites of the tongue of Cratinus the Bull-eater'.[192] At first sight, the representation of Cratinus in the plays of Aristophanes appears to have been transformed, as it were, from a wet blanket into a mystery cult. The immediate explanation is that when *Knights* was composed in 424 Cratinus and Aristophanes were deadly rivals in the comic competition, while in 405, when *Frogs* was composed, Cratinus was dead: he was now no danger to anyone and could be patronized or praised at will. So much we find in the comments of the scholiasts and of Sommerstein and Dover.[193] No doubt there is much truth in this: rival poets ritually battle it out with each other in old comedy just as they launch attacks on all or nearly all politicians—living politicians, that is.[194] This process is part of the rhetoric and the rituals of aggression characteristic of Old Comedy. I want to consider these Aristophanic references to Cratinus from a different perspective.[195] In *Frogs* Cratinus is identified with Dionysus, who is preeminently the Bull-eater:[196] for the cult title Taurophagos,

---

[192] μηδὲ Κρατίνου τοῦ ταυροφάγου γλώττης Βακχεῖ' ἐτελέσθη.

[193] Sommerstein (1981) on *Knights* 400: 'Cratinus, son of Callimedes, was the leading comic poet of the generation before Aristophanes, winning 9 victories between 453 and 423. He was now elderly, and while he remained a rival Ar. represented him as a played-out, drunken, incontinent, dirty man, though after death he is mentioned with respect (*Peace* 700 Κράτινος ὁ σοφός, *Frogs* 357).' Sommerstein draws on the parabasis of *Knights* and the scholia on 529 and 531.

[194] Normally (but not exclusively—Pericles in Eupolis, *Demes* and Cleon in *Peace* are exceptions) the dead politician is left alone.

[195] The other Aristophanic references to Cratinus are: *Acharnians* 848–53, Cratinus has an adulterer's haircut, like Artemon the wicked, is too swift in poetry, with goatish armpits; 1169–73, may Orestes the bandit take up some dung and throw it at Cratinus by mistake. While personal insult appears the motive here, Aristophanes may also imply poetic performance (Artemon was a famous target of Anacreon discussed in later scholarship, as noted by Athenaeus at 12.533e–534a), and Hegemon of Thasos describes in parodic verse his being pelted with dung by the audience—cited by Athenaeus at 15.698c–699a.5.

[196] Dover suggests that the term also characterizes Cratinus as larger than life, a man of 'Herculean' appetites. There are similar comments in the scholia on this line.

the scholiast compares Sophocles, *Tyro* fr. 668, 'Dionysus the Bull-eater'.[197] How has Cratinus become Dionysus?

Let us return to the wet blanket. The subject of incontinence in comedy deserves comment. Henderson (1991: 194) remarks that incontinence is a common problem for comic (as for other) old men. He argues that urination in comedy is used as part of the armoury of insult and scurrility: such is the case with the blanket of Cratinus. Henderson notes Philocleon's needs for a pot in *Wasps* 805–10, the old men in *Lysistrata* 402 and 550, and the accursed old man of Eupolis fr. 51. From another perspective, notes Henderson, to urinate on someone is to defile him: particularly important in this regard is *Frogs* 95–6, where Dionysus speaks of the poets who get a chorus, 'just once they have urinated on tragedy. A fertile poet you would not be able to find any more.' This passage, as Henderson and Dover reasonably claim, sets up an opposition between urinating on tragedy on the one hand and fertile poetry on the other, as if urination was allied to impotence. The allegation of Aristophanes against Cratinus appears to be different, as we shall see when we consider the parabasis of *Knights*: he used to be a fertile poet but now he is old and wets his blanket.

But Cratinus is also a drinker. The drunk's need to urinate is quite different from incontinence.[198] Even the gods pee onto soft

---

[197] Richard Seaford (private communication) suggests that Cratinus is both the bull and the bull eater, like Dionysus. The eating of his tongue is analogous to the probable eating of the tongue of the bull/Dionysus by the initiates in the mysteries, the tongue which is both a privileged part of the sacrificial animal and is also the vehicle for chatter and poetry: he compares the proposed consumption of the tongue of Odysseus in Euripides' *Cyclops* by which Polyphemus proposes to become more loquacious.

[198] For a medical opinion, Athenaeus (11.483f–484b, s.v. *kothon*, the Spartan cup) cites the letter of Mnesitheus of Athens (third century BC?) *peri kothonismou*: large quantities of unmixed wine at social gatherings seriously damage body and mind (*soma kai psuche*), but heavy drinking (*kothonizesthai*) a few days later purges body and mind. Daily drinking at symposia leads to a build-up of acid, the most natural disposal of which is through urination. The advice is (1) do not drink poor or neat wine or eat *tragemata* when drinking heavily, (2) do not go to bed before vomiting more or less, (3) when you have vomited enough, sleep after a brief bath; a hotter bath will help if you have not vomited enough. Athenaeus (15.665e–666a) reports that in later antiquity ἀποκοτταβίζειν was the term for the practice of drinking off an ἄμυστις (a cup drunk without taking a breath) of wine after a bath and then vomiting. The *Etymologicum Magnum*

covers after drinking Menaean wine, according to Hermippus fr. 77 (see above). The need for a chamber-pot is a regular feature of sympotic scenes, in comedy and elsewhere.[199] The pot introduces a note of bathos, but it is also associated with revelling. Comic examples of the chamber-pot at the symposium may be seen at *Frogs* 541–7 (a chamber-pot and sex for the master, the slave a masturbating voyeur) and Eupolis fr. 385.5, 'who first said "pot, boy" at the drinking bout?' At Aristophanes, *Dramas or Centaur* fr. 280, someone, perhaps Heracles, is told to get a *kados* and pee into it: wine jars have many uses, after all.[200] Too much revelling leads to mishaps.[201] Bed-wetting of course is a stage further than using the chamber-pot. When an old character is on stage, he may be incontinent, but he may also be something of a roué, still young at heart and an (over-) enthusiastic symposiast. The old man in comedy may display a vitality that is lacking in younger men: Philocleon illustrates this as a symposiast in *Wasps* and, I suggest, it lies behind Aristophanes' comments on Cratinus. As a drinker, he enjoys the symposium and other Dionysiac activity, the most notable of which is dramatic composition. I noted above Athenaeus 10.428e–429a on poetic composition: Epicharmus and Crates put drunks on the comic stage, Aeschylus did the same for tragedy. The biographical tradition even claimed that Aeschylus and Aristophanes were themselves drunks. Aristophanes fr. 688 and Phrynichus fr. 68 compared dramatic poets and poetry with wine. When Aristophanes

accords with Athenaeus in denying the practice to the ancients, but the view of Erasistratus of Iulis (a doctor of Ceos) that there were attendant dangers to eyes and intestines puts the practice at least as early as the third century BC. On *kottabos* and *kottabizein* = be sick [Athenaeus] see K. Schneider, *RE* II (1922), s.v. *kottabos*.

[199] See Athenaeus 1.4d, 'someone give me a chamber-pot, someone give me a flat-cake'; Aeschylus fr. 180 and Sophocles fr. 565 at Athenaeus 1.17c–d; a chamber-pot is not allowed at public dinners in the prytaneion of Naucratis (Athenae. 4.150a, from Hermeias).

[200] See Sparkes (1975). Add the anecdote about Euphorion the poet urinating into a *kiborion* at Athenaeus 11.477e.

[201] Mishaps may include, once again, other bodily fluids: Aristophanes, *Gerytades* fr. 157 τότε μὲν † σου κατεκοττάβιζον τὸ † | νυνὶ δὲ καὶ κατεμοῦσι, τάχα δ' εὖ οἶδ' ὅτι | καὶ καταχέσονται ('then they played *kottabos* against you(?), now they go on to hostile vomiting and I'm well aware that soon they will go on to hostile shitting'), and the river of diarrhoea at fr. 156.13. Note that the fluids in fr. 157 appear to follow the delights of *kottabos* (though the text is corrupt).

accuses Cratinus of bed-wetting he is in a sense recognizing him as a poet, albeit a poet no longer in control of his art or his bladder. Urination is more complex than Henderson would have us believe, for, beyond the rhetoric of aggression, urination—that is, the drunken production of bodily fluids—may further mental fertility, as we have seen at *Knights* 99–100. I turn now to the *Wine-Flask (Pytine)* of Cratinus.

5.6.1. The Wine-Flask of Cratinus

Aristophanes has more to say about Cratinus in *Knights*, in the survey of comic poets in the parabasis:[202]

Then he mentioned Cratinus, who once rushed through the simple plains in a flood of great praise. He swept away from their place and carried off oaks and plane-trees and enemies root and branch. Nothing could be sung at the symposium except 'Bribery with the fig-wood sandal' and 'Architects of well-founded songs'—to such an extent did he flourish. Now you look at him drivelling on and show no pity. His pegs have fallen out, the tension has gone and the strings are all loose. He's an old man dragging himself along, like Connas, with a withered garland and destroyed by thirst. What he should have got, in recognition of his earlier victories, was the privilege of drinking in the prytaneion. He shouldn't be drivelling but sleekly watching the plays by the statue of Dionysus.

The principal argument of the parabasis is that Cratinus, like the other rivals of Aristophanes, Magnes and Crates, is old and past his prime[203]—unable to compete with the new young

---

[202] Lines 526–36:

εἶτα Κρατίνου μεμνημένος, ὃς πολλῶι ῥεύσας ποτ' ἐπαίνωι
διὰ τῶν ἀφελῶν πεδίων ἔρρει, καὶ τῆς στάσεως παρασύρων
ἐφόρει τὰς δρῦς καὶ τὰς πλατάνους καὶ τοὺς ἐχθροὺς προθελύμνους·
ᾆσαι δ' οὐκ ἦν ἐν ξυμποσίωι πλήν, Δωροῖ συκοπέδιλε,
καὶ, τέκτονες εὐπαλάμων ὕμνων· οὕτως ἤνθησεν ἐκεῖνος.
νυνὶ δ' ὑμεῖς αὐτὸν ὁρῶντες παραληροῦντ' οὐκ ἐλεεῖτε,
ἐκπιπτουσῶν τῶν ἠλέκτρων, καὶ τοῦ τόνου οὐκ ἔτ' ἐνόντος,
τῶν θ' ἁρμονιῶν διαχασκουσῶν· ἀλλὰ γέρων ὢν περιέρρει
ὥσπερ Κοννᾶς, στέφανον μὲν ἔχων αὖον, δίψηι δ' ἀπολωλώς,
ὃν χρῆν διὰ τὰς προτέρας νίκας πίνειν ἐν τῶι πρυτανείωι,
καὶ μὴ ληρεῖν, ἀλλὰ θεᾶσθαι λιπαρὸν παρὰ τῶι Διονύσωι.

[203] The poets were not all of the same age. A passage of pseudo-Lucian, *On Longevity* (Testimonium iii Kassel–Austin (1983)) reports that Cratinus (who

poet. But consider the ways in which this criticism at the same time reflects on Cratinus as a fine poet. Aristophanes treats him quite differently from the tragic poets we have examined in earlier chapters, Morsimus and Melanthius, who have to be elbowed away from the fish-stalls by the demos, and Euripides whose verses need to be filled with comic foods. Cratinus, Aristophanes' chorus declares, had a rugged and abundant style, which popular support caused to flow like a mighty river, impressive but out of control. At the same time he operated entirely in a sympotic context. His impact was such that his songs were sung at the symposium, his verses spilling over from the public forum of the theatre to the private recitation. The scholia tell us these songs derive from the *Eumenides* of Cratinus.[204] The transition was a natural one, as we have seen.[205] The description of Cratinus' decrepitude maintains the sympotic theme (531–6):[206] he babbles (having evidently lost his facility in the discourse of Dionysus);[207] he resembles a broken

died in the late 420s) lived to the age of 94, Philemon to 97, Epicharmus to 97. It is unlikely that he was 94 in 423, for this would imply that he was 64 when he won his first victory in 453. Cratinus is simply older than Aristophanes, by at least a generation. Age apart, Cratinus was less decrepit than Aristophanes implied. In 425 his *Cheimazomenoi* came second at the Lenaea after *Acharnians*; and in 424, at the Lenaea, *Knights* won first prize, Cratinus came second with his *Satyrs*, and Aristomenes third with his *Wood-Carriers* (*Hylophoroi*). In 423, at the City Dionysia Cratinus won first prize with *Pytine*, Ameipsias second with *Konnos*, and Aristophanes third with *Clouds 1*.

[204] Fr. 70. *Eumenides* was emended by Fabricius to *Euneidae*, a better-attested play and suited to the composition of songs since its chorus may have been composed of harpists in the service of Dionysus Melpomenos, for whom there is inscriptional evidence. The following image of Cratinus the broken instrument may derive from *Euneidae* also. The suggestion of the scholion that the image is drawn from the construction of the couch (*kline*) has not found favour.

[205] The transition may have been assisted by his use of other genres: Cratinus used forms of parody in his *Euneidae*, according to Polemon (cited by Athenaeus 15.698c—see further Chap. 7). Other comic poets who combined genres were Hegemon, who wrote a comedy as well as his parodies, Hermippus, who composed parodies, iambics, and tetrameters as well as comedies, and Lynceus who wrote a comedy as well as sympotic letters.

[206] Contrasting with the light meal (*ariston*) of Crates who 'kneads extremely witty *epinoiai* from a very dry [or 'very loud'] mouth' 539: see Neil (1909).

[207] On the phrase *Dionysiakoi laliai* at Athenaeus 11.463c see above. Cratinus has got the balance wrong between drinking and discourse: cf. e.g. Antiphanes

lyre,[208] in other words a worn-out piece of sympotic equipment. As a man, he is old and broken, his victories a fading memory, like Connus who won victories at Olympia with his pipes.[209] Cratinus the symposiast with his withered garland and destroyed by thirst needs the care of his city—something to drink in the prytaneion. And rather than plays, he should have watched others from the auditorium beside the priest of Dionysus. This is an insulting picture which drives home the obsolescence of Cratinus. At the same time, we should note that Aristophanes recommends that Cratinus' devotion to the wine of Dionysus should be recognized in the special civic spaces of the prytaneion and the theatre, where he should sit sleekly[210] beside the statue of his patron god. For all its allegation of failing powers, this parabasis establishes Cratinus as a Dionysiac poet, a symposiast, a lover of drink and associate of his god.

Many of these points are taken up in the *Wine-Flask* of Cratinus, which, the scholiast tells us (see above), Cratinus wrote in response to the parabasis of *Knights*. Rosen (forthcoming) and Sidwell (1995) have recently discussed the relationship between the two plays, the latter in the much broader context of rivalry between Eupolis, Cratinus, and Aristophanes in the years 425 to 421.[211] Both scholars stress the importance of poetic rivalry in this debate. The supposed biographical detail is almost certainly exaggerated, if not invented. My concern here is limited to the

---

fr. 268, 'the man who fills himself too regularly becomes careless; if he drinks less he is an accomplished thinker', and Alexis fr. 304, 'I am not drunk to the detriment of my thought, but to this extent only, to be able to distinguish safely the sounds of the letters with my mouth'. (I have translated the transmitted text (διορίζεσθαι: διορίζεσθ' οὐ Meineke, supported by Kassel–Austin (1991), on which see Arnott 1996.)

[208] Or a broken couch, according to the scholiast.

[209] Cratinus himself described Connus as a (ridiculous?) symposiast at fr. 349, 'eat and give your belly joy so that hunger may hate you and Connus with his many garlands may love you'. Winkelmann thought Eupolis, *Dippers* fr. 77, 'with no *ariston* and nothing to eat, but with a garland', also referred to Connus (see Kassel–Austin 1986).

[210] On λιπαρὸν, Neil (1909) compares Cratinus fr. 1, in which Metrobius the father of Connus wishes he had been able to be feasted in sleek old age with Cimon. The polis itself is the recommended patron for Cratinus.

[211] Both suggest that some of the themes of *Pytine* may derive from exchanges in comedies prior to *Knights*.

sympotic themes of the two plays. In *Wine-Flask*[212] the two
Dionysiac activities of drinking and comic composition are represented as two of the poet's relationships, with his wife Comedy
and his mistress Drunkenness. A number of the surviving fragments (193[213] and 194,[214] possibly 195[215]) appear to come from
the complaints of Comedy against Cratinus. His neglect of her
reflects Aristophanes' suggestion that Cratinus, through old age
or for some other reason, was no longer writing comedies. These
three fragments link dramatic competition, the mixture of wine
with water, and sex. Fr. 196[216] also refers to the mixing of wine
and water. Fr. 197[217] may constitute the opening of a defence
speech by Cratinus.[218]

---

[212] The *pytine* of the title, according to Hesychius, is a woven *lagyne*, a flask
for wine, woven mainly by prisoners, who also made baskets and other woven
artefacts. Fr. 201 refers to the prisoners pitching the wine-flask, possibly a pun
on the use of pitch to seal the flask and on a metaphor for female sexual activity:
see Henderson (1991), 145–6. Hesychius also identifies a *pytine* as a chamber-
pot.

[213] In this corrupt fragment Comedy appears to be speaking. Charges are
made about the addresses of Cratinus to another woman, about his age, and
about a new development that is not clear. Kassel–Austin note Kaibel's suggestion that he has turned his mind to boys.

[214] γυνὴ δ' ἐκείνου πρότερον ἦ, νῦν δ' οὐκέτι. ('I was his wife before, but now no
longer'.)

[215] 'COMEDY(?): Now if he sees a nice young Mendaean wine (οἰνίσκον), he follows
him and dogs his steps and says "God, how soft and white! Will it take three?"'
Desire for Mendaean wine is represented as love for a young man—as we saw
above, poets developed the conceit of the similar natures of men and wine. On
the soft (*malakos*) Mendaean wine Kassel and Austin compare Athenaeus 1.29f;
on the soft (*hapalos*—the term used by Cratinus here) wines of Tarentum
Athenaeus 1.27c; on soft and white bodies *Birds* 668; and *Thesmophoriazusae*
191–2, the latter of Agathon dressed as a woman. 'Will it take three?' puns on
one of the proportions for the mixing of wine with water and probably on sexual
hunger—triumphant intercourse three times in succession (cf. *Acharnians* 994;
Birds 1256). This punning on wine and a lover may be compared with the visual
evidence gathered by Lissarrague (1990), 76–86 on wine-cups which resemble
the human body (they have bellies and lips) and on amorous images and inscriptions. Fr. 202, 'have you got your belly full of cobwebs?' may indicate that the
empty wine-flask was personified.

[216] '. . . carries equal measure with equal measure. As for me, I waste away.'

[217] 'Perhaps you are aware of the preparation that has gone on . . .'

[218] Fr. 200, 'but I do indeed give thought to my wickedness and foolishness'
(the fragment is corrupt), may be an expression of Cratinus' repentance.

Fr. 198[219] appears to echo *Knights* 526–8 on the image of Cratinus' poetry as a river. Far from fading away, it is still a mighty stream.[220] However, the river is very different, no longer a river in spate but the Attic Ilissos properly contained within a fountain. His mouth is the Twelve-spout fountain and the Ilissos flows in his throat. As Wycherley (1957)[221] has noted, Cratinus appears to have given three extra spouts to his version of the Athenian fountain Enneacrounos or Callirhoe. He flows abundantly, but the water of his poetry has become the drinking-water of Athens, the water mixed with wine at the symposium or drunk alone.[222] Other comic poets linked sympotic drinking with a mighty flood: Antiphanes fr. 228, 'tell me, what is life? Drinking I say.[223] You can see those trees which by the side of streams in winter spate are soaked by day and night grow big and beautiful, while those that oppose the flood are destroyed root and branch.' Pherecrates, *Crapataloi* fr. 101[224] wrote, 'whoever in the audience is thirsty can pour the mixture into a *lepaste* and drink down a whirlpool'. Cratinus avoids such an image: his verse pours forth abundantly but with civilized restraint and his drinking-water anticipates the image of the fountain as opposed to the muddied river in Hellenistic poetry.[225] Here the mighty fountain is more than the sympotic splash, but it is closer to the spring of words of Aeschylus at *Frogs* 1005 than the torrent of *Knights* 527–8. Kassel and Austin compare the last line of the fragment, 'he will wash away everything with his poems', with the drunken splashing of ideas by Slave A at *Knights* 99–100.

[219] 'Lord Apollo! What a flow of words! The springs are splashing away. His mouth has twelve spouts, the Ilissos is in his throat. What more can I say? If someone doesn't bung up his mouth, all this will be washed away with his poetry.'

[220] See Rosen (forthcoming) on this image in the exchange between Aristophanes and Cratinus: it may have originated with Cratinus.

[221] Pp. 137–42. Cf. Kassel–Austin (1983) on this fragment.

[222] For verbal inventiveness the phrase δωδεκάκρουνον τὸ στόμα is reminiscent of *Knights* 89, κρουνοχυτρολήραιον εἶ. But Cratinus is no water-drinker: see fr. 203.

[223] The question 'what is life?' and the answer 'drinking' is perhaps analogous to those statements of the Dionysiac mysteries which refer to life and death as taking on a new meaning for those who accept Dionysus.

[224] The fragment survives only in paraphrase.

[225] See esp. the end of the *Hymn to Apollo* of Callimachus; Horace, *Satires* 1.4.11, 'Lucilius cum flueret lutulentus'; and Rosen (forthcoming).

Fr. 199 comprises six lines of deliberation: 'how could anyone, how could anyone put a stop to his drinking, to his excessive drinking? I know. I will break his jugs (*choes*), I will strike down with lightning and reduce to ash his little jars (*kadiskoi*) and all the other pots to do with his drinking and he won't have even an *oxybaphon* for his wine.' Cratinus appears to be the drinker, but the speaker is less clear. It may be one of the well-wishers of Cratinus who is proposing the destruction of his drinking-vessels in order to remove temptation. But it may be a god. Two features are striking. The verb translated as 'strike down with lightning'[226] is very rare and, as Mendelsohn[227] has shown, appears to be used when the power of Dionysus is revealed. At Euripides, *Bacchae* 1103 the god strikes a pine tree; at Archilochus fr. 120, the poet declares, 'I know how to lead off the dithyramb, the fine song of Lord Dionysus, when my mind has been struck down by the lightning of wine'.[228] Too little survives to reveal how the god's power might be used to destroy his own vessels. Second, the overturning or breaking of such vessels is seen in other comedies as a warlike action against comic objectives. At *Acharnians* 983–7 (quoted in Chapter 3) War overturns the jars; at *Peace* 700–3 Cratinus is said to have died of rage when the Spartans broke a large jar full of wine.[229] It may be that a representative of Dionysus or the god of wine himself is attempting to contain the

---

[226] συγκεραυνοῦν.

[227] (1992), 105–24. He cites Archilochus fr. 120 and Euripides, *Bacchae* 1103.

[228] ὡς Διωνύσου ἄνακτος καλὸν ἐξάρξαι μέλος οἶδα διθύραμβον οἴνωι συγκεραυνωθεὶς φρένας. Cf. also the epigram of Marcus Argentarius, *Palatine Anthology* 9.246: ἐθραύσθης, ἡδεῖα παρ' οἰνοπόταισι λάγυνε, | νηδύος ἐκ πάσης χευαμένη Βρόμιον. | τηλόθε γὰρ λίθος εἰς σὲ βαρύστονος, οἷα κεραυνός, | οὐ Διὸς ἐκ χειρῶν, ἀλλὰ Δίωνος ἔβη. | ἦν δὲ γελως ἐπὶ σοὶ καὶ σκώμματα πυκνά, τυπείσης, | καὶ πολὺς ἐξ ἑτάρων γινόμενος θόρυβος. | οὐ θρηνῶ σε, λάγυνε, τὸν εὐαστῆρα τεκοῦσαν | Βάκχον, ἐπεὶ Σεμέλη καὶ σὺ πεπόνθατ' ἴσα. ('You were smashed, wine-jar that so pleasantly among the wine-drinkers poured Bromios from all of your cavity. From afar a stone came against you, deep-sounding like thunder, not from the hand of Zeus but from Dion. Laughter and many jests arose against you when you were struck, and much hubbub among the drinking comrades. I do not lament for you, wine-jar, who gave birth to Bacchus of the joyful cry, since you and Semele have suffered equally.') The epigram illustrates both the striking of a pot by 'lightning' and the representation of the pot as a body which can bring forth wine as a woman brings forth a child (cf. fr. 202).

[229] Sidwell (1995) would interpret this passage within the poetic rivalry between Aristophanes, Cratinus and Eupolis.

drinking excesses of Cratinus, in order to stimulate other activity such as comic poetry or the dithyramb.

Fr. 203, 'if you drink water, you would not give birth to anything wise',[230] is not certainly attested for this play, or even for Cratinus.[231] The fragment appears to connect wine-drinking and creativity, as does *Knights* 99–100, and to reject water-drinking as Slave A did at 89–90. Epicharmus opposed water-drinking explicitly to Dionysiac poetry at fr. 132, 'there is no dithyramb when you drink water'. The context for Cratinus' version is unknown. *Wine-Flask* illustrates a number of the connections between wine, water, and creativity that have been explored in this chapter. The play appears to have some 'Dionysiac' themes, even though the god is not explicitly mentioned: its subject-matter of the mixing and consumption of wine and the composing of comedy, the themes of the wisdom brought by wine, the special verb 'to strike with lightning', and the dangerous effects of alcohol. I make no claim that Cratinus was in any way unusual in pursuing Dionysiac themes and titles: he is simply an illustration of the ways in which the themes and associations found in Athenaeus might have been combined and exploited centuries earlier in comedy.[232] This book does not attempt to reconstruct

---

[230] This line was taken up in later antiquity in the description of the Dionysiac Cratinus in the *Palatine Anthology* 13.9 (Nicaenetus fr. V Gow and Page, cited by Athenaeus at 2.39c):

> οἶνός τοι χαρίεντι πέλει μέγας ἵππος ἀοιδῶι,
> ὕδωρ δὲ πίνων οὐδὲν ἂν τέκοις σοφόν.
> ταῦτ' ἔλεγεν, Διόνυσε, καὶ ἔπνεεν οὐχ ἑνὸς ἀσκοῦ
> Κρατῖνος, ἀλλὰ παντὸς ὠδώδει πίθου.
> τοιγάρ οἱ στεφάνων δόμος ἔβρυεν, εἶχε δὲ κιττῶι
> μέτωπον οἷα καὶ σὺ κεκροκωμένον.

('Wine is a great horse for the elegant poet, but if you drink water you would not give birth to anything wise. So spoke Cratinus, Dionysus, with the contents not of one wineskin on his breath but the scent of a large wine-jar. So it was that his house blossomed with garlands and he had brows like you, made yellow with the ivy.')

[231] See Kassel–Austin (1983).

[232] E. L. Bowie (1995), 122 observes, 'clever and theatrically effective though the idea of the *Pytine* was, it should not be interpreted as making a serious statement about the relationship between wine and the composition of poetry. It is a *jeu d'esprit* in which a typical ploy of Old Comedy, the personification of common phenomena in the audience's life, is ingeniously applied to the subject-matter that was already firmly at home in the genre.'

plays, but it does attempt, in this chapter, to provide some of the context for references to wine in the fragments of the lost plays. For the comic poet, whose plays, as Aristophanes says at *Clouds* 519, are inspired by Dionysus, there was always a creative tension to be exploited in the possible applications of wine and poetry between the semi-private symposium and the public festival which included comedy, between the ritualized control of drinking and the lack of control of drunkenness. In the next chapter I consider the consumption of food in a related but more problematic tension between ritual and lack of control—within the discourse of luxury.

6

Luxurious Eating in Comedy

This chapter explores the many foods that the Greeks on occasion identified as 'luxuries'. We shall see that rarely, if at all, is a food in essence a luxury as such, though almost everything can be presented as a luxury, either for pejorative purposes (which is usually the objective) or within a claim for beneficence. In the latter case, the language of 'luxury' is likely to be replaced by 'good things' (*agatha*), normally in order to avoid the pejorative associations of 'luxury'.

In the three previous chapters I have presented passages from comedies which might be considered to describe 'luxurious' foods and drinks, namely, the utopian dinners in Chapter 3, the special foods imported into Athens in Hermippus fr. 63, and the elite symposium in *Wasps*. In the latter an old man appears to be in need of re-education in the rituals of the institution in order to reach the levels of refinement (mainly in manners and etiquette) which he will find there. Do such levels of refinement constitute luxury? Certain forms of eating are often linked with luxury. For example, Andrew Dalby considers whether snails were a luxury in prehistoric Crete (p. 38); also 'honey set the example of a product in limited supply, easy to store, desirable for its flavouring qualities; essentially a luxury' (p. 47). Grapes, figs, and olives were luxuries (p. 49); wines and foreign foods contributed to the development of 'gastronomy' (pp. 93–112); northern Greece contributed to the development of luxury in the fourth century (pp. 152–7).[1] A range of senses of the term 'luxury' is employed here, the snail because it was imported; grapes, figs, olives, and honey because they were not 'staples'; gastronomy and northern luxury because the refined life of the rich supported by foreign influences is under consideration.

I adopt a very different approach to luxurious eating in this

---

[1] Dalby (1995).

chapter, for two reasons. First, ancient conceptions of luxury do not coincide with our own.[2] Second, the *discourse* of luxury came into its own in the late fifth and early fourth centuries—the very time in which most of the comedies discussed in this book were written—and new terms, *tryphe* and *hedypatheia*, lent impetus to the debate. Definition of luxurious foods is clearly needed, particularly since, as Dalby acknowledges (p. 49), much of the diet of the rich in ancient Athens rested on more refined forms of the foods that the poor consumed—finer barley, larger fish—together with a greater range and quantity. This was not a culture in which social distinctions were always marked by exclusive foods brought from elsewhere, though there were some, such as the Lydian *kandaulos*, as we shall see. This study of luxury is confined to Attic comedy, since too little remains of Sicilian to allow analysis.

It is in the city that luxury dwells in particular,[3] and it is the indulgent life of the city against which comedy, and indeed Plato, set the simplicity and integrity of country life. To a large extent luxury in ancient thought rested not on goods but on personal disposition and on the ability to control a person's desires. In his splendid study of desire in ancient Athens, Davidson (1997) has shown that in many texts of the fifth and fourth centuries the objects of desire were problematized because of concerns over the self-control of the individual. Consumption was an area of considerable anxiety, particularly in regard to the beautiful and desirable body—of a courtesan, a boy, or a large fish—for which

---

[2] Before the advent of the Industrial Revolution and the mass production of goods which might be marketed as luxuries, the discourse of luxury was, with some exceptions, negative, as Berry (1994) has shown. Sekora (1977) in his study of the Jews, Greeks, Romans, and British before the nineteenth century establishes the place of luxury in patriarchal cultures and highlights those who are particularly dangerous figures in this discourse, the tempter, the stranger, the interloper, and the foreigner—the kinds of people who were to be found in a large and populous city such as Athens. I discuss conceptions of luxury in Wilkins (1999).

[3] See Osborne (1987), 108–12 for a brief discussion of Athens, and Sekora (1977), 71 on Henry Fielding's *Tom Jones*: 'we shall represent Human Nature at first to the keen appetite of our reader in that more plain and simple manner in which it is found in the country, and shall hereafter hash and ragout it with all the high French and Italian seasoning of affectation and vice which courts and cities afford.'

large amounts of money might be paid in the competition of desire. If the consumer's desire ran unchecked, he might outrun his resources and face ruin; he might also lose his sense of right and wrong, both in the personal and the civic sphere. Davidson's case works particularly well for fish since, as he shows in his first chapter, fish was an *opson*, an addition to the basic cereal diet (*sitos*). In this division of the diet into two categories,[4] large fish were presented in texts which problematized eating into *the opson*, the supplement which, though tasty, was also perishable and expensive. Comedies and other texts returned repeatedly to scenes of eager buying and eating of large fish with unrestrained appetite. I return to fish in this and the next chapter, partly to develop two observations by Davidson, that all humans experience desire and that many Greeks loved the taste of fish. The audiences of comedy, when presented with gourmets fighting for the best fish, knew what the fuss was all about. The discourse of luxurious eating was not confined to comedy in the poetry of this period but extended to the genres of lyric (the *Deipnon* of Philoxenus) and to 'parody', the *Hedypatheia* (*Life of Luxury*) of Archestratus and the *Attic Dinner* of Matro, and to the sub-comic *chreiae* of Machon, all of which I discuss in this and the next chapter.

6.1. APPROACHES TO LUXURIOUS EATING

Five ancient approaches to luxury may be identified. The first four are negative and provide the criteria for this chapter. Two fragments from the elegies of Xenophanes, a poet from the Ionian city of Colophon of the late sixth and early fifth century, set a useful frame to the discussion, which is based on the *Deipnosophistae* of Athenaeus, by far the best synthesis of ancient approaches to luxurious eating.

Now the floor is pure, pure too the hands of everyone and the cups. A slave places woven garlands on their heads and lays out sweet-smelling perfume in a dish. The mixing-bowl stands full of good cheer and other wine is at hand, promising never to betray the drinkers. Honey-sweet it

---

[4] All Greeks ate *opsa* since the human diet cannot be exclusively built on cereals. Dalby (1995) admits (p. 49) that the poor ate olives and figs, as indeed they ate green leaves and lentil soup, all 'supplements' or *opsa*.

is in its jars and smelling of flowers. In the middle, incense lets off its holy fragrance, and there is water cold, sweet, and pure. At their side are yellow loaves, and the table of honour groans with cheese and rich honey. The altar in the middle is decked all round with flowers and song and feasting take over the house on all sides. First the men must cheerfully sing a hymn to the god with respectful tales and pure words, pouring libations and praying for the strength to do the right thing. These then are the most pressing things, not acts of hybris. To drink as much as allows you to get home without a servant unless you are really old. To praise the man who has much good to reveal when drunk, as far as his memory and eagerness for excellence will take him. To refrain from telling of the battles of Titans and Giants or of Centaurs, all fakes of earlier generations, or of violent civil strife. In these subjects resides nothing that is good. Better always to have good forethought for the gods.

(fr. 1 West=Athenaeus 11.462c–f)

The people of Colophon, according to Phylarchus, were originally tough in their training but ran aground on the reefs of luxury (*tryphe*). They made friends and allies of the Lydians and went out with their hair dressed in golden ornaments, as Xenophanes says: 'they learned useless softness from the Lydians while they were still free of hateful tyranny, and went to the central meeting-place wearing clothes of crimson, no fewer than a thousand all together, proud, taking pleasure in their handsome hair drenched in scent that was carefully prepared' [fr. 3 West]. They became so dissolute in their drinking out of hours that some of them saw neither the rising nor the setting of the sun . . . Theopompus says in the fifteenth book of the *Histories* that a thousand men went round the city wearing marine-purple garments, a thing at that time scarce even for kings and extremely sought after.

(Athenaeus 12.526a–b)

The first fragment describes an aristocratic gathering at which the correct observance of the rituals of the symposium is the prime concern, the second fragment pride before a fall, a moralistic approach that is taken further by the historians Phylarchus and Theopompus in the fourth century. For Xenophanes, an exclusive and aristocratic feast appears not to constitute luxury but good order, provided that privilege is properly controlled by the rituals of drinking. Order is threatened by impurity, betrayal, hybris, and the wrong kind of tale. In the second fragment, by contrast, the nobility of Colophon have begun to dress too extravagantly when on public business; they have yielded to 'useless softness' and have been influenced by their Lydian neighbours: this 'useless softness' is interpreted by Phylarchus as luxury (*tryphe*). In the late sixth or early fifth century Xenophanes exemplifies a concern over the display of personal wealth where there is no divine sanction or civic ritual within which to contain it. Already present in Xenophanes's approach to excess are a concern for self-control in two of the four areas most essential to life, namely food and drink, shelter and clothing.[5] Athenaeus in Book 12 gives many more examples of the reworking of these concerns by Herodotus and the historians of the fourth century such as Phylarchus, Theopompus, Heracleides of Pontus, and Timaeus. In this book Athenaeus addresses himself to the 'notorious' luxury (*tryphe*) of various peoples, among whom the Persians, Syracusans, and Ionians receive comic comment. Luxury in others is related to the excessive eating of such peoples as the Thessalians and Boeotians that I investigated in Chapter 2. The discourse of luxury also informs the ethnographic survey of Book 4 (in which Athens is shown to present herself as the city lacking luxurious eating) and the addiction to pleasure studied in Book 8, in which much Athenian excess is documented—luxury is a domestic as well as a foreign problem.

The first approach rests on the self-control which is needed to resist appetite and desire; this self-control might be tested by the desire for fish and the amorous pursuits of the symposium as set out by Davidson (1997), or by the elaborate sweet and savoury confections of cooks, many of them introduced from outside Athens. Luxury is thus not an intrinsic quality of an object or a food but is defined by the desire of the user to obtain and consume it. Such desire implies a certain level of wealth but, as we shall see, those who failed to exercise self-control were not necessarily the rich, but rather certain citizens, often young men and those in political office, the fish-loving politicians such as Callimedon, 'the Crayfish' and the subjects of Plato, *Perialges* fr. 106 'O god-like Morychos, how can you not be a demigod? And Glauketes the sole, and Leogoras, you who lead a pleasant life with nothing to worry about.' Davidson (1997) concerned himself principally with the appetites of the male citizen who failed to live by the codes of restraint. More vulnerable to appetite than the male citizen, however, were the other adult inhabitants of the city, the women, the

---

[5] See Berry (1994), 4–8, who, in a modern context, adds leisure.

foreigners, and the slaves.[6] These groups, together with the weaker male citizens, were considered particularly susceptible to desire and the temptations of luxury. Plato, in his discussion of eating (*Republic* 372d–e), sets out the evils of the luxurious city, which is seen as a city suffering from inflammation.[7] Once people have dining-couches and special foods and *hetaerae* and cakes they will want a vast number of servants and other good things and will never consider they have sufficient. The desire for these pleasures, if unchecked, damages both the city and the individual, as Plato demonstrates later in Books 8 and 9. In particular, the 'democratic' man, if he gives in to 'unnecessary' desires (which are further defined in regard to food at 559a–c), is besieged by the forces of appetite (559a–561e), and the 'tyrannical' man gives in completely to desire (573a–575a). To combat this problem, self-control (*enkrateia*), based on reason, is needed. Plato sets out the point at 430e–431c: the guardians should exercise prudence (*sophrosyne*), which is a form of order or control over certain pleasures and desires. Aristotle (*Nicomachean Ethics* 1145b8–12) endorses this: 'self-control and endurance are desirable and praiseworthy qualities, while lack of control and softness are weak and to be censured. The man who has self-control is also the one who stands by his reasoning process; the one without self-control abandons his reason.' Reason, for Aristotle, is the attribute of the Athenian upper-class male. The lower orders have other objectives: 'the many, those with the lowest tastes, suppose that the good is pleasure. They therefore embrace the life of enjoyment . . . The many are utterly servile in their choice of a life suitable for grazing animals. They come into the argument because many of those who are men of means lead a life similar to Sardanapalus' (1095b16–22).[8]

---

[6] Sekora (1977) has shown that the concept of luxury in a range of literary texts from different cultures (from the Old Testament to Smollett's *Humphry Clinker*) is built on the forces real or imaginary which threaten the established order and in their difference from it contribute to its clearer identity. In all cases considered that order is male and supported by appeal to a male figure of authority, the Jewish God, the male head of the household for Plato and Aristotle, the Stoic sage in later antiquity, and the squire in the England of the eighteenth century.

[7] Schmitt-Pantel (1992), 452 discusses this passage in the context of the contribution of *tryphe* to refinement: '*Tryphe* est donc un principe de l'évolution de l'humanité.'

[8] See below on this Assyrian king, perceived by the Greeks as the paradigm of the feminized oriental potentate.

Plato alludes to the role of desire in the oriental monarch at *Republic* 553c. Women are not to be trusted: Aristotle echoes conventional thought at *Politics* 1269b19–23. Speaking of the Spartans, he writes, 'the lawgiver wished to make the whole civic body tough and self-disciplined, and no one can deny that the men are so; but he overlooked the women, who give free rein to every form of intemperance and luxury'. In other states women have a liking for democracy and tyranny, expecting to dominate their husbands in the first and to prosper in the second (1313b32–8): in neither case do they keep their place, which is to be subject to the male (*Politics* 1259a37–1260a2). Being unable to control the power of reason (1260a12–13),[9] they are potentially more luxurious. Plato expresses similar opinions at *Republic* 431b–c: 'One would find many and varied desires, pleasures and pains in children in particular and in women and slaves and among the so-called free population in the many and the lower-class.'[10] There was always the fear that a man would let the side down, submit to the persuasion of other weak people, and fail to show that resilience and self-control which alone guarantee the moral order. Wealth based on landed property is threatened by luxury, for pleasurable goods are purchased whatever the cost.[11]

My second approach to luxury follows a developmental model, according to which the Greeks feared that, as they became more wealthy, so they became more luxurious and dissolute. They imagined a general decline in self-restraint. Athenaeus adds the Magnesians and the Sybarites to Xenophanes' Colophonians. Athenaeus (or rather his Epitomator) extends this model to the history of cooking in a remarkable synthesis apparently based on the Hellenistic work *On the Life of the Heroes in Homer*.[12] In order to make his heroes spend their time

---

[9] Unlike slaves, who possess no reason at all.

[10] Plato allows women guardians in his ideal state. His sentiments on women in the *Republic* are castigated by Annas (1981), 181–5. Women, slaves, and the lower orders are grouped together again at 395d–e as unsuitable dramatic characters for men to enact.

[11] On consumption see Davidson (1997) and C. Edwards (1993).

[12] On this work see the bibliography cited by Hunter (1983) on Eubulus fr. 118. Davidson (1997) reviews the debate on the absence of fish in Homer, within which scholars grappled with the rise in the estimation of fish from being a food of no regard in Homer to its luxurious status in the fourth century.

on fine deeds, Homer 'set up for all a life that was thrifty and self-sufficient' (1.8f).[13] He did this in particular by restraining the strongest desires and pleasures, to eat and to drink. The heroes were thus in control of themselves (ἐγκρατεῖς). The meat they received was roasted and normally beef—the process of boiling and the use of other meats were in principle more luxurious and excluded. Homer allows no one to eat fish, nor fruit, despite celebrating their abundance in *Odyssey* 7. Some concessions to elaboration were detected in Homer (1.25e): *Odyssey* 1.141, 'he lifted up dishes of all sorts of meats and served them' implies fowls, pork, and kid as well as beef, and 'varied preparation that was not uniform but excessive (*peritten*)'.[14] 'Thus emerged', concludes Athenaeus, 'the tables of Sicily and Sybaris, and of Chios.' This special reading of the *Iliad* and *Odyssey* derives from the Alexandrian debate on Homer, an offshoot of which was the reading of the epic according to the preoccupations of the third and second centuries BC. This is a literary discourse which located restraint in the past and lack of control in the present. Sicily was 'famous for its luxurious tables' (Athenaeus 12.518c); Sybaris had fallen because of its luxuries (12.518c–520c). Feeding into this model of development (which has little interest in chronology beyond using Homer as the benchmark for antiquity) are many elements of interest to comedy, in particular

---

[13] εὐτελῆ κατεσκεύασε πᾶσι τὸν βίον καὶ αὐτάρκη.

[14] Other foods not served in Homer (9a) include stuffed fig leaves, rich meat sauce, milk cakes and honey cakes (θρῖα καὶ κάνδυλον καὶ ἄμητας (καὶ) μελίπηκτα). In contrast, the non-Greek King Alcinous (in the *Odyssey*) was more inclined to the life of luxury (τὸν τρυφερὸν . . . βίον), and his Phaeacian people were exceedingly luxurious (τρυφερώτατοι). Even the suitors in the *Odyssey*, men who were hubristic and given up to pleasure, did not eat fish, birds, or honey cakes because Homer excluded 'the conjuring tricks of the cook' (τὰς μαγειρικὰς μαγγανείας). Homer has no garlands or perfumes. 'The refinements (περιεργία) of cooks and myrrh-sellers have increased . . . In full bloom too are the clever crafts of cake-making and the refinements to aid sexual intercourse.' Diners sat at mealtimes and did not recline (11f, 17f; cf. 8.363f, 10.428b). Portions at the feast were divided equally. Athenaeus' source appears to reflect some concessions to luxury in Homer, as if putting a counter-argument: the poet is aware of extravagant ways and wealth such as we have now (πολυτέλεια), but plays them down. There *is* passing reference to fish (some in metaphor); there is some catching of birds; but in general the poet omits the use of vegetables, fish, and birds because they imply gluttony (λιχνεία) and are not suitable for heroes to prepare. Similarly, boiled meat is implied in metaphors and in the ox-foot thrown at Odysseus.

the rise of the *mageiros*, apparently in Sicily (see Chapter 7), and the literary and dramatic elaboration of cooking methods by comic cooks and Archestratus. Since these were almost totally excluded from Homer, they represent a 'decline' into luxury.[15]

Plato, who shared, to a limited extent, comedy's interest in food, taps into this model of epic purity, commenting on the absence of fish in Homer (quoted in Chapter 7) and on the luxurious eating 'we now have'. Two comic fragments may also have done so. A character in Eubulus fr. 118 reflects on the absence of fish-eating and the boiling of meat in Homer—'meat they only roasted'—and, according to the Epitomator of Athenaeus, Antiphanes fr. 248 refers to Homeric cooking: 'he did not boil the meat or brains. He even roasted the guts. That's how ancient he was.'[16] Many comedies, as we shall see in Chapter 8, presented cooks who claimed ever-greater heights of artistry and elaboration over their predecessors. I do not know of one who compares his own cooking with that of the Homeric heroes, though the cook in Strato, *Phoenicides* borrows Homeric diction. An alternative developmental model is exploited by the cook in Athenion, *Samothracians* fr. 1, who shows how cooking is the supreme civilized art to develop from the savagery of primitive societies. The main comic counterparts of Homer are Hermippus frr. 63 and 77, which insert apparently luxurious foods and wines into hexameters, perhaps tempering them with the presence of Dionysus, and the parodies of Archestratus and especially Matro (see Chapter 7).

The third approach is built on restraint of the passions, by sacred and civic ritual rather than the ethical code of the past. We saw this approach in Xenophanes fr. 1 and in the parasite of Chapter 2, the sacred official whom Alexis appears to have converted into the comic scrounger at the luxurious tables of the rich. This approach is also prominent in the comic presentation of the prytaneion discussed in Chapter 4. Plutarch discusses the ritual containment of appetite in *Table Talk*[17] 2.10, where (642f) the topic is

---

[15] Dalby (1995) makes much of these developments but it is hard to chart the literary discourse against actual practice in Syracuse or Athens.

[16] Hunter (1983) on Eubulus fr. 118 notes the possibility of a monograph on Homeric cooking written early enough for Plato and Eubulus to use it—a much earlier work than the one summarized by Athenaeus.

[17] Plutarch's Συμποσιακά have a general bearing on this book since they are logoi on the symposium which present opposing arguments, and in that sense

the meal with equal distribution.[18] The opponents of such a distribution describe it as 'lacking in communality'[19] and 'unworthy of a free man';[20] the division of meat destroys the communality of 'drinking together and eating together',[21] where the shared company is more important than the physical satisfying of bodily needs; taking one's share by weight is like having it weighed out by the butcher (that is, as a mere commercial transaction). We share the song of the *aulos*-girl and the harp-girl, just as we share the crater or mixing-bowl, the 'unfailing spring of goodwill': this is good sharing since everyone enjoys as much as he likes, whereas with equal portions of meat the hungry diner has as much as the small eater. Homer's dinners[22] leave a man hungry and thirsty, and his kings are like penny-pinching Italian innkeepers (643d). The counter-argument is that the proposals for unequal shares are driven by greed. Plentiful—but equal—portions are needed. 'Sharing at the table'[23] is 'natural, not conventional, and meets a need that is necessary and not new or brought in for specious reasons'. Many of these terms are imported from earlier discussions in Plato and Aristotle.[24] We should not be surprised that both sides agree on the shared meal: it was rare for a Greek to eat in any other way, as we saw in Chapter 2. Greedy eaters set up war with the others, 'because I do not consider suspicion, snatching,[25] hand-contests, and elbowing to be a comradely and drink-sharing beginning of the feast' (644a): this is behaviour which leads to brawls.[26] The custom of equal distribution was abandoned when

resemble some of the argumentation of Athenaeus; at the same time, they give an angle on a food or eating practice which may be similar to the way in which a particular approach may be adopted in a passage of comedy—in praise of or opposition to a boastful chef, for example. Issues raised by Plutarch, as we shall see, were not original to him but are placed in a useful context and formulation.

[18] δαίς. On the equal share see Detienne and Vernant (1989), Loraux (1981), and Schmitt-Pantel (1992).

[19] ἀκοινώνητος.   [20] ἀνελεύθερος.   [21] συμπινεῖν καὶ συμφαγεῖν.

[22] Which were based on equal shares: see n. 18.

[23] ἡ περὶ τράπεζαν κοινωνία.

[24] See e.g. Plato, *Republic* 559a11–c1 on necessary and useful foods (quoted by Athenaeus at 12.511e–512a).

[25] ἁρπασμός.

[26] See Chap. 4 on the snatching of food. Plutarch here alludes to the lack of order and control that may befall a symposium if restraint is not imposed by ritual or personal morality. This was a danger behind Xenophanes fr. 1, Epicharmus fr. 148 and Athenaeus 8.363d, cited below.

'extravagant expenditure invaded dinners'.[27] The speaker suggests that 'cakes, *kandaulos*-sauce, and other *karyke*-style sauces and all kinds of dishes of pounded sauces and *opsa*'[28] could not be divided. 'Overwhelmed by their greed for these dishes and by luxurious living, they put aside equal shares. The proof of this is that even now sacrifices and public meals are run on the basis of equal shares because of the simplicity and frugality of the food.[29] Thus, to bring back equal shares is to restore thriftiness. If there are to be private portions, then that is the end of communality.' If we take each other's food why not each other's *hetaerae* and harp-players also? The most important aspects of this social occasion, says this speaker, concluding as did his antagonist, are 'words, toasts, and good feeling'. In this discussion Plutarch's contrasts of equal shares against appetite and equal shares against obscuring sauces establishes the ancient division between ritual (religious and social ritual guarantee equal shares) and lack of restraint or luxury.

Athenaeus brings together notions of ritual containment and our second model of luxurious development (8.363d):

the ancients, having conceived of the gods in human form, organized festivals accordingly. They saw that it was not possible for men to resist the desire to enjoy themselves, but that at the same time it was useful and beneficial to accustom them to living in good order and discipline. They thus set aside certain times when sacrifice to the gods would take place first, and only then would the men be released into relaxation. . . . Assuming then that the gods were nearby, they held their festivals in orderly and restrained fashion . . . It was not the custom among the ancients to recline but 'they dined sitting down'. In modern times, however, men pretend to sacrifice to the gods, and call friends and relatives to the feast, but in fact heap curses on their children, abuse their wives, make their servants weep, and threaten the crowd.[30]

Menander, *Dyscolus* 447–55 and *Drunkenness* (*Methe*) fr. 224 (quoted in Chapters 1 and 2) exemplify the elision of ritual with luxurious eating and appetite.

---

[27] ἐπεισῆλθον αἱ πολυτέλειαι τοῖς δείπνοις.

[28] πέμματα, κανδύλους, καρυκείας ἄλλας καὶ παντοδαπὰς ὑποτριμμάτων καὶ ὄψων παραθέσεις.

[29] ἀφέλειαν καὶ καθαριότητα. *Kathariotes* in *LSJ* has the sense of elegance as opposed to extravagant excess.

[30] See further Schmitt-Pantel (1992) 449–57 and Bruit and Schmitt-Pantel (1986) on the value of Athenaeus as a source.

The fourth approach, which Plutarch touched upon in *Table Talk* 2.10, is the opposition between the 'natural'[31] and 'useful' and the luxurious.[32] Plutarch pursues the question in 3.1, on the topic of garlands at the symposium. These represent 'luxury and sweet pleasure' (τρυφὴν καὶ ἡδυπάθειαν), it is asserted. Variety of flowers at the meal makes for pleasure (ἡδονὴ) and not piety (εὐσέβεια).[33] Flowers soon perish.[34] 'There can be no place at the symposium of philosophers for pleasure which is not combined with utility and which does not follow the lead of a natural appetite (φυσικῆς ὀρέξεως).'[35] An interlocutor suggests that flowers are natural, and not like purple-dye for clothes and perfume which are expensive:[36] they have simplicity and purity (τὸ ἀφελὲς ... καὶ καθαρὸν). Natural ἡδονή and χάρις, which flourish according to season, should not be dishonoured. Pleasure can be useful too. Doctor Tryphon's[37] case rests on the medical uses of flowers, particularly at the symposium: cooling ivy for intoxication, plant perfumes for countering the strength of wine, plants for opening up the vents (*poroi*) of the body. Saffron, henna, and hazelwort are gentle for drinkers. The perfumes of some flowers thin and separate the humours in the brains of drinkers.

Finally, 'luxury' has a democratic dimension, which is seen too in the polis as reconfigured in Old Comedy. The Athenian democracy prided itself on bringing to all citizens the good things that their political system had made available. Thucydides (2.38) has Pericles declare, 'we Athenians provide the most relaxation from toil for the spirit, in competitions and festivals observed throughout the year and in seemly private gatherings from which we derive the pleasure necessary to strike out painful things. Because of the size of the city, all the goods from all the

---

[31] On nature and necessity in relation to luxury see Sekora (1977).

[32] See n. 3.   [33] The polarity noted above.

[34] Like a number of luxury foods, in particular fish.

[35] A fine analogy follows: just as guests who are invited and uninvited friends of the guests are all welcomed equally (like Aristodemus who brings along Socrates also in Plato's *Symposium*), but the uninvited and unaccompanied guest is excluded, so pleasures associated with eating and drinking, if they are invited by nature and follow appetite, have a place at the feast, but the other pleasures that are not invited and have no reason are seen off.

[36] See Xenophanes fr. 3.

[37] On the personal name, derived from *tryphe*, luxury, see Arnott (1996) on Alexis, *Tokistes* fr. 232.

cities are imported here, and so it is that we enjoy the fruits of the goods grown here just as much as those from other men.' The oligarchic opponent of the democracy puts it similarly ([Xenophon], *Constitution of the Athenians* 2.7): 'through their rule over the sea the Athenians have various contacts in various places and have developed ways of feasting: whatever is pleasant[38] in Sicily or Italy or Cyprus or Egypt or Lydia or the Pontus or the Peloponnese or anywhere else, these they gather all together.' Braund (1994) discusses the phenomenon of luxury for the democracy on the basis of these and comic passages such as Hermippus fr. 63. These are striking statements, which suggest that democratic ideology demanded that good things should be available in profusion for all.[39] Both[40] add feasting and festivals as sources of eating and enjoyment for everyone. The term 'luxury' is not used (though [Xenophon's] 'whatever is pleasant' comes close to it), and these 'good things' are linked with proper religious and civic restraint. Braund argues that democratic ideology aimed to make 'luxuries' available to all, a utopian goal satirized in Plato, *Menexenus* 235c[41] and unlikely to be approved by Plato and Aristotle or by other opponents of the democracy. Braund (1994) calls these good things luxuries, though they do not so qualify under most of the criteria adopted in this chapter. The ideological point is, however, important since it makes clear that 'luxury' is not a concept linked only with the elite. Furthermore, opponents of the democracy could use the pejorative term 'luxury' or an equivalent in place of 'good things': Aristotle (cited above) claimed that the mass of the population was addicted to pleasure. Like the democratic regime, so Old Comedy, as we have seen in Chapters 3 and 4, sought to make 'good things', *agatha*, available to its own comic polis, for the benefit of

[38] 'Whatever is pleasant' draws on part of the language of luxury (see below).
[39] See the discussion in chap. 3 of Ceccarelli (1996), and Braund (1994) on political aspects of the plays of agricultural bounty such as Aristophanes' *Seasons*.
[40] Cf. [Xenophon] 2.9: the demos knows that each of the poor cannot offer sacrifice and feasts of set up shrines or run a great and beautiful city, and so has found ways of providing sacrifices, shrines, feasts and precincts. This passage is discussed at Chap. 3.6.3.
[41] 'I almost think I am living in the Isles of the Blessed, so skilled are the political orators.'

its favoured constituency, the protagonist, his chorus, and the audience. *Peace* 999–1009 exemplifies this, both in the supply of agricultural goods and in the dismissal of 'Morychos, Teleas, Glauketes, and all the other gourmets'. We have seen many comic passages dealing with foods coming to Athens in addition to Hermippus fr. 63, from *Wasps, Merchant Ships* probably, and from the end of *Acharnians*. These are *agatha*, not 'luxuries' as such,[42] normally, as I argued in Chapters 3 and 4, because they are provided by Dionysus and other benevolent gods.

These five approaches are illustrated in two books of Athenaeus which preserve a number of comic fragments on luxury, namely Book 4 on other peoples and Book 12 on luxury (*tryphe*) itself. As Schmitt-Pantel has shown,[43] most of these illustrations of luxury are drawn either from barbarians on the edge of the Greek world, such as Sardanapalus, the feminized king of Assyria, or from Greek cities which had declined at some time in the past, such as Sybaris. Luxury, bad government, kings, tyrants, or extreme democracy might each bring down a city or a people, especially if there was too much good living (*hedypatheia*) or pleasure (*hedone*). This approach, which sets out the moral dangers of luxury in a perpective of time, location, and gender, gained momentum towards the end of the fifth century, for example in the account of Sardanapalus by Ctesias (*FGrH* 688F1.23–8=Athenaeus 12.528–529d). Athenaeus preserves parts of Aristotle's work on the decline of Miletus (fr. 557 Rose = 12.523f) and possibly of Siris (fr. 584 Rose = 12.523c). Athenaeus' main points of reference are provided by the treatises *On Pleasure* by Theophrastus or Chamaeleon of Pontus and by Heraclides of Pontus.[44] The first work distinguishes the demigods at Troy, who suffered in no respect from luxury, from

---

[42] They are classified as luxuries by Athenaeus in the case of Polycrates of Samos (12.540c–d): 'Clytus the Aristotelian in his book on Miletus says that Polycrates the tyrant of Samos was driven by luxury to import goods from all sides, dogs from Epirus, goats from Scyros, sheep from Miletus, and pigs from Sicily.' This resembles Pindar's praise of Hiero (fr. 106 Sn.–M), cited with Hermippus fr. 63 at 1.28a. Tyrants can import whatever luxury goods they desire: under the Athenian democracy, similar goods are made available to all the people.

[43] (1992), 451–66.

[44] See 12.511c–d and 6.273c. On Heraclides see Gottschalk (1980).

'the people of today'. In the past life was 'unequipped'[45] and undiscovered.[46] This follows our developmental model and uses the formulation of discovery which we have noted in the speeches of parasites and boastful cooks.[47] Heraclides for the most part follows the tradition hostile to pleasure and luxury,[48] but offers one valuable example of the benefits of luxury: kings and tyrants control good things (*agatha*) and put pleasure first because they have tried everything. Furthermore, pleasure makes men more grand,[49] as can be seen in the Medes and Persians who demonstrate that those who honour pleasure and choose luxury (*tryphe*) are also braver and more lordly. Pleasure and luxury are a mark of freedom, and belong to the men of Marathon. Work is for slaves and the lower orders. This demonstration that Athenian luxury at the time of the Persian Wars brought the only victory over the Persians is an unusual counter-argument to the censure of luxury, perhaps to be related to the case for democratic luxuries. This is paradoxography, a new perspective on the Persian Wars to set beside Herodotus' presentation of the effete overcome by the lean and simple, Medes by Persians, Persians by Spartans and Athenians.

Athenaeus gives numerous examples of states who 'ran aground on the reefs of luxury' like Xenophanes' Colophon. Phylarchus, writing of the decline of Sybaris (Athenaeus 12.521d), imagined cooking to be part of the problem: any cook

---

[45] ἀκατάσκευος.   [46] ἀνεύρετος.

[47] Novelty was sought both in the Persian court and in Sybaris. Of the former Athenaeus writes (4.144b–c = Xenophon, *Agesilaus* 9.3), 'of the luxury of the king of Persia, Xenophon writes, "for the Persian king they travel round the whole country in search of something that he will find pleasant to drink, and ten thousand men work with skill on food he will find pleasant to eat".' On Sybaris, Athenaeus quotes Phylarchus (12.521d): any cook who invented a new dish was granted a year's patent to encourage competition in his skill. This is competitive cooking for palates, well beyond the requirements of hunger.

[48] Athenaeus (4.145a–146a) cites another account of dining at the Persian court which looks beyond luxury, from Heracleides of Cumae, *FGrH* 689 F 2. The king's separation from other eaters and drinkers is emphasized, but the organization and particularly the quantities of food are less excessive than appears. In fact, given his retinue, the king is not so much grand (*megaloprepes*) as economical and careful. For the range of Greek discussions on Persian food see further Sancisi-Weerdenburg(1995).

[49] μεγαλόψυχοι.

who invented a new dish was granted a year's patent to encourage competition in such skills, while there were tax concessions for eel-sellers, piped wines for export, and a liberal treatment of women. Numerous individuals too suffered like Sardanapalus, becoming either too feminine (Alcibiades[50] and Deinias the perfume-seller, who was so mired in luxury that he castrated himself)[51] or subject to women (Callias, the subject of the *Flatterers* of Eupolis, whose sufferings appear to have been discussed by Heracleides and others in the fourth century). Individuals might also be too monarchical, such as Philip of Macedon, Alexander, Dionysius, Demetrius Poliorcetes, Demetrius of Phalerum, and others. In Antiphanes fr. 185 (quoted in Chapter 1), a speaker prefers plain lentil soup to the fears and excess that beset King Seleucus, and in Menander, *The Fisherman* fr. 25[52] Dionysius, son of Clearchus the first tyrant of Heracleia, exhibits all the languor of a Sardanapalus:

He was a fat pig lying on his mouth.

He enjoyed luxury[53] of such a kind that he did not luxuriate for long.

I have one private desire, and this alone seems to me a death worth the dying for, fat as I am, to lie on my back with my many rolls of fat, talking little, short of breath, eating, and saying 'I am rotting away with pleasure'.

In Books 4 and 12 Athenaeus gives an unrivalled survey of cautionary tales on *tryphe*, the prominence of which, particularly in the authors of the fourth century, gives a splendid background to the exploitation of the concept in comedy.

6.2. TERMINOLOGY

The earliest terms relating to luxury are words with a broad reference to wealthy and gentle living that do not necessarily carry a pejorative force: *chlide, habrotes,* and *habrosyne*, with the associated epithets *habros* and *chlidanos*. Wealth and softness are common associates: that softness is later expressed as *malthakia*. In Xenophanes fr. 3, it is the useless *habrosyne* displayed by the

---

[50] So Eupolis, *Flatterers* fr. 171 and Pherecrates fr. 164.
[51] Heracleides of Pontus fr. 61.
[52] In fact three fragments grouped together.　　[53] ἐτρύφησεν.

wealthy that prompted the citation in Athenaeus' catalogue of luxury (*tryphe*). It is to the Ionians and peoples of the East in particular that the Greeks applied these terms. Later, the associations of 'pleasantness'[54] with good living, with the tastes of foods and wines, led to the formation of the term *hedypatheia*, the experience of pleasant things, luxury, first attested in Xenophon, of the Medes and Persians. While sweetness remains a term of the broadest application, all kinds of good and highly approved things being 'sweet' in comedy, *hedypatheia* was much more dubious, as was *tryphe*, luxury.

The term τρυφή appears to derive from the verb θρύπτειν, to break into bits, and refers in its earliest citations in Euripides, Aristophanes, and Plato to the broken-down nature of the sufferer who lacks the firm resolve and self-control, ἐγκράτεια, needed in a good man, but not to be expected in women and slaves. Thus, pseudo-Xenophon in his *Constitution of the Athenians* speaks (1.11) with full oligarchical horror of the luxury and grandiose life of Athenian slaves who are not controlled as they should be.[55] Aristophanes uses the term τρυφή as follows: at *Frogs* 21 Dionysus' question, 'is it not a sign of hybris and great *tryphe* that I [the god] have to walk and the slave to ride the donkey?', reflects a reversal of the order of god above slave. So too at *Lysistrata* 387, where the magistrate says that the '*tryphe* of the women has flared up', and has infected the men (405), order has broken down. A most indicative passage is *Clouds* 46–52: 'then I married the niece of Megacles son of Megacles, I a countryman, she a city woman. She was classy, luxurious (*tryphosan*), done up like Coesyra. When I married her, I slept with her and smelt of wine lees, crates of dried figs, fleeces, of surplus, and she of perfume, saffron and deep kisses, expense, gluttony, Aphrodite Colias, and Genetyllis.' The context is sexual,[56] the wedding of Strepsiades and a city woman, and it is the woman who has the appetite for both sex and food. She is aristocratic and has airs and is sexually provocative. When she worships the gods, it is to lesser fertility cults that she turns, and not the city's Thesmophoria festival designed for the

---

[54] The epithet ἡδύς.

[55] ἐῶσι τοὺς δούλους τρυφᾶν αὐτόθι καὶ μεγαλοπρεπῶς ἐνίους ('they allow their slaves to be luxurious and some of them to have a magnificent style of life').

[56] Softness and seduction are the subject of the *tryphe* at *Ecclesiazusae* 901, 973b.

propagation of babies.[57] While the husband smells of the country, the vintage, goats and sheep, and agricultural surplus,[58] she smells of perfume, saffron, sex, and expense. It is not that the husband is poor, but that his money derives from agricultural surpluses and is on the credit side, while the wife is a big spender. He is a producer, she a consumer. We shall see many close connections in comedy between expense and luxury, and many cases too of expenses located in the city, compared with which the country is a focus of economy and traditional values.[59] Those plays which portray agricultural paradises supported by the agricultural gods place a high value on abundance and the other things Strepsiades had in the country: this well-being may sometimes approach *tryphe*, but is not presented in terms of expense, for, as we have seen, the earth supports such endeavour *automatically*. The closest that such a play comes to luxury explicitly is *Wealth* 802–18, where the miracle begins with heaps of good things, transforms pottery to gold and silver and water to oil, and, in a flourish of comic earthiness, provides garlic instead of a stone with which to wipe your bum—what luxury![60] Luxury in Aristophanes extends beyond the term *tryphe*. The Athenian ambassadors to Persia at the beginning of *Acharnians* are softly reclining on wagons,[61] and drank unmixed wine from gold and glass (74).[62]

---

[57] The religious part of the city wife's *tryphe* is interesting—unfamiliar cults, albeit of Aphrodite, associated with sexuality, and perhaps similar to Eupolis, *Dippers* (*Baptai*), in which the Thracian goddess Cocyto was worshipped in some comic form. Fr. 78 of that play says, 'he is a man who is not lacking in luxurious charms nor the freshness of youth'.

[58] The farm surplus is not classified as a luxury, though it could be, as being above what was necessary: cf. Xenophon, *Oeconomicus* 5.2, the earth produces for farmers what men need to live on, and produces in addition what they need for luxuries (ἡδυπαθεῖν).

[59] The beginning of *Acharnians* is a well-known example. Buying is unheard-of in the country deme.

[60] τρυφή. In *Wasps* there is the *tryphe* of the dicasts at 551 who revel irresponsibly in their 'kingdom', of a young homosexual at 688, of Philocleon walking with a swagger at 1169, and again at 1455, where he is said to have been transformed into the luxurious and soft life (τὸ τρυφῶν καὶ μαλακόν).

[61] Line 70, μαλθακῶς κατακείμενοι.

[62] Barbarians value eating and drinking on a large scale—this might be gluttony rather than luxury—but the Persians also consume oxen baked whole in the oven (87)—that is, without the equal distribution of the Greek sacrifice. See Schmitt-Pantel (1992), Sancisi-Weerdenburg (1995).

Elsewhere in Old Comedy Ionia is described as 'luxurious and beautifully tabled' at Callias, *Cyclopes* fr. 8. Luxury is a likely theme of the *Malthakoi* (*Softies*) of Cratinus. The *Dippers* of Eupolis appears to have portrayed cross-dressing of men as women in an initiation cult (test. ii); fr. 78 describes one who 'is a man not lacking in luxurious charms nor the freshness of youth'.

6.3. COMEDY ON LUXURY IN ATHENS AND BEYOND

In Attic Old Comedy the concept of luxury among both Athenians and their neighbours appears well-established. The *Persians* of Pherecrates may have exploited this theme, both in its version of the 'Age of Cronos' (fr. 137, quoted in Chapter 3) and in fr. 138: 'you who pour forth mallow from your mouth and breathe hyacinth; you who chatter melilot, grin roses; you who have a kiss of marjoram and make love with celery;[63] you who laugh alexanders and walk larkspur; pour in some drink and shout the third paean as is our custom.' This sensual combination of physical actions internal and external to the body with plants resembles two other fragments, Eupolis, *Maricas* fr. 204, 'in possession of a seal and belching perfume', and *Flatterers* fr. 176, 'a man who smells of the graces, walks like a sexy dancer, excretes sesame cake, and gobs apples'. *Maricas* portrayed the politician Hyperbolus in the guise of a foreign slave, perhaps in a form analogous to Cleon/Paphlagon, the foreign slave of *Knights* with the uncontrollable appetite. In *Flatterers*, the chorus (fr. 174) celebrate the πολλή θυμηδία[64] available in the house of Callias, specified as κάραβοι καὶ βατῖδες καὶ λαγὼι || καὶ γυναῖκες εἰλίποδες 'crayfish and rays and hares and women of rolling gait'.[65] Whether or not *thymedia* signified luxury in the fifth century, the collocation of fish with a Homeric term for a feast and a term for cattle parodically applied to *hetaerae* at least imply that the developmental approach to luxury lies behind this fragment.

---

[63] Roses and celery were metaphors for the vagina: see Henderson (1991), 135–6.

[64] Θυμηδία ('gladness of heart') was a quality of the Homeric feast (*Odyssey* 16.389) and is the sense of well-being from which the Semonidean woman dislodges her man (Sem. 7.103). Photius glosses *thumedia* as τέρψις, τρυφή, εὐφρασία ('delight, luxury, good cheer').

[65] 'Of rolling gait' is a Homeric epithet for cattle.

While Athenians might be portrayed as foreign slaves, in Old Comedy and beyond Persians, Ionians, Sicilians, and Sybarites are presented as luxurious eaters, sometimes by convention— Sybaris came to stand for a quasi-mythical land of luxury since the city was destroyed in 511 BC—and sometimes with contemporary reference, as in the updating of Sybaris to the current city of Thurii in Metagenes, *Thuriopersians*. The tables of Ionia appeared in Callias, *Cyclopes* fr. 8 and of Syracuse and Sybaris in Aristophanes, *Banqueters* fr. 225. Phrynichus fr. 67, 'there was much *sybarismos* of pipers . . .' (whatever kind of music is meant by the term) is quoted for its luxury by the scholiast of Aristophanes, *Peace* 344, a passage proclaiming that when peace returns you can 'sail away, stay at home, have sex, go to sleep, attend big festivals, feast, play *kottabos*, live like a Sybarite[66] and cry out "hurrah! Hurrah!"'.[67] Quite what form the luxury takes in these last two passages is unclear. This scholiast also notes that Epicharmus used the term *sybarizein* (fr. 215), apparently in the sense 'to tell sybaritic tales'. This appears not to be a reference to the luxury of Sybaris in the Syracusan tradition.

Luxury in these fragments on food takes a number of different forms, normally of styles of eating rather than different foods and dishes, though we shall see some of these below. Antiphanes, *Oenomaus or Pelops* fr. 170 in the fourth century presents a Persian description of the differences between Greek and Persian eating which is similar to those found in *Acharnians*: 'What would Greeks do? They have tiny tables and chew leaves. There you'll get four tiny bits of meat for an obol. But among our ancestors they baked whole oxen, pigs, deer, and lambs. Finally, the cook roasted an amazing beast whole and served the Great King a—hot camel.' Apart from the surprise at the end, the Greeks have tiny tables, tiny helpings, and eat leaves.[68] They have far to go, it is implied by this speaker, to achieve luxury.

The discourse of the luxury was used in a number of comedies of the fourth century to present Athens as a city besieged by extravagant forms of dining. Pressures towards excess came from

---

[66] The scholiast notes that the term 'be a sybarite' may mean rather 'tell sybaritic tales'.

[67] This passage is discussed in Chap. 3.6.2.

[68] Leaf-eating appears to be the point of Callias, *Cyclopes* fr. 7 (I noted fr. 8 above): 'leaves make the end of the *deipna*, as indeed of the dancing-steps.'

within and without. The presentation of food in Athens as simple and food elsewhere (whether Greek or non-Greek) as excessive, extravagant, and exotic contributed to Athens' representation of herself as the city of restraint and good order. A number of examples are drawn from Book 4 of Athenaeus, who at 4.137e–f gives three models of restraint, two of which we have already met in Chapter 4. The first is religious ritual, illustrated by Chionides,[69] *Beggars* fr. 7 (in paraphrased form): 'whenever they serve a light meal (*ariston*) to the Dioscuri, they set on the tables cheese, puff pastry, tree-ripened olives, and leeks "in memory of their ancient diet".' This form of *theoxenia* exemplifies the way in which religion preserves the old virtues of the diet,[70] and avoids all sauces and non-traditional foods. Then, in public eating, 'Solon ordains that barley cake (*maza*) be provided for those eating in the prytaneion'. The third sanction is provided by the philosophers:[71] at the Academy a clever dish by an *opsopoios* ('fish-cook') was rejected 'because it was necessary to refrain from imports from afar', and at the Lyceum a cook who disguised one food as another was flogged for 'evil and perverse subtlety'. Athenaeus adds for good measure the restrained eating habits of the Spartans and the Cretans. While Crete appears to have been beyond the reach of Attic comedy,[72] Spartan eating is illustrated by Antiphanes, *Archon* fr. 46, 'you've been in Sparta? Then you must follow their customs. Go to the mess for dinner, make the most of their soup . . . your moustache. Don't look down on it and don't look for any more delights. In following their social practices, make sure you are old fashioned.'[73]

---

[69] 'Or whoever wrote the play attributed to Chionides.'

[70] We might compare the more extreme cases of the primitive meals eaten at the Anthesteria and Pyanopsia, on which see Burkert (1985), 240 and Plutarch, *Theseus* 22.

[71] The source is Chrysippus, *On the Good and on Pleasure: For Aristokreon* fr. 3 (*SVF* 3.198).

[72] With the exception of the remarkable fr. 5 from the *Geryon* of Ephippus.

[73] Athenaeus adds Cratinus, *Wealths* fr. 175: 'is it true then, what they say, that for all outsiders who go to Sparta, there is fine feasting in the *kopis*? And that in the public areas there are puddings hanging nailed up for the old men to bite with their teeth?' Also Epilycus, *Coraliscus* fr. 4, 'I think I'll go to the *kopis* at Apollo's temple in Amyclae, where there are many barley cakes and wheat loaves and very nice soup'. A *kopis* was a feast given to foreigners on certain festival days.

Athenaeus has selected these extracts to support his own case, but there is little comic comment on the dining of Sparta that does not conform to a context of religious festival and traditional or simple foods, none of which are 'luxurious'. Athenaeus presents Macedon and northern Greece as a major source of luxurious eating in the fourth and third centuries.[74] Two examples are given. The first is the feast of Caranus of Macedon described in the form of a letter sent by Hippolochus of Macedon in the early third century BC; the corresponding letter about an Athenian banquet does not survive, but Athenaeus tells us that it described a meal offered to the Macedonian tyrant Demetrius Poliorcetes by Lais the courtesan, in other words by a non-citizen woman to a non-Athenian ruler.[75] The lost letter was written by Lynceus of Samos, who also wrote the treatise on shopping noted in Chapter 4 and was himself a comic poet (though only one play is attested, a passage from which is quoted below).[76] The second is Anaxandrides, *Protesilaus* fr. 42, an anapaestic *tour de force*:

A: And if you do this as I direct we will receive you with dazzling banquets, in no way like the banquet for Iphicrates in Thrace. And yet they say it was an occasion of luxury and decadence. Along the marketplace purple cloths were strewn up towards the north side. The diners were gentleman accustomed to eating butter, a great multitude with

[74] On Macedonian eating see Dalby (1995), 152–7.

[75] Discussed in Dalby (1988) and Wilkins (1999). The letter is part of a correspondence on banquets between Hippolochus of Macedon and Lynceus of Samos, brother of Duris the historian and himself a comic poet (see below). Hippolochus explicitly compares performances at the feast with performers at the Athenian Anthesteria and contrasts the lavish presents from Caranus with eating herbs and studying philosophy with Theophrastus in Athens. On Caranus of Macedon see *CAH* 6².787.

[76] The best survey of Lynceus is Dalby (forthcoming). The work on shopping has a strong literary flavour. Lynceus writes (Athenaeus 7.313f–314a), 'not un-useful is it to stand by the fish-stalls and abuse the men who stare with intent and refuse to bring down their prices. Bring in Archestratus the author of the *Hedypatheia* or one of the other poets and recite his line, "the shore sea bream is a bad fish and never good" and—in springtime—"buy the tuna in autumn" and—in summer—"the grey mullet is amazing when winter comes" and many things of this kind. You will shoo away many of the customers and bystanders and if you do this will force the vendor to accept your estimation.' Lynceus draws both on the comic represention of the fishmonger and on the poetry of luxury living.

filthy hair. The cauldrons were of bronze and larger than cellars with room for a dozen beds. Cotys himself [77] had on his apron and carried in a soup in a golden pot; he had also tasted the mixing-bowl and was drunk before the drinkers. Their piper was Antigeneidas, the singer Argas, and Kephisodotus of Acharnae played the harp. They celebrated in song Sparta with its broad dancing floors and Thebes once more with its seven gates, varying the musical modes. As a dowry he received two herds of chestnut horses, a herd of goats, a golden shield, [. . .] a huge drinking-cup,[78] a jug of snow,[79] a pot of millet, a twelve-cubit bin of tassel hyacinths and a hecatomb of octopuses. This was how in Thrace, they say, Cotys put on a wedding for Iphicrates. Now the dinner at our master's house will be much more impressive and more dazzling than this. For what is lacking in our house, what good things? Not the scents of Syrian perfume or the breath of incense, the tender-skinned visions of barley cake,[80] wheat-bread, fine cakes, octopuses, tripe, fat, blood puddings, black soup, beet, stuffed fig leaves, pulse soup, garlic, whitebait, mackerel, sops for wine, barley gruel, soup, beans, grass peas, vetches, calavances, honey, cheese, puddings, wheat, nuts, and coarse-ground wheat; there will be baked crayfish, baked squid, boiled grey mullet, boiled cuttlefish, boiled murry, boiled gobies, baked tuna, baked wrasse, anglers, perch, dentex, hake, ray, flounders, dogfish, gurnard, shad [?], electric ray, slices of monkfish, honeycomb, grapes, figs, flat-cakes, apples, cornelian cherries, pomegranate, tufted thyme, poppy, wild pears, safflower, olives, pressed olives, milk cakes, leeks, two types of onion, puff pastry, tassel hyacinths, silphium stalks, silphium, vinegar, fennel, eggs, lentils, cicadas, rennet, cress, sesame, tritons, salt, fan-mussels, limpets, mussels, oysters, scallops, tuna. And in addition to this, an innumerable multitude of birds, ducks and pigeons, geese, sparrows, thrushes, larks, jays, swans, pelicans,[81] dabchicks, a crane . . .

[77] On Cotys see *CAH*[6] (1994), 461 (by Z. H. Archibald): there was import and local manufacture of high-quality luxury articles, judging by burials. These are discussed and illustrated in Fol (1989) and Cook (1989). Cups inscribed with the name of Cotys are discussed by J. Hind in Fol (1989), 38–43 and in chapters by B. Nikolov, G. Mihailov, and I. Marazov in Cook (1989).

[78] On the λεπαστή see Chap. 5.

[79] Snow for iced drinks is rarely attested before the Roman period, and perhaps a further respect in which Roman ideas of luxury are closer to Macedon than the Greek polis. Macedon of course offers good supplies of snow. On cold foods in hot weather see David (1994), who cites Gnathaina's jokes against Diphilus' 'frigid' comedy in Machon.

[80] For the ornate phrasing see on Antiphanes fr. 55 below.

[81] The identification is not certain: see Dunbar (1995) on *Birds* 882. *Larousse Gastronomique*, s.v., says that the pelican is eaten in some countries and has a

B: May that crane drill through the arse and ribs of this big-mouth and then strike him between the eyes.

A: And wines, you can have white, sweet, home-grown,[82] sweet-flavoursome, smoky . . .

The wedding of Iphicrates invites a comparison between his Athens and the Thrace of his wife. There is a crude, unrefined luxuriousness about the place, reminiscent of Caranus in the letter of Hippolochus and of Petronius' Trimalchio. The whole affair is a strange blend of lewdness, luxury, and dancing (line 5);[83] the purple cloth spread in the market-place evokes luxury both in itself and its novel location;[84] the leading men are 'butter-eaters', that is, eaters of a product of cow's milk.[85] This elite knows how to set itself apart but lacks refinement and restraint both in hair-care and administration of alcohol. The wedding is mainly distinguished for the size of vessels and quantity of food-stuffs, but aims for distinction in drinking-cups of precious metals.[86] The speaker presents the Athenian meal in competitive terms—theirs will be more impressive and more dazzling—

strong and oily flavour. Carniverous animals and birds are normally not eaten in the human diet.

[82] See Chap. 5 n. 72.

[83] βουβαυκαλόσαυλα. The *Etymologicum Magnum* defines *baukalon* as follows: 192.20 βαύκαλον· μαλακιζόμενον, τρυφερόν, ὡραιστόν ('softened, luxurious, a fop'), and the anonymous commentator on Aristotle, *Nichomachean Ethics* 1127b27 says βαῦκος γὰρ ὁ τρυφερός ὡς ὁ ποιητὴς Ἀραρὼς ἐν Καμπυλίωνι (fr. 9). βαυκά, μαλακά, τερπνά, τρυφερά (*baukos* means 'luxurious', as Araros the poet has it in *Campylion* fr. 9: '*bauka*, soft, delightful, luxurious'). On σαῦλον Photius offers τρυφερόν ('luxurious'). Kassel–Austin (1991) compare Aristophanes fr. 635, where the verb διασαυλούμενος is glossed by ἀβρυνόμενος καὶ διαθρυπτόμενος ('living a soft life and putting on airs'), and recalls the lewd dances of Aristophanes, *Wasps* 1173 and Euripides, *Cyclops* 40, of satyrs.

[84] Kassel–Austin (1991) compare Plutarch 527b on purple fabrics, expensive tables, and other superfluities (περιττά), and *Lycurgus* 13.3–4 in which the Spartan lawgiver is said to have ordained roofs of homes shaped with an axe so that *tryphe* and *poluteleia* have no place, as manifested by silver-footed couches, purple cloth, and golden drinking-cups.

[85] Kassel–Austin (1991) cite Pliny, *Natural History* 28.133 on butter, 'the most exclusive food of barbarian peoples which distinguished the rich from the masses'.

[86] The evidence for gold and silver cups in the area is extensive (n. 77). The comedy is taking the reality of Thracian life and distorting it. On one of the cups inscribed with the name of Cotys, he is 'son' or 'servant' of Apollo. Any ritual context is suppressed in Anaxandrides.

which envisage emulation rather than resistance to this foreign influence. The foodstuffs are listed broadly in the order of a meal, breads, tasty starters, fish, and tasty second tables,[87] and in an excessive form which emphasizes range, quantity, the delicacy of the early dishes (37–8), and many fish and birds that were not regularly eaten in Athens—the swan and the pelican. Luxury has arrived in Athens, albeit perhaps a more refined luxury than that found in Thrace.

Athenaeus puts Anaxandrides fr. 42 into perspective by citing Theopompus on Cotys and Iphicrates (12.531e–f). According to Theopompus, *History of Philip*, Book 1 *FGrH* 115 F31,

[the estate of Onocarsis] was one of those favoured by Cotys who, of all the kings of Thrace, particularly turned to pleasure and luxury (*hedy-patheias kai tryphas*). As he toured the country, he set up banqueting halls wherever he found a place shaded with trees and well supplied with running water. He visited them often, and whenever he was there, made sacrifices to the gods and met with his generals and was prosperous (*eudaimon*) and judged happy until he began to blaspheme against Athena and cause her offence [various sexual crimes follow].

Later in this work (Book 13) Theopompus turns to the great Athenian generals such as Iphicrates (*FGrH* 115 F115): '[Chabrias] was not able to live in Athens, partly because of his licentiousness and the extravagant cost of his style of living, and partly because of the Athenians. They are harsh towards everybody, and for this reason the most eminent citizens chose to live away from the city, Iphicrates in Thrace, Conon in Cyprus, Timotheus in Lesbos, Chares in Sigeum, and Chabrias himself in Egypt.'[88] Theopompus comments adversely on Cotys, Chabrias, and the democracy. He exhibits elsewhere strong opposition to the Athenian and other democracies,[89] but also reflects the tensions between personal extravagance and civic restraint.

Other comedies which commented on eating and drinking in Macedon appear to have included Strattis, *Macedonians or*

---

[87] On this order cf. Archestratus and Matro. On second tables see Chap. 5 and below.

[88] On Theopompus see further the discussion on Athenaeus, Book 12, below.

[89] On the lack of restraint of the Byzantine democrats see Athenaeus 12.526e–f.

Pausanias and Mnesimachus, *Philip*. In the first, fr. 29 contains a discussion on a local name for the grey mullet and the Attic name, *kestreus*, while fr. 30 mentions hot cuts of meat and fr. 32 belly portions of tuna. Whether or not Philip of Macedon was the target of Mnesimachus' play, *Philip* parodied a militaristic form of dining in fr. 7, commented on the greed of the Pharsalians in fr. 8, and on the fish-eating piper in fr. 10. Too little survives of either play to locate these fragments securely in the discourse of luxury.[90] Fr. 4 of the *Horse-Breeder* of Mnesimachus, which resembles Anaxandrides fr. 42 in length, in the choice of the enlivening anapaestic metre, and in presenting long lists of foods, does not reveal whether the meal is being held in Athens or elsewhere.[91] Both fragments exemplify long descriptions of foods and feasting which are consumed with a certain lack of restraint. The sheer length, like that of the speeches of boastful cooks looked at in Chapter 8, invites interruption and comment from an interlocutor, such as is provided in Anaxandrides fr. 42.

Athenaeus cites further fragments which distinguish Attic meals from those of other Greeks. Lynceus in fr. 1 of his *Centaur*, according to Athenaeus, made fun of Attic dinners:

A: Cook, the man who is making the sacrifice and giving me the dinner is from Rhodes, while I, the guest, am from Perinthus. Neither of us likes Athenian dinners.
B: Is there something unsavoury about Attica?
A: Yes, as if it were foreign. He serves you with a large tray which has five tiny little trays sitting on it. One of these holds the garlic, another a couple of sea-urchins, another a sweet cake,[92] another ten cockles, and the last a little bit of sturgeon. While I am eating one thing, the other guy is eating something else, and while he is eating something, I have polished off something else. I want both at once, my good friend, but what I want is impossible. I have neither five mouths nor five hands. Such dishes have a complex appearance but are quite useless as far as the belly is concerned. I spatter my lips, I don't actually fill my mouth with anything. What, then? Have you got some oysters?
B: Lots.
A: You will bring me a large tray of them, that and nothing else. Have you got sea-urchins?

---

[90] See further Arnott (forthcoming).
[91] See Chap. 7 for further discussion of this fragment.
[92] *Thrymmatis* appears to have been a crumbly kind of cake.

B: You can have another tray. I bought it myself for eight obols.
A: You will just serve us the food itself so that everyone has the same, not
  this for me and that for him . . .

What appears to distinguish Attic meals, from the Perinthian
point of view, is the range of foods on offer and the parsimonious
servings. We are given too little to evaluate the 'luxury' or otherwise of this meal, and whether the Perinthian or the Athenians or
both were ridiculed in the full play. It is worth noting, though,
that the Athenian meal does not satisfy the appetite, and that a
plethora of small dishes appears to be the reverse of the whole
animal a Persian would roast or the whole fish which luxurious
Athenians enjoyed. The Perinthian's criticism may in fact reinforce Athens' self-image of elegance and refinement tempered by
restraint and self-control.

Athenaeus continues his theme of distinctive Athenian eating
with Diphilus, *The Woman Who Left Her Husband* fr. 17.

COOK: Well, sir, how many are invited to the wedding in all and are they
  all Athenian or are some from the merchant quarter?
A: What's that got to do with you? You're the cook.
COOK: There is a guiding principle to my art, aged sir, to know in
  advance the mouths of those who are about to eat. For example, you
  have invited men from Rhodes. As soon as they come in, give them
  the chance to tear apart a great *silouros*[93] or *lebias*[94] that you have
  boiled—and make sure it is piping hot. You will please them much
  more with that than if you poured out myrrh-flavoured wine.
A: Yes, their *silouros*-eating[95] is very smart.
COOK: And if they're from Byzantium, soak everything you serve in
  wormwood and make everything as salt as the sea and with garlic.
  Because of the great number of fish in their waters, they are all
  clammy and full of thick liquids with a scum on top.

This fragment may simply link eaters with conventional characteristics of their home towns, but the Rhodians clearly fall within
our definition of luxurious, as diners unable to control their
appetite. Athenaeus' next example is Menander, *Trophonius*
fr. 351, whose speaker appears to be a cook.

---

[93] A large fish as yet unidentified: see Thompson (1947), 233–5.
[94] An unidentified fish: see ibid. 146.
[95] See Adespota fr. 1146 and Willis (1991).

The dinner is a reception for a foreigner. From where? This makes a big difference to a chef. Take the little foreigners from the islands. Brought up on fresh fish of every description, they are never attracted by salt fish; and if they do touch it, it is without serious intent. They are much more receptive to stuffed dishes and rich *karyke* dishes.[96] The Arcadian, conversely, does not know the sea and is attracted by little stewing-pots. If it's an Ionian in all his riches, I make a meal of *kandaulos*, which is food that leads to thoughts of sex.

The luxury of the Ionians was commonplace. I noted above comic references to their luxurious eating, for example in Callias, *Cyclopes* fr. 8: 'how goes Ionia with her luxury and fine tables? Tell me.'[97] Good living is found too in Antiphanes, *Woman of Dodona* fr. 91, 'a dweller of what place? Or is this a crowd of Ionians with their luxurious garments rushing up, soft and pleasure-loving?'[98] Menander's cook introduces two dishes, *karyke* and *kandaulos*, which are elsewhere linked with Lydia but this time appear to extend to the Aegean islanders and Ionians. On the former Athenaeus writes (12.516c),

the Lydians were the first to invent *karyke*, on the preparation of which many compilers of cookery books have pronounced, Glaucus of Locri and Mithaecus and Dionysius and the two Heracleides from Syracuse and Agis and Epaenetus and Dionysius, and again Hegesippus and Erasistratus and Euthydemus and Crito, and also Stephanus, Archytus, Acestius, Acesias, Diocles, and Philistion. Such are the writers of cookery books known to me. The Lydians also speak of a *kandaulos*. There were not one but three forms of this, so far did they train themselves in pleasure (*hedypatheia*). Hegesippus of Tarentum says that it is made from boiled meat, grated bread, Phrygian cheese, dill, and a rich meat stock.

There appear to have been sweet and savoury versions of these dishes, which were rich mixtures thickened with breadcrumbs.[99]

---

[96] κεκαρυκευμένα.

[97] Athenaeus continues (12.524f) with Hermippus, *Soldiers* fr. 55 and Aristophanes, *Triphales* fr. 556 on the soft living of the people of Abydos.

[98] πόθεν οἰκήτωρ, ἤ τις Ἰώνων τρυφεραμπεχόνων ἁβρὸς ἡδυπαθὴς ὄχλος ὥρμηται; The fragment asks about dress but employs three terms commonly applied to luxurious foods.

[99] See Dalby (1995), 111 and Arnott (1996) on Alexis fr. 178. Gulick and Arnott on this fragment translate *kandaulos* as 'pilaf', a meat dish thickened with bread and cheese. Dalby translates as 'sauce' but there is no evidence for its being added to meat, fish, or vegetables.

Lydian *kandaulos* and *karyke* entered the comic world, with explicit reference to Lydia, at least in Pherecrates fr. 195, 'grinding up an *abyrtake*[100] and Lydian *karyke*'. At an earlier date, in Lydia itself, the *kandaulos* probably had a ritual origin related to the death of a dog and the cult of the dead.[101] These dishes meet our criteria for luxury above all others. Reputedly once ritual preparations, they had become the classic *skeuasia* or elaborate confection of cooks and were taken from Lydia into the wide range of cookery and medical texts listed by Athenaeus, including, apparently the first cookery book known to us, by Mithaecus.[102] As far as Athenian comedy was concerned, this was a foreign (not necessarily Lydian) dish and one of the few which was an elaborately prepared mixture. So many of the other luxury foods we have seen appear to be better and more expensive examples of what was generally available in the diet—a large *silouros* in Lynceus fr. 1, for example. Fish, to which I turn below, best exemplifies such a luxury. Menander takes *kandaulos* a step further and links it with sexual desire. While *karyke* and *kandaulos* were known to the poets of Old Comedy,[103] their potential for exploitation as luxurious dishes appears to have been realized in parallel with the development of the *mageiros* in Middle and New Comedy. Even so, few citations survive, in addition to Menander fr. 351.

In Nicostratus, *Mageiros* (*Cook*) 16, the speaker appears to dismiss a man who 'didn't know how to make black broth[104] and never saw stuffed fig leaves and *kandaulos* or either of those ingredients for a *mattye*', while in Philemon, *Working His Way In*[105] fr. 63 the speaker claims, 'all the people in town can witness that I alone can make a black-pudding (*physke*), a *kandaulos*,

---

[100] On this preparation, also apparently of Eastern origin, see below.

[101] See Greenewalt (1976) and Harvey, 'Lydian Specialities, Croesus' Golden Baking Woman and Dogs' Dinners', in Wilkins *et al.* (1995), 273–85.

[102] See Dalby (1995), 106–7, 111.

[103] Pherecrates fr. 195, Aristophanes, *Knights* 343, the Black-Pudding-Seller knows 'how to speak and how to make *karyke*', the latter apparently a metaphor for elaboration and deception; there may be a pun on *kandaulos* at *Peace* 123 (according to the scholiast).

[104] This black broth appears to be not the feared Spartan version but a non-Spartan variety. See on Euphron fr. 1.8, discussed in Chap. 8.

[105] A play about a parasite? Cf. Philippides fr. 8, 'always flattering for crumbs and working his way in'.

eggs, stuffed fig leaves [the text is corrupt]. Where is the failure or the crime in that?' Each fragment lists complex dishes (with the exception of eggs) which mix and disguise their ingredients. The 'foreign' dishes of *kandaulos* and *mattye* (which I consider below) are listed beside *thria* (Attic stuffed fig leaves), which have no apparent connotations of luxury in, for example, *Acharnians* 1101 and *Knights* 954.[106] In Alexis, *All-Night Festival or Hired Workers* fr. 178,[107] a cook even claims to have invented *kandaulos*:

COOK: Next we will serve you some *kandaulos*.
A: *Kandaulos*? I have never eaten [. . .] or heard.
COOK: It is my own amazing discovery. Even if I put a very great amount of it on your plate, you will want to eat your fingers as well, so pleased with yourself will you be. We will make [?]
A: Sir, just make it white and keep an eye on [. . .].
COOK: Whenever, from our everyday foods, salt fish, fresh fish, meat, Sicilian dishes, straightaway [. . .], ? will serve a biscuit, an egg sliced on it, beestings, and a bowl of honey. I will slice and grill fresh new pieces of cheese from Cythnos. I will serve a little bunch of grapes, a little pudding, and some sweet wine in a cup. This sort of food always makes up the aftersport, while the main part of the meal—
A: Sir, get on with your 'aftersport'. Just leave me alone [. . .] with all your talk of *kandauloi* and puddings and Sicilian dishes [. . .] all pleasure.

Arnott brings out well the extravagant claim of this cook to have invented *kandaulos* and his peculiar diction, both of which are highlighted by his exasperated interlocutor. If Athenaeus (followed by Dalby 1995) accurately transmits the ubiquity of *kandaulos* and *karyke* in cookery books from Mithaecus onwards, and if those books reflect dishes that were eaten in Athens and elsewhere in the late fifth and fourth centuries, in comedy at least they appear to be comparatively rare. In two of the fragments under consideration they promote the appetite for food (Alexis) or sex (Menander) and for pleasure (Alexis).[108] In Nicostratus

---

[106] On *thria* see the scholiast on *Knights* 954 and Arnott (1996) on Alexis fr. 178.

[107] The last twelve lines of this fragment are corrupt. Arnott offers a possible reconstruction.

[108] In two others they are linked with excess, in Menander, *False Heracles* fr. 409 with a cook who shows no restraint and in Euangelus fr. 1 with a father of a bride who gives unwanted culinary advice.

and Philemon they appear with Attic stuffed fig leaves, and in the former with *mattye*. *Thria* might be made from meat, fish, or vegetables, *karyke* and *kandaulos* with meat or with sweet ingredients, *mattye* with meat, fish, birds, vegetables, or sweet components. All three dishes are elaborate confections of an apparently similar category: *karyke*, *kandaulos*, and *mattye* appear to qualify as 'luxuries' through their foreign origins—the *mattye* came from Macedon or Thessaly. Like *kandaulos*, *mattyai* also had erotic potential. Here, once again, we are dependent on Athenaeus and sources he quotes for most of the fragments, for the non-Athenian origin of the dish, and for the connection with sex. Since the *mattye* was eaten at the second tables during the symposium, an erotic element is perhaps not surprising.[109] We should, however, remember the connection of the erotic and the exotic in Menander's *kandaulos*.

The *mattye* was, according to Dorotheus of Ascalon, invented in Thessaly and made its way into Athens during the Macedonian occupation.[110] Here was a luxury 'from the most lavish of the Greeks', who 'emulated the Persians in luxury and extravagance'. The speaker in Machon, *Ignorance* fr. 1 credits the Macedonians with this foreign delight: 'there is nothing I like more than a *mattye*. Whether it was first the Macedonians who showed us Athenians this dish, or all the gods, I don't know . . .'[111] Athenaeus (14.663a–c) says that one derivation for the term *mattye*, now 'a rich food' based on 'fish, bird, vegetable, sacrificed meat, or cake', is from *mattein*, to knead (especially *maza*, barley cake).[112] This etymology follows the developmental model of luxury outlined above. Formerly a *mattye* was nothing more than a barley cake, now it has become a stimulating addition to the end of the meal. Athenaeus reinforces the idea by linking *mattye* with

[109] On the *mattye* and possible sexual overtones see the excellent survey of Arnott (1996) on Alexis fr. 208.
[110] Athenaeus 14.662f. Athenaeus discusses *mattuai* at 14.662e–664f. Dorotheus made this observation in his book *On Antiphanes*, demonstrating that some ancient writers on comedy concerned themselves with the food contained in the plays. Lycophron's book on comedy mentioned the poem of Archestratus, probably in relation to food or verse on food (Athenaeus 7.278a).
[111] The remainder of the fragment is corrupt. On the topos of the first discoverer see p. 78 n. 111.
[112] On the etymology see Arnott (1996).

sexual licence. Alexis, *Demetrius* fr. 50 provides an illustration: 'women, get this dish as directed and prepare it, have a feast, drink toasts, "peel away",[113] have your *mattye*.'[114] We saw above in Nicostratus, *Cook* fr. 16 that the *mattye* was one of the dishes with which a cook ought to be familiar. The same poet in *Driven Out* fr. 7 presents a cook who uses his *mattye* as a retort in a verbal attack he has received from a diner: 'COOK . . . very good, gentlemen, very good indeed. But with my *mattye* I will have such an effect on you that not even this guest will speak against me any more, I trust.'[115] The *mattye* helps to establish that the Thessalians were not simply gluttons, as we saw in Chapter 2, but also influenced Athenian eating, at least as far as comedy was concerned, and contributed to 'luxury'. Athenaeus returns to comedy with Alexis, *Running Together* fr. 216, 'I want to get hold of two chefs, the cleverest I can find in Athens. I am to be the host of a Thessalian and not in the Attic style nor sparingly . . .' [the rest of the fragment is corrupt]. 'The Thessalians are really good table men',[116] as Eriphus says in *The Peltast* fr. 6: 'this is not Corinth or Lais, my Syrian friend, nor the food served by hospitable Thessalian hosts, with which this hand is not unacquainted.'

There were evidently a number of 'made' dishes in the Attic comic kitchen, of which the 'foreign' *kandaulos*, *karyke*, and *mattye* were added to the native or long-established repertoire of

[113] See Arnott's note on fr. 50: the verb λέπειν also has an obscene sense, 'to masturbate', normally of men but perhaps here of women. On the next verb, ματτυάζειν Arnott observes, 'it would be astonishing if the speaker chose as the last in his series of increasingly forceful and vulgar expressions a verb which meant simply "make (or eat) the rich, spiced dish called ματτύη" '.

[114] Athenaeus also quotes Philemon, *Snatched* fr. 11, 'advise an unarmed man to be on his guard, and let a *mattye* cheer me up every three cups'; *Murderer* fr. 8, 'someone pour us a drink and make a *mattye* quickly'; *Beggar-Woman* fr. 71, 'he could have been stuffing himself all day, making and giving away *mattyai* there'; Alexis, *Fire-Raiser* fr. 208, 'when I find them busy I shout, "is someone going to give us a *mattye*?"'; Arnott (1996) on Alexis fr. 208 urges caution in reading sexual innuendo in Philemon frr. 8 and 11 and Alexis fr. 208 since the primary meaning of *mattye* is also present.

[115] The point made by the Cook in Dionysius, *Hit By a Javelin* fr. 1 is unclear: 'COOK: . . . so that on occasion when I make a *mattye* for these people, I hurry and make a mistake—and bring in one dish of the dead for the dead man.' The dead fish, bird, or animal in the *mattye* is clear enough, the 'dead man' not so.

[116] εὐτράπεζος is ambiguous between the meanings 'hospitable' and 'luxurious'.

thria and *muttotos*.[117] To these we may add general sauces (*katachysmata*), piquant sauces, *hypotrimmata* ('minces', literally 'ground-up fine'), and stuffings for cuttlefish and squid. One *hypotrimma*, called *abyrtake*, appears to have a foreign origin. In Theopompus, *Theseus* fr. 18 a traveller is advised, 'you will come to the land of the Medes where they make *abyrtake* from cress and leeks'. The foreign origin of the dish is not mentioned in a list of seasonings at Antiphanes fr. 140, though at Alexis, *Mandragorizomene* fr. 145 diners are said to go into a Bacchic frenzy over the dish.[118] This list hardly qualifies Attic cooking as a style that was *based* on rich mixtures, let alone sauces. Sauces in other cooking traditions, most notably the French, provide rich accompaniments to plain foods such as meats and white fish. Such sauces might be censured in literary and moralizing texts both for their richness and, more importantly, for their concealing of simple ingredients. The closest ancient Greek cooking appears to come to such sauces are the cheese preparations of Syracusan cooks denounced by Archestratus. To the best of my knowledge *Knights* 343, 'I can give speeches and make *karyke*', most closely approaches this notion of clever concealment, but the metaphor may go no further than mixing up in a clever way, that is, obscuring ingredients among themselves rather than adding them to a piece of meat or fish. Meat and fish appear to have been luxurious enough in this culture, with only occasional need for such additions as *hypotrimmata* ('minces') to provoke the appetite.[119] Meat and fish were supplements themselves, as Davidson[120] has shown so convincingly in his analysis of *opsa*, the tasty addition to the cereal base of the diet.

[117] A ground-up confection of cheese, garlic, honey, and leeks, which appears not to be a 'luxury' in *Peace* 242–54 or *Knights* 771.

[118] See Arnott (1996) on Alexis fr. 145.13.

[119] Dalby (1995), 106–7 offers a different picture, in which *kandaulos* and *karuke* are sauces.

[120] (1995); (1997), 3–35. He stresses fish as the *opson* above all others but in the comedies of the fifth and fourth centuries meat and vegetables continued to be classed as *opsa* (see e.g. Arnott on Alexis fr. 129.2). Many fragments offer lists of animal parts along with fish both in dinners and at the 'second tables': for comedy we should not push too far the contrast between meat (well regulated by sacrificial ritual) and fish (sold for enormous prices at market and provoking desire).

Before turning to the luxurious connotations of fish in Attic comic cooking, it is worth briefly noting the parameters set by Attic comedy to categories of diners who might eat luxuriously.

6.4. LUXURIOUS AND NON-LUXURIOUS DINERS IN ATTIC COMEDY

As I noted in Chapter 2, Attic comedy does not greatly concern itself with the poor, to whom luxurious eating is theoretically least accessible since their diet was most based on need and utility, on finding adequate calories, proteins, and vitamins to sustain life. To the poor we should add many of the inhabitants of the ancient city whose sustenance was periodically threatened by poor harvests and inadequate supply.[121] Comedy found a much more suitable category of consumer to whom luxuries were denied, namely the philosopher, who chose to deny himself the sweet pleasures of the table. I noted above the approaches of Plato and Aristotle to luxury and desire, and an anecdote quoted by Athenaeus on the expulsion of an over-ambitious cook from the Academy. Philosophers might be satirized for their asceticism, and there was scope too for challenging their sincerity in denying their appetite. In *Memorials* fr. 158 and *The Bag* fr. 133 Antiphanes satirizes Pythagoreans:[122] 'some miserable Pythagoreans happened to be nibbling shrubby orache in the gulch, and gathering wretched stuff like it in their bag', 'first, like a Pythagorean, he eats nothing animate, but gets for an obol a blackened bit of the largest barley cake he can and chews it'.[123] Pythagoreans are also the butt of Alexis, *Tarentines* fr. 223:

A: . . .
   the Pythagoreans, we hear, eat no fish nor anything else whatever that is animate, and they alone drink no wine.
B: Well Epicharides devours dogs, and he's a Pythagorean.

---

[121] See e.g. Garnsey (1988) and Gallant (1985) and (1991).

[122] Arnott (1996) on Alexis fr. 201 examines the comic presentation of Pythagoreans. Examples quoted here concentrate on the 'Pythagorists' or beggarly ascetics, who were imitators of the genuine believers known as *Pythagoreioi* or *Pythagorikoi*.

[123] *Bumble-Bee* fr. 63 appears to refer to Pythagoreans: 'garlic, cheese, an onion, a caper [. . .] all these for a drachma.'

A: But he kills it I suppose, so it is no longer animate. . . . . Pythagorean theories and subtle arguments and well-chiselled thought nourish these people, but their daily ration is this: one white loaf each and a cup of water. That's it.

B: You're describing a prison diet. Do all clever people live like this and endure such misfortunes I wonder.

A: No—these men live in luxury[124] compared with some others. Do you know that Melanippides is a disciple, along with Phaon, Phuromachus, and Phanos, and that they dine on one measure of barley meal every four days?[125]

In the *Woman Devoted to Pythagoras* fr. 201, Alexis writes 'their feasting will include dried figs, dried olives, and cheese. It is customary for the Pythagoreans to offer these in sacrifice.

B: By Zeus, that's the finest kind of offering there is, my good sir. . . . They had to withstand a frugal diet, dirt, cold, silence, gloom, and no bathing.'

It had already been suggested in Old Comedy that the asceticism of philosophers was not as sound as appeared. In Eupolis, *Flatterers* fr. 157, for example, someone says of Protagoras, 'Protagoras of Teos is indoors. The crook boasts of his theories of the heavens but eats the things of the earth.' Antiphanes took up the theme in *The Man Who Captures Runaways* fr. 87, 'neatly putting in a mouthful, by making his hand small to the viewer but full inside, like women do, he wolfed it down fully and fattily'. Similar appetite is shown at Aristophon, *The Devotee of Pythagoras* fr. 9, 'in the gods' name, do we think that those long-standing devotees of Pythagoras really wanted to be dirty or were happy to wear poor clothes? Not at all, in my view. It was of necessity, not by desire, all of it, that they found a good pretext for their frugality and fixed boundaries that would be useful for the poor. Now if you put in front of them fish or meat and they don't wolf it down, fingers and all, I'm ready to be hanged ten times.'[126]

The philosopher who above all others did not fall within the

---

[124] τρυφῶσιν.

[125] Arnott on this passage suggests that these four companions are not Pythagoreans but are satirized as paupers, Phyromachus possibly as a glutton.

[126] Frr. 10 and 12 continue the theme, 'as for being hungry and eating nothing whatever, imagine you are looking at [the parasites] Tithymallus or Philippides. He's a frog at drinking water, a caterpillar at enjoying thyme and herbs, at avoiding a bath, filth, a blackbird at spending the winter in the open air, a cicada

category of ascetic, as far as comedy was concerned, was Epicurus, whose endorsement of pleasure gave a ready opening to an improbable connection between philosophy and the consumption of fish. In Damoxenus, *Syntrophoi* fr. 2 (quoted in Chapter 8), a cook declares himself a pupil of Epicurus rather than of a cooking school and gives a long disquisition on the best conditions for fish-cookery, while in Baton, *The Fellow-Deceiver* fr. 5 a man, apparently a father, denounces an Epicurean who has advised a young man badly and led him to drinking and pleasure. The adviser stands by the teaching of Epicurus and claims that all philosophers are drunkards and, for all their abstract theorizing, easily and knowledgeably turn to food whenever a tender fish comes their way.[127] Parodies of philosophy of this kind bridge the gap between the ascetic with no interest in his body and, at the other extreme, the category of citizen most likely to be dedicated to pleasures of every kind, the young male, the *neoteros*. He (along with older men who ought to know better) is the person most liable to failures in self-control and most dedicated to the delights and desires of the flesh that Davidson (1997) has explored to such telling effect. The most abandoned of such citizens might be found in the *asoteion*, 'the residence of the spendthrift', who suffers that degree of luxurious unmanliness that undermines the male moral order from within by importing feminine or foreign self-indulgence.[128] Athenaeus (4.169b) notes the

at withstanding the heat and talking at midday, a dust-cloud at never anointing himself with oil, a crane at walking shoeless at dawn and a bat at never sleeping for a moment.' 'He said he went down to the realm of the dead to inspect each category, and the Pythagoreans differed greatly from the dead, for, he said, only they dined with Pluto in return for their piety. B: You're describing an easygoing god if he takes pleasure in being in the midst of filth. [. . .] And they eat vegetables and drink them down with water. No young person could endure their lice and poor clothes and dirtiness.'

[127] Parodies of philosophical schools and of general philosophizing abound in Middle and New Comedy. Numerous fragments reflect on the good life, which in comic perspective often includes eating and drinking. A notable example is Apollodorus of Carystus, *Inscription-Maker* fr. 5, in which the good life is identified as an absence of war and drinking for the under-thirties in Athens, revelling for the Knights in Corinth, boiling of cabbage in Megara, and mixing of wine in Euboea. This would be luxury (*tryphe*) and truly the life! On this theme in Middle Comedy see further Arnott (forthcoming).

[128] The *Asotodidaskalos* of Alexis is considered spurious: see Arnott (1996), 819–30.

term *asoteion* in Strattis, *Chrysippus* fr. 54: 'if there is to be no time for a shit nor for looking in at the house of a spendthrift nor for having the shortest chat when bumping in to someone . . .' As appetite overtakes him, the spendthrift fails to protect the wealth of the family.[129] Ctesippus son of Chabrias financed his *hedypatheia* by selling the stones of his father's tomb:[130] Menander uses the verb 'to wolf down', which recalls 'chewed up' in Alexis above. Food, drink, sex, property—everything is at the mercy of the appetite of the spendthrift.[131] Other spendthrifts are Pythodelus in Axionicus, *The Etruscan* fr. 1 and Polyeuctus in Anaxandrides, *Tereus* fr. 46: the latter is told, 'A: you will be called the rooster. B: Why, by the Hearth? Because I devoured my ancestral wealth like that fine fellow Polyeuctus? A: Not at all, but because you, a male, have been pecked to bits by females.' We see again the man who is dominated by women, as was Sardanapalus of old.

6.5. LUXURIOUS FOOD IN COMEDY: (I) FISH

It is well known that fish in many comedies, particularly of Middle and New Comedy, are the centre-piece of luxurious meals, served by the wealthy in profusion. They contributed to lavish entertaining in comedy to an extent that the imported dishes of *kandaulos*, *karyke*, and *mattye* never reached. Fish are *the* luxury food. Davidson has shown[132] that in the discourse of desire, one of my approaches to luxury outlined above, fish was the *opson* desired above all others and was the object of high

[129] On this theme Athenaeus cites two plays of Alexis, *Woman of Cnidus* fr. 110, 'that wretch Diodorus in two years has made his family property into a ball, so intensely has he chewed up the lot', and *Phaedrus* fr. 248, 'at leisure you say, at leisure. That little Epicharides in five days has made his family property into a ball, so intensely and rapidly has he rolled in up.'
[130] Athenaeus 4.165e, who proceeds to illustrate this failure in ancestral values in Diphilus, *Worshippers of the Dead* fr. 37; Timocles, *Demos-Satyrs* fr. 5, 'not even Ctesippus son of Chabrias has a shave three times a day any more. He dazzles the women but not the men'; and Menander, *Anger* fr. 264, *Sea-Captain* fr. 247.
[131] Verbs of consumption recur, 'wolf down' (καταφάγοι) in Menander fr. 247.4, 'chew up' (κατεμασήσατο) in Alexis, fr. 110.3. They are reviewed by Arnott (1996) on Alexis fr. 110.2.
[132] (1993), (1997).

spending, unrestrained eating, and lack of self-control in comic and other texts. A man who could not control his appetite for fish was in principle unlikely to be a good householder or a good citizen. I will first demonstrate comedy's exploitation of fish in the discourse of desire and then put that treatment into context.

Already in Old Comedy the rich Callias and his companions in Eupolis, *Flatterers* (frr. 160, 174) appear to be supplied with expensive fish; Bdelycleon in *Wasps*, as we have seen, is accused of anti-democratic leanings when he buys perch instead of *membrades* (488–99); in *Peace*, gluttons hated by the comic chorus will be elbowed away from the baskets of eels (1005–15); in *Frogs*, a rich man in disguise betrays his status by being seen at the fish stall. The overwhelming desire to consume is manifested in two senses in many fragments of Middle and New Comedy. First, to spend a small fortune on fish in the market. The desire to buy overrides all restraint and responsibilities both to the community and the self. This is the adverse side of the market, already noted in Chapter 4. The second desire is to eat the cooked fish as rapidly and at as high a temperature as possible.

The gourmet buying his fish at market became a topos of fourth-century comedy, to the extent that clever images were developed to vary the theme. In Alexis, *Demetrius* fr. 47 the gourmet threatens supplies like a winter storm: 'in the past, if the north wind or the south blew fresh on the sea, there was no fish available for anyone to eat. Now, a third winter wind has added itself to those two, Phayllus, and whenever he rushes down like a hurricane into the market,[133] he buys up the fish and goes off with the whole catch. All that is left as a result of this is a battle for the rest of us among the vegetable stalls.'[134] Phayllus is not otherwise known. Alexis refers to Callimedon at *Phaedo* fr. 249, 'god willing, you will be the market inspector, so that you can put a stop to Callimedon rushing down like a storm on the fish stalls the whole

[133] In the Greek, 'on the high seas' is echoed in the same place in the line by 'into the market': the natural wind unsettles the natural world, and thereby commerce, the human 'wind' comically disrupts the availability of fish.

[134] This fragment and Diphilus, *Merchant* fr. 31 (quoted below) make clear that fish and green vegetables are both in the same category of purchase, *opson*, which is supplementary to the cereal diet, with fish in nearly every case preferred. Phayllus is said to have cleared the market of fish, even the small fish discussed below.

day long. B: You're talking about a job for a tyrant, not a market inspector. The man is a fighter, and he is useful to the city.' This display of uncontrolled buying is particularly characteristic of politicians and the wealthy young. The politician Callimedon[135] at Antiphanes, *Fisherman* fr. 27.10–11[136] favours the red mullet and is currently consuming his property in order to get one.[137] Antiphanes lists similar difficulties in *Rich Men* fr. 188:

Euthunus,[138] with his sandals, signet ring, and perfume was calculating [verse corrupt] I don't know quite what. Phoenicides[139] and dear Taureas,[140] [verse corrupt], long-standing fish-eaters of the kind to guzzle down fish slices in the agora, almost died when they saw the state of affairs and took the fish shortage very badly indeed. They gathered people in groups around them [verse corrupt] that they couldn't live with it or tolerate the way that certain men among you should lay claim to the sea and spend so much money, while not the tiniest bit of fish was coming in. What then was the use of island-officers?[141] It should be possible to protect by law the safe transport of fish. But now today Maton has grabbed the fishermen and furthermore Diogeiton has persuaded them all to bring their fish to him. What he's doing is not democratic, gobbling it up like this. There were those weddings and drinking sessions by the young . . .

Whether the fragment draws on natural or political analogies, the focus is the problem of selfish greed, which threatens the community.[142] Such threats are explored by Davidson (1997), in particular in the speech of Aeschines, *Against Timarchus*. The purchase of fish, achieved through luxury and arrogant expense,

[135] Davies, *APF* 279, no. 8157. Callimedon, born perhaps around 370, seems to have been politically active in the period 345–318. He may have had Macedonian sympathies, but Davies shows that there is no support for this, and his son was nationalistic. See further Arnott (1996)—on Alexis, *Dorkis* (p. 1) and his index under 'Callimedon'—and *RE* 10 (1919), 1647–8.

[136] The fragment blends the delectable charms of girls and fish, as the bodies of both are offered for consumption.

[137] It has been conjectured that Red Mullet was the name of a courtesan; whether the object is fish or courtesan, the consumer displays reckless lack of control of desire.

[138] Apparently not in Davies, *APF*.   [139] Apparently not in ibid.

[140] Apparently not in ibid.

[141] There is a call in Sophilus, *Androcles* fr. 2 for 'fish inspectors'.

[142] There may have been particular problems of supply at certain times. Food shortages are attested, e.g. in the 320s: see Arnott (1996) on Alexis frr. 6 and 16.

may help to accentuate division between rich and poor, to which the demos may respond with wrath.[143] Since high prices reserve big fish for the better-off, the market can be seen as a focus of competition among the elite and a setting in which to display their power, through their dealings with the fishmongers. The most extravagant purchaser could leave with all the good fish. The expense could be problematic. The man who is unable to control his appetite will pay anything, and this desire in turn may be exploited by merchants, among whom in fourth-century comedy fishmongers are pre-eminent. Merchants are intrinsically dangerous in this regard, according to Plato, *Laws* 11.918d: 'the masses of the people are the opposite to these [people of moderation]. Their desires are desired beyond measure and if it is possible to profit by a reasonable amount they prefer insatiable profit. For this reason the tribes of *kapeloi*, merchants and innkeepers, are abused and beset by shameful insult.' Athenaeus collects a series of comic fishmongers who stimulate such desires in Book 6 (224b–228c).

I noted in Chapter 4 market stallholders who are particularly problematic in comic texts. Fishmongers form a special category of such vendors since their profiteering combines with the desperation of the buyer to satisfy his desire. The comic perspective resembles Plato's in this respect, though the poets added theme and variation to this moral and political discourse. In Antiphanes, *Young Men (Neaniskoi)*[144] fr. 164 the fishmongers are Gorgons from whom (5–7) 'I must perforce avert my gaze when talking to them, for if I look at them when they ask so much for such a small fish I am frozen solid for all to see'; in the *Wandering Jester* of Amphis (fr. 30), they are worse than generals for aloof inaccessibility and crouch in silence like Telephus until an unwary buyer dares to ask the price; in the *Man Who Has Got Glaucoma* of Alexis (fr. 16) the fishmongers have all the haughtiness[145] of generals in negotiating a price; in the *Polypragmon* of Diphilus (fr. 67) the fishmonger cheats by currency-switching; at Alexis, *Pylaeae* fr. 204 two men converse:

A: By Athena, I admire those fishmongers. How can they not all be rich men since they take on tribute worthy of the king (*basilikous phorous*)?

B: Just tribute you say? Don't they take a tithe of our estates as they sit in our cities, and rob us of entire estates on a daily basis?

In the *Lebes* of Alexis, frr. 130–1 necessary legislation is considered to control the fishmongers;[146] in the *Merchant* of Diphilus fr. 32 the buyer lacks control: 'I don't know that I've ever seen fish more expensive. By Poseidon, if you took 10 per cent from the price of them each day you would be far the richest of the gods. Yet if one of them were to smile winningly at me, I would pay up, albeit with a groan at how much he was asking. Well, I bought a conger eel and paid for it as much as it weighed in gold, as Priam did for Hector.' Fr. 31 of the *Merchant* puts the city's perspective:

A: This is the rule here in Corinth, sir, if we see a man continually buying fish in a big way. We ask him where his means come from and what he does. And if he has property whose income can meet his expenditure, we let him carry on enjoying that style of life. But if he is just then spending more than his property can bear, they forbid him to do so any more. Anyone who disobeys has a fine imposed upon him. If a man has nothing at all but lives lavishly, they hand him over to the executioner.

B: Heracles!

A: Because it is not possible for him to live without some criminal act, you see. Of necessity he will steal clothes at night and burgle through walls or be in league with men who do such things or be a blackmailer in the market or be a false witness.[147] We clear out that kind of person.[148]

B: Quite right, by Zeus! But what's that to do with me?

A: We have seen you buying fish every day, sir, with no moderation but sumptuously. No one can get their hands on anything like a fish because of you: you've brought all the city together at the vegetable stalls. We fight over the celery as if at the Isthmian Games. A hare comes into market. You've snatched it up instantly. As for a partridge

---

[146] There are more fishmongers at 7.309d (Antiphanes, *Timon* fr. 204 and Menander, *Ephesian* fr. 151).

[147] Alexis, *Heiress* fr. 78 describes the poor man who can only just afford fish and uses burglary to support his habit and see off rivals at the eel-stall.

[148] This is a comic version of the dangers set out by Plato at *Republic* 574d: the young man, overcome by appetite but lacking the income to meet his desires, turns to crime.

or a thrush, you can't even see one flying in the city any longer. You've pushed up the price of foreign wine no end.[149]

Other buyers in the fish market are the boastful cooks whom I examine in Chapter 8. They too may encourage the appetite of the young. In *Odysseus* of Anaxandrides (fr. 34) the cook compares himself with the artist (5–15),

for what other art, dear sir, burns the mouths of the younger generation so well, or has a better shoving of fingers or choking for fear of not being able to swallow at speed? Is not the market with all its fish the only maker of assignations? For what mortal who dines in company gets dry little fish or meagres bought in or a sprat? Tell me, please, how a boy in the prime of youth is to be seduced with charms and words if the art of the fisherman disappeared.

Athenaeus concludes his survey with the work by Lynceus of Samos entitled *The Art of Buying Fish*, which advised readers on how to deal profitably with the 'man-slaying fishmongers'.[150] I noted above this author's advice to cite Archestratus in order to disconcert the fishmonger who glares at his customers like the ones in Antiphanes fr. 164. The theme of the profiteering fishmonger is an important element in the discourse of desire; the comic poets were also at pains to show off ever-more inventive denunciations, just as they strove to display innovation in speeches by parasites and boastful cooks. Xenarchus' version in *Porphyra* fr. 7 makes the point particularly well, claiming that the fishmongers are far more inventive than poets when they think up practical dodges to sell bad fish: 'the poets are a waste of time. They invent not one novelty; each of them transfers the same stuff back and forth. Now when it comes to fishmongers, there is no class more philosophical, nor indeed more impious.' There follows a description of animated scenes between the fish-stalls.

Archestratus' *Hedypatheia* (*Life of Luxury*), which was probably written in the 360s,[151] is a touchstone both for buying fish at all cost and for enjoying it at the table. In fr. 15 the boar-fish should be bought whatever the cost; in fr. 21 the foxfish should be

---

[149] Add Timocles, *Spiteful Man* fr. 11 on Corudos deprived of his fish through poverty.

[150] This work is perhaps related to Archestratus' *Life of Luxury*, which is in places reminiscent of comic themes and preoccupations.

[151] Dalby (1995).

seized at the risk of life and limb if the seller will not sell it; at fr. 22 the 'dug-out from sand' should be swallowed quickly, to the point of choking; and at fr. 31 the *kitharos* takes pleasure in big spenders and in unchecked extravagance, the fish somehow acquiring the qualities of its consumer. Once the fish had been bought at great cost, it might be prepared according to recipes such as those of Archestratus or the boastful comic cooks[152] and preferably eaten with many fish of other species. There was no greater demonstration of wealth linked with appetite than to eat fish as hot as possible and in profusion. The most striking text on this theme is the *Attic Dinner* of Archestratus' fellow-parodist Matro.[153] Comic examples are provided by Anaxandrides fr. 42 (quoted above) and Eubulus, *Safely Returned* fr. 8, 'others who have taken on the gods(?) meet up with Crayfish [Callimedon], the only mortal who can swallow whole slices of fish from the boiling pans and leave not a thing'. There are many others. A burning-hot dish of squid might even be wished on an enemy to do him harm, such as Cleon/Paphlagon (*Knights* 934–40) or Antimachus the choregos at *Acharnians* 1150–61.

Fish in this discourse of consumption and desire is, as it were, an enemy within, because of its ability to stimulate appetite. Luxuries imported from abroad and conduct unbecoming an Athenian in other cities could be readily identified, but fish was an integral part of the Athenian diet. In order to understand this discourse we must put it into its cultural context. First of all, fish was not a luxurious food per se in ancient Athens. The misleading impression that it was a luxury might be gained if Davidson (1997), who makes much of the high cost of fish, were to be read with Gallant (1985), who argues for lower numbers of fish in the Mediterranean than had previously been supposed. Gallant tries to demonstrate, with a demographic approach based on figures for fish-catches from Greece, Turkey, and the Austro-Hungarian empire in the nineteenth and twentieth centuries, that there were too few fish in the ancient Black Sea and Mediterranean to feed the population sufficient calories per person per day to sustain life on a regular basis. He concludes (p. 44), 'its main function would have been to supply a source of sustenance during periods of food

[152] See Chap. 8.
[153] Both Archestratus and Matro are considered in detail in Chap. 7.

scarcity due to reduced crop-yields. In this way, it would have furnished a short-term solution to what would have been an endemic problem in the Mediterranean world.'[154] I believe a more accurate model than calories per day has been provided by Purcell, who stresses the unpredictability of fish supply which produces abundance and shortage. In some years the shoals arrive in abundance, in others they fail.[155] Fish were thus accessible to all, though not all the time. It is also clear from Gallant's figures and other Turkish figures for the Black Sea in the 1930s and 1950s that small fish such as anchovies and sardines often constituted between 40 per cent and 80 per cent of the catch. Thus, the fish that attracted the gourmets of ancient Athens and commanded high prices comprised only part of the supply. Anchovies, sardines, and small fish (in English 'whitebait') were often affordable for all.

This vital point is linked to another. There were many species of fish in the Mediterranean. Like birds, but unlike domestic and hunted quadrupeds, fish provided a huge variety of edible bodies. In ancient Greek, as in many other Mediterranean languages, the names of these hundreds of species were augmented by alternative and regional names. Since comedy delights in incorporating the myriad elements of foods in the material world into its text, many of these names were used, as Athenaeus attests in his gazetteer in Book 7. Lists of fish at banquets revel in all the variety—and do not necessarily reflect 'real' luxurious meals in Athens in the fourth century, where a few expensive fish may have sufficed. In addition to these many names, however, comic texts also refer to fish in generic cooking terms, as fish for boiling,[156] fish

---

[154] Gallant's conclusions have been challenged and modified by Purcell (1995), Gallo (1997), and Wilkins (forthcoming, d). Greaves (1999), 69–81, has used comparative modern evidence to challenge Gallant. Gallant's main objective is to demonstrate that fish were not a staple of the ancient diet and that there was no 'industry' in salted fish in the ancient Black Sea. Curtis (1991) opposes his argument on salt fish (Purcell, however, believes Curtis is too optimistic). For my purposes, fish was never more than a supplement, an *opson*, to the farinaceous staple of the diet (*sitos*). If Gallant had paid attention to the texts he would not have tried to prove what they all declare, namely that fish was supplementary.

[155] Gallant himself emphasizes this and hence does not claim that the supposed overall shortage of fish led to high prices.

[156] ἑψητοί. Cf. Athenaeus 7.301a: ΕΨΗΤΟΣ· ἐπὶ τῶν λεπτῶν ἰχθυδίων. . . . πληθυντικῶς δὲ λέγουσιν ἑψητοὺς κατὰ τὸ πλεῖστον ('Fish for boiling: a term applied to small fish . . . For the most part fish for boiling are referred to in the plural.')

for frying,[157] fish for cooking over the charcoal.[158] These fish, if no others, were, again, available to all when the supplies were good. In Alexis fr. 17 a character declares, 'we had some "boilers", I suppose you might call them spangled',[159] and at fr. 18, 'you haven't had a try at the meagres? Nor the sardines, nor even the boilers?'[160] At Aristomenes fr. 7 someone brings anchovies for an obol,[161] while at Aristonymus fr. 2.2 desperation is such 'that now there simply isn't any whitebait nor indeed a wretched anchovy'. The speaker at Alexis fr. 159.1–3 denounces the fishermen for 'catching little fish unworthy of free citizens, little sardines, little cuttlefish, and some fish for frying'.[162] A husband in *Ecclesiazusae* 55–6 spends the night farting after filling up with sardines, while the unsophisticated Philocleon at *Wasps* 1127–8 reports that he filled up on fish grilled over charcoal and soiled his clothes. The Black-Pudding-Seller in *Knights* (660–2) tries to bribe the assembly by promising to keep the cost of sardines below a drachma for a hundred. Even though the price may be absurd, the point is that these are cheap fish for ordinary citizens (this is a parody of statutory deliberation in the assembly over the supply of *sitos*, or grain, with the dietary supplement replacing the staple). The chorus in *Acharnians* can think of their Acharnian muse fanning the flames of the charcoal over which little fish (*epanthrakides*) are grilling (665–75). These fanatical countrymen appear not to view fish as luxuries for city people.[163]

Comedy, therefore, presents fish as a food eaten by a wide range of Athenians, with the choice of fish determined by price and

---

[157] φρυκτοί.   [158] ἐπανθρακίδες.

[159] Arnott's translation of the last phrase.

[160] On κορακῖνοι and τριχίδες and their low value see Arnott (1996).

[161] βεμβράδες might be anchovies or sprats: see ibid. on Alexis fr. 200.

[162] There are many other such fragments, e.g. Amphis fr. 22, 'a man who eats a meagre from the sea when a *glaukos* is available is not in his right mind'; fr. 26, 'a man who goes shopping for something tasty [. . .] and desires to buy radishes when he can enjoy real fish, is mad'; Aristophanes, *Danaids* fr. 258, 'turning to the fish-stalls he got little octopus and little sprats and little cuttles'; and Anaxandrides fr. 34.11. See also p. 327.

[163] Gallant (1995) suggests that there were few professional fishermen in ancient Greece and that most were part-timers seeking to augment a peasant or other income. If this is right, as it probably is, then the division in Aristophanes fr. 402 between the pure countryside and the criminal fishmongers of the city is a comic construction.

availability after the greedy have had the pick of the catch. The rarer, solitary fish such as the bream and the flatfish cost more because they were more difficult to catch than fish in shoals.[164] A speaker in Eriphus, *Meliboea* fr. 3 declares baldly, 'these things the poor cannot buy, the belly piece of a tuna or the head of a sea bass, or a conger, or cuttlefish, which even the blessed gods, I believe, do not turn up their noses at'. This picture is confirmed by two non-comic texts. Chrysippus wrote in his treatise *On Things Chosen For Their Own Sake*,[165] 'in Athens they scorn whitebait because of its abundant supply and declare it to be *opson* for beggars, while in other cities they rave over it even though it is inferior. Then again, here people strive to raise Adriatic birds even though they are of little use because they are much smaller than those back home. Conversely, people there import chickens from here.' Chrysippus illustrates both the cheapness of whitebait and the principle of luxury that is attached to imported foods. Archestratus rejects all whitebait as little better than excrement (fr. 9), except for the Athenian, caught at Phaleron. There is a discrepancy which I cannot adjudicate between Archestratus and Chrysippus over the valuation of Athenian whitebait, but that detail aside, Archestratus' *Life of Luxury* pursues the best fish in the best places, which might very rarely include small fish. Archestratus' luxurious fish-eating goes further than the import of the finest fish in sending the diner to each city where each fish is best in order to match quality with freshness.

The poem of Archestratus illustrates best of all the reasons for classifying fish as a luxury, namely their stimulation of appetite and desire and their cost if they are large or solitary species. In both parody and comedy, fish belong to the market-place where price is attached to them—hence the eager buying and selling I have just explored. Little interest is shown in the catching of fish—the stage before they come to market[166]—though

---

[164] Gallant (1985), who notes that even tuna-fishing can offer a poor return to the fisherman.

[165] Fr. 2 (*SVF* III, 195), quoted by Athenaeus 7.285d–e.

[166] Fishermen, in the few cases in comedy in which they, rather than fishmongers, are mentioned, are usually selling their catch—e.g. in Plato, *Feasts* fr. 28 and Alexis, *Odysseus Weaving* fr. 159 (cited above). Menander wrote a *Fisherman* or *Fishermen*, which may be an exception, as may Diphilus' original of the *Rudens* of Plautus.

some plays reflect on fish in the sea.[167] It is an important part of the thesis of Davidson (1997) that fish were a commodity with a beautiful body and that this luxurious quality had developed later than Homer, in whose poems fish are a natural resource, of interest only to the hungry.[168] Fish were creatures of the wild, in contrast to the cattle, sheep, goats, and pigs of the sacrificial order whose flesh was shared with the gods and divided in equal portions among the human participants. For Davidson, as for Detienne (1989), fish were not part of the sacrificial order; consequently they might be bought and consumed without the restraints of religious ritual or the equal shares which were an integral part of sacrifice.[169] There are exceptions to this separation of fish from sacrifice,[170] but the important point for the present discussion is that comic poets frequently drew attention to the disjunction between fish and sacrifice to the gods, often indeed claiming that the gods themselves took pleasure in this luxury food. The distinction between expensive fish and sacrificial meat is the point of Menander, *Drunkenness* fr. 224 (cited above); the speaker of Anaxandrides, *Cities* fr. 40 contrasts Greek and Egyptian religion (4–8): 'you bow down to the ox while I sacrifice it to the gods; you believe the eel to be the greatest god, but we by far the greatest of *opsa*; you do not eat pork, in which I take particular pleasure.'[171] Numerous fragments refer to the gods'

[167] The *Fishes* of Archippus may have explored the marine life of fish; some fragments describe fish dancing and playing; Archestratus fr. 23 and Antiphanes, *Butalion* fr, 69 reflect human fears of being eaten by fish if they are lost at sea.

[168] See p. 263–4, 313.

[169] Detienne (1989), 221; Wilkins (1993), 191–3; Davidson (1997).

[170] Athenaeus (7.297d) quotes Agatharcides, *European History*, FHG 3.192 on eel-sacrifice in Boeotia and (297e) Antigonus of Carystus on the offering of the first tuna to Poseidon if the catch was good at Halae in Attica. The offering of a *thynnaion* was a sacrifice to Poseidon. I doubt if this festival was unique in the Greek world. Durand (1989), 127–8 has identified the sacrifice of a tuna on a black-figure *olpe*—the interpretation is challenged by Sparkes (1995). We might also note the sacrifice of a bull at Delphi by tuna-fishermen (see Purcell (1995: 139) on Pausanias 10.9.3–4), preserved fish in the foundation myth of Phaselis (see Purcell (1995: 144) on Philostephanus of Cyrene, *De Asiae civitatibus, FHG* 3.28 = Athenaeus 7.297e–f), and the consumption of red mullet by women at the Attic festival of Haloa.

[171] Cf. Antiphanes, *Lycon* fr. 145, 'they say that the Egyptians are clever in various respects but particularly in believing the eel the equal of the gods. It is in fact much more expensive than the gods. For we can reach the gods simply by

taste for fish, once again implicitly breaking down the division between gods and men that I discussed in Chapter 1. I noted above Eriphus fr. 3, in which it is claimed that the gods cannot ignore the cuttlefish; the gods eat a banquet of fish in Epicharmus, *The Marriage of Hebe or The Muses* (see Chapter 7); at Philemon fr. 82.22–3 Poseidon supplies conger eels to the gods. There are many other examples of gods desiring fish as much as any human consumer, thereby confirming the extraordinary status of fish as a luxury and the universal desire for the savours and textures of the piscine body.[172] Archestratus once again puts the point most strongly. In fr. 15 the *kapros* or boar-fish is so delectable that the gods will blast anyone who passes it by at market, for many mortals are not allowed to see it, let alone taste it. The parodist would also have Hermes shopping at market for good barley flour (fr. 4), again converting the god of the agora into the consumer out shopping for luxuries.

6.6. LUXURIOUS FOOD IN COMEDY: (II) CAKES

The place of fish within the discourse of luxury is in some way comparable with the place of cakes. Both appear prominently in the *Deipnon* (*Dinner*)[173] of the dithyrambic poet Philoxenus of Cythera, which I discuss in detail in Chapter 7. I quote the poem in full as a touchstone of luxurious eating in verse.[174]

A boy with a nice softness[175] came in carrying water for washing the hands in a silver jug. He poured it and then brought in a garland that was double-woven from fine branches of delicate myrtle. (Fr. 836a)

Two slaves carried in for us a table, its face richly oiled, for others another, for the rest another, until they had filled the room. The tables gleamed in the high-lamped rays of light and were well-garlanded with flat dishes and side dishes(?) of saucers [. . .] and were luxuriating[176] in every kind of novelty[177] of the cook's art directed at good living, entrapments of the soul. Other slaves served us from baskets with barley cakes of snowy complexion, and following them came first not a stewing-pot,

prayer while it costs at least twelve drachmas—or more—just to sniff an eel. So it is [corrupt text] the beast is utterly sacred.'

[172] The gods' consumption of fish takes further the comic idea of their appetite for animal flesh which we saw exemplified by Hermes in Chap. 1.
[173] *PMG* 836.   [174] See the translation and comments by Dalby (1987).
[175] ἀπαλός.   [176] χλιδῶσαι.   [177] παντοδαποῖς τέχνας εὑρήμασι.

my love, but the most enormous [. . .]. Rich [. . .] eels [. . .] conger [. . .][178] full and to delight a god.[179] Following on came another as big containing a ray rounded like a shield,[180] and there were small cooking-pots, one with some dogfish, another with stingray . . . There was another . . . and rich from little squids and cuttle-octopuses, with their tentacles in soft tresses. After these there came in a hot [. . .] whole and as big as a table[181] [. . .][182] squid, my friend, and tawny gentle honey cakes came in. On top of these there were crumbly cakes of fresh green petals [. . .] puff pastries the size of a cooking-pot, a sweet-sour [. . .] is called the navel of the feast by you and me, I know well enough [. . .] by the gods a giant piece of tuna coming baked from abroad [. . .] sliced forthwith into the underbelly. If it had been for me and you to assist stalwartly at the task we would have been delighted. But where we fell short, the feast was laid on. [. . .] And still I, for it was not possible to speak truly of everything that was there, to you [. . .] hot entrails. And then came the intestine of a home-grown young sow, and the back of the pig and the loin and hot(?) and the whole head in two sections boiled [. . .] and served the [. . .] of a stewed kid. Then boiled trotters and with them white-skinned ribs and snouts, heads, trotters and pieces dressed with silphium. Then there was more meat boiled and roasted of kid and lamb and the sweetest lightly cooked entrails, the kind mixed from kid and lamb which the gods love. This [. . .], my love, you could eat and then hare and hen's chicks and [. . .] of partridge and doves and breads in soft folds. And as close companions of these there then came in tawny honey and milk curds, and the cheese—everyone would say it was soft, and I declared it so. When we comrades came to our fill of food and drink, the servants removed the food and slave-boys gave us water for our hands [. . .] and pouring on the warm water mixed with solvents and orris, as much as each wanted, and [. . .] linen towels, they offered ambrosial perfumes and garlands blossoming with violets. (Fr. 836b)

And you [. . .] receive this cup full of the fine dew [. . .] and may Bromios with his gift of this gentle shining liquid turn all to delight. (Fr. 836c)

And he(?) drank the draught like nectar in golden(?) [. . .] horned [. . .] (Fr. 836d)

And they brought back once more the [. . .] gleaming freighters that had gone away earlier and they were groaning with many good things which

---

[178] Four lines of the text are seriously corrupt.   [179] θεοτερπές.

[180] For the fish rounded like a shield cf. Archestratus fr. 13.3 on the *skaros*.

[181] Note the size of this fish and the fact that it is not cut up into (equal) portions.

[182] Three lines are seriously corrupt.

mortals now call second tables but the immortals the horn of Amaltheia.[183] And in the centre was set up a great delight for mortals, sweet white marrow, hiding its face in garments as fine as a spider's web, ashamed that you might see the dry [. . .][184] born of a sheep in the dry springs of Aristaeus that flow with honey. Its name was meal cake. And with their fierce hands they set to [. . .] their mouth [. . .][185] accepted whatever was given, which they call the dessert of Zeus. Then was served a safflower-mixed roasted wheat-oat-white-chickpea [. . .] confection in a glorious mixture [. . .] And to accompany it, a dough(?) [. . .] a yellow thoroughly parched cake and a sweet [. . .] and [. . .] round [. . .] too many to count and honeyed made without number of sesame. There was a cheese cake liberally smothered in milk and honey, a moulded meal-cake. There were cakes fashioned of sesame and cheese, cakes boiled in oil, with sprinkled sesame. Then chickpeas mingled with safflower blooming in their tender season, and eggs and almonds with soft skins [. . .] nibbled by children and other [. . .] nuts that befit a feast that is rejoicing in its wealth [. . .]. The drinking took its course and the *kottabos* games and the words shared by all. Here some smart new conceit was expounded and they were amazed at it and praised [. . .] (Fr. 836e)

The poem presents opulent dining in the ornate dithyrambic style which, as we shall see in Chapter 7, came to influence descriptions of food in Attic comedy in the fourth century and indeed may have influenced Aristophanes' compound dish at the end of *Ecclesiazusae* (1168–75).[186] Some of the dishes in the *Deipnon* 'come in', as if of their own volition: this may suggest plenty and is reminiscent of the self-cooking foods of the comic utopias, as is the largesse from the horn of Amaltheia. Both slaves and tables are sleek, and the tables luxuriate with novelty and pleasure. The desirable qualities of fat, texture, and temperature are stressed. There is much variety, too, in the textures of meat. In addition to the great variety of foods, the greatest ornamentation is reserved for the favoured items of the marrow and the beestings. The latter is fashioned into an *amulos* or meal cake. The ornate description gives pleasure additional to the food

---

[183] For the formulation 'the mortals call, but the immortals . . .' cf. Epicharmus, *The Marriage of Hebe* fr. 42, cited in Chap. 7.

[184] A line-and-a-half of the text are corrupt.

[185] There are lacunae in three successive lines.

[186] Aristophanes' dish 'comes in' as do dishes in Philoxenus and Matro; the food is piping hot, which in these texts indicates desirability. Ussher (1973) compares Rabelais and other texts for such dishes compounded of many words.

itself, and is perhaps parodied by Antiphanes in *Aphrodisios* fr. 55.7–11 in which a speaker describes a cake which is a mixture of the curdled milk of bleating goats, the streams of honey from the tawny bee and the flat chamber of Deo's daughter, 'luxurious in its thousand layers lightly combined.[187] Or should I say "flat-cake" and be done?'

Cakes in English, like *pemmata* in Greek, cover a broad range of confections which extend far beyond the highly crafted creations of literary cooks. Contrasting with these 'luxurious' confections are the cakes of religious cult. Some terms appear to be specific to a religious context, such as *pelanos*—strictly a liquid mixture of wheat, honey, and oil poured in offerings but sometimes baked solid. The *amphiphon*, it appears, was a flat-cake normally offered to Artemis,[188] and attested in Philemon, *Beggar-Woman or Woman of Rhodes* fr. 70, 'Artemis, dear lady, I bring you this *amphiphon*, my queen, and the libatory offerings', and Diphilus, *Hecate* fr. 27. The man in Pherecrates fr. 167, who has 'in his gluttony, eaten a *diakonion* when he already had an *amphiphon*', is eating in an unspecified context. Other cakes, such as *pemma* and *popanon*, appear in sacred and secular contexts. Cnemon at Menander, *Dyscolus* 450, for example, denounces the sacrificers for offering the gods incense, a *popanon*, and the inedible parts of an animal while they enjoy the best cuts (see Chapter 1). *Popana*, conversely, are part of the sympotic delights on offer in the utopian Athens of *Ecclesiazusae* (843). It is not clear that cakes counted as a luxury per se, any more than barley cakes or bread were luxuries—though very refined versions might qualify as such. Herodotus reports that the Persians thought little of Greek cakes. Conversely, Plato's Socrates twice classifies cakes as luxuries in the *Republic*. At 404d Attic *pemmata* are part of the luxurious life, along with Corinthian courtesans, fish, and Syracusan and Sicilian *opsa*, while at 373a they belong to the luxurious city in such company as hairdressers, poets, and swineherds. Plato's approach, which classifies most sympotic elements as 'luxuries' and advocates a vegetarian regime in which the only

---

[187] λεπτοσυνθέτοις τρυφῶντα μυρίοις καλύμμασιν.

[188] With, says Athenaeus (14.645a), torches round it. Gulick (1941) adds Pollux 6.75 and *Etymologicum Magnum* 95, the latter explaining the derivation by the full moon.

baking to be done should be of wheat into bread,[189] follows a definition of what constitutes a luxury that is much stricter than comedy or most of his contemporaries allowed.

Pemmata at formal mealtimes were eaten at the 'second tables', along with savouries, fruits, and nuts, during the symposium, as we saw in Chapter 5. The most common is the *plakous* or flat-cake. Athenaeus (14.641a) cites Dionysius, the disciple of Trypho the grammarian, on 'additional courses' (*epiphoremata*), which were introduced when the diet evolved from a single course set out before the guests reclined to 'many and varied' foods. Dionysius reflects the first approach above, the developmental model, but is not speaking only of cakes. Athenaeus has a list of cakes at 14.639b–648c,[190] which are served with fruits, nuts, and some savouries. Many comic examples appear to me, at least, to be better classified as 'sympotic' than luxurious, such as the cakes for the symposium at *Acharnians* 1091, 'fine-meal cakes (*amuloi*), flat-cakes, sesame-cakes, honey-cakes'.[191]

Some cakes appear in contexts which at least imply an element

---

[189] 372b3 πέψαντες.

[190] He cites various treatises on cakes, written over several centuries, and regional variations. Alexis, *Archilochus* fr. 22 cites the flat-cake of Paros as an excellent product for mortals; Sopater the *phlyarographos*, in his *Suitors of Bacchis* fr. 4 hails Samos as 'the flat-cake maker'. Other regional cakes listed by Athenaeus include the Cretan *glykinas*, the Syracusan *epikuklios* and *staitites*, the Spartan *kribanai*, the Sicilian *amorbites*, the Coan *paisa*. What Athenaeus in Book 14 classifies as a *pemma* is included in 3.110b in a list of breads in Epicharmus, *Marriage of Hebe* fr. 52, 'Epicharmus sets forth the kinds of breads, *kribanites, homoron, staitites, enkris, aleophatites, hemiartion*.' I do not think the two categories can always be distinguished. Thus the *enkris* is elsewhere described (14.645e) as a cake boiled in oil and soaked in honey, cited in Nicophon, *Encheirogastores* fr. 10, Aristophanes, *Danaids* fr. 269, and Pherecrates, *Crapataloi* fr. 99. The *tagenites*, or pancake, is noted by Athenaeus in Magnes, *Dionysus* fr. 2 and Cratinus, *Laws* fr. 130, both on hot pancakes giving off steam.

[191] Diphilus, *Telesias* fr. 80, 'A: Nibbles (*trogalia*), myrtle-berries, a flat-cake, almonds. B: I can have the sweetest dessert with those'; Archippus, *Heracles Gets Married* fr. 11 (in paraphrase) '[a table] groaning with honey-cakes (*itria*) and other *epiphoremata*'; Antiphanes, *Little Leptines* fr. 138.4, honey-cakes (among other *epiphoremata*); Alexis, *Philiscus* fr. 252 a flat-cake (among other sympotic items); Antiphanes, *Similars* fr. 172, 'a second table groaning with all sorts of cakes (*pemmata*).' Ephippus, *Cydon* fr. 13 offers a choice of cakes (the fragment is corrupt): 'and after the *deipnon* [pomegranate] seed, [. . .] chickpea, [. . .] broad bean, porridge, cheese, honey, sesame-cakes, [. . .] *mnous*, wheat cake (*puramis*), apple, nuts, milk, hemp-seed, mussels, barley water, Zeus' brain.'

of luxury. In Amphis, *Madness of Women* fr. 9 the developmental model is extended: 'A: Have you ever heard of the "refined"[192] life? B: Yes. A: That's just what this is. It's as clear as day. Milk cakes (*ametes*),[193] sweet wine, eggs, sesame, perfume, a garland, a girl-piper. B: By the Dioscuri, you've gone through the names of the twelve gods.' In Menander, *False Heracles* fr. 409, cake-making has taken over in a kitchen where the traditional roles are reversed, with the chef working on 'second tables' and his assistant on meat:

Cook, you have a most unsavoury air to me. This is the third time you've asked how many tables are we going to set up. We are sacrificing one little pig: what difference does it make to you whether we set up eight tables or two or one? I will lay one.[194] There are no *kandauloi* to make nor the kind of *karyke* mixtures of honey, fine flour, and eggs that you are accustomed to. Everything is now reversed. Now the *mageiros* makes the moulded cakes (*enchutoi*), bakes flat-cakes, boils *chondros*, and brings it in after the salt fish, and then the fig-leaf speciality and a bunch of grapes. Meanwhile, the female artisan is drawn up in line to compete with him and roasts bits of meat and thrushes as *tragemata*. Consequently the diner feasts on savouries and, when he's put on his perfume and garland, goes back to dining on honey-cakes—with thrushes.

In Nicophon, *Encheirogastores* fr. 6 an excessive number of bread and cakes appear to be listed: 'I . . . breads, barley cake, porridge, barley meal, rolls, spit-bread, honey bread, "poured on" cakes, barley water, flat-cakes, *dendalides*, pancakes.'

Some cakes in comedy appear to hover between sacred and secular. The *charisios*, one of those sharing the form of bread and cake, was, according to Athenaeus 15.668c, baked for *pannychides* or all-night festivals, at which celebrants danced and the winners were given the cakes.[195] Athenaeus cites two plays, somewhat

---

[192] ἀληλεμένον, 'of refined flour', milled, of flour producing finer breads and cakes, implying civilized refinement. The phrase is found also in Theophrastus, fr. 584A Fortenbaugh.

[193] The *ames* is a kind of flat-cake that is common in comedy: Athenaeus cites Antiphanes fr. 297, '*ametes* and meal-cakes'; Menander, *Suppositious Child* fr. 381; Telecleides, *Amphictyons* fr. 1.12.

[194] Reading παραθήσω μίαν (Bentley).

[195] Hunter on Eubulus fr. 2 explores the evidence for the *charisios* as either bread or cake.

unrevealingly. In Aristophanes, *Daitaleis* fr. 211 someone undertakes to send a *charisios* for the evening. In Eubulus, *Ankylion* fr. 1 someone else is baking a *charisios* victory-cake,[196] while in fr. 2 there is to be dancing all night and sympotic pleasures.[197] Sesame cakes, which often appear in sympotic lists, were also consumed at weddings, because they promote fertility, according to the scholiast on *Peace* 869.[198] Moschion in Menander, *Samia* 74 and 125 includes sesame cake in the preparations for his wedding.[199] The 'wedding' at *Peace* 869 is the less formal union of the protagonist with the *hetaera* Opora: 'The girl has had her bath and all of her bum is beautiful. The flat-cake is cooked, the sesame cake kneaded, and everything else is there. All that's missing is a penis'. Sesame cake appears in a luxurious setting at Eupolis, *Flatterers* fr. 176.3, 'he shits sesame cake', used of a man with extravagant airs (cited above).

While it is possible to propose a general definition of cakes as a luxury, as an additional and non-essential farinaceous element in a diet that could well restrict itself to bread and barley cakes,[200] in the way that Dalby (1995) identifies honey, for example, as a luxury, such a proposition—which coincides with my approach of what is necessary or useful—does not appear to have been adopted in comic texts, though it is by Plato's Socrates. We have seen that it is not always possible to distinguish cakes from breads, and that cakes are firmly embedded in religious and sympotic ritual, though they may appear in luxurious contexts, if the symposium or other occasions of eating may be so defined. Plato's Socrates singled out Athenian cakes as particularly luxurious, along with Corinthian *hetaerae* and Sicilian dining. These

[196] The fragment is obscure, but Athenaeus (who preserves it at 15.668c–d) implies that the victory in question was for those who had danced longest and therefore kept awake longest during a *pannychis* or all-night festival.

[197] The *pannychis* may resemble Dicaeopolis' sympotic pleasures at the Anthesteria in *Acharnians*. On the *pannychis* here see above, Chap. 2.

[198] On sesame cakes and weddings see Arnott (1996) on Alexis fr. 168; on cakes as slang for the female private parts, Henderson (1991), 144.

[199] Wedding preparations at Euangelus, *The Bride Unveiled* fr. 1 (quoted in Chap. 2) include moulded cakes (ἐγχύτους), *kandaulos*, and a little meal cake (ἀμύλιον).

[200] Barley cake (*maza*), as we have seen, is a staple and a 'cake' only in the sense of cereal ground and dampened, analogous to the term cattle-cake in English.

luxurious Athenian cakes do not appear to be reflected as such in Attic comedy, which does, however, mention the specialist *bread-maker* Thearion, identified in Plato's *Gorgias* (518b) as a commercial dealer along with Sarambus the Boeotian vintner and Mithaecus the Sicilian cook.[201] Dalby (1995: 109) identifies these three as 'non-Athenian contributors to the gastronomy of Athens'.[202] Specialist cake-sellers are rare in comedy—I know only of honey-cake-sellers[203] at Nicophon fr. 10. Plato's estimation of Attic cakes finds unlikely corroboration in Archestratus' *Life of Luxury* fr. 62, in which the discerning eater is advised that *tragemata* are not worth eating except for the flat-cake of Athens. Archestratus came from Gela in Sicily, and it is to that island that the next chapter is devoted. Attic comedy, as we have seen, often identified Sicilian meals as luxurious. Sicily had luxurious potential, not merely because it was not-Athens: it was a rich island with a number of tyrants who held court lavishly; it supposedly produced the first writer of a cookery book—Mithaecus—and it produced in Archestratus a poet whose work was related to comedy, both to the earlier Syracusan plays of Epicharmus and, later in the fourth century, to Attic comedy. As we shall see, Sicilian comedy and parody were as interested in the luxurious status of fish as were their Attic counterparts.

---

[201] Thearion is named in two plays with mythological titles, probably burlesques. In Aristophanes, *Aeolosicon* fr. 1 a speaker declares in tragic parody, 'leaving the bread shop of Thearion, where the foundations of the ovens are to be found, I have arrived here', while at Antiphanes, *Omphale* fr. 174.6–7 Thearion is declared to have shown the people how to cook oven bread.

[202] Behind Plato's censure of this trio lies perhaps concern at commercial suppliers taking over the provision of bread and wine that was traditionally provided within the family network, while the clever tricks of the cook encouraged by the book of Mithaecus may have been an unwelcome addition to the preparation of food by slaves and female members of the household.

[203] ἐγκριδοπώλαι.

7
The Culinary Literature of Sicily

This chapter examines representations of food in Sicily and Magna Graecia, both in literature and on the painted pottery of the region. The most important texts for this purpose are the comedies of Epicharmus, the parodic literature of Archestratus of Gela and others, and the cookery book of Mithaecus. These texts and painted pots were clearly influenced by their Athenian equivalents; there is some evidence that such influence was not a one-way process.

7.1. PUTTING THE FISH BACK INTO POETRY

Plato's Socrates declares at *Republic* 3.404b–d:

'You know that Homer feasts his heroes on campaign on neither fish— even though they were by the sea at the Hellespont—nor on boiled meat. They feasted on roast meat only, which would be particularly easy for soldiers. It is much easier to use a fire in many different places than to carry round cooking-pots.'

'Yes, very much so.'

'Nor, I think, did Homer ever mention sweet or savoury seasonings. Do not our athletes know this, that for the body that is trying to achieve fitness it is essential to keep away from all that kind of stuff?'

Socrates proceeds to the Syracusan and Sicilian cookery, Athenian cakes, and Corinthian *hetaerae* that we have just seen.

Plato is among the first to note the absence of fish in the Homeric diet.[1] His sequence of thought appears to be that Homer excluded from his poems those features of Greek life which—for the early fourth century at least—represented the life of luxury, the eating of fish, boiled meat,[2] and cakes, commercial baking,

---

[1] See 6.1 and Davidson (1997), 11–20, who gives a splendid analysis of this passage and the later interpreters of Homer.

[2] One ancient etymology of *opson* derived the noun from ἕψειν, to boil. Boiled

dining in the Sicilian style, and spending time at symposia with *hetaerae*. From the Homeric poets' point of view, epic was a form of poetry for which fish was not appropriate. The heroes of the *Iliad* and *Odyssey* conducted much feasting and sacrificing in domestic and military contexts, but fish-eating was reserved for those near to starvation.[3] In this section I trace the process by which fish were returned to epic verse, whether in the narrative style of Homer or the didactic of Hesiod. The insertion of fish into epic verse in the fifth and fourth centuries was to change heroic verse into hexameter parody, a form which became a minor genre in its own right and in the fifth century was related to comedy, probably first to Epicharmus who wrote (though not in hexameters) his magnificent tribute to fish, *The Muses or The Marriage of Hebe*, demonstrating therein the desirability of fish for diners at a wedding banquet of the gods. Homer's gods resembled his mortal heroes in abstaining from the eating of fish.

We do not know why fish were excluded from the heroic diet by Homer—the guess of Plato's Socrates is that they are unsuitable for athletes and soldiers—but in the innovative forms of poetry written in the fifth and fourth centuries certain fish were linked to the discourse of luxury and pleasure, as we saw in Chapter 6, often with a Homeric flourish. Thus Philoxenus adapted the phrase 'when we companions had reached a surfeit of drinking and eating' into his Dorian dithyramb, Matro brought endless Homeric phrases into his magnificent banquet of fish in hexameters, and Strato into a comic speech by a formulaic boastful cook (*Phoenicides* fr. 1). Alongside this literary panache, other cultural forms were inspired by fish, not least the hundreds of fish-plates that were painted in southern Italy during the fourth century. Related to fish-plates painted in Attica, these representations of the material world were painted on vessels apparently for use at table. We do not, however, know for sure either their true function or why some fish were portrayed and others not (many bream, few if any tuna). In this respect the fish-plates resemble the *phlyax* vases which represent comic dramas of southern Italy in the fourth century. There are many of them and

---

dishes might then fall into the same category of *opson* as fish. See ibid. 20–35 and esp. 32

[3] *Odyssey* 12.

many images, but no sure way of matching fish on plates with fish in texts or comic performances on vases with performances in the theatre or elsewhere. We have little idea which comedies we are dealing with, or in which performances or in which cultural contexts. These visual and poetic forms reflect the rich world of southern Italy and Sicily, whose cities represented their cultural identities powerfully and richly and experienced cross-cultural exchanges with the Greek homeland, and with Athens in particular. We will see, in this chapter, how the Greek-speaking inhabitants of this rich land surrounded themselves with these representations of comic and marine life.[4]

Sicily was a seductive island for Greeks from the motherland—Plato himself visited it on more than one occasion. Aeschylus had died there. But the traffic was not one-way. Vase painters as well as writers and philosophers demonstrate in their work a lively interaction and development of themes between the cities of the Greek mainland and those of southern Italy and Sicily. While this chapter concerns itself with literary form and representation, many of the writers discussed travelled from smaller islands and *poleis* to the large centres of Syracuse and Athens and brought with them new perspectives and approaches which had a significant impact on Attic comedy. Notable examples for this study are the dithyrambist Philoxenus of Cythera and the parodists Hegemon of Thasos, Archestratus of Gela, and Matro of Pitane. Travel itself—in the cause of seeking out the best fish in Aegean, Ionian, and Italian waters—forms the very subject-matter of Archestratus' poem. Representations of Athens in the last three of these texts offer a sharp perspective on the city's own representation of food in her culture. Not all of these poets had links with Sicily and southern Italy—only Philoxenus and Archestratus are reasonably certain—but Sicily also hosted the development of a further branch of literature on the subject of food, the cookery book of Mithaecus. The interrelations between poetry and drama and the Greek cities of Magna Graecia and Athens enabled oppositions and contrasts to be

---

[4] Davidson (1997) has written of the 'mania for fish' in Athens. If anything it was greater in Sicily and southern Italy, whose waters, Athenaeus tells us (12.518c), were rich in fish.

established and Athens to develop the notion of luxury increasing elsewhere in the Greek world and threatening her supposed frugality.

The history of Sicily and southern Italy in the period 500–350 BC is complex and often obscure, characterized by dazzling tyrants such as Hiero I and Dionysius I ruling Syracuse with a period of democracy intervening, major wars between the Greek cities and between Greeks, Carthaginians, and local Italic peoples in a maze of shifting alliances, and by the gradual Hellenization of parts of the Italian peninsula.[5] Of the texts to be studied in this chapter, too little is known of Syracusan comedy, of the comic poets (of Epicharmus, let alone his contemporaries and successors), or of the place of comedy in Syracuse to draw any conclusions about the role of comedy in that society. It appears that Syracuse had a large theatre at an early date. The tyrants are known to have had some interest in drama, but only small details are known.[6] As for Archestratus of Gela, whose home town was one of those destroyed by the Carthaginians, *The Life of Luxury* sheds little light on the background of its author.

In addition to their patronage of poetry the tyrants appear to have entertained lavishly at their courts, but much of the evidence is anecdotal and from a later period. Athenaeus draws on the *Hiero* of Xenophon for a series of reflections on plenty and pleasure at court. I discuss below anecdotes of Philoxenus at the court of Dionysius, some of which appear to have been exploited in Attic comedy. It is clear from Thucydides and others that Athenians had increasingly close links with a number of Sicilian cities during the fifth century, and it is probably through these contacts that Sicilian dining came to be of interest to Attic comedy, the genre most likely to comment on such matters. Since Syracuse was a democracy from 467 to 405, it is not surprising

---

[5] For a general survey of Sicily and southern Italy in the period 500–350 BC see D. Asheri, 'Sicily 478–431'; in *CAH*[5], 147–70, and the chapters in *CAH* 6[2] by D. M. Lewis on Sicily (pp. 120–55) and N. Purcell on South Italy (pp. 381–403).

[6] Hiero supported tragedy, or at least a production of Aeschylus, *Aetneans* in Sicily. Dionysius won a victory in Athens at the Lenaea, possibly with a comedy: see Kassel–Austin (1986) and Hunter (1983) on Eubulus *Dionysius*. The *Suda* records that Dionysius wrote a work *On the Poems of Epicharmus* (Epicharmus test. 15 Kaibel).

that eating in Syracuse, as far as Attic comedy was concerned, was not based on a court but on unspecified inhabitants. Attic comedy was not interested in Syracuse and Sicily for their own sake, but for their influence on Athens. In the area of food and eating these influences were three:[7] the supply of agricultural products, cheese and pigs, for example, in Hermippus fr. 63.9 (quoted in Chapter 4);[8] a lavish form of eating that (like other luxuries, as we have seen) appealed to the young, as seen in the 'Syracusan table and Sybaritic feasts' of Aristophanes' *Banqueters* fr. 225;[9] and the *mageiros* or specialist cook, who might, like Mithaecus, come from Sicily. An early example is to be found in Cratinus the Younger, *Giants* fr. 1: 'A: Do you see how sweetly the earth smells and fragrant smoke comes forth? Someone it seems is living in that defile, either an incense-seller or a Sicilian cook. B: Are you saying both have a similar smell?'[10]

It is difficult to assess how strong these influences were, but they were not peculiar to the discourse of comedy, for they are supported by other texts, albeit those pursuing a similar discourse of luxury.[11] The Old Oligarch refers to the 'pleasant' imports from Sicily,[12] and Plato, as we have seen, to Syracusan tables and Sicilian elaboration of *opsa*, to eating twice a day,[13] and to the Sicilian cookery book writer Mithaecus, whom he treats

---

[7] Four, if we believe the *kottabos* to be a Sicilian invention: see Chap. 5.

[8] Add Philemon, *The Sicilian* fr. 79, 'A: In the past I thought that Sicily produced this one special item, fine cheeses. I had also added by hearsay how one spoke of ornate Sicilian robes. B: I thought it produced household goods' (the text of the last line is uncertain).

[9] Eubulus fr. 119 (cited in Chap. 1.8) mentions Sicilian couches.

[10] Add Arnott (1996) on Alexis fr. 24; Epicrates fr. 6; Antiphanes fr. 90; Anaxippus fr. 1.3. See Chap. 8.

[11] Sicilian wealth and cooking became proverbial (see Arnott on Alexis fr. 24). The scholiast on *Knights* 1091 comments as follows on Aristophanes' invented *plouthygieia* ('health-wealth'): 'perhaps Aristophanes is alluding to the gifts to Muscellus and Archias when they were in the process of founding Croton and Syracuse and seeking to receive a good prophecy/report. The oracle predicted: "bringing with you the people who would colonize a land and a polis, you have come to ask Phoebus which land you should go to. But come, give thought: would you choose the wealth of fine possessions or most pleasing health?" Muscellus chose health, Archias wealth. Hence, they say, the people of Croton are more healthy and their city became the mother of many fine athletes . . . while the city of the Syracusans became extremely wealthy.'

[12] Quoted in Chaps. 4 and 6.   [13] *Epistle* 7.326b.

disparagingly in *Gorgias* (518b) along with other purveyors of the life of pleasure, Thearion the baker and Sarambus the wine-seller.[14] All three encourage superfluous physical pleasure at the expense of what is strictly needed (which is the concern of doctors). His criticism of Thearion and Sarambus appears to be based on an objection to commercial provision taking over what was traditionally provided within the family network, while the clever tricks of the kitchen encouraged by the text of Mithaecus and by cooks hired for special occasions were an unwelcome addition to the preparation of food by slaves and female members of the household. Bakers, wine-merchants, and cooks were of considerable interest to Attic comedy: I discussed bakers in Chapter 4 and the *kapeleion* in Chapters 2, 4, and 5. While there are no direct traces of Mithaecus in Attic comedy, writers and cooks like him appear to have influenced Middle and New Comedy and first left their mark in the late fifth or early fourth century. I explore their considerable influence in this and the next chapter. Much of the evidence is intensely literary and far from the heat of the kitchen. We shall consider below Plato, *Phaon* fr. 189, from an Attic comedy which quotes a cookery book in hexameters by one of the Philoxeni. For the present, I note an extremely speculative link between Attic comedy and Sicily. Aristophanes' last two plays, *Cocalus* and *Aeolosicon*, like many of their predecessors, appear to have contained an element of tragic parody. *Cocalus* seems to have been related to the *Camici* of Sophocles and *Aeolosicon* to the *Aeolus* of Euripides. Both tragedies were probably based on myths from the islands of the Western Mediterranean, *Camici* on the boiling of Minos in Sicily by the daughters of Cocalos, *Aeolus* on the king of Lipari and his incestuous children. In *Wealth* Aristophanes parodied the *Galatea* of Philoxenus (which was based on a Sicilian myth—see below). In his three last plays, then, Aristophanes chose subjects with Sicilian connections and allusions. The title *Aeolosicon* combines the name of a mythical king with the name of a slave or a cook: was Aeolus presented as a Sicilian *mageiros*? It is not certain that the name Sicon denotes a cook, let alone a Sicilian cook—Sicon appears to be the name of a non-specialist slave at

---

[14] Dalby (1995), 109 points out that Plato follows the standard tripartite division of the Greek diet into *opson*, cereal staple, and wine.

Ecclesiazusae 867—but the name belongs to cooks in Menander, *Dyscolus*[15] and Sosipater (see Chapter 8), and was derived from *Sikelos* in ancient etymologies.[16] *If* the last two plays were burlesques and *if* Sicon was a cook, then Aristophanes ended his career in a strikingly Sicilian mode.[17]

7.2.   DRAMA IN SICILY

Burlesque treatments of myth were a significant feature of the plays of Epicharmus, while later in the fifth century in Deinolochus and at the end of the fourth in Rhinthon burlesque versions of tragic myth in particular became the standard forms of comedy, as far as evidence for written texts is concerned. As early as Epicharmus,[18] the language of Aeschylus appears to have been reflected in Syracusan comedy. Productions of the *Aetnaeae* and *Persians* of Aeschylus at the invitation of Hiero are attested. The appetite for tragic myth in southern Italy is reflected in a large number of vase paintings (an early example of which is Euripides' *Aeolus*, painted by the Amycus Painter in about 410 BC), to which can be added the anecdote of Athenian prisoners singing extracts from Euripides to their Syracusan captors.[19]

We have seen that Attic comedy reflects not only the world around it but also itself. Syracusan comedy has not survived in sufficient quantities to demonstrate a similar feature on an extensive scale. What have survived, however, in profusion in Sicily and southern Italy are representations of comedy by vase painters. Sicilian and southern Italian painters (working in the comic tradition from 400 BC onwards, decades after Epicharmus) created many images of comedy. These images appear to have

---

[15]   See Handley (1965) and Gomme and Sandbach (1973) on 889.
[16]   Zwicker *RE*. 2A.2527. On the name see further Hunter (1983) on Eubulus fr. 126 and Arnott (1996), 825.
[17]   Burlesque appears to have played a much larger role in Old Comedy than the surviving plays lead us to expect. It appears to have been even more important in Middle Comedy. See in particular Hunter (1983), 22–30 and Nesselrath (1990).
[18]   Fr. 214.
[19]   On the vases representing tragedy see Trendall and Webster (1971), Kossatz-Deissmann (1978); Dearden (1988); Trendall (1991); and Taplin (1993).

been initiated in Athens but were then taken up enthusiastically by the southern Italian painters and developed in many forms. Oliver Taplin (1993) has revived the debate about how these vases relate to the history of comedy and how the comedies of southern Italy relate to Athens. He believes that the majority of the images portray Attic comedies performed in Sicily and southern Italy (I discuss his thesis below). The vases have a further significance for the present study, since they are often craters—bowls for mixing wine—which comprise part of the tableware looked at by diners as they ate and drank.[20]

Comedy in Sicily and southern Italy has a long history. To the best of our knowledge, 'comedy' as a dramatic genre existed in a recognized form in Syracuse long before it did in Athens,[21] and was, in ways that will be discussed below, independent of Athenian drama but cognizant of it. Arguments about priority are inconclusive, given our ignorance of Attic comedy before the official incorporation of comedy into competitive festivals in 486, the fragmentary nature of early Attic and all Sicilian comedy, and the absence of information on the circumstances of performance in Sicily and southern Italy. Furthermore, too little is known of related genres, such as mime and forms of drama that did not make their way into the textual tradition, if indeed they ever existed as texts. We simply do not know what was performed in the theatres of Magna Graecia in the late fifth and fourth centuries. I doubt that the answer is predominantly Attic comedies, as Taplin (1993) would have us believe, although he has persuaded me that Attic comedy strongly influenced the Sicilian and southern Italian theatre. Was there influence in the other direction? The attempt by von Salis to demonstrate Sicilian elements in Old Comedy has rightly not won acceptance, since he begs too many questions. The form of Old Comedy did, however, change, whether under Sicilian influence or not. I consider below various influences on Attic comedy, on both form and content, which may or may not have been decisive for comedy as a

---

[20] The vases also served a further purpose as grave-goods. Both drinking-vessels and fish-plates were deposited in tombs and some (even a large number of them) may have been made for that purpose: see Trendall (1989), 11–12 and Kunisch (1989), 43–9.

[21] Aristotle, *Poetics* 1448a29–34.

genre. These influences are well known, but are rehearsed here because they are central to the topic of the present study.

Estimates of Epicharmus are difficult[22]—his plays probably pre-dated nearly all Attic comedies and constitute some of the earliest manipulations of comic themes, but antiquity does not constitute influence.[23] His work is obscured by his reputation as an ancient sage.[24] He may have made advances in prosody.[25] Epicharmus mentions the iambic poet Aristoxenus in fr. 88 in a passage apparently about iambic poetry; the fragment is from a play entitled *The Masculine and Feminine Word* (*Logos and Logina*), though too little survives to indicate how the play was concerned with language and gender. One fragment (87) preserves a mild joke based on a misheard word.[26]

7.3. THE ROLE OF FOOD IN THE PLAYS OF EPICHARMUS

Food and eating are frequent subjects in the fragments of Epicharmus and the meagre remains of the other dramatic forms of the region, in particular the mimes of Sophron and the *phlyax* plays of Sopater.[27] Food appears to be as integral to these genres as to Attic comedy and will be presented by the categories followed in Chapters 1–6. Again, the majority of the fragments

[22] See further, on Epicharmus' possible links with Corinthian drama (Syracuse was a Corinthian foundation), on burlesque and political allusion, Pickard-Cambridge (1962) and E. W. Handley in Easterling and Knox (1985), 367–70.

[23] His plays were influential in Athens to judge from Plato's citations in *Gorgias* and *Theaeteus* 152e, but the latter passage is hardly representative since it avoids all Attic drama by declaring Epicharmus *the* comic poet and Homer *the* tragic poet.

[24] See e.g. the *Pseudepicharmea* (frr. 239–302 Kaibel). Various proverbial sayings are attributed to him, as they are to Simonides: both are credited, for example, with the *skolion* 'Good health is best' (*hygiainein men ariston*, *PMG* 890).

[25] Hephaestion comments helpfully (*Ench.* 8.2–3) on the anapaestic tetrameter catalectic. Though known as the Aristophanean, it could be traced back to Cratinus, Epicharmus in *Dancers* and *Victory Ode*, and Aristoxenos, the Sicilian elegist (considered also as a possible comic poet by Kaibel) who long predated Epicharmus.

[26] 'A: Zeus invited me to a feast (*g' eranos*) he was giving for Pelops. B: It's a vile *opson*, my friend, the crane (*geranos*). A: I didn't say crane, I said feast.'

[27] There is little reference to food in the few fragments of Rhinthon.

relating to food derive from Athenaeus, whose lexicographical interest found many unusual terms in the Doric dialect of Epicharmus. The material world was richly reflected in the lists of foods, nearly all fish, in the thirty-five fragments[28] of *The Muses or The Marriage of Hebe* and other plays.[29] Epicharmus created the earliest-known comic parasite. In fr. 34–5 of the *Hope or Wealth* he portrayed the Syracusan parasite, unwelcome, always eating, drinking his life away, and sycophantic, though with a ready wit to charm his host. The character expresses more strongly than in most of the Attic examples his poverty and inequality with others at the feast.[30] In fr. 37 the parasite is addressed, 'someone invited you to his dinner against his will but you ran there eagerly', and a parasite was also addressed in *Periallos* fr. 71. The *mageiros* appears to have been a character at least once in Epicharmus, in a form unattested in Old Comedy. A papyrus fragment of a commentary on Epicharmus preserves the phrase 'I am a *mageiros*'.[31] In Old Comedy, as far as we know from surviving plays and fragments, the *mageiros* never declares himself to be such on stage. He is either a character off-stage or his role is taken by the protagonist.[32] *Busiris* fr. 21 presents Heracles the eating machine, both language and physical detail adding to the comic effect. The subject of the play was probably the mythological encounter between Busiris, the cannibal king of Egypt, and Heracles: 'first, if you were to catch sight of him eating, you'd be a dead man. His throat roars within, his jaw rattles,

---

[28] Some 15% of all the 'genuine' fragments.

[29] The play is discussed below. Fish are also cited in frr. 28–32, 84, 89, 102, 114, 124, 138, 162, 164, 180, 211. Other foods: lentil soup, *Dionysuses* fr. 33; porridge (*poltos*), fr. 23; beans, fr. 151; parsnips, frr. 3 and 27; garlic and onions, *Philoctetes* fr. 134; mallow, fr. 153; mushrooms, fr. 155; summer vegetables, fr. 156; lettuce, fr. 158; marjoram, fr. 17; various vegetables (they are praised in fr. 159), frr. 159–61 and 204; gourds, fr. 154; meats, *Bacchae* fr. 19 ('wrapping up the chief in the caul'), *Thearoi* fr. 80, *Cyclops* fr. 82; a piglet, *Odysseus the Deserter* (fr. 100) and *Sirens* (fr. 124.3); birds, frr. 84, 157; nuts, hen's and goose's eggs, frr. 150, 152; figs, fr. 128; myrtle-berries, fr. 207. No fragments survive from the *Orua* (*Sausage*).

[30] Epicharmus' parasite is unlikely to have been identified by this term, even though a Homeric scholion attests its use in this play (fr. 36): see Chap. 2.

[31] Epicharmus, *CGFP* fr. 84.7.118 μάγειρος εἰμι. On the *mageiros* see Chap. 8.

[32] See Chap. 8. Did the *mageiros* of Epicharmus influence the later work of Mithaecus and Archestratus in Sicily?

his molar crashes, his canine has a creak, he sizzles in his nostrils, he waggles his ears.'

Agricultural themes are not well represented, though Columella 1.1 attests the contribution of Epicharmus to agriculture (Test. 5 Kaibel), and the *boukoliasmos*, or cowherd's song, which later influenced pastoral is attested in two plays (frr. 4 and 165). Public festivals are cited at frr. 100 and 231, dedications at Delphi in fr. 79, and animal sacrifice at frr. 118, 139, and 187.

The market-place does not appear in the fragments, though a number mention Sicilian coins (frr. 9, 10, 40), which possibly indicate commercial interest.

At least six fragments belong to the symposium. *Philoctetes* fr. 132, 'there is no dithyramb when you drink water', anticipates Cratinus fr. 203, while fr. 148 on violence generated by excessive drinking anticipates Eubulus fr. 93.[33] Luxury (*tryphe*) is not explicitly at issue in the fragments, though *The Muses or The Marriage of Hebe* might have explored this area and *Sirens* fr. 124 strongly hints at it:

A: In the early morning, at dawn, we grilled round whitebait, we had roast pork and octopus, and we drank it all down with sweet wine.
B: O dear, O dear!
A: One could talk of it as a meal.
B: Alas for your misfortunes!
A: In so far as there was one fat red mullet and two bonitos cut in half and the same number of doves and scorpion fish.

7.3.1. Fish in Epicharmus

Two plays of Epicharmus, *Earth and Sea* and *The Marriage of Hebe or The Muses* contained 'banquets with many fish', according to Aelian.[34] Kaibel suggests that *Earth and Sea* may have presented a debate over the relative merits of each element, rather as *The Fisherman and the Peasant* of Sophron may have done in mime;[35] while in Attic comedy the *Goats* of Eupolis and the *Beasts* of Crates put the case for animals and possibly the *Fishes* of Archippus for fish. All ten fragments refer to foods produced on land or sea, though no clear trace of Aelian's 'banquet of fish'

[33] The last two are compared in Chap. 5. Other fragments: 133, 174, 200 and (on Sybaritic tales, apparently, rather than Sybaritic luxury), 215.
[34] *On the Nature of Animals* 13.4. On the ἰχθύων πανθοίνιαι see below.
[35] Cf. Handley (1985), 370, within his discussion of Epicharmus (367–70).

survives. *The Marriage of Hebe or The Muses* has fared better.
The feast was described by a character—Kaibel suggests Hermes. Athena played the *enoplion* tune on her pipes for the
Dioscuri (fr. 75). There was an extensive fish banquet, with
many species named, and some or all of the guests, presumably at
Hebe's wedding feast, were gods. Athenaeus reports that *The
Muses* is a revised version of *The Marriage of Hebe*,[36] but it is not
possible to distinguish which parts belong exclusively to each
version. Tzetzes attests the presence of the Muses in the first
play.[37] These Muses, all apparently named after rivers and
daughters of Fatness and Fullness, imply richness based either
on land well-watered by rivers or perhaps (but less probably) on
a plentiful supply of freshwater fish. In fr. 42 a god or gods nar-
rate(s) a long list of shellfish that were brought in for eating:

[he/she] brought in shellfish of every kind, limpets, *aspedoi*, *krabyzoi*,
kikibaloi, sea-squirts, scallops, *balanoi*, murex, oysters closed up (to
prise them open is difficult, to eat them up easy), mussels, *anaritai*,
whelks and *skiphydria*, which are sweet to consume but sharp to bite
into, and long, round razor-shells. Also the black shell which is [. . .] for
children to hunt for shellfish. On the other hand, land-snails and
amathitides, which are little valued and cheap and which all mankind
calls 'man-avoiders' but we gods 'whites'.

The speaker comments on the ease or otherwise of eating shellfish, the ease of opening them, the qualities for eating and taste,
methods of collection, and cost. The most striking feature is the
divine speaker, who attends in great detail not only to fish but to
varieties available to the poorest human. These are not the great
fish discussed in Chapter 6. In this play at least one god is concerned with fish, and the whole gamut of fish at that. The play
appears at one level to be a celebration of the produce of the
seas around Sicily, and at another a mythological play about a

---

[36] (3.110b) *Muses* is a *diaskeue*. Only Athenaeus, Tzetzes, and Aelian (*Nature
of Animals* 13.4) cite *The Muses*. Fragments attested for the *Marriage of Hebe* are
42–3, 44, 45, 47, 49, 51, 52, 53, 54, 55–6, 57, 58, 59, 60, 61, 62, 63, 64, 65, 66, 67,
68, 69, 70; for *The Muses*, 42–3.9, 44.2, 46?, 48, 50, 51?, 52, 71, 72, 73, 74, 75.
Athenaeus records closely similar lines for each play in frr. 42–3, 47–8, and
49–50, explicitly noting the variation at 3.85e.

[37] (Fr. 41) 'Epicharmus in the *Marriage of Hebe* says the seven [Muses were]
daughters of Fatness and the nymph Fullness, Neilous, Tritone, Asopos, Epta-
pore, Achelois, Titoplous, and Rhodia.'

wedding feast where the gods ate foods normally reserved for mortals. Poseidon arrives at the feast with sea bream and parrot wrasse in Phoenician ships (fr. 54): 'Poseidon himself came, the commander, bringing in Phoenician merchant-ships the finest [the text is corrupt] sea breams and parrot-wrasses, even whose excrement it is not lawful for the gods to throw away.' This remarkable fragment appears to present Poseidon not as the lord of fish and monsters, terrifying to humans,[38] but as a Phoenician sea-captain with a cargo of fish for consumption by the gods.

The fish in these fragments are not all presented in the same format. Some are listed, 'there were lobsters . . .,' 'there were electric rays . . .' (57, 59); some are brought—for example by Poseidon; others enter, as if arriving as guests (53). The last resemble the fish of Matro's *Attic Dinner* who are presented as Homeric heroes.[39] We know nothing of the bride and groom, Hebe and Heracles. More importantly, the gods are portrayed eating foods, as would mortals at a human wedding feast. Gods may be imagined to eat like humans on the analogy perhaps of *theoxenia* or of the literary precedent of the Homeric banquet at the end of *Iliad* 1. Gods in Old Comedy, as we have seen, display a remarkable desire to eat almost any human food, though they concentrate on meat derived from sacrifice. This play resembles nothing known in Old Comedy, either in form or cultural content. A striking formal element for the history of comedy is the use of narrative and the long list—the latter a comparatively rare phenomenon in Old Comedy, much more common in later Attic comedy. This luxurious banquet in narrative form is difficult to parallel in Old Comedy as it has survived, with the exception of the utopian fragments discussed in Chapter 3. When combined with the testimony of Aelian on the importance of the 'fish banquet', the play is quite extraordinary. Athenaeus makes no explicit statement on the 'fish banquet', but of the thirty-five fragments in Kaibel's edition, twenty-nine are cited by Athenaeus.

Aelian goes on to say that 'feasts of fish'[40] were presented not

---

[38] On the 'sons of Poseidon' see Pease (1955) on Cicero, *De natura deorum* 1.62 (I am indebted to Matthew Leigh for the reference).

[39] See Degani (1995), 416–19.

[40] οὐ ῥαιδίως δὲ αὐτοῦ μνημονεύουσιν ἐν ταῖς ὑπὲρ τῶν ἰχθύων πανθοινίαις, ὧν τι καὶ ὄφελός ἐστι ποιητῶν θεμένων (ποιηταὶ θέμενοι Herscher) σπουδὴν ἐς μνήμην ἔνθεσμον, 'Επίχαρμος μὲν ἐν 'Ήβας Γάμωι καὶ Γᾶι καὶ Θαλάσσαι καὶ προσέτι καὶ Μώσαις, Μνησίμαχος δὲ ἐν τῶι

only by Epicharmus but also by Mnesimachus, a poet of Attic Middle Comedy, in his *Isthmionike*.[41] Aelian appears to mean literal feasts based on fish rather than 'feasts' of words which listed fish, since his context is the edibility of the *kallionymos* and the attempt of the poets to record every fish worth eating.[42] Athenaeus, as we have seen, amplifies Aelian's picture by quoting some of the list of fish in the *Marriage of Hebe or The Muses*. While he does not mention the *Isthmionike* of Mnesimachus, he attests to much listing, cooking, and consuming of fish in Middle and New Comedy.[43] Aelian passed over Attic Old Comedy; Athenaeus did not, but produces no more than hints of feasts of fish and the briefest of lists, some of them from the *Fishes* of Archippus, a play whose chorus, if it was anything like the birds of Aristophanes' *Birds*, represented a wide range of fish. Why does *Fishes* not constitute a list or full 'feast of fish'? One explanation is that Aelian did not know the play, but Athenaeus certainly did, for it formed the subject of a monograph he wrote (7.329c), and he cites in Book 7 parts of the conflict between humans and fish that constituted the agon. It is possible that few fish were listed in Archippus, but much more likely that a number were cited in one form or another but that the eating of fish was largely suppressed, as is the eating of birds in *Birds*. The chorus was not, for the most part, eaten in the plays of Attic Old Comedy.[44]

Ἰσθμιονίκηι. ('[Authors] do not readily mention it [the *kallionymos*] in their feasts on the subject of fish, the utility of which the poets have earnestly attempted to record properly, Epicharmus in *The Marriage of Hebe* and *Earth and Sea* and also *Muses* and Mnesimachus in *Isthmionike*.')

[41] The title might indicate a scene of celebration comparable to the divine wedding in *The Marriage of Hebe*.

[42] Athenaeus, probably drawing on a similar source to Aelian, confirms the absence of the *kallionymos* from Epicharmus (7.282d). On the complexities of identifying *anthias*, *elops*, *kallionymos*, and *kallichthys* in 7.282d see Thompson (1947), 98–9.

[43] Athenaeus fails to cite the *Isthmionike* but quotes a long fragment from another play of Mnesimachus, the *Horse-Breeder* (fr. 4), in which there was what appears to be a 'fish-banquet'. Forty-five species of fish are listed (31–45), along with some meats and vegetables, and diners are twice warned that the fish is getting cold (10, 28). Athenaeus (9.402d) introduces this and related fragments with 'the dinners spoken about in the comic poets provide the sweetest things for the ear to hear rather than for the throat', again emphasizing that feasts of foods are feasts of words.

[44] See Wilkins (forthcoming, b).

The *Marriage of Hebe or The Muses*, by contrast, presented both the listing and the consumption of fish. Aelian's phrase 'banquets of many fish', at least, implies consumption.

The wedding meal in the play of Epicharmus extended beyond the many varieties of fish. If we compare the foods in *The Life of Luxury* of Archestratus (a Sicilian poem on food from the fourth century), we find in both texts, in addition to an abundance of fish, lists of breads (Archestratus frr. 4–5, Epicharmus fr. 52) and birds (Archestratus 58, Epicharmus frr. 45–6). There are appetizers and hare in Archestratus, but no sacrificial meat in either text.[45] Fat, 'sweetness', and flavour come at a premium in Epicharmus (frr. 49, 50, 63, 68), as they do in Archestratus.[46] The gods do not avoid excrement in fish nor fish which eat excrement (frr. 54 and 61); they are concerned with seasonal factors (fr. 63) and with pickling fish (fr. 71), and Zeus and Hera reserve for themselves the desirable *elops* (fr. 71).[47] There is nothing in the divine meal which would appear to cause surprise if served at the table of one of the Sicilian elite—as we understand it from texts such as these. The meal is likely to have constituted only part of the play, as do the preparations for the cooking of fish by the boastful cook in Middle Comedy. How this element related to the rest of the play is unknown.

The evidence of Aelian and Athenaeus, such as it is, when set beside the surviving plays of Aristophanes and the fragments of Attic Old Comedy, suggests that the extensive eating of fish was not a major feature of Attic Old Comedy, but became so in Middle and New. In Old Comedy (apart from the special case of the chorus of Archippus), fish were not prominent, but were mentioned periodically as an element of the life of the polis which comedy reflects. Much feasting in surviving Aristophanes is based on agricultural produce, as are the utopian passages on banqueting.[48] Athenaeus' *Deipnosophists* provides in Book 7

---

[45] Meat may have been deliberately excluded in Athenaeus' selection: see Olson and Sens on Archestratus.

[46] Wilkins and Hill (1994), 22.

[47] The expensive *elops* is reminiscent of Archestratus' comments on sought-after fish and the lengths to which purchasers will go to acquire what they want: see frr. 15 and 21 and below.

[48] See Chap. 3, where I also discussed notions of the 'ancient life' in Old Comedy, whether imagined in the Age of Cronos or in Attic agriculture or enshrined

much of the evidence for fish in Old Comedy.[49] Old Comedy's most desirable fish is the Boeotian eel.[50] Small fish, such as *aphyae* ('whitebait'), are cited from, among others, Hermippus, *Demotae* fr. 14, Callias, *Cyclopes* fr. 10, Aristonymus, *Cold Helios* fr. 2 and Aristophanes, *Fryers (Tagenistae)* fr. 521,[51] large fish from Callias, *Cyclopes* fr. 6, 'a baked *kitharos*, a ray, and this head of a tuna, eels, crayfish, a grey mullet,[52] and this sea bass',[53] Archippus,[54] and Cratinus, *Trophonius* fr. 236, 'to eat no longer a red-skinned mullet at Aixone . . . nor the noble appearance of a sting-ray or a dreadful saddle-bream'.[55] A particular interest in

in religious ritual. Fish are not validated by antiquity in these ways, except fleetingly in the utopias and there only as 'fish', not by species, except in fr. 6 of the *Thuriopersians* of Metagenes which describes a utopian River Crathis. In fr. 171.49–50 of the *Wealths* of Cratinos, a play with utopian content, fish may offer themselves for consumption: see Kassel–Austin (1983).

[49] Gleaned from many books (7.277b–c). The fact that Athenaeus picks up a large number of the citations of fish in the surviving plays of Aristophanes may imply a good coverage of Old Comedy—but not necessarily.

[50] From Old Comedy Athenaeus cites *Acharnians* 889, *Lemnian Women* fr. 380, *Banqueters* fr. 229, *Knights* 864–7, *Clouds* 559, *Wasps* 510, Cratinus, *Wealths* fr. 171.50, Strattis, *Rivermen* fr. 40. Not all these citations concern the *eating* of eels.

[51] Other cheap fish: *Bembrades* (sprats or anchovies): Phrynichus, *Members of the Tragic Chorus* fr. 52; Aristomenes, *Quacks* fr. 7; Aristonymus, *Cold Helios* fr. 2; Aristophanes, *Old Age* fr. 140; Plato, *Ambassadors* fr. 131; Eupolis, *Goats* fr. 31. *Hepsetos* ('boiler'): Aristophanes, *Anagyros* fr. 56; *Dramas or Niobe* fr. 292; Archippus, *Fishes* fr. 19; Eupolis, *Goats* fr. 16. Some of these are the merest citation with little detectable interest in eating. *Skombros* (mackerel): Aristophanes, *Gerytades* fr. 189. Small cuttle etc.: Aristophanes, *Danaids* fr. 258.2; *Trichides*: Aristophanes, *Knights* 662; *Merchant Ships* fr. 426; Nicochares, *Lemnian Women* fr. 14, '*trichiai* and *premnades* [tuna] coming to the dinner in abundance'.

[52] *Lineus*, identified by Hesychius as a grey mullet.

[53] *Acharnos*, partially identified by Hesychius as a sea bass. Add Eupolis fr. 174 (below); Aristophanes, *Women Setting Up Festival Tents* fr. 491, 'with my belly full of bogues I went home'.

[54] *Fishes* frr. 18, 23, 'Egyptian Hermaeus is the foulest of fish-merchants. He forcibly skins monk-fish and dogfish and sells them off, and disembowels sea bass so they tell us.' Add Aristophanes, *Lemnian Women* fr. 380, 'to buy no head of a seabass nor crayfish, nor a Boeotian eel, nor a *glaukos* nor the underbelly of a tuna'; Plato, *Sophists* fr. 146, 'whether it be a dogfish or ray or eel'; *Alliance* fr. 164, 'boiled electric ray is a delightful food'; fr. 166.

[55] Cratinus, *Wealths* fr. 171.49–50, 'for I am your black female tuna, your male tuna, sea perch, *glaukos*, eel, and dogfish' (cf. n. 48 above). Add Strattis, *Atalanta* fr. 5, 'the underbelly of the tuna and a pig's trotter for a drachma', and *Macedonians* fr. 32 'sweet underbellies of tuna'; Theopompus, *Calaeschrus* fr. 24,

fish is characteristic of gluttons and those given to appetite and luxury,[56] who, in the words of *Peace* 810–11, are 'fish-eating Gorgons, skate-searching Harpies, foul ghastly crones, fish-destroyers with armpits like goats'.[57] Sometimes fish are listed with other foods,[58] at others the eating of fish is not at issue,[59] as we have already seen in the *Fishes* of Archippus, which combines the worlds of the human and the fish and even discusses a peace-treaty between them.

Naturally, it is difficult to judge what appeared in the lost plays. For all we know, the chorus of fryers in Aristophanes'

'underbellies of fish, O Demeter'; Aristophanes, *Telmessians* fr. 550; 'black-finned meagres'; Pherecrates, *The Forgetful Man* fr. 62, 'accompanying your little meagre and little sprats'; Aristophanes fr. 612, 'sea bass, the cleverest of all fish'; *Knights* 361 (sea bass); *Wasps* 493 (sea perch); Archippus fr. 17; Cratinus, *Odysseuses* fr. 154, 'a hot slice of sea perch'; Pherecrates, *Slave-Teacher* fr. 43, 'A . . . become a *kitharos* and move through the agora as a *kitharos*. B: A fine thing, a *kitharos*, and very much belonging to Apollo. A: But that's what's upsetting me, my good woman, because they say there is some evil in the *kitharos*.' The *kitharos* is unidentified but is assumed to be a flatfish: Thompson (1947), 114–15.

⁵⁶ See Chap. 6.

⁵⁷ Cf. *Frogs* 1068; Cratinus fr. 358, 'and if he were to have eaten a red mullet . . . of some glutton'; Strattis, *Lemnomedea* fr. 26, 'gulping down many large sea bream'; *Philoctetes* fr. 45, 'and then going to market they buy great fat sea bream and slices of soft round-sided Copaic [eels]'.

⁵⁸ e.g. Aristophanes, *Thesmophoriazusae* B fr. 333 and Pherecrates, *Slave-Teacher* fr. 50.

⁵⁹ A number of passages in Old Comedy concern the *nestis* or 'fasting grey mullet', one of the *kestreis* or grey mullets (see Athenaeus 7.306d–308d and Thompson (1947), 176 and 108–12): Ameipsias, *Apokottabizontes* fr. 1, 'I'm going to the agora to try and get a job. B: In that case you'd be less likely to follow me round like a fasting grey mullet'; Aristophanes, *Gerytades* fr. 159, 'is the colony of grey-mullet-men indoors? You know you are fasters'; Theopompus, *Luxury-Lover* fr. 14, 'and stand in line, my chorus of fasting grey mullets, entertained on greens like geese'. The fish appear to be for consumption at Archippus, *Heracles Gets Married* fr. 12, 'fasting grey mullets, *kephalos* grey mullets' and Plato, *Feasts* fr. 28, 'as I came out a fisherman met me with some fasting grey mullets, fish not fit for food and pretty poor in my view' (*kephalos* is another variety of grey mullet). Others concern the octopus (not for consumption?): Aristophanes, *Daedalus* frr. 195–197; Alcaeus, *Sisters Seduced* fr. 1; fr. 30; Eupolis, *Demes* fr. 117; Pherecrates, *Savages* fr. 14; (for consumption?): Ameipsias, *The Eater* fr. 6; Plato, *The Baby* fr. 100; Theopompus, *Aphrodite* fr. 6. A woman is threatened with being eaten by fish at Plato, *Cleophon* fr. 57, as is someone at Ameipsias, *Connus* fr. 8. Fish-cries: Archippus, *Fishes* fr. 16. Other issues seem to be the point in Plato, *Europa* fr. 44 and in some cases in n. 48–50 above.

Tagenistae, for example, may have fried a banquet of fish in their frying-pans. The *Flatterers* of Eupolis, which presented blackmailers attached to the powerful and wealthy Callias, is a more likely possibility for extensive feasting. Fr. 160, 'I have bought fish for only a hundred drachmas, eight sea bass and twelve gilthead', and fr. 174, 'by the side of this Callias much pleasure can be had—there are crayfish and rays and sea-hares and women of rolling gait', imply feasting and revelry which contrast with the parsimony of Callias' father who (fr. 156) 'was sparing before the war and bought cheap *trichides* only once, but when the troubles with Samos arose, meat for half an obol'. These and other plays of Old Comedy may conceivably have presented 'banquets of fish' that Athenaeus and Aelian failed to cite, just as Athenaeus omits details of the *Isthmionike* of Mnesimachus.

If we search for an explanation for the invasion of significant fish-consumption into Middle Comedy—as described in Chapter 6—differences in actual consumption, lower in Athens in, say, 420 BC than in 350 BC, are, for want of evidence from outside comedy, unverifiable and anyway unlikely. There may have been more fish in the seas off Syracuse than off Athens, but even if that were so, it does not explain what we find in Middle Comedy. We can at least make the case that the eating of fish which is to be found in Old Comedy, whether in the form of little snacks (*Knights* 662, *Acharnians* 665–75) or luxurious meals (*Wasps* 488–99, *Flatterers* frr. 160, 174) or lists, is less prominent than eating and feasting based on other products, in particular sacrificial and other animals and the products of the soil. Fish are, in fact, a potential comic resource, to be exploited later, along with the *mageiros* who also comes into his own in Middle Comedy. Changes in representation are likely to have been paramount, rather than changes in social practice. If we ask why fish was listed in profusion in the two plays of Epicharmus, explanations might include the importance of listing, the influence of the courts of kings and tyrants, and a comic tradition less tied to agriculture.

In a sense, in the fourth century Attic Comedy became more like her Sicilian sister, having earlier favoured communal festivity over the feasts of the privileged. Old Comedy may well have portrayed scenes of divine weddings in lost burlesque plays, but the plays that have survived suggest that the gods were starved rather than feasted (in *Birds* and *Wealth*), and there is no description to compare with the *Marriage of Hebe or The Muses* of Epicharmus, with its many varieties of fish.

The influence of Epicharmus on Attic Old Comedy could hardly have been direct, given the differences in date[60]—let alone on Middle Comedy—but whether by influence, direct or otherwise, or by coincidence, Attic comedy came to give a greater significance to fish and to the *mageiros*, who moved from the protagonist's sphere of operation to having one or more individual scenes in the guise of a full stock character. His materials changed to fish, which had not been the case in Old Comedy, where fish was consumed but the cooking of it a matter of little significance.[61] Three related developments played their part: the writing of texts on the cooking of fish, the impact of parody, and the invasion of hexameter verse by fish. If Epicharmus wrote his plays at too early a date to influence Old Comedy directly with his lists of fish for consumption and his *mageiros*, Sicily and other cities outside Athens played their part in writing recipe books and bringing food into hexameter parodies of Homer and Hesiod.[62]

Poetic influences too have a role to play. Little is known of the poetry of western Greece on fish, but small links can be made with Epicharmus. In *The Marriage of Hebe or The Muses* fr. 58 Epicharmus writes, 'and the sword-fish and the *chromis* which in the spring is, according to Ananius, the sweetest of all fish, and the *anthias* in winter'.[63] The fragment is preserved by Athenaeus at 7.282a–b, together with the corresponding passage of Ananius (fr. 5): 'Ananius says "in spring the *chromis* is best, and the *anthias*

[60] The dates of Epicharmus are not securely known. He may have written towards the end of the sixth century BC. Some fragments refer to events in the first quarter of the fifth century. Almost none of the fragments of Old Comedy date to this period.

[61] Though we have no evidence that there was no *mageiros* cooking the fish in, e.g. the *Flatterers* of Eupolis.

[62] We might add other Sicilian influences on Athens such as the impact of the rhetoric of Gorgias of Leontini and political appeals to Athens by some Sicilian cities in the 420s and later.

[63] The identification of the *anthias* was problematic for the sources of Athenaeus as he notes at 282d–e: see Thompson (1947), 14–16. Dorion identified it with, among others, the *kallionymos* which was discussed by Aelian in the passage cited above.

in winter, but of the fine *opsa* the prawn on a fig-leaf is best. Sweet too to eat is the meat of a nanny-goat in autumn and of a young pig to eat when men turn and tread the vintage . . .".' Over a century later Archestratus of Gela quoted Epicharmus in his hexameter version of the best lobster to eat in season.[64] Epicharmus also anticipated Archestratus in overtly identifying the name of a species in his verse (fr. 57.2), '*karabos* is the name' [of the crayfish]. In Attic Middle Comedy these interests came to Athens. The connecting link between Ananius, *The Marriage of Hebe or The Muses*, Archestratos, and the speech of a *mageiros* of Middle Comedy is a descriptive mode of narrative. *The Marriage of Hebe or The Muses* lacks the dramatic animation of much of Old Comedy, presenting instead narrative variations on names and species of fish and their taste.

7.4. THE *PHLYAX* VASES AND THE FISH-PLATES

The plays of Epicharmus demonstrate considerable sophistication in a number of technical features. We know less about his successors. Of Phormis almost nothing is known. Deinolochus appears to have been greatly influenced by tragedy, writing a *Komodotragoidia*, a *Medea*, *Telephus*, and two other plays, *Althaea* and *Amazons*. The first may have been wrongly attributed, while the tragic titles may have nothing in fact to do with tragedy. After Deinolochus we know of no dramatists until Rhinthon at the end of the fourth century. He is a writer of *phlyax* plays,[65] apparently inventing the form known as *hilarotragoidia*.

---

[64] Athenaeus quotes the two passages at 3.105a–b. His ostensible purpose is to show that the *astakos* of Archestratus is identical to the *karabos* of Epicharmus rather than to demonstrate the debt of Archestratus to Epicharmus. Epicharmus wrote (fr. 57), ἐντὶ δ' ἀστακοὶ κολύβδαιναί τε χὠς τὰ πόδι' ἔχει | μικρά, τὰς χεῖρας δὲ μακράς, κάραβος δὲ τοὔνομα ('There are lobsters and crabs and the creature that has little feet but long claws—crayfish is its name.'); and Archestratus (fr. 24.1–3), ἀλλὰ παρεὶς λῆρον πολὺν ἀστακὸν ὠνοῦ, | τὸν τὰς χεῖρας ἔχοντα μακρὰς ἄλλως δὲ βαρείας, | τοὺς δὲ πόδας μικρούς . . . ('But leave aside a lot of rubbish and buy the lobster, the one that has long claws that are also heavy, but little feet . . .')

[65] *Phlyax* is an Italian term for an actor in simple comedy or farce, according to Sosibius (*FGrH* 595 F 7 = Athenaeus 14.621f). The term is applied specifically to plays written by Rhinthon and others, and broadly to the Italian vase paintings that represent apparently comic scenes.

His plays almost certainly adapted Euripides, given the titles *Iphigenia at Aulis* and *Iphigenia Among the Taurians*, and he shows some metrical sophistication. A number of successors developed the form, not all in Sicily and southern Italy. Sopater of Paphos, for example, both a 'parodist' and 'writer of *phlyax*', put on plays in Alexandria in the third century and referred to Philoxenus in Sicily (fr. 22). The elements at work on these dramatists are local tradition, massive influence from Attic tragedy, and the local *phlyax* tradition, on which Athenaeus (14.621f) cites Sosibius. It is quite unclear how these elements fitted together and how this comic tradition related to the flourishing mimes of Sophron, Xenarchus, and others.

A further class of evidence comes into play between the works of Deinolochus, which date to the fifth century, and Rhinthon at the end of the fourth: the 200 to 300 *phlyax* vases whose masked characters reflect dramatic production. Given our concern with representations of fish, the hundreds of fish-plates painted in southern Italy in the fourth century also come into play here. Just as the dramatists are influenced by Attic tragedy, so the vase painters inherited both comic vases and decorated fish-plates from Athens. But they took that inheritance very much further, both in quantity and sophistication. It has long been recognized that, while the majority of *phlyax* vases represent local drama, a number, perhaps a significant number, reflect Attic comedies. The Athenian plays appear to have been incorporated cheerfully into local productions in theatres, in impromptu performances by travelling players, and in sympotic and related performances. Productions of local plays are not likely to have ceased in the large theatres such as those of Syracuse and Tarentum; it is much more probable that Attic comedy supplemented and enriched local forms. The vases attest feverish production and representation both of drama and of painted pottery. To an extent that is difficult for us to decipher, they supplement gaps in texts and written traditions, and they probably also reflect productions of types of play that do not derive from a tradition later preserved in texts, such as those of Epicharmus and Aristophanes.[66] Performances took place in many forms in many cities in many different

[66]   The textual base of Aristophanes requires no demonstration. The importance of the text in Epicharmus is demonstrated by his citation of Ananius and Aristoxenus and by the metrical interest shown by Hephaestion (see above).

contexts, not all of them local dramatic festivals such as the Attic Lenaea and Dionysia.

There appears to be a consistent interest in Attic tragedy from an early date. Hiero put on productions of Aeschylus, whom Epicharmus parodied; Deinolochus may have parodied Euripides, who was popular in Syracuse (see above). Tragedy was a major theme for the vase painters, both straight and in parodied form, while Rhinthon took parody some stages further. This level of activity marks a different use of tragedy in Sicily and southern Italy than in, say, Macedonia where, although Euripides and Agathon repaired to the court there—the former writing a play which incorporated the royal family—there was little if any local dramatic tradition onto which Attic tragedy could be grafted.

Tragedy and parody of tragedy are particularly prominent in Taplin's interpretation of the *phlyax* vases, rightly so, since his purpose is to demonstrate that the vases provide strong evidence that Attic comedy as well as tragedy was produced in Sicily. He argues for a level of sophistication in the vase paintings, whose visual representations of drama are often as clever as the representations of tragedy in Aristophanes. Both drama and vases operate at a high level, in his account.[67] A counterpoint to Taplin's analysis is offered by Bieber (1961). While she surveys tragic vases, her principal focus is on farce, on the extent to which performance in southern Italy before Atellan farce and Plautus anticipated those genres of the Roman Republican period. Thus, she identifies Epicharmus as a writer of 'mimes . . . travesty of mythology in some plays and travesty of daily life in others' (p. 129). Bieber uses the terms 'farce' and 'mime' loosely. I try where possible to keep separate Sicilian comedy, mime, *phlyakes*, *hilarotragoidia*, and Attic comedy, although I recognize both that there was likely to be much interplay between the genres and that representations of productions on vases cannot usually be assigned to a particular genre.

---

[67] Taplin attempts to show that Rhinthon introduced a new sophistication in about 300, implying thereby that sophisticated vases will tend to reflect Attic vases, but elements he attributes to Rhinthon (metre and adaptation of Euripides to an Italian format) are already clear in Epicharmus and Deinolochus. Nor is there any evidence that Epicharmus was merely of antiquarian interest in Sicily and southern Italy in the fourth century.

7.4.1. Comic Angels

Taplin (1993) selects some 100 from the 250 *phlyax* vases as being of interest theatrically, that is, depicting *specific* scenes as opposed to a general Dionysiac ambience. The inclusion of a stage is particularly important for this purpose (whereas the *phlyax* mask identifies all 250 vases), though Taplin's clearest example, a representation of Aristophanes' *Thesmophoriazusae*, does not include a stage.

The sophistication which Taplin argues for on southern Italian vases does not, in my opinion, depend solely on plays imported from Attica. Southern Italy had a lively tradition that welcomed Attic drama with open arms, whether performed in theatres or by travelling players, or—more likely—both. It cannot be argued from silence that some of Taplin's 100 relevant vases are not depicting indigenous dramas. Of Taplin's chosen vases, the 'Rio fish eater', the *obeliaphoroi*, and the 'Milan Cake-eaters' raise as many questions as they answer. It is not even the case necessarily that an Attic text on a vase (on the 'Milan Cake-eaters', for example) indicates an Attic play, though the case is stronger where iambic lines from a play are quoted, as on the vase of the 'New York Goose Play'. Taplin passes over the general Dionysiac content of many of the vases, but those themes form the content of much of Attic comedy, as we saw in Chapter 5, as does the interplay between comic and sympotic themes. His one exception before dismissing the Dionysiac vases is Dionysus looking at a female tumbler. But is she so different from some of the dancers in Aristophanes—at the end of *Wasps*, for example? Dionysiac themes on the vases may derive from Attic comedy, Sicilian comedy, and other forms of drama, or sympotic themes. Overall I believe there is much more varied dramatic activity in southern Italy than he allows, and that includes all the Attic influence that he adduces.

7.4.2. The Phlyax *Vases and Representations of Eating and Drinking*

Taplin has taken the argument that *phlyax* vase paintings reflect Italian productions of Athenian plays a good deal further.[68] It is possible to go too far in linking particular plays with vase

---

[68] I am not convinced that the vases are Italian representations of Attic plays put on in Athens—a possibility considered by Taplin (1987).

images, as Taplin and others have shown: few would see now the Sikon Painter's name vase as reflecting a production of the *Aeolosicon* of Aristophanes,[69] and Taplin doubts that an Apulian bell-crater[70] represents the *Dionysalexandros* of Cratinus. Some consideration of Trendall's 200 and more *phlyax* vases (1967) is instructive and relevant to our purpose. The vases fall into a number of categories: those reflecting performances of tragic and comic drama, the latter through the depiction of a stage, masks, and costumes in part or combination; and those related to the drama in various ways (apparently tragic scenes might be simply mythical, apparently comic scenes might be sympotic). Taplin has analysed how the vase painters negotiated the interrelation between the categories in ways that are analogous to intertextual references in the plays themselves. We are often not in a position to get the full impact. To take an example, on the Apulian bell-crater apparently illustrating the *obeliaphoroi*,[71] two male figures are carrying a spit holding either meat or a long loaf of bread. They are dressed in comic costume and masks and phalloi, and follow a female piper across a stage. A performance on a stage appears to be represented. Do the figures represent the chorus of Ephippus' Attic comedy *Obeliaphoroi*? Taplin points out (1993: 76) that they would be expected to wear identical masks if that were the case. Is this vase in fact a representation of an Attic vase (one of the few representing comedy) illustrating *obeliaphoroi*? That vase[72] is probably too early to represent Ephippus' play, nor does it represent either a stage or a female piper. The Apulian vase may have been painted as a tribute to or an improvement on the Athenian; it may have taken into account both the Athenian vase and the play of Ephippus; it may represent a south Italian play. The *obeliaphoroi* carried their bread in processions probably linked with Dionysus.[73] Is the god relevant here? He is certainly represented on many of the *phlyax* vases. Is it bread at all? If it is meat from a sacrifice, the possibilities extend

[69] As suggested by Trendall (1952).
[70] Trendall (1967), no. 23 = Berlin F 3047.
[71] Ibid., no. 34, St Petersburg, Hermitage Museum inv. 2074 (W. 1122), discussed by Taplin (1993), 73, 76, 113.
[72] Athens, Agora P23907, dating from the 390s = Trendall (1967), no. 12.
[73] Athenaeus 3.111b.

much further.[74] In short, we can see that one and possibly more aspects of eating, perhaps ceremonial eating, are represented in one or more forms of performance, with possible reference back to an Attic vase a decade or two older.

Multivalencies of this kind abound on the vases. To take another of Taplin's examples, an Apulian bell-crater represents a male and female figure, with a tray of food and a slave sneaking off with a flat-cake in his tunic. They are identified in Attic script as Philotimides, Charis, and Xanthias respectively.[75] A stage is represented. Part of the interest of the scene, as Bieber points out, lies in the contrast between the elegant names of the eaters (Man of Honour and Graceful Woman) and their grotesque masks (a *visual* joke), and in their absorption in their food while the slave escapes with a pilfered cake. On the reverse, Heracles holds up the earth in the place of Atlas while satyrs make off with his bow and club. No stage is represented on this side, which may indicate a satyr play performance. How do the two sides relate? To the common theme of theft? To comic and satyr plays put on at the same festival somewhere in Italy?[76] Many vases on the reverse have standard images, often two or three young men, or 'draped youths'. Some vases portray a *phlyax* actor and Dionysiac scene on the reverse, some a scene with Dionysus and a *phlyax* together. Do the Dionysiac scenes relate to dramatic or sympotic scenes? Do the satyrs stealing Heracles' bow constitute a 'Dionysiac scene'? For the combination of sympotic and dramatic, consider the banqueters with *kottabos* stand, masks hanging above them, Papposilenus under the table, and a Dionysiac scene on the reverse.[77] It is impossible to characterize these scenes as Attic or Italian in content, but Taplin (1993) should not lead us to characterize them all as inspired by Attic drama. Not even Attic script need necessarily indicate Attic subject-matter: either painter or patron may have opted for the Attic touch without suggesting that the play is Attic. Taplin (1993: 41–2) has a valuable discussion of Attic script on the vase he calls the 'New York Goose Play' (New York, Metropolitan

---

[74] Trendall noted the subject as 'off to the feast'.
[75] Trendall (1967), no. 45 = Milan, Moretti coll.
[76] So Dearden (1990).
[77] For examples of draped youths see Trendall (1989). The Papposilenus vase is Trendall (1967), no. 172 = Vatican AD 1 (inv. 17370).

Museum of Art, 24.9.104), and compares vases which portray Electra and name her, sometimes in Attic, sometimes in Doric script. Taplin is more confident than I am that the 'Goose Play' is Attic. Other vases are extremely difficult to interpret, like a Campanian bell-crater[78] which, with no stage portrayed, depicts a *phlyax* before an altar, a woman playing a pipe, and a second man sitting on a second altar and eating a fish.

The vast majority of the comic vases probably represent Sicilian or south Italian performances of some kind. The related scenes and sympotic scenes added by Trendall (1967) at the end of his list imply a certain tie-in with cultural life in the Italian cities. So the tuna-seller and his customer[79] appear not to be dramatic, since they wear no masks, phalloi, or costumes and do not stand on a stage. Nevertheless, Trendall notes their caricatured heads and suggests that an analogous vase of a woman watering a tuna, with a satyr standing nearby with a large knife may, in the person of the satyr, indicate a dramatic performance. Is this a representation of a mime such as Sophron's *The Tuna-Hunter*? Or of a comedy, given the genre's known interest in buying and selling and in fish? Even less certainty is possible in this case than with the *obeliaphoroi* vase, but there is a similar play between representations of everyday life and representations of representations, whether artistic or dramatic or drama-related. Everyday life, in the form of fishmongers and butchers, is a very rare subject for vase painters in this period.[80] In other respects, however, as Taplin points out, the *phlyax* vases abound with items from everyday life, baskets, sticks, food, altars, and so on: here the vase painters share comedy's interest in material objects.[81]

7.4.3. The South Italian Fish-Plates

Nearly all the *phlyax* vases are mixing-bowls and cups designed for the symposium. Only two in Trendall's catalogue are plates. We noted in Chapter 1 that plates are comparatively rare in both ancient texts and archaeological finds. The exception is fish-plates, some thousand of which are catalogued in McPhee and Trendall (1987). These plates appear to derive from 'Gallatin'

---

[78] Trendall (1967), no. 56 = Rio de Janeiro, Museu Nacional 1500.
[79] Ibid., no. 191, Cefalù 2.   [80] Cf. Sparkes (1962), n. 6.
[81] Taplin (1993), 34, 36; Neiiendam (1992), 56.

plates, normally painted in black glaze with decoration in Athens in the late sixth and early fifth centuries; in design they are concave with a central depression, an overhanging border, and a stand. In rare cases a small vessel, possibly an *oxybaphon*, has been found nearby which may have been used for holding seasonings for the fish.[82] Fish-plates proper were made in Athens early in the fourth century, most of them, apparently, for export to northern Italy and the Crimean Bosporus, though some have been found in the Athenian agora, some at Olynthus and at various other sites. Production appears to have begun in Sicily at about the same time, possibly influenced by Attic potters and painters, possibly by related Carthaginian ware,[83] and to have moved to Campania and Apulia later. Fewer than 200 Attic plates survive, compared with over 800 south Italian. Why were fish-plates so popular in southern Italy in the fourth century? The answer is beyond the scope of this book, but certain aspects are germane here.[84] Painters of the fish-plates can be linked with workshops producing other painted vases in the region; there are links too between fish-plates and bands of fish used as decoration on Apulian craters.[85]

While fish were considered suitable decoration on some mixing-bowls at the symposium, they were also considered suitable decoration for plates at the *deipnon*—if the plates were made for eating fish at dinner. Since many were found in tombs, some scholars have suggested that they were funerary ware, the fish representing in some form life after death or the journey of the soul after death. The argument has been used of the early Attic plates which incorporate the myth of Europa and the bull, and of a plate

---

[82] See McPhee and Trendall (1987), 22, 56, 63; Kunisch (1989), 49–61. Pollux 6.85 lists the *oxybaphon* under 'pots for seasonings', while at the same time noting its use for the *kottabos* game (cf. also 10.67 and 10.86). The *oxybaphon* appears to be a small shallow dish like a saucer (*Birds* 361), and may occasionally have been applied to a fish-plate itself—apparently at least in a graffito from Olynthus.

[83] There is no certain link with either. See McPhee and Trendall (1987), 18, 59–64; Kunisch (1989), 39–43.

[84] For fish in Greek art see Kunisch (1989), 64–140.

[85] McPhee and Trendall (1987), 54 link some Apulian plates with the workshops of the Darius and Baltimore Painters, some Paestan with the workshop of Asteas and Python (104–5).

which was found in the necropolis at Palermo with fishbones still lying on it. Others, however, have been found in a domestic setting—for example, two Attic plates at Olynthus—and since so many provenances are not known, certainty in this area is not possible. My limited observations are three. The Sicilians and south Italians represented fish extensively in various forms, which included accurate drawing of fish, sophisticated reflections of bodies in water, caricature, and playful design (fish leaping and a human face on a torpedo, for example).[86] Unless the plates were exclusively for funerary use—which neither McPhee and Trendall (1987) nor Kunisch (1989) believe—diners in the cities of Sicily and southern Italy had many representations of fish around them, presumably for use at *deipna*, just as for symposia they had representations of wine and the power of Dionysus.[87] I would draw an analogy with the *Marriage of Hebe or The Muses* of Epicharmus, in which fish are presented both as food for consumption and as guests at a feast—in a similarly multifaceted role. Both in Epicharmus and on the fish-plates, a wide range of fish are portrayed. The fish are not always easy to identify, but appear to include varieties of bream, wrasse, and perch, grey mullet and red mullet, gurnard, bass, angler-fish, some of the *sciaenidae* (the family which includes meagres), swordfish, flatfish, dogfish, the major cephalopods, and such shellfish as mussels, prawns, and the hornshell.[88] Secondly, McPhee and Trendall (1987: 59) have noted the stylistic similarity in the treatment of fish between the six oldest Sicilian plates and the 'Tuna-seller' bell-crater from Lipari, which, as we noted above, portrays the tuna-seller in a caricature analogous to the *phlyax* vases.[89] Thirdly, the oldest 'fish-plate', in fact the lid of a pyxis, portrays Nereids and sea-horses. Later plates too portray nonedible creatures such as sea-horses, Tritons, and dolphins, suggesting that it is the wealth and exoticism of the sea that is

---

[86] Ibid. 71, 75, 78; Davidson (1997), pl. 1.

[87] For artistic manipulations on the fish-plates see Kunisch (1989), 94–140 and cf. Lissarrague (1990).

[88] There are regional variations, scorpion-fish mainly in Athenian, more dogfish, flatfish, and cuttlefish in Apulian. The Italian plates illustrate more species than the Attic.

[89] The tuna-seller has chopped up the body of the tuna: on the fish-plates the fish are alive and their bodies intact.

portrayed as much as the fish on the plate of the diner.[90] Again, the artists appear to represent fish in ways analogous to Epicharmus.[91] His fr. 115, possibly from the *Pyrrha or Prometheus*, mentions 'the fine sea-horse-son of Poseidon'. The fish-plates, in short, reflect a culture in which the representation of fish in visual images and in comic verse was sophisticated and (given the surviving fragments of both pottery and comedy) extensive, at least in pottery. The evidence suggests that we should attribute this to local inspiration much more than to Attic painters or Attic comedy.

7.4.4. Phlyax *Vases and Fish-Plates*

The production of these forms of painted pottery in Sicily and southern Italy is dateable to the fourth century BC, specifically to the period in which no comedy has survived from the region. This appears to support Taplin's argument that much, if not all, the inspiration for comic scenes on south Italian vases came from productions of Attic comedy. It seems to me much safer to say that *some* inspiration did indeed come from Attic productions, whether performed in the region (as I believe) or in Athens itself. It is, after all, a dangerous argument from silence to suppose that indigenous comedy had died out. Comedy first appeared in Sicily, mime was popular here, comedies are attested for the early third century, and Plautus and Terence follow in Rome. All these forms attest Attic influence of some kind, as do, possibly, all the styles of vase painting, though the fish-plates are less certain. At the same time, all these forms display local development of Attic influence. I would prefer to modify Taplin's case and claim that, in these flourishing cities, artists bent on portraying comedy used the productions of the region, modified—perhaps greatly, perhaps less so—by Attic production. It is not, in my view, likely that comedy and mime in Sicily and southern Italy were confined to the texts and authors who have chanced to survive, or indeed to productions that used a text at all. As for the portrayal of fish, the painters, whether *phlyax* or the painter of the Lipari

[90] Kunisch (1989), 71–7.

[91] Cf. Nereids, seahorses and Tritons on the early Attic plates portraying Europa (McPhee and Trendall (1987), 28–9) and in Attic Middle Comedy Nereus as the *protos heuretes* of fish-eating (Anaxandrides, *Nereus* fr. 31, quoted p. 18).

tuna-seller or fish-plate painters from the great workshops and elsewhere, painted the fish that they saw all around them. Some of these probably came straight from the sea, some were artistic impressions, some were highly stylized. But the tuna-seller's tuna, like the parodic verses of Archestratus, probably came from somewhere between 'real life' and comedy. Archestratus, furthermore, provides a possible analogy. He draws on Epicharmus to a limited extent; he is cited in Attic comedy; but the interplay between his verses and contemporary comedy is difficult to identify.

There are no fish-plates in the surviving verses of Archestratus, and the only *oxybaphon* mentioned is a dish for appetizers (fr. 6), perhaps similar to the dishes called *embaphia* in Epicharmus fr. 70. It is to Attic comedy that we must look for the best surviving comment on a fish-plate. At Anaxandrides, *Odysseus* fr. 34.1–4 a fisherman says: 'the fine handiwork of artists is admired hanging up on *pinakes*, but mine is solemnly snatched up from the stewing-pot and instantly disappears from the frying-pan.' The term *pinax* is applicable to both painted panel and plate, and it is possible that Ananandrides' character puns on the two meanings.

7.5. ATTIC COMEDY AND THE COOKERY BOOK

While comedy and related forms of performance in Sicily and southern Italy were influenced by Athenian drama, so Attic comedy itself was subject to outside forces. This came about broadly for two reasons: comedy's continuing tendency to reflect all kinds of poetry, and cultural influences in Athens that promoted a change in the form of Attic comedy. Whether or not 'Middle Comedy' existed as a distinct form, Old Comedy transformed itself into New during the fourth century. For present purposes the term 'Middle Comedy' will be retained.[92] Early in the fourth century the representation of food in Old Comedy came under new influences from outside Athens, some from the Aegean—the parodies of Hegemon of Thasos and Matro of Pitane—but the majority from the West: the dithyrambs of

[92] On Middle Comedy see Webster (1953), Arnott (1972) and (forthcoming), Hunter (1985), Nesselrath (1990), Sidwell (forthcoming), and Handley (1985).

Philoxenos of Cythera, the cookery book of Mithaecus of Sicily or Syracuse (in prose), and the parody of Archestratus of Gela, together with other non-literary influences which I discussed in Chapter 6, the rich dishes of *kandaulos* and *karyke* from Lydia and the *mattye* of northern Greece. *Karyke* had been known to fifth-century comedy,[93] but was used—as far as we know—only as a metaphor and thus resembled other features of Old Comedy such as the stock characters of the *mageiros* and parasite, who had remained as potential comic material which was not to be exploited in Athens until the fourth century.

At the end of his life Aristophanes wrote two plays, *Aeolosicon* and *Cocalus*, which I mentioned above. At least one later scholar saw the former as a turning-point in the history of comedy: Platonius comments, 'it was the aim of Old Comedy to mock[94] the demagogues and jurors and generals. Aristophanes abandoned his customary mockery in great fear, and lampooned[95] *Aeolus*, the play written by tragic poets, alleging it was a bad play. Such then is the form of the Middle Comedy, of which examples are *Aeolosicon* and the *Odysseuses* of Cratinus[96] and many of the old plays which lack *stasima* and *parabaseis*.' Platonius appears to give tragic parody a new function, which had not been required, for example, in *Acharnians* and *Peace*, that of politically neutral material. It may be mere coincidence that both plays are set in the West.

A little earlier, Plato the comic poet[97] parodied 'the cookery book of Philoxenus'—the first time that a cookery book was lampooned in surviving Greek drama. Comedy had earlier parodied scenes of eating—the meal of Thyestes in the *Proagon* of Aristophanes, for example; the new development is a parody of a text devoted to cooking. Plato, *Phaon* fr. 189:[98]

---

[93] *Knights* 343.   [94] σκώπτειν.   [95] διασύρει.

[96] This play almost certainly dates to the 420s and its distance from the *Aeolosicon* of the 380s demonstrates the long period during which Attic comedy underwent significant change from 'Old' to 'Middle'. This is only one of a number of reasons which should prevent us from identifying too readily features that belong to 'Old' or 'Middle'. Rather, as I have done above, we should allow for potential features in 'Old' to await later 'Old' or 'Middle' for their full exploitation.

[97] His *Phaon* was written in 391, according to the scholiast on *Wealth* 179.

[98] Quoted as it appears in Athenaeus 1.5b–d.

A: Here in this lonely place I want to run through this little book to myself.

B: What is this work? Please tell me.

A: It is a new cookery book by Philoxenus.

B: Show me what it's like.

A: Then listen. 'I will start with the tassel hyacinth and finish with the tuna.'

B: With the tuna? It's the best thing to be placed there in the last rank.

A: 'Tassel hyacinths. Smother them in ashes, moisten with sauce, and eat as many as you can, for they make a man erect. So much for that. I will turn now to the children of the sea.'

[Then a little later he goes on:]

'A cooking-pot is not bad, but I think the frying-pan is better.'

[And a little later:]

'the perch, the speckled fish, the even-toothed dentex, and the jag-toothed dog-shark you should not cut up, for fear that the nemesis of the gods should blow down upon you. Bake them whole and serve. That is much the better way. The twisting octopus, if you beat it as necessary, is better boiled than roasted—if it is a large one. If, however, there are two baked, to hell with the boiled one I say. The red mullet does not wish to be a lover of the real man because she is daughter of Artemis the virgin and hates erections. Now the scorpion-fish . . .'

B: . . . can sneak up and strike your bum.

The parody appears at the outset to be in alphabetical format, though that order is abandoned[99] in favour of something like the order of a standard meal, appetizers such as tassel hyacinths followed by fish. The lonely place is presumably a location outside the city for quiet reflection or rehearsal of an important statement, often concerning love.[100] The speaker is reading 'Philoxenus', not, apparently, for its advice on cooking but with a view to its amorous applications, which coincides with the sexual content of the other main fragment of Plato's *Phaon* (fr. 188, quoted in Chapter 3). It is not clear from the fragment in which Philoxenus is under review whether the cookery book is itself a novelty or simply the latest product of the writer, and what form

[99] Citation in alphabetical order was used in the glossary of Zenodotus at the end of the fourth century and, much later, Athenaeus has it, for example, in his list of fish in Book 7. Elsewhere, the *Grammatical Tragedy* of Callias, an apparently parodic text, may be a dramatic parallel (Athenaeus 10.453c–f).

[100] Kassel–Austin (1989) compare Menander, *Samia* 94–5, 121–2, and Terence, *Andria* 406.

of instruction was given in the original (if there was one). The cooking of tassel hyacinths follows ancient practice, but the advice for fish concentrates almost entirely on the gods and aphrodisiacs at the expense of cooking. Cookery books are a novelty at this date; probably originating in Sicily,[101] they have come into comedy very quickly. All that survives of the genre is the odd sentence from the book of Mithaecus that Plato mentions in *Gorgias* (518b) and Athenaeus cites three times, twice for its treatment of fish and once for its recipe for the rich sauce *karyke*.[102] Plato's parodic cookery book is the only early example written in hexameters—no cookery books of that kind are known as early as 391, though they are a few decades later, at least in the *Life of Luxury* of Archestratus of Gela.What is known is the *Deipnon* of Philoxenus, the dithyrambic poem quoted in Chapter 6, which according to Athenaeus (1.5b), is the work parodied.[103] If Athenaeus is right, Plato converted the lyric, which elsewhere is strongly mocked, into the hexameter or 'parodic' genre. The earliest comic reference to a poem about food is, as we have seen, Epicharmus fr. 58, on Ananius, but Epicharmus' interest appears to have been in content, not, as here, in form.

Plato's adoption of a dithyrambic poem on food (if that is what he has done) was a novelty, but comic adaptation of dithyramb itself was not. The genre had long been fruitful territory for mockery in comic verse, as is exemplified in the *Clouds* and *Birds* of Aristophanes.[104] Novelty in dithyramb is the topic of Pherecrates, *Cheiron* fr. 155, and it is likely[105] that Philoxenus is the crowning example at the end of that list of terrible writers of

[101] It is possible that this cookery book of Philoxenus is being read in Sicily: in [Ovid], *Epistula Sapphus ad Phaonem* Phaon has travelled to the island. Knox (1995) on line 12 notes, however, that the *Epistula* is the first known evidence for Phaon's journey to Sicily.

[102] On the cultural background to the cookery book of Mithaecus see Wilkins and Hill (1996); on Mithaecus in Athenaeus (7.282a, 325a, 12.516c), Wilkins and Hill (1995), 431–2, and on the surviving fragments Dalby (1995), 109–10.

[103] Athenaeus may have found this information in the ὀψαρτυτικαὶ λέξεις (*Cookery Lexicon*) of Artemidorus of Tarsus whom he mentions immediately before citing Plato fr. 189.

[104] *Clouds* 335 is ascribed to Philoxenus, wrongly (see *PMG*). Aristophanes referred to some form of song that Philoxenus had introduced into cyclic choruses in fr. 953.

[105] The text of Plutarch is not absolutely clear on this point.

dithyramb.[106] Where Old Comedy mocked dithyrambic language overtly, it was the way of Middle Comedy to absorb dithyrambic language into itself,[107] sometimes in festive contexts.[108] Aristophanes seems to have incorporated some dithyrambic elements into his feast at the end of *Ecclesiazusae* (1164–83). It is all the more surprising, therefore, that Plato should have converted Philoxenus' lyric into hexameters—if that is what he has done.

At the beginning of the fourth century, then, Plato parodied 'a cookery book of Philoxenus'—by which we are apparently to understand a poem about a banquet—while Aristophanes parodied the *Cyclops or Galatea* of Philoxenus of Cythera in the parodos of *Wealth*. The *Cyclops or Galatea*, along with *The Genealogy of the Aeacidae*, *Comast*, *Mysians*, *Syrus*, and *The Wedding* are the known poems of Philoxenus of Cythera. Of these, the most influential appears to have been the *Cyclops or Galatea*, which is said to be a mythologized version of Philoxenus' relations with Dionysius I of Syracuse and his mistress. Uncertainty surrounds the author of the further dithyramb *Deipnon*—a poem of great significance for the present study— despite the clear statement in the epitome of Athenaeus (1.5b) that the *Deipnon* of Philoxenus *of Leucas* was the 'cookery book' parodied by Plato in *Phaon*. Later citations by Athenaeus suggest that the *Deipnon* was in fact written by Philoxenus of Cythera. If there was only one dithyrambic poet called Philoxenus, as Gulick, Webster, and Dalby believe, then both the *Cyclops or Galateia* and the *Deipnon* were linked to the court of Dionysius I of Syracuse.[109] The confusion is compounded by a series of comments on various Philoxeni by scholars of the fourth and third

---

[106] See Kassel–Austin (1989); B. Zimmermann, *Dithyrambos* (Göttingen, 1992), 122; Dobrov and Urios-Aparisi (1995).

[107] Nesselrath (1990), 241–66.

[108] See Handley (1965) on Menander, *Dyskolos* 946–53; Hunter (1983) on Eubulus fr. 75.

[109] Dalby (1995), 114–16, 246; Bilabel, *RE* 11 (1922), 941—the latter followed by Page, *PMG*. In most of his citations from the *Deipnon* Athenaeus attributes the poem to Philoxenus of Cythera (4.146f, 11.476e, 14.642f, 11.643d) or to Philoxenus *tout court* (9.409e, 11.487a, 15.685d); only in the Eptiome (which has many citations and complexities of attribution stripped out) is Philoxenus of Leucas credited in the context of the parody in Plato's *Phaon*, while at 4.146f Athenaeus explicitly casts doubt on the latter identification.

centuries BC.[110] Much of the evidence is anecdotal and links the author of the *Cyclops or Galatea* with the court of Dionysius I of Syracuse.[111] One or more Philoxeni were in the entourage of the tyrant and were implicated in two activities of great interest to comic poets, an affair with a *hetaera* (the mistress of Dionysius) and the consumption of foods—fish in particular. The earliest authority is Aristotle, who called Philoxenus a 'lover of dinners'.[112] Phainias of Eresus[113] explains the poem as a mythologized version of the love affair between Philoxenus and Galatea, with Dionysius playing the role of tyrant. In this account, both Dionysius and Philoxenus negotiate a mutual desire to eat a large mullet. Early in the third century Hermesianax, in his elegy on the love affairs of poets,[114] links Philoxenus of Cythera with Galatea and Ortygia.[115] Chrysippus[116] records Philoxenus' desire to eat food very hot and on his own,[117] while Clearchus[118] presents Philoxenus the *opsophagos*: he took selected flavourings to houses in his own and other cities in order to spice up the food; he ate greedily and, in Ephesus,[119] finding all the *opsa* for sale had been sold to a wedding party, he went uninvited to the celebrations and after the dinner sang his dithyramb *The Wedding*.[120] Clearchus cites the opening words of the poem in the form of a

[110] Most of them cited by Athenaeus immediately after Plato, *Phaon* fr. 189 at 1.5d–7a.

[111] For a bibliography of the following anecdotes see Arnott (1996), 139–41.

[112] Fr. 83 (Rose). Athenaeus continues (1.6d), '[Aristotle] also, I think, wrote "men make popular speeches to crowds, spending whole days in tales of wonder (*thaumasi*), and address those who have sailed down from the rivers Phasis and Borysthenes, having read nothing except possibly the *Deipnon* of Philoxenus, and only part of that"'.

[113] Quoted by Athenaeus at 1.6e–7a = fr. 13 Wehrli = *PMG* 816. Duris of Samos has Philoxenus of Cythera basing his poem on a shrine of the nymph Galatea which he saw near Etna (*PMG* 817 = *FGrH* 76).

[114] Fr. 7 Powell, quoted by Athenaeus at 13.598e.

[115] Not Syracusan Ortygia but Ortygia the grove near Ephesus where, according to the *Suda* (under the entry 'Philoxenus'; cf. Strabo 14.1.20), Philoxenus died. It is difficult not to see this reference to a name redolent of Syracuse as poetic artifice, since the reader first thinks of Philoxenus in Syracusan Ortygia, only to be forced to correct him/herself. A similar effect is to be found in Archestratus' reference to the River Selinus—not the Sicilian river but the Ephesian.

[116] Fr. 10 (*SVF* III, 200) = Athenaeus 1.5d–e.

[117] See Chap. 2.   [118] Fr. 57 Wehrli = Athenaeus 1.6a.

[119] Where he died? Cf. n. 115.   [120] *PMG* 828.

standard scholarly citation,[121] while the anecdotal material identifies the poet according to the topoi of glutton and parasite that
were analysed in Chapter 2. Clearchus compares the gluttony of
Philoxenus with that of Melanthius the tragic poet, one of the
targets of comic abuse in the *Peace* of Aristophanes.[122] Philoxenus
was further satirized in the third century by Theophilus (so
unnatural was he that he envied the neck of a crane, the neck
being identified as the seat of taste-buds),[123] and in the sub-comic
Chreiae of Machon (64–90 Gow), in which a long neck is again
sought and the pleasure of eating an octopus exceeds his concern
for his own mortality. Of these anecdotes, those of Phainias,
Duris, Hermesianax, and Clearchus refer to Philoxenus of
Cythera, those of Aristotle, Chrysippus, Theophilus, and
Machon to an unidentified Philoxenus (Theophilus identifies a
Philoxenus son of Eryxis, who may or may not be Philoxenus of
Leucas).[124]

It is not easy to see how the Philoxeni are to be disentangled
from each other given their similar areas of interest, their use of
an identical poetic form, their contemporaneity and the similar
place they share in the discourse of luxury. Maas[125] distinguishes
Philoxenus of Cythera, of Leucas, and Philoxenus the parasite,
but Clearchus clearly identifies Philoxenus of Cythera as a 'parasite'.[126] Dalby and others may well be correct in identifying
Philoxenus of Cythera as the author of the *Deipnon*, on the basis
of attestations of the fragments in Athenaeus; Maas and others
counter with the significant but somewhat subjective criteria of
metrical tedium and poor style in the *Deipnon*. Dalby's further
contention, that only the court of Dionysius could have parallelled

---

[121] οὗ ἡ ἀρχὴ Γάμε θεῶν λαμπρότατε ('The opening words of the poem are "O Marriage, brightest of the gods".')

[122] See Chap. 3.

[123] Athenaeus 1.6b. On the 'unnatural' desires of the glutton see Chap. 6.

[124] Further biographical anecdotes in the *Suda* and the Aristophanic scholia
describe Philoxenus of Cythera as enslaved by the Athenians with his compat-
riots in 424 and sold in Athens, where he was later taught by the dithyrambic
poet Melanippides before his trip to Syracuse. Whatever the reliability of the
detail, the biographer seeks to link the poet with Athens (as well as Syracuse).

[125] *RE* xx, 1 (1941) 192–3.

[126] Dalby (1995) likewise goes too far in distinguishing Philoxenus of Cythera
the poet from Philoxenus of Leucas the glutton: the anecdotes do not support
that division.

the scale of the feast in the *Deipnon*, begs several questions.[127] A number of points can, however, be made with confidence. Philoxenus or the Philoxeni with the dithyrambs *Cyclops or Galatea* and *Deipnon* made an impact with their content and style on Athenian and other comedy;[128] anecdotes attached to the dithyrambist(s) demonstrate the cross-fertilization of themes belonging to the discourse of luxury between prose authors of the fourth century and comedy and related genres.[129] The dithyrambist(s) was/were linked with the court of Dionysius I (himself allegedly a poet as well as a tyrant, and earning comic comment accordingly),[130] and provide an entrée into Athenian comedy for themes linked with tyrants which were to reappear during the Macedonian rule of Athens. While the identity of the work parodied in *Phaon* fr. 189 eludes us (a hexameter poem, a prose cookery book by a Philoxenus,[131] or the *Deipnon* of Philoxenus of Cythera or someone else), Plato's linking of cookery—largely fish-cookery—with sex places the fragment firmly in the discourse of luxury and appetite. His choice of hexameters has great significance. The only cookery book known from this period is the prose work of Mithaecus: we do not know whether a cookery book had been written in Hesiodic hexameters as early as the 390s, but such a book was written by Archestratus of Gela thirty years later—*The Hedypatheia* (*Life of Luxury*). Athenaeus[132] calls Archestratus 'the Hesiod or Theognis of *opson*-eaters', and the Hesiodic style of Plato fr. 189 has been

---

[127] He compares the phrase πλήρωσαν οἶκον ('they filled the house') in 836(b)2 with the description by Satyrus of the court of Dionysius (Athenaeus 12.541c) in which 'thirty-couch rooms' were 'filled with men feasting', but the possibly coincidental imitation of the verb πληροῦν is insufficient to identify the poem with the tyrant's palace. There is nothing in the *Deipnon* to suggest that there were any more than, say, ten diners, and we have no reason to think that meals with ten or even twenty diners were not on occasion held in Athens and Greek cities other than Syracuse.

[128] On Sopater fr. 23 see below.

[129] To the *Chreiae* of Machon we might add the *Characters* of Theophrastus. The prose authors cited above have a number of objectives in common with such historians as Theopompus and Heracleides of Pontus who were examined in Chap. 6.

[130] See Hunter (1983) on the *Dionysius* of Eubulus.

[131] Possibly not even by one of the Philoxeni if 'Philoxenus' had become a byword for an interest in food or writing about food.

[132] 7.310a.

noted.[133] There is no prima facie reason to suppose that Archestratus invented the cookery book in Hesiodic mode—even Athenaeus does not claim as much, for all his heralding the influence of Archestratus at the beginning of the *Deipnosophistae*.[134] There are some close similarities in advice and expression between *Phaon* fr. 189 and Archestratus: unless we date the latter to before 391,[135] then either Archestratus has imitated Plato's parody or a common hexameter source has been imitated by both of them.[136] Brandt[137] has shown that there is good reason to suppose that Plato and Archestratus drew on a hexameter source,[138] perhaps, Brandt argues, the object of Archestratus' dissent in fr. 62.12. It is impossible to say where this hypothetical poem originated,[139] but the literature on cookery that we do know about, Mithaecus in prose and Archestratus in hexameters, appears to be a Sicilian contribution to Greek literature, and a category on which Athenian comedy readily commented. If the version in Plato fr. 189 derives from a hexameter poem, adaptation of the original (the possible addition of aphrodisiacs, which suited the amorous subject of the play) was clearly much less radical than

---

[133] Dalby (1995), 116–18, notes the Hesiodic language and gnomic and didactic style of *Phaon* fr. 189.

[134] 1.4e. Other writers of works on food, including the details of Philoxenos, follow at 1.5a–b.

[135] Dalby (1995) gives reasons why we should not.

[136] Cf. 189.15 μή σοι νέμεσις θεόθεν καταπνεύσηι ('for fear that nemesis from the gods blows upon you') and Archestratus fr. 15.3–4 μή σοι νέμεσις καταπνεύσηι . . . ἀπ' ἀθανάτων ('for fear that nemesis blows upon you from the immortals'), 189.16 ὅλον ὀπτήσας παράθες ('bake whole and serve'), and Archestratus fr. 12.4 (identical); at fr. 38.3 Archestratus uses a version of the colloquial expression κλαίειν ἀγορεύω ('I bid you to weep' = 'go to hell') common in comedy and found in 189.19, and both poems share the expression 'children of the sea' (189.11; fr. 49.3).

[137] (1888), 125–7, after Meineke and Ribbeck. Olson and Sens (forthcoming) concur. On the relationship between comedy and gastronomic poetry see also Dalby (1995), 113–19.

[138] 'Terpsion', the supposed master of Archestratus, appears an unlikely candidate—even if he existed. On his *Gastrology* Athenaeus (8.337a–b) preserves only the iambic jingle ἢ κρῆ χελώνης δεῖ φαγεῖν ἢ μὴ φαγεῖν, well translated by Gulick '"Tis meet to eat or not to eat the tortoise meat'. Both Plato in fr. 189 and Archestratus concern themselves with 'normal' foods rather than the unusual tortoise and do not sacrifice instruction to clever rhyme.

[139] Though Plato fr. 189 with its attribution to the *Opsartysia* of Philoxenus does not imply Athens.

was adaptation of the *Deipnon* of Philoxenus from descriptive lyric into didactic poetry.

7.6. THE *DEIPNON* OF PHILOXENUS

The *Deipnon*, which is unusual as a dithyramb and has been viewed with suspicion by historians of the genre,[140] was written in the Doric dialect in the period between the comedies of Epicharmus and Attic Old Comedy on the one hand and 'Middle Comedy' on the other. It signals important developments,[141] not least since the dithyrambic form allows exuberant expression and elaboration. While the debt of Philoxenus to Epicharmus and Old Comedy is important, the *Deipnon* first deserves comparison with the advice of Xenophanes[142] for a well-ordered *deipnon* and symposium, since his elegy, a complete and self-contained description of the meal unlike anything in surviving Old Comedy, provides a model for Philoxenus. As we saw in Chapter 6, Xenophanes counsels restraint governed by ritual. The floor should be clean, along with the hands of the symposiasts and the drinking-cups; garlands are distributed; the crater expresses the good spirit of the feast; there is pure water and an altar and libations and hymns to the gods in pure words. Philoxenus has no interest in purity and piety, but his version shares features with the elegy in addition to providing a full description of the occasion. Hands are washed and garlands provided;[143] there are numerous attendants;[144] as far as we know, no *hetaerae*

---

[140] Sutton (1989), 70–3; Zimmermann (1989), 143–4.

[141] The text unfortunately is badly damaged in several places. I give an English version in Chap. 6. Dalby (1987) translated the poem with annotations.

[142] Fr. 1 West=Athenaeus 11.426c–f. For an English version see Chap. 6.

[143] There is no mention of these rituals in some comparable descriptions of banquets from the fourth century, such as Matro's *Attic Dinner*, the meal of Caranos in Hippolochus, or the wedding of Iphicrates in the *Protesilaus* of Anaxandrides.

[144] Xenophanes: πλεκτοὺς δ' ἀμφιτιθεῖ στεφάνους, ἄλλος δ' εὐῶδες μύρον ἐν φιάληι παρατείνει· . . . ἄλλος δ' οἶνος ἕτοιμος ('[a slave] places woven garlands on [their heads] and another lays out sweet-smelling perfume in a dish . . . Other wine is at hand'). Philoxenus: εἰς δ' ἔφερον διπλόοι παῖδες λιπαρῶπα τράπεζαν ἄμμι, ἑτέραν δ' ἑτέροις, ἄλλοι δ' ἑτέραν ('Two slaves brought in a gleaming table for us and another one for other guests. Other [slaves] another [table].')

are present.[145] In other respects Philoxenus is far from Xeno-phanes: his mode is narrative rather than prescriptive; the luxury of the setting[146] and the innovations of the cook's art offer pleasure and beguile the soul;[147] there is far more interest in describing foods than sympotic ritual; the casseroles and various dishes are said to be self-motivated.[148] Many of the foods, in particular the fish, are enormous, the ray the size of a shield,[149] a whole mullet the size of the table,[150] a huge slice of tuna with belly slices added, a whole boiled head [of pig?]. This is food for display, for demonstrating wealth in the size and variety of the foods rather than in the refinement sought in Archestratus.[151] Philoxenus introduces the textures of foods such as eels and parts of animals[152] and describes high-quality white barley[153]—these imply an approach to food as it is to be eaten and enjoyed as well as a vehicle for poetic elaboration. Overall, though, elaboration predominates, particularly in descriptions of breads and cakes.[154] In the first part of Philoxenus' meal,[155] where the expensive and high-status dishes of fish and meat are listed, three lines (17–19) are devoted to breads, the last of which, *phystai* or puff pastries,[156] are said to form the 'navel of the feast'.[157] For the 'second tables',[158] six lines (5–10) are devoted to an elaborately wrought meal cake, and a further ten (12–21) to more cakes (including another meal cake), which include a number of polysyllabic

---

[145] I am indebted to David Harvey for this observation.

[146] Lamps and tables are singled out at *PMG* 836(b) 1–5.

[147] [τράπεζαι] χλιδῶσαι παντοδαποῖσι τέχνας εὑρήμασι πρὸς βιοτάν, ψυχᾶς δελεασματίοισιν ('[Tables] luxuriating in every kind of technical inventiveness for living, in temptations for the soul').

[148] Cf. the automated food in the utopian fragments, *Acharnians*, and *Peace*, cited in Chap. 3.

[149] Cf. Archestratus fr. 13, the *skaros* has a body 'resembling a circling shield'.

[150] Matro's conger eel 'lay over nine tables'.

[151] Refinement in cooking and presentation, that is: see Wilkins and Hill (1994), 22–3.

[152] And softness: note compounds of ἁπαλός at 836 (b) 13 and 38 and (e) 21.

[153] Cf. Wilkins and Hill (1994), 40–1 on Archestratus fr. 4 and Arnott (1996), 425 on Alexis, *Mandragorazomene* fr. 145.

[154] See Chap. 6 for Philoxenus on cakes.

[155] *PMG* 836a–b.

[156] In some preparation that is obscured by textual corruption.

[157] There are more breads at lines 6 and 37.   [158] *PMG* 836(e).

creations.[159] The emphasis on cakes is striking and probably linked to their connection with luxurious eating.[160] It is not clear from the poem as Athenaeus has preserved it what Plutarch has in mind in his statement, 'Philoxenus the poet says . . . that of the meats the non-meats are the sweetest and of the fish the non-fish',[161] but artifice (whether of the cook or poet or both) is clearly indicated. The poem is narrated by one of a group (2) to a friend (7, 16, 35) and the narrator intervenes directly in matters of nomenclature (19) and appetite (which is aroused by serving tuna: 22–3). He is unable to match his narrative to the extent of the feast (24–6).

Just as Epicharmus adapted Ananius into his *Muses or Marriage of Hebe*,[162] so Philoxenus adapted from his comic predecessor into dithyramb the interest of the gods in food. 'What men call second tables, but the gods the horn of Amaltheia' (*Deipnon* 836e3–4) echoes *Marriage of Hebe* 42.10–11, 'all men call them "man-avoiders" but we gods "whites"'.[163] The poem departs from the *Marriage of Hebe* (though not from Epicharmus in general) in giving fish a significant but not all-embracing part in the meal and in introducing the appetite and complicity of the first-person narrator who is eager to join the waiters in carving up the belly-cut of tuna. The principal contrast with Old Comedy also lies in the eager participation of the narrator in the meal. Old Comedy was characterized either by the rapid dialogue of the protagonist—Dicaeopolis or Trygaeus—as the person in charge of the cooking who dismissed the antagonist from the feast, or by the dispassionate narration of utopian eating in which the focus is on the eagerness of the food to be eaten. These elements in Philoxenus herald the Attic development of the *mageiros* who can produce food pleasing to the gods and pleasing to the appetite.

---

[159] The details of which are obscured by textual corruption. I note that Athenaeus (1.5d) records (from an unnamed source) that certain (unspecified) cakes were named Philoxeneii after 'Philoxenus'.

[160] See Plato's remarks on confectionary at the beginning of this chapter, Chap. 6, and Athenaeus 14.639b–649c.

[161] *PMG* 836(f) = Plutarch *aud. poet.* 1.28.

[162] Both in trochaic tetrameters.

[163] The gods love the mixed sausage of kid and lamb (*Deipnon* 836(b)34), while some part of the conger (the text is corrupt) is pleasing to the gods (9).

At least three fragments of Antiphanes appear to allude to the *Deipnon*.[164] Two characters converse in *Parasite* fr. 180:

A: After this there will be here another great and noble, the size of a table—
B: What are you talking about?
A: —nurseling of Carystus, earth-born, seething—
B: Then aren't you going to tell me? Get on with it.
A: —I mean a casserole (*kakkabos*). Perhaps you might say a stewing-pot (*lopas*).
B: Do you think the term makes any difference to me? Whether some people take pleasure in calling it a *kakkabos* or a *sittubos*? All I know is you're talking about a pot.[165]

The ornate language of the first speaker, the *kakkabos* the size of the table and the *kakkabos* itself, which twice appeared in the *Deipnon* (836(b) 7, 11) are all reminiscent of Philoxenus, while the irritation of the interlocutor and the consideration of alternative terminology for material objects brings the ornate expression firmly into the comic tradition.[166] The dithyrambic poet's extravagance with the language of eating and drinking found comic echo in Antiphanes fr. 172, which also imitates the metres of the *Deipnon*.[167] This fragment explicitly curtails the description of the dinner and concentrates on the wine, second tables, and cakes. Antiphanes, *Tritagonist* fr. 207 comments explicitly on Philoxenus: 'The best of all the poets by far is Philoxenus. First of all, he uses special and novel terms all over the place. Then how well he mixes his lyrics with modulations and colour! That man is a god among mortals and truly knows the art of the muse. The poets now write wretched lyrics, ivy-woven, flower-flying fountain stuff woven in with wretched terms that produce outlandish results.' To be sure, Antiphanes may not be parodying the *Deipnon* of Philoxenus but the *Cyclops or Galatea* which, as we have seen, may have been written by a different Philoxenus altogether. Athenaeus, however, implies that the *Deipnon* is in question, since Antiphanes fr. 207 is quoted immediately after a substantial quotation from that poem (836(e)). Novelty of

---

[164] As does possibly *Ecclesiazusae* 1168–75.

[165] See Nesselrath (1990), 259; Dalby (1995), 114.

[166] Cf. Eubulus fr. 37 for a list of cooking-pots too long for the speaker to complete (cited in Chap. 1).

[167] On the trochaic tetrameters and dactyloepitrites see Kassel–Austin (1991), Nesselrath (1990), and Arnott (1996) on Alexis fr. 137.

language is what caught the attention of Antiphanes, precisely what we find in the *Deipnon*:[168] the power of language is a major concern of the poet[169] and of the symposiasts he is describing.[170] While the form and language of the *Deipnon* are the main object of attention, content also plays its part—the speaker in fr. 172 passes over all the details of the dinner, as Philoxenus had not done. We should also note the occasion of the *Deipnon*, a private banquet, of which there were to be far more in Attic Middle Comedy than there had been in Old, as far as we know. In another sphere we might compare Amphis, *Dithyramb* fr. 17, in which a speaker says that a new musical instrument, a small pipe called a *gingras*, is unknown in the theatre but beloved in symposia. It is yet to be introduced to the masses.

I turn now to a further poetic form, apparently composed by poets from outside Athens, which was to inspire further the representation of food on the comic stage.

7.7. PARODY IN HEXAMETERS

We have seen that the hexameters used by Plato in *Phaon* fr. 189 anticipated the *Hedypatheia* of Archestratus of Gela, probably by some decades. Archestratus wrote in the genre of 'parody'. While many admirers of Aristophanes will be familiar with the comic parody of tragedy in many ingenious forms,[171] less well known is the literary form of hexameter parody exemplified by Archestratus.[172] Some parodies appear to have been performed

---

[168] *PMG* 836e24: ἔνθα τι καινὸν ἐλέχθη κομψὸν ἀθυρμάτιον ('then a new saying was uttered, a smart and playful conceit').

[169] *PMG* 836b24–5 (text corrupt).

[170] *PMG* 836e23 πόσις δ' ἐπεραίνετο κότταβοί τε λόγοι τ' ἐπὶ κοινᾶς ('and the drinking came to an end, as did the games of *kottabos* and the word-games among the company').

[171] See e.g. Silk (forthcoming), Taplin (1986) and (1993), Rau (1967), Foley (1988). Since forms of eating and feasting are comparatively rare in tragedy, parody of tragedy often imports foods into tragic language. By contrast, there is no shortage of sacrifice and feasting in Homer, and so parody of Homer often chose to import into Homeric language either special categories excluded by Homer—such as fish—or anachronistic forms of eating.

[172] The surviving texts are collected by Brandt (1888). These parodies differ from such sub-Homeric poems as the *Margites* and *Battle of the Frogs and the Mice*, but share some features, not least the unattractive narrator and the trivialization of subject-matter.

in the public arena, while others, such as those by Archestratus and Matro, may have been written for sympotic presentation. Aristotle records[173] that the first writer of parody at Athens was Hegemon of Thasos, while Aristotle's successors identify him as a public performer of parody.[174] His only poem to survive is a self-deprecating parody in which the poet is pelted from the stage with excrement in Thasos, is given small rations by his wife, and is not fêted in his home island as he was in Athens where he won a prize of fifty drachmae. Athena addresses him as Foul Lentil Soup[175] and urges him to enter the contest.[176] Notable elements here are the mild scapegoating of Hegemon, the personal narrative, and the self-mocking presentation of the narrator, all of which will have analogues in the speeches of *mageiroi* and parasites in Middle Comedy. Explicit in the text are the prize, the performance, and the incentive of hunger which drives him to perform.[177] Inscriptions record parodic contests in the fourth century in Eretria; Degani has collected more from the Hellenistic and Roman periods.[178] Euboeus of Paros and Boeotus[179] are two further parodists of the fourth century singled out by Polemon.

Athenaeus' authorities are Chamaeleon of Heracleia's monograph *On Old Comedy* (fr. 18 Koepke) and Polemon's *Letter to Timaeus* (fr. 76 Preller),[180] texts which have a considerable importance for the history of comedy. Polemon traces hexameter parody back to Hipponax fr. 128 West[181] and to limited exploitation

---

[173] *Poetics* 1448a. Add Polemon at Athenaeus 15.699a = fr. 76 Preller.

[174] Chamaeleon of Heracleia (Athenaeus 9.407a–b = fr. 18 Koepke) provides a date: he records that Hegemon was performing his *Gigantomachia in the theatre* in Athens when news reached the city of the Sicilian disaster in 413 BC. Hegemon's style was 'shameless and actorly' (πανούργως καὶ ὑποκριτικῶς). Polemon, echoing Hegemon's own words, says that Hegemon was the first to perform *in competition in the theatre* (πρῶτος εἰσῆλθεν εἰς τοὺς ἀγῶνας τοὺς θυμελικοὺς Ἡγήμων (fr. 76 Preller = Athenaeus 15.699a)).

[175] Cf. the *phlyax* play by Sopater entitled *Lentil-Soup*.

[176] δεινὰ παθοῦσα, Φακῆ βδελυρά, χώρει 'ς τὸν ἀγῶνα.

[177] For the assimilation of the hungry poet with the parasite see Chaps. 2 and 8.

[178] *IG* XII 9, 189; Degani (1995), 414–15; Dover on 'parody, Greek' in *OCD*[3].

[179] On whom see Brandt (1888), 50–2.

[180] Athenaeus 9.406e–407d, 15.698b–699c.

[181] Μοῦσά μοι Εὐρυμεδοντιάδεα τὴν ποντοχάρυβδιν, | τὴν ἐν γαστρὶ μάχαιραν, ὃς ἐσθίει οὐ κατὰ κόσμον, | ἔννεφ', ὅπως ψηφῖδι [. . .] κακὸν οἶτον ὀλεῖται | βουλῆι δημοσίηι παρὰ θῖν' ἁλὸς

in Sicilian and Athenian comedy, noting Epicharmus, the *Euneidae* of Cratinus, and Hermippus, who is said to have composed parodies. Whether this refers to hexameter passages in such dramatic fragments of Hermippus as frr. 63 and 77[182] or to performances separate from comedy we do not know. Polemon does not specify. Hegemon himself produced a comedy, *Philinna*, whose only surviving fragment concerns the purchase and consumption of an octopus. Polemon's evidence for some cross-fertilization between parody and comedy appears to be confirmed both by Chamaeleon, who wrote of Hegemon's parody in his monograph on Old Comedy, and by the Alexandrian scholar Lycophron, the Hellenistic editor (*diorthotes*) of comedy, who commented on the correct title of Archestratus' poem in his *On Comedy*.[183] Furthermore, Athens was not the only centre in which parody was of interest. Alexander of Pleuron, the first *diorthotes*[184] of tragedy, wrote an elegy on parody in which he says parodists of Homer (Boeotus and Euboeus are named) were favoured in Syracuse.[185]

Parodies were written on a number of themes in addition to food, from the early *Margites* to the *Battle of the Frogs and Mice* (written in the early fifth century?), the *Gigantomachia* of Hegemon, and *The Battle of the Bath-House-Men* of Euboeus.[186] The

ἀτρυγέτοιο. ('Tell me, Muse, of the son of Eurymedon, the one with the whirlpool as big as the sea, the dagger-belly, who eats in no good order; of how he died a wretched death [. . .] by stoning, through the wish of the people, by the shore of the unharvested sea.') The hexameters of Hipponax, similar in content to the elegiac lines of Asius fr. 14 West (quoted in Chap. 2), are insulting, listing gluttony of the belly and a likely death by stoning, and not unlike Hegemon's poem. For Hegemon's mocking of himself we might compare Alcman fr. 17.4 *PMG*, in which the poet describes himself as *pamphagos*, though not rejected by the community.

[182] If fr. 77 is from a comedy. Fr. 63 is certainly dramatic since Athenaeus contrasts the *Phormophoroi*, a drama, with the iambic verse of Hermippus (15.700d).

[183] Fr. 19 Strecker=Athenaeus 7.278a.

[184] On the significance of the term and the importance of Alexander of Pleuron and Lycophron at Alexandria see Pfeiffer (1968), 105–22.

[185] Fr. 5 Powell=Athenaeus 15.699c.

[186] See P. Maas, *Parodos* (1), *RE* 18.4 (1949), 1684–6; Koller (1956), 17–32; E. Pöhlmann, 'Parodies', *Glotta*, 50 (1972), 144–56; Degani (1983); D. Gilula, 'Hermippus' Catalogue of Goods (fr. 63)', in Harvey and Wilkins (forthcoming); and the Introduction of Olson and Sens to *Archestratus* (forthcoming).

comic representation of food, however, is my present concern, to which parody in the late fifth and early fourth centuries appears to have contributed. Epicharmus, Cratinus, and Hermippus may have used hexameters in their comedies independently of a parodic 'tradition', particularly if it is true that Hegemon was the first to give public recitations in Athens. But we know that Hermippus composed other forms of poetry (West lists 'trimeters', tetrameters, and iambics of uncertain genre) and Hegemon, as we have seen, wrote a comedy. Athenaeus claims (1.5a–b) that both Matro and Hegemon wrote 'treatises on *deipna*'.[187] These are not otherwise attested, but if they existed then two prose texts may be added to the recipe book of Mithaecus, the *Deipnon* of Philoxenus, and the possible hexameter predecessor of Archestratus as inspiration for comic treatments of banquets in Athens in the fourth century.

In the early parodic texts, such as Hegemon, luxurious meals did not appear. This was to change with *The Life of Luxury* of Archestratus of Gela and the *Attic Dinner* of Matro of Pitane.[188] The poems differ in style, with Matro's developing elaborate descriptions of a feast in imitation of Homer, while Archestratus gives advice in the style of Hesiod on where to sail for the finest products, and with cooking instructions added. *The Life of Luxury* gives advice to two recipients, Moschus and Cleandrus. Sometimes the tone is polemical,[189] but normally they are directed both to a particular place for a particular item of food and to the best way to prepare it. The vast majority of foods are fish, but there is an important fragment on breads and some advice on the restricted size necessary for a decent symposium, on appetizers and what is needed for 'second tables', and for some meat-cooking.[190] Much of the advice could be followed by a cook in need of practical guidance, but here our concern is with the form of the poem. Archestratus, mindful of epic verse,

---

[187] δείπνων ἀναγραφαί.

[188] Matro composed other parodies, fragments of which are cited in Brandt (1888), 91–5. The first five maintain the themes of the *Attic Dinner* (foods served and a musical *hetaera*), while fr. 6 reviews the predecessors of Matro, among whom Euboeus is prominent.

[189] Against Pythagorean vegetarians (fr. 23), on Syracusan cooking (fr. 45), on the best wines (fr. 59), on Syracusan drinking (fr. 62).

[190] Sacrificial animals are not included.

nevertheless adapts Homer to a much more limited extent than does Matro.[191] He inherits from Epicharmus and Philoxenus gods endowed with a keen interest in imitating the eating practices of mortals: at fr. 4.6–7 '*if* the gods eat barley groats . . . Hermes must come and buy them [in Eresos]'; at fr. 4.16 Athens provides market bread for mortals;[192] the gods will be angry if you don't buy a boar-fish in Ambracia (fr. 15); the underbelly of the shark is a divine food (fr. 23); slices of the female tuna are 'like the immortal gods in form and stature' (fr. 37); a sea bass from Miletus is 'one of the children of the gods' (fr. 45). Further important playful elements are the choice of colourful or exaggerated language and the presentation of appetite as a powerful motivation. The first is exemplified in fish of exaggerated size (at fr. 12, the gilthead bream is ten cubits long)[193] and long neologisms such as 'stormy-petrel-locustish'[194] of the soul (fr. 23.14) and 'chatterers of empty boasts' (fr. 59).[195] The reader is encouraged to satisfy his desire for fish by any means, including theft (fr. 21). This elevation of desire characterizes the poem as an incitement against self-control within the discourse of luxury examined in Chapter 6. For this reason it was censured by Chrysippus and Cleanthes and frequently by Athenaeus.[196] The promotion of appetite coincides with those comic passages in which characters are ridiculed either for their greed or lack of self-control.[197] That failure of self-control is likely to be manifest in paying high prices, snatching or stealing food, and eating rapidly (eating at great temperature is not found in the surviving fragments of Archestratus).[198] The

---

[191] The borrowings of both poets are listed in Brandt (1888). See further Olson and Sens (forthcoming) on Archestratus, and Degani (1995) on Matro.

[192] Mortals also in 8, 15, 23.

[193] Giltheads in the Mediterranean now grow to a maximum of 60 cm. See also Dalby (1995), 227 on the enormous *karcharias* roasted whole at Plato, *Phaon* fr. 189.13.

[194] The adjective κεπφαττελεβώδης is an ingenious emendation by Bentley of κούφαν γε λεβώδη in MS A of Athenaeus (7.310e; of κούφην τε λεβώδη in the other quotation by Athenaeus at 4.163d). The first element derives from *kepphos*, a bird which is not certainly identified as a stormy petrel.

[195] Cf. Epicharmus fr. 46: herons have long and bendy necks, μακροκαμπυλαύχενες.

[196] See Wilkins and Hill (1994).

[197] See Chap. 6 on gluttons in pursuit of fish.

[198] Paying high prices, fr. 15; stealing, fr. 21; eating eagerly, to the point of choking, fr. 22.

desire of the big spender is not necessarily self-generated but may be stimulated by the fish itself (fr. 31): 'Now the *kitharos*, provided it is white and firm [and large?], I order you to stew in clean salt water with a few green leaves. If it has a reddish/yellow appearance and is not too big, then you must bake it, having pricked its body with a straight and newly sharpened knife. And anoint it with plenty of cheese and oil, for it takes pleasure in big spenders and is unchecked in extravagance.'[199] The fragment well illustrates the comic potential of Archestratus. The apparently didactic tone of the hexameters is undercut by the concluding remarks, which may sound a sarcastic note—the *kitharos* was not greatly favoured by nutritionists, and Archestratus elsewhere does not favour fish which need cheese sauce.[200]

Matro's *Attic Dinner* is a narrative of a meal held in Athens that is characterized by its lavishness, the vast quantities of food described, and its ingenious application of Homeric language to descriptions largely of fish and vegetables. Homeric characters such as Tityus and Homeric gods such as Thetis are converted into fish, often in ways of considerable subtlety, as Degani (1995) has shown.[201] Zeus has even taken on prawns as the subject of his song. Matro shares with Attic comedy the presentation of citizens whose greed is out of control. Xenocles the host gave many dinners of this kind; Chaerephon is the parasite just as he is in comedy, as too, probably, is Stratocles; the unnamed narrator cannot control his appetite—even when full (65–72):[202]

There was a gilthead, which is the finest fish among them all, a crayfish, and a lobster was eager to put on his breastplate at the feasts of the

[199] Archestratus presumably means that the fish enjoys big spenders because it tastes better when lavishly cooked.

[200] The fragment is quoted by Athenaeus at 7.306b. He cites an Apollodorus as authority for the *kitharos* as a fish sacred to Apollo, but the fish may be of no more interest to Apollo than in its name—lyre fish.

[201] The eel who boasts she has slept with Zeus owes something to the eel of *Acharnians* 885–94 (a parody of a *tragic* model) and something to the discourse of sex which presents women as objects for male consumption (see Chap. 1). Women are brought in for men to consume once they have eaten their fill of food at the end of the *Attic Dinner*.

[202] On the parasites see Brandt (1888), 57–8, and in general Chap. 2 above. The appetite of the narrator was a less prominent feature of the *Deipnon* of Philoxenus and appears also in the narrative of Trimalchio's dinner in the *Satyricon* of Petronius.

Blessed. On these the feasters launched their hands and put them in their mouths and pulled them this way and that. At their head was the lord sturgeon,[203] the famous spearsman, for whom, full though I was, I stretched forth my hand, eager to get a taste. To me it seemed to be ambrosia, on which feast the blessed gods who live for ever.

The enthusiasm for eating centres on the sturgeon or *elops*, the fish which in Epicharmus (fr. 71) was reserved for Zeus and Hera. Matro may be using Epicharmus as his model, and giving divine interest in this fish a new, secular twist. In Athenaeus' day Matro's poem was a rarity;[204] in the fourth century its impact on Attic comedy (if any) is difficult to detect. The comic poets appear to have been unwilling to take on this degree of Homeric parody and to have confined themselves, rather, to lists and other modes of describing excess. Matro in fact appears to constitute a stage too far for the comic representation of excessive dining. We shall see in Chapter 8 the cook in Strato's *Phoenicides*, but his Homeric phrases are dismissed as outlandish. Archestratus, on the other hand, did influence comedy and may himself have drawn on comic models. Olivieri (1939) has demonstrated a significant relationship between *The Life of Luxury* and both Epicharmus and Attic comedy. We noted above the dependence of Archestratus on Epicharmus in his description of the lobster;[205] to this we may add Archestratus on the saupe, a bad fish to be eaten in summer, possibly his lists of shellfish and breads, and possibly his citation of conger and 'fat dog', though the link is tenuous—many others may have composed verse on these foods—and may be coincidental.[206] The relationship between Archestratus and Attic comedy is complex because of uncertainties over dating. There are close correspondences between Plato, *Phaon* 189 and Archestratus;[207] Antiphanes, *Butalion* fr. 69 appears to present man-eating fish in a comic context analogous to Archestratus fr. 23.16; Eubulus, *Amaltheia* fr. 6.4–5 dismisses

---

[203] *Elops*, a fish not certainly identified as the sturgeon: see Thompson (1947), 62–3.

[204] 4.134d.   [205] Epicharmus fr. 57; Archestratus fr. 24.

[206] The saupe (*salpe*): Epicharmus fr. 63; Archestratus fr. 28. Shellfish: Epicharmus frr. 42–3; Archestratus 56. 'Fat dog': Epicharmus fr. 68; Archestratus fr. 21 'this is the fish they call fat dog in Syracuse'. Bread: Epicharmus fr. 52; Archestratus fr. 4. Conger: Epicharmus fr. 72; Archestratus fr. 18.

[207] See n. 136 above.

tassel hyacinths on side-dishes in a form similar to Archestratus fr. 6; there are correspondences in frying the small fry known as *gonos* in Archestratus fr. 9 and his fellow-parodist Hegemon of Thasos, in Hegemon's one known comedy *Philinna* (fr. 1). A character in Philemon's *Soldier* fr. 82.16–18 praises the conger-eels of Sicyon (praised by Archestratus in fr. 18) in terms reminiscent of Archestratus: 'the conger eel from beloved Sicyon which Poseidon brings to heaven for the gods—all who eat it would become gods.'[208]

Where the earlier parodists wrote on subjects which often depicted the narrator or an adversary in a poor or demeaning light, Matro and Archestratus wrote about the cultivated symposium, though with a poetic voice which is not neutral but open to charges of immorality. Matro's poem describes an *Attic* banquet, clearly one of those occasions where the imagined simplicity and abstemiousness of the Athenians gave way to luxury and desire. The fact that the author is not an Athenian may be significant. Archestratus grants Athens no special prominence but presents the city as one among dozens which might be visited by a gourmet with nothing to do but seek out the best fish. Polemic in Archestratus is directed at earlier cooks, but only Syracusan cooks are mentioned. The eating of food is more extensive in these two poems than anywhere else in surviving Greek literature, the eating of fish in particular. Even here little light is cast on the use of fish-plates, which were discussed above. For the most part fish are brought to table in their cooking-pots, *tagena*, *lopades*, *kakkabia*, and so on. Plates—*pinakes*—carrying fish (and perhaps other *opsa*) are cited at *Attic Dinner* 47, and silver plates for fatted geese at fr. 4. Archestratus, and Philoxenus too, seem to reserve 'plates' (*paropsides* and *oxybapha*) for tassel hyacinths and other appetizers.

To these parodic works we may add other forms which invade comedy from the world of the symposium: the verses and proverbs of Charmus of Syracuse, who adapted the language of Homer and tragedy to foods,[209] and the sympotic versifying of

---

[208] Cf. Archestratus frr. 4 and 15, the latter on the boar-fish which is also mentioned in Philemon fr. 82.

[209] Athenaeus 1.4a–b. His dates are unknown but he is cited by Clearchus of Soli, a pupil of Aristotle.

Cleanthes of Tarentum and of Pamphilus the Sicilian (the latter in trimeters).[210] Cookery books might also provide memorable or proverbial material. I noted above how, according to Lynceus of Samos in his treatise on shopping, the verses of Archestratus can be used to beat down prices at market:[211] the parodic text is taken to a market peopled with fishmongers very similar to those of Middle Comedy, who may be assailed by such apophthegms as 'the shore sea-bream (*mormyrus*) is a bad fish and never good' or 'buy bonito in autumn' [when buying in spring] or 'the grey mullet is wonderful when winter comes' [when buying in summer].[212] Such material, according to Clearchus,[213] could also be used for sympotic games of forfeit. All this material shares with comedy a representation of the everyday in a playful or ludic form masquerading as utility—Lynceus' treaty on shopping was ostensibly written to help those who experienced difficulty at the market (*dysonoi*), but has many affinities with the comic agora. Archestratus likewise promoted the buying of fish (frr. 15, 16, 20, 21, 22, etc.); this practical skill, to be placed beside the preparation and cooking of fish, while appearing innocuous to the modern reader might suggest temptations to a young man's self-control such as we saw in comedy in Chapter 6. The dangers of money probably lie behind Plato's criticisms of Thearion, Sarambus, and Mithaecus—who all offered services which ought not to be bought.

These writers bring new influences to Attic comedy from the rich linguistic world of the *deipnon* and symposium. Chapter 5 demonstrated the close links between sympotic features and Old Comedy and the exploitation of one by the other—the recitation of verses of Cratinus and Aristophanes at the symposium and conversely of *skolia* in comedy are two examples among many— but more have now been added. Where feasts were described in Old Comedy—agonistically at the end of *Acharnians*, extensively in the utopian fragments—the *mageiros* in Middle Comedy is imported to instruct and to boast about his prowess in preparing the feast; where hexameter parody in Old Comedy praised

---

[210] Athenaeus 1.4d. Dates unknown, though again the latter is cited by Clearchus.

[211] Compare Dalby (1995), 118 and (forthcoming).

[212] Athenaeus 7.313f–314a.   [213] Ibid. 10.457c–e.

Dionysus and his festive gifts of good and wine, such parody in the fourth century is developed outside comedy and, thus invigorated, invades comedy anew. New forms of instruction and first-person involvement combine with a broadening discourse of luxury to inform further the long speeches of *mageiroi* and their like. Middle Comedy was able to draw on the poetic products of Greek cities outside Athens to reinvent itself: where in Old Comedy Syracuse, Sicily, and Sybaris could be identified as centres of luxury and self-indulgence, in Middle Comedy cookery books in prose and Hesiodic parody, *mageiroi*, and the poetry of fish-eating could be incorporated as new sources of humour and a new outsider against which to set an ideology of plain eating in Athens that was under threat from young and other uncontrolled citizens, metics, and slaves. All of this is a comic discourse whose relation to 'real life' in the Athens of the fourth century, as opposed to civic ideology, is difficult to quantify. Given the level of innovation in writing about food in comedy as the genre evolved from Old to New, from a more civic to a more private focus, and revelled in what it found in dithyramb, parody, sympotic literature, and cookery books and was able to put into the mouths of such practitioners as the comic *mageiroi*, it would be dangerous to say that rich Athenians did hire more cooks, eat more fish, and consume more rich dishes. In many ways the comic discourse of eating may have been self-generating, and a mode of comic writing which reflected much broader changes in Athens than any increase in 'gastronomy'.

7.8. THE IMPACT OF PARODY ON ATTIC COMEDY

Along with the role of the *mageiros* as cook came the specialization of tasks—the *mageiros* is to be distinguished from the *opsopoios* (the man who prepared *opsa*, especially fish), the *trapezopoios* (the waiter or butler), and the *demiourgos* (the confectioner)[214]—and the establishment of schools of cookery, whatever they were. The writer of an *Opsartytika* might be influential as an individual or as the leader of a group of supporters. Clearchus of

---

[214] See Menander fr. 409, cited above, and Arnott (1996) on Alexis, *Crateia or Drugseller* (pp. 313–14).

Soli writes of 'the associates of Archestratus',[215] while Alexis, *Linus* fr. 140 has a cookery book written by a plain Simus. We know of two plays of the fourth century written by Dionysius of Sinope. The *mageiros* in his *Thesmophoros* fr. 2.24 declares, 'Archestratus has written [his book], has a reputation in some quarters, as if he has a useful contribution to put forward. For the most part he is ignorant and he has nothing to say. Do not listen to everything and do not learn everything [. . .].[216] It is not possible to speak of the art of the *mageiros* . . .' These comments appear to date to the period between the composition of *The Life of Luxury* and the statement of Clearchus. Archestratus has arrived in comedy very quickly,[217] both directly in what he has written and more broadly in the notice people have taken.[218] At a later date (unknown) a *mageiros* in Sosipater, *Perjuror* fr. 1.10–14 declares, 'there are only three of us still left, Boidion, Chariades, and I. Fart at the rest. B: What do you say? MAGEIROS: We preserve the school of Sicon.[219] He was the founder of the art . . .' In another New Comedy, Euphron's *Brothers* fr. 1, a similar *mageiros* appeared and, Athenaeus reports,[220] listed his predecessors, who include the Chariades of Athens just mentioned and Agis of Rhodes.[221] Anaxippus, *Behind the Veil* fr. 1.1–5 (also a New Comedy) has a *mageiros* declare: 'Sophon of Acarnania and Damoxenus of Rhodes became fellow students of the art. Labdacus of Sicily taught them, and they wiped out from the books the old much-vaunted seasonings.' He proceeds to stress the influence of Sophon in Ionia and to reveal (23–6) 'you will see me in the morning with books in hand searching out the detail of the art, just like Diodorus of Aspendos'—a Pythagorean ridiculed by Archestratus in fr. 23. The reading of Sophon is also reported by a *mageiros* in the *Benefactors* of Baton fr. 4, along with books

---

[215] Athenaeus 7.285c–d οἱ περὶ ᾿Αρχέστρατον.

[216] Two lines apparently about the emptiness of the written word are corrupt.

[217] Dalby (1995), 118 suggests that the *Archestrate* of Antiphanes may have something to do with Archestratus or a comically imagined sister, but this is far-fetched, not least because the name Archestratus is common enough in Athens.

[218] On his likely date see Dalby (1995), 400–12, modified by Olson and Sens (forthcoming). The *mageiros* in Dionysius, *Namesakes* fr. 3.19 declares, 'you are my student, I am your teacher', though the form of instruction is not given.

[219] See above on Sicon's possible links with Sicily.   [220] 9.379c–d.

[221] Agis may be the man who wrote a cookery book (Athenaeus 12.516c).

by Semonactides of Chios, Tyndarichus of Sicyon, and Zopyrinus. Whether or not these writers or their cookery books existed,[222] the combination of cooking with a related textbook is well established as a subject for comedy in the fourth century and beyond.[223] All but one of the books were written outside Athens.

Comedy's interest in cookery books extended also to recipes, particularly for the cooking of fish. At the same time it must be noted that many of the fourth-century fragments are not interested in the processes of cooking in any way but wish, rather, to list—fr. 4 of the *Horse-Breeder* of Mnesimachus is a notable example—and/or to identify social types. Some reasonably close links can be demonstrated between Archestratus and Middle Comedy, though it is not always clear which precedes the other. Clearly Archestratus imitated Epicharmus;[224] there are no clear signs of imitation of the *Deipnon* of Philoxenus, though Archestratus was interested in versification between genres, noting the unsuitability of the word *antakaios*[225] for hexameters (fr. 39). Archestratus took from Old Comedy two standbys, the Copaic eel and the sea bass of Miletus. He placed them beside other eels and sea bass in the Mediterranean, extending a simple identification of a fish with a place to its location in a wider natural setting.[226] Fragments of Middle and New Comedy which may owe something more than a passing reference to the recipes of Archestratus are fr. 1 of *Behind the Veil* of Anaxippus and fr. 1 of the *Locked-Up Women* of Sotades. The former[227] rejects previous

---

[222] They are attested by Pollux 6.70.

[223] Sophon is identified as a writer of cookery books, for what it is worth, in Pollux, but not in Athenaeus' lists at 1.5a–b or 12.516c. Many in the second passage come from southern Italy, though for most we have no date—e.g. Herecleides of Syracuse, Dionysius of Syracuse, Hegesippus of Tarentum. Sophon has a namesake at Athenaeus 14.622e who is contemporary with the Deipnosophists and recites a speech on feasting from the *Auge* of Eubulus, thereby resembling the Simus of Alexis, *Linus* who has tragic and cooking skills. This incident reminds us of the ludic nature of our main source for all this information, Athenaeus.

[224] Cf. n. 206–7.   [225] A sturgeon: see Thompson (1947), 16–17.

[226] On Copaic eels, *Acharnians* 880, among many other citations (see Chap. 1); on Milesian sea bass, *Knights* 361; contrast Archestratus frr. 8 (eels) and 45 (sea bass).

[227] Already cited above.

excessive seasoning of fish in favour of oil and gentle heat, as does Archestratus in frr. 35 and 45, while the latter concentrates on cumin, oil, green leaves, and brine in a way very similar to a number of Archestratus' recipes. The bonito is cooked in fig leaves in ashes, just as Archestratus recommends. There are other details which do not match, but it seems likely that Archestratus is the model: his knowledge of fish-cooking is prima facie much more extensive than Sotades'. Almost all of Sotades' fish appear in the *Life of Luxury*, as does the liking for the head meat of the *glaukos*. The final joke of Sotades' *mageiros* is 'this is my art. Nothing comes from recipes or memoranda.'

In the fourth and beyond comedy was changing in style and content and food was commented upon in a new way. There were new styles of cooking, and a new role was evolving for the *mageiros*, though to what extent comedy kept pace with such developments in the real world is difficult to say. Cooking was appearing in books and in a new way in poetry. There was an expansion in the parodic poem. Comedy referred to all of this, either coincidentally with its own transformation or as part of the transformation. As far as food in social rituals was concerned, there was now much less festivity (though still some) and more concentration on the details of the meal or symposium, which continued to be both public and private (funeral feasts, for example, and weddings). The presentation is, however, very different, though not totally different, if we take the utopian rather than festive passages as typical of Old Comedy. There was also more on the art of the cook and on the wittiness associated with that art. I consider it likely that in this area southern Italy played a large role.

The reading of the cookery book in Plato, *Phaon* fr. 189 is repeated later in the fourth century. In Alexis, *Linus* fr. 140[228] Heracles is offered various classics to read, including Orpheus, Homer, and Epicharmus, but chooses instead a cookery book of Simus,[229] who is said to be a clever man, a cook (an *opsopoios* or *opson*-maker), and a tragic actor (*hypokrites*). Of the actors he is the best cook, as people who have employed him can testify, and

[228] Date unknown.
[229] He is unknown. See Arnott (1996), *ad loc.*; Ghiron-Bistagne (1976), 356; Bain (1977), 217.

of cooks the best(?)[230] actor. This put-down,[231] whether or not applied to a figure of real life, as Arnott believes it must have been, also appears to return us to the complex relationship between comic characters such as the cook or parasite and tragic parody that was seen on the *phlyax* vases. Since both cooking and tragedy are major interests of comedy at this time, it is difficult to believe that the fragment concerns only professionals in those skills outside the theatre. Heracles who, stereotypically, is interested only in eating maintains the connection: in reply to Linus' observation, 'the man is obsessed with food', he says: '*say* what you like. Be quite clear that *I am hungry.*' Heracles does not appear to pay attention to the cookery book of Simus in this fragment, but by the fourth century the mythological eater could be imagined in a library in which such works sit beside texts of the great authors. The only culinary advice apparently available to the gods in Epicharmus' *The Muses or The Marriage of Hebe* were the tetrameters of Ananius. I have suggested elsewhere that the conditions were not sufficient in ancient Greece to generate the production of cookery books before the fifth century.[232] Mithaecus, or a near contemporary, was probably prompted to write a recipe book as an extension of the medical treatises of the Hippocratic and other schools, perhaps even of Croton. As the doctors came more and more to commit case notes and theoretical material to prose writing, some of it relating to diet, so instruction on how the food comprising that diet might be prepared became possible. Already in the Hippocratic *On Diet*, which Joly and others date to around 400, the author recognizes elaborate sauces, for example for fish.[233] As the fourth century progressed more cookery books appear to have been written, particularly in southern Italy and Sicily. I have tried to show in this chapter that the cookery book and Archestratus' parody, both of which came from Sicily, readily came to mind when a comic poet in Athens wished to give sententious views to his stock cooks. Similarly,

---

[230] There is a lacuna in the text.

[231] For parallel expressions see Kassel–Austin (1991), and Arnott (1996), *ad loc.*

[232] Wilkins and Hill (1996), drawing on the criteria of Goody (1982), 97–9, namely sufficient agricultural production to generate surplus, the ability to choose one mode of cooking over another and the written medium.

[233] See further the introduction of Olson and Sens (forthcoming).

other non-Attic poetry on food—the displays of 'Philoxenus' in dithyramb and Matro in parody—and sympotic literature (of which cookery texts *might* also have been part) also had a role to play.

The book of Mithaecus was put squarely in the discourse of pleasure by Plato in *Gorgias*, contrasting it with the utility of medicine, as we have seen. Only three fragments survive,[234] two on fish and a statement by Athenaeus (12.516c) that he gave a recipe for *karyke*, as did a number of cookery and medical texts (the latter including Diocles, Erasistratus, and Philistion) also listed by Athenaeus—from the late fourth century and thereafter. Mithaecus' fish and *karyke*, together with Archestratus' *Life of Luxury*, gave comic commentators on this tradition of recipe books a ready link with luxury. They appear not to have cited Mithaecus directly, perhaps because poetic form such as Archestratus provided was an added attraction. But from Mithaecus, Archestratus, and the other writers of cookery books cited in the comic fragments above the Attic comic poets also derived a new way of presenting the materiality of food, with new emphasis on the techniques and transformations of cooking and the ways in which these could be put into discourse. Thus it is that comedies of the fourth century and beyond developed the themes of cookery books and of reading and writing about the kitchen which was derived from them. The cook in Strato, *Phoenicides* fr. 1 is declared a sphinx for his diction expressed in sub-Homeric parody so obscure that it requires elucidation from the scholar-poet Philitas. Speeches by such linguistically gifted cooks are the subject of the next chapter.

[234] All quoted by Athenaeus: see Wilkins and Hill (1995); Dalby (1995), 109–10; introduction to Olson and Sens (forthcoming).

8

The Comic Cook

Cooking has been at the heart of this study of food in comedy. I now consider the comic cook himself, the *mageiros*, who prepared and cooked animals and other foods for the table and wished to tell other characters and the audience what he was doing, often in great detail. There appears to have been a significant transition from Attic Old Comedy, in which the protagonist, if anyone, organizes the cooking, to Middle and New Comedy, in which the cook becomes a stock character. This shift transformed the cook-protagonist from one who controlled the discourse and drove off any unwelcome *alazones* at the sacrifice or feast into an *alazon* or boaster himself.

8.1. THE GREEK *MAGEIROS*

The Greek *mageiros* was essentially a butcher who might specialize in one or more of three roles. He dismembered sacrificial animals; he sold meat in the market, and he was available for hire as a private cook. The best discussion of the roles of the *mageiros* is Berthiaume (1982), who demonstrates that the term is not found before the fifth century BC, and thence appears in historians, other literature, and inscriptions. Before this date there was, it appears, insufficient impetus to distinguish these roles with a technical term that set them apart from other assistants to the processes of sacrifice (and its by-product, the sale of meat) and cooking.[1] The earliest attestations are probably a dedication by a *mageiros* in Epidaurus[2] and Epicharmus fr. 84 *CGFP*.[3] The term

---

[1] Berthiaume reviews possible cases of such a specialist in Homer and dismisses Semonides fr. 24 West as an instance, arguing that the term *mageiros* is due to Athenaeus (15.659d–f) and not Semonides.

[2] *IG* IV², 1.144.

[3] 'I am a *mageiros*.' Sophocles fr. 1122 Radt, 'I am a *mageiros* and I season food cleverly', is not accepted as genuine.

slowly appeared in Attic Old Comedy and expanded rapidly in Middle and New, just as it expanded in inscriptions of the Hellenistic and Roman periods which related to civic and deme festivals.[4] Berthiaume may be right to link the evolution of the term with new developments in sophisticated eating, but this hardly accounts for all the sacrificial instances. Furthermore, the term was used in a large number of poleis. The term *mageiros* might thus be used at sacrifice alongside other terms such as *hieropoios*; it is a much more common term for a commercial butcher than *kreopoles* (meat-seller), and it became one of the terms for cook alongside the older and more specific *opsopoios*. The wide range of the term *mageiros* allowed the comic poets to use it both of agent of sacrifice and cook, to distinguish or merge at will the ritual agent and the specialist cook. The *mageiros*, in Athens at least, appears usually to be an agent for hire, whether for civic feasting or for a private *deipnon*. His role thus potentially combines the sacred, the commercial, and the pleasurable areas of ancient life, to which are added his own lively discourse.

Since sacrifice and cooking lie at the heart of comedy, the *mageiros* came to have a significant role, not least because the low social status accorded to him could be exploited in comedy's pursuit of its materialist interests in those parts of the life of the polis which carried great cultural significance. The presentation of the *mageiros* in Attic comedy changed with time, but any attempt to map that change onto social change in the polis is hazardous. The detailed studies of the comic *mageiros* by Rankin (1907), Giannini (1960), and Dohm (1964) highlight the problem.[5] The *mageiros* as a character appears—on the evidence available—not to have been on stage in Old Comedy (though there are numerous fragments which *may* indicate the reverse). This study is unable to determine whether the use of cook-*mageiroi* increased during the fourth century in Athens or not, or whether they remain an essentially literary phenomenon created by a change of focus from public to private life. It may be significant that, in

---

[4] Berthiaume (1982), 17–39, citing *LSCG* 33B 27–31 on the Lesser Panathenaia, *LSS* 10, on a deme calendar?

[5] Add Ribbeck (1882), 18–26; Latte, *RE* 14 (1930), 393–5; Fraenkel (1960), 408–16; Nesselrath (1990), 297–309; and Arnott (forthcoming); on Eubulus, Hunter (1983); on Alexis, Arnott (1996); on Menander, Gomme and Sandbach (1973) and Handley (1965) on *Dyscolus* 393.

reporting an incident of the sixth century, the arrival of Smindyrides of Sybaris as a suitor of Agariste at the Sicyonian court, Herodotus in the fifth century merely mentions his luxury, while a later source, Timaeus or another, adds a retinue of a thousand cooks and wildfowlers.[6] Berthiaume reviews other instances of the *mageiros* read into earlier history by the moralizing historians of the fourth century BC.

8.2. FROM *MAGEIROS*-PROTAGONIST TO STOCK CHARACTER

The comic cook is a familiar stock character of Middle and New Comedy, to be compared with the parasite, the mercenary courtesan, and the clever slave.[7] He is an *alazon*, a boaster inflated with a notion of his own importance.[8] That importance is not recognized by other characters, who mock the boaster on behalf of the audience. The *mageiros* ought to leave the stage as quickly as possible and begin to work in his hot kitchen, producing objects of desire with the labour of his own hands or those of his assistants and slaves. He should be out of the picture, while at sacrifice the *mageiros* is a manual worker, essential to the ritual but taken for granted.[9] This is what we find in *Peace* and *Birds*: the essential preparations for the sacrifice or meal are performed by the protagonist and his slave, while some of the fine detail is provided off-stage by the *mageiros*—if required. The protagonist is perfectly able to manipulate the material objects of the culinary world, the sheep, instruments of sacrifice, and pots and pans, and has little call upon the *mageiros*. The protagonist in *Peace* acts 'like a *mageiros*' (1017).[10] The *mageiros*, in a non-speaking role, is available when the whim of the protagonist takes him. Peisetaerus in *Birds* demonstrates this best when he calls on a silent *mageiros* (1637) to finish off the sauce which he has begun

---

[6] Herodotus 6.127.1; Athenaeus 12.541b–c.

[7] I presume that the number of parasites, courtesans, and slaves did not increase during the fourth century, any more than did the number of cooks. I believe it more likely that it was comic perceptions that changed.

[8] Athenaeus 7.290b: ἀλαζονικὸν δ᾽ ἐστὶ πᾶν τὸ τῶν μαγείρων φῦλον ('the whole tribe of cooks is boastful').

[9] Detienne (1989), 129–4.   [10] μαγειρικῶς.

to prepare for some birds.[11] In these respects Aristophanes exemplifies Berthiaume's thesis that the *mageiros* is called in only when needed by the organizer of the sacrifice. The sacrifice conducted by Trygaeus and his slave in *Peace* is very similar to that of the *mageiros* in the *Flatterer* of Menander.[12]

The fully fledged *mageiros* of the later comedy offers clear advantages that may not have been exploited in Old Comedy. If the role of *mageiros* is separated from the protagonist, then the cook or agent of sacrifice no longer benefits from full participation in the feast, whether the food, the sacrificial victim, or the sexual pleasures available at the accompanying symposium. Thus he might become a kind of reinvented *bomolochus* who steals the meat of sacrifice (see below); more, he must sublimate the pleasure of eating into discourse about what he can do for others; lastly, he is more a creature limited to the material world of the kitchen than the protagonist can ever be. The comic *mageiros* operates, furthermore, in the private domain to a much greater extent than does the protagonist of Old Comedy. He normally officiates neither at state festivals nor on behalf of himself, chorus, and audience, but cooks for hire to a private employer.[13] This private aspect allows him to prepare high-status foods such as foreign sauces and large fish to which the cook/protagonist had no access.[14] His high ambition leads to greater elaboration than straightforward 'feasting'. This expands the attention paid to provisioning (household stores and shopping), the work of the kitchen, and elaboration at table. His distance from the controlling discourse of the play allows the poet to work in a larger element of 'luxury' and a commentary on the 'development of gastronomy'. This has been picked up in recent

[11] Peisetaerus and Euelpides earlier went inside to sacrifice a goat, apparently without assistance (1055–7).

[12] *Peace* 937–1126 provides a whole scene, *Flatterer* fr. 1 only seven lines spoken by a cook. Each pursues its objective with reference to parts of the animal, the vital organs (*Peace* 1040, *Flatterer* fr. 1.1), the tongue (*Peace* 1060, *Flatterer* 1.5), thighs (*Peace* 1039), loin (1053), tail (1054).

[13] We shall see below at least one comic *mageiros* who may be working in a public cult, in Euphron fr. 1.

[14] The foreign sauces in question are *kandaulos*, *karyke*, and the preparation known as *mattye*: see below on Nicostratus fr. 16. The protagonist sometimes prepares sauces, *katachysmata*, and special dishes such as *mimarchys* but not, as far as I am aware expensive fish. The picture might look quite different if the plays of more poets of Old Comedy had survived. See below.

scholarship. Von Reden (1998) has argued[15] that Menander's *Dyscolus*, a play of New Comedy with a large role for the *mageiros*, reflects a real disquiet over the development in the polis of a money economy that might undermine the traditional ordering of society through social and religious ritual. In a discussion of the same play, Scodel (1993) has argued (from the perspective of theatrical history) that the sacrifice has been threatened by the more 'trivial' pursuit of food for pleasure. My argument is very different, namely that cooking, sacrificial and/or non-sacrificial, is a central concern of comedy from Epicharmus to Athenion, that the same artisan, the *mageiros*, works at both; that pleasure, a sensation shared by all human beings,[16] derives from the eating of meat and from the social coherence brought by sacrifice as well as from the gourmet's table; and that the tension between 'ritual' and 'pleasure' is, in comic discourse, always available for the comic poet to exploit. Thus Austin's[17] censure of Dohm (1964) for suggesting that there are no *mageiroi* in Old Comedy will not be applicable to this study: there may have been *mageiroi* in lost plays of the Old Comedy who were prototypes of the stock character of Middle Comedy; indeed, the Black-Pudding-Seller of *Knights* is a kind of *mageiros*; but the *mageiroi* of Dohm's study differ from those of Aristophanes' surviving plays in being no longer protagonists or equivalent. They have developed from the protagonist who dismisses *alazones* from his sacrifice and feast into *alazones* and bit players themselves.

In Old Comedy the protagonist is normally master of the sacrifice or at least of the provision of food, nearly all of which has been cooked. The following survey of the surviving plays of Aristophanes identifies (A) the protagonist who sacrifices and (B) preparation for a meal.

In *Acharnians* Dicaeopolis sets up the sacrificial procession of the Rural Dionysia (A) and organizes his slaves in cooking food for an apparently private meal with the priest of Dionysus at the Anthesteria (B). In *Knights* the Black-Pudding-Seller is a trader

---

[15] See Chap. 1: her approach is based on the development of a money economy.

[16] Davidson (1997), whose emphasis on expensive fish may reinforce the notion that 'luxury' in fourth-century cooking eased out the ritual cooking of sacrifice, brings out well the pleasure that all take in eating and drinking.

[17] Austin (1964).

in the surplus meat from sacrifice and boils up Demos as if he were an animal at the end of the play (A). In *Clouds* Strepsiades recalls his cooking of meat at the Diasia and Panathenaia and turns to feasting Pheidippides at 1212. The feasting (all off stage) is largely conducted at the sympotic stage (1353–8) (B). The same is true of *Wasps*, which concentrates on the preparation for the symposium (1216–49) and *deipnon* (1250–2) and the performance of the subsequent komos (B).[18] In *Peace* Trygaeus sacrifices a goat (A) and invites all non-military participants to his wedding feast (1305–57) (B). Peisetaerus in *Birds* also sacrifices a goat and prepares a wedding feast (AB). In *Lysistrata* a feast is provided (1182–246) though not explicitly by the protagonist (B). There is no feasting in *Thesmophoriazusae*. Though some aspects of the Thesmophoria are alluded to, including the fast of the second day, none of the major characters is responsible for the preparation of food. In *Frogs*, another exceptional play,[19] food is prepared *for* the protagonist Dionysus. The innkeepers of the underworld prepare food, the initiates roast pork, and Pluto prepares a feast for Dionysus and Aeschylus (1480) (B). In *Ecclesiazusae* Praxagora has all the institutions of the polis converted into outlets for food and wine and all are invited to the final feast (B). In *Wealth* the god Wealth is given a feast (795) (B) for which the protagonist has conducted the sacrifice (819–22) (A).

Backing up the influential role of the protagonist in the provision of food for the feasts of comedy are a series of slaves and servants, sometimes on stage, sometimes off stage. The slave of Trygaeus in *Peace*, for example, has many of the skills of the *mageiros*. Some of these assistants are called *mageiroi*.[20] At the same time, the protagonist is sometimes said to display the skills of the *mageiros*—and these sometimes extend beyond sacrifice to festive cooking.[21] Giannini[22] has collected a number of fragments

---

[18] In this play Bdelycleon organizes the meal and Philocleon celebrates the komos. Whichever is the 'protagonist', both dominate the action.

[19] Exceptional in this respect since the protagonist is a god?

[20] *Mageiroi* at *Birds* 1637 (the *mageiros* is told to make a sweet sauce) and *Frogs* 517 (he is bringing out slices of meat and the tables).

[21] *Acharnians* 1015, *Knights* 216, *Peace* 1017. Butchers (*mageiroi*) are mentioned at *Knights* 376 and 418, a *mageiros*'s knife in *Old Age* fr. 143; the son of a *mageiros* is attacked in fr. 409.

[22] (1960), 142–52.

from Old Comedy which describe a wide range of cooking skills, the performers of which, he suggests, may have been *mageiroi*. He may well be correct in some cases—but not all. The man shopping for food at Ecphantides, *Satyrs* fr. 1, 'whenever it was necessary to buy and eat boiled pig's trotters', is not a likely candidate since the *mageiros* (in later comedy at least) buys and cooks for others: he does not usually benefit personally from eating any more than he enjoys the sexual pleasures of the feast. Particularly promising examples presented by Giannini are Cratinus fr. 336, 'not every man is able to season the *glaukos* well',[23] and two plays of Pherecrates, *The Kitchen or The All-Night Festival* and *The Slave-Teacher*. In the first a fragment (fr. 70), apparently from the parabasis, contains the statement 'nobody ever saw a [female] *mageiraina* nor indeed a female fish-seller', and another (fr. 66), in the first person, has someone complaining of ashes in his eyes when he is blowing the flames. In the second (fr. 50) there is the exchange:

A: How can you tell us how the preparations for dinner proceed?[24]
B: Well, there is available for you a slice of eel, a squid, some lamb, a slice of black-pudding, a boiled trotter, a liver, a rib, a great number of birds, cheese in honey, a portion of meat . . .

In fr. 197[25] someone declares: 'now it's necessary to pour in the barley, to winnow it, to toast it, to steep it in water, to dehusk it, to grind it, to make it into barley cakes, to bake it, and finally to serve it.' These examples may suggest a *mageiros* at work,[26] or a protagonist and his attendants, as in the surviving plays of Aristophanes. It is conceivable that the *mageiros* played a different role in plays of Cratinus and Pherecrates than he does in Aristophanes, since other differences exist between them, such as the use of myth.[27] In the *Odysseuses* of Cratinus (fr. 150) the Cyclops displays the skills of the *mageiros*, though he is not explicitly called a *mageiros* (as he is in the satyric *Cyclops* of Euripides):[28] 'in return for which, I shall grab you stout-hearted

---

[23] οὐ πρὸς παντὸς ἀνδρός ἐστιν ἀρτῦσαι καλῶς. This appears to be a boastful claim to cook a large fish well.

[24] The line is corrupt.

[25] Which Meineke attributed to *Slave-Teacher*: Kassel–Austin (1989) do not concur.

[26] Though fr. 197 confines itself to the various processes that barley goes through from seeding to eating.

[27] Henderson (forthcoming).   [28] 397, Ἄιδον μάγειρος.

companions and toast, boil, grill over charcoal, and roast you and into salt-dip and vinegar-salt dip and garlic-salt dip will I dip you hot, whichever of you all seems to me to be most roasted, and gobble you down, my good soldiers.' *Mageiroi* may have prepared some of the meals in the utopian fragments quoted in Chapter 3, two of which come from different plays by Pherecrates.[29] Pherecrates described someone (a *mageiros?*) preparing foreign sauces (fr. 195): 'grinding an *abyrtake* and a Lydian *karyke*', and someone is told in fr. 183, 'prepare a *deipnon*, and you[30] sit down'. There are, then, significant differences between Cratinus and Pherecrates on the one hand and the surviving plays of Aristophanes on the other, the most notable of which are the claim over seasoning of a large fish, foreign sauces, and the Cyclops as the *mageiros* from hell. There is a prima facie case for a *mageiros* on-stage in Old Comedy, to be distinguished from the cook/protagonist.

All that the fragmentary evidence shows for sure, however, is that much cooking of food was performed and commented upon in Old Comedy, whether by a *mageiros* or not. No fragmentary play survives to an extent sufficient to indicate whether a prototype of the stock *mageiros* was developed, perhaps by Cratinus or Pherecrates or, conversely, whether a poet other than Aristophanes had protagonists who were masters of the sacrifice and feast. One of the last plays of Aristophanes, *Aeolosicon*, may have presented a composite of the stock character and protagonist *if* the Sicon of the title was a Sicilian cook and *if* he was the protagonist. The fragments of the play which refer to cooking are insufficient to settle this point.

As for the plays of Epicharmus (which may or may not have influenced Old Comedy), a character declared, presumably on stage, 'I am a *mageiros*',[31] and there are fragments in which the preparation of food and sacrifice may have been performed by a *mageiros*,[32] but there can be no more certainty than for Old Comedy. The skills of the *mageiros* are seen in a play with a mythical

---

[29] Aristophanes' contribution (not preserved) came from the *Fryers* (*Tagenistae*): was the preparation for the meal performed by the chorus?

[30] A different person?

[31] In a lemma from the text picked up in a commentary, possibly on the *Odysseus the Deserter* as noted in Chap. 7, n. 31.

[32] Giannini (1960), 141–2; Dohm (1964), 22–30.

title, *Sirens*, though the speaker is not a *mageiros* but one of the beneficiaries of the feast (fr. 124):

A: In the early morning, at dawn, we grilled round whitebait, we had roast pork and octopus, and we drank it all down with sweet wine.
B: O dear, O dear!
A: One could talk of it as a meal.
B: Alas for your misfortunes!
A: In so far as there was one fat red mullet and two bonitos cut in half and the same number of doves and scorpion fish.[33]

All that can be said for sure is that cooking was a distinguishing feature of both Epicharmus and Attic Old Comedy, and several elements that came to make up the *mageiros* of Middle Comedy were in evidence, perhaps in prototype form, in the fragments of Old Comedy. If Epicharmus had any influence in this respect, it appears to be distant and combined with other Sicilian developments of the late fifth and early fourth centuries discussed in Chapter 7.

The evidence of the extant plays of Old Comedy points to the performance of these tasks by a protagonist and his appointees. In surviving plays the protagonist appears in nearly every case to be the master of the sacrifice and of the feast. There is a gender differential, in that no female protagonist prepares food with her own hands. This may indicate either that the *mageiros*/protagonist is considered to have a quasi-sacred role based on sacrifice (women did not slaughter animals in antiquity),[34] or (a less likely possibility) that the female protagonists were too high in the social order to perform 'menial' tasks, in a way that their male counterparts were not. His or her control is augmented still further by the power to determine who will attend the feast. Thus, Dicaeopolis in *Acharnians* excludes from the feast Lamachus and from the peace associated with it an Attic farmer and a bridegroom. The chorus join him in the final komos (1231).[35] This

---

[33] On this passage see also Chap. 7.3.

[34] Though see Osborne (1993), 392–405.

[35] After the expulsion of the Attic farmer, the chorus remarks of Dicaeopolis (1037–46):

CHOR.: the man has found something sweet in his peace-treaty and doesn't look as if he will share it with anyone.
DIC.: Pour the honey over the black-pudding and fry the cuttlefish.

pattern, which includes the chorus and excludes adversaries, notably those prominent in war, is repeated in later plays, with the audience also added to those included and mean *choregoi* (sponsors) and officious persons excluded.[36] As I have indicated in previous chapters, the protagonist reconfigures the polis, excluding from the feast the prominent, particularly those prominent in war, politics, philosophy, and tragic poetry, and including the demos, represented by the audience. In this respect Old Comedy presents a polis analogous to the polis described by the Old Oligarch, in whose view the demos seek to expand their participation in communal feasting at the expense of the powerful:

as for sacrifices and shrines and feasts and holy precincts, the demos is aware that not each one of the poor is able to sacrifice and have a feast and set up shrines and live in a city which is beautiful and great and has worked out how to make these things available. The city sacrifices many victims at public expense and it is the demos that enjoys the feast and gets the victims. Some of the rich have gymnasia, baths, and changing-rooms run at their own expense, but the demos has built for its own use many wrestling quarters, changing-rooms, and baths. The rabble derive more enjoyment from these amenities than the wealthy elite.

([Xenophon] 2.9–10: cf. Chapter 3, n. 182)

Comedy has taken the participation and exclusion several stages further—to an extreme, in fact, since priests and gods (in *Peace*, *Birds*, and *Wealth*) as well as civic officers are excluded from the comic feast. There is no single model presented by Aristophanes, for the inclusion may be in festivals of Dionysus (*Acharnians*), in sacrifice and marriage, or in the combination of citizens and audience (*Ecclesiazusae*). The phenomenon also extends from his earliest surviving play to his latest. The best

CHOR.: Did you hear his loud ringing tones?
DIC.: Roast the eels.
CHOR.: You will kill me and the neighbours with hunger if you say such things with roasting fat and a loud voice.
DIC.: Roast these and brown them nicely.

It is not clear whether the chorus fear expulsion also or are playing up the excitement of the cooking scene.

[36] Cornford (1914) tried to identify those excluded with the dying god, but goes too far.

fate that can be imagined for a comic character is to share in the feast, the worst to be excluded and hungry. Thus the blackmailer in *Wealth* is desperately hungry (873)[37] and taunted with the smells of salt fish and meat (893–6), while Zeus and Hermes no longer receive good things and sacrificial offerings (1112–38) and are starving along with their priest (1174). This is the comic polis, a major reconfiguration of the historical polis. As we have seen, the politicians and tragic poets in Old Comedy are said to have eaten too well, to have enjoyed themselves too far at the expense of the demos. As emphasized in previous chapters, the pleasures of the feast are only subject to the negative discourse of luxury in Old Comedy if they are found at the homes of the wealthy from which the 'demos' are excluded. If any attempt is made in comedy to argue the case for restraint in eating and the moral rewards of poverty, as is splendidly portrayed in the character of Poverty (*Penia*) in *Wealth*, then other characters read famine for restraint (562) and send the heretic packing.[38]

The *mageiros* of Middle and New Comedy may have appeared in some of the lost plays of Old Comedy, but as far as we know he makes his entrée on to the Attic stage in the period 370–350. The comic *mageiros* does not necessarily introduce a diet of luxury at the expense of sacrifice and good order, as has sometimes been suggested. We have just seen that the protagonist-*mageiros* of Old Comedy combines the two. When the daughter of Dicaeopolis acts as *kanephoros* for the procession of the Rural Dionysia in *Acharnians*, carrying the basket of grains which conceals the sacrificial knife (253–4, 260), she tells her mother, 'O mother, hand me the soup-ladle for me to pour the soup over this flat-cake here'. Sacrificial ritual and consumption of food go closely hand in hand.[39] This principle will guide our consideration of Menander's *Dyscolus* below. At the same time, the switch from protagonist-*mageiros* to the comic cook as a stock character is a massive change. He is no longer in control of events, either on the fictional level within the play or on the metafictional level as

---

[37] βουλιμιᾶι.

[38] No one appears to be excluded in *Lysistrata*, *Thesmophoriazusae*, or *Ecclesiazusae*. Euripides is probably excluded in *Frogs*.

[39] The daughter's words also convey a *double-entendre* which anticipates the sexual theme of much of Dicaeopolis' instructions and hymn to Phales: see Henderson (1991), 144.

one who controls the discourse. That is not to say that the cook cannot continue to play a significant part in a play, as does Sicon in Menander's *Dyscolus*. But it does mean that he is no longer the beneficiary either of the feast or of the accompanying sexual favours of *hetaerae* or a new or reconciled wife that are often enjoyed by male protagonists.

The comic *mageiros*, once separated from the protagonist, is given a number of essential functions. The first is to cook for a social occasion, often the marriage which is at the heart of many plots in Middle and New Comedy.[40] The second is to deliver a long speech to an employer or an assistant. Nesselrath has suggested[41] that these speeches may not have been developed by poets before Alexis and that the early utterances of the character on stage were in anapaestic metre, in pseudo-dithyrambic and parodic language of the kind discussed in the last chapter, or in rapid exchanges.[42] The cook arrived with ornate or animated speech rather than long practical or theoretical discourses. Early examples of such enlivening of culinary details with metrical and poetic ingenuity are provided by Anaxandrides, *Aeschra* fr. 6, Eubulus, *Auge* fr. 14, *Leda or Spartans* fr. 63, *Orthannes* fr. 75, *Titans* fr. 108 and Antiphanes, *Parasite* fr. 180 (cited in Chapter 7), among others. Speech animated by rapid exchanges is exemplified by Antiphanes, *Philotis* fr. 221:

MAGEIROS: So I tell you to boil the little *glaukos*, as on other occasions, in salt water.
A: And the little sea bass?
MAGEIROS: Roast whole.
A: The sturgeon?
MAGEIROS: Boil in a sour mince.
A: The little eel?
MAGEIROS: Salt, origano, water.
A: The conger?
MAGEIROS: The same.

[40] Nesselrath (1990), 297.
[41] Ibid. 298–302.
[42] Nicostratus, *Cook* fr. 16, if this is part of a long speech by a *mageiros*, may pre-date some of the speeches of Alexis, as may Anaxilas, *Cooks*—if that play contained a speech by a *mageiros*. Ephippus fr. 22 (cited below) is another possibility. Arnott cautions (1996: 22), 'priorities of innovation among contemporary comic poets are usually impossible to assign'.

A: The ray?
MAGEIROS: Green herbs.
A: There's also a tuna cutlet.
MAGEIROS: You will roast it.
A: Kid meat.
MAGEIROS: Roasted.
A: The other.
MAGEIROS: The opposite.
A: The spleen?
MAGEIROS: Let it be stuffed.
A: The empty jejunum?
MAGEIROS: This man will be the end of me.

As Nesselrath concedes, not all these examples were necessarily spoken by *mageiroi*,[43] but if he is right, the poets of Middle Comedy first developed their new stock character not so much as a skilled artisan of the kitchen who could set out for a theatre audience advice similar to Archestratus—as does the *mageiros* of Sotades cited below—but as one who could present his skills with animation and flowery language.

Once the long speech was established, interlocutors often tried to interrupt the relentless harangue with such stock expressions as 'don't chop me up, chop your meat'.[44] An early ancestor of such an expression is perhaps to be found in Old Comedy in Pherecrates, *Miners* fr. 113.20–1.[45] Protagonist-*mageiroi* in Old Comedy—who were in control of the discourse—had not expatiated at length on their cooking skills. The fact that later *mageiroi* bore their listeners and are interrupted is a further indication of their demoted role in the play. Their speeches are tedious or in other ways unwelcome because the *mageiros* does not properly belong at the dinner or symposium. His job is to prepare or organize the preparation of food in a hot kitchen and make sure it is properly served to the diners. He is an artisan who mistakenly believes he can leave the kitchen, and who, furthermore, speaks of the kitchen in detail which is often irksome to his listeners,

[43] Cf. Hunter's caution (1983) on the fragments of Eubulus cited here.
[44] Discussed by Arnott (1996) on Alexis fr. 177.12 and Gomme and Sandbach (1973) on Menander, *Samia* 285.
[45] Spoken to a woman describing utopian dining in the underworld. Culinary language is not used, however: 'you will be the end of me if you stay here any longer, when you can all tumble down to Tartarus as you are.'

at least the listeners on the stage. He both imposes himself on the gathering and complicates the preparations by introducing extraneous and verbose material, whether in the flowery language of dithyrambic parody or in surveys of previous theory and its relevance to his own practice.

8.3. THE HEAT OF THE KITCHEN

The *mageiros* in Sotades, *Locked Up Women* fr. 1 appears to confine himself to the purchase of provisions, the preparation of food, and the heat of the kitchen; in short, the material world over which the cook presides:

First I got some prawns. I fried all these in a pan. A large sturgeon has been acquired. I baked the middle section and the other bits and pieces I shall boil up using a mulberry sauce. I carry in two huge heads of the *glaukos*, these in a mighty stewpot, lightly adding green herbs, cumin, salt, water, and some oil. After that I bought a really fine sea bass. It will be covered in oil and boiled in salt water with green herbs after delivering up the parts to be roasted on the spit. I purchased some fine red mullet and some fine wrasse. I tossed these onto the charcoal as they were, adding marjoram and oil and salt-water. In addition to these I got some cuttlefish and squid. A nice dish is boiled squid stuffed, as are the lateral fins of the cuttle gently roasted. To go with these I made a sauce of all sorts of green herbs. There were some boiled [. . .][46] after these. I gave them a vinegar and oil sauce to bring out the flavour. After these I bought a really fat conger and cooked it at a high heat in rather fragrant salt-water. There were some gobies and some little rock-fish: I snipped off their heads and smeared them with flour [. . .] I send on the same way as the prawns. A tuna by itself, a very fine creature, I covered just enough with oil and wrapped it in fig leaves, sprinkled it with marjoram, and hid it like a firebrand in a heap of ashes. With it I got some whitebait from Phaleron. Half a cup of water poured over is plenty. I cut up some green herbs nice and finely—plenty of it—and even if the jar holds two cupfulls, I tip it in. What's left? Nothing else. This is my art, derived neither from recipes nor from memoranda.

This is the practical cook giving details of his kitchen-skills, with no appeal to other skills that we shall meet below nor to written instructions. He cooks a vast range of fish, many of which are found in Matro's *Attic Dinner*. The meal appears to be a

---

[46] The text is uncertain.

lavish affair based on expensive fish, but the cook's interest is only in cooking technique. Modes of cooking are uniform, boiling or roasting and using oil, salt-water, and herbs in sauces. There are no elaborate dishes and the style is similar to that of Archestratus' poem, as I noted in Chapter 7. He is not interested either in the modes of serving or other details of the dinner—only in cooking. This is rare in the speeches of *mageiroi*. Philemon the Younger fr. 1 shares the focus on technique but makes clear what is assumed in most speeches, that there is more to being a *mageiros* than manual skills alone: 'leave it just as it is. For roasted foods, simply make the fire neither too slow (that sort of fire is for boiled dishes, not roast) nor too fierce, for then it burns what it gets at on the outside but does not get into the flesh. The *mageiros* is not merely one who comes to a client with a soup-ladle and cook's knife nor one who tosses fish into stewing-pots—no, thought is required in this job.' It is the claim to thought and theoretical study that characterizes the boastfulness of the later speeches of the stock *mageiros*. The cook seeks always to extend into new areas, while his interlocutor urges him to concentrate on his trade. In some plays the *mageiros* comes out of the house to describe what he has done or requires to be done in the kitchen or what must be bought at the market. Other plays present him on his way to an assignment armed with the tools of his trade. Menander, *Dyscolus* is a particularly good example, since the cook brings his own sheep and has to arrange to borrow necessary pots and pans. This gives much emphasis on stage to the material objects necessary to his trade.

Two plays of Alexis, who wrote a number of speeches for *mageiroi*,[47] appear to have made much of the purchase and cooking of food. In *Lebes*,[48] frr. 130, 131, and 133 discuss problematic fishmongers and fig-sellers, while fr. 132[49] lists the seasonings that the cook will need the hirer to supply. Fr. 129 contains the advice, probably of a cook,[50] on how to rescue a piece of pork that has been burnt when the heat of the kitchen has got out of hand. Arnott has brought out well the medical language that lies

---

[47] See Arnott (1996), 21–2.

[48] The pot of the title may not have been a cooking-pot but a receptacle for valuables, as in the *Aulularia* of Plautus: see Arnott (1996).

[49] Quoted in Chap. 1. [50] See Arnott (1996).

behind this advice. The assistant responds to the cook's elaboration with 'you appear to be a much better speech-writer than cook'. In *All-Night Festival or Hired Workers* there are four fragments in which a cook speaks. Fr. 179[51] once again lists the seasonings the cook requires; fr. 178[52] claims the invention of *kandaulos* and elaborately sets forth other delights, to the irritation of the hirer. Two fragments concern the heat of the food; in fr. 180 the boiled conger appears to be ready but the meat and trotters are not, while the *perikomma* (chopped meat) is ruined. In fr. 177 hirer and cook argue over how hot the food should be and whether the kitchen is adequate, again to the irritation of the hirer.

The fragments on cooking show more elaborate cooking than is found in Old Comedy and more interest in bringing an interior scene—from the kitchen—out onto the stage for verbal elaboration. Interruptions appear in both, for the cooking of Trygaeus was invaded by the priest and Dicaeopolis taunted Lamachus with the fragrant food he was denied. Both Old and the later comedy clearly wished to spin out the all-important moment when the cooked food signalled that the feast was ready and the wished-for occasion—the wedding or other event—was at last sealed with communal eating. The cook of Middle and New Comedy was at liberty to present himself as a wonder-worker with new inventions (Alexis fr. 178), as one able to turn disaster into success (Alexis fr. 129), or as the master of all, as does Sotades' cook with many kinds of fish. Some later cooks distanced themselves from the heat of the kitchen completely, as we shall see.

8.4. A SICILIAN INFLUENCE?

There are two forms of 'luxurious' cooking which the new *mageiros* appears to introduce: the cooking of large fish, and a non-Athenian, sometimes a Sicilian style. In the plays of Aristophanes the latter was a foreign influence to be dismissed along with other distractions of the young (*Banqueters* fr. 225). Foreign influences on cooks appear early—certainly in the first half of the fourth century. As we saw in Chapter 7, *Giants* fr. 1 of the

---

[51] Quoted in Chap. 1.   [52] Quoted in Chap. 6.

younger Cratinus presented a Sicilian *mageiros* producing fragrant smells in a chasm (the plot may have been mythological). In Antiphanes, *Dyspratos* fr. 90 Sicilian skills extend to cakes,[53] while the speaker of Ephippus, *Philyra* fr. 22 asks: 'A: Shall I cut up the ray and boil it? What do you say? Or shall I do it roasted, in Sicilian style? B: Sicilian Style.' The cook in Epicrates, *Merchant* fr. 6 declares, 'I am the next *mageiros* after them. Neither Sicily shall boast that it brought up such an cook[54] for fish, nor shall Elis,[55] where I have seen the finest meat of pigs browned by the flames of the fire.'[56] Note in the last fragment the claim to ability in fish-cooking, which competes with the best in Sicily, and (sacrificial) meat-cooking which competes with that at Olympia: the stock *mageiros* is master of the sacrifice as well as cook to the extravagant fish-eater.

The possible Sicilian influence on Attic comedy of the fourth century was considered in Chapter 7—the role of Mithaecus, of the parodic epic of Archestratus, and of other cookery books, in addition to the possible contribution of Epicharmus and Sicilian comedy. The fragments quoted above have not suffered a specifically literary influence, but identify a 'foreign' style which may derive from the comedies, cookery books, or way of life of the Sicilian cities. There is little evidence that Sicilian cooking made a large impact on the Greek mainland, apart from these discourses and the satirical reports of Plato in *Gorgias* and the *Republic*. Even in comedy itself, specific reference to Sicily is limited to the passages listed above. We saw in Chapter 6 other influences on Athenian cooking from outside, for example in Nicostratus, *Driven Out* fr. 7 and *Cook* fr. 16. In the former, Athenaeus tells us (14.664b–c), a cook describes his dazzling and well-ordered presentation of three meals, breakfast, dinner and, third, a *mattye* (from northern Greece) which will confound all his critics. Fr. 16 adds *kandaulos* to a *mattye* as part of the successful cook's repertoire. These non-Athenian elements in the meal, as I argued in Chapter 6, help to construct that Athenian

---

[53] 'Banquet-cakes spiced with the arts of the Sicilians.'
[54] *Artamos*. On this term see Berthiaume (1982), 10–12.
[55] Cf. Antiphanes fr. 233 and below.
[56] Again, there are traces of dithyrambic expression here: Nesselrath (1990), 299.

identity of simplicity and sparing cooking satirized by Lynceus fr. 1 (also quoted in Chapter 6). Occasionally the cook/protagonist of Old Comedy indulged in foreign delicacies, or at least dishes with foreign names (such as, for example, *mimarkys* at *Acharnians* 1112); in Middle Comedy that foreign element may instantly be proclaimed. The fact remains, however, that even in Middle and New Comedy attribution of foods or styles of cooking to specific places is rarer than a general expansion in elaboration and detail. *Mageiroi* claim or reject affiliation to 'schools' of cookery and to teachers who come from a wide range of Greek poleis, Acharnania, Rhodes, or Chios as often as Sicilian cities.

The favoured dish to prepare is often fish, as we saw in Chapter 6. In Old Comedy we have no surviving example of their preparation by the cook/protagonist. In 'Middle' the cook has come out of the closet. While, as far as we can tell from the comic fragments, he does not jostle with the gluttons and gourmets at the fish-market investigated in Chapter 6,[57] nevertheless he buys his ingredients from the market-place—indeed shopping is an important part of his function—and is himself hired from the agora, from the cook-stand or *mageireion*. The protagonist/cook of Old Comedy rarely had to bother himself about shopping; to be sure, Dicaeopolis and Trygaeus restore the agora and the selling of food to the war-torn polis, but in a fantastic form analogous to the automatic provision of food by the gods. Shopping does not appear to have been a concern for the protagonist/cook. In *Acharnians* Dicaeopolis famously rejects the city and claims that the basic materials for cooking—charcoal, vinegar (or cheap wine), and oil—were not bought with money in his rural deme. When he establishes his market through his miraculous peace-treaty he shows no more sign of using money, but has foods brought to him by outsiders eager to exchange foods for little return. Other protagonists in Old Comedy who concentrate on the provision of foods, Trygaeus in *Peace*, Peisetaerus in *Birds*, and Praxagora in *Ecclesiazusae*, also harness divine or political forms of provision and not the commercial markets.

---

[57] Though he may have done in Alexis, *Lebes*. See above.

8.5. THE BOASTFUL COOK OF MIDDLE AND NEW COMEDY

The speeches of boastful cooks preserved from later Greek comedy have been systematically studied by Giannini (1960)[58] and Dohm (1964).[59] The following discussion does not review all the speeches or seek to recast these studies, but selects examples which are significant for the themes of this book.[60]

8.5.1. The Transforming Power of Cooking

Cooking, as we have seen, lies at the heart of Old Comedy. In the surviving plays of Aristophanes at least, the cook/protagonist achieves his or her fantastic aims and seals success in communal feasting that s/he has organized, often with the assistance of generous provision by benevolent gods. On occasion the cooking itself may become fantastic. In *Knights* the Black-Pudding-Seller boils up the Demos and rejuvenates him, a magical form of cookery normally reserved to myth.[61] In *Acharnians* Dicaeopolis puts his head on a chopping-block, strictly that

---

[58] Giannini's approach is broadly chronological, as far as a chronology can be established for so many fragmentary plays. He lists the distinguishing characteristics of the speeches as: boasting (*alazoneia*), chatter (*lalia*), pomposity, sententiousness, novelty (εὑρεῖν), theft (κλέπτειν), zeal or officiousness, gossip, excessive familiarity, ingenuity, rivalry, rascality.

[59] Dohm's approach (pp. 84–93) is developmental, dividing the speeches into (a) monologues, (b) fragments containing a dialogue between one cook and another, and (c) fragments containing a full-blown dialogue between a cook and his employer or slave. Under (a) he lists Nicostratus fr. 7; Alexis frr. 84, 191–4; Axionicus frr. 4 and 8; Dionysius fr. 1; Sotades fr. 1; Philemon fr. 82; Archedicus frr. 2 and 3; Adesp. frr. 1072–3. Under (b): Antiphanes fr. 221; Ephippus fr. 22; Anaxilas fr. 19; Alexis fr. 138; Dionysius fr. 3; Philemon Junior fr. 1; Diphilus fr. 42; Euphron frr. 1 and 10; Machon fr. 2; Poseidippus fr. 28. Under (c): Epicrates fr. 6; Alexis frr. 24, 129, 153, 177–9; Dionysius fr. 2; Philemon frr. 42 and 63; Diphilus fr. 17; Menander frr. 351, 409; *Kolax* fr. 1; *The Arbitration* frr. 2 and 433–8; Lynceus fr. 1; Anaxippus fr. 1; Hegesippus fr. 1; Sosipater fr. 1; Euphron frr. 9 and 11; Baton fr. 4; Poseidippus fr. 1; Damoxenus fr. 2; Demetrius fr. 1; Strato fr. 1; Athenion fr. 1; Euangelos fr. 1; Nicomachus fr. 1; Philostephanus fr. 1; Adesp. fr. 1093.155–237; Plautus, *Pseudolus* 790–892.

[60] The tripartite division of the speeches by Dohm has been criticized: see Austin (1964); Griffith in *CR* 15 (1965), 273–6; Arnott, *JHS* 85 (1965), 182–4; Nesselrath (1990), 297–309.

[61] Cornford (1914), 41–4. Such myths may have appeared in comedy in burlesque—in the *Medea* of Strattis, for example.

of the *mageiros*,[62] in a comic version of Telephus' words in
Euripides' *Telephus*. At the same time we should remember that
the protagonist plays part of the role of *mageiros*, having just performed sacrifice at the Rural Dionysia—that is where he last used
the *epixenon*—and is set on sacrificing the 'kinsmen' of the chorus
of charcoal burners (326–7). It appears to be a comic motif that
the agent of sacrificial violence may himself be chopped up.[63]
Dicaeopolis' chopping-block is the same implement that the
Black-Pudding-Seller carries round in *Knights* as part of his
trade (152, 169). We are not told if Demos was chopped up before
being put in the pot and boiled for rejuvenation, but Demos suffers a version of the violence he was accustomed to visit on the
heads of politicians—albeit for a beneficial purpose. In *Acharnians* and *Peace* sexual intercourse with women is presented in
terms which merge their sexual submission into sacrificial cooking, from which the protagonist emerges rejuvenated. This
theme of the restorative powers of cooking continues into later
comedy, transformed into the boasting of the cook:

a desire has come over me to come out[64] and declare to earth and sky how
I prepared this dish (*opson*). By Athena, it's a pleasure to succeed in all
things. What a tender fish I had! And how I served it! Not drugged with
cheeses[65] nor in a flowery presentation. But when baked it was just like
it was when alive. I set the fire so low and gentle for baking the fish that
I won't be believed. What happened was just like when a chicken
snatches something too big to swallow. It runs all round, keeping an eye
on its prey and keen to swallow it down. The others chase her. So it was
in this case. The first of the diners who discovered the pleasure to be
found in the stewing-pot jumped up and ran off in a circle with the dish
in his hands and the others chased hard on his heels. You just had to cry
out. Some of them grabbed a bit, others nothing, others the lot. Yet I
had taken river-fish which feed on mud. If I had got something rare, a
little Athenian *glaukiskos*, O Zeus the Saviour, or a boar-fish from
Argos or from beloved Sicyon a conger which Poseidon carries up to
heaven for the gods, all those eating it would have become gods! I have

---

[62] The scholiast glosses: ἐπίξηνος καλεῖται ὁ μαγειρικὸς κορμός, ἐφ' οὗ τὰ κρέα
συγκόπτουσιν'. ('*Epixenos* is the name for the butcher's block on which they chop
up meat.')

[63] Cf. Handley (1965) on Menander, *Dyscolus* 398.

[64] From the kitchen?

[65] Cf. Wilkins and Hill (1994), 82–3 on Archestratus's censure of cheese
sauces.

discovered immortality. Those who have died, once they've just had a sniff, I bring back to life!

(Philemon, The Soldier fr. 82)

The speaker is a boastful cook par excellence who draws on rich themes in the comic tradition. He can cook like no other and create magical effects on the lowest-grade river-fish which gourmets would not usually touch.[66] Nor indeed does such a fish merit the attention of Archestratus.[67] This cook works his magic in precisely the ways that Archestratus recommends, through the avoidance of cheese sauces, gentle cooking, and the sourcing of particular fish in the best location. The power of desire that leads the eater to snatch food away from others also recalls Archestratus' advice to pay any price or even steal to achieve the heart's desire. But for Philemon's cook the extraordinary boasting extends to deification of the guests and the restoration of the dead to life.[68] These claims bring together human and divine consumption of fish in a form that we have seen in Epicharmus' *Marriage of Hebe*. In frr. 42–3 the gods appear to eat shellfish, in fr. 71 Zeus and Hera enjoy the sturgeon (*elops*), and in fr. 54 Poseidon brings parrot-wrasse and sea bream to the divine wedding banquet for the gods to consume, piscine excrement and all.[69] In Archestratus fr. 15 the gods have a keen interest in the consumption of the boar-fish.[70] The extraordinary powers of foods to feast the dead in the underworld were seen in some of the utopian fragments of Old Comedy.[71] The absurd boasts of the present passage, taken still further in Plautus' *Pseudolus*, where the chef can make his diners live for 200 years,[72] should not distract from the theme of the transformative power of cooking which can make the hungry full, the ordinary Athenian feel like a king, the individuals in a community combine in commensality—all of which were among the goals of many cook/protagonists in Old Comedy. Philemon has taken these themes further

---

[66] See Chap. 6 and Davidson (1997).

[67] See Chap. 6 for the culinary desire to name fish. Archestratus does not reject all river-fish, praising the *kapros* or boar-fish in fr. 15.

[68] The same may have been claimed in Bato fr. 4.7. Unfortunately the quotation ends abruptly.

[69] See Chap. 7.   [70] Wilkins and Hill (1994), 52–3.

[71] See Chap. 3.   [72] See Lowe (1985), 411–16.

in creating a *rhesis*, a speech to replace the literal rejuvenation of Demos in *Knights*. The power of the word will prove a major theme in the speeches of cooks that follow.

Other cooks may have claimed miraculous powers. Nereus of Anaxandrides' eponymous play is probably a cook who has taken on the name as well as the powers of the sea-god (fr. 31):[73] 'the first to discover the expensive great head of the *glaukos* sliced and the frame of the blameless tuna and all the other foods from the watery brine, Nereus, he dwells in the whole of this realm.' Whether or not this Nereus is the sea-god or a famous cook,[74] Anaxandrides has managed somehow to combine the god with cooking. He has taken Epicharmus fr. 54, in which Poseidon brought fish to the feast, a stage further—a god or his human namesake now prepares fish for the table. Unfortunately, no more of the play survives. The cook[75] in Alexis, *Crateia* fr. 115 combines miraculous claims with fanciful expression:

First, then, I saw some oysters clad in seaweed[76] at the stall of an old Nereus.[77] I got them and some sea urchins, because they are the prelude[78] to a dinner that is elegantly governed.[79] These out of the way, some little fish were lying there and trembling over what they were to suffer. I told them to have no fear as far as I was concerned, declaring that I wouldn't wrong even one of them, and bought a large *glaukos*. Then I got a ray, bearing in mind that when a woman puts her soft fingers close to the spines she must not suffer any hurt of this kind. For the frying-pan I had wrasse, some sole, a hump-backed prawn, a goby, a sea perch, a bream, and made it more gaudy than a peacock. For meat there were trotters, snouts, pig's ears, and liver wrapped in the caul, for it is ashamed of its livid colour. To these no *mageiros* shall come nor even

---

[73] See Euphron, *Brothers* fr. 1.6 below on the cook Nereus of Chios. For Anaxandrides fr. 31 see pp. 18 and 78 n. 111.

[74] See Nesselrath (1990), 301–2; Arnott (1996) on Alexis fr. 115.2.

[75] Who, Arnott suggests (1996: 313–14), may have been a cook in the competitive market-place, an *opsopoios* or *opson*-maker, or an alternative wonder-worker, a doctor. At all events, he denies that he is a cook (line 18).

[76] Arnott retains ἠμφιεσμένωι, against Kassel–Austin (after Koraes), who read ἠμφιεσμένα. If Arnott is right, then the fishmonger is clad in seaweed.

[77] A fisherman: see Arnott (1996).

[78] Sophilus fr. 7.1, 'there will be lavish belly-work (γαστρισμός). I see the prelude . . .'. Similar expressions are found at Philoxenus, *Deipnon* 836 (b) 19 Page, and Alexis fr. 178.15.

[79] πεπρυτανευμένου.

cast an eye on them. By Zeus he'll regret it if he does. No, I shall organize it all with wisdom, with polish, and with colour,[80] to such an extent (for I shall make the dishes myself) that I'll make the diners at times sink their teeth into the stewing-pots through sheer delight. I am prepared to reveal, to declare, even to teach for nothing the methods of preparation and [. . .]—if anyone wishes to learn.

This cook, if that is what he is, produces miraculous dishes that stimulate the pleasure of the consumer beyond normal limits, as did Philemon's cook in fr. 82. He also combines dinner with the functions of the prytaneion—his meal that is 'elegantly governed' borrows the technical term properly applied to the president of the prytaneion.[81] The cook aims to subvert the personal and political restraint on eating which I discussed in Chapters 6 and 4 respectively, and adds for good measure rhetorical exuberance with his prelude and his wisdom, polish, and colour. His miraculous powers reside partly in poetic skills. We might recall Xenarchus, *Porphyra* fr. 7 (cited in Chapter 6), in which it was claimed that the fishmongers were 'more philosophical' and more inventive than the poets. Many of the cooks who come out onto the comic stage attempt to display miraculous discourse as often as miraculous dishes. The poets were competing to present cooks who not only teased audiences with ever greater stimulation of the palates of young diners but also amazed them with their ingenuity.

8.5.2. Cooking in Society

Readers of Chapter 6[82] may have concluded that the cooks of Middle and New Comedy prepare food exclusively for the so-called gluttons of the elite. This is far from the case. The cook's powers are available to a much wider cross-section of Athenian society and the cook is often at pains to tailor his skills to his market.[83] To be sure, the *mageiros* belongs to the agora, offering himself for hire at the *mageireion*. Berthiaume[84] makes it clear that in the Greek polis the *mageiros* was hired to conduct sacrifices for both cultic and private occasions. As we saw in Chapter 1, in

---

[80] Terms also applicable to rhetorical style: see Arnott (1996).

[81] See Arnott's note.   [82] And Davidson (1997).

[83] Thus the cook of Alexis, *Crateia* fr. 115, quoted above, considered the needs of the female diner.

[84] (1982) 28–9, on *mageiroi* hired by religious bodies.

ancient Greece religion was not strictly separated from the commercial world. The comic poets do not appear to have put on stage *mageiroi* hired by temples or shrines. The comic *mageiros* appears to operate only in the private domain, but that is not to say that his commercial aspect, the fact that he must be paid for, is necessarily stressed. *Mageiroi* were at hand in *Frogs* and *Birds*, with no reference to fees or cooking for people who could afford the cost. As we shall see, however, *mageiroi* operated in a competitive market, in comic texts at least—hence the need to cry up their skills. A good *mageiros* is able to transform a social occasion, as the speaker of Hegesippus, *Brothers* fr. 1 demonstrates:

SYRUS: My dear sir, much has been said by many on the art of the *mageiros*. Either speak and reveal some new element that your predecessors did not have or stop chopping me up!

MAGEIROS: No, but believe, Syrus, that I am the only man of all of us to have discovered the perfection[85] of the art of the *mageiros*. I didn't just learn as a sideline in my two years wearing the tunic and cook's belt;[86] no, for the whole of my life[87] I have sought out and researched the divisions of the art: how many forms of vegetables there are, the habits of sprats (*bembrades*),[88] the many varieties of lentil soup. I repeat, the perfection. Whenever I chance to be working at a funeral feast, as soon as they come from the carrying-out procession dressed in black, I take off the lid of the pot and make them turn from tears to laughter. Such a pleasant sensation runs through their bodies, as if they were at a wedding.

SYRUS: After serving lentil soup and *bembrades*? Tell me.

MAGEIROS: They are a sideshow for me. But now if I can get the necessaries and just fit out the kitchen then you will see again the very same phenomenon as happened with the Sirens[89] long ago, Syrus. With a

---

[85] πέρας. Kassel–Austin compare Poseidippus fr. 26.17, Choerilus of Samos *SH* 317.3.

[86] Arnott (1996) describes the cook's clothing in his note on Alexis fr. 179.11.

[87] For the rhetorical formula οὐ . . . παρέργως . . . ἀλλά, Kassel–Austin (1986) compare *CGFP* 255.3; Menander, *Samia* 638; fr. 397.6; Thucydides 1.142.9; and Philaenis *P.Oxy* 2891, fr. 1, col. 1.3. Philaenis' treatise on the arts of love was compared with Archestratus' *Life of Luxury* by Chrysippus and Clearchus: see Wilkins and Hill (1994), 37–8.

[88] The anchovy or the sprat? See Thompson (1947), 32 and Arnott (1996) on Alexis fr. 200.3.

[89] A reference probably to the *Odyssey*, though plays entitled *Sirens* were written by Nicophon and Theopompus and a delectable meal is discussed in Epicharmus, *Sirens* fr. 124, discussed in Chap. 7.

savour like that, no one will be able simply to walk past this alley. Every passer-by will instantly stand open-mouthed at the door, nailed to the wall, speechless until one of his friends runs along with his nostrils bunged up and drags him off.

SYRUS: You're a great artist.

MAGEIROS: You don't know to whom you're chattering. I know well many of the audience here who have run through their money because of me.

The remarkable skills of this cook and their impact on the consumer can be parallelled only in the magical creatures of myth. The cook claims to work in three areas. His research is in cheap foods, vegetables, sprats, and lentil soup, but unlike many other comic characters and cooks, he knows of great variety in these categories, even in lentil soups. Then he can transform with his cooking one social occasion into another, a funeral as it were into a wedding, so pleasurable is the eating of his lentils and sprats. Once he is allowed full rein in a kitchen, then he can match the Sirens. In addition, the cook claims to have a remarkable effect on the audience. The cook/protagonist of Old Comedy prepared a feast for the communal consumption of the Athenian demos as reconfigured by comedy, sometimes including the audience. This cook (probably of the third century) leads elements of the audience to ruin. His mention of running through their money presumably indicates that rich members of the audience are at risk from his full repertoire in the kitchen. This is a notable development, for in the many excesses of the fish-loving elite discussed in Chapter 6 the audience itself was not normally prey to ruinous consumption that extended beyond fish to their own property.[90] The cook does not specify whether the wonderful smells from the kitchen rise from large and financially perilous fish or whether he works wonders on the smallest fish, just as Philemon's cook transformed the mud-eating fish of the river.

Hegesippus' cook was anticipated by the cook in Antiphanes, *Pro-Theban* fr. 216 whose fish-cooking is so delectable that even bronze nostrils would be insufficient to protect the consumer

---

[90] This is not the only link between the *mageiros* of Middle and New Comedy and the audience. At Adespota 1093.221–37 a *mageiros* comes on stage and regrets the comic scenes he has watched in which a thieving *mageiros* brings shame on both the art and its practitioners.

from temptation. The cook, in describing the delights of his dishes, resembles an enchanter who combines magical words with amazing actions (15–17). An interlocutor claims to see three people chewing (16), presumably in the audience. In addition to his occasional comments on drama[91] and on the audience, the cook is often concerned to ascertain within the play who he is cooking for and to make quite clear what he believes his role to be. The cook in Menander, *Shield* 216–35, who is sent away because death has interrupted plans for a wedding, illustrates the difficulties besetting the cook: 'whenever I get a job, either someone dies and I must go off with no fee or one of the women of the house gives birth after a secret pregnancy and suddenly there is no sacrifice.' The wedding is the major commission for the comic cook, but there are other occasions. Tailoring to the market is best illustrated by Diphilus, *The Painter* fr. 42, where the *mageiros* says:

Dracon, I wouldn't take you along to any commission where you will not complete the day setting up the tables[92] with a great mass of good things. For I never walk into a house until I test out who is making the sacrifice or why the dinner is being put on or what men he has invited. I have a diagram of all categories, which ones to hire myself to, which ones are to be avoided. Now as an example, if you like, take the category of the metic merchant. This sea captain makes a sacrifice to repay a vow. He has thrown overboard the ship's mast or has broken the rudder or has thrown out the cargo after taking in water badly. I let that sort of man go. He does nothing for pleasure but only so far as custom permits. During the libations he is calculating how big a share of the risk he can impose on his fellow-passengers, adding it all up, and each of them eats his own vital organs.[93] Another merchant has sailed in from Byzantium on the third day, suffering no misfortune having made a good passage, delighted that he has made ten or twelve drachmas to the mina. Chattering about his fees and belching up his loans, he looks for sex with the help of rough-trade pimps. As soon as he disembarks I sidle up to him,

---

[91] See e.g. Euphron fr. 1.35; fr. 10.15–16; Alexis, *Linus* fr. 140.12–16; Menander, *Shield* 216–18; Demetrius II fr. 1.1–2; Adespota 1093.221–37 (see previous note).

[92] On the *trapezopoios* or 'table-maker' see below.

[93] The text is unclear. Casaubon was probably right to prefer 'each eats the vital organs of his own sacrificial beast' to 'each passenger eats his own vital organs'. Failure of commensality appears preferable to self-cannibalism since the circumstances are hardly that grave.

shaking him by the right hand, reminding him of Zeus the Saviour, with the fixed intent of waiting upon him. Such is my way. Or again, a young man is in love, playing ducks and drakes with his money. I approach him. Other young men perhaps get up a subscription dinner, by Zeus, and throw into the pot [. . .] rubbing the fringes of their cloaks and crying 'anyone want to have a tasty bite in the agora?' I leave them to their cries. For I'll get blows in addition if I go, and have to work all night. If you ask them for a little fee one says 'first bring me the pisspot. The lentil soup lacked vinegar.' You ask again. 'You'll be the first cook to get a good hiding,' he says. I could list thousands of similar tales. But the place I'm taking you to now is a brothel. A *hetaera* is celebrating the Adonia expensively with other prostitutes. You'll stuff yourself with heaps of gifts and come away with the folds of your tunic packed full also.

The cook must adapt to the category of diner and even to the region from which he or she has come. I cited examples in Chapter 6, for example Lynceus, *Centaur* fr. 1, in which the cook is asked by a Perinthian who is dining at a sacrifice given by a Rhodian not to serve in the parsimonious style of the Athenians.

The most frequent occasions for which the comic cook appears to be hired are weddings, funerals, public and private sacrifices,[94] and parties for private individuals, young men, and *hetaerae* as we have just seen in Diphilus fr. 42—in short, the social occasions of Greek life.[95] Athenaeus identifies weddings and sacrifices as the area of operation for cooks (14.659d). A wedding is the setting for the *mageiros* in Menander's *Samia* (189–98). An officious father prescribes what is to be done in Euangelus, *The Bride Unveiled* fr. 1 in such a way as to invite the comment 'what an *alazon* the wretch is' from his interlocutor, presumably a *mageiros*.[96] Posidippus fr. 28 contains a lecture by a *mageiros* which transforms social settings into opportunities for boasting or *alazoneia*:

Student Leucon and you his fellow assistants! Every single place is suitable for talking about the art. Of all seasonings in cookery, the most

---

[94] Examples of public and private combined are the Adonia in Diphilus fr. 42; the feast of Aphrodite Pandemos in Menander, *Flatterer* fr. 1; an offering to Pan in Menander, *Dyscolus*.

[95] See Dohm (1964), 76–81.

[96] Quoted in Chap. 2. A further instance of a character speaking lines that might have been spoken by the *mageiros* is to be found at Menander, *Samia* 399–404.

potent is boasting (*alazoneia*). You will see this taking the lead in almost all skilled areas. Here is a commander of mercenaries who wears a breastplate made of metal plates or a dragon worked in iron. He looked like Briareos, but if it comes to it is a hare. If a cook with a group of assistants and students goes into the home of a private citizen and calls them all cumin-splitters and starvelings, instantly everyone cowers. If you put your true self across you'll leave skinned alive. Do then what I told you, give ground when nothing is at issue and study the palates of the guests. It's like sailing into a mercantile port, the ideal of the art is to sail in nicely to the harbour mouth. Now, we are working on a wedding. The sacrificial victim is an ox.[97] The father of the bride is eminent, eminent too the bridegroom. Their wives are priestesses to the goddess [. . .] There will be mystic dancing, pipes, all-night festivals, commotion. This is the race-track the cook's art must run. You just remember.[98]

8.5.3. *The Skills of the* Mageiros

Mageiroi are often at pains to distinguish their skills from those of lesser operatives. Such distinctions are less demarcation disputes than claims to skills above the ordinary or comment on the state of the culinary art. At Dionysius, *Thesmophoros* fr. 2 a *mageiros* stakes his claim:

by the gods, you have done me a great service, Simias, in alerting me to these matters. The cook must know well in advance of undertaking preparations for the dinner who he is to cook for. If he only has an eye on one thing, in what way is the *opson* to be made, and gives no foresight or thought to how it is to be served and when and how presented, then he is a cook no longer but an *opsopoios*.[99] That is not the same thing at all, but vastly different. For every general receives the title when he enters into his responsibilities, but the one who is able to manoeuvre in

---

[97] διακονοῦμεν νῦν γάμους. τὸ θῦμα βοός.

[98] Euphron, *Fellow-Ephebes* fr. 9 contains similar advice on how to deal with a varied clientele—with an amusing twist. When dealing with a dining club (*eranistae*), the cook must give them all they pay for and be scrupulously honest (because they pay well?), whereas at a wedding paid for by an old miser (the current commission of the *mageiros*) the cook must be 'murderous' and devour food and charcoal in order to get even with the old skinflint. The poet has taken the option of satirizing the miser over the young spendthrifts, again using the *mageiros*, for all his dubious morality, as an agent of social control. Misers and weddings are a major feature in the *Aulularia* of Plautus and *Dyscolus* of Menander, on which see below.

[99] A maker of *opsa* or a fish-cook. See Berthiaume (1982), 55, 76–77, and Chap. 7, p. 363.

difficulties and somehow see a problem through, he is the general, while the other is merely a leader. So in our line of work, anyone could prepare dishes, chop, boil sauces, and blow on the fire. The *opsopoios* is merely of that kind. The *mageiros* is something else. He knows the place, the season, the host, the guest, when and what fish to buy [. . .] you will always get roughly the same. But you won't always have the same elegance in the dishes, nor will the pleasure be equal. . . .[100] But that man who you said just now had experienced many lavish dinners—I'll make him forget them all, Simias, when I just show him a confection in fig leaves and serve him a dinner with the scent of the Attic breeze. He'll come fresh from the water of the bilges, stuffed with the regime of shipboard food, and I'll put him to sleep with my starter.

At Menander, *False Heracles* fr. 409 an employer seeking traditional simplicity puts a *mageiros* straight:

Cook, you have a most unsavoury air to me. This is the third time you've asked how many tables we are going to set up. We are sacrificing one little pig: what difference does it make to you whether we set up eight tables or two or one? I will lay one. There are no *kandauloi* to make nor the kind of *karyke* mixtures of honey, fine flour, and eggs that you are accustomed to. Everything is now reversed. Now the *mageiros* makes the moulded cakes, bakes flat-cakes, boils the *chondros* and brings it in after the salt fish, and then the fig-leaf speciality and a bunch of grapes. Meanwhile, the female artisan,[101] drawn up in line to compete with him, roasts bits of meat and thrushes as *tragemata*. Consequently the diner feasts on savouries and when he's put on his perfume and garland goes back to dining on honey cakes—with thrushes.

The cooks' skills are cried up in a competitive market, as a patron explains in Posidippus fr. 1:

When taking on a *mageiros* I have heard all the insults they said against each other in competing for work: one does not have a discerning nose for a cooked dish, another has a foul palate, another has polluted his tongue in unseemly desires[102] for flavourings, all salt, all vinegar, too sweet a tooth, too likely to burn the meat, can't bear the smoke, can't bear the fire. From the fire they turned to knives. This man here has been through the knives and the fire.[103]

---

[100] The cook spends some lines denouncing Archestratus and writers of recipes, for which see Chap. 7.

[101] δημιουργός.   [102] Cf. *Knights* 1284–5.

[103] Philostephanus in *The Delian* fr. 1 has a potential patron who declares to a cook: 'I am aware that you, Daedalus, are the best of all in your profession and

Some cooks boast of their training and culinary achievements, while others place these in the context of other skills thought necessary. The first skill is to be trained as a *mageiros*. Other skills follow. Claims conflict over what constitutes training. Some *mageiroi*, for example the speaker of Dionysius fr. 2 cited above, dismiss the use of books such as the *Life of Luxury* of Archestratus and other works, while others appeal to authority, particularly that of 'schools' of cookery.[104] The ultimate appeals to authority by *mageiroi* are to Nereus, the 'inventor' of fish-cooking in Anaxandrides fr. 31 (cited above), to Cadmus, who is said by Athenaeus[105] to have been a cook, to Harmonia a pipe-girl (surely a comic invention),[106] and to Coroebus, who was the first victor at the Olympic Games and a cook.[107] A cook in Damoxenus claims to be a pupil of Epicurus (cited below). Less ambitious than these is the claim made by the cook in Sosipater, *Perjurer* fr. 1:

MAGEIROS: Our art is not completely easy to despise, Demylus, if you think it through. But the whole thing is washed up and almost all claim to be *mageiroi* when they know nothing. The art is polluted by such people. Now if you take a true *mageiros* who has been correctly brought up from childhood into the trade and who has a firm grasp on the powers of the art and knows all the branches of knowledge systematically, then the matter will take on a quite different appearance to you. There are only three of us still left, Boidion, Chariades, and I. Fart on the rest.

DEMYLUS: What do you say? If I?

MAGEIROS: We preserve the school of Sicon.[108] He was the founder of the art. First he taught us to study the stars [. . .] and straight after that to be architects. He'd mastered all the treatises on nature, and on top of all these, he declared, was the art of war. Before we learned the art he urged us to learn these.

DEMYLUS: Do you have the ability to chop me down, dear friend?

MAGEIROS: No, but in the time it takes my slave to return from the

in your keenness of mind after Thibron the cook from Athens who has the nickname Perfection. I have come to pay the fee you demanded and bring you home.' The cook in Hegesippus, *Brothers* (quoted above) also claimed to have reached 'perfection'.

---

[104] See Chap. 7.   [105] See below.
[106] Athenaeus 14.658e–f.   [107] Ibid. 9.382b.
[108] Sicon is a common name among comic cooks. It seems likely that this school is fictional.

market I am going to scrutinize you a little about the trade so that we may take an opportunity to talk.

DEMYLUS: Apollo! What a labour!

MAGEIROS: Listen, dear sir. The first thing the *mageiros* must know is about the heavenly bodies and the setting and rising of the stars and when the sun rises for the longest and the shortest day and in what part of the Zodiac it is. For almost all our cooked dishes and foods take on different delights in different circumstances according to the movement of the whole universe. So the man who is master of such things and sees the perfect time uses each of his materials as is fitting, while he who does not know rightly walks into the mire. Then on the matter of architecture, perhaps you wondered what that had to do with our art.

DEMYLUS: I wondered?

MAGEIROS: Well I'll tell you anyway. To set out the kitchen properly and to get the light that is needed and to see which way the wind blows all are very important for our business. Smoke carried this way and that usually makes a difference to our cooked dishes. What next? I still have the art of war to go through . . .[109] I have the *mageiros* at least. Good order is a wise thing everywhere and in every art, but in ours it almost takes command. For to serve all the food and take it away again in good order and to see the right moment for these, when to bring them in more swiftly and when at walking pace and how the diners are doing with their meal and when it is right for them to serve the hot dishes, the following dishes, the medium cool and the completely chilled, all of these are determined by the studies of strategy.

DEMYLUS: You have shown me all the necessaries. Now buzz off and be quiet.

This *mageiros* stresses the theoretical background to practical cooking—the theory must come first even though the selection of foods by season might be considered simply a practical matter. While the choice of natural history and military strategy might make sense in the theorizing of the kitchen, a hot place where seasonal foods should be prepared swiftly in good order, there is an implication that the cook is supporting his inflated art with sciences of real importance. Natural history and strategy are areas of knowledge which were also used by the student of rhetoric.[110]

---

[109] A line or more is missing here.

[110] I am grateful to Emma Gee for directing me to Cicero, *De oratore* and Quintilian I.

A cook in the *Eileithuia* of Nicomachus[111] expands on the skills
of the cook which extend to painting, astronomy, measurement of
the earth, and medicine, which reveal 'the qualities and skills' of
fish. Medicine is the science that the cook of Nicomachus is
best able to adapt to his argument (fr. 1.30–8): 'there are foods
that produce wind, that are hard to digest, and some of which
wreak revenge rather than provide nourishment. Everyone who
dines on conflicting foods becomes irritable and loses self-
control. For such foods, medicines have been found from the
same source, which is a transfer from the art of cooking.' Strategy
is also needed. There is much common ground between this
speech and Sosipater fr. 1, which was written much later. There
is surprisingly little exploitation of medicine in these expansions
of the theoretical areas which the cook must grasp, given the close
relationship between cooking and medicine at this time. This
perhaps supports the assumption that these speeches are primarily tours de force of *alazoneia*, even if they make broad sense. In
other speeches theory is subsumed into crude analogy.[112]

Euphron, *Brothers* fr. 1 provides a striking example of how a
basic statement about a cooking school (on which see Chapter 7)
might be developed into a form of *alazoneia* that merges with the
long established *bomolochia* (the theft of meat from a sacrifice):

I have had many students, Lycus, but thanks to your constant mental
powers and spirit you are leaving my house as a full *mageiros* in less than
ten months and far the youngest. Agis of Rhodes alone baked a fish to
perfection; Nereus of Chios boiled a conger fit for the gods;[113] Chariades
from Athens made the white fig dish;[114] Lamprias was the first with
black soup;[115] Aphthonetus with black-puddings, Euthunus with lentil

---

[111] On whom Athenaeus comments (7.290e), 'he exceeds the actors of
Dionysus'.

[112] So e.g. Poseidippus fr. 29 on the cook Seuthes, 'Seuthes is according to
them a great private soldier. Don't you know, friend, that he appears in no way
to differ from a good general? The enemy hove up and the general of profound
genius [Gulick's phrase] stands firm and takes on the attack. The whole crowd
of drinkers is hostile to him. It moves *en masse*. It has advanced after waiting fifteen days for dinner, with a great momentum, all fired up, alert to when something will be served to grab at. Think of the great roar of that kind of crowd.'

[113] See above on Philemon fr. 82.

[114] On this dish see Arnott (1996) on Alexis fr. 178.6–11 and fr. 179.5.

[115] That is, black soup of a particular quality: the confection was familiar in
Athens and Sparta from an early date. See Arnott (1996), 425–6. The black soup

soup [. . .].[116] These men have become for us the second set of wise men after those Seven Sages of antiquity. As for me, I saw that most dishes had been pre-empted so I was the first to invent theft of such a kind that no one hates me for it but all take me on. Now you in your turn have seen this trick pre-empted by me and have invented your own signature dish, and this is yours. Four days ago [. . .][117] a lot of old men were sacrificing a skinny little kid after much time spent at sea. No meat was to be taken away either by Lycus or his teacher.[118] You forced them to provide two more kids. While they were busily looking at the liver you lowered one hand and stealthily threw the kidney quickly into the pot. You kicked up a great row. 'It's got no kidney!', they said. They bent down in search of the lost part. They sacrificed another victim. Again I saw you gulping down the heart of this second victim. You've long been one of the greats, depend upon it. You alone have invented the art of the wolf not gaping in vain. Yesterday you doused the flames with two raw spitted gut-sausages and warbled to the two-gut-stringed lyre. I noticed! The first stunt was a full play (*drama*), this one an amusing game (*paignion*).[119]

The theft of fruit is attested for early Spartan forms of comedy,[120] and the theft of meat from altars, the act of the *bomolochus*, has been reviewed with regard to Old Comedy in Chapter 2. Theft became a distinguishing mark of the *mageiros* in New Comedy, some forms of which are reviewed by Dohm (1964: 129–35). In this fragment, theft of meat by deception from the altar is described as both a *drama* and a *paignion*; the thieves celebrate their achievement, whereas in Old Comedy *bomolochia* had become a metaphor only, a byword for comedy of a poor grade from which the poet distanced himself. The thieving of the *mageiros* is a further element to add to his *alazoneia*, should a

---

contrasts with the white *thrion* in the previous line in precisely the way Alexis compared white barley cake with black soup at *Woman Drugged By Mandrake* fr. 145.7–8.

[116] The text is corrupt. A seventh name is lost here.

[117] The text is corrupt.

[118] Adapted from the formula 'the meat is not to be carried away [from the shrine]' which applied to a number of sacrificial rituals in the cults of Attica: Kassel–Austin (1986) compare *SIG*³ 1004.31 and 1026.10; *Wealth* 1138; and Theopompus fr. 71. Add Poseidippus fr. 2.3.

[119] On *paignia* see Davidson (forthcoming).

[120] See Sosibius, *FGrH* 595 F 7, in Athenaeus 14.621d–e: David (1989), 1–25.

poet wish to develop the part of his character which belongs to low-life.[121]

Euphron fr. 10 uses anecdote in a cook's *rhesis* in a form similar to that found in fr. 1 above—it is used to illustrate a particular aspect of the skill of the cook in question which will be drawn out to make a point.

MAGEIROS: I became a pupil of Soterides who first served to Nicomedes when he was on a twelve-day journey from the sea and desirous of an anchovy[122] in the middle of winter, such a dish, by Zeus, as to make all exclaim.

A: How is that possible?

MAGEIROS: He took a female turnip and cut it thin and long, imitating the appearance of the anchovy itself. He boiled it, poured on oil, added salt deftly, and sprinkled two thousand seeds in number of black poppy. Thus he satisfied the king's desire in Scythia. And when Nicomedes tasted the turnip he declaimed an encomium to the anchovy. The *mageiros* is in no respect different from the poet: for each of these two, the mind is their art.

Euphron fr. 10, unusually for a comic fragment, is set in the entourage of a foreign king, Nicomedes I of Bithynia.[123] The passage establishes the speaker's claim to his position by illustrating the skill of his teacher, who shines in his artifice and ingenuity and is able to meet the extraordinary demand of an exotic monarch. Nicomedes translates his pleasure into words, from which the speaker draws the general reflection that the art of cooking is as cerebral as the writing of verse. Food has become inspirational, like wine. This and the previous fragment derive from the third century, but a similar affinity between verse and cooking is seen

[121] See also Dionysius, *Namesakes* fr. 3.

[122] The species of fish is unclear. In the plural *aphuai* are whitebait, the young of several species.

[123] Bithynia was a kingdom with a coast and one (Greek) city at least was noted for its anchovies, Heraclea Pontica. It is not inconceivable therefore that the cook's narrative is based on some distinctive feature of Bithynian culture which the king was denied in his trip to the north of the Black Sea. For cooking at a king's court in a comedy, cf. the cook who is a sauce-maker (*abyrtakopoios*) at the court of Seleucus and composer of 'tyrant's lentil soup' at the court of the Sicilian Agathocles in Demetrius II, *The Areopagite* fr. 1. He also does wonderful things with capers. His ingenuity is such, he claims, that no actor could ever match it. As in Euphron fr. 10, the comic *mageiros* is often conscious of being very close to the comic actor. See below.

in the previous century, in Alexis, *Linus* for example. All of the speeches of comic *mageiroi* in fact depend upon the tension between cooking food and speaking words on the stage.

8.5.4. *The* Mageiros *as Wordsmith*

The cook sometimes comes a long way from the hot kitchen of his calling. Damoxenus, in *Syntrophoi* fr. 2, presents a cook who claims his master is Epicurus:

MAGEIROS: You see me, the student of the wise Epicurus, at whose side in less than two years and ten months I 'condensed', let me tell you, four talents.

A: What's this? Tell me.

MAGEIROS: I consecrated them. He too was a *mageiros* [. . .].[124]

A: A cook indeed!

MAGEIROS: Nature is the origin of all art.

A: Origin, you crook?

MAGEIROS: There is nothing wiser than work and it was an easy matter for one familiar with this theory because many elements combine. Thus when you see an uneducated *mageiros*, one who has not read all of Democritus, and the Canon of Epicurus, send him away with shit on his head for being outside the discipline. It is necessary to know this first, my dear sir, what the difference is between a *glaukiskos* in winter and one in summer, then to know what fish is most useful at the setting of the Pleiades and at the solstice. For the changes and movements are a terrible evil for men and create changes in the foods, you see. What is taken in the right season gives in return delight. Who pursues these things properly? And so cramps and wind develop and make the guest behave in an unseemly fashion. But with me the food that is brought in nourishes, is digested, and 'breathes out' correctly. So the juice[125] is gathered everywhere evenly into the ducts—

A: Juice?

MAGEIROS: says Democritus. Nor does constipation develop and damage the eater's joints.

A: You seem to me to have some knowledge of medicine.

MAGEIROS: Yes. And so does everyone who is into nature. But consider what the ignorance, by the gods, of modern cooks is like. When you see them making a salt-water sauce out of fish of contradictory

---

[124] The line is corrupt.

[125] For the idea compare Democritus, *Peri chumon* ap Diogenes Laertius 9.46 (Kassel–Austin (1986)).

qualities and grinding sesame onto it, take each of them in turn and fart on them.[126]

A: Me? What uses you put me to!

MAGEIROS: Well how could it turn out well when one essence is mixed with another and they grapple in disconsonant grips? Distinguishing these things is an art for the soul, not washing dishes or smelling of smoke. I don't go into the kitchen.

A: What then?

MAGEIROS: I sit nearby and watch. Others do the work.

A: And you?

MAGEIROS: I tell them the first principles and the results. 'The mince-meat is sharp. Ease up.'

A: You are a musician not a *mageiros*.

MAGEIROS: 'Tighten up. Harmonize the fire with the fast notes.[127] The first stewpot is boiling out of harmony with the others.' Do you understand the style?

A: Apollo!

MAGEIROS: Does it appear as an art in some way? I serve no food at random (do you understand?) but mix everything in harmony.

A: How?

MAGEIROS: Some things are linked to each other in fourths, in fifths or, again, in the whole octave. These I bring together by their intervals and weave them straightaway sympathetically with their courses. Sometime I stand and give an order, 'What are you fastening it to? What are you planning to mix with that? Look! You are drawing a disharmony! Won't you move on?' [. . .] Epicurus 'condensed' pleasure in this way. He chewed with care. He alone knew what the Good is. The men of the Stoa seek it all the time without knowing what it is. What they do not have and do not understand they can't give to another.

A: I agree. Let's pass over the rest. It's long been clear what that is.

The cook-philosopher is an engaging development of the *mageiros* theme, since Damoxenus has fused two elements which are often placed in opposition to each other in comedy and sub-comic genres. This is a most important point. In Old Comedy there is little exchange between philosophy and comic cooking. The first is presented as both absurdly abstract and as the preserve of pretentious, rich, and probably anti-democratic citizens. Philosophy is thus, as we saw in Chapter 1, deflated by the application of culinary materialism, which is often administered by

---

[126] Kassel–Austin (1986) compare Sosipater fr. 1.12.
[127] The meaning is unclear.

the protagonist in the interests of the comic polis. The material takes on the abstract, head to head. New Comedy is different. Comedy has lost much of its political bite and in the speeches of its *mageiroi* has integrated a particularly dubious version of philosophy into its discourse. Comedy thus mediates the two former opponents, as we have seen in Damoxenus. That is not to say that there is no longer scope for satirical jibes at philosophers. Athenaeus supplies various examples of Epicureans, Stoics, and Pythagoreans in difficulties with eating, either because their system of thought is based on the antithesis of mind and body and thus excludes the consumption of food unless absolutely necessary, or because the philosopher is unable to sustain his austere regime.[128] Archestratus too sneers at Pythagoreans in his parody of epic, with a specific jibe at Diodorus of Aspendus (fr. 23). Anaxippus, *Behind the Veil* fr. 1, presents a *mageiros* whom I have already quoted in Chapter 7. Later in that speech (27–42) the cook picks up the theme of adjusting foods to suit the consumer:

I will give you a taste of my inventions, if you like. I do not offer the same foods all the time to all. I order them directly in line with their way of life. Different foods are needed for lovers, for philosophers, and for taxmen. A young man with a girl in love eats up his ancestral estate: for him I serve cuttlefish and squid and a selection of eye-catching rock-fish choreographed with rich sauces. That sort of person is not interested in dinners but puts all his thought into love. To the philosopher I serve a ham or trotters, for the creature is greedy to excess; to the taxman *glaukos*, eel, and a bream. When Dystros[129] is near, I prepare lentil soup and make the funeral feast of his life dazzling . . .[130]

Naturally philosophy covers many areas of knowledge, and some of those touched on by Damoxenus' *mageiros* are more appropriate to a cook's theorizing than others. Seasonal variation as indicated by the stars is not out of place, nor is Epicurus' theory of pleasure, though the latter is severely distorted. Even music has *something* to do with cooking, at least as far as regards a notion of harmony—but the point made by the cook is obscure. Philosophy is one of the more recherché areas of knowledge to be attempted by a comic *mageiros*. More often, areas of knowledge

---

[128] See chapter 2 of Braund and Wilkins (forthcoming).
[129] A winter month in the Macedonian calendar: see Kassel–Austin (1986).
[130] For lentil soups at funerals cf. Hegesippus, *Brothers* fr. 1, cited above.

appropriate in at least one respect to the art of cooking are exploited. The most important areas are astronomy and medicine, the latter in particular for three reasons. First, the doctor is an expert who is also a comic figure of fun, apparently from an early period.[131] Secondly, the doctor shares with the cook the quality of miracle-worker. Thirdly, treatises on diet and even of cooking form a subset of medical writing. In a number of speeches the *mageiros* is referred to as a *sophistes*, a comic philosopher, one of the names for simple comic characters according to Athenaeus 14.621d, along with *phlyakes* and other regional variants.

Strato, *Phoenicides* fr. 1 introduces a *mageiros* who has transformed his discourse almost entirely into Homeric phrases. This enables the poet to exploit hexameter verse in a form in which Archestratus and Matro specialized,[132] and which may have been more widely exploited in Old Comedy, since the rivals of Aristophanes appear to have exploited epic where his preferred model for parody was tragedy. Athenaeus introduces this *mageiros*[133] through the discourse of the *mageiros* of Larensis, the fictional host of the *Deipnosophistae*. (On this *mageiros*, see below.) From the first words of the patron in Strato fr. 1 it is clear that the *mageiros* is a master of words:[134]

it is a male sphinx[135] that I have taken into my house, not a *mageiros*. I simply don't understand, in the name of the gods, a single thing he says. He's arrived with a provision of new phrases. When he came he

---

[131] Sosibius, *FGrH* 595 F 7, if Athenaeus is still quoting his words at 14.621d, records the foreign doctor as a character of a Spartan variant of comedy. See Pickard-Cambridge (1962), 134; Cornford (1914), 136–41; Arnott (1996), 313, 329, and (on Doric doctors) 420 and 430–2. On doctors in comedy see further Gil and Alfageme (1972), 35–91.

[132] See Chap. 7.

[133] The text is also preserved in a slightly different version with the first three lines missing and with more lines at the end in a Cairo papyrus of the third century BC: see Kassel–Austin (1989) and Kassel (1974), 121–7.

[134] The text translated is that of the papyrus combined with Athenaeus: see Kassel–Austin. Webster (1953), 145 suggests that the papyrus version is in fact by Philemon the Younger and Athenaeus' version an improvement by Strato. The matter is complicated, since it is to Philemon the Younger that the first four lines are attributed by Athenaeus at 14.659b (see previous note).

[135] On the combination of the Sphinx and the cook see Hunter (1983) on Eubulus, *Sphinx-Carion*.

instantly asked me, with an intense gaze, 'how many Meropan persons[136] have you invited to the dinner? Tell me.' 'I've invited Meropan persons to the dinner? You're insane. You think I know these Meropan persons? None of them will come. That, by Zeus, is the limit, inviting Meropan persons to dinner'. 'So there won't be a feaster present at all?' 'Philinus will come, and Moschion, Niceratus, and What's His Name and What's His Name.' I went through them. There was not one Feaster to be found among them. 'He won't be coming', say I. 'What's that? Not one?' He grew angry as if I'd done him an injury in not inviting a Feaster. It was very novel. 'So you're not sacrificing a ground-breaker?'[137] 'Not I', I said. 'Nor a broad-browed ox?' 'I'm not sacrificing an ox, you wretch.' 'Are you sacrificing sheep then?' 'By Zeus, not I.' 'Sheep-flocks?' 'Sheep-flocks? I don't know, *mageiros*,' I said, 'anything about them, nor do I wish to. I'm too much the peasant, so converse with me simply.' 'Don't you know that Homer said these things?' 'He was certainly at liberty to say what he wanted, *mageiros*. But what is that to us, in the name of Hestia?' 'In his words, attend to the rest that I have to say.' 'Do you plan to wipe me out in Homeric style?' 'I'm used to this kind of patter.' 'Well, don't use that patter when you're with me.' 'Am I to discard my policy? For your four drachmas?', he says. 'Bring here the sacrificial grains.' 'What?' 'Barley.' 'Why then, you lunatic, do you speak in convoluted terms?' 'Is the *pegos*[138] here?' '*Pegos*? Go suck someone's cock, or say more clearly what you want.' 'You are rash, old man,' he says. 'Bring salt. That is the *pegos*. Show me the holy water.' There was water available. He began the sacrifice and spoke thousands more words that no one, in Earth's name, would have heard, cuttings, portions, folds, spits. I had to get the books of Philetas to see what each of the phrases meant. I begged him to change his ways and use human speech. But not even Persuasion herself standing over him there would have persuaded him. I reckon he's a slave son of some godless rhapsodizer who filled himself with the phrases of Homer.

Homer was always a ready resource for the comic poets, as much for his content of sacrifice (and the absence of fish) as for his elevated language and metre. This cook, if nothing else, lays a strong claim to being the sacrificer of animals. It is very suitable that a fictional *mageiros* invented by Athenaeus in the second

---

[136] Strato sets up a pun between the Homeric epithet μέροψ (*merops*, which ancient grammarians understood to mean 'dividing the voice' or 'articulate') and citizens of the town of Meropis in the Aegean.

[137] See Kassel–Austin (1989). Athenaeus has 'Erusichthon'.

[138] Crystalized salt.

century AD should quote these lines, since the status of Homeric verse was so important to the scholarly tradition in which he was writing.

8.6. ATHENAEUS ON THE *MAGEIROS*

All the speeches of *mageiroi* listed by Dohm are quoted in Athenaeus. Once again this unusual author has preserved an element of ancient comedy that would be obscured to us if we relied only on papyrus fragments of New Comedy and the Roman versions of Plautus and Terence. The majority of the speeches are preserved in three important passages in Book 7, 288c–293e, Book 9, 376c–383f (with a supplementary section at 403d–406b) and Book 14, 658e–662d. The first two stress the *alazoneia* of the cook, while the last gives a historical perspective that attempts to place the *mageiros* in ancient culture. As in his history of the parasite, so with the *mageiros*, Athenaeus' account, for all its flaws, is the best that we have. The treatment in Book 14 traces the origins both of the *mageiros* in the polis and in comedy. For the former, Cleidemus the Atthidographer attests,[139] amid much dubious etymologizing, both the role of the priestly Kerykes as *mageiroi* (specifically cooks/butchers and agents of sacrifice) and an official body of *mageiroi* who were recognized by the polis and who 'gathered together the people'. Mythical origins are drawn from the *Sacred Scripture* of Euhemerus of Cos,[140] who says that Cadmus the grandfather of Dionysus was a cook.[141] This explanation might be compared with 9.382b, which identifies the first Olympic victor, Coroebus of Elis, as a cook. All of this is likely to be inventive conjecture (built in part on comedy),[142] but it sets the perameters well. The ancient cook was also, we are told, in charge of weddings and sacrifices; again, comedy provides much evidence. Finally, according to Athenaeus, the Greek comic cook is never a slave, with the exception of Poseidippus frr. 2 and 25, in the second of which one of the speakers appears to be a slave to a master-*mageiros*.[143]

---

[139] Fourth century BC.   [140] Fourth/third century BC.

[141] The link with Dionysus and the supposed influence of tbe Phoenicians on cooking presumably lie behind this tale.

[142] As Bertiaume (1982), 7, 11–12, 96 has explained.

[143] On this see Arnott (1996) on Alexis fr. 134, who broadly endorses Athenaeus' claim, and Dohm (1964), 68.

Slave cooks were a Macedonian development. I do not believe, in this mixture of Attic mythologizing and antiquarianism, that comic and non-comic material can be separated.[144]

The *alazoneia* of the *mageiros* is introduced in Book 7 in the section on the eel, one of the favoured ingredients of the *mageiros*, and in Book 9 in the section on the pig. The second is introduced by a figure who constitutes Athenaeus' own attempt to create a *mageiros* for his Deipnosophistae. Athenaeus' *mageiros* is ingenious in the manner of the later cooks Paxamus and the cook of Petronius, who are adept at the elaborate stuffing of animals and feats of ingenuity based on concealment. In the speeches from comedy which follow, the elements picked out in particular are *alazoneia* based on military bravado and thieving. The cook runs through the speeches of *mageiroi* from Posidippus, Euphron, Alexis, and Dionysius, some of which come close to promoting that *bomolochia* from which Aristophanes had distanced himself, in metaphor at least. Dionysius, *Namesakes* fr. 3 provides a typical example:

Come now, Dromon, if you know any clever or wise or polished feat in your work, make it clear to your teacher. Now I'm asking you to make a display of your skill. I am leading you into enemy territory. Run against them with courage. They number the meat distributed and keep you under observation. Make them tender and boil them well and confuse their numbers, as I say. Here is a solid fish. The guts are yours and if you displace a slice, that too is yours, while we are inside. If outside, it's mine. The insides and related parts have no number or test in their own right, but have the rank or station of mincemeat—these will delight us tomorrow, you and me. By all means give a share to the booty-seller so that you have a more well-disposed pat through the doorway. Why say more to one who knows so much? You are my student, I am your teacher. Remember these things and walk this way with me.

The *mageiros* of Athenaeus lacks the wit of his comic counterparts, but he is praised by the host Larensis for these quotations which are apparently preferable to recitations of such works of

[144] Athenaeus also mentions (14.659a–c) the *maison* and *tettix*, respectively, he says, the local cook and his foreign counterpart. Chrysippus, Polemon, and other ancient scholars were interested in the supposed Doric origins of these figures and Pollux refers to their masks (4.148–9). Nothing further is known of the influence of these figures on Sicilian or Attic comedy. See Dohm (1964), 12–22; Handley (1965), 37; Pickard-Cambridge (1962), 181.

literature as Plato's *Timaeus*. Athenaeus has in this way created a sympotic version of the comic *mageiros* who can entertain at table with the material invented by the comic poets for the stage.

8.7. THE *SAMOTHRACIANS* OF ATHENION

The most impressive of all the comic *mageiroi*, to my mind, makes a long speech in the *Samothracians* of Athenion,[145] one of the many poets in Kassel–Austin whose major contribution to the history of Attic comedy now rests on a speech by a *mageiros*.

MAGEIROS: Don't you know that the art of the *mageiros* has overall made the greatest contribution to piety?

A: Is it of that order of importance?

MAGEIROS: Very much so, you barbarian. It freed us from a bestial life without any sanctions and from intractable cannibalism and led us to order, attaching us to this life that we now lead.

A: How?

MAGEIROS: Listen and I'll tell you. Beset by cannibalism and many evils, a man was born who was no fool, the first[146] to sacrifice an animal victim. He roasted the meat. Now since the meat was sweeter than human meat they no longer ate each other but the sacrificed and roasted animal that they grazed. Once they had some experience of the pleasure of eating, from this beginning they advanced further the art of the *mageiros*. This is why even now, in memory of what went before they roast the vital organs for the gods with fire without adding salt.[147] For at that point they had not discovered its use for this purpose. So when they got a liking for it later they [. . .][148] with an eye on ancestral practice. And the one principle that has proved a life-saver for us all is our desire to add to our skills, and to augment the art of the *mageiros* still further with flavourings.[149]

A: This man is the new Palaephatus![150]

MAGEIROS: Next, as time passed, someone introduced the stuffed stomach and cooked a kid until it was tender, cooking it with a hot sauce of

---

[145] Written sometime before the end of the first century BC, since Juba referred to it (Athenaeus 14.660e).

[146] On the πρῶτος εὑρετής see Anaxandrides fr. 31 (quoted p. 18, cf. p. 78 n. 111).

[147] The absence of salt marks an important intermediary stage between a bestial life and civilized cooking: see Detienne (1979), 75–6.

[148] The text is uncertain.   [149] ἡδυσμάτων.

[150] On Palaephatus, *Peri apiston* see *FGrH* 44 and Nesselrath (1990), 217, n. 133.

trimmings, and giving it a nice tone,[151] heightened slightly with sweet grape juice; he rolled in a fish that was not visible to the eye, some green vegetables, expensive pickled fish, some rough-ground grain and honey. [. . .][152] because of the pleasure I am now describing each man restrained himself from eating a corpse any more. They now thought it right to live together; the people gathered together and civilized poleis came into being all through this art, as I have said, of the *mageiros*.

A: Sir, welcome! You are very close to my master there.

MAGEIROS: We *mageiroi* offer the first rites of sacrifice, we perform the sacrifice, we pour libations, by which more than anything the gods listen to us most for having discovered what most pertains to living well.

A: For piety's sake leave off and stop talking. The mistake is mine. Just come into the house with me, take up your pans, and make everything as it should be.

This cook, like so many of his predecessors, has made himself unbearable to his interlocutor—because he has extended his skills of artisan into the inappropriate area of anthropology, with a little musical analogy added for good measure. His account of human development from bestial and cannibalistic origins echoes many other accounts.[153] While this speech may be unwelcome to a man who is waiting to have a meal cooked, it is a splendid demonstration of the central place of sacrifice in the lives of the Greeks, and combines the sacrificial function of the *mageiros* with his other role as cook to discerning clients who require their food to give them pleasure, to be refined, and even to please with subtle concealment of some ingredients. This is an account of the development of Greek civilization based on sacrifice, with sophisticated cooking slotted into the picture. It is almost a comic version of the thesis of Detienne and Vernant (1989) in its linking sacrifice with civilization and the growth of cities. This cook looks at the large picture. For him, the heat of the kitchen is represented by the sacrificial flame and the transforming power

---

[151] The cook draws his metaphor from the *giggras*, a kind of pipe.

[152] The text is uncertain.

[153] Dohm (1964), 170–1 and Kassel–Austin (1983) compare, among other accounts, Democritus fr. 68 B 5.1 Diels-Kranz; Critias 43 F 19.1 Snell; Diodorus Siculus 1.18.1; and Lucretius 5.931–2 for the bestial life of early humans, and Plato, *Epinomis* 975a; Theophrastus, *On Piety* (in Porphyry, *On Abstinence* 2.27); Moschion 97 F 6.3 Snell; Diodorus Siculus 1.14.1 and 1.90.1; and Orphic fragment 292 Kern for the cannibalism of early humans.

of cooking improves all human society. The speech makes a strong claim for the developmental model of Greek cooking which I considered in Chapter 6; it also collapses the division between restraints imposed by religious and social ritual and the pursuit of pleasure which I have also explored in earlier chapters. It is entirely appropriate for a *mageiros* to put this case, since he is both the master of sacrificial violence and the cook for hire.

8.8. THE *DYSCOLUS* OF MENANDER

Athenion probably wrote very late in the Attic comic tradition. I conclude with a *mageiros* from the high point of New Comedy who combines ritual, pleasure, and civilization, but without a long speech—Sicon in the *Dyscolus* of Menander. *Mageiroi* in Menander appear to be well integrated into the action, and Sicon is no exception.[154] He is the master of sacrifice and elaborate cooking and detests the old misanthrope whose criticisms of people offering sacrifice we have met before. In two farcical scenes Sicon torments the old man by demanding pots and pans. These scenes give prominence to material objects which Sicon requires for his cooking. At the same time, Cnemon's resistance to commensality is the ultimate step too far in ancient Greece. He must be forced back into 'civilized' life by Sicon the cook.[155]

I have referred several times to the speech of Cnemon in which he denounces the indulgence of those sacrificing. As Handley (1965) has observed, this is subtly done: there are grounds for criticizing the wealthy sacrificers from the city[156] who have hired

---

[154] The cook in *Shield* (cited above) is deflected from his preparations for the all-important wedding. In *The Arbitration* the cook appears to have provided information both about past events and on scenes inside the house—in addition to crying up his skills. In *Flatterer* the cook supervises a sacrifice. The cook's role in *Misumenos* is unclear. In *Perikeiromene* 995–9 a cook is indoors ready to sacrifice a pig. In *Samia* a cook is hired for the wedding along with provisions from the market (190–5), to work with Demeas the head of household who is in charge of arrangements (210–11, 219–22). The cook arrives with requests for detailed information. His preparations are later interrupted by the furious Demeas (357–89). I cited isolated fragments from *Trophonius* and *False Heracles* in Chap. 6.

[155] 903 ἡμερωτέον, as Sicon says to Getas (Kassel's correction of ἡμερωτερος in the papyrus).

[156] Sostratus is said to have come with soft hands to the mattock, τρυφερὸς ὢν δίκελλαν ἔλαβες (766). Gorgias uses the language of luxury.

a fancy cook. Handley adduces a number of passages in which concern was expressed in the fourth century over excessive elaboration at sacrifice.[157] On the other hand, the speech against gluttony is made by the misanthropic central character. Furthermore, the woman who has hired the cook is a devotee of dreams and the religious life, apparently no glutton. The cook arrives with his sheep and makes much of the animal that is to be sacrificed—this is no purveyor of expensive fish to the ridiculously wealthy, but the agent of sacrificial ritual acting for someone who cannot make the sacrifice herself. The cook emphasizes the sacred nature of his work (644–6) and the initial sacrifice leads into a wedding celebration, symposium, and all-night festival.[158] There are only the smallest hints of excess (women's bibulousness), and the play concludes with the cook and slave tormenting Cnemon for absenting himself from the celebrations (891–969). The scene is farcical, since it repeats the earlier scene where Cnemon was asked to supply cooking-pots to the sacrificers (456–521), and rests on the material pots and pans which are the stock-in-trade of the *mageiros*, who seeks at the same time to insist on commensality. This cook may be boastful (at 490 he boasts of having thousands of customers in Athens) and have a ready patter (492–7), but he is most emphatically the agent of sacrifice. I argued in Chapter 1 that Menander was not a good choice of poet for those who sought to portray him as a conservative reflecting on the debasement of the ritual process. Rather, his Sicon incorporates those ambiguous aspects of the *mageiros* seen in many comedies. Menander—on the present evidence—appears not to have favoured the extended speeches of the boastful cook full of his own learning, but to have presented the *mageiros* as the caterer for weddings and other social occasions who insists on his own position and the practical aspects of

---

[157] See Handley (1965) on 447–54, quoting Theophrastus, *On Piety* (frr. 584A and 584D Fortenbaugh), among others.

[158] Sacrifice in Old Comedy sometimes leads from one purpose, such as the installation of Peace in *Peace*, to another, the 'wedding' of the protagonist. The *pannychis* in this play is a good example of the informal all-night celebration, in contrast with the *pannychides* of festivals. The men's symposium is also an improvised affair at the shrine of Pan, indicating once again that an *andron* and expensive furniture were not essential for a symposium. Rugs and informal seating were perfectly adequate (405, 420).

cooking,[159] with the odd dithyrambic elaboration inserted into his discourse (*Dyscolus* 946–53). Sometimes another character speaks of an animal or the provision of food;[160] on occasion the *mageiros* offsets the angry outbursts of the male protagonist, thus being 'integrated' into the play.[161]

Dyscolus provides the perfect example of a comic cook at work. Often a luxury hired to perform tasks which a household could perform itself—sacrifice and cooking of meals—he is needed this time because a woman is in charge. He claims to have many clients and uses flattery to get his way (492–6), and yet he forces the misanthrope back into social life. Cnemon had denounced the way that the Greek sacrifice had been hijacked by greedy humans and had denied all requests for cooking-pots (456, 506), even for the axe and salt necessary for sacrifice (506). But his distinctions were extreme and based on his minimalist approach to life. The Greek sacrifice was intimately connected with the consumption of meat and other foods and with drinking. Ritual and pleasure, offerings to the gods and communal consumption of food and wine, always went had in hand in Greek society. There was always an implicit tension between 'ritual' and eating, which for any human being with taste-buds is a sensual experience. Greek comedy built its approach to food and eating on that tension—Dicaeopolis in *Acharnians* enjoys the final feast as much as any of Menander's diners in *Dyscolus* are alleged to do—and exploited the myriad possibilities arising from it. The *mageiros* with his sacrificial and cooking equipment catered for pleasure and commensality, for what was essential to civilization and what might take civilization a step too far. He belonged to comedy because his status was low, his skills both practical and gloriously impractical, and his self-importance absurd. His killing of animals and his cooking, however, placed him at the heart of the Greek polis. Where there was no meat and no fire, there was no culture.

---

[159] *Trophonius* fr. 351, *False Heracles* fr. 409.

[160] Niceratus in *Samia* 399–404.

[161] 'Don't bite', says the cook's assistant to Cnemon (*Dyscolus* 467) and the cook to Demeas (*Samia* 384). On integration see Dohm (1964), 211–75; Giannini (1960), 181–92.

9
Conclusion

The time has now come for the *mageiros* to be elevated from 'cook' to 'chef'. The term borrowed from French confers upon the chef in English culture that claim to status and exclusivity on which his boasting and philosophizing is based. The *mageiros* is no mere 'cook', to be compared with humble assistants at sacrifice or women and slaves working at the domestic level. I have called him the 'cook' until now because my aim was not to rehearse once again the development of the stock character that has been presented in detail by Giannini (1960) and his successors. Rather, I have tried to tie him into the themes of this book and his predecessors in Old Comedy. As far as themes are concerned, the *mageiros* works in the kitchen with his equipment and prepares all the materials necessary for a meal, those derived from animals, fish, and plants. He has a defined social status, above that of slave but below that of the diners at the feast. At the feasts and sacrifices of the city it was he who normally slaughtered the animal, butchered it, and sold in the market-place the residue not needed by the deme or polis. As far as private commissions were concerned, he offered a higher level of sophistication at *deipna* than domestic and slave cooks could offer, and thus might well prepare food that could be described as luxurious. At this level too, he was likely to prepare at least as much expensive fish as high-status meat, both of which would mark off such a meal from the experience of much of the population. Finally, there are some indications in comedy and Plato that the chef-*mageiros* was particularly linked with Sicily and southern Italy. While we need not doubt that such chefs really existed, their numbers are likely to have been far fewer than comedy might lead us to think. The reason why they were so popular in Middle and New Comedy was precisely their utility in evoking the themes identified in this book. There is one indication that a *mageiros* appeared in a play of Epicharmus.

Chefs were not to be found in Old Comedy, even though the

oldest Attic comedy addressed itself frequently—I would claim, no less than Middle and New Comedy—to themes of eating and drinking. *Mageiroi* hover silently in the wings in *Birds* and *Frogs*, but the protagonists perform many of their functions. They sacrifice animals, they cook delicious food, they sometimes even buy and sell in the agora—in *Acharnians*, Dicaeopolis buys girls who are disguised as pigs; in *Knights* the Black-Pudding-Seller sells his tasty wares. These protagonists are said to sacrifice like a *mageiros* (*Peace* 1017–18), to serve food like a *mageiros* (*Acharnians* 1015–17), and to have the ability to offer political sweeteners like a *mageiros* (*Knights* 216). These protagonists have the skills of the *mageiros* because cooking lies at the heart of Old Comedy. The plots of the plays see to it that the protagonist and gods friendly to the city provide all good things for the people, and these good things are cooked with fragrant smells. Even in long descriptions of utopia and the automatic arrival of food, those foods are all cooked. The comic world is very much a world of culture as opposed to nature, and that culture is manifest in the cooking of food.

Food and cooking are at the centre of the comic world. The drinking of wine is not overlooked—on the contrary—but comedy adds to the wine and its drinking, which were the gift of its patron god Dionysus, the food that goes with it. It is the literary form in which food takes its rightful place along with the wine. Comedy is where food is to be found in profusion, redressing the imbalance in favour of wine that sympotic poetry and philosophy promoted. Eating and drinking were not separate activities in ancient Greece, even though the symposium was ritually divided from the *deipnon* part of the meal.

Comedy interests itself as much in domestic eating and drinking as in festivity and ritual eating. The focus in Old Comedy on domestic aspects of civic dining (in *Acharnians*, for example, on the private arrangements of Dicaeopolis at the Anthesteria, and in *Knights* on the prytaneion as a domestic hearth) made for an easy transition to the more domestic focus of Middle and New Comedy, where the *mageiros* normally cooks for a private commission. Athenaeus, who provided many of the fragments used in this book, has an instructive anecdote on public and private feasting, about Arsinoë, wife of Ptolemy II:[1]

---

[1] Arsinoë II Philadelphus, wife of Ptolemy II Philadelphus (see Thompson, 'Arsinoë II Philadelphus', *OCD*[3] 177).

Ptolemy founded many kinds of festivals and sacrifices, especially those for Dionysus. Arsinoë asked the man carrying the olive(?) branches what day he was celebrating and what festival it was. He answered, 'it is called the Lagunophoria.[2] The celebrants eat what is brought to them while they recline on improvised couches (*stibades*) and they drink, each from an individual flagon which each brings from home.' When he had moved on, she glanced at us and said, 'this is evidently a sordid gathering. Of necessity it is the meeting together of an indiscriminate rabble who are served with a stale feast that is quite unseemly.' If she had liked this kind of festival, the queen would not of course have tired of preparing the same festival food as is found at the Choes festival.[3] There they celebrate the feast individually, but the food is provided by the man who has invited them to the *hestiasis* [entertainment].[4]

Although Alexandria and monarchs have played a small part in this book, the anecdote about Arsinoë is instructive. In Athens in the late fifth and fourth centuries BC new cults were common, and, as far as we can tell, were readily absorbed into comedy. They do not appear to receive better or worse comment than established festivals. Arsinoë dislikes the informality of this new festival: comedy's concentration on such informality has been a theme of this book. Public and private, formal and informal cannot always be distinguished. Comedy concentrates on the small-scale, the offering of a little beast in *Birds* or a black-pudding in *Clouds*, over the great sacrifices of hundreds of beasts made at the major civic festivals, 'Informality' in a 'festival context'—in a private house, at a picnic, reclining on a *stibas*—lies at the heart of comedy. What Arsinoë dislikes in particular is the 'indiscriminate rabble'[5] who are celebrating. This indiscriminate rabble, in an Athenian context, is the demos, the people of the polis gathered together. Richard Seaford has shown how the Athenian democracy strove to organize civic institutions to replace earlier aristocratic forms based on the power of the individual. One powerful motor towards this end, according to Seaford (1994), were the cults and festivals of Dionysus, which mixed the people

---

[2] The Festival of the Flagon-Bearing.

[3] The second day of the Anthesteria.

[4] Athenaeus 7.276b–c = Eratosthenes, *Arsinoë FGrH* 241 F 1b. See also Fraser (1972) 2.344–5. The last two sentences are not quoted from Eratosthenes but are the comment of Athenaeus' speaker, Plutarch of Alexandria.

[5] παμμιγοῦς ὄχλου.

together indiscriminately.[6] Whatever Ptolemy was trying to achieve with his new festival, the Athenian demos used its festivals to consolidate its own power. Arsinoë could, in another context, be complaining about democratic aspects of Athenian festivals. Comic representations of them revel in such aspects. A major theme of this book has been the comic reconfiguration of the polis, in which comedy excludes from its feast the powerful (defined in a special way as politicians, priests and other officials, musicians, and tragic poets) and includes the demos, represented by the chorus and audience in Old Comedy. Later comedy has different ways of arriving at a satisfactory result for the final meal or komos.

Comedy is essentially 'festive' because it reflects on real festivals and on the fact that it itself was produced at festivals of Dionysus. It also extends festivity beyond formal festivals of the polis to the merrymaking that is the goal of the final scenes. In practice there is a great similarity between the end of *Acharnians*[7] (1084–94), the wedding at the end of *Peace*, and the wedding festivities at the shrine of Pan at the end of *Dyscolus*. This 'merrymaking', which in comedy focuses on eating and drinking, together with sex, is blended into general 'festivity',[8] sympotic activity, and komos.[9] In Chapters 2, 3, and 5 I tried to show that Ian Ruffell is mistaken in interpreting the symposium as a private affair to which comic poets opposed their own genre of comedy that was enshrined in the festivals of the Dionysia and Lenaea. Comedy appears to derive from the early Dionysiac komos, to retain versions of that komos in the festivity of Old Comedy, and to make much of it in the musical interludes between acts in New Comedy, which appear to have consisted, in some plays of Menander at least, in some form of komos.

---

[6] ἀνάμιγα.

[7] In which, in the words of Athenaeus' speaker, the man inviting people to the feast [the priest of Dionysus invites Dicaeopolis to the Anthesteria festival] provides a *hestiasis* for them.

[8] Which I discussed in relation to Theoria ('Showtime' or 'Attending the Festival'), in *Peace* in Chap. 3.

[9] A speaker in Ephippus, *Geryon* fr. 3 claims that at the Amphidromia, a ceremony to mark the acceptance of a baby into the home, it was usual to eat cheese, cabbage, lamb, doves, thrushes, finches, cuttlefish, squid, and octopus and to drink many cups of strong wine.

Ruffell is, however, correct in another respect. Comedy, or rather the dozens of comic poets writing over more than two centuries, did not have a fixed view on the relationship between their genre and the symposium. There certainly were aspects of the symposium that were linked with the elite, as Aristophanes classically portrayed in *Wasps*. Such aspects were always there to be exploited. I would expect that if we had access to whole plays that are now represented only by fragments, we would find that some sympotic passages discussed in Chapter 5 derive from comic symposia that were portrayed as excessive in various ways, and to be censured as manifestations of the lives of the irresponsible rich. The symposium was, it seems, an area for ideological debate.

This book has explored a number of cultural contexts that were strongly contested in comedy. Ritual, whether the strictly religious ritual of the sacrifice correctly performed, or social ritual with religious underpinning, such as correct drinking at the symposium, has often been contrasted with its reverse, with unrestrained eating and drinking, whether 'luxury', excessive consumption, or the deviant conduct of the parasite and *bomolochus*. I must emphasize that I regard these precisely as areas for comic debate. They are areas of social concern that comedy pursues in its own special discourse. It is because the boundaries between 'ritual' and a 'lack of restraint' are blurred that these matters are pursued so frequently. It is not easy in a complex society, for instance, to declare that a certain kind of eating or drinking is ritually pure and completely removed from pleasure. Can sacrifice to a god, followed by the consumption of meat (a comparatively rare treat for ancient Greeks) be declared ritually pure and removed from pleasure? Plato and Theophrastus did not think so.[10] Nor did Menander, hence Cnemon's complaints at *Dyscolus* 447–53 and the remarks in *Drunkenness* fr. 224.[11] The pleasure which I imagine Athenians experienced when they ate

[10] *Republic* 372e2–373c7, esp. 373c4–7; Theophrastus, *On Piety* frr. 584A and 584D Fortenbaugh.

[11] So too on the relationship between money and religious ritual. The two could be opposed to each other, as Aristophanes does in *Knights*, but money, as we have seen, was not separate from sacrifice. Animals were bought for cult sacrifice, meat and hides often sold after butchering, and temple precincts often leased to farmers.

meat after a sacrifice is, in my view, related to the pleasure comic characters embrace with approval when the comic action has brought them to the goal at the end of the comedy, namely feasting and well-being. It was easy enough to dismiss non-Athenians as luxurious, since Attic comedy was primarily concerned with Attica. Within Attica the merits of pleasure and luxury were open to comic discussion. Comedy's viewpoint is often clear, namely that comically approved persons are entitled to their pleasures—food, sympotic drinking, and sex—while certain others, who do not enjoy such approval, are not.

This is a book about 'discourse' and only periodically about 'reality'. I have explored Aristophanes' improbable claims about agriculture and feasting during the Peloponnesian War. I have also ventured to suggest that the symposium in reality was not confined to the elite, and that ritualized drinking was not denied to the majority of the male population. I believe Davidson (1997) is mistaken in implying that 90 per cent of the population drank wine on a commercial basis. That 'reality' is for historians of the period to establish. I have only approached 'reality' where I needed to clarify an aspect of the cultural background to comic discourse. That discourse is all-powerful, as I have tried to show. The comic poets stuffed their plays full with 'real' things, in particular the plants, animals, and fish on which the Greek city subsisted. These natural products which were to be found as foods in homes, markets, and festivals, were converted by comic discourse into something special, into something to be mentally relished by the audience which heard this reality converted into words and saw the characters on the stage making interpretative gestures and postures.

Comic discourse differs from most other discourses on food in Greek literature in concentrating first of all on food as well as wine, and then in revelling in the myriad kinds of plants and fish. Aspects of the discourse, such as the problematizing of ritual and pleasure, could be found in many other places, in philosophy, sympotic poetry, and history, for example. But the many species of cereal and the hundreds of species of fish? These were only to be found elsewhere in such specialist works as Theophrastus, *On Plants*, Aristotle, *History of Animals*, Dorion, *On Fish*, and certain medical texts—and in the sub-comic parodies of Archestratus and Matro. Fish, surely, were the ultimate challenge. Comic audiences witnessed characters listing and describing for the pot more fish than many of them ate in their own homes. This book has tried to show why fish were of such interest to the ancient Greeks. The comic poets built on this interest and applied their ingenuity to it. Novelty was a major objective for a comic poet, as Aristophanes makes clear in his parabases and a character in Antiphanes says in *Poetry* fr. 189. A new description of fish was always welcome.[12] It might come from a hungry character or a rich one, but once the boastful chef was established in Attic comedy, he was the person above all to serve it up to the comic audience.

[12] Rarely do such descriptions concern fish of fantastic proportions. The fish are described in profusion, but in the context of their normal size. Ephippus, *Geryon*, a play on a mythological theme, offers an exception. In fr. 5 Geryon is offered a fish the size of Crete by his subjects.

BIBLIOGRAPHY

AMYX, D. (1958), 'The Attic Stelai', *Hesperia*, 27: 163–310.

ANNAS, J. (1981), *Introduction to Plato's Republic* (Oxford).

APPADURAI, A., ed. (1986), *The Social Life of Things* (Cambridge).

ARNOTT, W. G. (1968), 'Studies in Comedy, 1: Alexis and the Parasite's Name', *GRBS* 9: 161–8.

—— (1972), 'From Aristophanes to Menander', *Greece & Rome*, 19: 65–80.

—— (1975), *Menander, Plautus, Terence* (Oxford).

—— (1996), *Alexis. The Fragments: A Commentary* (Cambridge).

—— (forthcoming), 'Middle Comedy', in G. Dobrov (ed.), *A Companion to the Study of Greek Comedy* (Leiden).

AUSTIN, C. (1964), *Gnomon*, 36: 748–51.

AVEZZÙ, E. (1989), 'Il Ventre del Parassita: Identità, Spazio e Tempo Discontinuo', in O. Longo and P. Scarpi (eds.), *Homo Edens* (Verona).

BAIN, D. (1977), *Actors and Audience: A Study of Asides and Related Conventions in Greek Drama* (Oxford).

BAKHTIN, M. (1968), *Rabelais and His World* (Bloomington).

BALDRY, H. C. (1953), 'The Idler's Paradise in Attic Comedy', *Greece & Rome*, 22: 49–60.

BALDWIN, B. (1976), 'Athenaeus and His Work', *Acta Classica*, 19: 21–42.

BEAVIS, I. (1988), *Insects and Other Invertebrates in Classical Antiquity* (Exeter).

BELARDINELLI, A. *et al.* (1998), *Tessere* (Bari).

BERROUET, L., and LAURENDON, G. (1994), *Métiers oubliés de Paris* (Paris).

BERRY, C. J. (1994), *The Idea of Luxury: A Conceptual and Historical Investigation* (Cambridge).

BERTHIAUME, G. (1982), *Les Rôles du mágeiros* (Paris).

BEYER, E. (1942), *Demetrios Phalereus der Athener* (Berlin).

BIEBER, M. (1961), *History of the Greek and Roman Theater* (Princeton).

BORGEAUD, P. (1988), *The Cult of Pan in Ancient Greece*, trans. (Chicago).

BORTHWICK, E. K. (1964), 'The Gymnasium of Bromios', *JHS* 84: 47–53.

BOWIE, A. M. (1993), *Aristophanes: Myth, Ritual and Comedy* (Cambridge).

BOWIE, A. M. (1997), 'Thinking With Drinking: Wine and the Symposium in Aristophanes', *Journal of Hellenic Studies*, 117: 1–21.

—— (forthcoming), 'Myth and Ritual in the Rivals of Aristophanes', in Harvey and Wilkins (forthcoming).

BOWIE, E. L. (1986), 'Early Greek Elegy, Symposium and Public Festival', *JHS* 106: 13–35.

—— (1995), 'Wine in Old Comedy', in Murray and Teçusan (1995), 113–25.

BRANDT, P. (1888), *Corpusculum Poesis Epicae Graecae Ludibundae* I (Leipzig).

BRAUND, D. C. (1994), 'The Luxuries of Athenian Democracy', *Greece & Rome*, 41: 41–8.

—— (1995), 'Fish From the Black Sea: Classical Byzantium and the Greekness of Trade', in Wilkins *et al.* (1995).

—— (1998), 'Herodotos on the Problematics of Reciprocity', in Gill *et al.* (1998).

—— and WILKINS, J., eds. (forthcoming), *Athenaeus and his World* (Exeter).

BREMMER, J. (1983), 'Scapegoat Rituals in Ancient Greece', *HSCP* 87: 299–320.

BRILLAT-SAVARIN, J.-A. (1970), *The Physiology of Taste*, trans. A. Drayton (London).

BROCK, R. (1990), 'Plato and Comedy', in E. Craik (ed.), *Owls to Athens* (Oxford), 39–50.

—— (1994), 'The Labour of Women in Classical Athens', *CQ* 44: 336–46.

BRUIT, L. (1995), 'Ritual Eating in Archaic Greece: Parasites and *Paredroi*', in Wilkins *et al.* (1995).

—— and SCHMITT-PANTEL, P. (1986), 'Citer, classer, penser: à propos des repas des Grecs et des repas des Autres dans le livre IV des *Deipnosophistes* d'Athénée', *AION ArchStAnt*, 203–21.

BRUMFIELD, A. C. (1981), *The Attic Festivals of Demeter and Their Relation to the Agricultural Year* (Salem).

BRUNT, P. A. (1980), 'Free Labour and Public Works', *JRS* 70: 81–100.

BURKERT, W. (1979), *Structure and History in Greek Mythology and Ritual* (Berkeley).

—— (1983), *Homo Necans* (Berkeley).

—— (1985), *Greek Religion* (Oxford).

BURNET, J. (1924), *Plato's Euthyphro, Apology of Socrates and Crito* (Oxford).

BURTON, J. (1998), 'Women's Commensality in the Ancient Greek World', *Greece & Rome*, 45: 143–65.

CAMERON, A. (1991), 'How Thin was Philetas?', *CQ* 41: 534–8.

CAMPBELL, A. C. (1982), *The Hamlyn Guide to the Flora and Fauna of the Mediterranean Sea* (London).

CAPPONI, F. (1979), *Ornothologia latina* (Genoa).

CARPENTER, T. H. (1986), *Dionysian Imagery in Archaic Greek Art* (Oxford).

CARRIÈRE, J.-C. (1979), *Le Carnaval et la politique* (Paris).

CARTLEDGE, P. (1990), *Aristophanes and his Theatre of the Absurd* (Bristol).

CECCARELLI, P. (1996), 'L'Athènes de Périclès: un pays de Cocagne? L'idéologie démocratique et l'*automatos bios* dans la comédie attique', *QUCC*, 83: 109–59.

COLE, S. G. (1993), 'Procession and Celebration at the Dionysia', in Scodel (1993), 25–38.

—— (1994), 'Demeter in City and Countryside', in S. E. Alcock and R. Osborne (eds.), *Placing the Gods* (Oxford), 199–216.

COOK, B. F., ed. (1989), *The Rogozen Treasure* (London).

CORNFORD, F. M. (1914), *The Origin of Attic Comedy* (Cambridge; 2nd edn. Gloucester Mass., 1968).

CRANE, G. (1997), 'Oikos and Agora: Mapping the Polis in Aristophanes' *Wasps*', in Dobrov (1997), 198–229.

CSAPO, E. and SLATER, W. J. (1995), *The Context of Ancient Drama* (Ann Arbor).

CURTIS, R. (1991), *Garum and Salsamenta* (Leiden).

DALBY, A. (1987), 'The Banquet of Philoxenus', *Petits Propos Culinaires*, 26: 28–36.

—— (1988), 'Hippolochus, The Wedding Feast of Caranus the Macedonian', *Petits Propos Culinaires*, 29: 28–36.

—— (1995), *Siren Feasts: A History of Food and Gastronomy in Greece* (London).

—— (forthcoming), 'Lynkeus of Samos', in Braund and Wilkins (forthcoming).

DARAKI, M. (1985), *Dionysos* (Paris).

DAVID, E. (1989), 'Laughter in Spartan Society', in A. Powell (ed.), *Classical Sparta* (London).

—— (1994), *The Harvest of the Cold Months* (London).

DAVIDSON, A. (1981), *Mediterranean Seafood*, 2nd edn. (Harmondsworth).

DAVIDSON, J. (1993), 'Fish, Sex and Revolution', *CQ*, 43: 53–66.

—— (1995), '*Opsophagia*: Revolutionary Eating in Athens', in Wilkins *et al.* (1995).

—— (1997), *Courtesans and Fishcakes* (London).

—— (forthcoming), 'Gnesippus *Paigniagraphos*: The Comic Poets and the Erotic Mime', in Harvey and Wilkins (forthcoming).

DAVIES, M. I. (1978), 'Sailing, Rowing and Sporting in One's Cup on the Wind-Dark Sea', in *Athens Comes of Age: From Solon to Salamis* (Princeton), 72–95.

DEARDEN, C. W. (1988), 'Phlyax Comedy in Magna Graecia: A Reassessment', in J. Betts, J. Hooker, and J. R. Green (eds.), *Studies in Honour of T. B. L. Webster, II* (Bristol), 33–41.

—— (1990), 'Fourth-Century Tragedy in Sicily: Athenian or Sicilian?', in J.-P. Descoeudres (ed.), *Greek Colonists and Native Populations* (Oxford), 231–42.

DEGANI, E. (1983), *Poesia Parodica Graeca*, 2nd edn. (Bologna).

—— (1995), 'Problems in Greek Gastronomic Poetry: On Matro's *Attikon Deipnon*', in Wilkins *et al.* (1995).

DETIENNE, M. (1979), *Dionysus Slain*, trans. M. and L. Muellner (Baltimore).

—— (1989), 'The Violence of Wellborn Ladies: Women in the Thesmophoria', in Detienne and Vernant (1989).

—— (1994), *The Gardens of Adonis*, trans. J. Lloyd (Princeton).

—— and VERNANT, J.-P., eds. (1989), *The Cuisine of Sacrifice* (Chicago), trans. P. Wissing from *La Cuisine du sacrifice en pays grec* (Paris, 1979).

DEUBNER, L. (1932), *Attische Feste* (Berlin; repr. Hildesheim 1966).

DOBROV, G., ed. (1997), *The City as Comedy* (Chapel Hill).

—— (1997a), 'Language, Fiction, and Utopia', in Dobrov (1997).

—— and URIOS-APARISI, E. (1995), 'The Maculate Music: Gender, Genre and the *Chiron* of Pherecrates', in G. Dobrov (ed.), *Beyond Aristophanes: Transition and Diversity in Greek Comedy* (Atlanta).

DOHM, H. (1964), *Mageiros* (Munich).

DOUGLAS, M. (1966), *Purity and Danger* (London).

—— (1971), 'Deciphering a meal', in Geertz (1971).

—— (1978), *Cultural Bias* (London).

—— (1982), *In the Active Voice* (London).

—— ed. (1984), *Food in the Social Order: Studies of Food and Festivities in Three American Communities* (New York).

—— (1987), *Constructive Drinking: Perspectives on Drink From Anthropology* (Cambridge).

—— and NICOD, M., (1974), 'Taking the Biscuit: The Structure of British Meals', *New Society*, 30/637: 744–7.

—— and ISHERWOOD, B. (1979), *The World of Goods* (London).

DOVER, K. J. (1968), *Aristophanes: Clouds* (Oxford).

—— (1978), *Greek Homosexuality* (London).

—— (1993), *Aristophanes: Frogs* (Oxford).

DUNBAR, N. (1995), *Aristophanes: Birds* (Oxford).

DURAND, J.-L. (1989), 'Ritual as Instrumentality', in Detienne and Vernant (1989), 119–28.

EASTERLING, P. E. and KNOX, B. M. W., eds. (1985), *The Cambridge History of Classical Literature*, I, *Greek* (Cambridge).

EDWARDS, C. (1993), *The Politics of Immorality in Ancient Rome* (Cambridge).

EDWARDS, M. (1993), 'Historicizing the Popular Grotesque: Bakhtin's *Rabelais* and Attic Old Comedy' in Scodel (1993), 89–118.

EHRENBERG, V. (1943), *The People of Aristophanes* (Oxford).

FARNELL, L. R. (1896–1909), *Cults of the Greek States* (Oxford).

FAUTH, W. (1973), 'Kulinarisches und Utopisches in der griechischen Komödie', *Wiener Studien*, 86: 39–62.

FEYEL, M. (1936), 'Nouvelles inscriptions d' Akraiphia', *BCH* 60: 27–36.

FERGUSON, W. S. (1944), 'The Attic *Orgeones*', *Harvard Theological Review*, 37: 61–140.

FINLEY, M. I. (1975), *The Use and Abuse of History* (London).

FISHER, N. R. E. (1993), 'Multiple Personalities and Dionysiac Festivals: Dicaeopolis in Aristophanes' *Acharnians*', *Greece & Rome*, 40: 31–47.

—— (1998), 'Gymnasia and Social Mobility in Athens', in P. A. Cartledge *et al.* (eds.), *Kosmos: Essays in Order, Conflict and Community in Classical Athens* (Cambridge).

—— (forthcoming), 'Symposiasts and Other Drinkers in Old Comedy', in Harvey and Wilkins (forthcoming).

FOL, A., ed. (1989), *The Rogozen Treasure* (Sofia).

FOLEY, H. (1988), 'Tragedy and Politics in Aristophanes' *Acharnians*', *JHS* 108: 33–47.

FOUCAULT, M. (1986), *The Use of Pleasure*, trans. R. Hurley (Harmondsworth).

FOURNEL, V. (1887), *Les Cris de Paris* (Paris).

FOXHALL, L. (1993), 'Farming and Fighting in Ancient Greece', in J. Rich and G. Shipley (eds.), *War and Society in the Greek World* (London), 134–45.

—— and FORBES, H. (1982), 'Sitometreia: The Role of Grain as a Staple Food in Classical Antiquity', *Cheiron*, 12: 41–90.

FRASER, P. M. (1972), *Ptolemaic Alexandria* (Oxford).

FRAZER, J. G. (1921), *Apollodorus: The Library* (Cambridge, Mass., and London).

GALLANT, T. W. (1985), *A Fisherman's Tale* (Ghent).

—— (1991), *Risk and Survival in Ancient Greece* (Stanford).

GALLO, L. (1989), 'Alimentazione urbana e alimentazione contadina nell' Atene classica', in Longo and Scarpi (1989), 213–30.

—— (1997), 'Lo sfruttamento delle risorse', in S. Settis (ed.), *I Greci: storia, arte, societa* (Turin), 2.ii. 423–52.

GARLAN, Y. (1980), 'Le Travail libre en Grèce ancienne', in *Non-Slave Labour in the Greco-Roman World* (Cambridge).

GARNSEY, P. (1988), *Famine and Food Supply in the Graeco-Roman World* (Cambridge).

—— (1999), *Food and Society in Classical Antiquity* (Cambridge).

GAUTHIER, P. (1976), *Un commentaire historique des Poroi de Xénophon* (Geneva and Paris).

GEERTZ, C. (1971), *Myth, Symbol and Culture* (New York).

GELZER, T. (1960), *Der Epirrhematische Agon bei Aristophanes* (Zetemata 23, Munich).

GENTILI, B. (1988), *Poetry and its Public in Ancient Greece: From Homer to the Fifth Century* (Baltimore).

GEORGOUDI, S. (1990), *Des chevaux et des boeufs dans le monde Grec* (Paris).

GHIRON BISTAGNE, P. (1976), *Recherches sur les acteurs dans la Grèce antique* (Paris).

GIANNINI, A. (1960), 'La figura del cuoco nella commedia greca', *ACME* 13: 135–216.

GIL, L., and ALFAGEME, I. R. (1972), 'La figura del médico en la comedia ática', *Cuadernos de Filologia Clasica*, 3: 35–91.

GILL, C., POSTLETHWAITE, N., and SEAFORD, R. (1998), *Reciprocity in Ancient Greece* (Oxford).

GILULA, D. (1995), 'Comic Food and Food for Comedy', in Wilkins *et al.* (1995).

—— (forthcoming), 'Hermippus' Catalogue of Goods (fr. 63)', in Harvey and Wilkins (forthcoming).

—— (1995a), 'Food—An Effective Tool of Amatory Persuasion: A Commentary on Mnesimachus fr. 4 KA', *Athenaeum*, 83: 143–56.

GOLDHILL, S. (1991), *The Poet's Voice* (Cambridge).

—— (1994), 'Representing Democracy: Women at the Great Dionysia', in R. Osborne and S. Hornblower (eds.), *Ritual, Finance, Politics* (Oxford), 347–69.

GOMME, A. W., and SANDBACH, F. H. (1973), *Menander: A Commentary* (Oxford).

—— ANDREWS, A., and DOVER, K. J. (1981), *A Historical Commentary on Thucydides* (Oxford).

GOODE, J. C., CURTIS, K., and THEOPHANO, J. (1984), 'Meal Formats, Meal Cycles, and Menu Negotiation in the Maintenance of an Italian-American Community', in Douglas (1984), 143–218.

GOODY, J. (1982), *Cooking, Cuisine and Class* (Cambridge).

GOTTSCHALK, H. (1980), *Heraclides of Pontus* (Oxford).

GOUREVITCH, D., and GRMEK, M. (1987), 'L'Obésité et ses représentations figurées dans l'antiquité', *Archéologie et Médecine*, 7: 355–67.

Gow, A. S. F. (1965), *Machon: The Fragments* (Cambridge).

Gowers, E. (1993), *The Loaded Table* (Oxford).

Graf, H. E. (1885), 'Ad aureae aetatis fabulam symbola', unpublished dissertation, Leipzig.

Greaves, A. (1999), 'The History of Miletus to the End of the Archaic Period', unpublished thesis, Leeds University.

Green, J. R. (1994), *Theatre in Ancient Greek Society* (London).

Greenewalt, C. H. (1976), *Ritual Dinners in Early Historic Sardis* (Berkeley).

Grimm, V. (1996), *From Feasting to Fasting* (London).

Gulick, C. B. (1927–41), *Athenaeus: The Deipnosophists* (Cambridge, Mass. and London).

Hägg, R. (1992), *The Iconography of Greek Cult in the Archaic and Classical Periods, Kernos*, Supplément 1 (Athens-Liège).

Habicht, C. (1997), *Athens from Alexander to Athens* (Cambridge, Mass.).

Handley, E. W. (1965), *The Dyskolos of Menander* (London).

Handley, E. (1985), 'Comedy', in P. E. Easterling and B. M. W. Knox (eds.), *The Cambridge History of Classical Literature*, I (Cambridge).

Hanson, V. D. (1983), *Warfare and Agriculture in Classical Greece* (Pisa).

Harding, P. (1987), 'Rhetoric and Politics in Fourth-Century Athens', *Phoenix*, 41: 25–39.

Harvey, D., and Wilkins, J. (forthcoming), *The Rivals of Aristophanes* (London).

Heath, M. (1998), 'Heroic Meal-Times', *Eikasmos*, 9: 215–18.

Heberlein, F. (1980), *Pluthygieia. Zur Gegenwelt bei Aristophanes* (Frankfurt/Main).

Hedreen, G. (1992), *Silens in Attic Black-figure Vase-Painting* (Ann Arbor).

Henderson, J. (1987), *Aristophanes: Lysistrata* (Oxford).

—— (1990), 'The *Demos* and the Comic Competition', in Winkler and Zeitlin (1990), 271–313.

—— (1991), *The Maculate Muse*, 2nd edn. (Oxford).

—— (forthcoming), 'Pherecrates and the Women of Old Comedy', in Harvey *et al.* (forthcoming).

Henrichs, A. (1990), 'Between Country and City: Cultic Dimensions of Dionysus in Athens and Attica', in M. Griffith and D. J. Mastronarde (eds.), *Cabinet of the Muses* (Chico), 257–77.

Henry, M. (1992), 'The Edible Woman: Athenaeus' Concept of the Pornographic', in Amy Richlin (ed.), *Pornography and Representation in Greece and Rome* (Oxford).

Herfst, P. (1979), *Le Travail de la femme dans la Grèce ancienne* (New York).

HOEPFNER, W., and SCHWANDNER, E. L. (1994), *Haus und Stadt im Klassischen Griechenland* (Munich).

HORNBLOWER, S. (1991), *A Commentary on Thucydides*, I (Oxford).

HUNTER, R. L. (1983), *Eubulus. The Fragments* (Cambridge).

—— (1985), *The New Comedy of Greece and Rome* (Cambridge).

JEFFREY, L. H. (1948), 'The Boustrophedon Sacral Inscriptions From the Agora', *Hesperia*, 17: 86–111.

KAIBEL, G. (1899), *Comicorum Graecorum Fragmenta*, I (repr. 1975).

KASSEL, R. (1974), 'Ärger mit dem Koch', *ZPE* 14: 121–7.

—— and AUSTIN, C. (1983–), *Poetae Comici Graeci* (Berlin and New York).

KEULS, EVA C. (1985), *The Reign of the Phallus* (Berkeley and Los Angeles).

KNOX, P. E. (1995), *Ovid: Heroides. Selections* (Cambridge).

KOLLER, H. (1956), 'Die Parodie', *Glotta* 35: 17–32.

KONSTAN, D. (1997), 'The Greek Polis and its Negations: Versions of Utopia in Aristophanes' *Birds*', in Dobrov (1997), 3–22.

KOPYTOFF, I. (1986), 'The Cultural Biography of Things: Commoditization as Process', in Appadurai (1986).

KOSSATZ-DEISSMANN, A. (1978), *Dramen des Aischylos auf westgriechischen Vasen* (Mainz am Rhein).

KUNISCH, N. (1989), *Griechische Fischteller* (Berlin).

LADA, I. (1999), *Initiating Dionysus* (Oxford).

LAMBERT-GÓCS, M. (1990), *The Wines of Greece* (London).

LEAKE, W. M. (1835), *Travels in Northern Greece* (London).

LISSARRAGUE, F. (1990), *The Aesthetics of the Greek Banquet* (Princeton: French version 1987).

LLOYD, A. B. (1975–88), *Herodotus: Book II* (Leiden).

LONGO, O., and SCARPI, P. (1989), *Homo Edens* (Verona).

LORAUX, N. (1981), 'La Cité comme cuisine et comme partage', *Annales ESC*, 4: 614–22.

LOWE, J. C. B. (1985), 'Cooks in Plautus', *Classical Antiquity*, 4: 72–102.

LUKINOVICH, A. (1983), 'Tradition Platonicienne et polemique antiphilosophique dans les *Deipnosophistes* d' Athénée', *Concilium Eirene*, 16: 228–33.

—— (1990), 'The Play of Reflections Between Literary Form and the Sympotic Theme in the *Deipnosophistae* of Athenaeus', in Murray (1990), 263–71.

MACDOWELL, D. M. (1971), *Aristophanes: Wasps* (Oxford).

—— (1993), 'Foreign Birth and Athenian Citizenship in Aristophanes', in Sommerstein *et al.* (1993).

—— (1995), *Aristophanes and Athens* (Oxford).

McPHEE, I., and TRENDALL, A. D. (1987), *Greek Red-figured Fish-plates, Antike Kunst* Beiheft 14 (Basel).

MANUEL, F. E., and F. P. (1971), 'History of Paradise', in Geertz (1971).

MARR, J. (1994), 'Don't Take it Literally: Themistocles and the Case of the Inedible Victuals', *Classical Quarterly*, 44: 536–9.

—— (1996), 'History as Lunch: Aristophanes *Knights* 810–19', *CQ* 46: 561–4.

MENDELSOHN, D. (1992), '*ΣΥΓΚΕΡΑΥΝΩ*: Dithyrambic Language and Dionysiac Cult', *CJ* 87: 105–24.

MICHA-LAMBAKI, A. (1984), *Η ΔΙΑΤΡΟΦΗ ΤΩΝ ΑΡΧΑΙΩΝ ΕΛΛΗΝΩΝ ΚΑΤΑ ΤΟΥΣ ΑΡΧΑΙΟΥΣ ΚΩΜΩΔΙΟΓΡΑΦΟΥΣ* (Athens).

MIKALSON, J. D. (1975), 'Religion in the Attic Demes', *AJP* 98: 424–35.

—— (1975a), *The Sacred and Civil Calendar of the Athenian Year* (Princeton).

MILLER, S. (1972), 'Round Pegs in Square Holes', *AJA* 76: 78–9.

—— (1978), *The Prytaneion* (Berkeley).

MINCHIN, E. (1996), 'The Performance of Lists and Catalogues in the Homeric Epics', in I. Worthington (ed.), *Voice into Text* (Leiden), 3–20.

MOREAU, J. (1954), 'Sur les "Saisons" d'Aristophane', *La Nouvelle Clio*, 6: 327–44.

MORTON BRAUND, S. (1996), 'The Solitary Feast: A Contradiction in Terms?' *BICS*, 41: 37–52.

MURRAY, O. (1982), 'Symposion and Männerbund', in P. Oliva and A. Frolíková (eds.), *Concilium Eirene*, 16 (Prague), 94–112.

—— (1983), 'The Greek Symposion in History', in E. Gabba (ed.), *Tria Corda: Scritti in onore di Arnaldo Momigliano* (Como), 257–72.

—— ed. (1990), *Sympotica* (Oxford).

—— (1990a), 'Sympotic History' and 'The Affair of the Mysteries: Democracy and the Drinking Cup', in Murray (1990), 3–13 and 149–61.

—— (1995), 'Histories of Pleasure', in Murray and Teçusan (1995).

—— and TEÇUSAN, M. (1995), *In Vino Veritas* (London).

MYNORS, R. A. B. (1990), *Virgil: Georgics* (Oxford).

NEIIENDAM, K. (1992), *The Art of Acting in Antiquity* (Copenhagen).

NEIL, R. A. (1909), *The Knights of Aristophanes* (Cambridge).

NESSELRATH, H.-G. (1985), *Lukians Parasitendialog* (Berlin/New York).

—— (1990), *Die attische Mittlere Komödie* (Berlin/New York).

NIAFAS, K. (forthcoming), 'The Origins of the Sanctuary of Dionysos Orthos', in Braund and Wilkins (forthcoming).

OBER, J. (1989), *Mass and Elite in Democratic Athens* (Princeton).

OGDEN, D. (1996), *Greek Bastardy* (London).

OLIVIERI, A. (1939), *Frammenti della Commedia greca e del Mimo nella Sicilia e nella Magna Grecia*.

OLSON, D., and SENS, A. (forthcoming), *Archestratus: The Life of Luxury* (Oxford).

O'REGAN, D. E. (1992), *Rhetoric, Comedy and the Violence of Language in Aristophanes' Clouds* (New York and Oxford).

OSBORNE, M. J. (1981), 'Entertainment in the Prytaneion', *ZPE* 41: 153–70.

OSBORNE, R. (1985), *Demos: The Discovery of Classical Attika* (Cambridge).

—— (1987), *Classical Landscape with Figures: The Ancient Greek City and its Countryside* (London).

—— (1993), 'Woman and Sacrifice in Classical Greece', *CQ* 43: 392–405.

PALOMBI, A., and SANTORELLI, M. (1960), *Gli animali commestibili dei mari d'Italia*, 2nd edn. (Milan).

PARKE, H. W. (1977), *Festivals of the Athenians* (London).

PARKER, L. P. E. (1997), *The Songs of Aristophanes* (Oxford).

PARKER, R. (1987), 'Festivals of the Attic Demes', Acta Universitatis Upsaliensis, *Boreas* 15: 137–47.

—— (1996), *Athenian Religion: A History* (Oxford).

PEASE, A. S. (1955), *M. Tulli Ciceronis De Natura Decorum* (Cambridge, Mass.).

PICKARD-CAMBRIDGE, A. W. (1962), *Dithyramb, Tragedy and Comedy* (Oxford).

—— (1968), 2nd edn., revised by J. Gould and D. M. Lewis, and (1988) with supplement, *The Dramatic Festivals of Athens* (Oxford).

PLATNAUER, M. (1964), *Aristophanes: Peace* (Oxford).

PÖHLMANN, E. (1972), 'Parodies', *Glotta*, 50: 144–56.

POWERS, W. K., and M. M. N. (1984), 'Metaphysical Aspects of the Oglala Food System', in Douglas (1984), 40–96.

PURCELL, N. (1994), 'Women and Wine in Ancient Rome', in M. McDonald (ed.), *Gender, Drink and Drugs* (Oxford/Providence RI).

—— (1995), 'Eating Fish: The Paradoxes of Seafood', in Wilkins *et al.* (1995).

RANKIN, E. M. (1907), *The Role of the Μάγειροι in the Life of the Ancient Greeks* (Chicago).

RAU, P. (1967), *Paratragodia* (Zetemata 45, Munich).

RECKFORD, K. J. (1979), 'Let them eat cakes', in *Arktouros: Hellenic Studies Presented to Bernard M. W. Knox* (Berlin–New York), 191–8.

REDEN, S. VON (1998), 'The Commodification of Symbols: Reciprocity and its Perversions in Menander', in Gill *et al.* (1998), 255–78.

RHODES, P. J. (1981), *A Commentary on the Aristotelian Athenaion Politeia* (Oxford).

RIBBECK, O. (1882), *Alazon* (Leipzig).

—— (1883), *Kolax. Eine ethologische Studie* (Leipzig).

—— (1885), *Agroikos. Eine ethologische Studie* (Leipzig).

RICHARDSON, N. (1974), *The Homeric Hymn to Demeter* (Oxford).

RICHTER, G. M. A., and MILNE, M. J. (1953), *Shapes and Names of Athenian Vases*, 2nd edn. (New York).

ROSEN, R. M. (1989), 'Euboulos' *Ankylion* and the Game of Kottabos', *CQ* 39: 355–9.

—— (forthcoming), 'Cratinus' *Putine* and the Construction of the Comic Self', in Harvey and Wilkins (forthcoming).

ROSIVACH, V. J. (1994), *The System of Public Sacrifice in Fourth-Century Athens* (Atlanta).

ROSLER, W., and ZIMMERMANN, B. (1991), *Carnavale e Utopia nella Grecia Antica* (Bari).

ROTROFF, S. I., and OAKLEY, J. H. (1992), *Debris From a Public Dining Place in the Athenian Agora, Hesperia* Supplement 25 (New Jersey).

RUCK, C. (1975), 'Euripides' Mother: Vegetables and the Phallos in Aristophanes', *Arion*, 2 (1975), 13–57.

RUFFELL, I. (forthcoming), 'Comic Ideas of Utopia', in Harvey and Wilkins (forthcoming).

—— (1998), 'Metatheatre, Metafestival and the Comic Symposium' (Oxford).

STE. CROIX, G. DE (1972), *The Origins of the Peloponnesian War* (Oxford), App. 29.

SALLARES, R. (1991), *The Ecology of the Ancient Greek World* (London).

SANCISI-WEERDENBURG, H. (1995), 'Persian Food: Stereotypes and Political Identity', in Wilkins *et al.* (1995).

SCHAPS, D. (1985–8), 'Comic Inflation in the Market Place', *Scripta Classica Israelica*, 8–9: 66–73.

—— (1987), 'Small Change in Boeotia', *ZPE* 69: 293–6.

SCHEFFER, CH. (1992), 'Boiotian Festival Scenes: Competition, Consumption and Cult in Archaic Black Figure', in Hägg (1992).

SCHLAIFER, R. (1943), 'The Cult of Athena Pallenis', *HSCP* 54 (1943), 35–67.

SCHMITT-PANTEL, P. (1992), *La Cité au banquet* (Paris and Rome).

SCHRÖDER, S. (1996), 'Die Lebensdaten Menanders', *ZPE* 113: 35–48.

SCODEL, R. (1993), *Theater and Society in the Classical World* (Ann Arbor).

—— (1993a), 'Tragic Sacrifice and Menandrian Cooking', in Scodel (1993).

SEAFORD, R. A. S. (1984), *Euripides: Cyclops* (Oxford).

—— (1994), *Reciprocity and Ritual* (Oxford).

SEKORA, J. (1977), *Luxury: The Concept in Western Thought, Eden to Smollett* (Baltimore).

SIDWELL, K. (1995), 'Poetic Rivalry and the Caricature of Comic

Poets', in A. Griffiths (ed.), *Stage Directions: Essays in Ancient Drama in Honour of E. W. Handley* (London), 56–80.

SIDWELL, K. (forthcoming), 'From Old to Middle to New? Aristotle's *Poetics* and the History of Athenian Comedy', in Harvey and Wilkins (forthcoming).

SHEAR, T. L. (1975), 'The Athenian Agora: Excavations of 1973–4', *Hesperia*, 44: 331–74.

SIFAKIS, G. M. (1971), *Parabasis and Animal Chorus* (London).

SILK, M. (forthcoming), 'Aristophanes versus the Rest', in Harvey and Wilkins (forthcoming).

SIMON, E. (1983), *Festivals of Attica* (Ann Arbor).

SLATER, N. (1993), 'Space, Character and ἀπάτη: Transformation and Transvaluation in the *Acharnians*', in Sommerstein *et al.* (1993).

SLATER, W. J. (1976), 'Symposium at Sea', *HSCP* 80 (1976), 161–70.

SOMMERSTEIN, A. (1980), *Aristophanes: Acharnians* (Warminster).

—— (1981), *Aristophanes: Knights* (Warminster).

—— (1985), *Aristophanes: Peace* (Warminster).

—— (1989), *Aeschylus: Eumenides* (Cambridge).

—— HALLIWELL, S., HENDERSON, J., and ZIMMERMANN, B. (1993), *Tragedy, Comedy and the Polis* (Bari).

SPARKES, B. (1960), 'Kottabos, an Athenian After-Dinner Game', *Archaeology*, 13: 202–7.

—— (1962), 'The Greek Kitchen', *JHS* 82 (1962), 121–37.

—— (1975), 'Illustrating Aristophanes', *JHS* 95: 122–35.

—— and TALCOT, L. (1970), *The Athenian Agora*, XII (Princeton).

SPYROPOULOS, E. S. (1974), *L'Accumulation verbale chez Aristophane* (Thessalonica).

STAFFORD, E. J. (1998), 'Greek Cults of Deified Abstractions', unpublished thesis, London University.

STRAUSS, B. (1986), *Athens After the Peloponnesian War* (London).

TAPLIN, O. (1983), 'Tragedy and Trugedy', *CQ* 33: 331–3.

—— (1986), 'Fifth-Century Tragedy and Comedy: A *Synkrisis*', *JHS* 106: 163–74.

—— (1987), 'Phallology, Phlyakes Iconography and Aristophanes', *PCPS* 33: 92–104.

—— (1993), *Comic Angels* (Oxford).

THOMPSON, D'A. W. (1947), *A Glossary of Greek Fishes* (London).

THOMPSON, H. A., and WYCHERLEY, R. E. (1972), *The Agora of Athens* (*The Athenian Agora* XIV) (Princeton).

TOD, M. N. (1948), *A Selection of Greek Historical Inscriptions* (Oxford).

TRENDALL, A. D. (1952), 'Paestan Pottery: Revision and Supplement', *BSR* 20: 1–53.

—— (1967), *Phlyax Vases*, 2nd edn. (London).

—— (1989), *Red-Figure Vases of South Italy and Sicily* (London).

—— and WEBSTER, T. B. L. (1971), *Monuments Illustrating Greek Drama* (London).

USSHER, R. G. (1973), *Aristophanes: Ecclesiazusae* (Oxford).

VAN NES, D. (1963), *Die maritime Bildersprache des Aischylos* (Groningen).

VERBANCK-PIERARD, A. (1992), 'Herakles at Feast in Attic Art: a Mythical or Cultic Iconography?', in Hägg (1992).

VEBLEN, T. (1899), *The Theory of the Leisure Class* (London).

VERNANT, J.-P. (1989), 'At Man's Table: Hesiod's Foundation Myth of Sacrifice' and 'Food in the Countries of the Sun', in Detienne and Vernant (1989), 21–86 and 164–9.

VERSNEL, H. S. (1987), 'Greek Myth and Ritual: The Case of Kronos', in J. Bremmer (ed.), *Interpretations of Greek Mythology* (London), 121–52.

—— (1993), *Inconsistences in Greek and Roman Religion II: Transition and Reversal in Myth and Ritual* (Leiden).

VETTA, M. ed. (1983), *Poesia e simposio nella Grecia antica: Guida storica e critica* (Rome and Bari).

VICKERS, M. (1974), 'A Kottabos Cup in Oxford', *AJA* 78: 158.

VIDAL-NAQUET, P. (1981), 'Land and Sacrifice in the *Odyssey*: A Study of Religious and Mythical Meanings', in R. Gordon (ed.), *Myth, Religion and Society* (Cambridge).

VIEIRA, E. (1988), *The Taste of Portugal* (London).

VILLARD, P. (1992), 'Boire seul dans l'antiquité grecque', in M. Aurell, O. Dumoulin, and F. Thélamon (eds.), *La Sociabilité à table* (Rouen).

VON SALIS, A. (1905), De Doriensium ludorum in Comoedia Attica vestigiis (Dissertation Basle).

WALLACE, P. W. (1979), *Strabo's Description of Boiotia: A Commentary* (Heidelberg).

WARNER, M. (1985), *Monuments and Maidens* (London).

WEBSTER, T. B. L. (1953), *Studies in Later Greek Comedy* (Manchester).

—— (1956), *Greek Theatre Production* (London).

WEHRLI, F. (1969), *Die Schule des Aristoteles*, vol. 9 (Basle).

WEST, M. L. (1966), *Hesiod: Theogony* (Oxford).

—— (1972), *Iambi et Elegi Graeci* (Oxford).

—— (1974), *Studies in Greek Elegy and Iambus* (Leiden).

WHITEHEAD, D. (1986), *The Demes of Attica, 508/7–ca. 250 BC* (Princeton).

WHITEHEAD, T. L. (1984), 'Sociocultural Dynamics and Food Habits in a Southern Community', in Douglas (1984), 97–142.

WHITTAKER, M., 'The Comic Fragments in their Relation to the Structure of Attic Old Comedy', *CQ* 29 (1935), 181–91.

WILKINS, J. (1992), 'Public (and Private) Eating in Greece 450–300 BC', in H. Walker (ed.), *Oxford Symposium on Food and Eating: Public Eating* (London), 306–10.

—— (1994), 'The Regulation of Meat in Aristophanes' *Knights*', in H. Jocelyn and H. Hurt (eds.), *Tria Lustra* (Liverpool), 119–26.

—— (1999), 'Disorder and Luxury at the Feast', *New Comparison* 24: 5–22.

—— (forthcoming, a), 'Athenaeus and the *Fishes* of Archippus', in Braund and Wilkins (forthcoming).

—— (forthcoming, b), 'Edible Choruses', in Harvey and Wilkins (forthcoming).

—— (forthcoming, c), 'Food Preparation in Ancient Greece: the Literary Evidence', in L. Hurcombe and M. Donald (eds.), *Gender and Material Culture* (London).

—— (forthcoming, d), 'Les Poissons faisaient-ils partie de la diète antique?', in J. N. Corvisier (ed.), *Médecine et démographie dans le monde antique* (Arras).

—— and HILL, S. (1994), *Archestratus: The Life of Luxury* (Totnes).

—— and —— (1994a), 'Fish heads of Ancient Greece', in H. Walker (ed.), *Look and Feel: Studies in Texture, Appearance, and Incidental Characteristics of Food* (Totnes).

—— and —— (1995), 'The Sources and Sauces of Athenaeus', in Wilkins *et al.* (1995).

—— and —— (1996), 'Mithaikos and Other Greek Cooks', in H. Walker (ed.), *Cooks and Other People: Proceedings of the Oxford Symposium on Food and Cookery 1995* (Totnes), 144–8.

—— HARVEY, D., and DOBSON, M. (1995), *Food in Antiquity* (Exeter).

WILLIS, W. H. (1991), 'Comoedia Dukiana', *GRBS* 32: 331–53.

WINKLER, J. (1990), 'The Ephebes' Song: *Tragoidia* and *Polis*', in Winkler and Zeitlin (1990), 20–62.

—— and ZEITLIN, F. (1990), *Nothing To Do With Dionysus?* (Princeton).

WOODFORD, S. (1971), 'The Cults of Heracles in Attica', in *Studies Presented to George M. A. Hanfmann* (Mainz).

WYCHERLEY, R. E. (1957), *The Athenian Agora III: Literary and Epigraphical Testimonia* (Princeton).

ZEITLIN, F. (1990), 'Thebes: Theater of Self and Society in Athenian Drama', in Winkler and Zeitlin (1990), 130–67.

ZIELINSKI, T. (1931), *Iresione I* (Leopoli).

ZIMMERMANN, B. (1992), *Dithyrambos* (Göttingen).

ZWEIG, B. (1992), 'The Mute Nude Female Characters in Aristophanes' Plays', in A. Richlin, *Pornography and Representation in Greece and Rome* (New York and Oxford), 73–89.

SUBJECT INDEX

Macedon 221, 287, 348, 409

Machon 64 n. 58, 170, 259, 347, 348 n. 129

mageiros 30–6, 46, 66, 68, 83–4, 87–91, 101–2, 114, 145, 165, 166, 180, 181, 266, 271, 277, 282–8, 292, 298–9, 304, 307, 309, 313, 316–17, 321, 326, 329–31, 337, 342, 351–2, 357, 361–414

material (foods as) 1–51, 211, 212, 218, 222, 231, 313, 321, 337, 368, 371–2, 404, 412–13, 415, 420

Matro 15, 35, 38 n. 146, 85–6, 201, 259, 265, 281 n. 87, 299, 313–14, 324, 341, 355, 357, 359–61, 368, 382, 420

mattye 287–8, 342, 372, 385

Melanthius 107, 141, 250, 347

Menander 171

Miletus 160, 193, 270

mime 332–3, 337, 340

Mithaecus xxv–vi, 170, 284–5, 306 n. 186, 311, 312, 314–17, 321, 342, 344, 348, 357, 362, 367–8, 385

money xxiv, 9–11, 59 n. 31, 105, 170, 171, 373, 386, 419 n. 11

Morychus 70, 77, 141, 211, 270

Morsimus 101, 141, 250

Nile 119 n. 68, 130, 153, 154

Old Oligarch (pseudo-Xenophon *Constitution of the Athenians*) 53, 56, 141, 161–2, 269, 273, 316, 378

opsa 165, 167, 170, 188, 191 n. 187, 212, 259, 267, 289, 293, 294 n. 134, 300, 302, 307, 312 n. 2, 316, 331, 346, 348, 361, 363, 388, 396

pannychis 55, 60, 64, 309–10, 396, 413

parasite 44, 71–87, 93, 94, 145, 179 n. 128, 186 n. 164, 188, 242, 265, 271, 298, 321, 342, 347, 355, 359, 367, 371, 408, 419

peace 103–55

Persia 271, 273, 276, 287, 307

Pherecrates 375–6

Philochorus 40–1, 116, 153, 211–14, 244 n. 185

philosophy xvii, 2

Philoxenus (author of the *Deipnon*) 15, 17, 35, 85 n. 135, 86, 186 n. 164, 207 n. 13, 231, 259, 304, 313–14, 317, 341–2, 344–54, 357, 361, 365, 390 n. 78

phlyax 313, 320, 331–41, 367

Phylarchus 57, 260–1, 271

Pindar:
  fr. 106: 270 n. 42
  fr. 124: 238, 243 n. 182
  fr. 126: 159
  fr. 128: 235

Plato xxvi, 51, 57, 76, 258, 262–3, 266, 273, 290, 307, 310–11, 314, 316, 320, 344, 368, 415, 419
  Cratylus 403a: 126
  Critias 108 n. 22
  Gorgias 451e: 168, 170, 177 n. 122, 241 n. 175
  Laws 666a: 220
    918d: 186 n. 162, 296
  Menexenus 235c: 269
  Phaedrus 276d: 245 n. 188
  Politicus 111 n. 31
  Republic 372d–e: 262
    404: 312
    574d: 297 n. 148

Plautus 56, 64 n. 59, 68, 302 n. 166, 333, 340, 383 n. 48, 387 n. 59, 389, 396 n. 98, 408

Plutarch:
  Moralia 527b: 280 n. 84
    620c: 217 n. 67
    623d–625c: 239 n. 159
    642f: 265
    656c–657a: 239 n. 159
    714b: 176
    1098b–c: 116 n. 52

poetry:
  (comic) 40–51, 72, 76, 78, 99–102
  (elegiac) 212, 222, 235, 330
  (iambic) 212, 222

the poor 13–16, 89–90, 300–2

prytaneion 77, 79, 84, 100–1, 144, 174–83, 249, 251, 263, 265,

INDEX LOCORUM

This index contains only comic passages. For other authors see subject index.

DATE DUE